AF361501

Improvisation, Creativity, and Consciousness

SUNY series in Integral Theory

Sean Esbjörn-Hargens, editor

Improvisation, Creativity, and Consciousness

Jazz as Integral Template for
Music, Education, and Society

Edward W. Sarath

Published by State University of New York Press, Albany

For information, contact State University of New York Press, Albany, NY
www.sunypress.edu

Production by Diane Ganeles
Marketing by Anne M. Valentine

Library of Congress Cataloging-in-Publication Data

Sarath, Edward.
   Improvisation, creativity, and consciousness : jazz as integral template for music, education, and society / Edward W. Sarath.
      p. cm. — (SUNY series in integral theory)
   Includes bibliographical references and index.
   ISBN 978-1-4384-4721-6 (hardcover : alk. paper)
   1. Music—Psychological aspects.   2. Improvisation (Music)   3. Jazz—Instruction and study.   4. Interdisciplinary research.   5. Wilber, Ken.   I. Title.

   ML3838.S19 2013
   781.65'11—dc23   2012027592

10 9 8 7 6 5 4 3 2 1

Contents

Contents

PART III. CHANGE

Illustrations

Acknowledgments

Inasmuch as it would be impossible to acknowledge all the individuals to whom I owe gratitude, the following list is partial at best. I begin with a big thanks to my colleagues, past and present, in the Department of Jazz and Contemporary Improvisation at the University of Michigan: Geri Allen, Andrew Bishop, Vincent Chandler, Gerald Cleaver, Sean Dobbins, Michael Gould, Marion Hayden, Robert Hurst, Andy Kirschner, Mark Kirschenmann, Bill Lucas, Frank Portolese, Ellen Rowe, Stephen Rush, Martha Travers, Roland Vazquez, and Dennis Wilson, with the fondest memories of my friend, colleague, and ascended jazz master Donald Walden, always close to my heart. Great appreciation goes to Paul Boylan, Dean of Michigan's School of Music for the first half of my tenure there, for creating a climate conducive to asking big questions in a field not always conducive to such, to Professor Donald Sinta for supporting me in those fragile early years, and Senior Vice Provost Lester Monts for his ongoing support and inspiration for a number of projects as well as commitment to diversity and the arts. Special thanks to Richard Mann for being such a great colleague and cohort in bringing consciousness studies to the academy, to Henryk Skolimowski for his inspiring wisdom and support of my work, and to David Liebman for being a great inspiration and mentor throughout my professional career.

All appreciation to everyone who worked with me in launching and sustaining the International Society for Improvised Music, including Douglas Ewert, Mitchell Gordon, Maud Hickey, Betty Anne Younker, Karlton Hester, James Ilgenfritz, Billy Satterwhite, Michael Nickens, Ladonna Smith, India Cook, Jin Hi Kim, Stephen Nachmanovitch, Kate Olson, Bill Johnson, and Sarah Weaver.

Thanks as well go to Terri Adams, Kwasi Ampene, Molly Beauregard, Judith Becker, Dan Barbezat, Phillip Bowman, Mirabai Bush, Marionette Cano, Rui Carvalho, Mark Clague, Richard Crawford, Allan Combs, Nancy Cook, Robert Culver, Diana Denton, Jane Dutton, Shekinah Errington,

David Elliott, Jeff Evans, Kaeli Ferguson, Regina Ferguson, Marilyn Fitzpatrick, Robert Forman, Monte Fowler, James Froseth, Kyra Gaunt, Terry Glazer, Elliott Ginsberg, Tracey Goetz, Phillip Goldberg, Freda Herseth, Carol Hutchins, Frank Hueser, Lorin Hollander, Fritz Kaenzig, Paul Kantor, Sharon Kardia, June Katzen, Christopher Kendall, John King, Oliver Lake, Susan King, George Lewis, Joseph Lukasik, David Lynch (the filmmaker), David Lynch (the music promoter), Larry Livingston, Sunanda Markus, John Matlock, Isabelle Matzkin, Andrew Mead, Margaret Mell, Jack Miller, Marie McCarthy, Charlie Miklin, Theo Morrison, David Myers, Martin Mueller, Janne Murto, James Newton, Kate Noble, Eric Nystrom, Pauline Oliveros, Patricia Olynyk, Craig Pearson, Stacey Printon, Jane Pitt, Lenore Pogonowski, Robert Quinn, Guthrie Ramsey, John Rapson, Bennett Reimer, Carlos Rodriquez, Bobby Roth, Sue Shand, Daniel Sher, George Shirley, Stephen Shipps, Henryk Skolimowski, Julie Smigelski, Michael Sternberg, Larry Stevens, Joseph Subbiondo, Richard Tarnas, Fred Travis, Walter Turkenborg, Adam Unsworth, Jeff Vornhagen, Christopher Waterman, Peter Webster, Peter Westbrook, Susan Wilnus, Jackie Wiggins, Michael Wheeler, Paul Willis, Pierre Woods, Reggie Workman, Karen Wolff, Charles Young, and Arthur Zajonc.

To the scores of students who came through my classes through the years, I thank you profoundly and hope that you learned as much from me as I from you. And to those of you who chose to pursue the BFA in Jazz and Contemplative Studies pathway, please know that I will always regard you as among my true heroes.

Thanks to SUNY Integral Theory series editor Sean Esbjörn-Hargens and SUNY senior acquisitions editor Nancy Ellegate for having faith in me and for their help in bringing this book to fruition. Special appreciation goes to Ken Wilber as the predominant contemporary exponent of integral thought. It is almost as if the theory were originally designed for music, even if musical application of it has been so far elusive.

Deepest gratitude goes to his Holiness Maharishi Mahesh Yogi, without whose vision of wholeness and gifts of ways it might be fathomed, very little of this book could have been written. I believe his elucidation of the collective, field aspect of consciousness that unites all of humanity and beyond is among the very most important ideas of our times and I hope this book does justice to it. I have also gained considerably from my encounters with Andrew Cohen, Harry Palmer, Don Alberto Taxo, and Jaggi Vasudev and their spiritual teachings and convey my great appreciation for their gifts.

Finally, my most heartfelt appreciation to my wife Joan Harris, the light and love of my life, for being by my side every moment in this project, arguments about hyphenation and punctuation notwithstanding, and our journey together.

The following chapters are based on material previously published:

Chapter 3: Ed Sarath, "Meditation, Creativity, and Consciousness: Charting Future Terrain within Higher Education," *Teachers College Record* 108, no. 9 (2006): 1816–1841; and Ed Sarath, "Meditation in Higher Education: The Next Wave?" *Innovative Higher Education* 27 (2003): 215–234.

Chapter 6: Ed Sarath, "A New Look at Improvisation," Journal of Music Theory 40, no. 1 (1996): 1–39.

Chapter 10: Ed Sarath, "Is the Paradigm Shifting Without Us?" *International Journal of Music Education* 25 (1995): 29–37; and Ed Sarath, "Improvisation and Curriculum Reform," in *The New Handbook of Research on Music Teaching and Learning,* edited by Richard Colwell and Carol Richardson (New York: Oxford University Press, 2002).

Chapter 11: Ed Sarath, "Jazz, Creativity, and Consciousness: Blueprint for Integral Education," in *Integral Education: New Directions for Higher Learning,* edited by Sean Esbjörn-Hargens, Jonathan Reams, and Olen Gunnlaugson (Albany: State University of New York Press, 2010).

Chapter 12: Ed Sarath, "Improvisation, Consciousness, and the Play of Creation," *Ultimate Reality and Meaning* 30, no. 1 (2007): 33–53.

Introduction

> The future of the Earth depends on a change of consciousness . . . and the change is bound to come. But it is left to (humans) to decide if they will collaborate for this change or it will have to be enforced upon them by the power of crashing circumstances.
>
> —Mirra Alfassa, quoted in Allan Combs,
> *Consciousness Explained Better: Toward an Integral Understanding of the Multifaceted Nature of Consciousness*[1]

That humanity has arrived at a crossroads of historical significance by now requires little elaboration. The question is how, or even if, we will navigate our way through this critical juncture.[1] On one hand, issues such as climate change and environmental devastation, widespread poverty and disease, drought and famine, terrorism and increasingly sophisticated means of warfare, economic disparity and instability, along with a broad complex network of sociocultural challenges raise unprecedented questions about the sustainability of civilization as we know it.[2] On a more optimistic yet scarcely less daunting note, individuals and communities across the globe have unprecedented access to an ever expanding knowledge base that transcends disciplinary, cultural, historical, and geographical boundaries. While often spawning the overwhelming morass of data that exacerbates the alienation and disconnectedness that pervade much of contemporary life, this broad spectrum of resources—were it to be effectively harnessed—might be the source of newfound solutions to the present challenges.

Although some may be inclined to think that the present slate of crises, particularly in regard to global warming and related consequences, has progressed beyond the threshold of reversibility, I have faith in humanity's ability to dig deep into its wellsprings of ingenuity and invoke levels of understanding and action that enable not only survival but entirely new kinds of progress. Almost a half century ago, Buckminster Fuller predicted that *Homo sapiens sapiens* would approach a point at which two options—as expressed in the title of his book *Utopia or Oblivion*—would be available.[3] To encapsulate Fuller's central premise: There will be no middle ground—the kind of change required for mere survival will be of such scope as to catapult human civilization onto a new evolutionary plateau. Echoing the viewpoints of a growing contingent of more recent thinkers, I believe that at its core this transformation will occur on the level of consciousness, which in this book I approach in terms of the creativity-consciousness relationship.[4]

By creativity I refer to such qualities as inventiveness, interaction, the ability to synthesize new forms of knowledge from diverse sources, and the emergence of an individual voice or style within a discipline. Consciousness pertains to self-awareness, transcendence, realization of wholeness and interconnectedness, noetic experience, and the wide range of feeling and emotion that are thought to distinguish human beings from other species. Expanding upon these working definitions from the stand-point of an emergent worldview called Integral Theory, I will view the two realms as inextricably linked aspects of an unbroken, inner-outer whole-ness. "[F]or the first time," remarks Ken Wilber, commonly regarded as the leading contemporary exponent of integral thought, "the sum total of human knowledge is available to us—the knowledge, experience, wisdom, and reflection of all major human civilizations . . . are open to study by anyone."[5] Within this cross-disciplinary expanse, one of the most impor-tant contributions of Integral Theory is its capacity to embrace both the timeless insights of "the ancient shamans and sages" as well as the latest "breakthroughs in cognitive neuroscience,"[6] thereby bridging the interior and exterior realms that are often seen as inherently competing with one another. From this vantage point, we will see creativity as an exterior entryway and consciousness as an interior entryway to this inner-outer totality. This in turn gives rise to a conception of spirituality that, in encompassing this totality, transcends denominational boundaries, mani-fests in all areas of life, and is entirely compatible with—without, as some insist, being reducible to—science.

I develop two central themes related to the impending creativity-consciousness, integral revolution that tend to elude much of the thinking about this kind of paradigmatic change. One is that it will need to take place within, and be driven by, our educational systems if is to manifest on any significant scale in society at large. No other public agency has as much contact with as much of the population and thus the capacity to shape thinking and behavior as our schools. Unfortunately, by inhibit-ing inquiry—both practical and theoretical—into the interior, transcendent dimensions of human nature central to creativity and consciousness development, our educational systems have arguably perpetuated the very paradigm that needs to be transformed. Second is that the arts uniquely embody integral properties and will play a key role in this educational and societal shift. Within the arts, moreover, the creativity-consciousness relationship is uniquely embodied in the improvisation-based musical art form of jazz, pointing to the potential for this idiom to assume leadership in the arts-driven integral revolution.

Why jazz? Why, among the infinite array of musical genres that exist, is jazz a primary candidate for transformational catalyst? What might jazz-driven change look like?

Much of my focus in answering these questions will be on the jazz process scope, although I will also consider the idiom's rich structural aspects as they work in tandem with the process realm. Two aspects of the process realm are key. First is jazz's improvisatory core, which integrates a wide array of other processes—including composition, performance, and various kinds of theoretical analysis—that are also central to creative growth in music and beyond. This improvisation-based creative foundation will be shown to promote penetration beyond the idiom's discipline-specific boundaries and openings to the broader musical landscape, wide-ranging interdisciplinary connections, and innermost dimensions of consciousness that shape creative expression and growth. Whereas much of academic and commercial thinking and practice are bound by a highly fragmented conception of the musical landscape as comprised of innumerable, discrete stylistic compartments, an integral musical perspective views these as inextricably linked areas within a broader whole. The central pulse of the musical world, moreover, resides in the melding of genres, at which point the purpose of engagement in any given area is to realize it not as self-confining destination but self-transcending tributary. Here I am reflecting from a Western vantage point and do not suggest that this syncretic melding that is exemplified in jazz—which has been called the "first world music"[7]—necessarily represents an evolutionary thrust applicable to all musical cultures. Nor is this to suggest that the tributary, once its boundaries are transcended, then discards its unique features—which in the case of jazz include its rich expressive range, collective interactive features, propulsive rhythmic foundations, and other traits that evolved from the idiom's African American roots. Rather, these are "transcended and included," to invoke a central integral axiom, in the broader musical syncretism.[8] Jazz's improvisation-based process scope renders it a uniquely powerful tributary that flows not only into the overarching musical ocean but the broader oceans of creativity and consciousness. A template emerges that can inspire and inform this same self-transcending movement not only in other musical genres but wide-ranging fields in and beyond the arts.

This leads to a second aspect of the jazz process scope. The jazz tradition boasts a long legacy of leading artists, including Alice Coltrane, John Coltrane, Herbie Hancock, Charles Lloyd, John McLaughlin, Sonny Rollins, Wayne Shorter, and Mary Lou Williams, who engaged with meditation and related methodologies for growth of creativity and consciousness in order to integrate the transcendent experiences glimpsed during their musical excursions more fully into their work and lives. We will see that improvisation and meditation, even if the first occurs in the turbulence of creative activity and the second in silence, share important common features and invite mutual engagement. Meditation, viewed here as an anchor for a broader spectrum of spiritual growth, is thus regarded as an important aspect of the jazz process spectrum, in so doing broadening the integral template the idiom brings to the overall educational and societal evolutionary spectrum.[9]

Preliminary signs of jazz-driven, integral change may already be evident in what is sometimes called the New Jazz Studies. Here fields as diverse as business, education, law, medicine, sociology, and sports have begun to look to the idiom's creative foundations as a guide to greater creativity within their own boundaries. Columbia University, for example, includes jazz in its liberal arts core curriculum to model important sociocultural dynamics that are important aspects of, as Robert O'Meally puts it, "what it means to be educated in today's world."[10] However, in that the New Jazz Studies tends to stop short of the realm of consciousness, I propose the advent of "Integral Jazz Studies," where consciousness shares the stage with creativity, as the next evolutionary wave in this jazz-inspired transformation. Here it should be emphasized that, while implicit in these considerations is the commonly invoked idea of the arts as an enhancement to creativity and performance across disciplines, Integral Jazz Studies does not confine its scope to that relatively small realm of artistic function. Rather, Integral Jazz Studies penetrates to the core of the arts as among the most foundational realms of human endeavor, the importance of which needs to be recognized on its own terms, and not only as embellishment for other areas of life. This is in no way to dismiss the importance of arts-driven creative expansion in all areas of inquiry, but to situate it within a broader transformational mission for the arts—both of which are embodied by jazz.

An additional theme emerges as a by-product of this investigation of jazz's integral features. This has to do with possible shortcomings in integral discourse, where the arts and creativity in general, and music and improvised music in particular, tend to not assume the importance that is implicit in the theory itself. In other words, although the interplay of spirituality, art, and science—long held as the "Big Three" pillars of human endeavor—is a key integral precept, not only do the arts tend to be somewhat subordinate in the ongoing dialogues and publications that comprise the integral conversation, but within the arts, music and particularly improvised music receive scant attention. In exploring jazz as an embodiment of integral principles, not only is this oversight addressed and rectified, but in so doing, new insights may be unearthed that shed light on these patterns and thus contribute significantly to the evolution of integral thought.

In a single stroke, an inquiry into the integral properties of jazz in turn helps restore integral precepts to integral discourse and thereby lays groundwork for delivering the integral vision to a world in urgent need of a blueprint for the future.

A look at the circumstances that led me to the present formulation of these ideas will shed further light on the more in-depth investigation that will unfold throughout the course of the book.

My Story

In 1987, I was appointed to the music faculty at the University of Michigan to establish a program in jazz studies. I came in with bold ambitions: First, I would bring jazz and improvised music to the majority of students and faculty at this top-ranked, largely classical performing arts school, a task that I estimated could be completed in a few years. Colleagues outside of music are often surprised to learn the extent to which the primary creative processes of improvisation and composition are absent from the experience of most students and faculty, with interpretive performance being the primary task of the majority. I was convinced that I could expand this highly specialized orientation fairly quickly, and if this happened at Michigan, the entire field would shift. Once this was accomplished, I would then bring meditation and consciousness studies to the entire campus, which I calculated would take a few more years—at which point I figured I would sail through the tenure process. After all, how could anyone not be excited about these ideas and the benefits to be reaped by students and faculty alike?

It did not take long before I realized that, in fact, there were more than a few who did not share my enthusiasm, and that I would have to significantly revise my timetable. While I managed to make fairly significant inroads on both improvisation- and meditation/consciousness-related fronts, earning tenure along the way, I saw firsthand the glacial pace of change in the academic world, perhaps best expressed in the statement: "It is easier to move a cemetery than change a curriculum."[11] As I persisted in my efforts, I realized that it would not be enough to design new educational models, but it was also necessary to catalyze new kinds of thinking and dialogue that would cultivate receptivity to any such practical initiatives. Which, exemplary of the delineative and diagnostic facets of the integral framework, meant the articulation of a clear and compelling vision of a new approach, as well as an analysis of the prevailing model's limiting practices and conceptual underpinnings.

This hit home early on in my teaching of improvisation to classical musicians. Although jazz was central to my job description, I had designed unique approaches to not only jazz improvisation but also stylistically open improvisation that provided classical (and other) musicians "user-friendly" entryways into the process. Instead of imposing external style constraints at the outset, my approach elicits a creative flow from whatever style backgrounds musicians bring to the process. Once that flow is established, multiple parameters of refinement can follow through the introduction of melodic, harmonic, rhythmic, and other style-specific constraints.[12] In addition to offering coursework of this nature to students, I formed a faculty improvisation ensemble in hopes of providing my classical colleagues with hands-on experience in this historically central approach to music making and, as will be also explored, musical understanding. While students and faculty alike would commonly report some degree of fulfillment even from their initial improvisatory attempts, and furthermore noted positive benefits that transferred to their interpretive performing such as greater freedom, expressivity, and sharper listening skills, I became acutely aware of an important deficiency that needed to be addressed.

This was the view of improvisation, regardless of what it had to offer, as an embellishment to interpretive performance. In other words, even though improvisation was in earlier times central to the classical tradition, and in one form or another has always been the most predominant practice in the musical world at large, academic musical culture has long been grounded in an object-mediated aesthetic that is sadly out of touch with this central facet of musical reality. By object-mediated, I mean that the basis of musical meaning and worth is the composed-notated composition, not the creative process.[13] Thus, while the composed work represents the central aesthetic locus, the composition process, as noted earlier, remains relegated to a scant few. Improvisation fares even worse within this orientation, not only excluded from the curriculum with the exception of jazz coursework, but often dismissed as a less evolved sub-species of composition and thus occupying a marginalized status in the aesthetic hierarchy in the field. Therefore, while improvisation might be enjoyable and uphold a kind of therapeutic role for those interpretive performers open to expanding their horizons through this process, the idea of it upholding the transcendent, spiritual function that has long been attributed to the arts, and is central to an integral aesthetics, was and still is quite foreign.[14]

Presaging the integral analysis that will begin in part 1, this view of improvisation in musical academe is confined to exteriors and oblivious to the interior richness in this powerful aspect of creative expression. And as elusive as this appreciation of improvisation's transcendent properties might be for interpretive performers when engaging with the process from a stylistically open standpoint, I found the idea that improvisation when situated within a culturally grounded, style-specific context, such as jazz and its African American underpinnings, to be even more remote to their experience. At a moment in history when the need for a cross-cultural awareness has never been more urgent, and when few fields embody this to the extent of music, I was struck by the extent to which an academic discipline could, in deviating from the creative and diverse thrust of the musical world, fall so short in light of these values.

As I will emphasize repeatedly, the problem is *not* the European classical repertory, the greatness of which is beyond the debate. Nor is it the interpretive performance tradition that has stemmed from it. The problem is the extent to which the part has overtaken the whole, where a tiny slice of musical practice has been conflated with the totality and impeded the broader connections to be made to equally great musical regions. While it would be a while before I fully grasped the complicated nature of the reform that would be necessary, two things began to become clear to me early on. First was that the kind of change needed and I believed was possible would be a win-win affair; musical study had everything to gain from diversifying its horizons. Second was that this change would need to involve more than a horizontal expansion of the existing model if the gulf between musical study and the musical world were truly to be bridged; it would need to take on vertical dimensions. In other words, wedging in electives in improvisation and more diverse kinds of musical engagement atop the reigning foundation, which has characterized much of the reform efforts that have prevailed, would be inadequate.[15] Only through wholesale overhaul of the model from its conceptual, curricular, and cultural foundations on up would the necessary reform take place.

Among the important inroads I made in the conceptual realm include one of the first consciousness-based accounts of improvisation and composition processes to appear in the literature, which is the basis for chapter 6.[16] As John Sloboda, Christopher Small, David Elliott, and others note, musicology—consistent with the object-mediated paradigm—has largely ignored investigation of the creative process and instead has focused on resultant works and related structural and historical concerns. I advanced a model that not only broached the moment-to-moment decision making sequences invoked by improvisers and composers, but revealed the two processes as contrasting pathways to transcendent experience. In the curricular realm, I designed an improvisation-based musicianship course, among the first jazz offerings to be accepted as part of the core curriculum for classical music majors.[17] As an alternative to conventional approaches to music theory and aural skills that focus largely on writing exercises and analysis, my class would cover basic tonal, modal, and rhythmic materials through the hands-on, creative, and integrative approaches that are not only unique to jazz but increasingly emphasized by educational theorists. Written and analytical work would not be supplanted in my approach but rather situated within a broader epistemological scope. Approaching the jazz idiom, moreover, as *writ large* not only would unite a wide swath of processes—including composition, performance, and multiple kinds of theoretical analysis—but yield openings to wide-ranging musical sources from around the globe, including those from the European classical lineage. The design of the class was based in several key principles to an integral approach to music, which harkens back to points made here earlier, that also pose important ramifications for education at large. First is the need to step back from style categories and view the musical landscape, and the skills needed for its navigation, in terms of processes and structures. One then returns to style categories—which I prefer to think of as process-structure regions within a broader process-structure musical wholeness—and seek the richest sources for the skills identified, according to criteria such as hands-on, creative application, integrative learning, and contemporaneous approaches as entryways to tradition. This procedure reveals that a process-structure region called *jazz* looms large as a fertile source for musicianship skills.[18]

Again, the point is not to endorse jazz as a self-confining destination but as a self-transcending gateway that connects musicians with the central creative and aesthetic pulse of today's musical world. The fact that, furthermore, the idiom also spawns connections beyond music, including the innermost dimensions of consciousness, would lead to further innovations. Central to these was the integration of meditation and related practices in my classes in order to further expand the tools students could use for not only musical but broader personal development. In 1997, I was a fellow in the first year of the American Council of Learned Societies (ACLS) Contemplative Practice Fellowship program,[19] the purpose of which was to promote the use of interior methodologies in college and university classrooms. Having had extensive practical experience in meditation and having made preliminary pedagogical inroads in this area, I used this opportunity to design a course called Creativity and Consciousness. Now meditation would not be ancillary, but rather a primary process in a class devoted to the practical and theoretical study of consciousness. After teaching this class for a few years, a further possibility occurred to me—to create a curriculum that enabled students to gain more significant grounding in the meditation/consciousness studies realm. I drew up a proposal for a Bachelor of Fine Arts in Jazz and Contemplative Studies degree, which would be the first of its kind in or beyond music at a mainstream public institution. As I was about to discover, any resistance that I might have encountered in striving to bring improvisation to the classical musical world would pale compared to what I was about to face.

At first, the proposal met with a kind of curious silence when it first appeared on the curriculum committee agenda. No one really knew what to make of it. Since I had been a member of the committee for several years, I had established fairly good connections and credibility with a number of other members. Most colleagues had come to appreciate me as a consistent generator of new ideas, as long as they remained within limits (e.g., my aforementioned musicianship class aside, outside the core curriculum). But now the bar would be raised because, while the proposed curriculum would not impact the schoolwide core, it introduced components that for many would be unthinkable: meditation practice not only in the classroom but implicit in the name of a degree program.

I managed nonetheless to make a fairly convincing case to the committee, citing the ACLS initiative, the growing body of research into the benefits of meditation practice, and the rich intellectual connections to be drawn from the area of consciousness studies.[20] The proposal sailed through by a 12-3 margin. This was an encouraging first step, and I naïvely wondered if the next, and more critical hurdle, would be as easily over-come. This would entail the proposal being ratified by the full music faculty, consisting of over a hundred colleagues. Since, generally speaking, proposals that passed the curriculum committee would tend to be rubber stamped by the full faculty, and the period following the initial committee vote was silent, I could not resist getting my hopes up. Several uneventful weeks passed. And then, a few days prior to the big vote, all hell—or perhaps from another vantage point, all heaven—broke loose.

It began with a colleague raising entirely reasonable questions about the validity of students sitting in silence during class time, how meditation might be graded in a credit-bearing academic class, who would be qualified to provide meditation instruction, and precedents for this work at other institutions. I replied to each of these concerns, pointing out that class time spent in group meditation was relatively small (although students would be expected to sustain regular individual practice outside of class), a wide-range of assessment criteria—including the same kinds of reading, writing, and discussion elements found in conventional classes—would factor into grading, that local meditation centers would be among the instructional resources tapped, and the overarching movement afoot to bring this work into the academic sector. I had also formed a cross-campus advisory committee of colleagues interested and experienced in this work who would contribute.

It did not take long, however, for the exchange to escalate in intensity, with a handful of faculty members mounting a sustained attack against the proposal, while a smattering of others expressed support. I was up late most every evening replying to the latest emails that were forwarded to the faculty listserve. I was struck early on by the fact that resistance and support did not break down according to any sort of anticipated party lines. Colleagues from areas generally thought of as more conservative in the field were as likely to express support as resistance, with important advocacy coming from key faculty in the orchestral ranks. One declared that this was a "cutting edge idea at the forefront of educational thought." In response, someone from another area, evidently concerned about what might seem to be a return to the educational experiments of the 1960s, complained that "this would set the School back 50 years!" While an otherwise perfectly legitimate expression of an individual predilection for keeping education current, that this faculty member's academic focus was on music of 200 years ago confounded the issue considerably. Not to be outdone, another colleague decried the proposal by proclaiming "one could accomplish the same thing (as meditation) with Prozac!," further adding to the lively and imaginative nature of the discussion.[21]

Some of the more perplexing remarks aside, a high point in the dialogue came when a highly respected colleague declared to the full faculty that this was one of the very few meaningful dialogues about the educational process that he had experienced in his entire academic career. When the room erupted in applause, not only did I feel encouraged about the prospects for a favorable vote, but by the possibility that I may have made a contribution far more important than the proposal in question by catalyzing penetrating dialogue and thinking in a field in which such has long been absent. Following a protracted debate that riveted the school for a period of weeks, the curriculum passed by close to a two-thirds majority.

In many ways, this book is a commentary on the Jazz and Contemplative Studies curriculum and its broader ramifications since not only would it open up new horizons in my own work and what could be offered to our jazz students, it also provided a template, one with the improvisation-meditation interplay at its core, for crossing the exterior-interior divide that could be applied across fields, and which in my view represents the future of education.

Weaving Tradition-specific and Trans-traditional Threads

It was only in retrospect that a particularly significant ramification extending from the establishment of the Jazz and Contemplative Studies curriculum would come into view. This involves the delicate balance between what might be called *tradition-specific* and *trans-traditional* engagement that is central to both contemporary musical and spiritual life. Just as today's musicians navigate their ways through an ever-expanding range of influences, practices, and pathways, today's spiritual landscape presents an equally exciting, if daunting, array of options that the increasing number of individuals who identify as spiritual (whether religious or not) encounter. And just as tradition-specific grounding in music, particularly when it encompasses the process-structure breadth of jazz, can provide a strong foundation that supports trans-traditional musical journeys, tradition-specific spiritual grounding can uphold the same function when it comes to trans-traditional spiritual explorations. By trans-traditional spirituality, a concept about which Robert Forman has elaborated extensively,[22] I refer to penetration beyond the boundaries of a traditional spiritual pathway not only during the moment of spiritual practice but in one's overarching vision, where the totality of practices and knowledge of our time are seen as potential sources of inspiration and guidance. While this orientation may sound exemplary of a contemporary spiritual sensibility, particularly to those within the steadily growing constituency that self-identifies as spiritual-but-not-religious, it is important to recognize both benefits and challenges inherent in it, two of which are common to trans-traditional musical growth.

On one hand, access to diverse spiritual and musical resources may enhance growth simply due to the possibility for engagement with a broader methodological scope. It is also important to recognize that trans-traditional engagement has always been an organic part of musical and spiritual evolution, even when access to diverse sources was far less than it is now. In other words, even the most seemingly intact lineages are the result of contact with and melding of diverse influences. Mozart heard Turkish military music and it influenced his composing and thus European classical music; the confluence of Mahayana Buddhism and Daoism spawned Zen. As advances in travel, information technology, and an increasingly global economy have made boundaries between cultures and knowledge radically more porous in today's world, it would be inevitable that this kind of syncretism accelerate.

The result of which are two significant challenges. The first is likely obvious, having to do with tendencies toward "superficial skimming," where musicians and spiritual aspirants, having access to an unlimited spectrum of options, end up cobbling together a "bit of this and a bit of that," thus compromising the regular practice and focus in a lineage that can be the source of deep grounding. *Many shallow wells*, a Zen proverb reminds us, *do not yield water*. At the same time, the opposite extreme, where seclusion in a particular pathway renders one oblivious to the broader world, can be equally limiting.[23] The plight of many classical musicians, whose process scope is confined to interpretive performance, is a musical case in point, with the many instances of religious fundamentalism revealing a commonly acknowledged parallel in spiritual life. We will see, in fact, that the interior mechanisms of these predilections are remarkably similar.

A second challenge of trans-traditionalism, while arguably the basis for the first, may not be as evident. This has to do with the potentially compromised conceptual scope that frames musical and spiritual journeys. Tradition-specific sources tend to be repositories for more complete accounts of interior-exterior wholeness, even if sometimes shrouded in dogmatic misinterpretations, than those that often emerge from trans-traditional engagement. I concur with Wilber and other integralists who contend that, while progress may result from engagement with transformative practices regardless of worldview, when grounded in a comprehensive account of the relationship between individual consciousness and cosmic totality, progress may be optimal.[24] Therefore, in the forging of a spiritual-but-not-religious identity, which I regard as an important if partial evolutionary stride, liberation from dogma may also have severed connections with deep principles along these lines that might be unearthed not by retreating from traditional lineages but by penetrating more deeply into them. In music, traditional lineages are where deep processes and structures in the musical world, which will be examined as grounded in transcendent dimensions of consciousness, tend to be housed.[25] Jazz's rhythmic and collective improvisatory foundations, and European classical music's repository of composed repertory, are primary examples. I believe an integral musical vision, similar to its spiritual counterpart, has the capacity to retain sight of these and other treasures while at the same time promoting wide-ranging creative confluence. Moreover, it reveals that depth in both realms is mutually dependent; one's apprehension of traditional richness is directly predicated on contemporary vitality and individuation, which is equally enhanced by tradition-specific grounding.

I consider myself deeply fortunate to have had strong tradition-specific and trans-traditional grounding in both my musical and spiritual pursuits. In music, jazz has provided me with a tradition-specific base that has significantly informed, and been informed by, broader improvisatory and compositional excursions and trans-traditional musical studies. My studies in European classical music are also important to this base. In my spiritual journey, I encountered Integral Theory—which is unmatched as a trans-traditional resource—after many years of grounding (which continues to evolve) in a Vedantic meditation lineage taught by His Holiness Maharishi Mahesh Yogi. What has come to be known as Maharishi Vedic Science provides not only an elaborate system of transformational practices, including foundational and advanced meditation methodologies among a wide range of psychosomatic modalities, but a conceptual framework that presents among the most extraordinary accounts of cosmic wholeness and interconnectedness that I have encountered. At the core of this framework is Maharishi's commentary on the Rig Veda called the *Apaurusheya Bhāshya*, from which extend extraordinary insights into the role of human creativity and consciousness in fathoming that reality.[26] Grounding in this tradition-specific vision has been key to my gaining fluency with the trans-traditional, integral vision, and in certain instances to my ability to critically examine and recommend modifications to it.

Conceptual and Practical Ramifications

To gain a brief look at both conceptual and practical ramifications of this grounding:

Among the most important aspects of the integral vision is its acknowledgment of the nondual relationship between human consciousness and the cosmic wholeness. The Sanskrit term *advaita* translates as "not two," meaning that there is no separation between individual and universe in the broader scheme of reality. Just as a wave is a localized manifestation of the ocean, individual consciousness is similarly inseparable from the cosmic intelligence that gives rise to the entire creation. *Yoga*, while often reduced to physical postures, refers to the union of wave with its eternal source, or personal self and transcendent Self. While nonduality in one form or another is central to most of the world's wisdom traditions, the Vedantic lineage of India may provide among the most expansive and intricate accounts of it. In his chronicling of the strong influence of Vedanta on American culture, Phillip Goldberg suggests that it is because of the nondual foundations of this lineage, an idea common to highly diverse traditions, that it elicits ecumenical embrace.[27] When Ralph Waldo Emerson, who was deeply impacted by his study of Vedanta, states "the currents of the Universal Being run through me; I am part or particle of God," he could be speaking from most any spiritual or religious perspective.[28] In no way is this to succumb to a naïve perennialism that overlooks significant differences between religions, but rather to identify a unifying precept in which, exemplifying an integral perspective, difference is situated within an overarching wholeness of nondual consciousness.

Unfortunately, the nondual premise is not nearly as prevalent as it might be in much integral discourse—the day-to-day conversations and publications that fall under the heading "integral."[29] I believe this reflects an imbalance in the trans-traditional/tradition-specific interaction, with greater emphasis on the first at the expense of the second, which again is consistent with the spiritual-but-not-religious movement in contemporary society. Let us examine a particularly promising practical application, one that is intimately linked with jazz, that extends from the nonduality premise to illustrate its importance in the broader educational and societal transformation.

Central here is the idea of intersubjective or collective consciousness. Jazz musicians commonly report a melding of artists, listeners, and environment in peak, improvisatory performances, as if they become "one mind," or a single creative organism that is unified by a common creative, or spiritual, thrust. Meditators commonly report experiences along similar lines, where group practice tends to elicit deeper experiences than those invoked in individual practice. An emergent body of research on collective meditation may provide empirical support for this. Among the most compelling studies involves a project convened in a large urban area involving 4,000 meditators from across the nation and world who gathered for a two-month period in the heat of the summer, when crime is at its peak, with the prediction being that a group this size would enliven coherence and harmony in the environment resulting in decreased crime. With the cooperation of public officials, several parameters of quality of life were measured during the length of the program, showing that not only reduced crime, but significantly reduced accidents and illness occurred during this period. When the program ended, and practitioners returned to their homes, the results lingered slightly, and then the numbers returned to normal.[30]

That this and other studies, including several that suggest collective meditation may quell fighting in war-torn regions, have been published in a number of peer-reviewed journals suggests strongly that the phenomenon warrants serious consideration for further research and application.[31] The basic theoretical premise is that consciousness, contrary to a materialist perspective, is not localized within the individual psychophysiology but in fact is a collective, intersubjective phenomenon, and that enlivenment of this intersubjective field can radiate positive effects in the environment. Some have even postulated that this could emerge as a possible antidote to terrorism, and in chapter 12 even more far-reaching ramifications will be considered.[32]

Although there is no denying the provocative nature of this idea, it is difficult to imagine a clearer example of the role of "anomalies"—findings or possibilities that defy accepted premises—which Thomas Kuhn identifies as catalyzing the paradigm shifts that have been central to "scientific revolutions."[33] In one discovery after another, receptivity to anomalous possibilities by one or a few innovators—as opposed to kneejerk resistance by the majority—has been seen as key to progress. This receptivity, and thus potential for innovation, tends to be weak and needs to be enlivened in education and society if the full potential of human creativity and consciousness is to be harnessed. Here a continuum might be noted that illustrates the intimate connection between conceptual framework and practical exploration and application.

From the conventional scientific materialist standpoint that is prevalent in the academic world, the idea of collective consciousness is completely anomalous; an untenured assistant professor or doctoral student would be wise to keep quiet about any interest in this area. From the standpoint of prevailing integral discourse, where general receptivity to intersubjectivity is found, the idea of harnessing its practical ramifications remains nonetheless peripheral; mention is scarce, for example, of group meditation studies even if overall interest in meditation is widespread.[34] From an integral perspective that is grounded in the nondual relationship between individual consciousness and cosmic wholeness, receptivity to this possibility increases dramatically, because now a conceptual backdrop of sufficient scope is in place that not only easily accommodates the idea of collective mind, but is also able to view it as *both* an emergent property of individual consciousness and, more significantly, a more foundational stratum of cosmic wholeness from which individual consciousness differentiates. Here it is noteworthy, then, that the aforementioned collective meditation projects are not only grounded in the practical methodologies brought to light by Maharishi Mahesh Yogi, but in the conceptual account of nondual wholeness he has articulated that illuminates this among other practical applications that might be possible.

The point is not to endorse a particular meditative pathway or philosophy but rather to underscore important principles that will undergo elaboration throughout the book. Foremost among them is that overarching worldview directly shapes where we look for solutions to problems and avenues for progress, and also what doors remain habitually closed to further exploration. I view the meditation/intersubjective consciousness relationship as among the most promising and exciting ideas of our time, but unless the conceptual backdrop against which conventional and nonconventional ideas alike are considered expands beyond what generally prevails, this and other possibilities will not receive adequate attention. In chapter 4, intersubjective consciousness will be considered as one among roughly 10 consciousness-related phenomena that have been subjected to rigorous scientific study and issue near fatal challenges to materialism while strongly compatible with the integral nondual vision. Unfortunately, the academic world tends to be hostile to anomalous findings or ideas, and this research therefore minimally informs higher education discourse.

Were the academic world a site where the most penetrating thinking and dialogue about the broader purposes of education and human potential prevailed, in essence an environment predicated on critical investigation of worldviews—including its own—I believe much greater receptivity to these and other challenging possibilities would be found. Here an axiom might be stipulated as a guide: The more expansive the inquiry into the farthest reaches of human nature and reality, the broader the spectrum of practical exploration that might ensue.

Ultimate Reality and Meaning as Gateway for Nondual Discourse

The Society for the Study of Human Ideas on Ultimate Reality and Meaning, or URAM for short, has been formed to promote this wide-ranging inquiry.[35] By providing a forum for open exploration of the biggest questions of human and cosmic existence, URAM invites individuals to come together from widely varying perspectives and, much like jazz's relationship with the broader musical world, transcend their respective entryways and realize the enlivened meaning, sense of purpose, and understandings that stem from this quest. The realization of spirituality and science, long at odds with one another, as self-transcending entryways that unite in a common wholeness is among the important manifestations that might stem from URAM inquiry, particularly when conducted from an integral perspective. The possibility of an intersubjective consciousness, dimensions of individual consciousness that transcend the physical body, capacities for remote cognition, and the many other phenomena that—sometimes classified under the heading "psi"—have been studied and pose strong ramifications for scientific and spiritual understanding alike might shift from anomaly to avenue for progress.

Humanity has reached a juncture where solutions to the unprecedented challenges it faces will only come from full-out investigation of the farthest dimensions of human nature and creative and spiritual potential. URAM inquiry may thus be considered as important to sustainability and progress as the multitude of environmental, economic, and sociocultural interventions that are also essential.

To be sure, not all readers will be inclined toward URAM inquiry, with detractors found even within the integral community. Integral theorist Steve MacIntosh, for example, is explicit in his convictions that the biggest questions about ultimate reality should be relegated to the confines of religion, with Integral Theory instead concerning itself with philosophy.[36] Not only—the thinking goes—does this broader inquiry invite dogmatic interpretations, examples of which one does not have to look far to find, presumed limitations in the capacity of human consciousness to fathom the deepest mysteries of human existence and cosmic reality may suggest that time and energy are more fruitfully invested elsewhere.

With the greatest respect for these concerns, I believe they reflect a limited vision and that the way forward is not to evade URAM inquiry but to embrace it as fully as possible. For one thing, even if this kind of investigation risks dogmatic interpretations, the decision to impose boundaries on what ought and what ought not comprise integral (or any kind of) exploration is rooted in its own metaphysical assumptions about the nature of reality and human consciousness. To deny URAM inquiry may be to supplant a familiar dogmatic risk (e.g., fundamentalist religion) with one whose myopic tendencies may remain hidden but no less problematic. We will shortly consider the materialist science worldview as an example. Many in the liberal population, including those of the spiritual-but-not-religious persuasion, find exceedingly difficult the idea that science may be prone to a fundamentalism that is not only as rigid as that found in religion, but possibly as detrimental to the future of our world. An integral perspective reveals that extremism is possible in all fields, and ways this extremism may be rectified. An integrally informed approach to URAM reveals the solution to religious and scientific extremism not, as some would have it (particularly in regard to religion), to pull back from the respective domains but to deepen engagement in them in order that self-confining understanding opens up to self-transcending synthesis.

And, to address the second concern, even if there are limits to human understanding about the ultimate nature of reality, few would deny that humanity has likely not come close to any such threshold, and that with each increment of new understanding may extend insights and solutions important to sustainability. An example of which was considered a moment ago involving practical potentialities resulting from a newfound understanding of intersubjective consciousness.

Moreover, URAM inquiry need not be regarded as an attempt to delineate a single, static account that is to hold from here to eternity, but rather as an ongoing process of constructing provisional theoretical platforms that are subject to ongoing critical scrutiny and from which future exploration might follow. And if, indeed, human consciousness is inextricably linked to the cosmic wholeness, a tradition-specific precept that is also trans-traditionally compatible, as well as remarkably compatible with the expanded vision of science that the integral framework invites, then URAM inquiry inspired by this age-old precept is neither frivolous or useless but in fact a direct manifestation of the intrinsic urge in the human psyche to fathom its deepest and most expansive nature. To ignore, or worse, inhibit this inquiry—which it must be emphasized must entail both practice and study—may be tantamount to repressing the most foundational aspect of what it is to be human.

A New Kind of Jazz-inspired Swinging

Inasmuch as the degree of critical self-reflection possible is directly predicated on process breadth, the jazz-inspired integral framework may be among the most viable platforms for investigation of the biggest questions regarding human potential and reality—at a time when the need for such is unprecedented. Combining rigorous attention to technical and analytical detail, robust creative engagement through a rich, multilineal process scope, and deep penetration to the innermost dimensions of consciousness that is accessed through both parts-to-whole, improvisation-based and whole-to-parts, meditation-driven engagement, jazz enables a kind of *swinging* between scientific, artistic, and spiritual realms that charts the educational and societal terrain of the twenty-first century. This swinging not only delineates the outer boundaries of an expanded scope of human experience and growth, it also delineates within those boundaries a highly differentiated tapestry that renders the paradigm optimally transformative, inclusive, and self-critical. It provides awareness a powerful conduit through which it may flow and integrate rich strata of experiences, influences, and knowledge, in a single stroke not only accessing an unprecedented range of possibilities for growth, but also examining those possibilities from a wide-angle lens that is also uniquely capable of critically examining itself. The delineative scope of the model is matched by powerful diagnostic tools. Previously rejected anomalous ideas and possibilities—once relegated to the outermost fringes, if not altogether banished, of an impoverished collective imagination—may now assume center stage and be subject to close consideration as potential avenues to progress. Language-bound categorical attachments, including to jazz itself and the litany of other labels that compartmentalize the musical world, and those such as *science*, *spirituality*, and *religion* that uphold a broader compartmentalization, are dissolved, with the regions within wholeness they designated recognized as self-transcending gateways rather than self-confining destinations.

When this paradigm moves from music to the overall educational enterprise, it may then be transmitted to society at large, at which point the heightened moment-to-moment creative decision making processes of the adept jazz improviser in a trio or quartet format may come to characterize the creative decision making activities of the seven-plus-billion-member planetary improvising ensemble called Humanity.

Overview of the Book

Part 1 provides both a comprehensive introduction to the basic premises and tools of Integral Theory and a preliminary look at how they are illuminated from a jazz-inspired integral perspective. Chapter 1 introduces the Four Quadrants map of cosmic wholeness and corresponding levels, lines, stages, states, and types that are central to the theory. Chapter 2 explores improvisation as a parts-to-whole vehicle for all-quadrants integration. Chapter 3 explores meditation as a complementary whole-to-parts pathway toward the same goal. Chapter 4 considers the evolutionary dynamics by which individuals and systems achieve this integration over time, with special focus on conventional patterns in education and musical study that will need to be addressed if these areas are to uphold important roles in the broader integral revolution.

Part 2 undertakes a more comprehensive integral reading of jazz by examining it in terms of the processes, structures, and evolutionary considerations broached in part 1. Chapter 5 begins with a look at tendencies in academic jazz studies, which in inhibiting creative exploration—patterns that are directly inherited from the just-considered conventional musical study and education at large—deviates from the integral thrust of the jazz tradition in important ways. Chapter 6 probes the inner mechanics of the improvisation and composition processes that are core jazz, revealing each as contrasting, culturally mediated pathways to transcendent experience that are rooted in different models of temporal conception. Here we come to the processual core of Afrological and Eurological musical-cultural frameworks. The interactive dimensions of collective improvisatory creativity, drawing upon the principle of intersubjective consciousness, are examined in chapter 7, further underscoring the Afrological aesthetic. Chapter 8 turns to the issue of style development, revealing the evolution of the personal voice and collective style periods to be rooted in the same mechanics—the merging of first-person transcendent impulses, second-person sociocultural influences, and third-person exterior grounding. These considerations come together in chapter 9, where an integral reading of jazz sheds new light on the idiom's emergence as a powerfully syncretic force in the musical world, setting the stage for a closer look at how its self-transcending features may also impact the broader educational and societal landscapes.

Part 3 deals with paradigmatic change. Chapter 10 explores what an integral school of music would look like, one that harnesses the self-transcending capacities and not only bridges the gulf between musical study and the musical world, but provides a template for integral inroads beyond music. Chapter 11 goes into the particularly elusive nature of paradigmatic change in overall academe, providing a framework called Deep Inquiry that aims to catalyze an entirely new conversation and receptivity to integral principles. Chapter 12 moves from education to the planetary ramifications of these ideas, where a continuum of jazz-driven anomaly centering is considered that lays groundwork for a post-integral understanding of the musical world and human creativity and consciousness.

PART I

————————

CREATIVITY, CONSCIOUSNESS, AND THE INTEGRAL VISION

Overview

What is Integral Theory? What does it have to offer personal and collective development, particularly at this juncture in human history when questions about sustainability loom as never before? What are the prospects of integral approaches being adopted in education and society, and what might the new models look like? Why is jazz uniquely equipped as a catalyst for integral reform?

These questions launch an exploration of what I believe is among the most promising blueprints available for understanding and navigating our way through this complex moment in history. Synthesizing insights from an extraordinarily wide range of disciplines, Integral Theory offers an account of the nature of the human being, human development, and reality that is unprecedented in scope. As the preeminent integral philosopher Ken Wilber notes, by placing what "the various cultures have to tell us about human potential—about spiritual growth, psychological growth, social growth"—within a "composite, comprehensive map,"[1] Integral Theory both delineates wide-ranging vistas for growth as well as enables deep penetration into the practical and conceptual obstacles to change that often impair progress. Particularly prominent among these delineative and diagnostic capacities is the integral bridging of spirituality and science, the conventional polarization of which often suggests that the realms are paradigmatically irreconcilable. Integral Theory provides a framework that breaks this impasse. As will be seen, the improvisation-based art form of jazz makes important contributions to this and other integral unifying capacities, and in probing the integral features of the idiom, we will further see how this exploration in turn sheds new light on the integral framework itself.

23

While it is easy to be overwhelmed by the sheer expanse of the integral framework, I present in this opening section three primary lenses, or constituent maps, through which its basic premises may be readily grasped: structure, process, and evolutionary dynamics. Structure pertains to things, processes to activities, and evolutionary dynamics to the patterns that govern growth over time. These are inherent facets of the following one-sentence definition of the theory: *Integral Theory maps the inner-outer dimensions of human being and cosmic wholeness, the processes that promote navigation and integration of this wholeness, and the evolutionary dynamics by which systems evolve over time.*

The four chapters in this opening section are based in the three basic themes. Chapter 1 explores the inner-outer structural expanse in the form of the AQAL (pronounced ah-qwal) framework—the acronym for "all quadrants, levels, lines, states, and types"—that many integralists utilize as a central integral map. Chapters 2 and 3 take up the process realm through, respectively, improvisation-driven and meditation-driven integral growth. There these methodologies are seen as *writ large*, in other words, as anchors for, respectively, wide-ranging creative and spiritual engagement that will aid individuals and communities to navigate their ways through, and achieve oneness with, the inner-outer wholeness. The dynamics of how this evolution unfolds over time, with a particular emphasis on collective development within knowledge areas, will be the focus of chapter 4.

While the boundaries between the three lenses sometimes blur, with for instance structural criteria exhibiting process and evolutionary properties, I believe they nonetheless provide general categories within which the considerable detail that comprises the theory may be grouped and assimilated.

Therefore, while this opening section may be the most information-dense in the book, readers should not feel obligated to master all that is presented in it before proceeding to subsequent parts, but instead are encouraged to keep in mind the three overarching categories—which are contained in the one-sentence definition of Integral Theory—and how the concepts encountered fit within them. In so doing, they will have access to a basic framework that enables navigation of forthcoming material, much of which will reinforce the earlier concepts. It might be added that readers encountering Integral Theory for the first time need not feel disadvantaged, as the material is presented with no assumptions of prior conversance. The same holds for readers without formal musical backgrounds. Everyone has musical instincts and aptitudes, if not latent capacities for musical expression.

Chapter 1

The AQAL Framework

This chapter introduces the AQAL framework and closely related first-, second-, and third-person perspectives or realities as primary tools that map the interior and exterior dimensions of the human being and cosmic wholeness. The purpose of human development is to realize oneness with this totality, which is synonymous with growth of creativity and consciousness, or spiritual evolution. By gaining a sense of not only the overarching scope of this wholeness but also its highly differentiated nature delineated through the AQAL lens, we begin to grasp the inclusive and transformational power of the integral vision. We also gain an appreciation of the importance of process diversity in navigating this scope, to be taken up in the next two chapters, and the complex evolutionary dynamics inherent therein in the final chapter of this opening section.

Integral Structural Maps

The integral structural realm construed most broadly spans the interior (subjective experience) and exterior (objective, physical) dimensions of human nature and the cosmic totality—from galaxies, mountain ranges, and ecosystems to belief systems and structures in consciousness. It is important to emphasize the unified nature of this wholeness and the foundational role consciousness plays in it. "Kosmos"—spelled by Wilber to reflect Pythagoras' conception of the universe—is neither reducible nor epiphenomenal, as materialists would have it, to exterior, physical reality, nor is it adequately understood, as dualists hold, as consisting of ontologically separate subjective/interior and objective/exterior domains.[2] Rather, these are inextricably linked within a nondual wholeness, the capacity for oneness with—as posited by the world's wisdom traditions— is the driving force for human spiritual development. Spirituality, then, is not limited to interior experience and growth but involves interior and exterior integration, the very inner-outer synthesis that defines the creativity-consciousness relationship as previously noted. Unfortunately, the nonduality premise has not always assumed the centrality in integral discourse that it warrants, and in hopes of addressing this, I propose *general* and *strong* nonduality premises to bring a more nuanced approach to this realm. The first acknowledges the inextricable link between individual consciousness and cosmic wholeness; the second takes a further step and posits that individual creativity and cosmic creativity are rooted in the same underlying mechanics, an admittedly provocative proposition that I believe not only exhibits strong coherence on localized scales but poses extraordinary ramifications for creativity-consciousness understanding and development.[3]

The inner-outer integral scope enables entirely new approaches to emerge in specific disciplines as well as education at large. Underscoring this point in the field of ecology, Sean Esbjörn-Hargens and Michael Zimmerman note that whereas conventional "ecology and ecological discourse," in their emphasis on the physical environment, "have mostly excluded an explicit recognition of interiors and their development . . . Integral Ecology studies interiors in addition to exteriors (and) how those interiors develop within organisms in general and humans in particular."[4] The fact that the integral approach does not exclude exteriors but integrates them within a broader inner-outer scope—thus exemplifying the integral principle of "transcend and include"—cannot be overemphasized, for this will be key to the broader educational transformation that is needed.[5] As Esbjörn-Hargens, Gunnlaugson, and others point out, the integral approach, unlike other alternative educational visions, does not jettison conventional approaches but situates the best of these within an expanded and inclusive vision.[6] And as briefly noted in the introduction, what I propose as Integral Jazz Studies similarly differs from Conventional and New Jazz Studies by including their terrain within a broader interior-exterior scope.

The AQAL Framework

The integral structural range is commonly mapped through a model Wilber calls AQAL, which is short for *all quadrants, lines, levels, states,* and *types. Quadrants* pertains to his Four Quadrant map of the cosmic wholeness. As Wilber emphasizes, this is useful as long as one keeps in mind the age-old adage that "the map is not the territory," but rather a representation of the territory. As illustrated in Figure 1.1, *Upper Right* pertains to exterior, objective reality, *Lower Right* to interobjectivity, *Lower Left* to intersubjectivity, and *Upper Left* to interior, subjective realms. Inasmuch as

INTERIOR STRUCTURES	**EXTERIOR STRUCTURES**
UPPER LEFT: "I" • Individual, subjective interior • 1st person	**UPPER RIGHT: "It"** • Individual, objective exterior • 3rd person
LOWER LEFT: "We" • Collective, inter-subjective interior (can also be exterior) • 2nd person	**LOWER RIGHT: "Its"** • Collective, inter-objective exterior • 3rd person

Figure 1.1 Four Quadrants (after Wilber).

the Quadrants are interpenetrating—within each one can locate all four—they are best understood in relationship with one another. The individual physiology, for example, is an objective, exterior structure, represented by the Upper Right, in relationship to the overall environment, which is a collective, interobjective exterior structure corresponding to the Lower-Right quadrant. Right-hand quadrants pertain to exteriors, left-hand quadrants to interiors. The Lower Left represents the intersubjective realm of experience that results from the collective interactions between human beings, thus taking us from the physical, exterior domains of Upper-Right and Lower-Right quadrants to more interior dimensions. The Upper-Left quadrant represents even further inward terrain of individual, subjective reality, including cognitive, emotional, intuitive, sensory, and transpersonal or transcendent experience.[7] Optimal human development—growth of creativity and consciousness—entails achieving "oneness with all quadrants," or the full interior-exterior scope of cosmic wholeness.[8]

First-second-third-person Perspectives

The quadrants are commonly condensed to first-, second-, and third-person perspectives or realities, with third-person pertaining to the objective/physical realm, second-person to the intersubjective/sociocultural, and first-person to the interior-subjective.[9] Wilber's reference to these as the "three faces of Spirit" reflects the nondual perspective of the infinitely diversified universe as manifestations of *lila*, or what Vedantins call cosmic "play." First-second-third-person realities are primordial differentiations within this play that are the basis for the "Big Three" domains of, respectively, spirituality, art, and science that thinkers through the ages have acknowledged as pillars of human endeavor.[10] That the present analysis differs from those of Wilber and other integralists in its first-second-third-person correlations ought not obscure the foundational importance ceded to these realms from both integral perspectives. Whereas the tendency is to link first-person with art, second-person with spirituality, and third-person with science, I equate first-person with spirituality and second-person with art (and maintain the third-person/science correlation); the rationale for this will be taken up in chapter 3.[11] Most important is that because it spans inner-outer wholeness, engagement with spiritual, artistic, and scientific realities promotes the oneness noted previously that is characteristic of optimal growth. Whereas exclusion of spirituality, marginalization of the arts, and an emphasis on science and scientific approaches characterize conventional education, integral education is predicated on the balanced interplay of the three realms, both within a given field and across the overall educational spectrum.

Quadratic and Quadrivium Applications of the Quadrants

It is important to understand two applications of the Quadrants, which can also apply to corresponding first-second-third-person perspectives (even if the terminology used is quadrant oriented). Wilber originally conceived the Quadrants from what in retrospect may be called a *quadratic* vantage point—that is, a delineation of the infinitely differentiated regions of cosmos that emerged within the universal wholeness. This may be thought of as a whole-to-parts perspective. More recently, a *quadrivium* perspective has entered the integral conversation as a way of mapping the capacity for a given field, or developmental line, to achieve all-quadrants integration from a parts-to-whole angle.[12] So whereas the quadratic application illustrates the diversity that arises from unity, the quadrivium application illustrates how any given part of that diversity, which in the present analysis will pertain to a given area of the knowledge base, serves as a pathway that connects with that wholeness to achieve all-quadrants integration. A quadratic map or application will therefore begin with Upper Left—in that, as will be seen, interior, subjective experience at its core is most directly aligned with cosmic wholeness—and proceed in a counterclockwise direction to reveal how Lower-Left, Lower-Right, and Upper-Right domains cumulatively unfold (e.g., Lower Left integrates Upper Left, Lower Right integrates Lower and Upper Left) from this wholeness. Quadrivium applications will conversely begin with Upper Right, exterior, objective reality and proceed in the opposite direction to show how exteriority can open up to interior-exterior unity. And in terms of the three perspectives or faces of spirit: Quadratic maps move in a first-second-third-person direction, quadrivium maps proceed third-second-first. In the next chapter we will consider a complementary way of visually representing all-quadrants integration.

A brief look at the Quadrants and corresponding first-second-third-person realms in terms of jazz will illuminate the capacities of the idiom to play a key role in this integration. Approaching this from a quadrivium perspective, where movement around the quadrants begins with Upper Right and proceeds in a cumulative, clockwise direction: The neurophysiological and technical aspects of playing an instrument and stylistic norms of the idiom are examples of Upper-Right, third-person, exterior-objective phenomena. Lower-Right (also third-person, but now *interobjective*, exterior) phenomena include the pitch systems, rhythmic languages, formal structures, and other facets of the broader musical world. In exploring how a genre such as jazz opens its horizons to the broader musical landscape, we will—in addition to a process-based exploration—view key structural aspects of this in terms of music theorist Leonard Meyer's *syntactic* and *nonsyntactic* parameters.[13] Syntactic parameters are harmony, melody, and rhythm—or pitch-rhythmic language structures. Nonsyntactic elements include density, dynamics, timbre, tessitura, and silence. Different genres may be differentiated, from a structural perspective, in terms of their respective syntactic/nonsyntactic content and configurations. For example, the form of jazz known as *bebop* differs from the late-Romanticism of European classical music along some (but not all) harmonic parameters, and more dramatically along rhythmic lines, to note two syntactic differences. Prominent nonsyntactic differences include density and timbre. As awareness opens up from discipline-specific to intradisciplinary musical conception, thus moving from Upper-Right confinement to Lower-Right grounding, it apprehends syntactic and nonsyntactic building blocks in more fluid and diverse forms and thus is more able to navigate the mosaic of possibilities in the broader musical world.

Lower-Left, second-person (intersubjective) phenomena include the wide-ranging sociocultural factors that shape personal and collective style evolution as well as impact collective style evolution. The interactive structures and relationships that comprise a jazz group may also be considered part of the second-person, Lower-Left scope that has been of increasing interest in progressive business, medicine, educational, and other circles in recent years. Further creativity-consciousness, or all-quadrants development, thus involves enhanced receptivity to extramusical influences, which meld at subtle levels of consciousness with the expanded and more fluid syntactic/nonsyntactic grounding also characteristic of this growth.

Upper-Left, first-person (interior, subjective) phenomena include the rich emotional aspects of jazz and transcendent experiences commonly invoked by jazz artists. The drummer Ronald Shannon Jackson provides characteristic testimony of a heightened Upper-Left experience when he speaks of "a level of playing which we reach that is the same thing that (is achieved through) meditation and yoga." Merging "the physical, the spiritual and the mental," he continues, "the state I am talking about even transcends emotions. It's a feeling of being able to communicate with all living things."[14] The idea of a state that "transcends emotions" need not be construed as one that is devoid of feeling, but rather one that penetrates to the subtlest dimensions of feeling and over time enables the full range of human emotional capacities—from the joys, anxieties, inspiration, and interpersonal love of everyday life to the ecstasy and unconditional love for the entire cosmos that for many are invoked only occasionally—to be enlivened and flow in the untold ways that are possible. Jazz is a powerful conduit for this range of emotional experience.

The jazz tradition, as noted earlier, boasts a long legacy of leading innovators who engaged with meditation and other contemplative disciplines in order to more consistently invoke transcendence and integrate it in their work and lives.[15] Exemplifying all-quadrants, creativity-consciousness integration, this involves integration of the rich spectrum of exterior structural influences—including third-person syntactic and nonsyntactic elements in diverse and fluid configurations and second-person sociocultural influences—along with enlivened first-person experience. We will in the next two chapters begin our probing of how improvisatory creativity and meditation practice work in tandem to facilitate this all-quadrants, quadrivium synthesis, underscoring the idiom's transformational and unifying potential. We will also explore the ramifications of this from a nondual perspective, in which enlivened first-person inner experience is understood as the alignment of individual consciousness with cosmic intelligence that is the source of creation—at which point the boundaries between inner and outer collapse, save for their purpose as designations of entryways to this extraordinary wholeness.

Lines, Levels, States, and Types

Running through the Quadrants is a broad spectrum of *developmental lines*, which might be thought of as pathways, or grooves, that serve as channels for this kind of growth. These are very much akin to the educational psychologist Howard Gardner's notion of "multiple intelligences." Gardner posited that human intelligence is multifaceted, comprised of linguistic-mathematical, logical, kinesthetic, musical, spatial, interpersonal, and intrapersonal aspects, and that everyone has different propensities for each.[16] Thus, one can be highly developed along certain lines and less developed along others, which as Wilber elaborates at length makes it possible for an individual to consistently invoke deep experiences in meditation that are suggestive of significant transpersonal growth, yet be less developed within emotional, interpersonal, or other areas.[17] That individuals who display exceptional creativity, or experience what appear to be extraordinary episodes of transcendent awareness, may appear in other areas of life even dysfunctional does not therefore invalidate the peak moments invoked in certain lines of attainment; it simply confirms that considerable growth along one pathway can occur without commensurate growth along another. This supports the argument for line-rich programs of development. Here it is important to recognize that distinctions between lines and processes can blur, because processes are the means through which one progresses along any given line, and many lines—as will be seen with improvisation and composition in music—are at once pathways, thus structures, as well as processes. This, however, does not undermine the general utility of structure-process distinctions as a conceptual entryway into Integral Theory.

Developmental lines are not only individual phenomena but can manifest on collective scales as well, with every field of study, education at large, and society as a whole serving as developmental lines in that they are capable of growth toward more expansive, diverse yet unified evolutionary stages. Each of these, moreover, may be thought of in terms of what integralists, after Arthur Koestler, call *holons*, which are wholes within wholes—structures that at once subsume constituent structures and are in turn subsumed by composite ones.[18] Atoms are not only subsumed by molecules, compounds, and infinitely larger structures within the physical world, they are also in the opposite direction composite wholes that subsume increasingly miniscule subatomic phenomena. Jazz may similarly be thought of as a developmental line within music that exhibits holonic properties in being not only integrated within the broader developmental lines of the arts and the overall knowledge base, but also encompassing numerous constituent lines, including its pitch and rhythmic structures and improvisatory and compositional pathways. And because, as we will see, jazz is line-rich within its own borders, it has the capacity to significantly impact the broader domains within which it is a constituent part.

Next is the precept of *levels*, which are enduring developmental stages or structures that may be achieved within a given development line. As Wilber emphasizes, levels/stages are therefore not to be confused with the temporary glimpses of higher stages or levels of experience, which are *states*, along a given line that may be invoked, as in the peak experiences of consciousness noted earlier. Levels/stages are permanent stations of growth, states are fleeting episodes of experience that lie beyond one's current "center of gravity," or the prevailing station/level/stage of growth at any given point in one's development.[19] States are ephemeral while stages or levels/stages are enduring, and the consciousness line is among those in which distinctions between the two are most prominent. Indeed, as Rhea White and Michael Murphy have observed in sports, the desire to more consistently and permanently integrate transcendent experience, invoked in passing glimpses of transcendence during their respective forms of creative engagement, may underscore why jazz musicians, athletes, and many other individuals engage with systematic meditation practices.[20] It is one thing to invoke peak, transcendent experiences occasionally, it is another is to permanently integrate this expanded awareness so that one's work and life are grounded in a higher stage development, or higher center of gravity.

Types pertain to qualities such as masculine and feminine that may be identified within a variety of disciplines and which manifest on exterior and interior scales.[21] Collective, improvisatory, modal music making will be seen as a manifestation of the feminine and also what George Lewis identifies as an "Afrological" wave within the musical landscape. Heide Göttner-Abendroth echoes the views of other feminist thinkers who surmise that artistic expression in matriarchal societies tended toward collective, spontaneous, improvisatory, and inclusive approaches.[22] In contrast, individual, compositional, tonal (and post-tonal) musical creativity, as well as the interpretive performance tradition that it has spawned (which while often collective, as in string quartets or symphony orchestras, is predicated on works that were created individually) may be seen as a manifestation of the masculine and correlated with the "Eurological" wave.[23] Jazz, while at its core an Afrological phenomenon, uniquely straddles these contrasting and complementary musical types/waves, and has thus evolved a composite structural expanse that exhibits strong properties of the differentiated wholeness we will see as characteristic of integral evolutionary trajectories. This will be viewed in terms of both the idiom's pitch and rhythmic languages, the first not only encompassing but also integrating a formidable portion of the modal/tonal/post-tonal spectrum of the musical world, the second encompassing, among other features, the notion of *time feel* or *groove* that is among the most pervasive facets of global musical practice. The origins of this latter feature in African and African American musical cultures is illuminated by what Jeff Pressing called "Black Atlantic Rhythm,"[24] perhaps the most recent significant manifestation of which has prompted Guthrie Ramsey to declare ours the "Age of Hip Hop."[25] Jazz's important role in the delivery of Black Atlantic Rhythm to the global musical landscape will be considered as fundamental a contribution to cross-cultural syncretism as the idiom's improvisatory foundations. As will the fact that, among the thousands of musical genres that might be identified in the world, none combines the primary creative processes of *both* improvisation and composition to nearly the extent found in jazz.

In taking our analysis to the interior dimensions of the structural realm, we will correlate the emergence of the Afrological in contemporary musical practice with the emergence of the "divine feminine" that is increasingly prominent in contemporary spiritual discourse.[26] Collective improvisation reflects a decidedly feminine thrust, and while one need not look far for small ensembles centered in this kind of creativity—indeed, small groups that in one way or another improvise together comprise the most prevalent musical configuration in the global landscape—what has not yet emerged to any notable degree are large, stylistically open improvisatory frameworks. Drawing on my own work with this framework, I predict this musical embodiment of the divine feminine to be a defining aspect of the integral musical era.

In considering these surface features as manifestations of transcendent, or archetypal, feminine-masculine impulses, we will see that jazz embodies not only the broad interior-exterior expanse of the integral vision but the capacity for richly detailed analysis within that expanse. The idiom's intricate third-person/Upper-Right exterior aspects, fertile integration of second-person/Lower-Left sociocultural influences, and capacities for first-person/Upper-Left transcendent experience—or states—and uniting of improvisatory and compositional lines, along with corresponding Afrological/Eurological, masculine/feminine types, present powerful pathways for awareness to embark on an all-quadrants journey. The first-person dimension, moreover, is where the nonduality premise illuminates the extraordinarily broad scope of this inner-outer journey, even if it essentially renders these very notions dysfunctional. For the archetypal impulses that originate in the innermost realms of consciousness, as Richard Tarnas' massive analysis of the relationship between human experience and planetary alignments shows, correlate with cosmological configurations, to the point where the boundaries between cosmos and psyche, and exteriority and interiority, disappear. When he asks—"What could be more *outer* than cosmos? What more *inner* than psyche?"[27]—he illuminates the limitations in language in depicting the nondual oneness of reality. He also may delineate the next major frontiers of scientific and spiritual inquiry.

Nonetheless, we do the best we can with these language-bound descriptions of reality, just as we do with musical genre categories. Jazz, having long honed its category-transcending properties—where categories are realized as entryways to a broader wholeness—gives rise to an integral vision that applies these principles across fields. And as will be shortly considered when we turn to process, improvisation and meditation are key vehicles for this.

Structures in Consciousness

Let us conclude our structural overview with a brief look at structures in consciousness. Here Maharishi Vedic Science illuminates core principles. First is the understanding of consciousness as consisting of a personal, relativistic *self*, which is the rational mind that guides much everyday thinking and action, and a transcendent *Self* that is its unbounded, non-localized source. In transcendent or heightened states of consciousness, the self merges with the Self; in ordinary consciousness, the self instead becomes bound or overshadowed by relativistic *objects of perception*, which are thoughts, feelings, actions, or sensory perceptions. The merging of self and Self in heightened states represents a *self-referral* condition of consciousness; the disconnection between self and Self, resulting in bondage to relativistic objects, represents an *object-referral* condition. Higher stages of consciousness development involve the enduring capacity for self-referral, self-Self union to be sustained even in the midst of the most turbulent engagement with objects of perception. Integralists have noted that these stages—three most prominent among which are *subtle, causal,* and *nondual*—have been acknowledged in a wide range of spiritual traditions across the world. Chapter 3 will go into these points more fully.

Among the ramifications of this analysis are its enhanced delineative and diagnostic faculties, both central to paradigmatic change as noted earlier. This reveals the surface fragmentation and inhibited creativity-consciousness process breadth of conventional paradigms as overlying manifestations of underlying object-referral proclivities that result from the divide between personal and transcendent Self. Integral paradigms, on the other hand, will be seen to exhibit integrative, process-rich surface features that are grounded in underlying self-Self union. Where the integral perspective truly shines, moreover, is in its capacities to illuminate second-person connecting realms in which the respective tendencies manifest in contrasting sociocultural patterns of perception and practice. For example, the process dearth that characterizes the surface of the conventional musicianship paradigm of musical study will be seen as underpinned by attachments to second-person culturally mediated notions of time, interaction, and meaning, which are further rooted in the self-Self split in the first-person domain. The overlying integration and breadth of the integral jazz paradigm will be seen as optimally conducive to contrasting culturally mediated perspectives and first-person self-Self integration.

Summary

While there is nonetheless a lot to grasp in this consideration of the integral structural scope, a jazz-inspired integral perspective brings these diverse facets together within a single, coherent framework that is readily apprehended, vivifying Wilber's reminder that all of these aspects "are, right now, *available in your own awareness*."[28] While quadrants, lines, levels, states, and types may manifest in external forms, they are also interior phenomena that, as creativity and consciousness develop, become increasingly clear, accessible, and subject to attention for further growth. The richly differentiated analysis of these facets enabled by the integral account may be seen as the identification of a powerful circuitry through which awareness can flow as it achieves interior-exterior union. Here the integral precept of scope, nuance, and coherence may be underscored—that among the ways integral theory excels is not only by mapping the overarching interior-exterior spectrum of human nature and cosmic wholeness, but also in illuminating rich differentiation within that spectrum and patterns that, manifesting on both local and global scales, reveal this wholeness to be extraordinarily coherent. The purpose of human existence is to connect with the cosmic wholeness, which means rendering the various lines of engagement that comprise human life as self-transcending pathways that lead toward this end. Humanity has lost sight of this goal, and the extent to which it is restored—which again must happen in our educational systems—is directly predicated on the extent to which awareness is able to swing freely between the most detailed and localized concerns of everyday life and the biggest questions of cosmic reality.

As much as jazz may help delineate this expanded vision from a structural angle, it is the idiom's process realm where this spectrum is traversed and the idiom's integral features and transformational capacities become most evident. As we turn to this realm, we encounter a cumulative thrust in this analysis in that, because process and structure are intimately related, one cannot broach one without bringing the other into play. Therefore, in probing the process domain we will not ignore structure but gain an expanded understanding of it.

Chapter 2

Improvisation-driven Growth of Creativity and Consciousness

What is it about the jazz process scope that renders the idiom an integral transformational agent? This chapter replies to this question with an exploration of the improvisatory foundations of the jazz process spectrum, as well as more general process-related integral principles. As will be seen, it is not only that jazz is among the most improvisatory art forms that exists, but also that its improvisatory core supports and integrates an exceptionally wide range of creative engagement, including composition, performance, and various types of theoretical inquiry. This poses important ramifications for not only musical growth but the overall educational enterprise, as aspects of this broad spectrum may be located in many if not all fields. Let us keep in mind that the purpose of engagement in any field from an integral perspective is to realize the field as avenue for all-quadrants, creativity-consciousness development. Jazz's improvisatory core underlies a wide creative spectrum that uniquely exemplifies this principle within and beyond the arts.

We will consider this improvisation-based spectrum as a *parts-to-whole* approach to all-quadrants, creativity and consciousness development, which when complemented by *whole-to-parts* meditation-driven growth, also an important aspect of the jazz tradition to be considered more fully in the next chapter, encompasses an even wider process template for this integration. We will further see that, also in line with integral precepts, inherent in both aspects of the jazz-inspired process scope are strong transformational and hermeneutic/interpretive aspects. In other words, improvisation and meditation have the capacity to not only elicit temporary shifts (states) and enduring growth (stages) in creativity-consciousness experience, but in so doing also open up new ways of understanding and perspectives. In this way, the two processes also uphold the delineative and diagnostic functions that are necessary for paradigmatic change.

We begin with a look at the prevailing orientation in integral process discourse, a key principle of which is that engagement with diverse epistemologies, or what is called "Integral Methodological Pluralism,"[1] is key to achieving interior-exterior, all-quadrants synthesis. Noting that improvisatory creativity, while exemplary of methodological pluralism, has eluded the attention of integral theorists, we then turn to the expanded horizons that comprise the jazz-inspired integral process scope. Here a complementary map to the Four Quadrants is presented that charts the all-quadrants growth of creativity and consciousness driven by this extended process scope. Distinctions between creativity as it occurs within and beyond the arts are among the insights revealed in the analysis and comprise the final section of the chapter.

Prevailing Integral Process Conceptions

The jazz-inspired integral perspective supports and extends upon a central principle in integral thought—that engagement with diverse epistemologies, or ways of knowing, hence processes, is key to traversing and uniting interior and exterior domains, which was examined in the previous chapter in terms of the all-quadrants or first-second-third-person synthesis. It is not enough to identify the terrain to be covered, nor even the routes—or developmental lines—along which one traverses that terrain; it is also necessary to access the process vehicles that are adequate for the various kinds of journeys to be made. Third-person objective reality is most directly fathomed through the objective, empirical epistemologies of science, second-person intersubjective reality through a variety of interactive and creative modalities (hence an important place for the improvised performing arts), and first-person subjective reality through meditation and other contemplative disciplines usually associated with the spiritual realm. These are just a few of the many processes or epistemologies that come under the umbrella of Integral Methodological Pluralism. In short, the more diverse the epistemological spectrum—the ways of knowing and being that comprise our daily existence—the greater the capacities for all-quadrants synthesis.

Among the benefits of this growth is the ability to transcend surface boundaries that commonly separate areas, including those such as spirituality and science that appear to be at such odds with each other, and understand even the most seemingly disparate realms as united in an overarching wholeness. Here is where the transcend and include principle,[2] key to the integral vision, comes into play, where penetration beyond surface features of a domain does not entail discarding that domain but situating it within a broader unity. We have already encountered this principle in the idea of style categories as self-transcending entryways into a broader musical ocean rather than self-confining destinations. And in connecting with that ocean, the stylistic entryway does not compromise its integrity, and in fact gains depth and vitality. The same holds for all fields of knowledge, with process breadth key to this level of engagement.

The process realm is thus of enormous importance in the integral framework, and in light of the emphasis Wilber and other integral theorists have placed on this principle, the idea advanced in the introduction that this area nonetheless has been overlooked in integral discourse may appear difficult to support.[3] If anything, the opposite problem might seem to be a more pressing concern, in that integralists identify such a broad process spectrum as useful, if not necessary, to personal growth that it can be difficult to select from this slate a manageable program of "Integral Life Practice" that suits one's needs and time constraints.[4]

We will begin to address this concern shortly, with further elaboration provided in the coming chapters. First, however, several points might be noted that support the idea that the process domain has not received the attention it warrants. For one thing, among the key aspects of AQAL—all quadrants, levels, lines, states, and types—no processes are included. Although there is no denying that process engagement is implicit in some of these facets, particularly developmental lines, the absence of process as one of these AQAL subheadings reflects and at least subtly reinforces a structural orientation.

Even more supportive of the case is a continuum of marginalization in integral discourse where within the general subordination of creativity and the arts, compositional forms such as painting, sculpture, and architecture in the visual arts receive greater attention than the performing arts, and within the performing arts, improvisatory creativity has been largely excluded. Therefore, I do not believe it unreasonable to conclude that while Wilber and other integralists at times offer powerful testimony regarding the transformational impact of the arts in human development, important facets of art making have yet to significantly inform these deliberations.[5] The omission of improvisation in music is particularly conspicuous given not only the ubiquitous role of this process in global musical practice, but also the ubiquitous place of music in world culture, and reflects an orientation whose limitations extend far beyond music. To exclude improvisation is to exclude an essential aspect of human nature and creative potential. The uniquely broad jazz process spectrum, unmatched in and beyond the arts due to its improvisatory foundations, both illuminates these shortcomings and expands the scope of Integral Methodological Pluralism.

The Jazz-inspired Integral Process Scope

> Integral Theory maps the interior-exterior scope of the human being and reality, the diverse processes that enable traversing and integrating this scope, and the evolutionary dynamics that govern this growth over time.

Central to this process scope is the interplay of parts-to-whole and whole-to-parts trajectories. The first is improvisation driven, the second meditation driven. Improvisation, in other words, motivates transcendence and holistic integration from immersion in activity, meditation from the unmanifest wholeness of silence. The richness and power of this interplay is further underscored when improvisation and meditation are understood not as isolated procedures but as anchors for corresponding systems of practice. Let us first provide working definitions of these two processes, to be further elaborated on in subsequent chapters (meditation in chapter 4, improvisation in chapter 6).

Improvisation may be defined as spontaneous creativity with little or nothing planned in advance. It is perhaps best understood in relationship to compositional creativity, which is essentially an ongoing planning endeavor. Whereas composition occurs in a series of discontinuous episodes than can span days, weeks, or months in the completion of a work, improvisation occurs in a single, continuous creative episode. Whereas composers usually work alone, improvisation—which can certainly happen in solitude—often occurs collectively. Whereas compositions are created at times and places that are different from when they are presented to audiences, improvisation involves simultaneous creation and performance/presentation.[6] In chapter 6 we will see that underlying these surface, exterior differences—the third-person domain—are more foundational distinctions at second-person cultural and first-person transcendent levels. The point is not that improvisation is superior to composition, and from an integral perspective we will see that both uphold important waves or lines of musical practice. Nor is this to deny that both lines have evolved from a common improvisatory ancestor. However, by understanding them as distinct means of expression and creativity/consciousness development, we can also organize them as part of a coherent system. Which brings us to what I call a *systematic* approach to improvisation as an anchor for the parts-to-whole, jazz-inspired process trajectory.

This includes multiple approaches to improvisation (e.g., style-specific, as in jazz, or Hindustani, or Baroque styles; stylistically open, or free, where no style parameters are set forth in advance), composition, performance, and various kinds of theoretical inquiry (harmonic analysis, historical, aesthetic, cognitive studies, and personal reflection). Lingering notions of improvisation as an undisciplined, whimsical, "anything-goes" kind of activity are thus dispelled and replaced by a rigorous framework of study and practice that—while certainly including robust, exploratory play—encompasses a wide spectrum of study. Inherent in this spectrum is the interplay between *emulative* and *exploratory* process functions that we will see are essential to all-quadrants, creativity-consciousness integration. Emulative activity reinforces normative knowledge and promotes skill development within a field; exploratory extends the boundaries of a field. While creativity is often seen in terms of a largely exploratory thrust, both are essential to integral development. "It is difficult to see how a person can be creative," states Mihalyi Csikszentmihalyi, "without being both traditional and conservative, and rebellious and iconoclastic."[7]

Meditation, a whole-to-parts methodology, is a procedure by which awareness experiences deeper dimensions of itself, sometimes described in terms of the merging of a personal self, that in ordinary consciousness has lost sight of its transcendent moorings, with the transcendent Self that is its source. We will consider a primary form of meditation to be silent, sitting practice, which serves as an anchor for a broader range of methodologies that might include contemplative approaches to reading, writing, creative expression, interpersonal relationship, and environmental communion. Hence, as a counterpart to systematic improvisation and its broad spectrum of creative engagement, systematic meditation practice encompasses a broad range of contemplative engagement. In chapter 3, I will identify as a further criterion for systematic meditation the grounding of practice in a particular contemplative lineage and its cultural and philosophical/theoretical roots, even if informed by the diverse spiritual influences that are inevitable in our times.[8] Most important to the present discussion is the breadth and synergistic interplay of the various contemplative activities that comprise the systematic approach.

To briefly preview the extramusical ramifications of this model: While the fact that different individuals have different needs will direct them to different aspects of the respective process spectrums, the complementary improvisatory/meditative anchors of the parts-to-whole and whole-to-parts interplay may provide a framework that helps organize the broad methodological scope of Integral Life Practice (ILP) into a manageable program. Most individuals will benefit from some kind of regular engagement with the two anchors (improvisatory creativity, either in or beyond the arts, and meditation) and may then select aspects of the respective process systems that serve their particular needs at a given time. We therefore begin to glimpse a response to the aforementioned concern regarding the often-overwhelming slate of growth practices that are recommended in ILP.

If the scope of improvisation-based and meditation-based trajectories is formidable in its overarching range, that within this range of diverse processes might be identified further richness—the just noted distinctions between improvisation/composition lines being a prominent example—further underscores the power of this process spectrum. This exemplifies the scope, nuance, and coherence that are key to the integral framework's transformational potential. Awareness thus has avail of a robust conduit through which it can flow in both parts-to-whole and whole-to-parts directions in its quest for all-quadrants, creativity-consciousness growth.

Let us now look at key indicators of this development.

Indicators of Creativity and Consciousness Development

Figure 2.1 shows creativity development to be measured in terms of what I call the three extrinsic "I's" of integral creativity: *invention, interactivity,* and *individuation. Invention* entails the capacity to generate and realize ideas. *Interaction* is characterized by heightened sensitivity, listening capacities, and ability to adapt spontaneously to one's environment. *Individuation* is the cultivation of a distinctly personal voice within a field. We will see that as an individual voice emerges that is grounded in, and reflective of, both contemporaneous and interior, transcendent dimensions, growth in this direction takes on self-organizing qualities. In other words, individuation elicits self-motivational and self-navigational (abilities to chart their own pathways) tendencies in practitioners, which in turn fuel further individuation.

Consciousness development is measured here in terms of self-realization, diversity intelligence, and critical inquiry faculties. Self-realization refers to the degree of transpersonal penetration as the self fathoms its true nature as an aspect of the Self that is the source of Being. Diversity intelligence pertains to capacities to experience and appreciate the multitude of connections—disciplinary, multidisciplinary, multiethnic/cultural, spiritual—as inextricably linked aspects of the ever-evolving self-Self structure. Critical inquiry involves the capacity to step back and critically examine both exterior phenomena and the subjective vantage point, again the self-Self union (or disunion) from which one engages in the analysis. Although our focus is on creativity and consciousness development as catalyzed by a given line or area of activity as it is approached integrally, the ramifications for broader growth in these dimensions are likely evident.

CREATIVITY			CONSCIOUSNESS		
Inventiveness	Interactivity	Individuation	Self-realization	Diversity awareness	Critical inquiry faculties
• generation of ideas • mind-body integration • craft development	• ability to adapt and respond to environment • listening capacities	• evolution of personal voice • self-organizing growth	• self-referential consciousness • heightened clarity insight, compassion, love, well-being, oneness	racial, ethnic, cultural, gender, spiritual, creative diversity awareness	• self-mediated • object-mediated • anomaly centering • reflection and self-organizing growth

Figure 2.1. Indicators of Creativity and Consciousness Development.

Let us consider how an integral view of these creativity-consciousness features expands upon, and sometimes modifies, conventional perspectives of them. Two general points may be noted at the outset. First, whereas the integral always embraces exteriors and interiors, thus the entire first-second-third-person (or all-quadrants) spectrum, conventional research tends to focus on exteriors at the exclusion of interiors. This leads to a second point, that conventional perspectives tend to therefore view areas in isolation, which is inevitable when phenomena are only considered in terms of exteriors, whereas the integral inner-outer synthesis enables an understanding of connections between phenomena. In this way, all facets of the creativity-consciousness spectrum are not only seen as interconnected, but more importantly, they are all enlivened in the parts-to-whole, whole-to-parts creativity-consciousness developmental thrust.

Creativity research, for example, with a few notable exceptions, tends to avoid transcendent experience, even though many creative practitioners—jazz musicians foremost among them—regard these dimensions as important aspects of the process.[9] Instead the focus is on "psychometric" problem solving, "biometric" correlations between mind and brain that are enlivened during creative activity, and "historiometric" influences of time and place on creativity, among other angles.[10] The integral viewpoint situates these within a more expansive framework.

Creativity research also exhibits exterior confinement when it limits itself to products at the expense of processes, as evident at times in conventional music education research.[11] A result, which is perhaps inevitable, is the tendency to assess creativity in terms of degree of "novelty," which is another exterior consideration that limits the broader significance of creativity as revealed in an integral perspective. I believe the novelty criterion is a kind of ontological blind alley that raises more questions than it answers and narrows the scope of considerations that come into play in our hopes to understand this important aspect of human experience and potential.

This becomes apparent when, from the integral standpoint being advanced, creativity is understood as much an interior process as an exterior result. From this perspective, we shift our gaze from product to transformational process and ongoing development, which does not neglect product but situates it within a broader range of considerations. The futility of the product/novelty premise is underscored in the recognition of the possibility that, in a given moment, the exact replication of an action, idea, or structure that one may have enacted previously may still be a profoundly creative act due to the fact it is rooted in an integrative, transcendent state of awareness that enables such an expression to manifest not as the result of conditioning but radical, mindful presence. While this argument, in a limited capacity, might be extended to illuminate creativity in interpretive performance of classical repertory, important distinctions might be noted—prominent among which are that the interpretive performer has no choice as to whether or not to play a given idea (which has already been fashioned by the composer), whereas the improviser does. This is not to suggest interpretive performance is devoid of creativity, a point that we will take up shortly.

Shifting our attention from exterior product to interior process, and its interaction with product, we are then also able to see the exquisite silence of *pure consciousness*,[12] in which there is no exterior product, as a form of creativity. Pure consciousness, to be explored more fully later, is the experience of nothing but consciousness itself, a state at once pristinely silent and devoid of mental content, yet radiantly wakeful. At this point the issue of whether or not something is creative is replaced by two more far-reaching, and in my view, productive principles: First is that everything is creative, and second is that creativity can be cultivated through diverse process engagement and corresponding structural study. Every facet of reality, or as Whitehead might term it, "occasion of experience," is creative. And creativity can evolve. And, therefore, instead of attempting to delineate parameters by which a given phenomenon might or might not be deemed creative, our attention goes more toward delineating parameters that define how individuals, and fields, may grow creatively.

When it comes to consciousness research, an integral perspective similarly cedes great importance to interior dimensions that tend to be neglected, if not downright dismissed, in conventional research. While it is interesting to note that a much more robust cadre of consciousness researchers who firmly embrace interiority is found in consciousness studies than creativity studies, "materialism of one sort or another," which Daniel Dennett describes as "a received opinion approaching unanimity" in academic circles, continues to overshadow nonmaterialist perspectives.[13] We will explore materialist and nonmaterialist perspectives further in the next chapter.

Diversity, included as noted earlier within the consciousness domain, also takes on broader dimensions from an integral perspective. Typically construed largely in terms of demographics (e.g., race, ethnicity, gender), diversity from an integral viewpoint also encompasses knowledge dimensions, which can be thought of in terms of processes and content. Integral Methodological Pluralism, considered previously, exemplifies epistemological or process diversity. Moreover, the integral perspective takes diversity to its innermost foundations, where inherent in growth of creativity and consciousness are tendencies to embrace, if not thirst for, engagement with diverse ethnic, racial, cultural, gender, intellectual, and other expressions. From a general educational standpoint, among the important ramifications from the integral perspective are that interdisciplinary and transdisciplinary exploration are intrinsic to learning models that encompass the process-structure scope necessary for creativity and consciousness growth, thereby establishing an interior foundation for multiethnic/cultural and other kinds of integration. This perspective yields particularly important ramifications for musical study given the urgent need for the field to broaden its monocultural horizons, and prevailing tendencies for such efforts to amount to little more than "superficial skimming" of diverse sources. "Multicultural music education," Terese Volk reminds us, ought not to be approached as "a musical supermarket" where students gain "a touch of this and a taste of that."[14] However, without establishment of the internal basis for genuine multicultural infusion—which requires at the very least the situating of improvisation studies at the core of the musicianship model, and ideally also incorporates meditation practice—the supermarket syndrome is inevitable. Diverse structural integration requires diverse process foundations (not just cursory exposure to improvising and composing). When these foundations are intact, musicians begin to perceive the multiethnic riches of the musical world, and their cultural backdrops, as just as intimately connected to their artistic growth as the influences of their own cultural heritage. To deny diversity is to deny a fundamental aspect of one's own being, which the premise of consciousness as nondual and intersubjective reminds us is more than a fashionable metaphor but a direct commentary on the very nature of consciousness.

Critical inquiry is another area within the consciousness domain for which an integral approach provides an expanded perspective. Much along the lines of John Dewey's perspective, we will view this as synonymous with critical *thinking* and critical *reflection*, sharing his view that these are essential aspects of educational development.[15] However, whereas conventional approaches to these areas tend to focus on third-person, objective-exterior thinking processes, with some second-person, intersubjective consideration, an integral approach is unique in both extending each of these domains beyond conventional parameters and, most notably, taking the critical reflection enterprise into the innermost, first-person dimensions of consciousness.

This can be understood in terms of the enlivenment of three kinds of critical inquiry faculties, corresponding respectively to third-person, second-person, and first-person realities, the totality of which is central to paradigmatic change. Rigorous engagement in the kind of wide-ranging, third-person/craft studies (technical and theoretical) that are characteristic of an integral approach allows familiar and new concepts and skills to bump up against one another, thereby dislodging conditioned patterns and yielding composite structures that shed new light on prior ones. I call this *object-mediated* critical inquiry. *Process-mediated* critical inquiry, second-person oriented, also upholds a kind of liberating function due to the sheer movement of awareness inherent in robust creative activity, which is exemplified in a systematic approach to improvisation. Most unique to the integral framework is first-person, *self-mediated* critical engagement. Here awareness takes recourse, through meditation, to a realm of consciousness entirely transcendent of mental activity.

Accordingly, whereas the conventional approach focuses on critical examination of one's own and others' beliefs and assumptions, an integral framework also involves penetration to *strata of consciousness that lie deep beneath those considerations.* How can critical reflection occur without access to domains of mental activity that underlie those at which ideas and convictions take hold? That conventional critical inquiry discourse has not posed this question suggests that it is deficient in the very enterprise it seeks to elucidate.

A view of critical inquiry from this expanded perspective may shed new light on debates among conventional researchers in the area. It supports the idea shared by Dewey that critical thinking is an inherent potentiality in human awareness, one that needs nurturing,[16] by revealing the capacity as directly related to the self-referral foundations of creativity and consciousness. In other words, the merging of the relativistic *self* with the transcendent *Self* that is its source, characteristic of transcendent or higher states and stages of creativity-consciousness development, is the basis for human self-awareness, of which critical inquiry faculties are a direct manifestation. This in turn supports the idea that development of these faculties may be generalized so that manifestation in one area might apply to another. Although, as Betty Anne Younker notes, recent decades have seen embrace of the view that critical thinking is field specific, with the recognition that "knowledge of subjects and not some general ability to think well differentiates experts and novices,"[17] the integral perspective's recognition of interior foundations points to underlying common ground. In no way, however, is this to suggest that field-specific knowledge is unnecessary to critical reflection in that field—as always, the integral vision cedes a place for the broadest range of engagement.

The interplay of the three approaches (object-/process-/self-mediated) contribute to a critical faculty that is particularly important to paradigmatic change—what I think of as *anomaly centering*. This involves shifting some idea, finding, or possibility at the outermost fringes of one's imagination to front and center where it can be critically scrutinized and either embraced as a platform for further exploration (which is highly unlikely as long as the anomaly remains uncentered), dismissed as nonviable, or tucked away for further consideration. As considered in the introduction to the present volume, Thomas Kuhn's analysis of scientific revolutions revealed receptivity to anomalous possibilities as key to important strides.[18] Here it thus interesting to note educational tendencies to herald discoveries of the past, yet impede the exploratory dynamism that gave rise to them. The parts-to-whole/whole-to-parts process thrust of the jazz-inspired integral framework provides a powerful means for rectifying this problem and upholding robust critical-inquiry faculties.

This process scope gives rise to an axiom that clearly distinguishes conventional from integral notions of critical thinking: *The extent to which practitioners may critically examine their work and the field at large is directly predicated on the extent to which engagement in a discipline situates that field within the broader knowledge base, which must always include the innermost dimensions of consciousness.*

Engagement in the parts-to-whole/whole-to-parts process scope therefore provides a unified framework in which important groundwork for critical thinking and the array of other creativity-consciousness faculties is established. That conventional academic institutions proclaim strong commitments to areas such as innovation, diversity, and critical thinking, but minimally recognize these as inextricably linked, underscores this point and suggests ways the integral framework can greatly impact the educational enterprise. This will become further evident as we consider in our overview of creativity-consciousness indicators how process breadth promotes structural breadth, a look at which underscores connections with the previous chapter.

Process Breadth Drives Structural Breadth

Music theorist Leonard Meyer's classification of basic musical elements into syntactic and nonsyntactic parameters provides a useful tool for understanding core structural facets in music that may also have wider applicability.[19] As noted in chapter 1, syntactic elements are harmony, melody, and rhythm—in essence, musical pitch-rhythmic structures. Nonsyntactic parameters include density, dynamics, timbre, register, and silence; these might be understood as upholding an expressive function that augments the structural function of pitch-rhythmic, syntactic elements. Different musical genres may be distinguished from one another according to their different configurations of syntactic/nonsyntactic elements. Jazz, for example, while sharing some syntactic common ground with European classical music in the realm of harmony, also differs significantly in this syntactic realm and even more in that of rhythm. It also differs along a number of nonsyntactic parameters. The pitch systems of Indian music and other traditions that divide the octave into more than the 12 chromatic tones of Western music represent further kinds of syntactic distinctions between wide-ranging genres.[20]

When process breadth is limited, awareness is confined to contact with syntactic and nonsyntactic elements in style-specific configurations, which is adequate to gain competency in a given genre, but little more than that. However, when the central pulse of the contemporary musical world is seen to lie not in discrete style regions but in their melding, this illuminates the need for a broader kind of access that enables transcendence (and inclusion) of boundaries. Here is where the jazz process scope excels, which sheds light on why the genre has been called the first world music. Or, as the composer György Ligeti has put it, jazz is most aptly defined as "a combination of things—it is not African, nor Irish nor French, not even American—it's everything all together, the first musical expression to be multicultural."[21] An even more nuanced conception enables appreciation of the syncretism Ligeti underscores, as well as the strong roots, notably its Afrological and African American foundations that he may not quite adequately appreciate, atop which Eurological and other streams were integrated, that make this syncretism possible, a syncretism for which process breadth is unquestionably central.

Jazz's rich parts-to-whole trajectory, which includes not only improvisation and composition, but also multiple approaches to these core modes of expression, promotes syncretism through contact with basic elements in diverse and fluid configurations. As a result, practitioners grounded in this process scope will inevitably penetrate beyond style boundaries, even if their final destinations may or may not fall within those boundaries. When meditation and thus whole-to-parts engagement is added, following the lead of many jazz innovators, capacities for expanded diversity and fluidity of perception are all the more enhanced. Musicians whose process spectrum is confined to interpretive performance, as has defined the majority of practitioners over the past two centuries in European classical music, have no such boundary-transcending capacities.

Meyer's syntactic/nonsyntactic distinctions also enable us to identify a useful process hierarchy. Improvisation and composition, considered earlier as differentiated lines, are now united in their classification as *primary* creative processes because they involve creating with all syntactic and nonsyntactic and elements. In other words, improvisers and composers can generate harmonies, melodies, rhythms, and infinite kinds of densities and textures. Interpretive performance, by contrast, where most parameters have already been fashioned by composers, often centuries and continents removed from performers' time and place, allows invention with only a few nonsyntactic elements (e.g., dynamics, tempo, timbre). Interpretive performance is thus characterized as a *secondary* creative process, the parametric basis for which enables us to counter arguments, such as that advanced by Carol Gould and Kenneth Keaton, that the more overt form of improvisation that occurs in jazz differs from the more subtle improvisation that occurs in fine interpretive performance only in degree, but not in kind.[22] In fact, because jazz improvisers manipulate all syntactic and nonsyntactic elements, and interpretive performers only a few nonsyntactic, the kinds of improvising differ paradigmatically—both in degree and kind.[23]

Also to be considered are analytical and technical studies as *ancillary* creative processes that promote primary and secondary creative development. Why are these creative to any extent? Because they involve profound ingenuity when it comes to deciding which areas to study, in many instances involving the fashioning of one's own exercises (for instrumental technique), and devising ways of integrating them into the resultant voice. The possibility will also be explored of individuals who, with grounding in primary and secondary creativity, focus on some area—such as scholarship—within the ancillary domain as a central career emphasis. When this focus is informed by substantive prior primary-secondary grounding, then the previously construed ancillary activity now becomes a site for primary and secondary creativity within its own horizons. This represents a very different scenario than generally occurs, where ancillary and secondary creativity assume center stage without such grounding. From an integral standpoint, the central purpose of analytical and craft studies is to serve primary creativity, not to assume centrality of their own.

Most important is that all three process realms are necessary to integral development, and the point is not to delineate a values hierarchy but rather a cognitive hierarchy that allows us to organize this process scope into a coherent and comprehensive system of study—that which comprises the systematic approach to improvisation.

The jazz-inspired integral process scope provides the tools for this inquiry and growth. In order to illustrate this new and expanded process and process-structure spectrum, a complement to the Four Quadrants will be in order. Whereas the current graphic excels in depicting the scope of wholeness from a structural, quadratic standpoint, it falls short in its capacities to show how process breadth can drive the growth in a given area of endeavor—or developmental line—toward all-quadrants, quadrivium integration. I believe the complementary map excels in this regard.

A New Jazz-inspired Integral Map

Figure 2.2 reconfigures the quadrants by not simply aligning them vertically, but also depicting them as part of cumulative developmental stages, or levels, in creativity and consciousness growth within a given field. In other words, any discipline may be realized as a parts-to-whole vehicle for all-quadrants or third-second-first-person integration (listed in reverse numerical order to represent the parts-to-whole trajectory), and this map traces its stages of progression. Each underlying level represents a more expansive kind of awareness that transcends and includes that or those overlying it. Therefore, the opening up of awareness at Level IIA to the intradisciplinary spectrum does not replace discipline-specific grounding of Level I, but integrates it within the more expanded scope. The same holds with Levels IIB (integrates IIA and I) and III (integrates IIB, IIA, and I). Note that the expanded structural scope of each level is accompanied by an expanded process scope, the representation of which is among the map's key features.

The progression correlates generally with modern (Level I), postmodern (Levels IIA and IIB), and integral (Level III) development. The respective stages of cultural evolution will be considered more fully in the next chapter, where we will distinguish between *astructural* and *structural* postmodern paradigms. Were the Quadrants to be viewed in isolation and awareness depicted as lodged in the Lower Left with access to Upper Right and Upper Left subordinate, this would correlate with an astructural postmodern orientation (which tends to prevail in humanities) that privileges cultural influences over surface structural features and transcendent dimensions. That, by contrast, the new map integrates terrain of Lower Right and Lower Left with ever more cumulative awareness indicates a structural postmodernism which, unlike its astructural counterpart, celebrates the cultural without compromising surface and interior realms.

Note the arrows to the right that depict the complementary parts-to-whole and whole-to-parts trajectories of improvisation and meditation. Reflecting the fact that systematic improvisation practice includes both exploratory and emulative processes of various kinds, corresponding

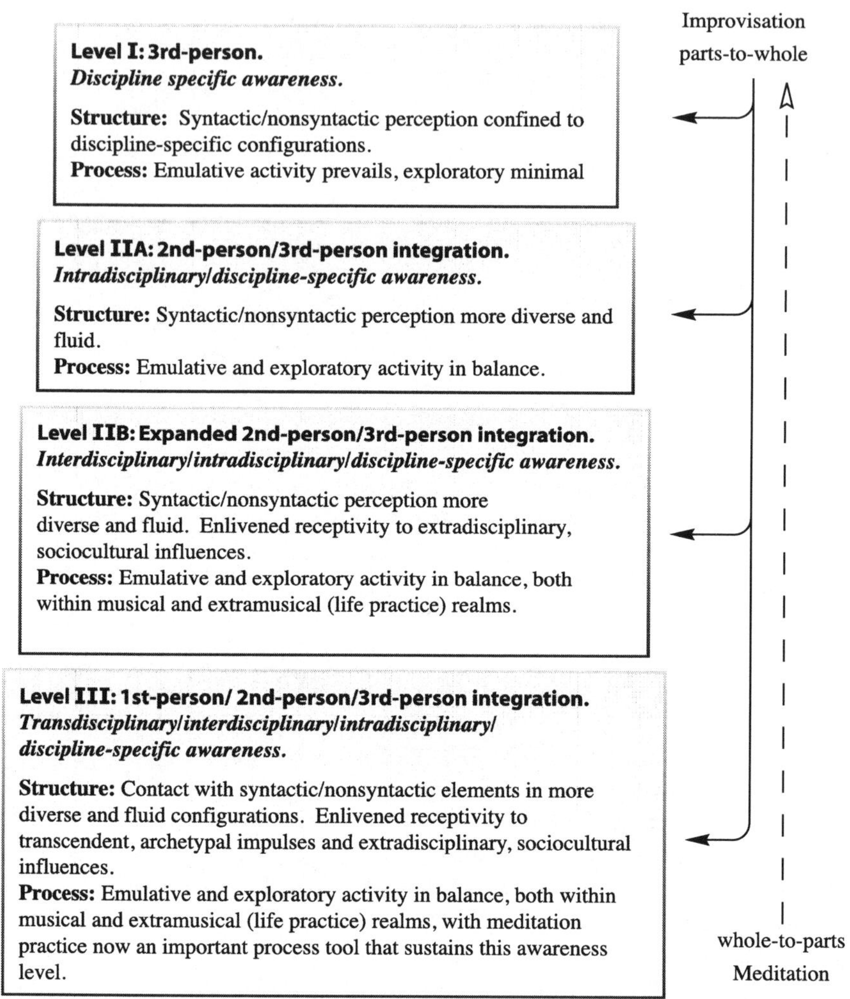

Figure 2.2. Four Levels of Creativity and Consciousness Awareness.

arrows are shown to indicate emulative-driven horizontal establishment of knowledge and skills at each level. Exploratory processes catalyze vertical penetration, which always requires emulative activity for enduring integration. Note also that the shaft extending from the whole-to-parts meditation arrow is perforated; this is because the cumulative parts-to-whole trajectory indicated in the diagram is not conducive to adequately showing how meditation promotes cumulative growth in the opposite, whole-to-parts direction. This would require overlying boxes to be increasingly larger to represent first-/first-second/first-second-third-person integration rather than the opposite. However, I believe the general idea of how meditation-driven growth complements that which is improvisation-driven is sufficiently represented.

It is also important to realize both linear and nonlinear aspects of this integration. From a linear standpoint, the degree of enduring grounding in any subsequent stage is predicated on the degree of grounding in prior stages. At the same time, reflecting nonlinear growth, influences from glimpses of later-stage terrain may be had early on in the process and significantly enhance prior stage grounding. One could as well acknowledge a kind of spiral effect in which grounding in prior stage processes and structures continually deepens with subsequent stage access, reminding us that more important than firm objective criteria that define level-specific grounding is progress along the respective parameters. Just as style categories are approximations of regions within an interconnected landscape, developmental stages are approximations of plateaus, defined by general process and structural indicators, within an ongoing continuum of growth.

Let us now proceed to a level-by-level analysis with these principles in mind. We will use music as a primary lens, with distinctions between classical and jazz paradigms providing an initial point of departure prior to a more jazz-oriented perspective as more expansive stages are considered. However, at all junctures, cross-disciplinary ramifications should never be far from view.

Level I Awareness: Discipline-specific

Level I (third-person/discipline-specific) awareness is where process and structure breadth, and thus overall creativity-consciousness development within a given line, are minimal. This is exemplified in music in the highly specialized division of labor that has engulfed European classical music for the past two centuries, even if a more integrative and comprehensive profile prevailed earlier. In the prevailing model, improvisation is virtually extinct, composition relegated to a small minority, and interpretive performance comprises the exclusive task of a large majority. Hence, secondary creativity is the guiding force and primary creativity is marginalized or excluded. With compromised process engagement comes compromised structural engagement. Awareness is dominated by the structural features of age-old repertory whose syntactic and nonsyntactic elements

Level I features		
Process	**Structure**	**Indicators of creativity/consciousness development**
Emulative function prevails, exploratory absent or marginalized	Awareness overshadowed by normative syntactic-nonsyntactic configurations	**Creativity:** Inventiveness, Interactivity, Individuation limited. **Consciousness:** Object-referral attachments prevail that impede self-Self integration, diversity intelligence minimal, critical inquiry faculties minimal.

Figure 2.3. Indicators of Level I Awareness (Modernism).

were molded into place centuries and continents removed from twenty-first-century musicians' time and (for Americans) place, thus precluding contact with basic elements in fluid forms, and abilities to perceive the idiom as a self-transcending gateway to the broader landscape. As a result, the basic conditions for creative growth—as measured by inventiveness, interactivity, and individuation—are absent: Limited processes as well as materials accessed impair the capacity to generate and realize ideas, to spontaneously adapt to one's environment, and most radically, to evolve a personalized voice that is at once contemporary, informed by diverse influences, and grounded in transcendent experience.

From the standpoint of consciousness, even when transcendent experience is invoked in the act of performance, it is not an all-quadrants experience that is informed by the rich array of processes and structures identified by the integral scope. Awareness, in other words, has no adequate conduit through which to flow whereby intradisciplinary elements from the broader musical world, interdisciplinary elements of the broader knowledge base, and transdisciplinary, archetypal impulses can intermingle and promote a truly broad and self-transcending artistic understanding. As a result, diversity awareness is inevitably compromised as the richness, depth, and beauty of the broader musical landscape is obscured when viewed through this incomplete lens and its structure-bound assumptions. In other words, when music is perceived largely as a phenomenon of works that are composed by one contingent and performed by another, the idea of an improvisation-driven paradigm, in which the creative and transformational impact is rooted in the spontaneous unification of musical functions, remains highly elusive. As a result, the broader musical world is seen as a foreign, hostile entity that needs to be kept safely at a distance if the integrity, or perhaps more apt, "purity" of tradition is to be ensured. To fathom the ethnocentric tendencies inherent in this perspective requires no great power of imagination.

And perhaps the most serious casualty of the process dearth at the core of the classical model is the resultant limited capacity to critically examine these patterns and their origins. Limited means to connect with the broader landscape ensures limited capacities for practitioners to step back and examine their field as part of a larger entity. Underlying this is the limited contact with basic elements in diverse and fluid forms, as a result of which the experience of familiar and new configurations bumping up against one another and dislodging conditioned assumptions and patterns is undermined.

Anomalies are not centered but tend to be rejected. From the standpoint of self-mediated critical inquiry, awareness does not penetrate to the delicate interstices where fluid forms meld with the individual voice. Self-motivation is compromised—there is little to reflect upon if one cannot see the individual voice emerge in one's work—as are limited self-navigational faculties. Any self-driven movement tends to be directed toward discipline-specific growth, not broader development. An example of this is the dependence on institutional resources in the classical field, as opposed to greater independence in the learning processes of jazz musicians.

Musical study is a primary example of "paradigm blindness," or as it might also be put, "a paradigm that does not realize itself as a paradigm."[24]

Level IIA: Intradisciplinary/discipline-specific Synthesis

Level IIA awareness unites discipline-specific grounding with intradisciplinary experience. Accordingly, whatever stylistic area serves as a point of departure is now realized as a tributary that flows into, and is in turn informed by, the broader musical ocean. As will be seen, the move from Level I to Level IIA awareness represents a highly significant juncture in the model as it indicates the first stage of liberation from discipline-specific attachments. Key here is not only the introduction of the primary creative processes of improvisation and composition, but because they are approached in a systematic manner, the establishment of the interplay between exploratory and emulative functions within each of these process lines. Subsequent movement to Level IIB, by contrast, is but a relatively small step that will occur spontaneously following IIA. Neither this awareness level (IIA), nor those that follow, are available to the Interpretive Performance Specialist due to the significantly curtailed process scope of that profile. However, restoring this process scope to its prior breadth and situating it within a contemporary structural context can easily rectify this problem. Limited forms of awareness level IIA are available through the conventional jazz education paradigm, and thus the reference to jazz as the musical vehicle that is unmatched for this and all-levels growth presumes a conception of the idiom as *writ large* or integral—in other words, encompassing the broad process and structure scope that renders it a robust gateway to global musical practice. That jazz provides a framework for this self-transcending growth exemplifies an important principle not only for the next evolutionary strides in classical music, but in a variety of fields, as these can also gain from jazz-inspired process rejuvenation.

Let us go into this a bit: In their style-specific work, jazz musicians replicate (in their craft studies) and creatively manipulate (in their style-specific improvising and composing) conventional harmonic,

Level IIA emergent features (in addition to those of prior level)		
Process Emulative and exploratory functions now coexist in balance	**Structure** Perception of syntactic-nonsyntactic elements in more abstract, fluid and diverse forms.	**Indicators of creativity/consciousness development** **Creativity:** Expanded inventiveness, interactivity, and evolution of individual voice. **Consciousness:** Growth of self-realization, diversity intelligence, and critical inquiry faculties

Figure 2.4. Emergent Indicators of Level IIA Awareness (Postmodern A).

melodic, rhythmic, and other elements characteristic of the genre. When they augment this with improvising and composing that takes them to broader (than jazz) musical regions, they add to their creative palette new groupings of fundamental elements. This process is not theoretically driven—creative musicians are not consciously thinking about the types of parameters they employ or encounter, they are simply allowing their creativity to flow and to take them to new musical territory. However, the analysis of this in terms of syntactic and nonsyntactic elements enables us to begin to understand its inner workings and how creative exploration not only promotes greater fluidity and diversity through sheer structural expansion, but also through the relationship of old and new structures that, upon bumping up against one another, spawn yet newer possibilities. A device I commonly use in my teaching, both for beginning improvisers and advanced style-specific improvisers, is to use nonsyntactic elements as catalysts. Therefore, when musicians are asked to improvise with elements such as density, or duration, or tessitura, they begin to break down conventional conceptions of these elements. And because conventional conceptions are often bound to syntactic conventions—for example, harmonic structures often accompanied by particular kinds of timbral and textural practices—enlivened nonsyntactic exploration can quickly enliven syntactic exploration.[25]

Whereas Level I engagement is dominated by secondary creativity, as in interpretive performance, which is inherently emulative in nature, Level IIA brings in primary creativity and the emulative/exploratory interaction uniquely possible through the systematic improvisatory and compositional engagement found in jazz writ large. Normative boundaries are both reinforced and transcended through this process scope.

From a structural vantage point, this process breadth enables contact with basic syntactic and nonsyntactic elements in varied and fluid forms, giving rise to the variety of benefits considered earlier as characteristic of creativity and consciousness development. Enhanced inventiveness, interactivity, and individuation comprise creative growth. In other words, expanded access to musical building blocks in fluid forms enhances capacities to generate ideas, adapt to musical surroundings, and evolve a distinctly personal voice.

A framework more conducive to the flow of awareness from concrete to subtle domains emerges, promoting growth of the self-awareness that is one of the three facets associated with consciousness growth. The first seeds for diversity intelligence also begin to sprout at this level as liberation from style-specific attachments (a constituent form of discipline-specific confinement) reveals genres as self-transcending tributaries that flow into a broader musical ocean and which, as waves that float atop its surface as well as dissolve into its recesses, are in turn sustained by this contact with the source. Revealing style dissolution to be as important as style reification, Level IIA awareness sees the musical ethnocentrism that prevailed at Level I give way to a thirst for exposure to diverse forms. And once one experiences even a single new paradigm and begins to recognize there is more to human creative expression than one's localized area, the seeds for receptivity to wide-ranging possibilities are sewn. One need not directly experience every form of music being made—were this even possible—to evolve a profoundly intradisciplinary musical awareness. Rather, the liberation from conditioned attachments to a single, most familiar genre coupled with infusion of influences from the overall musical world establishes an inner receptivity to diverse genres that will promote deep engagement as one's musical journey proceeds. As the personal voice begins to be experienced as a reflection of both one's inner and outer worlds, a deep level of intimacy is established with new sources of knowledge. The notion of contrasting musical paradigms may now be more than a politically correct slogan, but something that is directly linked to one's most profound sense of musical being and purpose. This inner grounding will make possible strong connections to wide-ranging and important exterior developments. For example, the infusion of influences from time feel–based improvised music and contemporary improvisation based in European roots provides a lens into George Lewis' delineations of Afrological and Eurological streams.[26] It is but a small step for this to blossom into a broader diversity awareness, that of Level IIB, which extends beyond musical boundaries and includes a celebration of the cultural backdrops that significantly shape the mosaic of musical styles that comprise the ocean from which they emerge and return. The discipline-specific/intradisciplinary nexus that is established at IIA is thus a highly significant juncture in the scheme.

One can easily see how the same expanded contact with basic elements that promotes diversity intelligence enhances critical inquiry faculties. To reiterate the aforementioned axiom: One cannot critically examine a domain without transcending it. When musicians are able to step outside the normative syntactic/nonsyntactic configurations of their area, contacting new configurations, they are able to view their genre from a distance in comparison to other genres and the broader musical world. This represents an initial form of anomaly centering that is a central object-mediated critical inquiry catalyst. Preliminary glimpses of self-mediated critical inquiry, even if it does not fully take shape until Level III when perception further opens to the abstract realms at which the self is able to fathom underlying tendencies that shape beliefs and our relationship with them, are also had at this level. The first significant expansion of the process/structure scope at this level produces a notable increase in the self-organizing nature of one's growth, which will only grow further at Level IIB.

One can thus see the significance of Level IIA awareness in the parts-to-whole trajectory as it represents the first increment at which one begins to liberate from conditioned, style-specific attachments. At which point, openings to Levels IIB and III are virtually inevitable.

Level IIB: Interdisciplinary/Intradisciplinary/Discipline-Specific Synthesis

The defining feature of IIB awareness is receptivity to not only expanded discipline-specific and intradisciplinary influences, but now those of an interdisciplinary nature. Musicians, in other words, are now more open to how the ever-evolving personal voice is informed by not only musical forces but the sociocultural environments in which they live and work. Music becomes a direct reflection of these environments, as a result of which it takes on higher degrees of meaning and purpose.

Level IIB process considerations

From a process standpoint, the parts-to-whole trajectory and its systematic improvisatory and meditation anchors begin to work more closely in tandem since creativity now penetrates more fully beyond the boundaries of music. Exploratory and emulative process functions, while of a disciplinary nature at Level IIA, now also take on crossdisciplinary or interdisciplinary dimensions. Whereas Level IIA emulative and exploratory activity involve musical processes, IIB emulative and exploratory activity also includes extramusical processes, which in turn catalyze further structural expansion. Emulative activity at this level involves the regular routines of life—adequate rest, exercise, proper diet, positive relationships, among others—that most individuals regard as essential to success in their work and well-being. Csikszentmihalyi helps dispel the notion of the creative individual as "tortured genius" as a "myth (stemming) from Romantic ideology," noting that creative innovators in many fields attribute stable life circumstances as important to their work.[27] However, practitioners also acknowledge the importance of periodically breaking free from routines and thus augmenting emulative activity with new kinds of

Level IIB emergent features (in addition to those of prior levels)

Process	Structure	Indicators of creativity/consciousness development
Interdisciplinary emulative and exploratory processes (e.g. life experience)	Awareness now more open to *extradisciplinary* structural influences.	**Creativity:** Individuation informed by extra-disciplinary, sociocultural influences. **Consciousness:** Enhanced self-realization, diversity intelligence, critical inquiry faculties.

Figure 2.5. Emergent Indicators of Level IIB Awareness (Postmodern B).

exploratory experiences. These might entail travel, exposure to new kinds of ideas and studies, trying different foods, new hobbies or recreational activities, among others. Naturally, the emulative/exploratory scope and balance will differ from one individual to another, and at different times in their development.

And with each new activity or process, new structural influences— sociocultural, political, economic, environmental, and so forth—from the world at large are integrated into the creative process and impact creativity and consciousness development within and beyond the primary discipline. As Charlie Parker famously stated, "if you don't live it, it won't come out of your horn."[28] Depth of creative expression, in other words, depends on depth of experience both within one's field and in life as a whole. The question of how this transformation of extradisciplinary influences into disciplinary expressions occurs brings us to the IIB structural realm.

Level IIB structural considerations

Whereas intradisciplinary creativity as we saw involves the transformation of broader, field-specific influences into the localized realm of the field (e.g., multi-stylistic musical influences into style-based practice), now a new kind of transformation must be addressed—that involving influences from an entirely different domain being metabolized, as it were, into the materials of music. Much as herbivores transform nutrients from plants into their massive musculoskeletal systems, every place visited, every person encountered, every food eaten, every thought or idea entertained, every discipline practiced—these and the rest of the infinite spectrum of life experiences become part of a rich interior repository that shapes the individual creative voice. Essentially paraphrasing Parker's comment, musicologist Paul Berliner notes that jazz artists often view their expressions as "a distillation of their experiences with life."[29] Since everyone has different life experiences, their inner reservoirs will differ, as will their creative expressions.

The very contact with syntactic/nonsyntactic building blocks in diverse and fluid configurations that enables intradisciplinary integration is also key to interdisciplinary integration. Here fluid perception of disciplinary, syntactic/nonsyntactic influences works in tandem with fluid perception of extradisciplinary influences. The greater the fluidity of perception, the greater the receptivity to influences from life experience and the capacity for these to shape musical melding. At their core, syntactic and nonsyntactic elements are vibrational impulses that have differentiated into musical language structures, and the subtler the awareness of these structures, the greater the receptivity to extramusical influences molding their formation. This promotes growth along all parameters of creativity and consciousness.

INDICATORS OF IIB CREATIVITY-CONSCIOUSNESS GROWTH

From the standpoint of creativity, all the three "I"s are enhanced by a broader sphere of influences and fluidity. More influences shape invention, greater fluidity enhances interactivity, and both scope and fluidity contribute to individuation, which now takes significant strides in being shaped by extramusical factors.

From the standpoint of consciousness, awareness gains at this level an even more expansive and differentiated conduit through which to flow as the self progresses in its merging with the Self and integrates the terrain encountered along the way. The "I" expands beyond its "It" and "Its" orientations to now also encompass "We," at which point development of diversity intelligence expands considerably. Where intradisciplinary/interobjective awareness opened the door to seeing the discipline as part of the broader field, interdisciplinary/intersubjective awareness now situates all of that within the broader knowledge base. In the arts, this means awareness of the all-important ethnological, cultural context that shapes artistic style. Now one begins to see overlying Level I features, and their Level IIA syntactic/nonsyntactic underpinnings as shaped by sociocultural forces, at which point the Afrological and Eurological waves of musical practice come into view as important aspects of today's musical topography. Anything but flat, the musical world requires identification of its important contours if it is to be successfully navigated. Afrological and Eurological streams, while certainly not the only ones, are essential for Western musicians to access the central syncretic current, and an important reason for this is their respective improvisatory and composition processes. Level IIB awareness brings an important interior shift to this aptitude, where cursory interest in contact with the cultural diversity underlying this synthesis opens up to a genuine thirst for deep grounding—where, for instance, non-African American musicians delve into the Afrological as if it were as much a part of their heritage as the Eurological (or whatever other cultural lineages one might identify as ancestral). Because, in fact, it is.

From the standpoint of critical inquiry, by situating the discipline in yet another stratum of the knowledge base, one is able to further step back from it and objectively scrutinize it. Cross-cultural anomalies (e.g.,

Afrological principles such as collective improvisation, embodied Africanisms, etc., for musicians from largely a Eurological background) are centered, as they bump up against and aid liberation from familiar assumptions and promote object-mediated critical faculties. Level IIB awareness represents a further step toward self-mediated critical inquiry, where the self fathoms the self-Self juncture from which beliefs and assumptions first differentiate and are thus prone to dissociation. Reflection, which is the fulcrum for self-organizing development, takes further strides as its expanded inner platform now takes on sociocultural dimensions, thus revealing greater meaning and significance in one's work, as well as possibly lingering obstacles, and areas for further growth.

But it is not until Level III transdisciplinary awareness is established that these faculties fully blossom.

Level III: Transdisciplinary/all-levels Synthesis

What is meant by the term *transdisciplinary*? Relatively new in the educational lexicon, and highly prone to varied conceptions, the idea tends to be defined in relationship to its multidisciplinary and interdisciplinary predecessors.[30] Multidisciplinarity involves the juxtaposition of fields, reflective of the core liberal arts premise that exposure to diverse disciplines produces well-rounded individuals. Interdisciplinarity takes the next step and interweaves perspectives of diverse disciplines within an approach to a given problem or field. Transdisciplinarity takes a further step and recognizes a stratum of experience that is transcendent of disciplinary jurisdictions. While not all transdisciplinary commentary views this experience as vertical penetration into deeper levels of consciousness, an integral perspective on transdisciplinarity, particularly one that is informed by the jazz-inspired parts-to-whole/whole-to-parts interplay, uniquely illuminates this point.[31]

From the standpoint of process: Parts-to-whole transdisciplinary awareness is accessed through creative engagement in which one transcends (and includes) surface, Level I features, intradisciplinary IIA structures, and interdisciplinary/intersubjective IIB influences in a level of experience in which these phenomena are perceived as faint impulses of consciousness as it differentiates at the subtlest scales. Perception here must be understood as largely intuitive and feeling based, and it is only in retrospect that intellectual analysis comes into play in any significant way. Whole-to-parts transdisciplinary experience is directly invoked in the pure consciousness of meditation, where awareness accesses a stra-

Level III emergent features (in addition to those of prior levels)		
Process	**Structure**	**Indicators of creativity/consciousness development**
Meditation key to sustaining transdisciplinary grounding, thus sustaining both parts-to-whole and whole-to-parts process trajectories.	Receptivity in awareness to archetypal structures	**Creativity:** Individuation further enhanced by archetypal influences. **Consciousness:** Broader fabric for self-realization, expanded capacities for diversity intelligence and critical inquiry.

Figure 2.6. Emergent Indicators of Level III Awareness (Integral).

tum of unmanifest Being, characterized by the juxtaposition of the most pristine, contentless silence, and the most radiantly wakeful awareness of only awareness itself. The purpose of meditation, as noted previously, is to allow the conscious mind, the self, to experience deeper levels of awareness from which it originates. The "pure consciousness event" is the most foundational form of this self-Self unification, an experience that Robert Forman describes as "wakeful, contentless (though non-intentional) consciousness" in his argument that this experience is core to spiritual and mystical experience across wide-ranging traditions.[32] "The boundary that I put on myself," as a new meditator describes this experience, "became like a mesh, a net, it became porous and then just dissolved, only unbroken pure consciousness or existence remained."[33] That it is difficult to imagine how these two conditions—extraordinary silence and stillness, and extraordinary wakefulness—can coexist confirms our arrival at a point in human experience that clearly defies language. One must experience it directly; verbal descriptions offer at best an approximation, which is not to therefore declare such analyses futile but simply to place them in proper perspective.

Meditation, while an important enhancement to prior stages of growth, is indispensable to enduring Level III awareness within a discipline. The interplay of robust parts-to-whole creative engagement, anchored in systematic meditation and its diverse constituent processes, and whole-to-parts growth rooted in systematic meditation practice provides an optimal framework for cultivating this level of perception and understanding.

Process functions take on new dimensions here in that meditation can uphold both emulative and exploratory roles. It is emulative in providing repeated exposure to transcendent experience. It is exploratory in its capacity to open up new vistas of transcendence and wholeness. When viewed in terms of the broader contemplative continuum characteristic of systematic meditation, moreover, more robust exploratory dimensions may be noted that transcend boundaries of expectations. It is important to recognize that boundaries between Level IIB exploratory processes, those involving new life experiences, and Level III exploration may dissolve at times; for example, new modes of human relationship or communion with environment can comprise either.

At Level III, the principle of process hierarchy, explored from a disciplinary perspective at Level IIA (improvisation and composition as primary modes of creativity), meets its whole-to-parts counterpart as silent meditation is seen as an anchor for the broader contemplative continuum.

Level III Structural Considerations:
Archetypes as Subtle Impulses in Consciousness

As awareness swings between the pristine silence of pure consciousness in meditation and the turbulence of creative engagement, perception of the delicate junction point at which the finest strands of differentiated creation emerge is enlivened. Following the work of psychologist C. G. Jung, we will regard the primordial impulses that originate at this junction point as *archetypes*. Here it might also be noted that Jung regarded the "collective unconscious," which is roughly synonymous with what I am calling intersubjective consciousness, as the transcendent ground from which archetypes originate. Because they retain their transcendent nature even at highly differentiated strata of creation, archetypal impulses, when expressed in art works, myths, and dreams, can invoke a transformational experience. "The creative process," Jung wrote, "consists in the unconscious activation of the archetypal image, and in elaborating and shaping this image into the finished work." In so doing the artist translates it into the "language of the present," directing awareness in perceivers "back to the deepest springs of life."[34]

Note similarities with Wilber's depiction of the transformational function of art, which for him is "art in its original and highest meaning," as the "wrestling of Spirit into matter." As a result of which the artwork then reminds us of "our own higher possibilities, our own deepest nature, our own most profound ground," which we are then "invited to rediscover."[35]

As will be explored in greater depth in chapter 8, archetypes need not be thought of as discrete or static metaphysical structures, or perhaps ethereal versions of their surface manifestations, and can simply be understood as the first sproutings of differentiation from unmanifest, undifferentiated wholeness. Archetypes are the interior impulses in consciousness that give rise to surface manifestations. This does not mean that surface structures resemble their archetypal underpinnings in any way. Jung, at times misunderstood by integralists and others on this point, reminds us that "the archetypal representations (images and ideas) mediated to us by the unconscious should not be confused with the archetype itself." In other words, archetypes "are very varied structures which all point back to one essentially unrepresentable basic form. The archetype belongs to the invisible, ultraviolet end of the psychic spectrum." Every exterior archetypal expression therefore "differs to an indeterminable extent from that which caused the representation,"[36] which is the cosmic wholeness that is the source of creation. Jung's surmising that archetype and atom are "two different aspects of one and the same thing"[37] not only affirms his dynamic conception of this stratum of creation from which archetypal impulses originate, but is also consistent with a nondual vision. While all creativity is informed to some degree by archetypal impulses, we will consider as "archetypally rich" those expressions that uniquely elicit a transformational impact by, as it were, reminding the consciousness of the perceiver of the transcendent origins it shares with the archetypal impulse.

It should therefore be emphasized that the conception of archetype being advanced is compatible with a variety of parallel concepts—including the subtle energies recognized by healers, the transcendent *devatas* in Vedantic cosmology, which correlate with the spiritual entities or intelligences recognized in shamanic and other indigenous traditions, and interpretations of quantum physical reality that recognize an underlying stratum of creation where matter and consciousness are revealed to profoundly intersect. When the physicist David Bohm describes the atom "as a poorly defined cloud, dependent for its particular form on the whole environment, including the observing instrument," he points in this direction. That "one can no longer maintain the division between the observer and the observed" directly corroborates with Jung's unity of atom and archetype. And just as a subatomic element will "behave as much like a wave as a particle,"[38] archetypal impulses may be thought of as processes as much as structures. I will therefore favor this kind of dynamic terminology—archetypal *impulses*, or *energy*—over the more static notion implicit when the term is used as a noun. In short: exterior expressions are rooted in interior impulses in consciousness, and the archetypal concept is among the variety of ways this relationship has been understood.

The archetypal principle will be examined shortly as an important criterion for distinguishing between artistic and extra-artistic creativity. The basic idea is that the abstract surface materials of the arts are particularly conducive to archetypal expression and thus able to evoke an aesthetic, transformational response. Combined with the previously considered attributes of parts-to-whole process richness, the transformative capacities inherent in an artistic idiom such as jazz are further underscored.

LEVEL III CREATIVITY AND CONSCIOUSNESS GROWTH INDICATORS

These principles of expanded depth and fluidity of perception, exemplified in archetypal perception, reveal even further growth along the three "I"s of creativity development, with inventiveness largely impacted by the first, interactivity by the second, individuation by both.

In terms of consciousness development (self-realization, diversity intelligence, critical intelligence): We have already glimpsed these features of Level III self-realization in the access to subtle domains of perception through creativity and meditation. It is here that the self merges with the Self and engages with objects—at subtle and manifest levels—from this vantage point. Diversity intelligence takes its next developmental strides as the sum total of diversity parameters—including disciplinary, creative, intellectual, ethnic, racial, cultural, processual, spiritual—are seen as forms of differentiation from undifferentiated wholeness. Level III archetypal perception now allows more substantive awareness of the Afrological and Eurological currents that are understood as ethnocultural from a IIB standpoint and in terms of syntactic/nonsyntactic configurations from a IIA standpoint by revealing these currents as underpinned in the first, primordial strands of feminine (Afrological) and masculine (Eurological) differentiation from undifferentiated wholeness. An important facet of this Level III understanding will be considered in chapter 6 in the contrasting types of temporal consciousness that underpin improvisation and composition processes. There we will see improvisation as driven by a nonlinear or inner-directed conception that is uniquely conducive to the collective interaction of improvisatory, process-mediated creativity. Composition will be seen as rooted in a linear, expanding conception that is uniquely conducive to the construction of large-scale, architectural forms, and thus as an object-mediated creative process that is generally undertaken not collectively but in solitude. Level III awareness illuminates these two modes of time conception as contrasting pathways to transcendence that underpin the contrasting ethnocultural streams that come into view with IIB awareness, the corresponding syntactic/nonsyntactic configurations revealed at IIA awareness, all of which underscore the richness of the jazz process scope, in which improvisation and composition coexist.

Here a point to which we will return repeatedly is that the transcendence-based, archetypal analysis of Level III combined with overlying process and structural considerations underscores the foundational nature of the Afrological line to the Afrological-Eurological synthesis. In other words, in response to the argument that jazz and other African American music represents a kind of horizontal merging of African and European influences, or the integration of African into the European framework, I believe a more complete assessment reveals a different vertical alignment, where the Afrological provides the foundation. "The emerging African American genres," notes Samuel Floyd as he describes the confluence of these streams even as far back as the nineteenth century, "were not formed by the insertion of African practices into the formal structures of European music, as conventional wisdom would have it." Rather, they resulted from the superimposition of European forms on the "rich and simmering foundation of African religious beliefs and practices. The foundation of the new and syncretized music was African, not European."[39] The present process-structure analysis not only strongly supports this assessment, but illustrates how the deeper the analysis goes into transcendent regions, the more it becomes evident.

Critical intelligence is optimal at Level III. Object-mediated critical faculties are promoted by the nesting of the discipline within the underlying and more expansive three levels. A host of anomalies associated with consciousness development are encountered, including expanded capacities such as remote cognition, discarnate consciousness, psychokinesis, collective consciousness (all to be explored further in chapter 4), with access to optimal tools for centering these ideas. Of particular relevance to this book will be parallels between enlivenment of collective consciousness through group improvisation and group meditation. Group improvisation represents a central feature of an integral music aesthetics, and group meditation shows promise as an important integral sociospiritual vehicle. In the latter realm, as noted in the introduction, a promising body of research suggests that large groups of meditators can generate a harmonizing effect in the environment that results in significantly reduced crime, accident, and illness rates. Inasmuch as improvisation and meditation are central anchors to the jazz process scope, the argument for the idiom as a central catalyst for delivering the integral vision to society may be further strengthened by these two innovations.

Self-mediated critical intelligence also becomes optimal with Level III awareness as the self is now fully able to navigate the delicate interstices at which thoughts, and thus assumptions and beliefs, first differentiate and, if *self-referral* awareness succumbs to *object-referral* attachments (to be explored more fully in the next chapter), dissociate into what ultimately may become rigid ideologies. The problem is not the ideologies, which are but thoughts that have become static or calcified, nor is the solution to abandon beliefs, which would be tantamount to abandoning thinking. Rather, the solution is to ground awareness in the source of thought, so that the critical awareness of these tendencies—accompanied by the critical strategies of overlying levels—is heightened. At which point, belief systems may be experienced not as rigid truth claims that are to be adopted by every person from here till eternity, but as provisional conceptual platforms from which further exploration is possible that either confirms the validity of the platforms or not. The "not knowing" proclaimed by mystics in diverse traditions does not, contrary to common misconception, refer to a passive stance when it comes to the nature of reality. Rather, it indicates a profound and direct noetic apprehension of the cosmic wholeness, from which—partly because this extraordinary knowing defies, and is thus easily distorted, by language—individuals are able to sustain the dynamic, self-critical relationship with conceptualizations of such.

An understanding of Level III perception also enables an important distinction to be made between transcendent experience as it occurs within and apart from integral, process-rich frameworks. It must be kept in mind that transcendence can be invoked in any activity and is to be celebrated as a possible glimpse—therefore a temporary state—that presages higher developmental stages. But without sufficient process breadth and thus access to the second-person process-structure matrix, awareness lacks a conduit through which this heightened first-person experience may flow and inform, and be informed by, the first-second-third-person, all-quadrants totality that is necessary to enduring, Level III stage development. With limited means for transcending and thus critically examining the pathway that leads to the experience, practitioners are prone to erroneously conclude theirs is the sole, or at least superior, avenue to this peak episode. The result is a kind of aesthetic fundamentalism that is remarkably similar to religious fundamentalism. Just as religious fundamentalists become overshadowed by denominational dogma as the most valid account of spiritual reality, musical fundamentalists become overshadowed by tradition-specific conventions as the most valid account of musical reality. Other avenues are excluded or marginalized, and therefore instead of a synergistic, integral mosaic that exemplifies the power of diversity, a narrow range is privileged and ultimately threatens the vitality of the system. Conventional musical study is a primary example of this in centering the secondary creativity of interpretive performance within a single cultural lineage and subordinating the primary creative processes of improvisation and composition that are not only key to multi-cultural infusion but all-levels awareness integration.

The integral framework thus reveals ethnocentrism and aesthetic/spiritual extremism to be systemic problems with common, process-deficient roots. Viewing this from the standpoint of both the Four Quadrants and the four levels of the jazz-inspired framework: Impeded contact with basic elements in fluid and diverse configurations confines awareness to Level I/Upper Right by precluding the cultivation of an individual voice informed by IIA/Lower Right broader musical influences and IIB/Lower Left extramusical influences. This compromised musical and cross-cultural embrace is reinforced by deep object-referral attachments characteristic of incomplete Level III/Upper Left experience. Engagement in the field is rendered self-confining rather than self-transcending. Happily, the framework also reveals how the restoration of process breadth—and here it must be emphasized that the systematic improvisation spectrum at the heart of the jazz idiom is essentially that which prevailed in earlier stages of the European classical tradition—can rectify the problem. The disciplinary or stylistic point of departure now becomes a tributary that flows toward increasingly broad vistas of knowledge, culminating in the inner-outer wholeness that defines the integral approach.

Let us close this chapter with a look at what the arts may uniquely contribute to this growth.

Distinguishing between Artistic and Extra-artistic Creativity

Although creativity is commonly associated primarily with the arts, recent years have seen increased interest in creativity across fields. An integral vantage point reveals ways artistic creativity may be unique, thereby both underscoring conventional wisdom and expanding contemporary application. In exploring these possibilities, the point is not that artistic creativity is superior to that in the sciences, humanities, business, and other fields, but simply that a more nuanced understanding of this core aspect of all fields will enable us to better understand how the arts may inform and inspire cross-disciplinary creation. Nor is this to suggest that the purpose of the arts is primarily to facilitate creativity in other areas; it is an important area of human endeavor and evolution unto itself. Therefore, returning to a jazz lens, it is not enough for fields to adopt jazz-inspired approaches within their disciplinary horizons, as valuable as this may be. It is also necessary for practitioners to engage more directly in listening, studying, and possibly even gaining hands-on experience in jazz-related music making as these become available.

A central premise is that artistic materials tend to be more abstract in nature than the materials of disciplines outside of the arts (with some notable exceptions), which renders artistic expression more conducive to the expression of transcendent, archetypal content. Musical sounds, visual images in painting and sculpture, and physical movements in dance are abstract, symbolic, and forms of creation characterized by what Koestler has termed "preverbal" or "prerational levels of mental activity. . . . Creativity begins where language ends."[40] This renders the arts uniquely conducive to interior, parts-to-whole movement of awareness since, as seen earlier, all phenomena are multidimensional, with the abstract surface features of the arts underpinned by even more abstract and fluid transcendent structures. An artistic idiom such as jazz, which combines abstract materials and a robust creative scope that includes primary, secondary, and ancillary creative processes working synergistically, provides awareness with a particularly receptive conduit through which to flow. Not only do such materials invite complementary process-based whole-to-parts/meditation-driven integration, they also invite what might be termed structure-based whole-to-parts integration in that transcendent properties are retained even in surface forms that comprise, to reiterate Jung, "the language of the present." Awareness is then led back to the transcendent depths from which it and archetype both originate.

Jazz thus embodies what Suzanne Langer considered "the real power of music," which to her was the prototypical form of art, "in the fact that it can be 'true' to feeling in a way that language cannot, for its significant forms have that ambivalence of content which words cannot have." Music, as an artistic medium that is "tinged with affect, tinged with bodily rhythm, tinged with dream," exists beyond the "pale of discursive thinking," rendering it a vehicle for vital "emotional and organic experience."[41]

This is not to deny that biologists, astronomers, engineers, corporate strategists, physicians, economists, and practitioners in many other areas may invoke abstract imagery in their creative activities. However, practitioners in these areas cast their ideas in either concrete materials or language, thus inhibiting the archetypal richness and transformational impact in the resultant expressions. I therefore do not suggest that the composition of a sonata or making of a painting are intrinsically more creative than the design of a toilet seat, or recycling system, or articulation of a theory about the underpinnings of the material world. However, it is possible to distinguish between the functions of these kinds of creative products, from which we can make an important observation: artists contact abstract, interior imagery and express this in abstract, surface forms, thus fulfilling an *aesthetic* function. Practitioners in other fields contact abstract, interior imagery and express this in concrete (physical, or language-bound) forms, thus fulfilling more of a *utilitarian* function. The arts provide surface structures as well as processes that are conducive to the archetypally rich expressions central to aesthetic knowing. The situation is perhaps analogous to reaching into a body of water with one's hands to quench one's thirst; by the time the hands reach the mouth, most of the water has been lost. Unique to the arts are huge buckets that allow significant amounts of archetypal imagery to be retained and expressed at highly differentiated levels of creation.

Another way of thinking about artistic and extra-artistic creativity is in terms of two contrasting functions: problem solving and creative expression. Creative problem solving occurs in frameworks that are externally delineated, whereas creative expression involves frameworks that are of one's own design. For example, geologists do not design rock formations, archeologists do not design ancient ruins, biologists do not design life forms, but all of these practitioners creatively solve problems by studying and fashioning theories that expand our understanding of these areas. By contrast, painters and sculptors design visual works, musicians sonic structures, dancers physical movements, and novelists literary forms. Reminiscent of the distinctions between primary and secondary creativity in music, where improvising and composing enable melding of basic materials in ways that interpretive performance does not, we can say that creative expression enables a melding of materials that is not available in creative problem solving. Abraham Maslow distinguished between A-needs and B-needs, the first comprised of necessities for survival, the second with broader emotional, aesthetic, and spiritual requirements. Problem solving fulfills A-needs, creative expression B-needs.[42]

What about extramusical areas such as mathematics and physics, whose surface materials are not only abstract but whose functions might be considered as much of an aesthetic nature as utilitarian? Physicists have been known to regard the elegance—the sheer beauty and coherence—of a theory as being as important as its ultimate viability. The extraordinary imaginative and exploratory facets that comprise this work are exemplary of Cziksentmihalyi's notion of "autotelic" engagement, where intrinsic rewards rooted in the process equal or overshadow any sort of exterior products.[43] How does one assess these modes of extra-artistic creativity in comparison to that of the arts?

This question is further illuminated when we examine what appear to be powerful parts-to-whole properties inherent in this work, where creative engagement leads to transformations in consciousness. Franklin Wolff was among a number of thinkers who attributed to mathematics a transcendent function, leading to his conception of "mathematical yoga." Asserting that "mathematic is that portion of ultimate truth which descended from the upper hemisphere . . . into the *Adhara* with minimum distortion and thus became the Ariadne thread by which we may ascend again,"[44] Wolff provides a clear depiction of archetypal integration. (Here transcendent is upper; *Adhara* is the Vedantic term for a "container" into which transcendent impulses are infused.) In other words, as Imants Baruss elucidates, "mathematics is the purest expression of the transcendent within the ordinary, dualist consciousness, and can be used as the most direct means of access to the transcendent."[45]

Here we are reminded of the provisional nature of language-bound categorizations. Headings such as arts, science, and spirituality are approximations of regions that both originate and flow back into an overarching wholeness. This does not render such categorizations entirely futile, provided we are vigilant in realizing their limited applicability. Physics and mathematics, for example, may be located closer to the intersection between art and science than other scientific areas and point to a possible creativity continuum that helps us understand ways in which certain artistic and certain extra-artistic domains differ from each other considerably, as well as those in which distinctions are more nebulous.

And even ceding that there may be points where the lines blur, this more nuanced analysis may still help identify distinguishing criteria. For example, the previously noted facets of mathematics and physics aside, an important question still must be addressed that may underscore differences between these domains and the arts: While it is one thing for specialists in these areas to invoke these heightened experiences of creativity and consciousness, what about those not versed in these areas or engaged in this work? In other words, even if practitioners contact abstract imagery in their work, this does not mean this imagery is retained in the ultimate manifestation of the work, which in terms of mathematical or physical theories is linguistic-analytical. Most of us do not attend physics and mathematics lectures or read corresponding literature to invoke the kind of experience we may gain through listening to musical recordings, concerts, or visiting art museums. Whereas we are not generally inclined to verbally explain the purpose of a particular musical or dance improvisation in order to derive great meaning from the experience, the meaning of mathematical and physical theories—the creative products of those fields—is tied to such linguistic explanation. It is one thing to invoke some transformation in consciousness during creative activity; it is another for the resultant creative expression to elicit that affect in the perceiver. This is where I believe a case may be made that the arts are indeed unique.

This, however, should not obscure the possibility that certain fields outside the arts are rich parts-to-whole vehicles for those engaged in those areas. For one thing, even if the integral education revolution is jazz-driven, it will be important for areas outside of the arts to establish early prototypes. Here the complementary whole-to-parts aspect of mathematics might be noted in support of this argument, where—just as jazz artists complemented their creative work with meditation practice—Wolff regarded meditation practice as an important component of his mathematical yoga.[46] Whatever degree of transcendence might be invoked through mathematical practice would be enhanced by stepping outside the realm of even this abstract form of mental engagement and allowing awareness to unite with its transcendent source unfettered. This underscores the possibility of establishing, through some version of this interplay, a "culture of interiority"—a culture of self-transcending engagement—not only in the arts but across fields, even if some may be more intrinsically conducive to this than others. Coupled with what might be termed a "culture of spontaneity,"[47] a phrase Daniel Belgrad applies to post–World War II society as its improvisatory sensibility expands, but which is every bit as applicable to a given field, we see that the process scope of the arts has much to offer in this regard, particularly that of the improvisation-based musical art form called jazz.

Summary

The power of the integral framework is not only its expansive vision of human nature and potential but the range of perspectives and resources it brings together to promote realization of this vision. In asserting that the purpose of human existence is oneness with the inner-outer, cosmic wholeness, which is synonymous with creativity and consciousness development, it is only natural to infer that the purpose of engagement in any area of endeavor is to realize it as a vehicle for this development. Complementing the Four Quadrants model in chapter 1 that nicely portrays the structural aspects of this growth, a jazz-inspired map was introduced that illustrates the central role process plays in it. A systematic approach to improvisation, which subsumes multiple approaches to improvisation, composition, performance and theoretical inquiry, was seen as upholding parts-to-whole movement toward this goal. This was analyzed as the expansion of discipline-specific engagement to encompass intradisciplinary, interdisciplinary, and transdisciplinary/transcendent grounding. A preliminary glimpse was gained of meditation practice—to be considered more fully in the next chapter—as a whole-to-parts catalyst. Identification of a variety of attributes of creativity and consciousness development—including enhanced inventiveness, interactivity, and individuation pertaining to the first, and heightened self-realization, diversity awareness, and critical inquiry faculties related to the second—points to a new paradigm of musical study and education at large.

In addition to the delineation of new vistas characteristic of an integral vision, the jazz-inspired framework was also seen to uphold a diagnostic function in illuminating how conventional models fall short of all-levels synthesis. The process-deficient paradigm of musical study and its focus on interpretive performance of European classical music provided a good example. Excluding the primary creative modalities of improvising and composing and placing secondary and ancillary creativity at the center, the model is constrained by self-confining rather than self-transcending movement of awareness. Instead of an integral conception of musical styles and disciplines as tributaries that originate in and flow into a boundless musical ocean, the conventional perspective of them as separate and competing prevails. When the self-transcending melding is placed at the center, both tributary and source are vitalized, and the very sustaining of tradition that custodians of the conventional model so desperately seek is possible. Ironic indeed is that not only the solution to the problem the very process breath that was once central in the European lineage whose preservation is sought, but that the primary source of this process breadth today is a genre—jazz—that tends to be marginalized in musical academe. Chapter 10 will consider how an overhaul of the field will enable the European classical tradition, the greatness of which has never been at question, to take its next evolutionary strides. But until its epistemological foundations are restored, the prevailing model will be threatened by a host of patterns that comprise a *creativity/diversity/ critical inquiry crisis*, among the most problematic aspects of which are aesthetic extremist tendencies that share a common inner mechanics with religious fundamentalism.

Although the integral analysis may at times appear excessive in its illumination of shortcomings, it is essential to keep in mind the newfound levels of joy, creativity, fulfillment, and transformation that are possible through this kind of deep diagnostic work and which would not be without it. The integral revolution requires more than horizontal modification of existing approaches, it calls for nothing short of vertical reconstruction of paradigms from their foundations on up. This point is underscored as we turn our attention to meditation as a whole-to-parts vehicle within the jazz-inspired process scope that is essential to this vertical penetration and growth.

Chapter 3

Meditation-driven Growth of Creativity and Consciousness

What is meditation? What is its role in creativity-consciousness development? How does it work in tandem with improvisation to promote this growth? What are the traditional landmarks of meditation-driven, creativity-consciousness development as defined by spiritual traditions? What insights might be brought to light on this growth from an integral perspective, particularly one that is informed by improvisation-based musical art?

These questions launch our inquiry into the meditation-driven, whole-to-parts process trajectory that complements the parts-to-whole movement outlined in the previous chapter. We begin by defining meditation, then probe the inner mechanics of practice and transcendent experience, which will be followed by a consideration of enduring stages of development. The culminating nondual stage launches the final section of the chapter, involving reflections on the self-referential dynamics of consciousness that underlie meditation and improvisation as manifesting on both localized individual and cosmic scales. This premise, central to the strong nonduality thesis and related account of Ultimate Reality and Meaning, provides an expanded conception of the wholeness from which, and toward which, meditation and improvisation—particularly when both are approached systematically—drive creativity and consciousness development. A fuller understanding of the jazz-inspired integral process spectrum bolsters the argument for the transformational template that the idiom yields for music, the overall educational enterprise, and society at large.

Defining Meditation

Meditation is a process whereby the mind transcends ordinary thinking and sensory engagement and experiences deeper, more silent and expansive levels of consciousness. During meditation, as Charles Alexander describes it, "mental activity gradually subsides and increasingly refined levels of thought and feeling are experienced."[1] Swami Durgananda puts it more poetically, characterizing meditation as "the most reliable way I know to touch the tenderness of pure being."[2] "With a correct meditation technique," Hari Sharma and Christopher Clark observe, "the human mind will settle down effortlessly to [a] silent state, motivated by the mind's natural tendencies."[3] Meditation can thus be thought of as a means by which one dives deep into the inner ocean of consciousness, connection with which often remains dormant in day-to-day life, in order that this contact may inform the various dimensions of daily life.

Heightened mental clarity, self-awareness, unconditional love and compassion, interconnectedness, inner calm, and noetic experience are among the benefits commonly associated with meditation practice.[4] Over time, these qualities may begin to manifest in activity outside of meditation, thus underscoring that the primary purpose of meditation is not to escape the sometimes turbulent and stressful realities of life, but to enhance capacities for fully engaging in all areas of life. Indeed, a primary goal in most meditation traditions is to render all of life a meditation— a life lived with greater happiness, love, awareness, creativity, sense of interconnectedness, meaning, and capacities to contribute productively to the world, at which point, the question "what is meditation?" is perhaps more aptly framed, "what is not meditation?"

Helpful to responding to these questions is to realize, as Daniel Goleman reminds us, that a variety of meditation practices exists.[5] And while most everyone will benefit from one form or another, different individuals will have different needs in this realm. In the previous chapter, we examined a systematic approach to meditation that included silent sitting practice, which is perhaps the form most commonly associated with the idea of meditation, and an array of more active modalities such as contemplative approaches to reading, writing, movement, creativity, interpersonal interaction, and environmental communion. As stated earlier, the idea is not that everyone will engage with the entire spectrum on a daily basis, were this even possible, but that the combination of regular silent sitting practice and some kind of active practice, which might alternate between various kinds of active modalities, offers formidable grounding in the system to promote a robust conduit for awareness to flow in the whole-to-parts direction that complements parts-to-whole improvisation-driven growth.

Let us go into why silent meditation, two predominant forms of which are mantra-based and breath-based practices, may serve as an anchor for the broader contemplative continuum. A *mantra* is a sound that is "heard" mentally and promotes deeper levels of awareness that are transcendent of thought and thus even the mantra itself. Commonly misconstrued as a form of mental concentration, where—the thinking goes—by intently focusing on repetition of the mantra, awareness is somehow lulled into a transformed state of consciousness, correct mantra practice is rooted in entirely different principles. Here the central premise is effortless, wherein gently allowing the awareness to be with the mantra, the mantra can undergo transformation, including complete dissolution, as consciousness connects with the spacious wholeness that is its true nature.[6] Effective mantra-based meditation practice may involve but a few iterations of the mantra even in the course of a lengthy and deep session.

Breath-based practice involves allowing attention to follow the cycles of inhalation and exhalation of the breath, which promotes an experience of mindfulness. Tendencies to exert excessive effort in this procedure, paralleling misconceptions about mantra practice, are sometimes elicited in the common instruction to "focus on the breath."

The main principle behind silent, sitting meditation is that it involves a more complete withdrawal from ordinary mental, physical, emotional, and sensory engagement, thus allowing awareness to most directly and completely fathom its innermost dimensions, what Sharma and Clark term the "source of thought."[7] The exquisite silence, coexisting radiance of being and wakefulness, and mind-body oneness of pure consciousness thus provides a foundation that can inform the rest of the contemplative continuum and promote a channel through which transcendent being can flow into more active realms of life.

Within the systematic meditation framework, further guidance may also be helpful by distinguishing between what I have elsewhere categorized as *formal*, *nonformal*, and *quasi-formal* approaches to practice.[8]

The formal approach includes those in which practice occurs in the context of a spiritual lineage, which thus makes available resources for expert instruction, communities of practitioners, advanced programs and retreats—all of which are often regarded by longtime meditators as essential to their staying with practice. Formal practice is also enriched by the cultural, historical, theoretical context that is inherent in meditation lineages. Among the many examples available include Transcendental Meditation and Self-Realization Fellowship from the Vedanta tradition; Siddha Yoga from the Kashmir Shaivism tradition; Zen, Mindfulness, and Tibetan practices from Buddhism lineages; and various Christian, Judaic, and Islamic meditation practices from the Abrahamic traditions.

Nonformal practices include any activity that may or may not be undertaken from a contemplative perspective, such as the more active modalities (e.g., contemplative approaches to reading, writing, movement, etc.) that comprise the systematic meditation spectrum outlined earlier, but which are approached with contemplative intention. Quasi-formal practice includes meditation that is extricated from its formal lineages, as in learning meditation from a book, video, online, from a friend, or self-constructing a practice. An ideal program of systematic meditation practice will combine formal and nonformal approaches, with quasi-formal engagement recommended only in the absence of formal instruction resources. The point is not to privilege certain approaches over others but simply to delineate the range of options so that individuals may make informed choices. Ultimately, many of the processes that comprise Integral Life Practice can be situated along this epistemological scope, particularly when one takes into account the overarching, and constituent, whole-to-parts/parts-to-whole relationships.[9]

And as a variety of spiritual thinkers, such as Elizabeth Lesser, Phillip Goldberg, and Robert Forman suggest, grounding in a formal tradition provides a foundation for navigating the morass of trans-traditional possibilities that define the contemporary spiritual landscape. This grounding may also provide a basis for dealing with the evolutionary dynamics that are inherent in the meditative journey.[10]

Let us turn to the inner mechanics of meditation practice, in so doing further elaborating on the integral conception of consciousness, followed by a consideration of developmental stages.

Self-reference: Uniting Personal *self* and Transcendent *Self*

The inner mechanics of meditation may perhaps be best understood in terms of the union of two aspects of consciousness. One is a personal aspect of consciousness, or *self*, the other is a more expansive, transcendent (also called universal, unbounded, eternal—to use a few terms one might encounter) *Self*.[11] The personal self is the aspect of consciousness that discerns, decides, evaluates, and guides much of daily existence. Mental functioning or experience of a more intuitive nature corresponds more to the transcendent Self, which is often spelled with the upper-case *S*. Pure consciousness, as we will consider shortly, involves dissolution of the personal self and complete immersion in the transcendent Self, exemplifying the self-referential capacity for consciousness to curve back on itself that is the basis for creative and spiritual experience and growth. Buddhist objections to the notion of a transcendent Self might be noted; I believe these are largely a question of semantics, although in some instances, materialist-influenced misinterpretations of Buddhist principles.[12]

Distinctions between the two facets of consciousness are often made through comparison with the wave-ocean relationship. As Sri Aurobindo states, the "(individual self) or ego are like the crown and dome jutting out from the waves while the great body of the building is submerged under the surface of the waters."[13] Lama Govinda similarly writes that "the universal consciousness . . . is compared to the ocean, on the surface of which currents, waves and whirlpools are formed, while its depth remains motionless, unperturbed, pure and clear."[14] Whereas the personal self is localized in time and space and inextricably linked to the psychophysiology, the transcendent Self, which again subsumes the personal self, is immaterial and transcends time, space, and physiology.

The self-Self structure of consciousness sets the stage for a consideration of contrasting states and stages of consciousness, which, as we have seen, correspond with contrasting degrees of creativity. In ordinary consciousness, the self experiences itself as disconnected or dissociated from the Self and thus, ungrounded in the transcendent source that is the basis for freedom and spontaneity, is prone to conditioned patterns as it clings to relativistic objects of perception—what Alexander defines as "thought, perception, and action."[15] Fred Travis describes the condition of consciousness where awareness is "identified with thoughts and actions" as "object-referral," which is the opposite condition of consciousness to *self-referral*, and equates with the habituated patterns discussed in the previous chapter that result from limited process engagement.[16] Hence, ordinary consciousness equates with Level I (third-person, objective-exterior) awareness, where creativity is minimal, as considered within the multitiered scheme introduced in the previous chapter. Heightened/transcendent consciousness, corresponding to Level III awareness, brings an enlivened first-person, interior-subjective dimension into play. Here the self experiences itself as grounded in the Self and thus free from conditioned patterns and capable of greater fluidity, clarity, inventiveness, spontaneity, and other characteristics of optimal creativity. As Alexander describes it, the self "is no longer identified with or overshadowed by the boundaries of the changing values of thought, perception, and action."[17]

Two general categories of transcendent states are pertinent to this discussion, one that is invoked in meditation, the other in the midst of active, creative engagement. Meditative transcendence, embodied in the experience of pure consciousness, is a form of undifferentiated wholeness; active transcendence is a more differentiated wholeness, and we will shortly see that ordinary consciousness is a dissociated condition of consciousness. Active transcendence thus can be thought of as a temporary glimpse of Level III, all-tiers functioning, in which creativity and consciousness within a given developmental line are optimal. We will later consider more enduring manifestations of active transcendence, first as noted in the *individuation* that characterizes regular experiences within the context of a discipline, and then in the permanent enlightenment or self-realization that pervades all of one's experience. The following diagrams and discussion illustrate these distinctions and how meditation enhances the capacity for the integration of transcendent experience in life as a whole.

Ordinary Consciousness

First is the antithesis of transcendence, which is ordinary consciousness. As Figure 3.1 indicates, here the personal self is experienced as disconnected or dissociated from its unbounded source, the Self. As a result, the self seeks grounding wherever it can, which usually means relativistic—rather than transcendent—phenomena, and thus becomes overshadowed by conditioned attachments to objects of perception. Objects of perception, as previously noted, can be thoughts, actions, sensory perceptions or emotions. Shortly we will see that in heightened consciousness the self-Self union is possible along with engagement with objects of perception. Unless that state is invoked, one is prone to attachments that limit overall creativity and vitality as well as that within a given discipline. Govinda states, "it is just this objective occupation with the phenomena of the world" that makes us "become their slaves."[18]

Examples include the music improviser who relies on stockpiles of acquired clichés and thus compromises individuality and interactivity and is incapable of sustaining the interest of listeners and fellow musicians; the physician who is attached to conventional interpretations of symptoms and is thus prone to misdiagnosing a patient who presents those symptoms but in reality is afflicted with a completely different disease; and the basketball player who is bound by standard moves and thus easily thwarted by opponents. These are all examples of what Ellen Langer calls "mindlessness," corresponding to Level I awareness in the creativity-consciousness continuum considered in the previous chapter.[19]

As noted earlier, ordinary, object-bound Level I awareness results from a limited process spectrum and generally involves an overbalance of emulative activities. While exploratory processes will begin to enhance

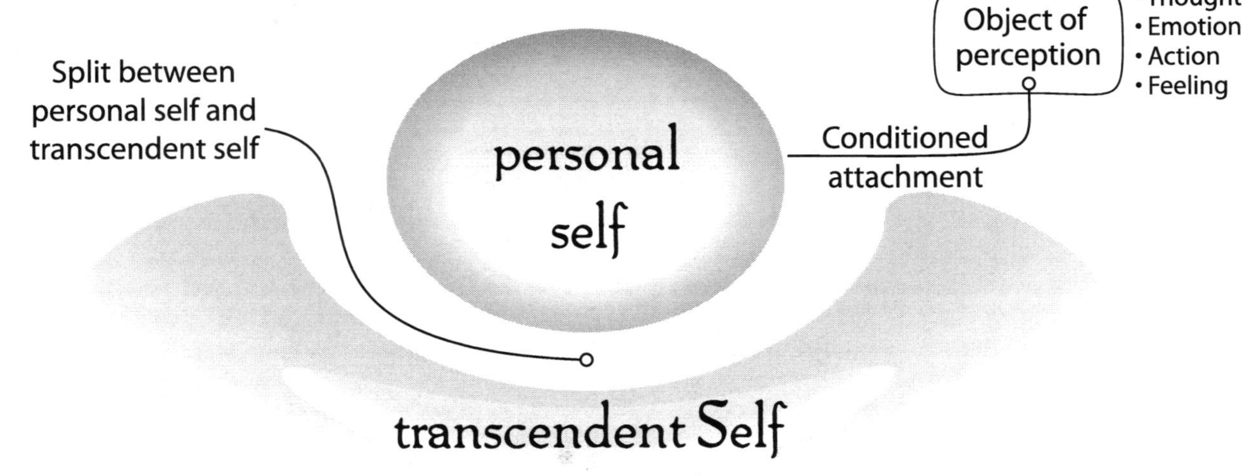

Figure 3.1. Ordinary Consciousness.

the capacity for liberation from Level I attachments, the addition of meditation to the epistemological/process palette enables optimal access to heightened Level III consciousness, the epitome of creativity and consciousness development.

Heightened Consciousness in Meditation: Accessing the Continuum from Its Core

Meditation enables access to a core kind of transcendent experience that is invoked apart from mental-physical-emotional-sensory engagement and exemplifies the notion of transdisciplinary experience as it manifests in silence, illustrated in Figure 3.2. Note that, unlike in ordinary consciousness, here the self is connected with the Self. Meditation allows the surface, thinking mind to penetrate beyond the day-to-day flurry of concerns and chatter and connect with its innermost, silent core. Where the surface of the ocean is active and turbulent, its depths are silent. Same with our minds, even if the hectic pace of modern life has rendered many oblivious to the possibility of a silent mind. But this aspect of mind has never been absent—it is the foundational nature of the mind, of which many have lost sight and to which access needs to be restored. Meditation is a means for accomplishing this, "a procedure for allowing the excitations of the mind to gradually settle down until the least excited state of mind is reached."[20]

Whereas ordinary consciousness is dominated by object-referral tendencies, meditative transcendence epitomizes the self-referral capacity inherent in human consciousness—the capacity for awareness to be aware of itself.[21] As considered earlier, this capacity for consciousness to curve back on itself, to be conscious of being conscious, may be the feature that most distinguishes the human being from other species. *Homo sapiens sapiens* denotes the evolutionary capacity by which the human being, as Ervin Laszlo has put, "not only knows, but knows that he knows."[22]

Meditation, Laszlo continues, permits the experience of "nothing but [one's] self-referential nature, empty of compelling contents," suggesting that this practice enables a further degree of self-awareness.[23] Fred Travis comments on this experience of "pure consciousness" from a trans-traditional perspective:

> The prevailing Western view is that an individual cannot be aware without being aware of something. In contrast, the subjective traditions of the East—the Vedic tradition of India

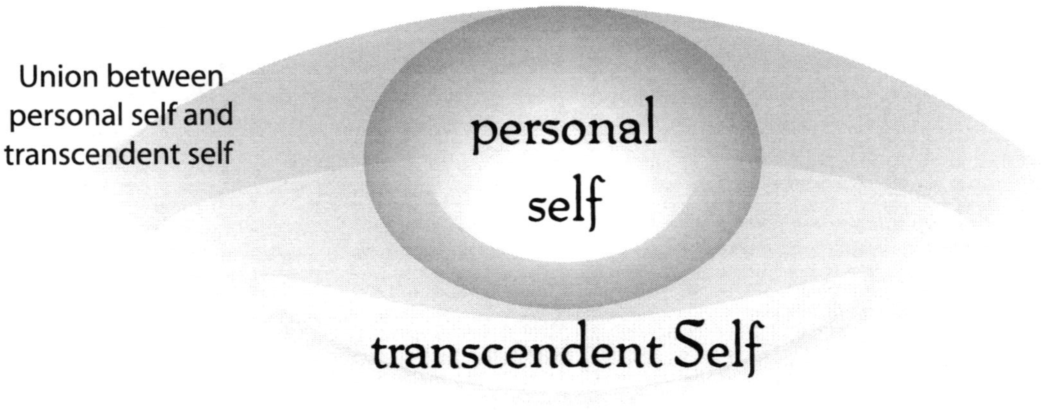

Figure 3.2. Transcendence in Meditation.

and the Buddhist traditions of China and Japan—include formalized meditation techniques predicted to lead to the direct experience of a foundational state of self-awareness devoid of mental content.[24]

While Hindu Vedantins call this *turiya chetena*, Buddhists call it *shunyata*, and Jewish mystics *ayin*, among the many ways this has been described.[25] Combining a radical emptiness devoid of content with the most exquisite wakefulness where awareness is radiantly aware of itself, the "pure consciousness event," as already seen, is often characterized as both a dissolution of the ordinary sense of individuality and the emergence of a more expansive sense of "I."[26] W. T. Stace describes this experience as an "apparent fading away, or breaking down, of the boundary walls of the finite self" so that one experiences a merging with "an infinite or universal ocean of being."[27]

Even individuals new to meditation can glimpse this kind of internal union:

> The thin boundary that had previously divided individuality from this silent consciousness began to dissolve. *The 'I' as a separate entity just started to have no meaning.* The boundary that I put on myself became like a mesh, a net, it became porous and then just dissolved, only unbroken pure consciousness or existence remained.[28]

When this young practitioner marvels that "the feeling after that state is incredible," we get a sense of the ultimate significance of meditation—which is to promote the capacity for transcendent experience not just during meditation but in all of life so that one can enjoy greater creativity, fulfillment, and be of greater service to the world.[29] In other words, the purpose of withdrawing from ordinary physical, mental, and sensory engagement through meditation is not merely to find reprieve from the vicissitudes of everyday life. The ultimate purpose is to serve as a vehicle for a fuller kind of integration in which enlivened interior grounding is integrated with complete engagement in all aspects of life. As Govinda terms it, we do not seek through meditation practice an "annihilation of sense-activities or a suppression of sense-consciousness," but rather "the removal of arbitrary discriminations, attachments and prejudices" so that we can engage in the world more freely and creatively.[30] Meditation enables us to pacify our mental activity, or "incessant inner soliloquy and reasoning," and redirect our inner vision from the manifold to the unified, from the intellectual to the intuitive, from the individual to the universal."

Over time it is possible to be so "pervaded by this universality that when we return to the contemplation of the small, the single, the individual, we shall never lose the meaning and connection with the whole and shall not fall back into the error of egohood."[31]

Egohood, of course, refers to the personal self disconnected or dissociated from its source and overshadowed by objects of perception in ordinary consciousness.

Another way of thinking about these principles is in terms of the evolutionary thrust from undifferentiated to differentiated wholeness. Meditation exemplifies undifferentiated wholeness in that it involves withdrawal from engagement with objects. But, as Govinda emphasizes, the purpose is to carry that transcendent wholeness into the realm of differentiated experience.

Active Transcendence

Active transcendence involves heightened consciousness amid some kind of otherwise ordinary mental, physical, or sensory activity. This can be thought of as a temporary glimpse of what in Vedanta is called *sahaja samadhi*. Whereas *samadhi*, synonymous with pure consciousness, exemplifies what Forman calls "introvertive mysticism," *sahaja samadhi*, in which "a silent level is maintained within the subject along with (simultaneously with) the full use of the human faculties," characterizes "extrovertive mysticism." Here a "permanent" transcendent experience is found to "last even while one is engaged in activity."[32] Consistent with the principle of meditation as a whole-to-parts methodology for creativity-consciousness integration, Forman makes a case that the introvertive experience lays groundwork for the extrovertive. The possibility for enduring integration, commonly described as enlightenment, will be taken up shortly.

At first glance, the capacity for transcendence outside of meditation may seem counterintuitive. It is one thing to experience heightened awareness, wholeness, unconditional love and well-being, and other attributes of transcendence when withdrawing from mental, emotional, physical, and sensory engagement; it is, one might think, quite another to invoke this kind of experience in the midst of action. However, a look at testimonies from athletes, musicians, and practitioners in other fields reveals that, in fact, such experiences are possible, whether or not one happens to be engaged in a program of formal meditation practice.[33]

Russian weightlifter Yuri Vlasov cites instances where "all suddenly becomes quiet within you. Everything seems clearer . . . than ever before, as if great spotlights had been turned on. There is no more precious moment in life than this."[34] Tennis star Billie Jean King's testimony along these lines is even more dramatic, as she describes peak experiences as "a perfect combination of . . . violent action taking place within an atmosphere of total tranquility. . . . When it happens I want to stop the match and grab the microphone and shout, 'That's what it's all about.' Because it is. It's not the big prize I'm going to win at the end of the match, or anything else."[35] Jazz musician Ronald Shannon Jackson describes it as "a feeling of being able to communicate with all living things."[36]

Literature on these kinds of experiences suggests that they often are fleeting and difficult to invoke at will.[37] Or they are invoked consistently in a particular activity but not readily integrated into the totality of one's life. Michael Murphy and Rhea White note a tendency among athletes who, after having invoked powerful, perhaps life-altering transcendent experiences, pursued meditation as a more systematic means for tapping into these states not just during sports but in the full spectrum of life's activities. "Sport by its very nature promotes this heightened [experience], but meditation can help it develop. Several well-known athletes, among them Bill Walton, Joe Namath, rodeo rider Larry Mahan, and Billie Jean King, have testified to the help meditation has given them."[38] At this point, the combination of athletics and meditation, just as the combination of improvised music and meditation, provides a form of the very whole-to-parts/parts-to-whole template that I propose is central to integral education. I will later explore parallels between athletics and art, suggesting that athletics, a field that—albeit for different reasons—is as academically marginalized as improvised music, is a kind of art form that is rich in creative (many sports are highly improvisatory) and transcendent properties and may play an important if unexpected role in the expanded epistemological landscape of the future academy.

Figure 3.3 illustrates the inner mechanics of active transcendent experiences and may help provide a clearer sense of how the whole-to-parts/parts-to-whole interplay may optimize the capacity to invoke them.

Comparing 3.3 with previous diagrams, we see that whereas in ordinary consciousness (3.1), the self is disconnected from the transcendent Self and thus attached to objects of perception (thought, sensation, action), and in meditative transcendence (3.2), the self unites with the Self, but withdraws from engagement with objects, in active transcendence (3.3), the self is both united with the Self and also engages with objects. This "is classically described," as Alexander portrays it, "as 'non-attachment,' not in the sense of being withdrawn, but because it [the self] is no longer identified with or overshadowed by the boundaries of . . . thought, perception, and action."[39]

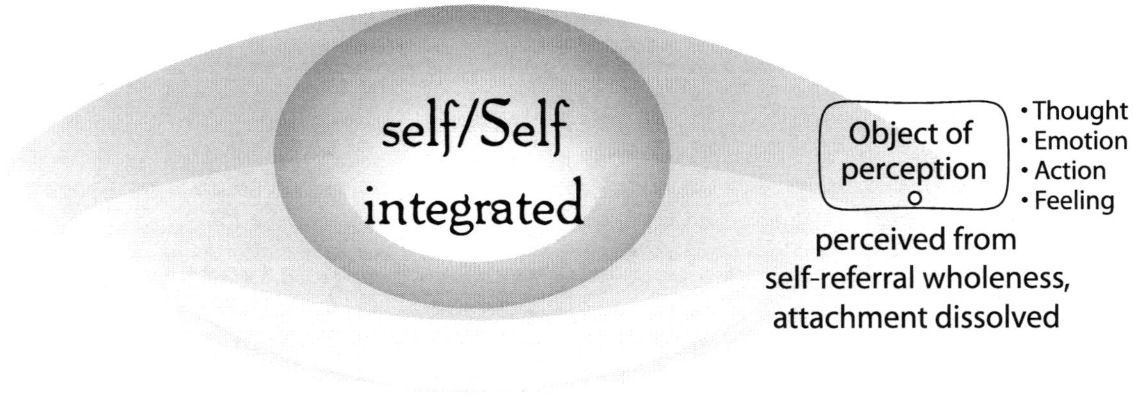

Figure 3.3. Active Transcendence.

These experiences are not only important as temporary instances—or states—of peak performance within a given time, place, and activity, they are also significant as a glimpse of what may become a permanent kind of functioning at a higher developmental stage. The term *enlightenment* refers to a level of consciousness development in which transcendence is enduring; grounding of the personal self in the transcendent, eternal Self is the basic condition of consciousness and pervades every moment and every activity—waking, sleeping, and dreaming—of every day. In Alexander's words, "when awareness no longer alternates between the bounded ego and the underlying Self and instead becomes permanently established in [transcendent] consciousness, the first stable stage of higher consciousness is gained."[40] Put another way, the alternation of activity (bounded ego) and meditation (contact with Self) represent states of awareness, and the permanent union of these experiences represent higher stages of consciousness growth.

We will shortly consider three enduring higher stages, each of which are characterized by significant openings in the nature of their self-referential grounding and corresponding perceptions of relativistic objects. Prior to this, however, let us explore what might be thought of as a transitional kind of development that may promote movement from the temporary transcendent states invoked in meditation and peak experience to permanent integration. Here we return to the notion of individuation broached in the previous chapter. Individuation can be thought of as a kind of enlightenment, or enduring self-Self integration, within a specific discipline. Even if this integration is provisional and has not yet manifested in life as a whole, it is significant in indicating a formidable degree of inner-outer union within a given field.

Individuation as Line-specific, Provisional Enlightenment

At first glance, Jung's characterization of the interior-exterior integration that comprises the basis of individuation may suggest he is talking about a developmental stage synonymous with enlightenment. "Individuation means becoming a single, homogenous being, and, in so far as 'individuality' embraces our innermost, last, and incomparable uniqueness, it also implies being one's own self. We could thus translate individuation as 'coming to selfhood' or self-realization."[41]

The integration of the "unconscious into consciousness," with Jung's notion of unconscious comparable to our notion of transcendent Self, seems particularly congruous with permanent grounding in transcendent being.[42] Jung, however, despite a long-standing interest in Eastern thought, appears hesitant to accept the extent of integration that is central to Eastern (and other) notions of higher stage development. The prospects for faculties of the conscious mind such as "exclusion, selection, and discrimination"—which Jung asserts "are the root and essence of everything that lays claim to the name 'consciousness' "—to coexist with grounding in "universal consciousness"—which "so far as we know is equivalent to a state of unconsciousness"—appears to be the point of contention.[43] Instead of these faculties being heightened in this union, Jung erroneously seems to conclude that they would be undermined due to the fact that "the unconscious has swallowed up ego-consciousness."[44] On the other hand, as Harold Coward has pointed out, Jung elsewhere suggests greater receptivity to the capacity for a stage of consciousness development in which these seemingly competing functions might coexist, further confusing what might be inferred of Jung's stance regarding the individuation-enlightenment relationship.[45]

We can circumvent these debates. Instead of attempting to either equate individuation with, or distinguish it from, enlightenment, let us simply situate the idea within a broader developmental scheme that culminates in enlightenment. Thus, where Jung uses the term "to denote the process by which a person becomes a psychological individual, that is, a separate, indivisible unity or whole," we will think of this as the emergence of a distinct, individual voice that is grounded in transcendent values *within a given discipline or developmental line*.[46] Thus, Victor Mansfield's statement that the "[t]he point of individuation is to become who we are meant to be, the expression of our authentic self, not some clone of another person or the expression of collective values" could apply not only to the discovery of one's ideal career path, as he intends, but also the evolution of an individual voice within that path in accordance with the usage at hand.[47] For this to happen, the self-transcending engagement in a field that characterizes all-levels experience as presented in the previous chapter is necessary. Awareness confined to the discipline-specific level is precisely that which is susceptible to "cloned" behavior. Even awareness that attains the cross-disciplinary level but has not yet gained transcendent grounding is still somewhat prone to collective conditioning. When these overlying levels of engagement are grounded in transcendent experience, our individual voice in our field will be informed by these levels but free from their binding influence, allowing, as Mansfield puts it, "[o]ther aspects of our wholeness (to) reveal talents and potentials that are essential to becoming who we authentically are."[48]

The arts exemplify the emergence of an authentic, individual voice, and improvised musical art is particularly suited as a template for growth across artistic and extra-artistic lines. Recall Jung's definition of artistic creativity as the "activation of the archetypal image" and the fashioning of it "in the language of the present, whereby it leads us back to the deepest springs of life."[49] The archetypally informed language of the present is the individuated voice, whose evolution the arts can help foster in a variety of fields.

Individuation in this context is promoted by consistent experiences of transcendence that are informed by strong discipline-specific (third-person), intra- and interdisciplinary (second-person), and transdisciplinary (first-person) grounding. Epistemological diversity is central to this growth. Thus, for musicians, style-specific and stylistically open improvisation and composition processes that allow awareness to span the four tiers is essential. Interpretive performance, the primary activity for a very large constituency in musical academe and in the professional classical music field, may serve as a destination that a musician arrives at as a by-product of the individuation process, but which in itself is inadequate—due to its limited process expanse—to serve as a pathway to this kind of growth. The goal may not necessarily be the path. Indeed, as we have seen, only improvising and composing allow the contact with basic musical elements in fluid configurations, which can then be molded into style structures upon interaction with the myriad relativistic influences of one's time and place and transcendent influences from deep in the psyche, that are the basis for a distinctly artistic voice.[50] Most musicians for whom interpretive performance remains an aspect of their musical identity will sustain their grounding in improvisation and composition that was important to their realization of this identity.

As this voice emerges, practitioners view their art as a direct reflection of the interior-exterior totality of their being. Their impetus for engaging in the activity shifts from relativistic incentives (e.g., remuneration, recognition, social contacts) toward what Csikszentmihalyi refers to as an "autotelic" impulse—an incentive that is rooted in interior rewards.[51] An integral perspective enables us to probe these interior rewards at their innermost core, which is the primordial drive for consciousness to be whole, for the personal self to (re)unite with the transcendent Self that is its source. In chapter 8, we will explore how the totality of musical and interior-exterior extramusical influences of one's life are, as it were, metabolized into musical materials that comprise the personal voice and thus remind awareness of its interior origins. For present purposes, we need only acknowledge that this transformation takes place, and that the resultant individuated voice thus serves as a vehicle for self-Self infusion within a given activity.

Although, as I suggest, the arts are a robust conduit for individuation, this can manifest in all areas. Engineers, corporate visionaries, classroom teachers, athletes, office managers, conflict mediators, news correspondents all evolve individual styles and thus—upon engaging in diverse top-down/bottom-up epistemologies—begin to perceive these styles as gateways toward self-Self wholeness. And from this basic framework, they are able to supplement their process scope as needed and relevant to include areas that are organically related to not only growth in their fields but in their lives at large—as both domains are inextricably linked.

And if one's primary occupation can be realized as a developmental pathway toward individuation, an important fulcrum for Integral Life Practice is gained, as this can serve as the locus for parts-to-whole development via enlivened improvisatory and compositional creativity in the field. This may then be augmented by engagement in jazz and the broader realm of arts in one capacity or another. A corresponding program of systematic meditation will then provide the complementary whole-to-parts trajectory. In this way practitioners in wide-ranging areas may be able to navigate their way through the often overwhelming morass of practices that can easily confound spiritual aspirants in this day and age. Even with the helpful organization of modalities into a few core modules within the Integral Life Practice framework, this challenge in my view remains unresolved.[52] I believe that the framework for individuation proposed here provides a viable alternative. Atop the core whole-to-parts/parts-to-whole framework that is comprised of creative activity within the field and meditation practices, additional modalities may be integrated as part of a unified, self-developmental matrix that is rich in coherence and meaning. Instead of attempting to construct a piecemeal methodological template from an endless assortment of possibilities, the rendering of one's primary career activity as a pathway for individuation provides a kind of organizing framework around which a diverse spectrum may be incorporated. And because all aspects resonate with the needs of the individual and with each other as a unified system, they are readily sustained. Some practices, such as meditation and career work, will be done on a regular basis. Others may be done periodically. When integrated as part of a synergistic, individuation-driven system, a routine will emerge that may be effortlessly and joyously sustained.

Enlightenment

To be sure, the move from line-specific individuation, where all-levels transcendence is invoked consistently within the context of a given activity, to the permanent grounding in transcendence that defines enlightenment—

described by Alexander as "the permanent, uninterrupted coexistence of transcendental consciousness along with waking, dreaming, and deep sleep"[53]—represents an enormous evolutionary stride. It appears that in any era this is achieved by but a few individuals—who may previously have not achieved individuation in a specific field. Is this kind of development really possible? While one can grasp the possibility of increasing capacities for transcendence in a given activity, what does it mean to sustain permanent grounding transcendence in all areas of life—described by Alexander as "the permanent, uninterrupted coexistence of transcendental consciousness along with waking, dreaming, and deep sleep"?[54] A consideration of this kind of potential may yield an entirely new and expanded context for understanding the arts in conjunction with meditation in human development.

Among the most compelling support for the idea of enlightenment is research conducted by Daniel Brown, in which he found remarkable similarities across spiritual traditions separated by wide-ranging historical, geographical, and cultural boundaries for higher stages of development that include the basic parameters for enlightenment.[55] A number of theorists, including Alexander and Wilber, have mapped these stages along a developmental continuum that extends beyond Piaget's preoperational, concrete operational, and formal operational stages, and generally acknowledge three discrete stages of enlightenment. Integralists term these as *subtle, causal,* and *nondual.*[56] It is not just that the general notion of permanent grounding in, rather than fleeting episodes of transcendence, is widely shared, but that a sequence of stages is reported to unfold across cultures within the general scheme, providing a more nuanced and compelling account of this evolutionary possibility. Wilber comments on these remarkable findings:

> Taken together, these various approaches—conventional and contemplative—seem to point to a general, universal, and cross-cultural spectrum of human development, consisting of various developmental lines and stages that, however otherwise different their specific cultural or surface features might appear, nevertheless share certain recognizable similarities or deep features.[57]

As we briefly examine these stages, it is also noteworthy that we may be seeing the beginnings of a new wave of neurobiological research that supports the notion of enlightenment, even if the obstacles to this work—namely, access to large populations of enlightened individuals—

are formidable. While neuroscientific research into meditation is by now fairly abundant, this has largely involved the study of subjects during actual meditation practice.[58] Much less research has been done on aspects of longtime meditators' experiences outside of meditation, particularly regarding reports of transcendent experience invoked in activity, let alone those suggestive of enduring higher-stage cultivation. Needless to say, inherent in objective measurement of active transcendence that is invoked on an occasional, fleeting basis are significant research challenges. However, when subjects report sustained periods of transcendent experience, even if these subjects are harder to find, the situation is highly conducive to scientific study. One such study, conducted by a team of researchers led by Fred Travis, is particularly promising in this regard.

Travis and his colleagues sought long-term practitioners who report sustained episodes of what is called "witnessing" in sleep or in daily activity.[59] Witnessing arises when the personal self liberates from attachments and, grounded in the transcendent Self, experiences engagement with objects of perception as though through the lens of a detached, perhaps more aptly analyzed as unattached, observer. "When pure consciousness is continuously maintained along with activity," Alexander notes, "then it also functions as a silent 'witness' to that activity."[60] Travis and his team noted that subjects who reported this quality on a consistent basis scored higher along a variety of consciousness-development parameters—moral reasoning, happiness, emotional stability, inner orientation, and lower anxiety—as well as measuring higher frontal EEG coherence, alpha gamma power ratio, and more efficient cortical responses than a control group.[61]

> Though many scientifically minded people may consider enlightenment either imaginary, impractical, or simply outside the boundaries of scientific investigation, the implications of these data are that enlightenment may be operationalized. Laboratory experimentation can help us make progress in this arena as seen by responses during unstructured interviews, supported by factor analysis of scores on psychological tests and brainwave patterns during tasks.[62]

Witnessing is one of the preliminary indicators of the first stage of enlightenment, which I will refer to using the Vedantic terminology of *turyatit chetana*.[63] Whereas the previously considered *turya* is a stage, a temporary episode of transcendence, *turyatit* is enduring. This is synonymous with *sahaja samadhi*, or what Wilber refers to as the "subtle" developmental stage. Brown's taxonomy, as noted earlier, locates parallels to this and other higher stages across wide-ranging traditions. *Bhagavad chetena*, the causal stage, follows *turyatit*. Here perception, permanently liberated from attachments to objects, opens up to the subtle strata of creation—sometimes called the "finest relative"—from which objects originate.[64] Whereas in the first stage of enlightenment, *turyatit chetana*, "the material world," as conveyed by Alexander, "may still be viewed as essentially lifeless and inert," *bhagavad chetana* involves an entirely new "level of not only perception but feeling" that is characterized by "greater love and joy for the object, which in turn facilitates still deeper appreciation of the object."[66]

Such perception may manifest in a variety of ways, from the perception of objects as "transparent structures of soft, satiny light (unlike harsher, normal day light), through which the very essence of life appears to flow,"[66] to a deep sense of communion with the source of creation, to communion with transcendent intelligences or spiritual entities that is sometimes reported as characteristic of this level of perception. Psychologist Gary Schwartz is among the most recent scientific researchers to probe these latter phenomena in depth.[67] The causal stage may also see extended capacities of consciousness, or *psi* phenomena (e.g., remote cognition) for which compelling empirical support is beginning to manifest. Evans-Wentz: "[T]elepathy, or the transmission of thought naturally, i.e. without the cumbrous mechanism[s] [acknowledged by] Western science, has been . . . a matter of common knowledge . . . for unknown ages for the *yogin*."[68] This is not to suggest that some of these capacities may not manifest far prior to the causal stage; extrasensory channels that are characteristic of this stage may, in a limited capacity, begin to open before one's consciousness is fully established at that stage. This, of course, can be confusing and even distracting for the spiritual aspirant. As Evans-Wentz emphasizes, any such capabilities must be appreciated as by-products of higher stages of consciousness development, even if serving as a preliminary temptation along the spiritual path. "[I]t happens again and again in the lives of the Siddhas that the initially desired magic power becomes worthless in the moment of its attainment; because in the meantime the much greater miracle of the inner 'turning-about' has been achieved."[69]

The ramifications of the causal stage and associated perceptual phenomena for artistic creativity are significant in that this is the level of the creativity-consciousness continuum where archetypal impulses reside and enable artistic expressions to resonate with transcendent beauty and transformational capacities. The culminating stage in Vedanta, which again corresponds to the apogee acknowledged in most traditions, is *brahma chetana*. This is the stage of nondual, or unity consciousness. The Sanskrit term *advaita* translates as "not two," meaning that individual conscious-ness now experiences itself as the undivided totality of cosmic intelligence and creation. Now the personal self is so fully grounded in the eternal, universal Self that it is not only freed from object-referral attachments, it has taken the next evolutionary stride of permanently experiencing all of creation—"all levels of mind and objective reality," notes Alexander—"in terms of the Self."[70] Maharishi Mahesh Yogi explains that at this stage "the experiencer and the object of experience have both been brought to the same level of infinite value, and this encompasses the entire phenomenon of perception and action. The gulf between the knower and the object of his knowing has been bridged."[71] An advanced follower of his who appears to have established this level of being reports the prevailing experience that "I am the entire universe. When I look at anything, I see conscious-ness . . . I see subjectivity which has taken a form, which has adopted an appearance of matter."[72]

Durgananda reports a vivid, if fleeting, glimpse of this develop-mental stage upon an encounter with her teacher, Swami Muktananda, where "I could feel the earth, the sky, and even the galaxy inside me. In that moment, I understood, with a surety that was both terrifying and exhilarating, that there is only one thing in the universe: Awareness and that Awareness is me."[73]

Prior to this stage, even if the liberation that defines the first stages of enlightenment has been achieved, a dualist condition of consciousness still prevails whereby one experiences inner and outer worlds as ontologi-cally distinct, even if intimately linked. What distinguishes ordinary dual-ity, then, from transcendent duality in *bhagavad chetana* is that relativistic objects bind perception in the former stage, whereas perception is liber-ated from those bonds in the latter (still dualistic, if partially liberated) condition. With the subsequent establishment of nondual awareness in *brahma chetena*, liberation from objects occurs within the awareness that the Self is the source of all creation.

We thus once again arrive at the primacy of subjectivity as the ground of all being and the capacity to experience this reality in increas-ingly direct ways as creativity and consciousness evolve. Nonduality is a kind of evolutionary end goal, progress toward which is driven by this reality, and grounding in which permits the most profound apprehension, at which point, all quadrants are revealed to be a facet of the Upper Left. This is in absolutely no way to suggest that the exterior world is illusory or has no ontological significance, rather that consciousness is the primary ground from which creation emerges, at which point differentiated whole-ness prevails. The sequence of stages delineated herein may be seen as a progression toward this nondual, though highly differentiated awareness of Kosmos.

Ordinary consciousness, in which one is bound by some relativistic object and oblivious to the true nature of the Self, is the furthest removed from nonduality. Episodes of transcendence, either within or outside of meditation, represent the first steps toward unification by liberating perception from the object, albeit only temporarily, and providing initial grounding of the perceiving self in the transcendent Self. Then the enduring self-Self integration of *turyatit* manifests, involving permanent liberation from objects of perception. A more refined and thus differentiated perception of objective reality, atop the self-Self union, characterizes *bhagavad chetana*. *Brahman chetana* involves a further step in experience as both objective and subjective reality, heretofore perceived as separate, are realized as inseparable aspects of eternal Being, the Self that knows no other. The ability to perceive the entirety of creation in terms of the Self represents the apogee of differentiated wholeness.

Integral Perspectives on Enlightenment

Integral Theory presents a powerful framework for bringing this kind of understanding and experience into the educational world due to its capacity to acknowledge and synthesize diverse perspectives. Consciousness and its evolution is not only an Upper Right, neurobiological phenomenon, as materialists would have it. It is also a Lower Left intersubjective affair, and of course an Upper Left subjective interior phenomenon. The integration of higher-stage developmental methodologies such as meditation within the academic world will require this all-quadrants perspective, both from the standpoint of integrity of and advocacy for this level of educational innovation. Meditation without corresponding theoretical models will not suffice, nor will, needless to say, theoretical models without practical methodologies—a third-person educational "experiment" that scarcely anyone will deny has failed horribly in terms of the kind of human development that is possible, and urgently needed, in our schools. Chapter 11 will go into the essential interplay between practice and theory within the context of meditative development, suggesting new terrain for the emergent contemplative studies movement. Integral education, as argued previously, does not downplay the need for theoretical understanding, and this holds as well for the realm of meditative practices. In a single stroke, this principle will allow for a degree of internal integrity in this new academic terrain that also enhances external credibility, enhancing the capacity of education to bridge the long-standing exterior-interior divide that separates conventional from integral learning models.

Complementing the previous description of enlightenment, which may be viewed as representative of the classic account, integral discourse has sown the seeds in recent years for a more expansive view. When Wilber defines enlightenment as "oneness with the realization of all stages and major structures that are in existence at any given time in history," he adds to the mix two central points that suggest the need for rethinking on this topic.[74] First is that some evolutionary stages or structures, most notably the intersubjective/intercultural (Lower-Left) phenomena that are the basis for postmodern thought, are relatively recent developments. As are the various psychosocial stages that comprise the GlobalView spectrum of Spiral Dynamics. "How could somebody 2,000 years ago be enlightened, since some of the stages, like systemic GlobalView, are recent emergents?"[75] This does not mean, Wilber continues, that "a person's realization today is . . . Freer than Buddha's . . . but it is Fuller,"[76] referring to a kind of lateral growth that is inherent in differentiated wholeness, which complements the vertical penetration and integration that appears to unite classic and integral conceptions of enlightenment. And the assertion that "a 1,000 year old path today, by itself, can no longer be the carrier of full Enlightenment" need not be taken as a devaluation of the tools that that path has to offer the contemporary spiritual aspirant.[77] "As human consciousness evolves, so does enlightenment!"[78] proclaims Allan Combs. As I will argue in chapter 11, this emergent conception may, in fact, illuminate the value of age-old practices and corresponding theoretical models, as well as the need to supplement them with a broader range of methodologies that address the broader developmental spectrum. That the arts may make key contributions to this process represents a further contribution of the integral perspective on enlightenment.

Music and Higher Developmental Stages

Let us briefly surmise, even without a large pool of musicians (or practitioners in any field) who have attained these stages, how musical perception might manifest at the three levels.

At the subtle stage, *turyatit*, awareness liberates from object-referral attachments and thus engages with objects from the much more fluid and expansive perspective of self-Self union. Manifestations in terms of both direct musical engagement and overarching musical understanding may be noted. Recalling our features of creativity: Inventive capacities are strong because of both peak mind-body integration and self-Self merging, the latter of which entails connection with an expansive reservoir of ideas, influences, impressions, and internalized knowledge. Peak interactivity is due to the fluidity of contact with all objects. One can see how these faculties might thereby promote individuation.

In terms of consciousness: Naturally self-Self integration, which is now permanent, is optimal and thus the witnessing quality that prevails in all areas of life also prevails in musical engagement. Peak diversity awareness manifests in important ways. Most prominent is the liberation from tendencies in academic and commercial circles to think of the musical landscape in terms of discrete style and disciplinary categories and realize these as provisional process-structure regions within an overarching musical wholeness, which itself is realized as an aspect of the broader wholeness of consciousness. Just as the personal self is at this stage realized as but a wave atop the eternal and infinite ocean of the transcendent Self, localized areas of musical practice are recognized as waves atop a musical ocean. Or, as tributaries that flow into that ocean. With this stage of development, the axiom—All Music is World Music—becomes a living reality. The entire musical landscape is available to the creative artist who is permanently grounded in the Self.

Here an important caveat must be articulated. That is, this heightened understanding requires that the self-realized individual at the subtle stage sustains, or at least has had, adequate creative grounding. It is possible, in other words, for an Interpretive Performance Specialist to achieve enduring self-Self realization characteristic of the subtle stage with no experience in improvisation or composition. Such an individual, however, will have skipped over the individuation phase that can only occur with such creative grounding and thus, while having evolved extraordinary expressive skills within the highly localized area of interpretive performance, will not be capable of the apprehension of the wholeness of the musical world. It is even possible for such an individual to harbor exclusionary tendencies, for these require process-rich frameworks, along with corresponding studies, to be neutralized.

However, for reasons that will be increasingly apparent with a consideration of subsequent stages, I believe that this scenario will be rare, and perhaps increasingly so as improvisation and composition make their way back into the process scope for most musicians. Indeed, even without ready access to these processes (e.g., through conventional musical studies), the musician who approaches higher stages of consciousness evolution will be spontaneously drawn to a broader creative process scope that enables the individual creative voice to manifest. When the self unites with the Self, the creative thrust of the cosmos permeates one's being with a force that cannot be denied and thus must find an adequate channel. For many, this gravitation toward improvisation and composition will happen early on in the spiritual-musical path. This does not mean, however, that interpretive specialists who become improvisers and composers and at some point permanently self-realized will discard interpretive performance. Rather, they may include this as part of their musical activity, and it is even possible for it to be prominent in what they do. But now this highly localized form of expression is arrived at, and informed by, a broader range of engagement, which is the foundation for specialized and comprehensive musical profiles alike. I believe that the majority of fully realized musicians will center their creativity in the primary activities of improvisation and composition.

At the causal stage, *bhagavad chetena*, awareness opens up to finer levels of perception of musical processes and structures, and thus the faint transcendent or archetypal impulses that originate in the most foundational regions of consciousness and give rise to surface forms. Here is where, in addition to the qualities that emerge at the subtle stage, heightened degrees of expressivity, sensitivity, and feeling will manifest due to the expansion of the heart that characterizes, and catalyzes, growth to this level. And because awareness at this stage is so deeply attuned to the archetypal realm, an even more nuanced personal voice may manifest that is particularly reflective of both transcendent and relativistic aspects of time and place. Now the artist is even more drawn toward improvisation as this process provides the means for harnessing these impulses in real time, aided by the collective consciousness comprised of fellow musicians and listeners. Awareness of the contours of the musical landscape, such as Afrological and Eurological streams, come more clearly into view, as these are now understood as rooted in contrasting yet prominent transcendent impulses. If musicians at the subtle/*turyatit* level, if not already deeply engaged with improvisation, will be strongly drawn to it, those at the causal/*bhagavad* stage will regard improvisation as central to their musical being. The idea of a musical existence in which the spontaneous connection with one's deepest creative impulses—and those of fellow musicians, and transmission of these to listeners, whose own deep impulses flow and inform the performance—is absent is as foreign to musicians at this stage as the idea of a life without water is to fish.

In nonduality, *brahma chetena*, where all of creation is experienced as one's own consciousness or self, which is now realized as cosmic in nature, the transformational capacities of musical expression take further strides. Now abilities to enliven collective consciousness between performers and performers and listeners are optimal, which places improvisation as an even more central mode of expression. The individual-cosmic oneness invoked in one's own awareness manifests spontaneously in interactions with other musicians and the audience.

In terms of overall development, the nondual stage is where contemporary trans-stylistic engagement is situated at the overlying tier of a tri-level framework. The middle tier is one already considered, in the tradition-specific engagement that characterizes conventional practice. However, in nondual consciousness, an underlying tier comes into view, having to do with grounding in the primordial nature of sound and music as preserved in various traditions across the globe. A prominent example is the Hindustani tradition and its time theory that equates the structure of its *ragas* with time of day. The basic principle is that the very differentiation of primordial cosmic vibrations into the frequencies of the daily cycle—morning, afternoon, evening and constituent divisions—also manifests in the frequencies of the intervallic structures of the *raga*.[79] Skilled performance of the *raga*, of which it is noteworthy improvisation is central, enlivens those frequencies and the transformational effect of the *raga*.

In their inquiry into these subtle dimensions at which sound and energy intersect, musicians established in nondual consciousness will likely grapple with the possible limitations of the tempered tuning, or equal temperament, of Western music in eliciting these effects. Equal temperament enables the octave to be divided into 12 equal parts, giving rise to the 12 notes of the chromatic scale and the rich system of harmony unique to Western music. Pure tuning, on the other hand, while precluding harmonic complexity as we know it, enables far more extensive division of the octave and thus what from a Western perspective are called "microtones" but from many other musical cultures are naturally occurring tones with, as nicely underscored by Alain Danielou, unique expressive and transformational capacities.[80] The point is not, as some suggest, that tempered tuning is inferior to or less "spiritual" than pure tuning, but simply that the different pitch systems are capable of different effects. I therefore do not suggest that Western musicians who naturally and rightly master the tuning system of their culture and attain nondual grounding will tend to relinquish this aspect of their background. Rather, they will complement their contemporary musical expressions and explorations with studies of one or more pure tuning traditions in which primordial connections between sound, consciousness, and environment may be uniquely preserved. A possible outgrowth of this may be the emergence of musical pitch languages that integrate aspects of tempered and pure tuning in new ways.

As the previous analysis shows, meditation-driven, whole-to-parts growth of creativity and consciousness invites complementary improvisatory engagement just as the opposite was seen to hold in the previous chapter. The nondual developmental stage, because it represents a culmination of growth in both improvisatory and meditative or creativity and consciousness dimensions, is particularly significant to our coming full circle in understanding this relationship. A brief examination of correlations between these phenomena on individual and cosmic scales, while admittedly ambitious, will shed further light on the improvisation-meditation relationship and lay further groundwork for examination of practical ramifications for education and society.

Self-reference as Individual-cosmos Connecting Principle

Recall that extending from the general nonduality thesis, which views individual and cosmic intelligence as inextricably linked, is a strong nonduality thesis that identifies a common mechanics underlying this relationship. The central premise: The very curving back of consciousness onto itself that underlies individual creativity is also at the heart of cosmic creativity.

Among the most explicit accounts of the strong nonduality thesis may be found in the Vedantic tradition of India, with its notion of *lila*, or cosmic play.[81] The basic concept is that the eternal, unbounded field of cosmic intelligence curves back on itself and creates primordial vibrations, or sounds, which are the building blocks of the manifest creation. As Peter Westbrook describes it,

> [T]he creator, Brahma, is completely alone, without a second. At the moment of creation, the first boundary [or differentiation] occurs within the unbounded value of Brahman by virtue of his being aware of one thing—himself. This act of awareness . . . turns the unity of the Self into the trinity (of) subject, or perceiver, the process of perception, and the object, known in Sanskrit as *rishi, devata,* and *chandas,* or *adhyatmika, adhidaivika,* and *adhibhautika.* . . . The manifest world (emerges) from the interactions occurring within the field of consciousness.[82]

Parallels with a variety of creation accounts may be noted, including the Pythagorean premise of how from the One emerges the Three and then the many, and the Daoist conception as articulated by Lao-Tse:

> Tao gave birth to one
> One gave birth to two
> Two gave birth to three
> Three gave birth to all myriad things.[83]

Similarities with ancient Egyptian cosmology might be noted, where, as John Anthony West points out, "*Tum* (transcendent cause), becoming conscious of itself, creates polarized energy. One becomes simultaneously Two and Three."[84] Westbrook further suggests connections to the Christian trinity, where the Father correlates with the subject, the Son with the object, and the Holy Spirit as the process or "flow of consciousness between them."[85] The subject/process/object interplay in the neo-Vedantic account will be considered shortly as corresponding closely with the subjective, intersubjective, objective, or "I/We/It"/first-second-third-person facets of Integral Theory. By conceiving of second-person intersubjectivity as a process impulse (within the subject-process-object trinity), we expand our understanding of this realm as correlative with creativity and the arts as well as the broader realm of human interaction. This will also support a revision of prevailing correlations in integral circles between first-second-third-person realities and, respectively, art, spirituality, and science to spirituality (first), art (second), and science (third).

The age-old view of sound, and thus music, as a direct manifestation of the self-referral dynamics by which the cosmic intelligence creates points us in this direction. Again, it is Indian thought in which particularly vivid accounts appear to be found. As described by the Hindu sage Abhinavagupta, largely regarded as the seminal figure in the establishment of the Kashmir Shaivism tradition, the primordial vibrational impulse—or *spanda*—that is the "essence of all" is rooted in the capacity of consciousness to "double back" on itself, in other words, "its capacity for self-referral," as a result of which, "there always *arises a spontaneous sound*."[86]

In more recent times, Maharishi Mahesh Yogi has elaborated on how creation unfolds in a sequential nature from this self-referential generation of primordial frequencies or sounds. He cites the hymns of the Vedic literature as the manifestations of a "mechanics of transformation of self-referral intelligence into the ever-expanding material universe." The primordial sequences of differentiations are "available to us in countable stages in the structure of Rk Veda." In other words, "the sounds of the Vedic Literature" manifest in its syllables, verses, and chapters, just as "all the material and nonmaterial expressions of creation have specific frequencies."[87] In his *Apaurusheya Bhāshya*, he takes a further step in illuminating the "mechanics of transformation" within the unmanifest, silent "gaps" by which "the creative and evolutionary processes of the diverse universe," which are the play of self-referral intelligence, give rise to these frequencies, which are the building blocks of music.[88] Sound, in other words, is a manifestation of primordial frequencies, which are fluctuations in an underlying, eternal field of self-referral consciousness that is awake within itself. In every moment of creation and on all scales of creation, the *samhita*, or wholeness, upheld by the interactions of *rishi*, *devata*, and *chandas* impulses is found, and the more awareness is open to the subtle levels of these interactions, which are lively in the gaps, the more profound the creative expression.

Here we come upon an extraordinarily subtle juncture in the cosmic wholeness at which the foundational intersections between the most seemingly disparate phenomena—music, mind, and matter—are located. The "sequential emergence of discrete energy levels and corresponding frequencies that finally leads to a continuum of frequencies in Condensed Matter Physics," Maharishi continues, is indistinguishable from the "Vedic Frequencies" that sequentially unfold from "the transcendental level of Nature" and manifest in musical sound.[89] Jung also indicated an understanding in this direction, one that suggests a broader conception of the archetypal impulse than is often associated with his thought, when he surmised that "psyche and matter," because they coexist in the same world and therefore must originate in "irrepresentable, transcendent factors" are likely "two different aspects of one and the same thing."[90]

But the strong nonduality thesis and its underlying self-reference principle invite us to take an additional step that poses particularly significant ramifications to the music-cosmos connection. Generally speaking, the idea that music uniquely embodies the most fundamental impulses of creation has been framed from a structural vantage point, as in the aforementioned Hindustani view of musical sounds as primordial vibrations, or the notion of music of the spheres in the West, where systems as diverse as planetary orbits and the periodic table of the elements are seen as correlating with the musical overtone series.[91] The nonduality, self-reference principle enables us to add a process component to the mix, where the curving back of cosmic intelligence onto itself comprises the most primordial level of process reality. Structural reality consists of the primordial frequencies that are in turn generated from this movement. It is not insignificant that process underlies structure in this scenario, a principle whose pedagogical ramifications will be explored later. It is also consistent with ideas advanced by "process philosophers" such as Alfred North Whitehead, Henri Bergson, and more recently the physicist David

Bohm, for whom the universe is understood as a kind of cosmic flux rather than static phenomenon.[92]

As individual creativity and consciousness evolve, "Kosmic intelligence and creative energy," states the spiritual teacher Andrew Cohen, "consciously act through the awakened human being."[93] A farther step that might be inferred from the strong nonduality premise, one that is resonant with Cohen's background as a jazz drummer, is to understand the cosmic self-referential process as *improvisatory* in nature. It is interesting to note that the idea of *lila* is often portrayed as a capricious, almost whimsical venture on the part of an eternal cosmic intelligence that, able to choose to either create or not create, chooses the first. Ananda Coomaraswamy, summarizing various traditional accounts, describes *lila* as "a kind of game and dalliance"[94] on the part of the creator; William Sax refers to it as "mere sport," or "amusement."[95] Rabindranath Tagore muses that in their shared "self-willed joy, there is something in common between the *lila* of childhood and the works of God."[96] And thus from unmanifest, cosmic intelligence, the first impulse of differentiation may be thought to constitute a form of improvisatory play.

Just as musicians spontaneously generate ideas through the self-referential curving back of individual awareness onto itself, might the cosmic intelligence spontaneously create the universe, and possibly multiple universes, through the same self-reflexive folding back of consciousness? As speculative as this individual-cosmic connection may be, it represents an attempt, however rudimentary, at giving further shape to the strong nonduality thesis of the integral framework—or any, such as those of the world's wisdom traditions, that lay claim to nondual foundations. If the revolution in creativity and consciousness is to be adequate to the challenges of our times, this kind of inquiry will be necessary as it expands the conceptual space within which new insights and practical applications may manifest. Furthermore, if this individual-cosmic connection holds, even in part, then the ramifications for not only musical study but education at large are extraordinary. For the absence or inhibition of improvisatory development might be seen as entailing nothing less than inhibiting an intrinsic aspect of how individuals connect with the cosmic wholeness. When one further considers the participatory role of human consciousness in cosmic evolution, which is inherent in the strong nonduality thesis, exclusion of improvisatory creativity might be seen as impeding cosmic evolution. All of which underscores the transformational potential when this core process is embraced in the educational enterprise.

Additional support for the self-referential core of the strong nonduality thesis may be found in the coherence it exhibits on localized scales.

As to be explored shortly, individual improvisation and meditation practices may be understood as different forms of self-referral consciousness that, based on the very sequential unfolding of creation on a cosmic scale glimpsed earlier, give rise to highly synergistic systems of study that may similarly be organized sequentially. The analysis of this premise will call for two revisions in the integral first-second-third-person, or I/We/It trinity that maps the sequential unfolding and organization. The first entails modifying prevailing correlations between first-, second-, and third-person domains and, respectively, art, spirituality, and science, to spirituality (first-person), art (second), and science (third). The second entails a broadening of typical conceptions of the second-person domain whereby "We," or intersubjectivity, is seen as a manifestation of the cosmic process impulse. In other words, subject/intersubject/object becomes subject/process/object.

Meditation and Improvisation as Manifestations of Self-referral Consciousness

Let us begin by recalling notions of systematic approaches to meditation and improvisation and their respective continua of differentiated forms. Recall that anchoring these continua are, respectively, the pure consciousness of silent meditation, the wholeness of which then can flow more freely and completely through various kinds of active contemplative engagement, and free improvisation, the wholeness of which then flows, and itself thereby undergoes differentiation, through engagement in various kinds of musical creativity.

This becomes evident when meditation, improvisation, composition, and performance are placed along a continuum of manifestations of self-referral awareness. As Figure 3.4 illustrates, meditation is a self-mediated transpersonal process, improvisation is a self-mediated primary creative process, composition is an object-mediated primary creative process, and interpretive performance is an object-mediated secondary creative process. Meditation, in its core experience of pure consciousness, is the most direct manifestation of self-referential awareness in *silence,* and thus represents the most foundational alignment (one that supports the infinite diversity of silent and active spiritual experience and development) between human spirituality and cosmic spirit. Meditation is thus characterized as a *self-mediated transpersonal process,* the term *transpersonal* in this context utilized to differentiate the silent nature of meditation from the active nature of creativity. Were the active meditation spectrum to be mapped in 3.4, which we refrain from doing for the sake of clarity, they might be seen as forms of *object-mediated* transpersonal processes in that, for instance in the domain of contemplative reading, the process begins with *a priori* constraints unlike silent meditation.

Improvisation, in its core experience of free improvisation, is the most direct manifestation of self-referential awareness in *activity*, and thus represents the most foundational alignment (one that supports the infinite diversity of creative experiences and development) between human creativity and cosmic creativity. In other words, recalling the idea of *lila* as just noted as cosmic improvisation, cosmic intelligence, in its first and most primordial impulse to differentiate, transforms from pure unmanifest subjective reality to manifest a process dimension in its curving back on itself. Improvisation on human scales is therefore deemed a *self-mediated* primary creative process. Why self-mediated? This is illuminated when a continuum from self-mediated to object-mediated engagement is identified within the improvisatory realm somewhat similar to what was just considered within the realm of meditation (silent to active forms): free or stylistically open improvisation is most self-mediated, improvisation within preordained constraints is more object-mediated.

However, improvisation is never as object-mediated as composition, which is characterized as an *object-mediated* primary creative process because, as discussed in chapter 6, moment-to-moment decisions are shaped more by cumulative structure than in improvisation, due to the expanding, linear nature of compositional time conception.

Interpretive performance is an object-mediated *secondary* creative process because the composed-notated work, and thus foundational creativity, has already been accomplished prior to its realization. The descriptor *object-mediated* in the latter two instances should not be confused with object-referral attachments, which as an indicator of ordinary consciousness is possible in all four of the processes along the continuum. The designations here refer to heightened or transcendent states in each realm.

How does this enable, as noted previously, revision of prevailing correlations between first-second-third-person realities and art, spirituality, and science to first-person/spirituality, second-person/art, and third-person/science? The first-person/spirituality link is rooted in the fact that pure consciousness—at once exquisitely silent yet radiantly wakeful awareness of nothing but awareness itself—is human consciousness in its most unmanifest, undifferentiated form and correlates with unmanifest cosmic intelligence, or eternal Spirit. In other words, pure consciousness is pure subjectivity, which equates with the "I" of the I/We/It integral trinity. In no way is this to suggest, of course, that art is devoid of spirituality, but

Meditation	Improvisation	Composition	Interpretive performance
Self-mediated trans-personal process	Self-mediated primary creative process	Object-mediated primary creative process	Object-mediated secondary creative process

Figure 3.4. Distinctions Between Various Processes According to Self-Mediated and Object-Mediated Parameters.

that its process-oriented nature, most embodied in improvisation, renders it a second-person vehicle. Correlations between third-person reality and science, both pertaining to objective reality, are retained and require no commentary.

At this point, correlations may be also drawn with the *rishi*, *devata*, *chandas*, or subject, process, object differentiations of Maharishi's *Apaurusheya Bhāshya*, an important facet of which is the recognition that these primordial impulses of creation interact to yield not only the macro domains of spirituality, art, and science, but the most infinitesimal points of creation. Exemplifying the principle of *anoraniyan mahato-mahiyān*, which translates as "smaller than the smallest and bigger than the biggest," the subject, process, object interaction and its *samhita*, or resultant wholeness that is more than the sum of the parts, upholds all aspects of the cosmic totality.[97] Spirituality, art, and science not only interpenetrate each other, particularly when these disciplines are practiced integrally, in the course of a six-week meditation retreat, or concert tour, or design of a magnetic resonance imaging device, but in every nanosecond and subatomic impulse in the tiniest fabrics of time-space, and in the centuries-long evolutionary trajectories of knowledge areas. And because the *samhita* of *rishi*, *devata*, and *chandas*, or first-second-third-person realities, or spirituality, art, and science, is at the basis of both human consciousness and cosmic intelligence, developmental models can be constructed that harness this interaction and provide a powerful conduit through which awareness may flow and grow toward integral wholeness.

This takes our understanding of the unique nature of jazz-inspired integral process scope to an entirely new level.

Nested Synergies

Figure 3.5 illustrates the jazz process spectrum (minus meditation at the moment), which essentially consists of a systematic approach to improvisation mapped vertically. With each (overlying) stage of differentiation, (underlying) prior processes are not jettisoned but included—which means that they exist in increasingly differentiated forms along with the processes they spawn. Practitioners may thus benefit from the synergistic relationship between any two or more processes at each differentiated stage. In other words, while engagement with improvisation by itself will be of value to musical growth, this engagement and growth when informed by composition will be enhanced, and further enhanced when performance and then the various modes of craft come into play. All of which, of course, are enhanced by their coevolutionary relationship with improvisation.

This alignment illuminates the many kinds of synergistic relationships possible in systematic improvisatory engagement. One could, for example, identify improvisation-composition, improvisation-performance, or improvisation-theory relationships as among the many two-pronged synergistic interactions that are possible. And then when adding further combinations, an even broader spectrum is evident. Awareness, thus, has avail of a truly rich circuitry through which it can flow in its parts-to-whole integration.

This conception may be thought of as a musical correlate to Wilber's "Great Nest of Being," which is his reconception of Arthur Lovejoy's Great Chain of Being, so modified in order to show that higher stages of development integrate aspects of prior stages.[98] Hence, a process-mediated "Great Chain of Musical Being" characterized by increasingly differentiated, synergistic engagement with primary, secondary, and ancillary creative modalities—key to optimal self-transcending navigation of the musical landscape.

And when meditation is added to this analysis of the jazz process spectrum, even greater synergistic nesting is evident that underscores capacities for both parts-to-whole and whole-to-parts flows of awareness. While the variety of meditative practices that comprise a systematic mediation approach are not included for the sake of clarity, one can infer that these are part of the picture, giving rise to a truly rich process tapestry. And because, as has been emphasized, process breadth drives structural breadth, these diagrams could be extended to include structural dimensions, an example of which will be provided in chapter 9.

Important ramifications for musical study extend from the analysis that suggest the need for a radical revision of conventional approaches. First, whereas improvisation and composition are typically excluded from not only the curricular core but their upper structures, now they are shown to be foundational. Whereas conventional models are typically fragmented, this model is not only richly integrated, it exhibits both lateral and vertical kinds of integration. From a vertical standpoint, foundational processes, because they include in seed form more differentiated processes, at each stage inform, and are informed by, the totality. For example, when one engages in free improvisation within the nested synergies context, as opposed to freely improvising with minimal supportive skills in composition, performance, and theory, one accesses a conduit through which the process thrust may flow upward into any of the more differentiated areas, and can also flow back to inform it to promote greater

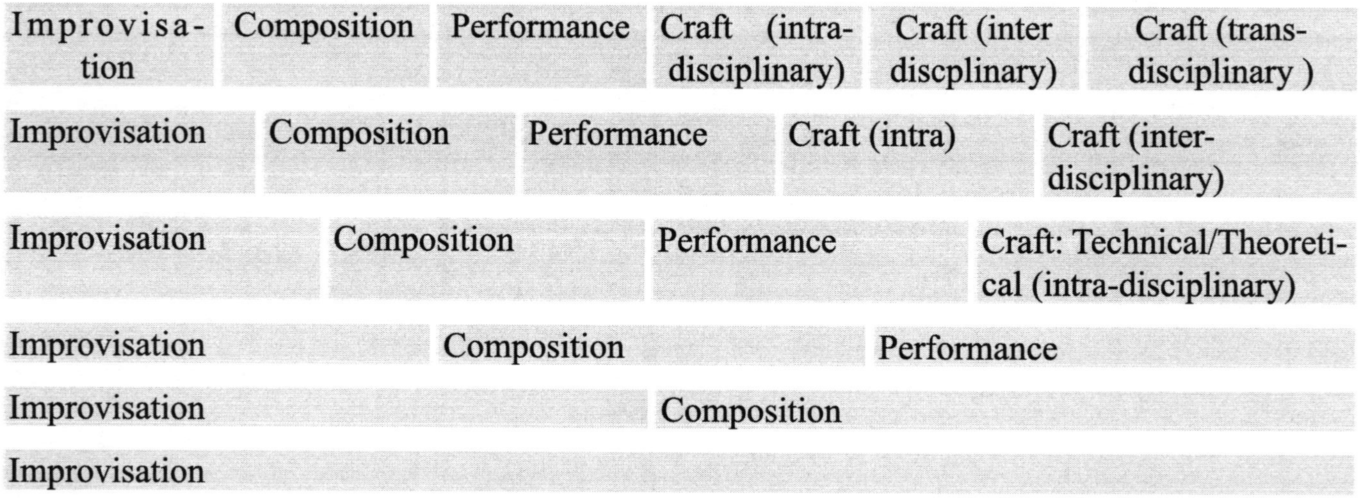

Improvisation	Composition	Performance	Craft (intra-disciplinary)	Craft (inter discplinary)	Craft (trans-disciplinary)
Improvisation	Composition	Performance	Craft (intra)	Craft (inter-disciplinary)	
Improvisation	Composition	Performance	Craft: Technical/Theoretical (intra-disciplinary)		
Improvisation	Composition	Performance			
Improvisation	Composition				
Improvisation					

Figure 3.5. Nested Synergies: Primary, Secondary, and Ancillary Creative Processes.

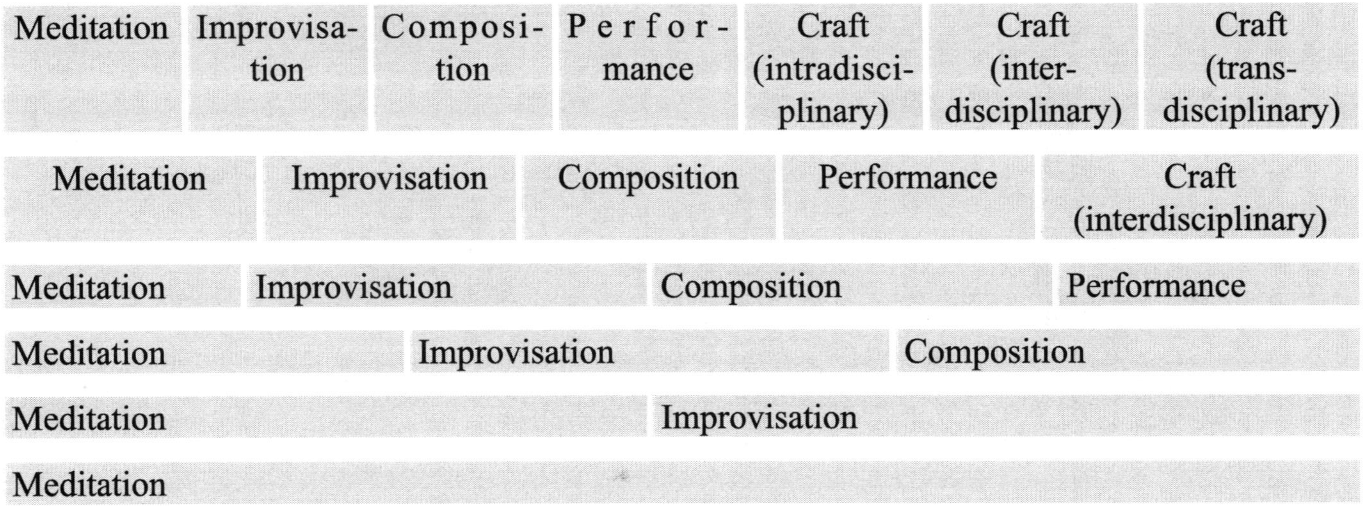

Figure 3.6. Nested Synergies Expanded: Meditation and Primary, Secondary, and Ancillary Creativity.

development. From a lateral standpoint, most evident at the most differentiated (overlying) level of the system, any given process is intimately linked with any other process. For example, theoretical inquiry, which all too often happens in isolation, now is connected with primary and secondary creativity. It is important, however, to realize that this kind of lateral connection is made possible by vertical alignment that proceeds from holistic to more localized processes. That process underlies structure, and process-mediated creativity underlies object-mediated creativity, holds on cosmic scales, where we see that process is a more primordial differentiation from the cosmic intelligence than objective reality, and on localized scales.

The nested synergies principle thus sheds light on the richness of both jazz process and structure scopes. Process is likely more obvious, with systematic approaches to improvisation and meditation (which we regard as part of the idiom's process range) and their constituent processes readily aligned according to the least-differentiated to more-differentiated scheme. Less immediately evident is the idiom's structure realm. To preview the more complete analysis that chapter 9 will present: Jazz's rhythmic-pitch spectrum spans considerable portions of that of the overall musical world, even if falling short of the idiom's process expanse in comparison to that of global practice. In the rhythmic domain, jazz's grounding in Black Atlantic Rhythm and time feel languages position it as a predominant global rhythmic stream. In the realm of pitch, jazz not only encompasses significant aspects of the world's modal/tonal/post-tonal continuum, particularly when the idiom is construed writ large to include its many offshoots, but it integrates much of this within a single performance, and sometimes within a single piece. Though it could be argued that European classical music spans as great, if not a greater, pitch spectrum, access to this tends to be fragmented and linear. Hampered by a kind of taboo on tonal or modal approaches, current composers are often driven by an ethos of aversion to past practices. Jazz improvisers-composers, on the other hand, move fluidly between past and highly innovative present application, thereby exemplifying the nested synergies principle not only in pedagogical models designed around this, but in actual creative practice.

Were jazz to be endorsed as a transformative musical force solely due to its unmatched process scope (which is untouched by the European division of labor, falling at the other end of the scale), the case would be overwhelming just along these parameters, a point that will be underscored when we differentiate improvisation and composition in chapter 6. When we include its structural aspects, it is strengthened even further, and here let us note the synergistic relationship between the broader process and structure realms as well as between any two or more components within those realms. Accordingly, advocacy of jazz as an integral transformational agent is based not only in its immediately evident, and clearly unmatched, process scope, but its process-structure scope. This underscores the significance of African American music in overall American musical culture and the global musical landscape.

Ultimate Reality and Meaning as Essential to Integral Inquiry and Development

While not everyone may be inclined to embrace the idea that individual creativity and consciousness are rooted in the same mechanics underlying those by which the cosmic intelligence creates the infinitely diverse universe, I believe that even the localized coherence revealed in the previous analysis—that which manifests on human scales—presents a compelling and important case for the importance of improvisatory creativity and meditation, particularly when approached systematically, in music and education at large. If these processes individually offer extraordinary benefits, then both their synergistic interplay as manifest in parts-to-whole and whole-to-parts trajectories considered in the previous chapter, and the nested synergies considered earlier, underscore what is possible when engaged with in tandem. A powerful alternative to the fragmented, creatively deficient, and ethnocentric horizons of conventional musical study emerges, one that does not require discarding the treasures of the past but rather is capable of situating them within the explosive, yet integrative diversity of the present.

And for those who, inspired by the strong nonduality thesis, are inclined toward the possibility that, indeed, these shared (individual and cosmic) self-referential foundations may hold, seeds are planted for a vastly expanded role for these processes in human creative and spiritual development. At this point the question—Why improvise?—takes on entirely new meaning. We improvise because it is an intrinsic aspect of the human psyche, which is an intrinsic aspect of the cosmic order with which the human psyche is inextricably linked. This analysis not only gives substance to Henryk Skolimowski's proclamation—"We create because the Cosmos is creating through us, we create because we are an outreach of the creative Cosmos"[99]—it may also invite paraphrase: "We improvise because we are an outreach of the improvising Cosmos." When we add the structural component—the fact that the primordial building blocks of creation are sounds that emanate from cosmic, improvisatory play—the nonduality-based argument for improvisation-based musical art as transformational agent is further strengthened. To neglect improvisation in musical study, music within the arts, the arts within the overall educational enterprise is to impede core facets of human being from blossoming. To neglect meditation is to similarly neglect a core facet of human nature and its inextricable link to cosmic totality. In my view, the stakes are raised for any critique of musical academe and education at large, and any vision for the future, to place these processes front and center.

As I have intimated in the introduction, I believe the time has come to situate all areas of human endeavor, which means all educational disciplines, within the context of Ultimate Reality of Meaning inquiry. Any inherent limitations in the capacity for human awareness to apprehend cosmic mysteries notwithstanding, the very fathoming of these boundaries holds vast potentialities for discovery and growth. Aversion to this due to reservations about succumbing to a murky metaphysics only replaces one metaphysical stance with another. That even Wilber himself vacillates on this point underscores the ambivalence and possible confusion in integral discourse surrounding this inquiry. On one hand, he admonishes us to beware the "myth of the given" and the lure of metaphysical assumptions, as they are, we are told, capably replaced by an "integral post-metaphysics"[100]—the central idea being that higher developmental states and stages (and thus realms of cosmic wholeness) are not ontologically pregiven, as "independent levels of being that are lying around waiting to be seen by humans," but rather are co-created by the "knowing subject."[101] To a certain extent, there is no conflict between these assertions and a strong nonduality premise; they, in fact, are potentially consistent with a dynamic, participatory vision of consciousness in cosmic evolution. However, they still beg the question—are there not likely inherent features of human consciousness, such as its self-referral nature, that, if it is indeed a manifestation of cosmic intelligence, it has inherited from this source and that thus endow it with this co-creative, participatory potential?

If Wilber's response to this is "yes," as would be mine, then that points to the very metaphysical, ontological pregivens he and other integralists dismiss as myth (but which I believe must be embraced). If his answer is no, then how does he justify his statement that no "spiritual philosophy can do completely without any *a priori* forms (no philosophy can); but the fewer the better."[102] It is difficult to wonder if the aversion to such forms is not largely arbitrary, thus reflecting the kind of unexamined, default metaphysics he eschews. How few prior forms, in other words, is few enough to satisfy this ostensibly necessary aspect of spiritual reality?

How many is too many, thereby pushing us past the threshold where we succumb to the "myth"? Would not even a single *a priori* assumption or given—for starters, that human consciousness is a manifestation of cosmic intelligence—be enough to significantly undermine any aversion to pregivens?

I believe robust URAM inquiry driven by jazz-inspired, parts-to-whole/whole-to-parts process breadth would yield a framework that centers this kind of analysis and enhances critical integrity and consistency. The marginalization of human improvisatory creativity in integral discourse might well be recognized as consistent with its marginalization of cosmic improvisatory creativity. Jorge Ferrer is another important thinker who, like Steve MacIntosh, resists venturing into URAM terrain yet whose contributions may be enhanced by it. Advancing an elaborate case for an "irreducible religious pluralism,"[103] he advocates an aversion to universalizing principles in order to avoid tradition-specific dogma as well as to illuminate the capacity for individual creativity in spiritual development. While important points are made in these arguments, notably Ferrer's elucidation of the extent to which such universalizing has largely evaded critical analysis in transpersonal psychology circles, I believe the fulfillment of his vision—which is a participatory spirituality whereby individuals fashion unique pathways to wholeness—lies not in the retreat from the problematic terrain, but a fuller commitment to this terrain that is possible through whole-to-parts and parts-to-whole engagement.

Ferrer's notion of a single spiritual "ocean with many shores" is an example of an incomplete parts-to-whole approach that never quite fathoms the whole, which as I have noted is a common tendency in integral circles.[104] While seeking to avoid the same kind of metaphysical dogma that Wilber eschews, in never quite reaching the whole, we are left deeply unsatisfied as to what the features of the source from which this pluralism emerges might be that enable such creativity. If the ocean, to paraphrase Ferrer using his own imagery, is only approached by land, the manner in which both water and soil emerge from a unified wholeness that both gives rise to the shores and is shaped by them will remain arbitrarily off-limits. The very "participatory turn" that Ferrer and others advocate in contemporary spiritual understanding is impeded because of a limited understanding of the individual-cosmos relationship that enables such participation in the first place. Instead of a robust participatory ontology, we are left with, at best, a participatory hermeneutics whose foundations are always vague due to what might be assessed as a politically correct, and clearly metaphysical, assumption about limitations in human consciousness to probe this realm.

This point may be underscored by comparison with another line of participatory thought, that advanced by thinkers such as Skolimowski and David Skrbina, which is rooted in the panpsychism premise that consciousness and matter are linked at all levels of creation; in not shying away from a mechanics that underlies individual and cosmic creation, this may allow a basis for a fuller participatory conception.[105]

"An important function of Integral Theory," Michael Zimmerman reminds us, "is to provide a coherent narrative of cosmic, terrestrial, and human development. Ideally, such a narrative is informed by multiple perspectives, including artistic, spiritual, ethical, scientific, and political."[107]

The way forward is not withdrawal from URAM inquiry but rather an all-out commitment to it that utilizes the full spectrum of integral conceptual and methodological resources. And, as pointed out, any sort of cosmic narrative or related conceptual frameworks need not be approached as rigid and impervious to question but simply as provisional platforms that promote further investigation and that are subject to critical inquiry at every step of the way. If, as the previous analysis attempts to demonstrate, the model exhibits coherence at local and universal scales, this may be among the criteria that suggest further exploration is warranted.

The rigorous attention to detail, robust creative exploration, and deep penetration into the innermost realms of consciousness, which are inseparable from the farthest reaches of the cosmic wholeness, inherent in the jazz-inspired integral process scope exemplify the best of conventional education while at the same time laying groundwork for entirely new educational vistas. The time has come to harness this process breath and engage in robust parts-to-whole and whole-to-parts swinging that can render this inquiry optimally dynamic, self-critical, joyous, and productive; to deploy the heightened inventive, interactive, individuative, transcendent, and self-critical faculties that are enlivened in ways that open up new vistas for imagining and transforming our world. Let us not fear inquiry into the biggest questions about human and cosmic existence but follow in the footsteps of the great artists, scientists, and mystics who not only derived great meaning in this intrinsic aspect of human evolution but at times unearthed important insights that enhanced day-to-day life. Having now explored parallels between improvisation and meditation on localized and cosmic scales, a conceptual backdrop against which their shared capacities to enliven intersubjective consciousness might be appreciated has come more fully into view. The next step is to gain a stronger grasp of the dynamics by which new ideas move from the outskirts of thinking to the center so that they can be more completely examined and developed.

Summary

We have now taken up two of the three primary lenses—structure, process, and evolutionary dynamics—that comprise our introduction to a jazz-inspired perspective of Integral Theory. Chapter 1 dealt with the interior and exterior dimensions of the integral structural scope, chapter 2 the parts-to-whole, improvisation-driven process scope (with some consideration of meditation), and this chapter the whole-to-parts, meditation-driven process scope (with some consideration of improvisation), that work in tandem to traverse and integrate the inner-outer, creativity-consciousness spectrum. Higher states and stages (subtle, causal, nondual) were seen as landmarks in creativity-consciousness development, with not only each individual plateau rooted in the self-referral dynamics of consciousness, but the means by which cosmic wholeness gives rise to the infinitely diverse creation also rooted therein. From the general nonduality thesis that recognizes the inextricable link between individual consciousness and cosmic wholeness, we thus took the further step of delineating a strong nonduality thesis in suggesting that human improvisation is a manifestation of cosmic improvisatory play. While this is admittedly speculative, that it gives rise to the nested synergies of the jazz process scope, whereby (viewing it in terms of its creativity spectrum) improvisation, composition, performance, and various modes of theoretical inquiry might be seen as sequentially differentiated manifestations of self-referral awareness, provides an example of localized coherence that poses compelling ramifications for musical study and beyond. Now the systematic approach to improvisation, which includes this total synergistic scope, takes on greater significance as a core platform for self-transcending engagement, as does the systematic approach to meditation that promotes the same. For the richly differentiated circuitry extending from these process trajectories, through which awareness may flow in parts-to-whole and whole-to-parts directions in the quest for all-quadrants, creativity-consciousness growth, may now be seen as more than a powerful tool for individual evolution, but as a conduit through which cosmic intelligence flows and informs, with human consciousness as a channel, the totality of creation.

We now turn to the complex patterns that govern—and sometimes impede—individuals, communities, and knowledge systems as they invoke transformation in this direction.

Chapter 4

Integral Evolutionary Dynamics

This chapter covers the third of our three primary integral lenses, the evolutionary dynamics by which systems develop over time. It elaborates upon two general principles, both of which have already been encountered in a variety of forms, and introduces further considerations that enhance our grasp of the paradigmatic change that is among the central themes of the book. First is that evolution progresses from less-differentiated to more-differentiated wholeness, or toward greater diversity within unity. This is true of a wide range of phenomena, from biological systems, cultural systems, to the stages of consciousness growth considered in the previous chapter. Second—most prominent in human knowledge systems—is that the thrust toward differentiation often gives way to dissociation, where a part becomes severed from, and in turn may view itself as competing with, the whole. Object-referral attachments that prevail in what was considered ordinary consciousness provide a clear example. At this point the task becomes one of restoring the dissociated part to, as Wilber has put it, a more healthy differentiation status.[1]

Epistemological diversity—engagement with diverse methodologies such as systematic approaches to improvisation and meditation—was seen as an important means for accomplishing this on an individual scale, as this dislodges conditioned patterns and cultivates more holistic, integrated functioning and understanding. However, it is important to recognize that dissociated tendencies can be so deeply rooted, comprising what integralists, after Jung, call the "shadow,"[2] that they need to be carefully diagnosed and approached through corresponding modalities. Generally defined as the repository of repressed emotions and anxieties, shadow patterns left unaddressed may manifest in various kinds of pathologies, and Wilber, even while emphasizing meditation as among the most important tools for personal growth, concedes that it in itself is ill-equipped to address certain kinds of shadow structures. Western psychotherapy, which he points out has been long regarded in meditation circles as outmoded and unnecessary, may at times be among the most effective interventions.[3]

Although shadow considerations are generally taken up from the standpoint of individual development, they are also important to collective development, as in a given developmental line or discipline, or—more broadly—the transformation of educational and societal systems that is needed in our times. It becomes apparent that the same expanded epistemological scope that is needed for individual growth naturally will promote some degree of collective change. However, the need for careful diagnosis of the broader shadow patterns prevailing in collective systems may be even more complex due to the expanded array of factors involved. As we will see in our look at overall education and musical studies, where change is often confined to surface modifications, the dissociative, shadow patterns in these areas are often multitiered, manifesting in both outer and inner forms, and an understanding of this is absolutely essential for paradigmatic change—that entailing both horizontal and vertical reform. As noted previously, horizontal change entails modification of the existing paradigm, vertical entails fundamental restructuring, as in the enduring access to interior dimensions of awareness that comprises creativity and consciousness development.[4]

Among the powerful tools Integral Theory brings to this work are the various developmental scales that have emerged from areas such as psychology, sociology, and cultural studies. Two in particular will inform our analysis of the musical landscape and academic musical training. One is the progression from premodern to modern, postmodern, and integral stages of cultural evolution. The other is that which proceeds from egocentric to ethnocentric, worldcentric and integral stages of self-development emerging from the work of psychologists Carol Gilligan, Jane Loevinger, Suzanne Cook-Greuter, and other integral theorists.[5] Closely intertwined with these models is the range of philosophies of consciousness—including dualism, materialism, and integralism[6]—that has followed its own developmental progression and exhibits patterns whereby differentiation has taken the extreme step of dissociation. We will see that education and musical studies have inherited patterns from the materialist worldview, where tendencies in the sciences and humanities to reduce consciousness to a neurobiological substrate, even amid empirical findings that corroborate with age-old and far more expansive conceptions of consciousness, have significantly constrained the scope of study. Just as scientific materialism reduces mind to brain at the exclusion of transcendent dimensions of human experience and reality, educational materialism reduces learning to ingestion of information and musical materialism reduces musicianship to interpretive performance of already composed repertory, all at the expense of broader creativity and consciousness development.

If the jazz-driven integral revolution is to take hold in education and society, these dissociative tendencies must be rectified in the broader academic spheres in which its integral features will need to be harnessed.

Cultural Evolution

We begin with premodern, modern, and postmodern stages of cultural evolution, to which integralists add an integral stage in which salient aspects of prior stages are united in a more expansive vision. It is important to emphasize that these stages are framed from largely a Western cultural viewpoint, and thus any global ramifications that might be inferred should be approached with caution. We will proceed from a quadratic or whole-to-parts perspective in order to more clearly grasp the evolutionary trajectory from undifferentiated to more differentiated wholeness, as well as the dissociative tendencies that would take hold. These will be seen in terms of various kinds of *quadrant absolutism* that relate to the respective phases. We will also identify a closely related evolutionary trajectory in the area of philosophy of mind as it progresses from dualist to materialist and then integral stages of understanding.

Premodern, Modern, Postmodern, and Integral Cultural Evolution

Premodernism may be understood as Upper-Left absolutism in that prior to the emergence of the scientific method as we now know it, aspects of the physical world were understood largely in terms of mythical/magical forces and later dogmatic interpretations of scripture or church doctrine. Therefore, an overarching and crudely fathomed subjectivity prevailed. Though "premodern cultures certainly possessed art, morals and science," Wilber observes, "these spheres tended to be relatively undifferentiated." Galileo, for example, "could not look freely through his telescope and report the results because art, morals and science were all fused under the Church," which "defined what science could—and could not do."[7] With the onset of modernity, "the differentiation of the value spheres" placed rational inquiry, undertaken apart from a religious viewpoint, at the vanguard of social progress. Thinkers could now investigate the world around them "without fear of being charged with heresy or treason."[8]

While this capacity for objective, rational inquiry resulting from the differentiation of spirituality, art, and science set the stage for a wide range of progressive reforms, ranging from "liberal democracy, the end of slavery, the growth of feminism, and the staggering advances in the medical sciences," it did not come without a cost.[9] In fact, the three "value spheres did not always just peacefully differentiate," Wilber continues, "they often flew completely apart." He further explains:

> The wonderful differentiations of modernity went too far into dissociation, fragmentation, and alienation. As the value spheres began to dissociate, this allowed a powerful and aggressive science to begin to invade and dominate the other spheres, crowding art and morals out of any serious consideration in approaching "reality." Science became *scientism*—scientific materialism and scientific imperialism—which soon became the dominant "worldview" of modernity.[10]

Hence, Upper-Left absolutism gave way to Upper-Right absolutism. Scientific materialism, which at its core is a perspective of the nature of consciousness and thus the human being as either reducible to, or rooted in, a physical substrate, will be taken up in depth shortly as it exerts an enormous influence on the academic world.

If modernity privileged third-person epistemologies or ways of knowing and objective/exterior reality at the expense of the first-person domain, postmodernism may be generalized as the championing of the second-person, intersubjective realm—the Lower Left quadrant. Whereas modernism and its structural orientation presume that inherent in the forms of works of literature or art are timeless, transcendent features that might be gleaned by individuals across cultures, post-structural/postmodern thought shifted the locus from the work to the aspects of percipients' (listeners'/viewers'/readers') time and place that shape interpretation. In other words, knowledge, reality, and meaning are not intrinsic to the features of created objects but rather are culturally constructed, or inferred by percipients according to their particular backgrounds. Just as with modernism in science, where the differentiation that first manifested in dualism would take the extreme, dissociative step of materialism, the postmodern differentiation in the cultural relativistic sphere similarly dissociated. In its quest "to embrace surfaces, champion surfaces," as Wilber describes it, postmodernism succumbed to "glorification of surfaces and surfaces alone." In "making the culturally relative features the entire story," many postmodernists ended up denying "depth altogether" within a "flatland" conception of human nature and development.[11] The idea of transcendent reality would not only be rejected as an oppressive myth when ascribed to the structural features of a given work or expression, it would be categorically dismissed from an overall account of human nature and reality. Therefore, in advocating the importance of diverse perspectives—and attempts to avoid the privileging of any single perspective—postmodernism has, albeit unwittingly, exempted itself from these seemingly noble guidelines and indeed privileged itself as the most viable perspective, in so doing perpetuating the very hierarchical stratification of knowledge systems it seeks to dethrone.

Postmodernism, then, at least as generally construed, can be seen as Lower-Left absolutism, privileging cultural relativistic reality. However, an integral perspective enables us to distinguish between the prevailing dissociative, *astructural* postmodernism, and a *structural* postmodernism in which recognition of Lower-Left cultural relativistic factors do not overshadow the possibility that Upper-Right structural features of works, and Lower-Right creative disciplines, might inhere transcendent facets that are the source of meaning.[12] By contrast, differentiation in the cultural relativistic sphere does not take the step of dissociation but simply transcends and includes structural premises. At this point, the boundaries begin to blur between the postmodern and the integral, where the limited and exclusionary tendencies of prior stage dissociation are sifted out, the unique contributions of these stages are celebrated, and thus all-quadrants unification is achieved. We will see in our consideration of the musical world where subtle yet not insignificant criteria may be noted that help distinguish these two later stages and reveal the unitive power—its scope, differentiated nuance, and coherence—of the integral.

In any case, it is postmodernism of the deconstructive type that tends to prevail in the academic humanities, and materialism that prevails in the sciences, both of which reject interior realities that are central—along with exteriors—to the integral. The integral stage of cultural development, corresponding to an integral view of consciousness, is an all-quadrants perspective. Upper-Right mind-brain correlations, privileged by materialists, Lower-Left cultural influences, privileged by postmodernists, are not rejected but located within a broader vision that also celebrates Upper-Left interior, subjective reality. If movement to this stage is to be achieved, vigilant introspection into the dissociative patterns—the collective shadow—that constrain the current model will be needed. We begin with what I think of as a *Matrix of Materialism*, where tendencies to privilege exteriors at the expense of interiors is evident across highly diverse fields.

Matrix of Materialism and the Collective Shadow

As already glimpsed, cultural evolution and philosophy-of-consciousness evolution are closely intertwined. This is underscored by a look at the scientific materialist worldview, which is the philosophy-of-consciousness that prevails in the academic world and influences far more than the sciences.

Materialism may perhaps be best understood in comparison to contrasting worldviews. Dualism, which may be seen as a precursor to materialism that took hold in the modernist turn, holds that mind and matter, interior and exterior, or subjective and objective realms are fundamentally separate. This premise is commonly associated with the work of the French philosopher René Descartes and captured eloquently in biologist Stephen Jay Gould's famous description of religion and science as "non-overlapping magisteria."[13] Although dualism, at least in theory, permits the harmonious coexistence of interiors and exteriors, materialism privileges exteriors and categorically subordinates interiors by either reducing them to—in other words, defining them as "nothing but"—a neurobiological substrate, or attempting to explain them as a by-product of that substrate. Two primary strands of materialism might be identified.

Its most extreme form is reductionism, no clearer articulation of which is found than Francis Crick's and Christof Koch's statement: "The problem of consciousness, in the long run, can be solved only by explanations at the neural level."[14] In other words, mind is reducible to, and thus nothing but, brain. Transcendent experience, spirituality, and notions of nonphysical dimensions of reality are illusions that are explicable in physical terms. Crick elaborates: "You, your joys and sorrows, your memories and your ambitions, your sense of personal identity and free will are in fact no more than the behavior of a vast assembly of nerve cells and their associated molecules." And issuing the ultimate materialist *coup de grace*, he concludes: "You are nothing but a pack of neurons."[15]

Situating, as many materialists do, this reductionist account of the human being and notions of any intrinsic meaning in human existence in a cosmological perspective, Stephen Weinberg asserts that the more we learn about the brain, the subatomic underpinnings of the physical world, and their emergence in the moments following the Big Bang, the more we realize our universe as "pointless."[16] Concepts such as soul, or spirit, or of a transcendent purpose to life and existence are remnants of an outmoded kind of thinking that humanity would do well to outgrow. Attempting to console us, he admits, "[t]he reductionist [materialist] worldview is chilling and impersonal." But we must accept it as it is, "not because we like it, but because that is the way the world works."[17]

Recent years have seen a general retreat from reductionism toward a more moderate form of materialism called *epiphenomenalism*, or *emer-*

gentism, that yields, albeit partial, openings to interiority.[18] Here consciousness is still viewed as rooted in a physical substrate, but as nonreducible to that substrate. "Consciousness," Searle writes, "is caused by lower-level neuronal processes in the brain . . . [and because] it emerges from certain neuronal activities, we can think of it as an 'emergent' property of the brain. . . . [B]ut . . . it cannot be explained simply as a summation of the properties of these elements."[19] Judith Hooper points to a further aspect of epiphenomenalism, the capacity for consciousness, once emerged, to exert a "downward influence on the brain's psycho-chemical machinery, pushing the atoms and molecules around."[20] Experiences such as love, hope, anxiety, and joy may have physiological correlates and origins, but they represent emergent properties of consciousness that are not entirely explicable in physicalist terms. The human being, then, is more than "a pack of neurons."

Taking the materialist perspective in its more generalized terms, which are prominent when compared with the integral perspective, we can analyze materialism as largely confined to Upper Right and Lower Right with Lower-Left and Upper-Left realities as illusory or subordinate. Or put another way, third-person exterior/physical reality is privileged—at the expense of second-person intersubjective and first-person interior/subjective and dimensions—and thus dissociated from the broader wholeness. An integral understanding of consciousness does not privilege any particular quadrant but rather sees the phenomenon as encompassing all quadrants. Now, from the standpoint of nonduality, one could argue that Upper Left is primary, for all of creation originates in cosmic spirit or subjectivity. This would be a quadratic perspective on the quadrants. However, this still cedes an important place for the various differentiated regions—the remaining three quadrants—that emerge from the cosmic Upper Left. It also invites a complementary quadrivium, or parts-to-whole, perspective where all quadrants are self-transcending gateways to all-quadrants wholeness. The materialist exclusion of all but the Upper-Right (or arguably Right-Hand) quadrants enables no such integration.

Let us look further into deficiencies in the materialist platform as it shapes practice in much of the academic world and thereby confines the boundaries of consciousness exploration to but a small spectrum of what is possible and needed. And will be seen, what are being inherited across fields include not only limited conclusions about the nature of the human being and reality, but limited methodological scope leading to such conclusions. The platform, in other words, is built on both shaky ontological and epistemological ground.

Hard and Harder Problems for Materialism

To begin, materialism is theoretically problematic, as indicated in the "hard problem of consciousness" framed by materialists themselves. While reductionism, in essentially positing that a wide range of human experience—and even consciousness itself—are illusory, and only the physical is real, represents a kind of extremism that even most materialists find untenable, the epiphenomenalist alternative is not without its difficulties. "How could a physical system," wonders David Chalmers, a seminal thinker in framing the hard problem, "give rise to conscious experience?"[21] Because a response to this question has been so elusive, Chalmers confesses to considering dualism, despite its virtually taboo status in materialist circles, as the only viable option. "I resisted mind-body dualism for a long time, but I have come to the point where I accept it, not just as the only tenable view, but as a satisfying view in its own right."[22]

I believe the various manifestations of self-awareness that an integral viewpoint identifies pose further challenges to the materialist perspective. If it is difficult enough to fathom how the phenomenon of self-awareness in general—for example, Damasio's notion of "core consciousness," or Chalmers' "phenomenal consciousness,"[23] might be epiphenomenal to a physical substrate, I believe difficulties only increase when one takes into consideration heightened or transcendent states of self-awareness. As explored in the previous chapter, these can be understood as part of a continuum, at one end of which is the experience of pure consciousness, where awareness curves back on itself in the silence of meditation and experiences nothing but content-free, undifferentiated self-referential consciousness. That such experiences are initiated through mental techniques and then not only transcend those techniques to access dimensions of mind devoid of thought, but also result in profound neurobiological changes, is far more coherent with the idea that consciousness, not matter, is primary than the idea that consciousness is reducible or a by-product of the material. When we move further along the continuum and consider capacities for active transcendence, where heightened self-awareness now occurs in the midst of engagement with relativistic objects of perception, we encounter further dimensions of the hard problem. In chapter 6, I will take this reasoning an additional step and, in distinguishing between improvisatory and compositional pathways as contrasting, temporality-mediated pathways to transcendent experience, suggest that only a consciousness that is ontologically transcendent of the physical world could exhibit this range of self-referential properties.

From an integral perspective, the inherent conundrum in the hard problem thus lies not in the evasiveness of a convincing reply, but in the flawed nature of the question itself. "How does the self-aware entity emerge from deeper and more elementary physical processes?" asks the physicist Fred Alan Wolff in his challenge to the very assumptions underlying the question. "The answer is, it doesn't, and this is very difficult to deal with in today's reductionist science." Pointing instead toward a nondual vision, he asserts that "one eternal consciousness"[24] is the ontological ground of reality, an idea that is compatible with what mystics from the world's wisdom traditions have been asserting for millennia.

Further shortcomings of the materialist view may be noted. That it is incoherent with most individuals' day-to-day perception of reality, including experiences of love, anxiety, joy, and transcendence, do not in themselves suffice to dethrone the platform but certainly must be taken into consideration and added to the broader analytical mosaic. The same holds for the extent to which materialism flies in the face of accounts of consciousness posited by the world's wisdom traditions, with a conspicuous absence in materialist literature of addressing such accounts—which one would presume to be a basic protocol for philosophical inquiry. This is not only suggestive of an ethnocentric orientation, it also reflects a serious lapse in critical inquiry faculties, as does the entirely spurious conclusions it draws from its primary source of empirical evidence—findings that show mind and brain to be intimately connected. The problem is not that the findings are flawed, but that they could just as readily be interpreted to support an integral account of consciousness that at once embraces the discoveries of cognitive neuroscience and age-old wisdom of mystics who also acknowledge dimensions of consciousness that transcend the physical. Correlation does not mean causation—just because consciousness correlates with physical, objectively measurable parameters does not mean it is reducible to or caused by those parameters.[25] Have not materialists taken a leap of logic that conveniently supports their perspective but entails weak critical faculties and thus weak science? While none of these points taken individually may be sufficient to topple the paradigm, taken collectively they issue formidable challenges to the model, which are exacerbated in light of the absence of a compelling supportive rationale for the model.

Furthermore, an entirely new kind of challenge to the materialist platform can be cited that, particularly when coupled with the previous arguments, issues what may well be fatal blows to the ideology. What is most ironic is that this challenge comes not from spiritual traditions—

even if highly consistent with their perspectives of reality—but from science itself, in the form a wide range of empirical findings that strongly suggest human consciousness to be nonmaterial in nature.

The Collapse of Materialism: Overview of Research into Extended Capacities of Consciousness

In the early 1990s, the philosopher Daniel Dennett's *Consciousness Explained* was widely hailed as a landmark articulation of the materialism platform. More recently, psychologist Allan Combs, with his coyly titled *Consciousness Explained Better*, and his cohort Charles Tart, author of *The End of Materialism*, join the ranks of an increasing number of thinkers who believe the collapse of the materialist paradigm is imminent, if not long overdue. Perhaps no greater threat is posed to the materialist worldview than the rapidly expanding body of empirical research that strongly points to dimensions of consciousness that transcend the neurobiological substrate to which materialists either claim consciousness is reducible, or from which it emerges.

At least 10 types of findings might be identified, within each of which scores of studies have been conducted—which the psychologist Dean Radin in the late 1990s claimed to total in the thousands—at institutions including Princeton University, Duke University, University of Virginia, Maimonides Hospital, Bell Labs, Stanford Research Institute, and the U.S. military. These include:

Remote cognition, which as defined by Robert Jahn and Brenda Dunne at the Princeton Engineering Anomalies Research (PEAR) laboratory, consists of "the acquisition of information about locations remote in distance and time and inaccessible by any known sensory communication channel."[26] Even with "intercontinental distances of several thousand miles, there is no discernible deterioration in the signal-to-noise ratio. . . . If, as sometimes postulated, some form of physical wave propagation, such as electromagnetic waves or geophysical waves, were involved, an inverse fidelity of the information on that distance would be expected."[27] No such effect was seen, and "the specificity and replicability of individual operator signatures and the degrees of statistical significance argue forcefully against chance occurrence"[28] in these experiments. Among the most compelling support for remote cognition may come from research conducted by the Defense Department in response to reports during the Cold War that the Soviets were investigating these capacities. University of Oregon physicist and longtime psi skeptic Ray Hyman chaired the National

Research Council that was charged with investigating these phenomena. After reviewing the data, he concluded that the "statistical departures from chance appear to be too large and consistent to attribute to statistical flukes of any sort. . . . I tend to agree that . . . real effects are happening in these experiences."[29] Psi effects, affirms Radin, have appeared in an extraordinary range and quantity of experiments, leading "virtually all scientists who have studied the evidence, including the hard-nosed skeptics, to agree that something interesting is going on that merits serious scientific attention."[30] This has caused many researchers to shift their attention "from proof-oriented experiments" to "process oriented questions," such as "How does it work?"[31]

Psychiatrist Elizabeth Mayer, perhaps most aptly characterized as "skeptic-turned-critical advocate," closely examined a variety of psi capacities, including studies in Dream Telepathy conducted at Maimonides Hospital in New York City, where subjects have shown the ability to invoke experiences that corroborate with experiences of others through no known sensory channels. Suggesting that "when people disengage from the mental processes affecting their waking life, a vital capacity to transfer information from one person to another through dreams is freed to express itself in dreams," this work represents a "major new episode in the study of anomalous cognition."[32]

Psychokinesis is the capacity for mind to influence matter, which has been studied extensively at the PEAR laboratory as well as by Stanford physicist William Tiller, who has shown repeatedly that meditating subjects are able to consistently cause the pH balance in a solution, both in close proximity and also at great distances, to rise or fall through sheer intention.[33]

Discarnate consciousness is consciousness without a physical substrate, including that which survives bodily death. This manifests in several forms. Perhaps the most compelling support for this are the reincarnation or rebirth studies that began with the psychiatrist Ian Stevenson at University of Virginia, and which is the basis for the establishment of the Division of Perceptual Studies at UVA Medical School. A typical scenario involves children who report vivid recall of places they have never visited but claim to be of a prior existence, who are then led to such places by a team of researchers, as the children identify locations and in some cases specific individuals, knowledge of which is inexplicable through conventional protocols. That in many instances children recount a specific incident, often an accident, from a past existence and are born with a scar or birthmark on the corresponding part of the body, adds an additional parameter of corroboration. Also studied in the UVA laboratory are *near death experiences*, in which subjects report the sensation of awareness separating from their physical body and reporting veridical information that would not have been accessed otherwise.[34]

The psychologist Jenny Wade, reviewing this work in her framing of a "holonomic theory of consciousness," concludes: "Although reincarnation has not been proven, validated empirical evidence from a variety of sources suggests that a physically transcendent source of mind—i.e., a personal consciousness capable of escaping the boundaries of the body—does, in fact exist." Combined with research that suggests capacities of consciousness for "nonlocal transmission of thoughts, dreams, and visions outside linear time," these findings underscore the inadequacy of a "purely materialistic epistemology."[35]

Empirical research supports the possibility already encountered of *intersubjective*, collective dimensions of consciousness, among the most dramatic and perhaps provocative evidence for which in terms of practical application are studies of the effect of group meditation on the environment. The physicians Hari Sharma and Christopher Clark, closing their book on Ayurvedic approaches to health with consideration of this as a collective health intervention, cite findings that show significant decrease in "crime rate, traffic accidents, and illness" during a three-week period when several thousand meditators engaged in intensive daily practice together. They also cite a number of other experiments in which the effect was replicated, including neutralization of military conflict in the Mideast.[36] Radin and a team of researchers may have provided a form of cross-parametric corroboration of this effect when they set up random event generators, devices that are designed to measure field coherence by detecting deviations from ordinary random event firing, in the vicinity of meditation halls and found small but discernible readings on their equipment that correlate with strategic points in the group meditation practice. Now the idea that harmonizing effects may positively impact human behavior may be matched with psychokinetic, mind-matter interactions. Random event generator (REG) research has also shown that events that attract considerable worldwide attention, such as the Super Bowl and Academy Awards, register discernible fluctuations, strongly indicative of some kind of field effect. These results from events known in advance led researchers to set up REG sites that would run continuously in order to detect fluctuations in unforeseen events. The terrorist attacks of 9/11 revealed dramatic results.

The idea of a collective field aspect of consciousness is also closely linked to the biologist Rupert Sheldrake's notion of *morphic resonance*, where, as he has found in numerable studies, animals in disparate locations seem to be able to transmit to one another information and abilities to master tasks.[37] His work suggesting nonlocal linkage between animal and human consciousness may also be noted.[38]

Most recently, the psychologist Daryl Bem has conducted studies in the area previously called *precognition* and now called *retrocausation* that suggest consciousness may transcend the linear progression of time, and a future event may not only be fathomed in advance, but might even influence a past event.[39] Richard Tarnas' massive analysis of correlations between important periods of discovery, sociocultural turbulence, and specific planetary alignments presents among the most recent and compelling support for the age-old science of astrology, some form of which is found in many traditions across the world (e.g., *Jyotish* is the branch of the Vedic knowledge that deals with this), lending further support to the link between individual consciousness and cosmic wholeness.[40]

Perhaps most radical are University of Arizona psychologist Gary Schwartz' findings that support the idea of contact with spiritual intelligences or entities through psychic mediums, corroborated through arranged "visits" of these in carefully monitored light-proof chambers where high-tech equipment is capable of detecting photon activity at extraordinarily low scales. Consistently, photon activity increased dramatically at times when entities agreed to "show up."[41]

In no way is this to suggest that every single study of psi, or extended dimensions of consciousness, is impeccable, nor even that taken as a totality, they represent incontrovertible proof of nonlocal, intersubjective, dimensions of mind. However, following William James' wisdom regarding this work, where he argues that one need not examine every crow in the world to prove that not all crows are black—one need only find a single white crow—it clearly appears, as the philosopher David Ray Griffin states in his comprehensive assessment of these findings, that there seems to be little doubt that "white crows abound."[42] Combining this with the compatibility of the findings with the direct experiences of much of the population, widespread intuitions about the spiritual dimensions of the human being, the elaborate theoretical models of consciousness in various spiritual traditions that make room for these capacities (much materialist literature is notably lacking in reference to Eastern models of mind), the case for materialism seems increasingly untenable.

Though Weinberg and other materialists are quick to dismiss these kinds of findings—which he shows no indication of having seriously examined—as "superstition," Thomas Etter of the Boundary Institute justifiably redirects the same charge back at those who remain sheltered from the growing body of evidence: "When a belief is widely held in the face of overwhelming evidence to the contrary, we call it a superstition. By that criterion, the most egregious superstition of modern times, perhaps of all time, is the 'scientific' belief in the nonexistence of psi."[43] Parallels between religious fundamentalism and what Colgate astrophysicist Victor Mansfield calls "scientific fundamentalism"[44] are ever evident, further underscoring the pattern of quadrant absolutism—where but a portion of the cosmic wholeness, in this case the Upper-Right, exterior physical world—is privileged at the exclusion of the Upper-Left, subjective interiors that in fact underlie the Upper Right.

Dueling Dualisms and Nondualisms

It is important in distinguishing integral and materialist perspectives on the nature of consciousness to clarify two common points of confusion regarding their respective notions of dualism and nondual integration. The first involves distinctions between the materialist conception of mind-body unification and the integral unification of subjective and objective realities. While materialists rightly claim mind and body are one, a claim integralists share, they stop short of a broader subjective-objective unity that is key to the nondual integral vision. In other words, materialists reject dimensions of consciousness transcendent of the physical, and therefore their resolution of mind-body duality is confined to a localized integration that is not to be confused with integral nondualism and its unity of subjective and object realms on both localized and cosmic scales. It is also important to realize that materialist tendencies to dismiss perspectives that acknowledge physically transcendent dimensions of consciousness as dualistic are based on the a priori assumption that matter is primary, and therefore notions of consciousness transcendent of matter can only be dualist. The possibility that consciousness might be primary is not even remotely on the materialist radar screen. It must be thus emphasized that the integral perspective, which holds that consciousness is primary, is decidedly not dualist but nondualist, and rooted in a conception of unity that vastly differs from the localized coupling of mind and body held by materialism in not only expanse, but foundations.

This sheds light on a hidden ethnocentrism in the materialist platform, where the viewpoint has been articulated largely in response to the dualist philosophy commonly associated with the French philosopher Descartes with little or no mention of Eastern models that had resolved mind-body dualism, as well as the broader dualism, millennia prior.[45] One senses in reading much materialist literature that Western accounts of consciousness are the only ones worthy of serious consideration, which is notably similar to attitudes among conventional musicologists toward non-European musical traditions. An even more serious problem for materialists extends from this approach. For in defining itself in contrast to Cartesian dualism, it backs itself into a corner where it must choose between two deeply flawed options.

The first is reductionism. If mind and body are not separate but one, then the question of the fundamental nature of this unity must be answered. What, in other words, is the common source that what appear to be different realms of mind and matter are in fact manifestations of? To reply that consciousness and matter comprise the fundamental nature of reality at all scales, which is panpsychism, is not an option for materialists because it would then admit to the existence of consciousness even in what is generally regarded as inanimate matter. Nor is the idea that consciousness or spirit is foundational, which is idealism or integralism, because this disintegrates the entire materialist edifice. Therefore the only option is that matter is the primary substance, to which mind is reducible. This flies in the face of all logic and experience, which is why a retreat from reductionism has been evident in recent years within materialist circles.

But this leaves epiphenomenalism, with its equally insurmountable challenges, as the last resort. For now the hard problem of consciousness—that of how mind could emerge from a physical substrate—comes back into the picture. If the hard problem is difficult enough when it comes to explaining conventionally acknowledged human capacities such as love, hope, inspiration, creativity, and self-reflection, it is even more challenged to explain the extended capacities of consciousness considered here earlier. Unless the taboo against dualism is lifted, the only viable option for the materialist is the integral perspective and the principle that consciousness is primary. In a single integral stroke, the mind-body unity of reductionism is sustained, the hard problem of epiphenomenalism is resolved, a worldview emerges that is consistent with most people's experience and quest for meaning, compatibility with conventional and unconventional empirical research is achieved, and perhaps most important—a broader range of future exploration is possible than either reductionism or epiphenomenalism would likely promote.

Dismantling the Matrix

Although held by a remarkably small portion of society, and spanning a remarkably small time span even within the Western intellectual and cultural framework, scientific materialism has nonetheless held sway and exerted an enormous influence that extends far beyond the sciences. Just as materialists reduce consciousness to a physical substrate and reject interiority, postmodern cultural theorists reduce reality and meaning to sociocultural influences, and conventional educational systems reduce knowledge to information and data at the expense of broader creativity-consciousness development. This in turn directly shapes tendencies in academic musical study to reduce musicianship to interpretive performance and analysis of already-composed repertory to the detriment of creativity. The aversion in much creativity research to interior dimensions of consciousness, thus favoring more exterior facets of creativity such as problem solving (psychometric), society (sociometric), and physiological (biometric) considerations is another example.[46] Even religious fundamentalism, while often at odds with science, exhibits materialist tendencies in reducing spirituality to superficial, literal interpretations of scripture and denomination-specific doctrine at the expense of genuine transcendent union. Misconceptions in contemporary Buddhist circles of the notion of *anatta*, or "no self," as the absence of a transcendent Self rather than as the illusory nature of the egoic, personal self is yet another example in the realm of religious thought and can be seen as a form of fundamentalism in the exclusive ramifications that have been drawn from the error.[47] That even integral discourse, in its marginalization of process and favoring of object-mediated perspectives of art, is not immune from tendencies to favor objective, exterior phenomena speaks to the sheer power and pervasiveness of the materialist thrust.

Shifting from the aforementioned quadratic to a quadrivium standpoint that helps illuminate parts-to-whole evolution along a given line, all these instances can be understood as confinement of engagement and understanding of a given line of inquiry to the Upper-Right quadrant and its focus on exterior, objective features. Where the integral framework excels is not only enabling identification of this diverse spectrum of materialist, dissociative tendencies, but also how neutralizing of these tendencies does not jettison the key contributions that have nonetheless been made in these fields. As noted earlier, integral understanding of mind embraces the contributions from neuroscience without succumbing to the Upper-Right absolutism or dissociation that often prevails. The same holds when it comes to postmodernism and its championing of culturally relativistic reality. While Wilber has come under attack for his sharp critiques of the limitations of postmodern absolutism, detractors often overlook his equally strong endorsement of postmodern contributions as an important part, just not the totality, of the larger evolutionary story. His advocacy of this realm, in fact, at times even dwarfs in strength the relativistic perspectives of postmodern absolutists who, incapable of critiquing their own position, advance only a monodimensional viewpoint. Integral Education similarly does not reject or marginalize the conventional, third-person learning that it critiques, which as Esbjörn-Hargens and Gunnlaugson note sometimes happens in holistic and other alternative educational approaches, but integrates it within a broader first-second-third-person synthesis.[48]

But it is the integral uniting of science and religion, arguably the most polarized realms in today's world, where Wilber's contributions are particularly noteworthy. This is evident not only in his insights into the underlying dynamics—in essence, "an epidemic fixation" on the respective (scientific and spiritual) realms and epistemologies—that sustain the conflict, but also in his vision of what is possible when this "marriage of sense and soul" is achieved. As long as religion clings solely to Upper-Left subjective/interior perspectives, it will remain confined to a "mythic level of spiritual development," thus ever fueling tendencies in science to confine itself in its Upper-Right, objective/exterior corner where it hones its own exclusive truth claims. In response, the entrenchment of science fuels tendencies toward religious fundamentalism. Both realms "need to grow up" and adapt an "orienting framework that allows and encourages a spacious view of the role for science and spirituality" alike as equally important players in the integral synthesis.[49] Until this happens, religious and scientific extremists alike, perceiving themselves as under attack, will only more stringently fortify themselves in their separate quarters.

Art as Unifying Thread

It is also interesting to note that Wilber declares religion, when understood from an integral perspective, as a potential "conveyer belt" that leads toward a unifying platform for the domains. Due to its capacities to unite earlier developmental stages within an ever-evolving continuum of development (whereas materialist science continually jettisons the past in favor of "today's latest findings"), religion has the capacity to lift the lid of the "pressure cooker" that has been steadily building from the tensions between scientific and religious extremism.[50] While the widespread nature of spiritual/religious experience and engagement in contemporary society might be cited in support of this view, I believe a case may be made for another of the Big Three pillars of human endeavor to play an even more prominent galvanizing role in the emergent synthesis. I am talking, of course, about the arts, which have nothing near the divisive history of religion yet are just as widespread across the world's many cultures.

This brings us back to the improvisation-based art form of jazz as a leading catalyst for integral paradigmatic change. As we have seen, jazz's robust parts-to-whole/whole-to-parts process spectrum offers powerful resources to transcend attachments to categories that perpetuate divisions, and also broaches far-reaching questions regarding nonduality and the nature of ultimate reality that invite a highly nuanced science-spirituality synthesis. If jazz is to serve as a catalyst for this kind of change, however, it will be necessary to realize the extent to which academic jazz studies has not been immune from the very materialist thrust that has engulfed overall musical studies and education at large. We gained a fairly clear view of overall musical materialism in the previous chapter, and will go into how this has impacted jazz studies in the next. In the meantime, let us close the chapter with a look at materialist patterns in education as a whole in order to establish a context for that discussion.

Integral Overview of the Educational Landscape

The history of educational criticism may be generally seen as a legacy of appeals for education to move from a largely third-person, objective/ exterior orientation—where knowledge and education are construed primarily as the ingestion of facts and information—to a broader vision of human development. This is not to deny that conservative arguments, particularly in reaction to attempts at expansion of learning models in the 1960s and 1970s, have not been advanced that are leery of such reform, but that the most prominent critical voices have been those seeking an expanded vision. As Ron Miller points out, these voices can be traced back much further than the educational thrusts driven by the "human potential movement" of the mid-twentieth century, and indeed extend back over two centuries through the work of a group of "innovative, dissident educators" that included Jean-Jacques Rousseau, Johann Heinrich Pestalozzi, and Friedrich Froebel in Europe and a number of Transcendentalists in the United States.[51] "[T]he end of education is not reason per se," asserted Froebel, "but rather the happy, unified man [sic] who need not keep his instincts and impulses chained down, for they are functionally a part of the integrated man at peace with himself, his universe, and his God."[52] An important common thread in this early work is the unfolding of the moral, creative, and spiritual faculties latent in students—hence, properties of Left-Hand quadrants—and liberation from constraining third-person objective focus. Few were more scathing than Emerson about educational tendencies that prevailed in nineteenth-century American schools that countered this aim. "We are shut in schools and college recitation rooms for ten to fifteen years and come out at last with a belly full of words and do not know a thing." It is only the student "who holds the key to his own secret."[53] Similar sentiments were expressed by Henry David Thoreau, William Ellery Channing, and A. Bronson Alcott, who defined the province of the instructor as the "awakening, invigorating, directing rather than the forcing of the child's faculties upon prescribed and exclusive courses of thought."[54]

Here it is important to dispel any possible confusion over why conventional education is considered third-person, which we have also associated with physical reality: Key is the objective/exterior orientation and the exclusion in the educational process of the innermost, spiritual dimensions of the subject: consciousness. Therefore, even though it could be argued that rote memorization constitutes subjective activity, the locus of engagement is not the interior foundations of subjectivity but simply the ingestion of objects of perception. Opening up of the educational landscape to include problem solving, grappling with abstract ideas, discussion, and reflection represents the beginnings of second-person engagement. First-person education is grounded in direct experience of the transcendent Self, exquisitely silent and devoid of mental activity other than the radiantly wakeful self-referral awareness of awareness itself.

As I will argue in the next chapter, which will consider jazz education's repression of creativity and individuality, solutions necessary for first-second-third-person synthesis will require not only robust creative exploration, but also rigorous emulative grounding—the interplay of both comprising a cornerstone to an integral model that distinguishes it from what, as noted earlier, integral educators have categorized as holistic, alternative, and transformational approaches. While these unconventional approaches counter the third-person overemphasis on "acquisition of knowledge and cognitive development,"[55] they sometimes tend to err in the opposite direction, resulting in unbalanced first-person and/or second-person engagement. All are regarded as essential in the integral paradigm, a principle that is uniquely illuminated in the first-second-third-person process scope of jazz.

Twentieth-century educational criticism saw the beginnings of movement in this direction early on in the work of Alfred North Whitehead, whose *The Aims of Education*, despite its brevity, set the stage for much subsequent thinking. Among the insights Whitehead contributes include a three-pronged sequential trajectory he called the "Rhythm of Education" that proceeds from Romance, an initial exploratory-intuitive phase, to a phase of Precision, involving more detailed, analytical engagement, both of which culminate in a stage of Generalization, where they are integrated. In declaring that "[a] stage of precision is barren without a previous stage of romance,"[56] Whitehead in a single sentence issues a central critique of tendencies in education that prevail to this day. He also delineates a powerful principle through which third-person objective mastery and second- and (albeit to a lesser degree) first-person interior and creative engagement can enhance each other in a synergistic fashion. Chapter 10 will consider an approach to musicianship training that I have designed and utilized for many years that follows this sequential thrust. Whitehead presages the emphasis that would later come to the fore in much educational thinking when he places front and center the inherent limitations of formal schooling to provide all the knowledge needed, a point that however relevant in regard to the 1929 knowledge base is exponentially more so today. "If Methuselah did not become an educated man," he quipped, in comparing what could be learned in that alleged 800-year life span compared to the 80 or so most of us get, "it was his own fault."[57] Self-sufficiency must therefore be considered a paramount educational aim. In at once recognizing the value of classics, yet also acknowledging that they must be made relevant and approached and applied through the lens of the present, Whitehead demonstrated the kind of reasoned approach to the notion of canonical knowledge that has much to offer current debates. As does another of his patent mottos that directly pertains to this question of currency: "Knowledge does not keep any better than fish."[58]

John Dewey's famous "experiential continuum" can be seen as a further articulation of Whitehead's nonlinear, sequential premise, where again the heavily analytical approaches that prevail require broader, more unified interior-exterior engagement.[59] Although less explicit than Whitehead, who ascribed as important to education a religious goal—which he construed broadly it must be emphasized—interior development is implicit in Dewey's otherwise pragmatic vision. While less so in the work of Jerome Bruner, Dewey's emphasis on "process," particularly given his focus as a psychologist on science education, further pushed thinking away from an exclusively third-person focus in an area that is particularly prone—and understandably so given the integral correlation with science and third-person reality—to such. Seeking to counteract the emphasis in much of school learning and assessment upon "explicit formulations, upon the ability of the student to reproduce numerical or verbal formulae," he stressed the development of faculties such as intuitive thinking that are highly valued among mathematicians, physicists, biologists, and others in scientific areas.[60] His articulation of the importance, moreover, of cultivating capacities "to learn how to learn" presaged an important theme in later educational thought that is of particular relevance in today's world.[61]

Important contributions were made by other psychologists around the mid-twentieth century, even if these, perhaps reflective of the general revolutionary spirit that took hold in society at large around that time, stressed more the importance of providing students latitude for creative exploration than a balance with the analytical evident in other literature. Carl Rogers has joined other humanist psychologists as part of an important educational voice, perhaps exemplified in his characterization of prevailing tendencies in schools as the "mug and jug" approach. Viewing the teacher as the jug, which pours information into the passive receptacle, the student who is the mug, education leaves little "place for their [students'] feelings [or opportunities] to choose or initiate their own learning. It is only by chance that students learn anything that that has meaning for their lives."[62]

Maxine Greene is among the prominent advocates for the importance of the arts as vehicle for cultivating imagination and creativity in education and society, a position that appears even more under assault as we enter the second decade of the twenty-first century. "What happens to that imaginative creation," she asks in 1985, "in the face of pressures" to shift our educational gaze toward ensuring "our nation's technical and military primacy?"[63] We will see that an integral framework helps reconcile the apparent tensions between pragmatic and economically driven educational incentives and the broader ideals Greene and other visionaries endorse. The same holds for the all-important area of diversity, for which Greene has also argued forcefully and insightfully. Foreshadowing another theme to emerge in greater prominence in more recent years, she advocates diversity as not only an ethical imperative, but as a part and parcel of educational growth for all through the establishment of "spaces of excellence where diverse persons are moved to reach for the possible."[64] Howard Gardner's theory of Multiple Intelligences laid the groundwork for the notion of diversity to move from largely demographic considerations to an embrace of the different ways in which different people, according to their individual propensities, learn. Consisting of musical, logical-mathematical, linguistic, spatial, interpersonal, intrapersonal, and bodily kinesthetic intelligences, the basic idea is that each individual possesses strengths and weaknesses in one or more of these areas. By diversifying the educational landscape from its long-standing focus on logical-mathematical knowing, again what integralists consider third-person approaches, the prospects are heightened that more individuals would be empowered by having their strengths honored, at which point they could develop their weaknesses from a standpoint of greater integrity and confidence.[65]

Later Gardner would reflect on the possibility of spirituality qualifying as an eighth intelligence, hinting at an integral turn in his work.[66] As Helen and Alexander Astin confirm in their landmark survey of spiritual dispositions among college students and faculty, this is clearly an area of intense interest in the educational population. One would think, then, that it would assume equal prominence in the curricular and other deliberations that comprise academic discourse.[67] While ways that this might manifest would begin to take shape with the Contemplative Studies movement that was launched in the late 1990s,[68] that these experiences have not been foreign to educators so attuned is suggested in bell hooks' account of her classroom experiences that exemplify her notion of "engaged pedagogy." Conveying that "[a]fter twenty years of teaching, I can confess that I am the most joyous in the classroom, brought closer to the ecstatic than by most of life's experiences,"[69] she points to the transformational potential inherent in teaching for not only students but instructors themselves, a theme echoed in the work of Parker Palmer.

John Miller's "education for the soul," Diana Denton's "phenomenology of the heart" combined with her strong meditative pedagogy, and Robert London and Sam Crowell's contemplative approaches to engagement with the natural world are further examples of the growing body of attempts to bring a more systematic and explicit first-person dimension to the educational endeavor. While some examples of this work more closely embodies the full scope of the integral vision than others, as a whole it reflects important movement in this direction by traversing what I call the "exterior-interior" divide that has long separated conventional education from what education can, and arguably ought to, be. Accordingly, the first comprehensive volume on integral education, published in 2008, may be seen as arriving at the crest of an ever-growing wave of movement toward first-second-third-person synthesis.[70]

As inspiring and informative as this latter work is, a sobering fact must be kept front and center in our awareness. That is, despite these educational visions and corresponding innovations, they represent notably small and isolated compartments within an academic world that remains deeply entrenched in third-person, objectivist-materialist approaches.

The Matrix of Materialism continues to constrain education to a small portion of what it can, and must, be. Integral education in its ultimate manifestation will ground rigorous intellectual inquiry, and robust creative, physical, emotional, interpersonal engagement, in penetration to the innermost dimensions of consciousness through systematic meditation practice. While a shift to this approach represents one of enormous proportions, clear delineation of the scope, nuance, and coherence of the integral vision, combined with adept diagnostic activities that shed light on underlying patterns that preclude growth will make it possible.

Musical Materialism in Context

The need for these strategies is illuminated when we recognize the extent to which the Matrix of Materialism manifests in musical study, a field that one might expect would exemplify the integral expanse. However, as considered in the previous chapter, the division of labor that has engulfed the field has removed the primary creative processes of improvising and composing from the process scope of the majority and instead centered on secondary and ancillary creative engagement. Instead of a curricular and cultural orientation where, as is taken for granted in visual arts education, all participants engage as generators of work that reflects their distinctly personal visions, musical academe is centered around work that is created by a tiny minority, most of whom lived centuries prior and continents removed from our time and place. Integral diagnostic tools enable a deep probing of the "musical shadow" and reveal that the ramifications of a program in the arts that is creativity deficient are far more serious than limited means for self-expression, fulfillment, and career opportunities. Not only are musicians deprived of the creative skill set and its inventive, interactive, and individuative aspects that are key to artistic success and fulfillment, the model also inhibits a continuum of deficiencies that include inhibited musical understanding, a deeply ingrained and systemic ethnocentrism at a time when multiethnic/multicultural embrace has never been more needed, and—perhaps most seriously of all—impaired capacities for critical awareness of the very paradigm in which these shortcomings are inherent and inevitable. The integral model illuminates the multitiered nature of this "creativity/diversity/critical inquiry" crisis, laying groundwork for how it may be rectified and give way to an extraordinarily exciting paradigm of musical study and practice. Chapter 5 will examine how jazz education has both inherited materialist patterns from overall musical studies and also has the capacity to rectify these patterns and invoke an integral transformation within its own horizons, in doing so emerging as a catalyst for broader musical and educational change.

Summary

Our third integral lens, evolutionary dynamics—the patterns and trajectories that govern development of individuals and systems over time—ties together the structure and process considerations of prior lenses in profound ways and completes our account of the transformational capacities of the jazz-inspired integral framework. Let us refresh our memories as to the essence of Integral Theory in order to put this into context: *Integral Theory maps the inner-outer dimensions of human being and cosmic wholeness, the processes that promote navigation and integration of this wholeness, and the evolutionary dynamics by which this growth occurs over time.* From this perspective, the purpose of any given area of endeavor—or developmental line—can be seen as synonymous with the cosmic purpose that might be deduced from the age-old nonduality principle—to evolve toward differentiated wholeness, or diversity within unity. Integral evolutionary dynamics as we have just seen illuminate how this thrust is sometimes punctuated by tendencies toward dissociation, which when manifesting on not only individual scales but in entire disciplines are collective manifestations of the shadow. Scientific materialism, which has exerted a pervasive influence on the entire educational world, including musical studies, is a particularly prominent example. Where Integral Theory excels is in expanding the conceptual framework so that this form of extremism, along with postmodernism and other aspects of the materialist matrix, can be seen as developmentally incomplete, and appreciated for their partial contributions, as opposed to being categorically dismissed. Scientific materialism is science that has not yet penetrated beyond its Upper Right entryway to all-quadrants synthesis; postmodernism is cultural understanding that has not yet penetrated beyond its Lower Left entryway toward that same goal.

The jazz-inspired integral framework brings powerful delineative and diagnostic tools to the mix that illuminate these patterns and identify solutions. And as we are about to consider, these tools can be directed at jazz itself, which in its foray into the academic world has not been immune from the overarching materialist influence. Needless to say, this orientation must be closely examined and addressed if the broader continuum of reform is to manifest.

PART II

JAZZ: AN INTEGRAL READING

Overview

This part of the book brings jazz and the unique insights into the genre illuminated by an integral perspective into closer focus. Chapter 5 begins with a look at the conservative orientation of jazz education in musical academe and how it has inherited "materialist" tendencies—or confinement to third-person, exterior dimensions—from its broader musical and extramusical environments. We then shift our focus in chapter 6 and explore the inner workings of the primary creative processes of improvisation and composition. Commonly understood as slower and faster versions of composition, we identify foundational distinctions in the realm of time perception that reveal the processes to be contrasting expressive and culturally mediated avenues to transcendent experience. At which point, the jazz process scope may be seen as significantly more expansive—essentially encompassing two major developmental lines—than even previously thought. Chapter 7 continues the exploration of improvisation by viewing it from a complex systems perspective, which in underscoring the collective aspects of improvised performance further illuminates distinctions between improvisatory and compositional paradigms—both of which unite in jazz even if the idiom is more grounded in the first. This analysis also sheds further light on how an intersubjective, field aspect of consciousness may be enlivened in improvised performance.

Chapter 8 probes the realm of style evolution, examining personal and collective style development to be rooted in a shared inner mechanics. As individual artists "individuate"—evolve a distinctly personal voice that integrates both exterior aspects of their time and place with interior dimensions of consciousness—they inform the overarching stylistic fabric, with innovating artists ushering in quantum shifts in that fabric due to the alignment of expressions unique to their personal style revolutions with receptivity in collective consciousness to these particular developments.

Chapter 9 brings all of these considerations together in the style known as *jazz*, which is explored as an archetypally rich process-structure region in the contemporary music landscape that is unprecedented in both its synthesis of diverse influences and impact on broader musical practice.

Chapter 5

Jazz and the Academy

<blockquote>

You'll notice that I stress a great deal improvising and inspiration, rather than approaching creativeness from the vantage point of the finished work of art. . . . We need a different kind of human being to be able to live in a world which changes perpetually, which doesn't stand still.

—Abraham Maslow, *The Farther Reaches of Human Nature*[1]

</blockquote>

In the fall of 2003, I was a participant in a symposium convened by Harvard University's Law and Business Schools called Improvisation and Negotiation.[2] Perhaps ironically given the theme, jazz musicians comprised a distinct minority at the event, with the majority consisting of psychologists, sociologists, lawyers, corporate leaders, and colleagues from other fields beyond music in which interest in improvisation as key to optimal performance has been on the rise. I was deeply impressed by the level of dialogue about a process that I, and much of the jazz community, tend to take for granted as unique to our domain. As a jazz musician who teaches at a classically oriented institution, moreover, I greatly appreciated being part of an academic gathering in which my work was not viewed as peripheral but central to the discourse. I commonly stress to my graduate students that the marginalized status of jazz and improvised music in musical academe is not a clear barometer of the rising appreciation for this kind of creativity not only in the broader academic world but also in an increasing number of professional circles. Thus, my students are exposed to their share of commentary similar to this chapter's epigraph from Maslow in hopes of inspiring them to appreciate the importance of what they do in the broader scope of things. Maslow, indeed, is a treasure trove for such inspiration, as when he further exhorts the need for educational systems to "create a new kind of human being who is comfortable with change, who enjoys change, who is able to improvise, who is able to face with confidence, strength, and courage a situation of which he has absolutely no forewarning."[3] And nothing tops my all-time favorite: "We must develop a race of improvisers, of here-now creators."[4]

From an integral perspective, it might also be argued that we need to develop a race of "peak experiencers," to invoke another important aspect of Maslow's thought, this pertaining to the experience of transformed episodes of consciousness in which sense of self, clarity, wholeness, mind-body integration, inner calm and well-being, and a variety of other faculties are heightened.[5] Hence, the interior dimensions of the creativity-consciousness relationship, at which point the New Jazz Studies—championing the creativity component—gives rise to what I propose as Integral Jazz Studies. As previously discussed, jazz musicians report vivid episodes of such heightened states, and it is thus no surprise that the tradition boasts a long legacy of leading artists who have significantly delved into contemplative practices and studies in order to enhance this dimension of their work and lives. And thus in addition to the common acknowledgment of Maslow as the founder of the humanist psychology movement, his work might also be regarded as important to the emergence of the integral jazz movement.

It is from the standpoint of the creativity-consciousness relationship and its interior-exterior, integral dimensions that this chapter explores jazz's journey into the academic world, the arena in which its integral properties, if harnessed, have the capacity to yield considerable impact on the broader educational mission, and by extension, society. In so exploring, we will make full use of our integral delineative and diagnostic faculties. For, as we are about to see, as rich as jazz might be in its inherent integral properties, academic approaches to the discipline have been strongly shaped by the overarching materialist patterns inherited from the broader musical and extramusical academic knowledge base. These will need to be identified and addressed if the field is to uphold the transformational function of which it is capable.

Overview of Jazz Education

In order to understand how materialist or self-confining third-person tendencies have taken hold in jazz study, it is first essential to acknowledge how the marginalized status of the idiom in musical academe, at least in part, contributed to them. Jazz not only brought to the academy a vastly different and expanded process spectrum that departed from the norm, it also introduced Afrological musicocultural features to which the prevailing Eurological culture was not receptive. To ignore the issue of race in any assessment of the situation would be a significant oversight. Between what LeRoi Jones reminds us was the "unbelievably cruel" circumstance of slavery dating back several centuries and reminders to what Karlton Hester candidly identifies as a musical "bigotry" still evident well into the twenty-first century, a topic to be explored in some depth, the dynamics of race in the broader society have clearly played out in musical academe.[6] It is thus not surprising that jazz was overtly scorned and at times entirely forbidden, as Bruno Nettl points out, in university music departments.[7] Oliver Lake recounts that this even included extracurricular jam sessions: "They didn't consider jazz as music, and if they heard you playing jazz, you would be admonished. We would have to wait until all the instructors were gone, and then we would start jamming."[8] Dave Brubeck, reflecting on the early days of his college circuit performances, recalls "controversies at the institutions as to whether or not we should be allowed to play." Underscoring entirely uninformed notions that playing jazz is somehow damaging to musical instruments, Brubeck adds that "[s]ometimes I would be led to an old, beat-up piano for the performance when there'd also be a great grand piano backstage that they wouldn't let me go near."[9]

A Field Ascending

In light of the exterior obstacles jazz education has had to overcome, one perhaps gains an enhanced appreciation of the strides the field has made, which in fact may even underscore the integral properties of the music itself. Most every music school or department now offers credit-bearing jazz coursework, with many offering undergraduate and graduate degree programs in the genre.[10] A burgeoning body of jazz research that deals with the pedagogical, theoretical, historical, and aesthetic aspects of the music has made its way into some of the more receptive existing journals as well as spawned the creation of jazz-based outlets.[11] Strong appeals have been issued by organizations such as the National Association of Schools of Music and National Association for Music Education for jazz and improvisational experience to be included in the training of all music majors.[12] Many American high schools, in addition to one or two large jazz ensembles, also include small jazz ensembles and coursework in jazz improvisation and history. Junior high school jazz ensembles are now more the norm than the exception, and elementary school jazz groups are no longer the novelty they once were.[13] Jazz education outside the United States has also made great progress, with many major conservatories throughout the world offering jazz curriculums.[14] In Europe, strong activity is found at both the conservatory level and in the many community or private jazz schools that offer jazz instruction to citizens of all ages—a phenomenon that is less common in the United States.

Two international jazz education organizations evolved from, and in turn have helped to galvanize, this breadth of activity. The International Association of Jazz Education (IAJE), which was formed in the 1960s, had a worldwide membership of over 7,000, and attracted more than that number of participants at its yearly conventions before folding due to financial mismanagement in 2008.[15] The International Association of Schools of Jazz (IASJ), founded in 1989 by saxophonist David Liebman, has expanded from a largely European membership to include schools from all corners of the world.[16] Alongside the growth of these organizations, a robust jazz education industry has made available an endless supply of books, videos, software, and other resources intended to enhance the learning process. That top professional jazz musicians, despite in many cases having limited academic credentials, have become increasingly involved in all these levels of activity—performing and teaching at IAJE and IASJ meetings, publishing instructional methods, presenting workshops for jazz programs while on tour, and in increasing numbers, holding faculty appointments at colleges and universities—points to a growing symbiosis between jazz education and the professional jazz world.[17]

From all appearances, jazz education is alive and well. Just as the music has from its earliest days been played throughout the world, it is now also taught in educational institutions throughout the world. Former stereotypes of jazz as an undisciplined, unsophisticated form of musical expression, tainted by the dubious environments in which the music in its earlier days was often played, have been countered by highly systematic learning models that aim for a level of musicianship which arguably surpasses, particularly in its breadth of skills, that achieved in any other genre.[18] When in early 1987 the U.S. Congress proclaimed jazz to be a "national treasure," jazz educators could rightfully claim at least some of the credit for this recognition due to their efforts in promoting the awareness of the idiom in not only the academic world but society at large.[19]

While from this standpoint, one has every reason to be proud of the growth of jazz education and optimistic about its future, it is also important to recognize the limiting tendencies that have inhibited the growth of the field and severed it from the creative thrust of the overall jazz world. At this point, the question arises: Are these to be attributed primarily to the materialist/structuralist tendencies of the European classical environments in which jazz programs evolved, or the orientation of jazz educators themselves?

From an integral standpoint, the answer is both, and the quest to render jazz study as integral as the field at large requires attention to both realms.

While nowadays it is difficult to imagine a music department or school that forbids its students from curricular or extracurricular jazz activity, ample indicators of continued institutional marginalization may be cited. Perhaps most notable is the fact that, despite the idiom's rich foundational skills, jazz remains largely excluded from musical academe's core curriculum. Short units on jazz, which generally do not involve hands-on contact with the music, may be found in core music theory and history sequences, but full semester coursework in jazz improvisation, theory, composition, or arranging are relegated to elective status for all but jazz majors. Because music curricula tend to be filled to the brim with conventional requirements, leaving little time, space, or energy for electives, the result is that the majority of music majors—for whom interpretive performance and analysis of European classical repertory is the focus—continue to graduate with little or no hands-on engagement with jazz. This is most conspicuous in the case of American music students gaining certification to teach music in American public schools. As David Baker points out, "one or two courses in jazz"—which appears to be the best-case scenario, with many teacher certification programs including no jazz training—is not sufficient "to be able to adequately teach this music."[20]

Other forms of marginalization include the disproportionately small number of jazz faculty members at most schools compared to classical faculty,[21] and that jazz research has scarcely penetrated the pages of some of the more prominent music research (history, theory, aesthetics, cognition) journals. The combination of these factors contributes to an overarching subordination of jazz in academic musical culture that is arguably the biggest impediment to the growth of jazz education. Within every community, institution, and field is an overarching cultural orientation that is an emergent by-product of, as well as reinforcement for, the totality of curricular, organizational, demographic, conceptual, and other factors that comprise a given community. This cultural orientation reflects the dominant attitudes and proclivities of its constituents and serves as a backdrop against which myriad policy decisions are made—regarding curricular requirements, hiring, funding, scholarships, space allocation, faculty and student recognition—on a day-to-day basis. In musical study, jazz—the idiom that most comprehensively integrates the two primary creative processes in music—is a cultural outlier as well as a curricular outlier.

In reaction to these external, environmental constraints, it was inevitable that jazz educators would adapt by conforming to the overarching, materialist orientation that prevails in musical academe at large. This has manifested in two primary ways: One is through the privileging of large, conducted ensembles such as the jazz big band, where improvisation is minimal and interpretive performance, which we saw as the central means of music making in musical study at large, prevails. Second is through narrow, normative approaches to improvisation and composition that inhibit creative exploration. While jazz education, unlike European classical training, would not completely do away with improvisation, it would confine this central creative process to a largely emulative focus whereby, if unwittingly, the innovative thrust that has driven the evolution of jazz—exploration of new possibilities, infusion of diverse influences, and cultivation of individuality—would be compromised. "The type of jazz performed in the university," notes Nettl, "does not really correspond to the important types of jazz heard in the real musical world."[22] Graham Collier, Eric Nisenson, Charles Fowler, Pat Metheny, Stuart Nicholson, James Lincoln Collier, David Borgo, Mark Dresser, and Charlie Haden are among other artists and thinkers who have expressed concerns about the conservative horizons of jazz study.[23] Collier, a British composer, educator, and author, has provided among the most outspoken critiques of the field in his provocative report, *Jazz Education in America*, where he sums up these tendencies by what he calls an emphasis on a generally nonchanging "middle zone" of the jazz tradition—primarily characterized by a focus in "bebop" and "big band swing."[24]

As will be seen, these critiques do not suggest that the solution is to replace the past-based, emulative orientation with a contemporaneous, exploratory emphasis, but rather call for a synthesis that is very much in line with the integral perspective, and which—when in place—spawns openings to the interior dimensions of consciousness that fulfills the interior-exterior integral scope.

Will the Real Jazz Tradition Please Stand Up?

Here four views of tradition might be noted to illustrate this point. These correspond to the evolutionary trajectory delineated earlier that proceeds from modernist to postmodernist, with two stages included, to integral phases of development. As shown in Figure 5.1, the modernist perspective, which characterizes the conventional model, views tradition in terms of a linear, chronological sequence of developments, which includes a

Four views of the jazz tradition	
Conventional/modern	Tradition as linear sequence of events that is mastered by retracing timeline of history. Strong sense of canon. Guiding axiom: Grounding in the past is necessary for charting new territory.
Postmodern (astructural)	Locus of meaning and expression resides in the processes and materials of the current time and place. Pedagogy oriented toward the present. Experimentation is of greater value than emulation. No canon or foundational body of works except what is deemed as such by each individual.
Postmodern (structural)	Locus of meaning and expression lies in the dynamic interplay of present-based exploration and past-based emulation. There is a canon, but it is continually evolving, and must be accessed through the lens of the present. Strong sense of cultural origins of the music. Guiding axiom: Just as grounding in the past informs contemporary explorations, contemporary explorations inform grounding in the past. One can only fathom the past to the extent one has evolved an individual voice.
Integral	Unites structural post-modern synthesis of past-present, emulative-exploratory interplay within expanded framework that views tradition as originating in, and evolving toward, spiritual foundations of consciousness.

Figure 5.1. Four Perspectives of the Jazz Tradition.

strong sense of canon, or emblematic repertory, and thus advocates musical training that follows that timeline and corresponding mastery. Although this approach is often endorsed as securely grounded in traditional practice, a more nuanced look suggests that few if any jazz masters actually developed according to this sequential trajectory. Here it must be emphasized that the modernist assessment is relative to the respective line; modernism along the jazz line differs significantly from that along the classical line in that the first engages the majority of musicians with improvisation and composition—albeit in largely style-specific approaches—while the second excludes the processes altogether.

A second, *astructural* postmodern (review chapter 3) view of tradition departs radically from the first and, consistent with poststructural sociocultural theory, rejects the privileging of structural considerations—as in stylistic norms—and instead emphasizes the exploration of new possibilities and the evolution of a personal voice that is reflective of the circumstances of one's time and place. Naturally, advocates of the modernist approach are quick to claim that without grounding in the past, musicians will lack the grounding needed for contemporary exploration, while the astructural postmodern reply is that the evolution of the jazz tradition has always been driven by an exploratory thrust, and this needs to be an important aspect of musical training even at an early age.

A third reading of tradition, recognizing the partial validity in both modern and postmodern views of tradition, provides a synthesis. Grounding in the past is a necessary part of growth; robust creative, contemporary exploration is equally necessary. But the first does not necessarily precede the second in a linear fashion, rather the two approaches must inform each other from early on in the course of artistic development. The more the personal voice emerges, the more one has access to an interior framework for meaningful embrace of the past, which in turn enables present-based exploration and individuation. What has eluded modernist thinking is that the capacity to fathom the treasures of the past is directly predicated on the degree of individuation that has been achieved. What has eluded astructural postmodern thinking is that the degree of individuation that is achieved is directly predicated on the degree to which one has apprehended what has come before. Modernist insistence that, in this dynamic interplay, past grounding must precede present exploration reflects an incomplete understanding that has been inherited from the Eurological perspective.

Once the aspiring artist is grounded in this dynamic emulative-exploratory, present-past interplay, a conduit for connections to the realm of consciousness is in place. At this point, a fourth, integral understanding of tradition comes into view, which is closest to the pathway of the great jazz innovators.

Conventional jazz studies, where emulative approaches have over-shadowed the exploratory thrust, is thus constrained by a modernist view of tradition. Although the process deficiency underlying this modernism is nothing compared to that found in overall musical study, because jazz studies includes primary creative processes of improvising and composing while the broader field does not, both share the same underlying tendency to inhibit creativity. Here the modern/postmodern/integral evolutionary sequence is applied in a quadrivium manner, where jazz education and musical studies are assessed relative to their own capacities for parts-to-whole development. From a quadratic perspective, jazz study might be placed at a high modernist stage due to its inclusion of the primary creativity that overall musical studies excludes. Most important is that both have severed themselves from the diversity of the broader musical landscape.

One need not look far for guidance from leading jazz artists as to how jazz studies may break free from its modernist moorings. Yusef Lateef supports the importance of the emulative when he affirms the central importance of individuality in the jazz tradition: "That's the nature of this music, African American music, to sound like yourself. This has been presented to us by people like Lester Young, Coleman Hawkins, John Coltrane, and on and on."[25] Lester Bowie, trumpeter and pioneering figure in the Association for the Advancement of Creative Musicians, echoes these sentiments when he emphasizes that "innovation, creativity, moving forward, being contemporary (and) maintaining the individual voice have always been essential aspects of the jazz legacy."[26] Art Farmer hints at how the exploratory works hand-in-hand with the emulative: "You heard someone play something you liked, you thought about how you wanted to sound, and you went home and worked on it." Douglas Ewart further underscores this point. "In trying to forge new ground," as he describes the aspirations of musicians in Association for Advancement of Creative Musicians (AACM) circles, "cats were not in any way trying to undermine" the past.[27] In other words, while musicians may consciously strive for "a true departure from what had gone before," this does not mean a lack of reverence to the work of the masters. The same interplay of creative intention and respect for the past is evident in the words of AACM cofounder Muhal Richard Abrams: "We were deliberately breaking some rules. To us, Bird and them were people who broke ground. We copied them religiously, but that was not the end; we didn't sacrifice our individualism to do it."[28]

Pat Metheny provides a particularly compelling articulation of the emulative-exploratory interplay that is key to movement toward an integral understanding of tradition when he urges that students regard the past and mastery of "the fundamentals of the music as central and essential," yet that they also capture the "the emerging sound of [their]

OWN generation of musicians."[29] What has been overlooked is the exploratory component, which Metheny emphasizes needs to be cultivated during the time when it is ripe in students' development. Noting that musicians early in their development have access to "a certain kind of energy that is really valuable, rare" and which often inspires music that sounds "nothing like anything that has ever been heard before," he urges that students "listen to THAT with the same attention and curiosity that [they] reserve for [their] heroes on records."[30]

If anything, the intention to explore and find one's voice in the present enlivens, rather than compromises, receptivity to the repository of treasures that are to be found in any artistic tradition. Accordingly, the common notion of aspiring musicians engaging exclusively in extensive emulation of their distant predecessors before dealing with the music around them—the thinking being that exploration of new possibilities is neither valid nor productive without mastery of the past—is largely unfounded either theoretically or in actual practice. Yes, aspiring jazz musicians have always engaged in rigorous study and practice to gain the extraordinary skills needed to excel in this demanding art form. But more often than not, the primary sources of inspiration, as well as learning resources (e.g., books, exercises, repertory) derived as much from current musical artists and developments as those from the distant past. John Coltrane, a seminal jazz innovator, was exposed to a variety of technical resources of past and contemporary origins—including scales and exercises from diverse musical traditions—early in his training.[31] Instead of isolating themselves from the musical pulse of their time and place and approaching tradition in a linear, chronological manner (e.g., one begins with the 1930s, then proceeds to the '40s, etc., eventually reaching the present), artists have more commonly approached tradition in a nonlinear manner where creative exploration and rigorous emulative practice went hand-in-hand.

And in many instances, exposure to some cutting-edge, present development has a transformational impact that borders on a kind of spiritual awakening, which thus renders the exterior, musical experience as a gateway to interior grounding that points toward an integral approach. David Liebman, as a teenager hearing Coltrane—who by then had clearly emerged as one of jazz's major innovators—describes this kind of experience in quasi-religious terms.

> My first, really great experience with jazz was going to Birdland when I was 14. I saw Mulligan and Count Basie. But then I saw Coltrane. And that was a definite revelation. . . . I

mean that was the impetus and inspiration to want to play the saxophone in that kind of way. . . . I didn't know what jazz meant at the time; I had no idea of what he was playing. But the power was incredible, and it took me right away. I was 14, and I already was convinced that this was an amazing thing that was happening.[32]

Coltrane himself reports a similarly inspirational experience when, at age 19, he first heard Charlie Parker, whose bebop excursions were then at the cutting edge of the genre. The experience, as "Trane" recounts, "hit me between the eyes."[33] Again, we see the all-important transformational impetus of a present development in the evolution of one of the most extraordinary musical innovators of the twentieth century. This developmental trajectory was equally true of Parker himself—to continue this line of thought through the lens of the jazz saxophone lineage—who in his teens idolized and emulated Lester Young, a leading innovator at that time. Parker did not, upon hearing "Prez," shut himself off from the work of the present master and first seek those influences from which Prez evolved. Rather, he went right to Prez as the most immediate source, further exemplifying the centrality of the present as a lens to tradition.[34] I believe it is not unreasonable to conclude this has been more the rule than the exception with most artists.

And when musicians glimpse this kind of impact in the music of others, it is only natural that they seek this in their own music, at which point, aspiring artists engage in intensive emulative and exploratory work not only with the intention of gaining requisite skills, but to cultivate an individual voice that will reflect the inner-outer totality of their being and similarly have a transformational impact on listeners.

The significance of a present-based entryway to tradition is that it comprises engagement with musical materials in more fluid forms—in other words, configurations of elements that have not yet crystallized into the codified, normative structures that comprise much academic study—and therefore provides a robust conduit for movement of awareness toward first-second-third-person synthesis. Here is where improvisatory study that includes both style-specific and trans-stylistic, or rigorous adherence to idiomatic harmonic and rhythmic parameters along with wide-ranging excursions, is essential. It is difficult to imagine that Coltrane, in his legendary practice regimens, did not regularly launch into territory yet uncharted—how else would his ground-breaking activity manifest? While the importance of these improvisatory flights tends to be diminished in conventional education circles—with their perhaps being dismissed as self-indulgent, undisciplined lapses in focus—I believe they serve as essential moments where rigorous, systematic skill acquisition, which again is all-important, is integrated into the individual voice. Robust second-person creative exploration may even pave the way for deeper grounding in third-person technical and theoretical dimensions by unearthing ideas in undifferentiated forms that require specific kinds of practice and study to be molded into shape.

At this point, present-based exploration and rigorous craft development become part of a creative infrastructure that promotes receptivity, if not overt pursuit, to first-person interior development, which is keenly evident in the jazz tradition. Charles Lloyd, Mary Lou Williams, Alice Coltrane, John Coltrane, Herbie Hancock, Charles Gayle, John McLaughlin, Kenny Werner, Paul Horn are among the many jazz artists whose engagement in interior spiritual practices as directly informed and organically linked to their creative work is well known.

Nonetheless, whereas the evolution of the jazz tradition, just as with the classical tradition, was driven by this integral, self-transcending thrust, which is nothing less than the cosmic evolutionary thrust toward differentiated wholeness, jazz studies, like classical studies, has departed from this core aspect of tradition. What is ironic is that adherents to conventional models in both fields tend to defend their position in the name of upholding tradition. Restoration of both the parts-to-whole creative scope and complementary whole-to-parts consciousness aspect of the jazz tradition to jazz studies yields a first-second-third-person template that serves as both catalyst and prototype for integral paradigmatic change in music, education at large, and the overall knowledge base.

Conventional Jazz Research

Whereas conventional jazz studies is modernist in orientation, again in relationship to the postmodern/integral nexus of the jazz tradition, conventional jazz research reflects a postmodern horizontal expansion, with but only preliminary signs of integral verticality. Horizontal expansion is evident in the increasingly interdisciplinary nature of the research, limited verticality pertains to dearth of exploration of the spiritual dimensions of the music. In no way is this to suggest spirituality is not mentioned; it comes up fairly regularly.[35] What is lacking is systematic investigation of the transcendent function of jazz's process scope—the inner mechanics by which improvisation, composition, and performance catalyze transformed consciousness. Parallels might be noted here with the neglect of the process dimension in musicology at large, where as John Sloboda points out, emphasis on the structural and historical facets of resultant works have superseded investigation of "the moment-to-moment psychological history of the genesis" of ideas that comprise those works.[36] Whereas elaborate syntactic (e.g., the structure of altered dominant chords, harmonic substitution, polyrhythmic practices, etc.), historical, cultural, and aesthetic analyses abound in jazz research, little such inquiry has been pursued into the creativity-consciousness relationship that is central to the idiom's transformational impact. As such, interiority, even if mentioned, risks being reduced to metaphor, subject to dismissal as subjective artistic musing rather than appreciated in its ontological significance. Chapter 6 will provide among the first in-depth explorations of this realm. As I have intimated in previous chapters, jazz's spiritual dimensions not only corroborate with research into human consciousness, but also suggest areas for further research.[37]

Closely related is another limiting facet of conventional jazz scholarship, having to do with "anti-essentializing" tendencies inherited from postmodern thought. In other words, because of the postmodern privileging of sociocultural criteria in shaping meaning and knowledge and aversion to transcendent dimensions of human nature and reality, the idea is eschewed that inherent in the psyche of an individual, or more particularly, an ethnicity or race, might be a deeper essence. One reason for this is concern with racist inferences that might be drawn by those so inclined: If deeper facets, those that transcend cultural and obvious physiological differences, might be identified to distinguish ethnic and racial groups, this invites discriminatory predilections for the inherent superiority or inferiority of particular races. The problem is that this thinking fails to recognize a far greater unity, and diversity in unity, that is possible; one that the nondual, integral perspective brings into play and which will be central to integral jazz research. The basic premise is that since individual consciousness is a manifestation of the cosmic wholeness, and therefore all of humanity unites in a collective consciousness, we are all black, white, red, yellow, and all the other skin colors and races/ethnicities linked to them. Just as, which Jung has pointed out in his concepts of *anima* and *animus*, we are all female and male, and just as spirituality, art, and science contain each other. The surface features by which individuals, groups, and disciplines are labeled and distinguished from one another are those that predominate, but underlying these distinctions is a grounding in the ocean of collective consciousness where all unite, of which the individual consciousness of every individual is but a wave.

Therefore, within this expanded conception of unity, it is now possible to also identify deep essences—or transcendent/spiritual impulses—

that are uniquely embodied in the psyche of consciousness of a particular race or ethnicity without that becoming a criterion for ultimate differences, because, again, ultimately all are part of an underlying wholeness. At this point the stakes are raised when it comes to the diversity imperative: To deny the contributions of any given race, ethnicity, culture, or gender is to inhibit the evolutionary progress for both the totality of humanity, and one's own self.

The importance of black music in not only American but global culture now takes on new significance, because it may be understood as more than surface practices and structures—as important as these are—but as encompassing transcendent dimensions of human consciousness seeking an outlet for expression. An expanded basis emerges for appreciating an assertion such as William Banfield's of the foundational place of black music in "modern sound and living culture," and why he is right in describing this not as "an ancillary happening or fragmented cultural strand, or musical movement off to the entertaining side or separated from thinking" but in fact as "*the* game changer in modern musical sound."[38] Black music is a game changer because of the totality of its surface features and underlying, transcendent richness, which as outlets for its expression began to manifest, resonated deeply with not just black consciousness but planetary consciousness. As I have suggested in my analysis in the previous chapter, I believe the investigation of the transcendent dimensions of the jazz process spectrum, with the link drawn between human and cosmic improvisatory creativity, yields an opening to this broader kind of investigation and—while certainly challenging postmodern assumptions that may be held by many jazz researchers—enables greater support for their efforts to illuminate the richness and importance of jazz not only in the broader musical world, but in global culture.

Let us turn to what has been called the New Jazz Studies as a preliminary indication of this broader vision that, while sustaining postmodern aversion to interiors, sets the stage for subsequent movement to an integral jazz studies paradigm.

The New Jazz Studies

The New Jazz Studies, unlike what the heading implies, does not concern itself with broaching new musical terrain in the preparation of future generations of jazz artists. Rather, the heading refers to the burgeoning interest in jazz as a vehicle for fostering cross-disciplinary creative awareness. Robert O'Meally, reflecting on the incorporation of jazz in Columbia

University's campus-wide undergraduate curriculum from this perspective, clarifies:

> What is new here is the conviction that jazz is not just for players and aficionados who can count the horns and the boxes of the music "from Bunk to Monk," . . . but that knowing about jazz and its cultural settings is part of what it means to be an educated man or woman in our time—this regardless of a student's own specific major or field.[39]

Among the fields in which this thinking is most prominent is business, where it is not unusual for jazz musicians to be invited to corporate gatherings to talk about the inventive and interactive aspects of their work and its ramifications for productivity, innovation, and team work.[40] It is not that CEOs break out instruments in impromptu jam sessions at these meetings, but that they consider—as in the aforementioned Improvisation and Negotiation conference at Harvard's Law and Business Schools[41]—application of the inventive and interactive aspects of jazz to their business environments. The same principles apply to a number of other fields that have looked to the genre for creative inspiration and guidance. Paul Haidet cites parallels between jazz and the physician-patient relationship.[42] Kabir Sehgal looks at jazz as a model for democratic systems of government, with focus on the distributed leadership that is evident in a jazz group.[43] The Canadian government provided over $4 million in funding for a project called Improvisation, Community, and Social Practice, the purpose of which is to explore the improvisatory core to much human interaction and personal and collective-social scales.[44] David Brown draws connections between jazz and architecture, suggesting that if architecture were more informed by jazz, it might be better equipped to reflect the improvisatory nature of everyday life.[45]

What bears emphasis is that *knowing about jazz* need not be confined to a distanced theoretical and historical understanding of the genre, but may also involve direct incorporation of its spontaneous, inventive, interactive, unifying, and self-transcending principles in one's work and life. In other words, knowledge of jazz can help us *discover jazz* in many other activities.

Placing the New Jazz Studies within an integral, evolutionary context, it can be seen as largely a horizontal or lateral expansion of convention, with preliminary signs of vertical movement. It is horizontal in the sense that while, as noted, it does not impact the training of aspiring jazz musicians, it does presume an expanded appreciation of the robust creative, interactive, and individuative, as well as cross-disciplinary, aspects of the genre. Whereas conventional jazz studies aims to train jazz artists, New Jazz Studies applies jazz principles across fields. Limited signs of vertical development are evident in the fact that when business executives talk about the need to explore new horizons, take risks, embrace anomalies, transcend conventional roles, and to encourage the evolution of individuality among management and the workforce, they are looking at some of the very creative aspects of jazz that, while conventionally marginalized, embody its parts-to-whole thrust. In this sense, the New Jazz Studies may be equated with postmodern development, which we saw to exhibit materialist tendencies in privileging cultural relativistic influences yet also represent preliminary movement toward interior domains. That this thinking, however, has not significantly crossed the exterior-interior divide into the realm of consciousness suggests confinement to a horizontal locus that is mediated by the reigning exterior/materialist orientation.

Integral Jazz Studies

How does Integral Jazz Studies differ from New Jazz Studies, or for that matter Conventional Jazz Studies?

An integral perspective reveals clear and fundamental distinctions. Whereas conventional Jazz Studies is largely oriented toward third-person, discipline-specific engagement in the training of aspiring jazz musicians, New Jazz Studies, as just examined, concerns itself with application of principles of jazz creativity to creativity across fields.

Integral Jazz Studies, exemplifying the transcend-and-include premise axiomatic of the integral vision, unites the terrain of Conventional Jazz Studies, Conventional Jazz Research, and New Jazz Studies within an expanded approach to musical and extramusical inquiry. Rigorous third-person, discipline-specific grounding coexists with robust second-person creative, and thus intra- and interdisciplinary exploration and deep first-person penetration to the innermost dimensions of consciousness yield both an entirely new template for jazz artistry and creativity-consciousness development across fields. Reflecting both horizontal and vertical expansion, the improvisatory foundations of creative development and meditation-based foundations of consciousness development emerge as central facets not only of musical study but overall educational and social practice. Resulting from the jazz-driven shift from self-confining to self-transcending engagement in a field, where it is realized not as an exterior destination but gateway to inner-outer synthesis, wide-ranging benefits—

including inventiveness, interactivity, and individuation in the creativity realm; and self-realization, diversity awareness, and critical inquiry in that of consciousness—are enjoyed by practitioners in highly disparate disciplines. The divisiveness and alienation that is all too prevalent in contemporary life is replaced by holistic and unifying understanding. Ethnic, racial, gender, creativity, cultural, ideological, and spiritual differences can begin to be healed. This promotes newfound openness to innovative, consciousness-based approaches to dealing with environmental and other challenges.

Integral Jazz Studies also brings into the educational environment a new kind of inquiry into the Big Questions that is framed through the lens of a nondual understanding of consciousness. This yields openings for scientific, spiritual, philosophical, and other communities to come together and find common ground that otherwise remains elusive. Key is the interplay of parts-to-whole and whole-to-parts approaches. Conventional educational discourse is not only parts-driven but also parts-confined, with weak capacities for self-transcending expansion that ultimately fathoms wholeness. In other words, the academic enterprise is largely preoccupied with exterior detail, which is where disciplines appear most different from one another, and thus incapable of connecting with the underlying terrain of consciousness in which all domains unite and originate. If musical style categories such as jazz and classical are riddled by ideological conflict, one can see the intractability of the spirituality-science divide. And because whole-to-parts inquiry, that which begins with this expansive understanding of consciousness and then probes its various differentiated manifestations, is virtually nonexistent, capacities for bridging these divides are further undermined.

Here the importance of the Association for Advancement of Creative Musicians, considered briefly earlier, is noteworthy as among the closest embodiments of the integral jazz paradigm, even if the organization went to great lengths to avoid confinement to that or any label. Launched in the 1960s as a quest to galvanize and empower African American musicians in the face of a host of economic, racial, and artistic challenges, the AACM sustained performance programs, a school, and community outreach initiatives in the realization of its vision. Several facets of the vision are distinctly integral. One is its rich process spectrum, spanning a robust exploratory spectrum that placed from the outset great emphasis on originality, grounded in wide-ranging approaches to improvisation and composition, which was complemented by rigorous emulative grounding (which may arguably have been somewhat subordinate in the case of some members in the organization's early years). The AACM charter also ceded an important place for spiritual practice and development. Hence, what I have been calling the integral parts-to-whole/whole-to-parts interplay has been well centered.[46]

Because the musical thrust of the AACM, further embodying integral premises, transcended category, the AACM also carefully considered its use of terminology. Although jazz was clearly an important aspect of the movement, the term, if used at all, was situated within the broader expanse of Great Black Music as the overarching gateway through which its musicians accessed the broader landscape. "We play the blues, we play jazz, rock, Spanish music, gypsy, African, classical music, contemporary European music, voodoo . . . everything that you'll want," states AACM cofounder Muhal Richard Abrams. Because in the final analysis, "it's 'music' that we play: we create sound, period."[47]

While the impact of the AACM on the evolution of jazz and twentieth-century music was highly significant, it is interesting to note, although not surprising, that neither its music or vision has been even marginally embraced in conventional jazz education.

Integral Jazz Studies is directly inspired by the AACM's self-transcending vision that sought connections not only with the broader musical landscape but the overall knowledge base. Accordingly, Integral Jazz Studies not only embodies parts-to-whole and whole-to-parts engagement and inquiry through its musical creative spectrum, it yields a framework for dialogue that can inspire this across fields. Chapter 10 will examine how the parts-to-whole/whole-to-parts interplay provides a basis for an entirely new vision for a twenty-first-century school of music, where the very diversity of scope Abrams notes provides a radically new vision for the field. As already intimated, and to be explored more deeply in the coming chapters, African American music offers extraordinary process and structural tools that promote this kind of exploration and synthesis. Chapter 11 will take a further step and consider how the parts-to-whole/whole-to-parts interplay of the integral jazz paradigm can impact change in the broader educational arena. Considered there is a three-tiered model for an entirely new educational conversation that I call Deep Inquiry.

A brief overview of the terrain broached in a Deep Inquiry Group, or DIG, is in order: Three corresponding questions guide the progression of thinking and dialogue along the three tiers, which, consistent with the integral perspective, span the first-second-third-person, or modern, postmodern, and integral spectrum. From a conventional, modernist vantage point, where education is presently lodged, the prevailing question is largely discipline-specific: *What is the nature of knowledge within a given field?* From a postmodern vantage point, the question expands to encompass the entire educational spectrum: *What does it mean to be an educated individual in the twenty-first century?*

From an integral perspective, the breadth and inclusivity expands further and shifts its locus from outer to inner: *What is the nature of the human being who is being educated?*

It is here that the integral framework brings to the conversation the nondual relationship between human consciousness and cosmic wholeness, rendering education a site where the biggest questions imaginable about Ultimate Reality and Meaning are no longer relegated to the periphery but placed front and center, providing a backdrop for the extraordinary kind of inquiry and experience that is necessary for creativity and consciousness development. It is not just that the integral academy will encourage talk about the Big Questions, it will also deploy diverse epistemologies that enable an expanded realm of direct experience. Improvisation and creativity across fields, meditation, including collective practice to enliven group dynamics of consciousness, a variety of other psychosomatic methodologies, along with conventional analytical engagement will constitute a vastly overhauled academic environment.

When John Coltrane declared his commitment to awaken in humanity a reverence for "the divine in a musical language that transcends words,"[48] he laid groundwork for this transdisciplinary, nondual perspective through his intra- and interdisciplinary innovations whereby the boundaries of jazz expanded to the overall musical landscape and beyond. The nondual relationship between individual and cosmos need not be detached from the broader spectrum of knowing and creating; it is inextricably tied to it. "When you improvise," reflects John McLaughlin, among the generations of artists who were deeply inspired by Coltrane, "what are you saying/singing? You sing about your life and your relationships with the beings around you, the Earth and the cosmos itself—the all."[49]

The present juncture in human history calls for us to place these considerations front and center if there is reason for optimism about the future. For in this process, newfound understandings about human creativity and consciousness evolution may give rise to new solutions to the problems in the world that otherwise will remain hidden from in the current category-bound and externally oriented thinking that prevails. The arts in general, and jazz in particular, have important contributions to make to the centering of the farthest dimensions of the integral interior-exterior spectrum.

But if jazz studies is marginalized in musical studies, one might ask, which is marginalized in the academy at large, how will the jazz-inspired educational and societal transformation come about? This may be thought of in terms of what complex systems theorist Edward Lorenz proposed as the "butterfly effect."[50] A butterfly flapping its wings in Brooklyn can set in motion minute patterns of turbulence which, as James Gleick describes it, gradually build up into "dust devils and squalls and continent-sized eddies which only satellites can see,"[51] thereby having the capacity to impact the weather in Bombay. Therefore, crossing the exterior-interior divide in a single field, however localized, establishes a precedent that, because of its paradigmatic significance, may inspire parallel initiatives in other areas. The jazz-inspired integral musicianship paradigm that becomes the basis for musical studies may thus impact far more than music as it breaks the ice, so to speak, in bringing expanded creativity and, more dramatically given the third-person orientation of education at large, consciousness studies and its meditative methodologies into the classroom. If this precedent can be set in one academic area, it can take hold, with astute leadership on administrative, faculty, and student levels, across fields. And when the academic world invokes this integral revolution, it is but a small step for it to manifest in the world at large.

Summary

The conservative orientation of jazz education underscores the influence of the Matrix of Materialism and its emphasis on third-person, exterior epistemologies at the expense of second-person creative and first-person interior experience and development. The very orientation in overall musical studies that renders jazz marginalized has, perhaps ironically, but also understandably, been adopted as that which guides jazz education. We saw that aspects of this orientation shape conventional jazz scholarship as well, further indicative of the scope of the prevailing paradigm. Accordingly, the field falls far short in realizing its integral potential and thus emerging as a transformational catalyst in the broader spheres of music, education, and society.

Compared to any other field in music or overall education, however, jazz studies is most closely situated—or put another way, needs to invoke the least degree of change—to realizing the inherent integral potential within its own boundaries and thus assuming this transformational function. Our next step in gaining an integral understanding of the idiom takes us deep into its two primary creative processes: improvisation and composition.

Chapter 6

Invention

Improvisation and Composition as Contrasting Pathways to Transcendence

There is a music that must be composed, there is another that can only be improvised.

—Steve Lacy, *Findings: My Experience with the Soprano Saxophone*[1]

In the summer of 1979, I attended a meditation retreat in the wooded hills of western Massachusetts. Toward the end of a long and particularly deep session, an image appeared in my mind's eye, the significance of which would not become evident until several years later. The image was of an exquisitely ornate geometrical shape, the details of which, as vivid as they were at the time, faded from my awareness not long after the event. But what did not fade was the experience of wholeness, clarity, and a kind of noetic insight—a sureness that far transcended any kind of understanding possible through analytical inquiry—about musical creativity that would become central to my work. To be more specific: This was the understanding of improvisation and composition as fundamentally distinct processes, not just differing in their obvious surface features, but as grounded in contrasting transcendent principles originating in the innermost dimensions of consciousness. How this kind of knowing might have been transmitted through the visual image may forever elude me. But what will never dissipate is the knowledge itself, which has served as the basis for the integral account of musical creativity being advanced in this book.

While Lacy's comment is directly in line with my experience, it is important to realize that this perspective departs from conventional tendencies to view improvising and composing as essentially the same process undertaken at different speeds. More particularly, improvisation is generally viewed as an accelerated form of composition, thus not only inviting deeply ingrained tendencies to dismiss improvisation as a less-developed subspecies of composition, but in so doing also reducing two developmental lines to a single pathway. The extricating of improvisation from this common classification, in providing a more nuanced conception of musical creativity, is not to deny important ways the processes intersect, nor that what we think of as improvised and composed music emerged from a common ancestor that could only have been improvisatory, nor is it to cast one process above the other. Rather, it is to illuminate an important evolutionary development in musical practice marked by the differentiation of two highly distinct yet complementary modes of expression. And in so doing, our understanding of the richness of jazz, unmatched among contemporary idioms in its integration of the two lines, expands apace.

My central idea, which I call *nonlinear time dynamics*, is that improvisation and composition are rooted in fundamentally contrasting modes of temporal perception that serve as contrasting pathways to parts-to-whole, transcendent experience. Improvisation is driven by a moment-to-moment, *inner-directed* conception, compatible with what is sometimes referred to as *nonlinear* temporality, where the localized present is intensified and relationships to past and future events are cognitively subordinate. Inner-directed conception is the basis for the spontaneous inventive and interactive aspects that are at the heart of improvised music aesthetics. A very different type of temporal experience, which I call *expanding* conception, where past-future relationships from any point are cognitively magnified, drives composition. Expanding conception is key to the large-scale temporal projections that are central to the architectural richness of much composed music. The processes therefore primarily differ not in degree, or the speed at which they are undertaken, but in kind, in the more fundamental dimension of temporal directionality.[2] We will see that these contrasting modes of first-person, Upper-Left experience correlate with contrasting second-person, Lower-Left cultural sensibilities, which in turn give rise to contrasting third-person, Upper-Right/Lower-Right surface musical features: two different types of time cognition, two pathways to transcendent experience with correspondingly different expressive results.

The chapter begins with a look at the conventional conception of improvisation as accelerated composition and why the contrasting conditions of the two processes, even prior to investigation of underlying distinctions, reveal this understanding to be misguided. Also considered is why this perpetuates the marginalization of improvisation in musical study and research. We then turn to the relationship between time and consciousness to show how temporal perception differs between ordinary and heightened/transcendent states of consciousness. This sets the stage for a look at how improvisation and composition mediate transformations in consciousness through contrasting temporal mechanisms. Improvisation will be examined in this regard from both stylistically open and style-based perspectives, with consideration of the way the cyclical, pitch-rhythmic frameworks upon which jazz musicians improvise mediate temporal experience. The chapter closes with a look at the cultural ramifications of these contrasting models of artistic production, which support the idea of Afrological and Eurological streams broached earlier.

Why Improvisation Is Not Accelerated Composition

As noted in earlier chapters, the musical world in academic circles has been viewed through the lens of the composed work, or the art object, reflecting the influence of the overarching Matrix of Materialism that prevails in education at large. Several important limitations extend from this orientation. First is that both improvisation and composition are excluded from the overall core curriculum of musical training, and with jazz and composition majors as notable exceptions, the resultant identity of most students and faculty—and thus the culture—of musical academe. Though at first glance one might think that at least composition, in an artistic paradigm rooted in a composed-music aesthetic, would be an important part of musical study for all students, the modernist notion of the masterwork as some sacred product that can and ought to be fashioned by a select few runs deep in musical academe, thereby relegating even compositional activity to a distinct minority.

Consistent with this object-mediated aesthetic is a corresponding orientation in music research, where emphasis on the structural facets of works and related historical and cultural contexts far overshadow inquiry into the creative process.[3] It is therefore inevitable that, in the occasional investigation of musical creativity that does occur, improvisation is considered an accelerated subspecies of composition. Bruno Nettl for example, suggests that improvisation and composition might be considered, respectively, "rapid and slow" versions of composition.[4] Paul Berliner, in his widely acclaimed book *Thinking in Jazz*, marvels that "few experiences are more deeply fulfilling for improvisers than the compelling, all-absorbing nature of composing music in performance."[5] David Elliott refers to improvising as "the process of composing a musical work in real time," and advises listeners to attend as much to "what is being composed on the spot" as "how it is performed."[6]

There appears to be some logic to this thinking and it is important to understand both its underlying rationale yet also why it is misguided. One reason to define improvisation as sped-up composition might be to counter the idea that the creative flow of style-specific improvisers, jazz musicians in particular, is little more than the regurgitation of stockpiled clichés.[7] The improvisation-as-composition perspective may also help dispel notions of improvisation as a haphazard, undisciplined mode of expression that is inherently deficient in terms of sophistication, formal coherence, and aesthetic worth. Instead, the argument goes, the improviser in a single creative episode replicates the creative decision making process of the composer, who fashions ideas not in a single, continuous attempt but in a series of discontinuous episodes that may span days, weeks, and months.

The problem, however, with both lines of reasoning is that, in privileging composition as the ideal against which improvisatory musical expression is to be measured, the very concerns being addressed are exacerbated. For example, when Phillip Alperson suggests that the evaluation of an improvisation—which he defines as "the creation of a musical work while it is performed"—take into consideration "what has proven to be possible within the demands of improvisatory musical activity,"[8] one senses the presumption of a norm that improvisation is inherently incapable of achieving, at which point our only recourse is to appreciate the noble attempt. As a result, appreciation of the full richness of improvisation (as well as composition) will be limited. In other words, as long as improvisation is seen as a subspecies of composing, it will be seen at best as a kind of spurious creative endeavor that perhaps occasionally manifests in remarkable feats, while reservations linger that music made up on the spot will never measure up to that which has been thought out over time—in other words, where composers took the time to really *get it right*. "Improvisation," according to the composer Luciano Berio, "may be of therapeutic value to uptight performers," but lacks the capacity inherent in composition for "coherent discourse that develops along multiple levels."[9] As a result, this important, improvisatory expressive stream in the musical world will remain marginalized in research programs, curricular models, arts advocacy initiatives, diversity discourse, and cross-disciplinary exploration of creativity and the creativity-consciousness relationship.

An integral look at improvisation and composition reveals a much different picture, where improvisation is understood not as a subspecies of composition, but rather the two processes are seen as underpinned by differing cognitive mechanics that render them contrasting expressive vehicles and parts-to-whole pathways to transcendence. In essence, there are multiple ways to "get it right."

We have already considered in chapter 2 surface distinctions between the two processes that strongly suggest the need to rethink prevailing notions. Whereas compositions are created over a series of discontinuous creative episodes that can span days, or more often weeks and months, and which take place at times and places separate from those where pieces are presented to audiences, improvisation happens in a single continuous episode, where performance occurs in the same time and place of creation. Whereas composers usually create alone, improvisation—which certainly happens in solitude—often happens collectively. Improvisatory collectivity, moreover, brings together not only multiple musicians, but musicians and audiences in the act of performance.

We can thus begin to see how vastly differing surface conditions might give rise to significantly different expressive results that might correlate with different cultural sensibilities. This will be underscored further on when we link the inner-directed, nonlinear conception of improvisatory time with spontaneous, interactive musical cultures and the expanding, linear temporality of composition with work-centered cultures. Prior to going into the interior distinctions that underlie these contrasting paradigms—which come together in jazz—it is important to clarify some points.

First, the claim is not that there are no points at which improvisation and composition intersect, nor that improvisers cannot invoke compositional strategies or composers improvisatory strategies in their creative activities. Rather, large portions of musical practice are distinguishable according to these principles and thus support Lacy's contention that "there is a music that must be composed, another that can only be improvised." That these principles generally hold even amid the wide range of compositional and improvisatory strategies that might be identified underscores this point. This includes, within the compositional, Beethoven's extensive reworking of materials, Schubert's more rapid style, and on through recent methods involving aleatoric or indeterminate strategies as well as technologically driven approaches to composition,[10] and in the improvisational, free, or open improvisatory formats in which nothing is planned in advance as well as those involving preordained constraints such as jazz chord changes, Arabic *maqam*, or Hindustani *raga* and *tala* structures. While the boundaries between the general process categories may blur at points, they hold up in an overwhelming range of the creative expanse and thus support the proposed distinctions. Even in the emergent, jazz-driven integral era, where the idiom's current juxtaposition of the processes opens up to a more complete synthesis, at which point boundaries between them will at times indeed become nebulous, there will still be clear instances of distinctions between improvisatory and compositional creativity that is among the idiom's salient features. An understanding of temporality/culture-rooted distinctions will enhance appreciation and understanding of the significance of both improvisatory/compositional melding and retention of discrete natures.

Second is that while what have emerged as improvisatory and compositional streams per se may be distinguished from one another, they both may be seen as differentiated aspects of a common improvisatory ancestor. Again we encounter our core integral evolutionary trajectory whereby from undifferentiated or less-differentiated wholeness emerge increasingly differentiated phenomena. This is evident in music both from historical and practical vantage points: Naturally, the earliest forms of musical expression—whether as posited by Ellen Dissanayake, Steven Mithen, and others, this evolved from early mothers cooing their infants, or Darwin's idea that music originated in mating calls[11]—had to have been improvised, with composition evolving first in the form of gestures that were repeated and codified, and notation a relatively recent development. A similar trajectory may be evident on a practical scale in the composition process, where early on composers may improvise to generate ideas prior to seizing one or another and capturing it in notation.

But the moment the composer stops, steps outside the creative flow to reflect upon, capture, and structure as part of a larger work a moment that had just passed, a new kind of temporal consciousness begins to take shape that is the basis for a very different line of creative expression than that whereby the artist sustains a moment-to-moment flow throughout a single creative episode. And while the compositional line has assumed exclusive centrality in the academic world, to the point where an improvisatory line is either dismissed as inferior or irrelevant, most of the musical world has retained its improvisatory foundations, which with the advent of jazz and the broader realm of contemporary improvised music that it has spawned has evolved to unprecedented heights.[12]

From their common, undifferentiated improvisatory origins, two contrasting expressive pathways have emerged that inform each other in profound ways. We thus gain a new and expanded perspective on the systematic improvisation principle introduced in chapter 2, in which a broad spectrum of processes are understood as differentiated forms of improvisation. The differentiation of composition at a deep level in this scheme lays groundwork for newfound understanding of the creative and spiritual diversity of the contemporary musical world in general, and the jazz idiom in particular.

Contrasting Conditions Promote
Contrasting Temporal Conceptions

I begin my analysis presuming a collective, open improvisatory format (no preset constraints) in that this ideally illuminates the distinctions I seek to make. Taken up later will be improvisation within preordained frameworks (e.g., jazz chord changes and time feels), which is where improvisation-composition distinctions may be most clear. Then considered will be temporal dynamics of improvisation in solo, unaccompanied formats, which is where improvisation may seem to most closely intersect with composition. Even here, however, important differences may be identified that shed light on the inner dimensions of the respective processes.

A look at the inner mechanics of the processes lays preliminary groundwork. Inspired by Eugene Narmour's and Leonard Meyer's "implication-realization" model,[13] we can identify an aspect of the generation of ideas that is arguably common to much if not all creativity, and thus applied to music represents a point at which improvisation and composition have not yet differentiated into discrete operations. Though implication-realization principles were originally framed to illuminate how listeners assimilate and find coherence in musical ideas, they are equally applicable to the improvisatory and compositional processes of the artists creating the music. The basic premise when articulated from the vantage point of the creating artist is that at any given musical moment, or point of realization, subsequent future possibilities, or implications, are inferred. Over time, a chain of events unfolds in this way. In other words, an event sounds at moment A, the creating individual generates one or more possible successors, one is selected at moment B to yield resultant structure AB, from which in turn subsequent implications are inferred at moments C, D, E, and so on, to yield an ever-expanding composite structure.

Where improvisation and composition diverge is in how ideas or events are conceived in relationship to one another in time. In short; composition promotes a cumulative conception of the event chain, where AB gives rise to ABC, which then gives rise to ABCD, and then ABCDE, and so on. Improvisation, on the other hand, is driven by a more nonlinear conception that is more aptly represented as AB BC CD DE and so on. In other words, improvisatory decisions are made according to more localized detail, which gives rise to an entirely different kind of architecture and interaction. Jonathan Kramer, while not speaking of improvisation per se, compares nonlinear temporality to a Markov chain, in which "a series of antecedents [contributes] to the probability of a consequent event. In a first-order Markov chain, an event is understood as 'chosen' on the basis of probabilities suggested by the immediately preceding event." When more distant predecessors mediate events, indicative of a higher Markov order, "the greater the linearity. Total nonlinearity corresponds to a zeroth-order Markov chain, in which each event is understood as completely independent of preceding events."[14] I suggest that while varying degrees of nonlinearity are possible in composed music, the discontinuity of the process makes inevitable some degree of reinforcement of linear relationships, where the continuous, uninterrupted flow of improvisation is more conducive to nonlinearity. Therefore, even though linear and nonlinear distinctions might be inferred within the compositional line, when we view improvisatory and compositional processes together, we can generalize that the improvisatory falls further in the nonlinear direction.

Another way of thinking about this is to view compositional decision making processes as mediated by the accumulation of everything that has been created up to any given point in time, whereas improvisatory decision making is more driven by the very recent past and present. Compositional conception is thus called expanding because it enables attention to relationships from any given moment to proximal or distant past and future points, whereas improvised time is inner-directed due to its orientation toward the localized present and subordination of large-scale relationships. Expanding conception corresponds to linear, inner-directed to nonlinear. It should also be added that linear and nonlinear distinctions denote entryways to a transcendent wholeness that, regardless of entryway, exhibits properties of a nonlinear, complex system. Hence, improvisation employs a nonlinear gateway to nonlinear complexity, composition a linear gateway to nonlinearity.[15]

The two kinds of decision making are directly rooted in the contrasting conditions of the two operations. Composers—due to the discontinuity of the process—can pause, step back from the work, have a cup of tea, walk the dog, all the while reflecting on the relationship of any point in time in a work to any past or future point. The longer the time spent outside of the *timescape* of the work—the real-time flow that is experienced by playing or mentally performing the music—the more that a cumulative conception can develop and inform any subsequent creative decision.[16] A kind of reversible conception, moreover, is also available to composers, which allows them to proceed to some future point in the work and reflect on, and possibly alter, prior material from that vantage point. And then alterations made to past material may suggest changes to later material. Temporal discontinuity also enables composers to isolate a small section of a work and attend to its every detail over days or weeks or longer. These strategies make possible large-scale symmetries such as, for example, the sonata-allegro movement of the classical symphony, as well as what Kramer categorizes as "moment" forms, where "the order of moments is seemingly arbitrary," and yet events are bound together by a kind of overall "logic."[17] Even when the sense of overt relationship, through motivic development, or recapitulation of ideas, between materials in a sequence is consciously inhibited, the cumulative and reversible aspects of an expanding temporality may be essential to a composer's conceiving of such logic (save for instances where stochastic or random processes are involved). In fact, the greater the discontinuity in a piece, and the more a composer steps back to reflect on the evolution of a work, the more difficult it is to attend to each moment as uninfluenced by an ever-growing cumulative awareness of materials. Therefore, while the saxophonist Evan Parker sees less of a need to view "improvisation as something different from composition" but rather more "as opposed to notated music," I believe the discontinuity of the composing process, and the inevitable reflection upon and cognitive reinforcement of linear temporal relationship, is the more important defining and thus distinguishing factor.[18]

Improvisation's continuous flow promotes inner-directed conception and entirely different expressive capacities. Now invention and performance occur simultaneously, enabling a unique unification of performers, listeners, and environment. The improviser, having no provisions to pause and edit, makes a complete musical statement in a single attempt. And because there is no changing the past, and the future is always unknown, awareness is drawn to the moment at hand as the locus of engagement.[19] In collective improvisation formats, moreover, the necessity to attend to unpredictable input—and the potential for what I have called *interfering implications*[20]—from improvising colleagues serves as additional impetus for inner-directedness. In other words, in any given moment, two or more musicians may infer contrasting subsequent future schemes, at which point temporal conception must remain keenly in the moment if the musicians are to sustain the intricate listening and adaptive strategies that are key to improvised creativity. Composers usually create alone and thus need not contend with the multiple input sources that improvisers confront. Therefore, when for improvisers awareness is not rooted in the localized present, due to what will shortly be seen as object-referral attachments to future points (conditioned patterns), their capacity to retrieve content from the inner reservoir, and to perceive and respond to spontaneously arising information generated by improvising colleagues, is limited. "If it's one person," reflects Christian Wolff, "then it's one kind of thing. If it's more than one, then you're constantly in dialogue with other people."[21] If the unification of performers, listeners, and environment that we have posited is central to an improvised music aesthetics and transformational function is to be achieved, the complex network of variables necessary for this to happen must be unified within the heightened experience of the localized present.[22]

To be considered later is a further factor that directs time conception toward the localized present in much improvised music, that found in the cyclic pitch-rhythmic frameworks (such as jazz chord changes and time feels, or, say, Hindustani *raga-tala* cycles) common to many improvisatory traditions. Cyclical reiteration of the underlying structure undermines the sense of large-scale temporal projections and thus promotes intensification of the localized present moment. Even if the underlying pitch-rhythmic structure undergoes considerable change from one iteration to the next, the dominant effect is that of a recurring framework that enlivens localized present perception rather than directing awareness toward large-scale temporal projections between a moment and its past and future.

This is not to suggest that the improviser is entirely oblivious to the past, or perhaps to some overarching cumulative structure, nor is incapable of planning and then executing ideas that extend far into the future. Subordinate temporal conceptions are also available to the improviser that enable such strategies. Inspired by the work of the philosopher Edmund Husserl, I call these *retensive* and *protensive* conceptions.[23] Retensive conception involves retaining awareness of previously realized material and reiterating it at some future point. Protensive conception involves a kind of advance planning where the improviser imagines some future scheme and seeks to realize it. While retensive and protensive (RP) strategies are possible, they will always be secondary in improvisation given that they run counter to the prevailing inner-directed temporality of improvisation that is based in the essential conditions of improvised performance. This is particularly true of collective improvisatory formats in which the interfering implications of improvising colleagues pose particularly formidable obstacles to these kinds of strategies. In no way is this to dissuade improvisers from pursing these strategies—I believe, in fact, that they are part (along with heightened inner-directed capacities) of the evolutionary development of the improvisatory stream—but simply to acknowledge that improvisers will never be able to invoke these approaches to the extent possible in composition. Therefore, Noam Sivan's compelling advocacy of a "compositional approach" to free improvisation, which essentially may be seen as the activation of retensive-protensive faculties, must still be distinguished in its ultimate expressive impact from composition per se.[24] By the same token, composers will never be able to invoke nonlinear, lower-order Markov relationships to the extent that is possible in improvisation, which is not to suggest that attempts in this direction will not yield interesting results and thus ought to be abandoned.

Even from this preliminary overview of contrasting conditions, modes of temporal conception, and expressive results, we begin to glimpse contrasting aesthetic paradigms—or musical worldviews, which we will later consider as reflective of contrasting extramusical worldviews. Without this understanding, musicians whose experience is confined entirely to composed music will remain inclined to look askance at music improvised, which translates directly into educational policies and models that privilege that which is composed (although, because even composition is often excluded in the structuralist orientation of musical study, this privileging comes in the form of interpretive performance of composed works). And from an improvisationcentric perspective, one might be equally inclined to dismiss music in which spontaneous creativity among performers to generate and mold all aspects of musical structure in the presence of listeners, who often become inextricably part of the creative process, is absent. An integral vantage point, on the other hand, circumvents these limiting and exclusive notions and celebrates the confluence of diverse practices and worldviews as part of an overarching evolutionary thrust that enables contrasting streams to enhance one another and unite within an overarching and richly differentiated unity. Integral musicianship is thus rich in both improvising and composing experiences.

If this approach is to come about, however, a multitiered understanding is needed, one that reveals surface activity as a gateway to interior, transcendent experience. Because of the Matrix of Materialism considered in previous chapters, the association of aesthetic-spiritual richness exclusively with the composed music paradigm is too deeply ingrained in musical study. The situation is not terribly unlike politically correct attempts at an ecumenical religiosity when deep down convictions of superiority and exclusivity linger. Let us thus consider improvising and composing as contrasting parts-to-whole pathways to transcendence and, particularly when complemented with whole-to-parts meditative methodologies, development of consciousness and spirituality.

Improvisation and Composition as
Contrasting Pathways to Transcendence

How do improvisers motivate a shift from ordinary to transcendent awareness? How do composers invoke this shift? In order to answer these key questions, we first need to examine the intimate relationship between music, time, and consciousness.

Music, Time, and Consciousness

Music not only unfolds in time, but as Erik Christensen asserts, "music creates time," a point that is also implicit in investigations by Kramer, Barbara Barry, and others of the way temporal conception is mediated by musical structures and processes.[25] Generally speaking, these and other explorations into the temporality-music relationship are made exclusively through the lens of composed-notated music. Accordingly, Kramer's notion of nonlinear or vertical time, in which pieces (mostly late-twentieth-century works) elicit an experience of heightened presence in which past and future relationships are subordinated, bearing resemblance to my conception of improvisatory, moment-to-moment temporality, may at first glance point to instances where the two streams—the compositional and improvisatory—come into close proximity, if not unite completely. However, this still leaves, as noted earlier, large portions of the musical world that might fall more clearly within one or the other temporal classification. The same applies when considering the cultural historian and philosopher Jean Gebser's mid-twentieth-century inquiry into the temporality-music relationship, where he states: "The new music—and everything points to this—is in a position to abolish previous time forms. In its mode of expression it seems to approach timeless music."[26] Again the focus is largely on composed works, with Gebser drawing upon reflections of composers and theorists on such works, including those of Stravinsky, Hindemith, Schoenberg, and Krenek to observe a shift from the linear time inherent in tonal repertory toward more nonlinear temporal structures promoted by polytonal and atonal pitch languages.[27] "In music," Kramer states in underscoring a point central to Gebser's earlier analysis, "the quintessential expression of linearity is the tonal system."[28] Constituted by a "set of complex hierarchic relationships between tones, supported by durations, dynamics, timbres, etc. . . . the tonic [central pitch center] and tonal relationships conspire toward one goal: the return of the tonic, finally victorious and no longer unchallenged by other keys."[29] As composers explored alternative pitch languages that undermined these hierarchies, which in turn manifested concurrently with new formal propositions, the temporality invoked in the emergent music shifted.

Still, to underscore an earlier point, differences in improvised and compositional form may still be upheld even as the transformation of pitch and formal structures pushed temporal conception in a nonlinear direction. Arguments notwithstanding regarding how close the nonlinearity of contemporary compositional structures might at times approach that of improvisatory structures, that a general retreat in Eurological composition from completely atonal practice, which may have reached its apex a half century ago, supports my contention that large portions of music—with computer-generated composition and improvisation possibly exempt from these differentiations—may be distinguished according to these principles.

A look at the relationship between temporality and consciousness may illuminate these points. Central here is the correlation between contrasting temporal capacities in ordinary and heightened states of consciousness with the contrasting temporal conceptions of improvisation and composition.[30]

Time Is Perceived Differently in Different States of Consciousness

The basic idea is that in ordinary consciousness, a linear, sequential conception of time prevails, where localized present moments are experienced as discrete events in a past-present-future flow. In heightened or transcendent states, two kinds of time perception are possible. One is a linear, sequential flow of discrete "now" or present moments that is similar to that accessed in ordinary consciousness, the other is an overarching sense of an eternal present, where past and future connections are subordinate.[31] We can understand the correlations between state of consciousness and temporal conception in terms of the differing relationship between personal self and transcendent Self in ordinary and heightened states. In ordinary consciousness, as discussed in chapter 3, the personal self is disconnected from the transcendent Self and thus bound by relativistic objects of perception. These object-referral attachments manifest in bondage to past-present-future relationships between events. In heightened consciousness, the union of self and Self allows freedom from object-referral attachments and thus linear (past-present-future) temporal bonds, more akin to the lower-order Markov chain noted previously. However, this does not mean individuals invoking heightened or transcendent experience are oblivious to linear relationships—let us always bear in mind that transcendence allows both freedom from and access to objects—but rather that they are simply not bound by them.

Temporal experience and consciousness are thus intimately linked, if not indistinguishable concepts. When the contrasting temporalities of improvisation and composition are added to the mix, we encounter a wide range of musical temporalities that illuminate temporal distinctions between the processes as well as establish a framework for understanding musical creativity and the diversity of the musical world. We will see that ordinary consciousness in improvisation, for example, differs not only from heightened consciousness in improvisation, but also from ordinary and heightened consciousness in composition. Our goal of invoking heightened consciousness through music now takes on a more nuanced look, as does the unique capacity for jazz to fulfill that goal.

Our next step is to probe the mechanics by which inner-directed or nonlinear temporality of improvisation catalyzes transcendent experience, which brings us to the heart of nonlinear time dynamics.

Nonlinear Time Dynamics: Inner-directed Conception as Vehicle for Transcendence

[T]he patterns [were] well-known and everybody [was] playing them. . . . I knew what it took to learn them but I just couldn't stomach it. . . . When Bud Powell made them, fifteen years earlier, they weren't patterns. . . . Jazz got so it wasn't improvised anymore.[32]

—Steve Lacy

Inflated Points

In order to understand how the inner-directed conception of improvisation motivates transcendent experience, it is necessary to understand how object-referral, conditioned patterns, primary features of ordinary consciousness (the antithesis of transcendence), are constructed and dissolved within this temporal flow. The key principle here is that because musical ideas manifest in time, conditioned ideas will occupy time frames that run counter to the overarching directionality of the operation at hand. Therefore, because as noted earlier the conditions of improvisation direct attention toward the innermost boundaries of the localized present, improvisers in ordinary consciousness are prone to conditioned patterns that thwart this inner-directed movement. Instead of sustaining a moment-to-moment awareness, awareness is instead overshadowed by *inflated points* that expand the boundaries of the localized present and preclude spontaneity. In heightened consciousness improvisation, these inflated present boundaries collapse to yield the greater inner-directedness that is key to optimal inventiveness and interactivity. We will shortly consider the correlate in ordinary consciousness composition, where within the expanding temporal conception that drives the process, conditioned patterns manifest in *weak spans* that confine temporal projections to a modicum of what is possible.

Nonlinear time dynamics illuminates how this transformation from inflated points to collapsed points occurs in improvisation. In examining this we will delineate parameters that define the localized present, which we will see is more productively fathomed as a cognitive construct rather than one measurable by the clock.[33] To begin, imagine a sequence of improvised ideas in time, where one musical object—sound or silence— follows another. Now imagine this sequence could be hypothetically stopped so that small moments within it could be examined much like the workings of a single cell in a biological organism might be examined under a microscope. What I believe one would find are transformations in perception of moments as either resulting from prior moments, or as generators of subsequent moments. In other words, ideas tend to be either understood—perceived as meaningful or logical—as either products of their past, or sources of their futures. In any given sequence of ideas or objects—sounds and silences—some will be understood as generating moments and others as resultant moments. The length of the localized present may be measured as the time span that elapses between generating moments. The contents that are encompassed within this time span comprise a musical *event*. And, because as consciousness transforms an idea that was previously understood solely as a product of its past may in turn be also understood as a generator of future moments, different states of consciousness give rise to varying numbers of events that might be perceived within a given unit of time as measurable by the clock. With higher consciousness comes higher frequency of event perception. At this point spontaneity, inventiveness, and interactivity—key facets of improvisatory creative expression and impact—increase. Chapter 12 will examine the planetary ramifications of this idea in considering the need for the transformation of unsustainable ecological and sociological patterns on a global scale to avenues for progress.

Let us return to the implication-realization model considered earlier for a closer look. Imagine an idea sounding at moment n that generates implications, or possible successors, $n1$, $n2$, $n3$ and so on. Imagine a resultant event n-$n3$, defined as such because moment $n3$ is the point in time at which awareness shifts from perception of objects $n1$, $n2$, and $n3$ as resultant from generator n to perception of $n3$ as a new generator of its future possibilities. This perceptual shift from realization/generator to implication/successor back to realization/generator comprises a *cognitive event cycle*. The rate of transformation within a given unit of clock-time is called *event cycle frequency*. Heightened consciousness, because of its capacities for dissolution of time-bound attachments, enables greater event cycle frequency—and thus creative decision making moments—than ordinary consciousness within a given unit of time. If the event n-$n3$ just considered is mediated by the inflated points of ordinary consciousness, it might be experienced as the shorter n-$n1$ in transcendent consciousness due to the neutralization of inflated temporal projections and collapse of ordinary present boundaries atop the waves of the inner-directed flow.[34]

It is important to emphasize that higher event cycle frequency indicates a condition of greater freedom, one of greater differentiation within wholeness in which conditioned patterns, which in ordinary consciousness are not realized as creative choices but rather regurgitated responses, are transcended *and included* within the broader slate of options that open up. This helps us redirect our gaze when it comes to the parameters that define creativity, where exterior concerns such as novelty that have dominated conventional exploration of musical creativity give way to interior considerations, such as degree of self-Self integration.[35] Certainly, improvisers functioning from high degrees of this integration will have access to a much-expanded palette of musical materials, and thus capacities for novelty. But they will also be more highly attuned to the needs of a particular musical moment, which may at times call for a reiteration of some idea the improviser has played before, and possibly many times. If this idea is expressed from deep self-Self union, it will be capable of as powerful and magical an impact as any that appears to be radically novel; it will be as if the improviser had just unearthed some treasure for the first time. By the same token, an idea whose surface features appear novel but which is not realized from a deeply integrated consciousness will be devoid of any kind of transformational impact.

Therefore, while a creative statement made at any given moment by an individual in heightened consciousness may involve surface features that he or she may have played many times, and thus superficially may resemble the mindless regurgitation of inbred clichés that Lacy rightly laments in the epigraph to this section, it is important to realize the two scenarios are considerably different. Creative substance needs to be measured not by degree of exterior novelty but by interior integration of consciousness. "I'm always a little distrustful of the criticism," states Larry Polansky as he points in the direction of this inner locus, "that 'If you improvise long enough, you're just playing your licks.'" Rather, "if you're a smart enough musician, that's just a way to something else." To which Christian Wolff adds, "even if you may do things you've done before, you're still doing them with complete presence at the time you're doing them."[36]

This analysis should dispel any confusion about the importance of emulative engagement in creative development. Rigorous internalization of the very idiomatic conventions that Lacy found it difficult to "stomach" may, in fact, be genuinely part of the emulative process scope, which when sustained in tandem with robust exploratory studies, will help dissolve tendencies toward conditioned regurgitation of the content assimilated. Complementing these aspects of parts-to-whole creative growth with engagement in meditation practices that ground the entire enterprise in consciousness will promote optimal growth. Meditation also helps ground awareness in the transcendent interstices from which sounds emerge, and the temporal perception of sounds may be rendered optimally inner-directed and event-cycle rich.

Mind the Gap

Here we return to the idea of the "gap" from Maharishi Mahesh Yogi's commentary on the Rig Veda, the *Apaurusheya Bhāshya*, which illu-minated the silent, unmanifest junction points between the primordial sounds, or frequencies, that emerge from the eternal field of self-referral consciousness and give rise to the infinitely diverse creation. The Vedic literature is thought to be a direct manifestation of this inextricable link between sound and form, whereby the syllables that comprise the verses and chapters of this literature directly reflect the sequential unfolding and differentiation of the vibrational building blocks of the manifest world. The transformation of one syllable, or sound, to the next involves its disso-lution into the gap from which it emerged and its successor subsequently emerges. The gap is at once abstract and unmanifest—*atyānta-abhāva*—and at the same time a site of infinite dynamism—*anyonya-abhāva*—where interactions occur between the three impulses of *rishi*, *devata*, and *chandas*—or subject, process, and object—and the *samhita* that is their composite wholeness.[37] Recall also that these may be correlated with first-, second-, and third-person dimensions of wholeness central to Integral Theory, which are the core impulses underlying spirituality, art, and sci-ence. The *Apaurusheya Bhāshya* illuminates the interplay between these impulses as manifesting in every grain of creation, thereby exemplify-ing the principle of *anoraniyan mahato-mahiyān*—bigger than the big-gest and smaller than the smallest—where the structuring dynamics of wholeness may be seen at infinitesimally small scales as well as cosmic scales.[38] The transcendent, primordial frequencies from which originate subjective, processual, and objective, or first-, second-, and third-person realities (recall our analysis in chapter 3 where the integral intersubjective realm was shown to be a manifestation of the process domain) are active in the silent gaps between fluctuations in an eternal source of creation.

How does this relate to improvisation? Because in the transcendent experience that is invoked within the inner-directed, nonlinear flow of improvisatory creativity, and its breaking down of time frames into constituent present moments that characterizes heightened event-cycle frequency, awareness is grounded in the gaps and thus the holistic, structuring dynamics that govern cosmic and—never losing sight of the nonduality premise—individual creation. Inner-directed perception represents enlivenment of a fullness in each present moment that is grounded in the totality, or *samhita*, of *rishi*, *devata*, and *chandas* interactions. When, by contrast, temporal perception is dominated by the inflated points of ordinary consciousness, this fullness is weakened and the transformational power of improvisatory expression significantly compromised.

Here it is also important to not conflate inflated points of ordinary consciousness improvisation with the kinds of temporal projections that enable profound compositional choices; because of the overarching inner-directed flow of improvisation, no degree of temporal inflation would be enough to yield compelling compositional strategies. Perhaps ironically, it is only when inflated points are neutralized, and inner-directed conception is enlivened, that the aforementioned retensive-protensive strategies, which are the closest approximations improvisation can make to large-scale compositional construction (which ought not be considered an improvisatory ideal, nor spontaneous interaction a compositional ideal), are optimal. In order to escape, as it were, the gravitational pull toward the localized present that is inherent in inner-directed, nonlinear perception, one must first ride its waves and penetrate to its core. At this point, limited, though interesting and not unfruitful expressive capabilities of a compositional nature may become part of the improviser's creative palette.

Nonlinear time dynamics may thus be summed up as the principles that govern the potential by which improvisers contact the silent, transcendent gaps that underlie surface musical processes and structures. This is not to suggest that the gaps are only active, or contacted, in the overt spaces between sounds, as when a wind instrumentalist takes a breath or space is used as part of the creative flow. The silent nature of the gaps refers to their eternal, unmanifest nature, which is present, and thus can be accessed, even amid the most intensive surface turbulence.

To explain this another way: A long sustained tone that, in its surface manifestation, consists of unbroken sound can be created as a result of extremely high event-cycle frequency, where the improviser at the initial point of realization has no intention of playing a long tone but as awareness continually returns to new generative points, and thus new event boundaries, chooses to continue the sound. The resultant long tone, in this case, is not a product of a decision made at some relatively distant past point, but a dynamic series of moment-to-moment decisions—each of which are richly grounded in the fullness of the transcendent gaps in which the transformation of awareness from the idea at hand as result of its predecessor to generator of new possibilities occurs.

However, the use of overt silence in the improvisation process can help enliven this awareness, as well as further expand the improviser's surface creative palette. Here I might also mention the system of "silence studies" that I use in my improvisation teaching that help students shift from ordinary conception to heightened inner-directedness. The first step is to urge them to shift their thinking about music whereby instead of considering sounds central, silence is central and thereby sounds are interruptions atop an underlying field of silence. I have them create music in which spaces of silence comprise as important a part of the creative fabric as the sounds that are made. With practice, it is possible to create improvisations that make use of fairly lengthy stretches of time in which no sound is being made but the music retains extraordinary vitality.[39]

Let us close this section with questions that often arise regarding the initial catalyst for transformed temporal perception and thus consciousness in improvisation. This will underscore the complementary functions of improvisation and meditation. Does this transformation originate with the creative activity of improvisation, whereby movement of temporary conception toward the heightened experience of the present motivates dissolution of inflated points and thus transcendent experience? This shift may thus be seen as point-driven, through the heightened sense of the localized present. Or might it work in the opposite direction, where perhaps a propensity for transcendent experience and the heightened span aspect of the present—a facet of which is heightened localized present experience—impacts the dissolution of inflated point perception?

In fact, transformed consciousness can be motivated by either of these parts-to-whole or whole-to-parts angles. From a parts-to-whole perspective, the dissolution of inflated points can be seen as the shattering of conditioned logic patterns, the cognitive threads that keep ordinary awareness in place, allowing a more transcendent experience to flow. The inflation of localized present perception happens to be how conditioned patterns manifest in the temporal tapestry of improvisation; in composition, where time flows differently, conditioned patterns manifest in weak spans. In both instances, this top-down dissolution is reminiscent of rumination on a Zen koan, which as neuroscientist/Zen practitioner James Austin points out "in itself has no literal meaning" and can even seem nonsensical. However, when one "cleaves the layers of unconscious and preconscious mental processes" it is possible to make "direct sense out of apparent nonsense."[40] The resultant resolution of the koan is often characterized by a sudden flash of insight, which is nothing but the integration of consciousness, made possible by the liberation from, in this case, the layers of mental associations and attachments that confine awareness to ordinary consciousness. For the personal self is but a wave that floats atop the transcendent ocean of Being, which may shine through at the removal of the slightest obstacle that obscures this connection.

Creative Composition: Transcendence through Expanding Conception

Weak and Robust Spans

The contrasting conditions of composition give rise to a very different experience of time, yielding different types of conditioned pattern deconstruction than occur in improvisation. Just as we saw with the improviser, the composer realizes an idea at moment A and generates one or more possible successors that direct awareness to some future point in time (and possibly backward in time to some prior moment in the piece). However, whereas the improviser infers future possibilities within an inner-directed or nonlinear flow, the composer infers future possibilities within an expanding, linear flow. This directly impacts how conditioned patterns manifest and how they need to be neutralized. Whereas in improvisation, due to the inner-directed or nonlinear flow of time, conditioned patterns manifest as *inflated points*—in other words, temporal projections that impede the quest for the smallest possible conceptions of the localized present—in composition, conditioned patterns manifest instead as *weak spans* in the quest for the most expansive temporal conceptions. Thus, whereas improvisers seek to break down inflated points and corresponding time frames, composers seek to expand the boundaries of weak spans into more robust and broader temporal projections.

How does this happen? We begin with the inherent tendency in the expanding conception to exert an outer-directed cognitive pressure against the boundaries of the localized present. This inherent tendency is enlivened by the discontinuity of the composing process. With each exit from the timescape of the work, the composer runs through the piece in his or her mind, and in each moment, ponders, senses, and imagines temporal relationships between each moment and its predecessors and offspring. Composers, as all creative practitioners, can imagine more freely than they can actually realize—in other words, composers can conceive of temporal expanses away from pencil and paper that, at least at first, are not readily conceived in the actual iteration of ideas. Thus, during this moment, composers extend the boundaries of the localized present in an expanding direction. Composers can also avail themselves of precompositional strategies, which serve as correlates to trans-stylistic constraints imposed by improvisers, in order to expand their horizons and free up from conditioned conceptions. These might include mapping out formal proportions, number of movements, pitch material, dynamic ranges, density categories, and so forth. As with improvisation, these serve to deconstruct logic patterns that confine awareness to ordinary consciousness.

As a piece unfolds, the cumulative form increasingly mediates the composer's awareness state. As composers reflect on a work's expansive temporal relationships, they stretch the moderate temporal projections characteristic of ordinary consciousness to dimensions that are unfamiliar. The awareness is driven to more expansive and fluid states of consciousness that can accommodate these kinds of temporal demands; these of course are in the direction of greater transcendence. In other words, the ever-accumulating form places demands upon temporal awareness that increasingly require taking recourse toward more transcendent levels of experience in which past, present, and future are unified in an overarching presence. However, since transcendent awareness subsumes the object of perception of ordinary consciousness, and thus all corresponding phenomena, the sequential relationships of the localized present are still experienced, but now along with transcendence. In this way, transcendence in composition is structure-mediated, that is, driven by the large-scale temporal relationships conceivable in the process. The localized present perception continually expands as the work develops, placing greater and greater demands on the awareness to assimilate the growing temporal expanse, driving awareness toward the transcendent platform of overarching present awareness where these extraordinary temporal projections can be grasped.

Whereas exploratory processes in improvisation involve the inward collapse of the localized present, in composition this transformation involves the outward collapse of these boundaries. Weak spans in composition are the result of object-referral attachments that constrain temporal awareness to smaller rather than larger time frames, thereby running counter to the expanding temporal flow. When weak spans are "deconstructed," thus giving way to larger temporal conceptions, the constituent elements of these spans may be subsumed within, albeit in passages which may differ considerably from the initial conception of this material, the overall form of the work. The key is freeing up from the attachments to these ideas and perceiving them as more pliable. In improvisation, the rendering of inflated points as more pliable enables the uncovering of constituent moments, and thus corresponding musical objects, which may have previously (in nondeconstructed states) been conceived as part of larger, even if conditioned, ideas. Robust spans are instances of more differentiated wholeness in that they consist in longer time frames in which constituent moments are informed by the whole. Therefore, the transformations in creative awareness, and corresponding deconstructive processes in improvising and composing yield two very different ways in which musical ideas are linked together in time.

It is also important to emphasize that even though composition is driven by more of a surface linear temporal conception than is improvisation, this ought not to suggest that this process is more prone to ordinary consciousness, nor that improvisation, driven by surface nonlinear conception, is more prone to heightened consciousness. It must be remembered that heightened consciousness offers two layers of temporal conception—linear, sequential, localized present experience, and nonlinear, overarching presence. Composition thus moves from a linear surface to a nonlinear-linear synthesis, mediated by the linear, in heightened states; and improvisation moves from a nonlinear surface to a nonlinear-linear synthesis, mediated by nonlinearity, in heightened states.[41]

Two contrasting temporal conceptions, two pathways to transcendence, two contrasting expressive and aesthetic models: Improvisation and composition differ in far more than the speed at which they are undertaken. Understanding distinctions between these processes paves the way for an enhanced understanding of the richness of the musical world. Jazz, juxtaposing and integrating the two processes to an extent unmatched by any other contemporary genre, thus has the capacity to serve as a unique gateway to the global, multimusical expanse. In order to gain a fuller sense of this, let us look at how these principles manifest in the context of preordained improvisatory structures that are found in jazz and other style-specific improvisatory genres.

Improvisation within Pre-established Formats:
Jazz and Beyond

Much improvised music involves the use of an underlying format, or what the artist-researcher Jeff Pressing has termed the *referent*.[42] Jazz artists improvise on the harmonic-rhythmic frameworks of the compositions they play.[43] Common practice is to state the theme, which is composed, and for group members to take turns playing improvised solos on the harmonic and rhythmic parameters that accompanied the theme. Bruno Nettl compares this to improvising formats in various world musics including Indian *ragas*, the *maqam* and *dastagh* modal structures of the Arabic world, and various musics of Native North Americans.[44] Though significant differences in improvised performance practice must be acknowledged from one culture and idiom to another, there may be aspects common to all or much improvised music that use an underlying format. One such aspect may involve the challenge of adhering to the constraints of the format while maintaining spontaneity and interactivity.

Here an apparent contradiction may seem evident, however, with the spontaneity premise and the improviser's quest to neutralize inflated points, or the past-future temporal constraints of the format. The jazz improviser playing in bar 1 must have some awareness of an upcoming harmonic shift in bar 4, and in fact must have some awareness of the harmonic sequence as a whole in order to most fully create within this context. Would not awareness of the past-future dimensions of the improvising structure conflict with the intensification of the present?

The key to addressing this question is the capacity for the improviser to conceive of the referent both in a moment-to-moment manner *and* as a kind of teleological (past-present-future) structure. The interplay of inner-directed and retensive-protensive temporalities, as optimally enabled in heightened awareness states, allows these contrasting yet complementary conceptions to occur. I will look at how this works largely from a jazz perspective, and then reflect upon how the principles delineated might apply to other improvisation formats.

Deconstructing Time Frames within Referent-based Improvisation

Inner-directed conception within a referent context occurs in three ways. The first involves the deconstruction of implications, or inflated points, exactly as occurs when the improviser plays without previously established parameters, as has been outlined up to this point. The only difference now is that the implication fields inferred from each realized event will include the constraints of the referent. However, within such constraints—for example, an approaching harmonic shift—the artist may still deconstruct temporal associations, and so conceive of constituent presents and events and adapt to spontaneous developments. Thus when a jazz or rock improviser approaches the IV chord on a blues tune, or the Hindustani sitarist approaches *sam*—the first beat of the *tala* cycle—the slate of implications generated will include the respective constraints of the referent, as well as the artist's predispositions in dealing with such constraints. Despite the apparent likelihood that more challenging constraints promote greater tendency toward conditioned functioning, improvisers creating within the context of a referent are in no way limited in the extent to which they may project and deconstruct implications and thus invoke inner-directed conception.

A second aspect of inner-directed conception in referent-based improvisation involves the transformation of the referent itself. The harmonic-rhythmic formats of jazz, for instance, are both precise and at the same time ambiguous, lending themselves to continual transformation while still providing the improviser strong syntactic underpinnings. In other words, any given parameter may be realized in a virtually infinite variety of ways. A jazz pianist may let a single harmonic structure sustain throughout the time frame designated for that chord to sound, or play the chord rhythmically, or not at all, or use a three-note cluster voicing, or a seven-note voicing with extensions and chromatic alterations, or a melodic fragment, and so forth. The possible choices of the bassist are similarly wide ranging. Furthermore, within a time feel many interpretive layers exist; for example, playing 4/4 with a 2 beat, "broken swing feel," or other approaches and their infinite combinations. Moreover, the rhythm section can lay out and let a saxophonist play unaccompanied, with the underlying harmonic structure upheld even in a single melodic line. Thus the possibilities for invention while still upholding a chord sequence are virtually unlimited. In addition to deconstructing personal inferences, as might the "free" improviser, the referent-improviser also deconstructs the constraints of the referent itself in uncovering new layers of temporality and consciousness within a given improvising format.

When looking at other improvising formats from this perspective, the nature of the referent becomes an important factor in the degree to which referent-deconstruction occurs. In this regard, jazz and North Indian improvisation might be examples of highly malleable referents that could undergo significant transformations while still clearly delineating syntactic parameters. A less malleable referent might be found in much rock music, where the improvisational component and the acceptable inventive options open to the performer are generally more confined. Various forms of concert music improvisation using entirely different sorts of referents also involve differing degrees of deconstructive potential, either in the artists' implications or in the format itself.[45] David Cope contrasts Lucas Foss' UCLA Improvisation Chamber Ensemble of 1957, which "worked primarily from charts indicating only initial ideas (e.g., motive, rhythm, pattern] needed to create a work" with formats such as the "improvisation boxes" of Berio's *Circles* (1960) or Duckworth's *Pitch City* (1969), which provided improvisational latitude of a different and more constricted nature.[46] In the first movement of Foss' *Etudes for Organ*, the performer "varies an exactly-notated motor-rhythm single line melody by freely repeating note groups" representing yet another degree of improvisational constraint.[47] Improvised ornaments in Baroque performance might represent an even narrower spectrum of creative possibilities.[48]

A continuum thus emerges where at one end total improvisation with little or nothing planned in advance is found, while the other end includes musics with greater compositional content. At the latter extreme, even interpretive performance of repertory, moreover, might be considered as a species of improvisation. For even in works entirely composed, performers will have some degree of creative options through volume dynamics, inflection, tempo, frequency of vibrato, and other expressive nuances. While interpretive performers do not change the pitches or rhythms delineated by the composer, they certainly deconstruct personal interpretive patterns in seeking spontaneous renditions of pieces they have already played countless times. Interpretive performance might then be seen to involve temporal principles similar to those defining improvisation within a highly detailed referent. This is not to subscribe, however, to the argument, such as that advanced by Carol Gould and Kenneth Keaton, that interpretive performance is a form of improvisation that differs from more overtly improvisatory formats such as jazz only in degree, but not in kind; in other words, that the two forms of expression are not paradigmatically different.[49]

This view may be easily countered by a closer look at the situation. Recall from chapter 2 Meyer's taxonomy of syntactic and nonsyntactic elements. Syntactic elements are harmony, melody, and rhythm; nonsyntactic include density, dynamics, timbre, tessitura, silence, and other elements that, in themselves, are not style specific. Interpretive performers' improvisatory creativity is limited to a few nonsyntactic elements of timbre, dynamics, and tempo, so they cannot manipulate or invent harmonic, melodic, and rhythmic structures. Improvisers are able to invent or manipulate all parameters. The improviser's resultant individual voice will thus be shaped by the interaction of the full scope of syntactic/nonsyntactic elements and the myriad extramusical influences that shape personal and collective style evolution, which will be explored further in chapter 8. While interpretive performers may evolve personalized styles in, say, the way they interpret repertory, they, unlike improvisers, are not able to develop personalized harmonic, melodic, rhythmic languages. For this reason, we refer to improvisation, along with composition, as primary modes of creative musical expression, and interpretive performance a secondary mode of creative expression.

The Cyclical Nature of the Referent

A third aspect of referent-based improvisation that may impact inner-directed conception is its cyclical nature; the harmonic-rhythmic format of jazz, for example, or the Hindustani *raga* or Arabic *maqam*, repeat throughout a performance. How might this impact inner-directed temporal experience? The answer has to do with the way repetitive structures can obliterate the sense of cumulative structure and, in fact, intensify the experience of the present. This effect may be somewhat similar to what Herbert Simon describes as "flattened hierarchies" resulting from repeating ostinato patterns[50] or the musical forms cited by Jonathan Kramer that, because they have "no changes of structural import," direct awareness toward the "vertical time of the work."[51] However, as considered previously, the jazz format may undergo dramatic changes within the context of extensive repetitions, and so it is important to distinguish improvised music with cyclical referents from compositions that engender vertical conception through repetition or other strategies.

In fact, it may be the coexistence of (possibly great) change and cyclical repetition that imbues such improvised music with unique, transcendence-inducing temporal mechanisms. Therefore, inner-directedness may result not only from moment-to-moment temporal deconstruction, both of internally generated implications and the referent itself, but also from the cyclical nature of the referent. Furthermore, that transcendence-inducing properties are thought in some musics to be inherent in the structure of the referent (the intervallic makeup of the *raga* being one example, various African drum patterns being another) may suggest further parameters for transformations in consciousness inherent in improvised music.[52]

Heightened present awareness and inner-directed conception are therefore possible not only in improvising formats with past-present-future dimensions; certain formats may in fact have inherent properties that further promote such conceptual states. A key principle in this regard is the dual capacity in heightened consciousness for the present to be experienced as both a point and an overarching span, with the corresponding retensive-protensive (RP) strategies enabled by heightened states.

One RP strategy is the enhanced ability to conceive of the referent as a teleological structure within any given iteration of the cycle, so that for example an idea stated in bar 4 of a 32-bar form can be sustained, or recalled in bar 24 or some other later point. Heightened consciousness also enables the RP capacities to develop a motive over multiple "choruses" (which are repetitions of the referent), or the capacity to attend to the overall shape of a solo by, say, consciously employing contrasting textures in relationship to what was played several choruses earlier. Thus, heightened RP conception is a by-product of heightened inner-directed conception; by penetrating into the point value of the present, the improviser gains access not only to liberated point-present conception, but also to temporal expanse.

Here, however, it is important to emphasize several points. One is that the demands of moment-to-moment information processing in a dynamic, collective setting will tend to inhibit sustained RP conception, since not only the malleability of the referent but also interfering implications necessitate attending to the localized present. Inner-directedness will tend to prevail instead. Moreover, such collective referent-improvising conditions are conducive to more generalized rather than detailed RP conception. An example of the former is in attending to the overall shape of a solo, its general evolution from sparse to dense, soft to loud, sense of length, and climatic points. An example of a more detailed RP strategizing is the use of motivic development, where the improviser establishes a melodic idea and then sustains the basic shape while transforming its intervallic structure, contour, direction, or simply repeating the basic shape on another pitch level. Pervasive in European classical composition, a commonly cited example is found in Beethoven's Fifth Symphony, in which extensive material is derived from the initial four notes of the piece. This sort of motivic development, however, is not nearly as common in jazz improvisation. With notable exceptions—Coltrane's solo on his piece "Impressions," Oliver Nelson's on his "Stolen Moments"[53]—jazz improvisers, somewhat akin to what composers call "through-composed" strategies, tend rather to spin out streams of constantly changing ideas, each of which might serve as a melodic motive to be developed sequentially, but which more often than not is followed by a contrasting idea.

Why might this be? I believe the reason is clearly the cyclical nature of the jazz referent, which combined with the need to constantly contend with interfering implications, performers' awareness is directed more to localized present moments as relatively autonomous from past and future than toward longer range temporal strategies. The fact, however, that jazz musicians utilize motivic development in their compositions, and here it is important to keep in mind that jazz artists are almost universally improvisers and composers, suggests that the discontinuous composition process enables musicians to thwart the inner-direct thrust and invoke more robust RP conception than usually occurs in improvisation.

This is not to suggest that motivic development is antithetical to jazz improvisation, or perhaps in some way undermines the essence or expressive capacities of the music. In my view, this is, as noted earlier, a relatively uncharted frontier in the organization of improvised melodic materials that has much to offer in terms of expanding what can be done atop chord changes. To this end, I have developed strategies that utilize not only conventional motivic practice in jazz formats, but also multimotivic development whereby improvisers are asked to establish and evolve two or more motivic sequences in the context of harmonic progressions. Here is where composition can inform improvisation, and where the Eurological, architectural stream can inform the Afrological, referent-based, collective improvisatory stream, as the two unite in the grand, multimusical synthesis that defines the central current of the musical landscape.

Solo Improvisation and Extemporaneous Composition as the Closest Points of Intersection

While I believe the preceding analysis enables a strong case to be made for foundational distinctions between composing and collective improvising, such a case is admittedly more difficult when it comes to differentiating solo, unaccompanied improvisation from composing. "[F]or me," states Evan Parker, this poses a "special problem . . . precisely because it was one mind at work and none of those qualities of group improvisation."[54] In other words, where the constraints of collective improvisation, due to the necessity for improvisers to deal with streams of interfering implications, tend to inhibit RP conception, inhibitions that are arguably magnified in time-feel based improvising, would not the unaccompanied improviser, free from the need to contend with input of improvising partners, be able to invoke this conception quite readily and thus create exactly as does the composer?

Two compositional approaches might be noted in response to this question. If we view the situation through the lens of discontinuous composition, which is far more conducive to RP strategies than even unaccompanied improvisation (which is more conducive to them than collective improvisation), a case for distinctions may still be upheld, even if the boundaries are more nebulous than those separating composing from group improvising.

However, what about what might be termed extemporaneous composition, where, as legend has it, Mozart and Bach would spontaneously improvise entire works and then recall and notate their improvisations, thereby casting them into compositions? A short answer might be that, indeed, these are instances where a form of improvisation and a form of composition intersect. But even were we to concede this point, the broader distinctions delineated in this chapter still pertain to vast portions of improvisatory and compositional practice that can be seen as substantially contrasting. For one thing, whether or not these extraordinary accounts are valid, the vast majority of compositional practice more resembles Beethoven's ardent reworking of materials into a finished product over a series of many, discontinuous creative episodes than the rapid, let alone extemporaneous, creativity sometimes alleged. Moreover, even conceding that certain instances of solo improvising and extemporaneous composition may be indistinguishable, it may be possible to also maintain that other instances where, for instance, the artist invokes a lower-order and thus more nonlinear Markov process that is unique to improvisation may suggest that distinctions be upheld. Elsewhere, I have elaborated on this more fully.[55]

Again, even conceding special exceptions, I believe the general distinctions pertain to much musical practice and thus are important in understanding contrasting musical streams in the musical landscape. Let us turn to differences in descriptions of transcendent experiences by composers and improvisers that are consistent with this analysis.

Comparing Composers' and Improvisers' Descriptions of Transcendent Experiences

Further support for the idea of contrasting temporalities may be found in the differing descriptions of transcendent experience offered by composers and improvisers: composers' descriptions are structure-mediated, improvisers' are process-mediated. Brahms, for example, spoke of "rare, inspired moods" where "measure by measure the finished product is revealed to me . . . clothed in the right forms, harmonies and orchestration."[56] Mozart reflected on instances where "the whole, though long, stands almost complete and finished in my mind, so that I can survey it, like a fine picture or a beautiful statue, at a glance."[57] More recently, Paul Hindemith has asserted that composers who are incapable of conceiving "in the flash of a single moment [a] composition in its absolute entirety, with every pertinent detail in its proper place, are not genuine creators."[58] These testimonies clearly indicate the conception of large-scale temporal projections, or robust spans, characteristic of heightened expanding temporality. Even if, as testimonies of other composers suggest, such total glimpses are more the exception than the norm, formidable large-scale conception, and corresponding expanding and reversible temporality, inevitably come into play as a piece takes shape.

By contrast, improvisers' descriptions of peak experiences, as we have seen from statements quoted in previous chapters, indicate transformations in consciousness mediated by process, not musical materials. Recall, for example, jazz musicians' testimonies as to the merging of players and listeners and environment cited in previous chapters. Wholeness, or overarching presence in improvisation, is not mediated by musical structures, but by spontaneous processes and interactions. Were this not the case and indeed improvisers functioned as real-time composers, the ramifications for collective improvisation would be disastrous. Why? Because conception in a single instant of large-scale sections, let alone entire improvisations, by all or even a few ensemble members would result in a colossal case of interfering implications. Improvising is driven by a radically different yet equally miraculous conception than that of the composer.

Temporality, Language, and Culture

A further area of support for the notion of contrasting temporalities involves the relationship between temporality, language, and culture. The inner-directed conception of improvisation and expanding conception of composition are musical manifestations of broader patterns in a given culture that also manifest in language. This point poses important ramifications for the argument for a conjoining of Afrological and Eurological streams in Western music, from which, as considered in the introduction, receptivity to further global streams is possible in the growth toward a grand synthesis.

In foreshadowing this broader connection, Judith Becker essentially reiterates the central theme of this chapter in emphasizing that "more than a single idea of time" is represented by the world's musical traditions. "Some music may be strongly linear with a dynamic thrust forward that compels movement from the beginning to the end. . . . Other music may be basically cyclical, like the American blues form."[59] Becker then goes on to equate the cyclic nature of Javanese gamelan music with the cyclic nature of Hindu-Buddhist cosmology, which is rooted in a nonlinear sense of time. Here the "immediacy of the present as against the demands of the past or future"[60] prevails, which bears close resemblance to the notion of inner-directed conception I put forth. Moreover, the sense of eternal timelessness, which as mentioned earlier I also identify as characteristic of time perception in transcendent states, is also equated with the nonlinear sense of time.

Becker and others link nonlinear temporality with language, further suggestive of a temporality-culture relationship. "Balinese, Javanese and Indonesian are all tenseless languages" where the "sense of linear, progressive time" is subordinate. "Most Indo-European verbs have past, present or future—often combined with aspectual markers—in every utterance. If the speaker of Javanese wishes to indicate temporality, he must add a separate time word such as 'before,' 'now,' (or) 'after'. . . . Temporality has to be consciously superimposed upon an utterance if a speaker feels it necessary."[61] John Broomfield notes similar qualities "in the language of the Native American Hopi," where "there is no reference to time. The grammatical forms which appear to correspond to our tenses distinguish not times but different kinds of information."[62]

Dorothy Lee notes similar aspects in what she calls the "nonlineal" language structures of the Trobriand Islanders. "There are no tenses, no linguistic distinction between past or present. There is no arrangement of activities or events into means and ends, no causal or teleologic relationships."[63] In contrast to the goal-directed aspects of Western temporality, which may be correlated to the architectural forms of Western classical music, there "is no lineal development, no climax."[64] Kramer concurs, adding "South Indians, many African tribes . . . [and] the Quiche Indians of Guatemala" to the list of cultures in which nonlinearity appears prominent, thus remarking that the music of these cultures, "not surprisingly, is also nonlinear."[65]

Admittedly, it is important to proceed with caution when extrapolating from these highly generalized observations specific correlations between cultural patterns and musical practices. Perhaps most problematic is the idea of dividing temporal-linguistic correlations into Western and non-Western orientations, the inherent tendency to privilege the West in this perspective not the least of its problems. Nonetheless, the compatibility of these connections with the broader themes of this analysis clearly invites some degree of consideration, and the Western/non-Western duality may provide at least a viable point of departure even if it only partially holds. Christopher Small has provided possible groundwork here in his correlations between the ascent of industrialization in the West and the decline of improvisation, developments that correspond notably well from a chronological standpoint.[66] Thus a direct link may be seen between specialized roles—the division of labor—in society and in music.

Concomitant with industrialization are tendencies toward dissolution of community, disconnection from the natural environment, and either rejection of spirituality or separation of spirituality and other facets of life—aspects that appear to have manifested first in Western society before spreading to other parts of the world. Ken Wilber notes that the concept of reincarnation, perhaps a notion that most clearly distinguishes materialist and nonmaterialist conceptions of the human being, is common to virtually all the world's wisdom traditions, including earlier stages in Christianity, with the conspicuous exception of the past few centuries of religious thought in Western industrialized society.[67] Accordingly, the advent of a repository of musical compositions in the European classical tradition whose architectural richness (which must be kept in mind is among a broader range of parameters from which one might assess musical worth) is arguably unprecedented in the history of the world's music, thus exemplifying an object-mediated aesthetic, is directly compatible with the materialist orientation of the Western industrialized worldview.

The point is neither to valorize nor denigrate industrialization, nor to in turn suggest that the musical paradigm that it spawned is either unmatched in its greatness, as some would have it, or somehow tainted as others might contend. Rather, we appreciate musical traditions on their own terms as well as reflective of the power of art to transform broader influences into meaningful forms of expression. As much as we abhor much of the circumstances—slavery, racism, oppression—out of which jazz emerged and which certainly influenced its evolution, we appreciate the music in its own right, with corresponding awareness of its broader circumstances as indicative of the extent to which artistic practice is mediated by intersubjective, cultural forces as well as transcendent dimensions of consciousness. Temporal conception is a direct reflection of cultural sensibilities as well as a conduit for archetypal impulses. Until we recognize "temporal linearity," which Kramer describes as among "our most accepted and comfortable concepts," as "not a necessary aspect of human existence but a cultural creation," we may be prone to dismiss other cultures and their creative expressions "as primitive."[68] And until we realize that cultural creations are manifestations of transcendent as well as relativistic forces, our appreciation of coexisting and contrasting streams, and the significance and complexities related to their melding, will be limited.

Time, Types, and Shadow

A context emerges for exploring the integral precept of types, which are generally construed in terms of masculine and feminine orientations, within the realm of music. Here improvisation and composition may be correlated, respectively, with feminine and masculine types, which in turn enable us to draw such correlations with two central cultural streams of Afrological (improvisatory, feminine) and Eurological (compositional, masculine) musical practice. How might such correlations be justified? While the idea that different surface practices may be rooted in differing underlying or subtle archetypal impulses is more important than how these impulses are labeled, Heide Göttner-Abendroth's idea of a "matriarchal aesthetic" suggests support for the proposed correlations. Informed by mythological and archeological evidence, she surmises that ancient women-centered rituals, within the structures at hand, lent themselves to ample latitude for freedom of expression, spontaneity, and improvisation. Matriarchal art "is not a thing but a process, a praxis in which the subject speaks in actions and thereby changes the subjective and objective world."[69] As society became more patriarchal in nature, "the ingenious fabric woven of social politics, psychology, science, and aesthetics . . . was unraveled into its individual threads, which became the individual formal categories of reason that replaced the ecstatic unity."[70] The impulse toward freedom of expression and gesture, collective interaction, and dissolution of boundaries between participants and between ritualistic expression and life at large that she equates with the feminine is fundamentally different than the orderly, hierarchical, and rational nature of the patriarchal, suggesting correlation with the improvisatory/Afrological/feminine versus compositional/Eurological/masculine distinctions we are drawing in music.

The significance of these correlations in the present context is twofold. First of all, they not only enhance our understanding of jazz as a genre that straddles the two streams to an unprecedented degree, but also that of the broader musical world, as these streams are important tributaries that flow into the central syncretic current. While the astructural postmodern perspective may subordinate the tributaries in favor of the resultant confluence, the integral celebrates both tributaries and central melding. And inasmuch as even the postmodern, let alone the integral, eludes musical academe, an essential site where integral musical values may be inculcated and transmitted to the overall educational field, an understanding of streams as manifestations of integral types may serve a second important function. This is the need to penetrate deeply into the musical shadow, defined in chapter 4 as the repository of dissociated patterns in individual and collective musical consciousness that shape prevailing assumptions about the nature of music, musical worth, and musicianship studies. If movement from the current modernist/ethnocentric orientation to postmodern/worldcentric and integral/cosmocentric stages is to occur, these patterns must not only be identified as multitiered in nature but also rectified as such.

We have already seen how the integral framework excels in this way. Viewing this now through the more complete understanding of improvisatory and compositional creativity that has been articulated: Upper-Right distinctions between the paradigms consists of the surface features of the processes. Whereas composition occurs in a discontinuous temporal flow comprised of discrete creative episodes spanning days, weeks, or months, improvisation occurs in a single, continuous flow. Whereas composition is a solitary activity that takes place at times and places different from those of performance of resultant works, improvisation, which can be solitary, is often collective, merging time and place of creation, and not only performers/creators but listeners in a unified artistic event.

From a Lower-Right perspective, we see these processes as the basis for contrasting streams in the musical world. From a Lower-Left perspective, we see these streams as shaped by cultural influences, with the improvisatory primarily fueled by Afrological influences, the compositional by Eurological. From an Upper-Left perspective, we can appreciate these cultural expressive streams as contrasting pathways to transcendent experience, with the domain of temporal cognition the interior mechanism through which heightened consciousness is invoked. We can also appreciate from this vantage point the two streams—the Afrological/collective improvisatory and Eurological/compositional—as manifestations, respectively, of feminine and masculine archetypal impulses.

This multitiered understanding of the contrasting paradigms points to the need for multitiered change in musical study if the field is to house both streams, let alone open up to others. It also reveals the prevailing object-mediated orientation, which we must remember not only excludes improvisation but is so object-bound that *it also excludes the composition process for all but a distinct minority*, to be multitiered. In other words, improvisation-deficient and fragmented learning models, as limiting as these commonly noted problems indeed are, must be recognized as but the tip of an ethnocentric/gendercentric/epistemocentric iceberg that also includes corresponding fragmented and object-mediated organizational structures, research terrain, and hiring/promotional criteria and incentives. David Elliott: "[T]he aesthetic concept of music as a work- or object-centered art has become so familiar that many people . . . fail to recognize its historicity, let alone its force." They then proceed to "evaluate all music making," and approach all aspects of the field, from this standpoint.[71]

Reform measures must be grounded in close attention, on the part of individuals and communities, to all these parameters. They must also, because music and thus musical paradigms are physically and emotionally embodied, involve engagement among students, faculty, and administrators alike in somatic work that enables psycho-emotional-physical grounding in Afrological style features—particularly that of globally pervasive Black Atlantic Rhythm. This reform will require close examination and alteration of exnomination language practices—for example, headings such as New Music and Art Music—that suggest diversity and inclusivity yet in practice are quite narrow and exclusive. Academic New Music concerts rarely include improvisation in general and Afrologically rooted improvised music in particular; Art Music usually refers to Eurological composed-notated repertory. This more expansive musical vision will also call for corresponding arts advocacy models that, instead of—albeit unwittingly—perpetuating the reigning value system to the broader society, transmit expanded values. As noted earlier, not only does conventional, object-mediated arts advocacy perpetuate patterns that, in fact, are antithetical to the arts (e.g., ethnocentrism, inhibition of creativity), it also arguably exacerbates, rather than rectifies, broader challenges to sustainability. For the ecopathology that threatens the physical environment is inseparable from, and thus fueled by, the ethnopathology and epistemopathology that are sustained in the prevailing paradigm of musical study.

There is no denying that this assessment may seem harsh. However, an integral perspective holds that while nothing short of this kind of delineative and diagnostic work will be adequate to the reform needed, extraordinarily exciting gains are possible were it to be implemented. Fundamental distinctions between improvisation and composition are a necessary part of this. Whereas, as we have noted, musicology has neglected the creative process in favor of a focus on structural (e.g., formal, historical, cultural) facets of resultant works, an integral musical vision places process front and center. Identification within the process realm of two developmental lines where there were thought just to be one illuminates the self-transcending power of the jazz idiom, which is unmatched in its incorporation of both processes. This at once enables improvisation to be extricated from typical classification as a subspecies of composition and also sets the stage for a heightened appreciation of composition and the treasures it has produced, treasures that could have only come about through the surface conditions and underlying temporal, cultural, and archetypal principles that define the process.

Summary

In considering improvisation and composition as fundamentally distinct expressive and transformational pathways, multiple threads have been woven into our jazz-inspired integral vision and its delineative and diagnostic functions.

First, the parts-to-whole process trajectory is seen as more richly differentiated, contributing to our core principle of scope, nuance, and coherence. The identification of two contrasting pathways to transcendence further underscores the idea for the genre as a transformational template. The notion that improvisation underlies composition, seen earlier on both localized and cosmic scales, is underscored in this analysis as improvised and compositional lines are seen as differentiated extensions of an improvisatory ancestor.

Pedagogical ramifications also extend from the analysis in its support for the idea of a systematic improvisation study as a means that integrates the broadest array of musical pursuits. Recall that important to that model was multiple approaches to improvisation, a point underscored here, as well as composition, performance, and various types of theoretical inquiry.

Further groundwork is also laid for a closer look at the evolutionary trajectory of the musical world, where improvisation and composition are central to postmodern and integral stages. Whereas the astructural postmodern eschews retention of the processes in traditional and thus fairly discrete forms, the integral embraces both the melding of processes and the importance of intact tributaries that both inform this melding and constitute sources of important music.

Let us now probe the unique facets of the improvisation paradigm further, viewing it as a complex system in which players, listeners, and the many facets of the time and place of performance are unified in the individual and collective consciousness of all present. The capacity for individual transcendence to catalyze, and become magnified in collective transcendence, represents a central aesthetic premise in the emergent integral era, and when viewed as complementary to its counterpart in large group meditation, suggests an important way the arts can help define a new paradigm of understanding and practice for education and society.

Chapter 7

Interaction

A Systems View of the Improvisation Process

What is interaction? What is its role in integral creative development? Is interaction merely the exchange of ideas, or information, or material resources? Or might it entail a kind of merging that transcends these levels of exchange? Stephen Nachmanovitch equates peak improvised interaction with "an intimacy that cannot be reached through words or deliberation, resembling in many ways the subtle, rich, and instantaneous communication between lovers,"[1] suggestive of the spiritual nature, and function, of sexuality central to a variety of Eastern spiritual traditions. Michael Murphy, referring to Tantric practices, states that "in erotic union, joy overflows, erasing boundaries between lover and beloved, deepening the care of each other for the other."[2] He quotes a woman who relates an experience where she and her husband "recognized each other, not merely from an objective point of view, but as though we were one entity, or one field. There was no obstruction or delineation between us."[3] Murphy points out that this kind of communion "does not depend on sexual intimacy," but can manifest in a range of human interaction. Something along these lines appears to be a common experience among improvisers. Ronald Shannon Jackson cites "a level of playing characterized by a feeling of being able to communicate with all living things."[4] Leroy Williams reflects on moments when "you and your instrument are one. It's almost like there's no separation. It's like you're in tune with the universe."[5]

Where improvisation may be unique in achieving this oneness is its merging of a variety of aspects of a given time and place of performance. It is not just the invoking of peak or transcendent experience, as much as this is to be celebrated. It is the invoking of peak experiences within a real-time, collective format, where musical ideas are generated by artists and perceived by listeners simultaneously, and where the entire creative episode is influenced by the infinite array of influences that comprise the totality of the event. Composition, for all its expressive richness, is not capable of yielding this kind of result, just as improvisation, as I have suggested, is not capable of producing the kinds of architectural forms possible in composition (which is not to suggest improvisation does not produce its own architectures).

This real-time unification will be explored from two angles, which correspond with the parts-to-whole/whole-to-parts interplay introduced earlier. A parts-to-whole (PW) perspective reveals the unification to be information-driven, that is by the sounds and interactive gestures that comprise moment-to-moment music-making. Whole-to-parts (WP) integration is of a very different nature, proceeding from the collective consciousness of all participants. We will appropriate a complex systems view of the improvisation process and see how collective consciousness is enlivened through parts-to-whole coherence and profundity, which in turn feeds back to enhance moment-to-moment engagement from a whole-to-parts direction.[6]

The previous analysis of the PW/WP interplay on an individual scale therefore now opens up to a collective perspective, where group improvisation shares common principles with group meditation.

What Is a System?

A system is a network of components that function synergistically around a common goal.[7] An ecosystem is comprised of the various life forms and materials, such as plants, animals, soil, and bacteria, whose exchange of energy and resources sustains the collective vitality. A human relationship system consists of two or more individuals who complement each other and support each other's growth and the growth of the relationship. An improvised music system consists of players, listeners, and an environment that, as described earlier, merge in peak performances into a collective unity. When the components of a system are integrated, a wholeness results that is greater than the sum of the parts, and which in fact feeds back to enhance the vitality of each of the parts, whose enhanced integration in turn further promotes the vitality and integrity of the overarching wholeness.

The degree of complexity in a system is determined by the diversity of its components. The more diverse the parts, the greater the challenges and thus elaborate the mechanisms required for unification. The improvised music system is highly diverse and yet has the capacity to achieve and sustain unity through its complex network of interactive processes.

Four basic aspects of complex systems thought figure prominently in this regard: *information, feedback, self-organization,* and *hierarchy.* In considering the interplay of these elements from an integral perspective, where consciousness plays an important role, we not only gain insights into the aesthetic underpinnings of improvised music, but we also reveal in the improvising system an exemplary model of complexity.

Information

Information can be thought of as a kind of interactive currency, or unit of exchange, be it a type of behavior or expressive gesture, which is transmitted from one component of the system to another. Information in improvised music can be thought of as spanning multiple levels. At the surface, information consists of musical ideas or materials, the syntactic and nonsyntactic elements (see chapter 2) generated by performers that comprise musical expressions. Information also consists of environmental, cultural, personal, and transpersonal influences, as well as experiences of transcendence or ordinary consciousness. The enlivenment of an intersubjective field aspect of consciousness, an example of collective transcendence, may be thought of as a kind of information. In chapter 4, we encountered empirical research that supports the idea that consciousness is not localized in the brain but in fact exhibits nonlocal, collective properties, which thus poses considerable ramifications for not only improvised music but also for many kinds of performance.

Of particular relevance to improvisation is the degree to which listeners participate as dynamic contributors rather than as passive bystanders to the music making. Listeners generate surface information in the form of applause, movement, verbal gestures of approval, laughter, and when they are less engaged, fidgeting, or coughing. Listeners, as connected to performers through the intersubjective field of consciousness, also convey more subtle information, as in their emotional and mental states, which might be shaped by their cultural and environmental contexts. Economic depression or uncertainty, political unrest, war, and weather can all shape the psycho-emotional disposition of an audience, which artists can sense. Finally, where listener information unites with that of performers is in their capacity to contribute to the enlivenment and intensification of the field aspect of consciousness in transcendent states. Listeners can intensify this field effect due to fact that they usually greatly outnumber performers (although most improvisers are able to offer sobering accounts of exceptions to this!).

Feedback

How does information flow within a system? Here the principle of feedback comes into play. Feedback is the means through which a system, or a component of a system, assimilates and responds to information from another component or system. An organism existing in an ecosystem undergoing draught conditions must feed back—in other words, register and respond to—the scarcity of water in order to survive. In human relationships, individuals must be sensitive and able to adapt to fluctuations in the behaviors and needs of their partners. Improvisers need to perceive and respond to constant streams of highly unpredictable information, revealing formidable feedback requirements. We will shortly examine the capacity to invoke inner-directed conception and transcendent experience as the core feedback mechanism for both localized and collective information.

Feedback is the mechanism through which information flows and enables a system to integrate within itself. When feedback is strong, more information flows and thus a wider range of interactive factors can unify the system's parts. When feedback is weak, the range of unifying factors is limited, and the system remains fragmented.

Creative athletes, business negotiators, teachers, therapists, and improvisers exhibit feedback qualities in their ability to adapt to minute and spontaneous fluctuations in their environments.

A correlation is evident here with the idea of self-referential union, where the self curves back on the Self as considered in chapter 3 as the basis for transcendent experience and creativity. From this standpoint, self-reference is a kind of core feedback mechanism at the level of consciousness that promotes more differentiated kinds of feedback to occur at surface levels of creativity. The more robust a system's feedback mechanisms, the more information can flow and unify the various components of the system, which directly determines the self-organizing properties of the system.

Self-organization

Systems are self-organizing to the extent that the evolution of the system is driven internally with minimal dependence on exterior input. From an integral perspective, the basis for this internal drive is twofold. A self-organizing interpersonal relationship is one that, through strong communication (feedback and flow of information) between the partners, spontaneously adapts to challenges and promotes increased well-being for both individuals. A self-organizing business can adapt to rapid fluctuations in the marketplace and thrive as an individual entity, capacities that the corporate visionary Peter Senge describes as characteristic of "learning organizations."[8] In self-organizing improvising systems, musicians generate ideas that engage and thus integrate listeners within the creative process, and in turn listeners feed back information of various types to the musicians to further enhance communication flow and integration of the various components of the system. In all of these and other instances involving human interactive systems, collective properties emerge from the localized levels of information exchange to further feed back and enhance the self-organizing properties of the system. Our analysis supports David Borgo's reflection that "freer forms of improvisation lie perhaps closest to the ideal of a self-organizing system. Their bottom-up style emphasizes the capacities for adaptation and emergence; they accentuate creativity-in-time and the dynamics of internal change."[9] However, this should not suggest that improvisation in referent-based formats (e.g., jazz, or Hindustani music) are not capable of high degrees of self-organization; when performers in these formats invoke optimal creativity, they are capable of invoking the same degree of self-organizing dynamics in their respective settings as free improvisers.

But if we move to the opposite end of the improvisatory spectrum, viewing improvisation as *writ large*, we recognize musical formats such as in European classical music involving interpretive performance of fully notated compositions, where improvisation is minimal but not entirely absent, as minimally self-organizing; rather, the organizational impetus is external in the form of the notated work as guide for creativity, and when a conductor is involved, an additional external constraint is added that further inhibits self-organizing functioning. This explains why, as Frank Barrett points out, organizational systems visionaries will find jazz more than classical music as exemplary of the creativity and innovation increasingly regarded as essential across fields.[10]

From the kind of self-organization exemplified in improvising systems emerges the principle of hierarchical/macrohierarchical stratification.

Hierarchical/macrohierarchical stratification

All systems or systems components are part of a broader scheme of systems, in which any level functions both as constituent of a larger level, and also as a component within which constituent parts may be found. Again we encounter Arthur Koestler's concept of *holon* to refer to this dual-faceted nature of systems.[11] The holonic properties of a cell are evident in that it is both a constituent of an organism, which is a constituent of a population of organisms, which is a constituent of an ecosystem, a planet, and so on. It is also a composite system within which molecules, atoms, subatomic elements exist. This hierarchical configuration of holon levels upholds the evolution of each level. And the greater a system's self-organizing properties, as previously described to be dependent upon strong feedback and information flow, the greater its capacity to both contribute to and benefit from, and thus integrate within, the broader scheme. When we look at holons as constituent systems that are integrated within an increasingly broad spectrum of composite systems (e.g., a cell as part of an organism, which is subsumed within a population, and so forth), we refer to what Ervin Laszlo calls its *macrohierarchical* integration. When we consider holons as composite systems within which constituent levels exist, we refer to their *microhierarchical* integration.[12] Macrohierarchical integration is parts-to-whole; microhierarchical is whole-to-parts.

That the improvised music system exhibits both kinds of integrative properties is evident when each holonic unit, viewing this from a macrohierarchical perspective, becomes subsumed as a constituent part of the next composite level. It must be emphasized that this is more than a passive kind of integration, where two things that were experienced as disconnected are now experienced as connected. Rather, this integration also allows the self-organizing, integral qualities of each level to flow and be infused by each other. Emergent wholes are informed by, and in turn, inform, constituent parts and the boundaries between the two dissolve. To be considered shortly is the capacity of the single artist to catalyze this integration beginning with that which occurs in his or her own awareness, which then transmits unifying tendencies to the ensemble, which in turn transmits these to listeners. What must be emphasized is not only that the unified performers-listeners level feeds back its wholeness in the form of enlivened collective consciousness to the constituent parts, but that each localized integration feeds back its degree of wholeness to the part(s) that informed it.

When the improvising system is fully self-organizing within its domain-specific boundaries, it becomes subsumed within the broader musical landscape by serving as a receptive conduit to (broader musical) influences and also fueling musical practice, which is followed by the same receptivity to fueling of creative, transformational awareness in the broader society. And if one subscribes to the strong nonduality thesis, with its participatory role for human consciousness in cosmic evolution, the macrohierarchical integration of the improvised music system extends from planetary to universal scales.

A closer look at how this happens illuminates the key role upheld by heightened creativity and consciousness in the individual improviser.

How the Single Improviser Can Motivate Systems-wide Integration

We begin by looking at the improvising system as consisting of four levels:

1. Individual musician within an improvising ensemble

2. Ensemble level

3. Ensemble-audience level

4. Ensemble-audience-environment totality

At each tier, the degree of enlivenment of the four qualities of complex, self-organizing systems just discussed determines the degree to which that tier will be subsumed by and thus transmit integral, self-organizing values throughout the micro- and macrohierarchy. In other words, optimal information, feedback, and localized self-organization at each level promote optimal micro-/macro-self-organization. Self-organization in the consciousness of a single improviser, which entails the self curving back on itself and realizing its more expansive self-Self nature, serves as a powerful catalyst for the broader, systematic integration. As discussed by now extensively, self-referential, transcendent awareness renders the improviser's time conception more inner-directed, thus enabling optimal inventiveness, interactivity, individuality, which enables optimal information flow. This level of self-organization can motivate the integration of the next level, the ensemble, and beyond through a variety of factors.

From a localized standpoint, we begin with what I propose as a *cognitive fractal*, where in the movement from ordinary to heightened consciousness the breaking down of composite time frames as conceived in the former to the more differentiated temporal conception of the latter yield constituent events. The greater the cognitive event-cycle frequency, the greater the number of cognitive fractals in any given time frame as measured by the clock. These events, or heightened present moments, that are unearthed in this process may be seen as the psychological correlate to fractal patterns identified by chaos theorists in physical systems. The idea of a cognitive fractal may lend support for Borgo's analysis of fractal patterns in the improvisations of Evan Parker, Peter Brötzmann, and Derek Bailey; whereas the search for such patterns in the realm of sound, as measured digitally and then analyzed mathematically, represents a structural inquiry into the fractal realm, my idea reflects movement toward a process-oriented conception that might be seen to underlie the structural.[13]

The essential idea is that a highly sensitive and self-integrated ensemble member can trigger a number of types of responses in the ensemble that may promote heightened collective engagement and transcendence. Simply the act of heightened attentiveness to subtle detail may transform a mundane musical interaction into a catalyst for new ideas. Just as individuals are prone to conditioned patterns, groups are prone to conditioned ways of performing together, and these group behaviors are strongly supported by conventional roles and expectations of instruments in group formats. Thus, when an individual in heightened consciousness breaks free from his or her own patterns and plays something new or particularly inspired at a given moment, this may trigger similar breakthroughs in other players. Even fellow ensemble members with marginal interactive skills (due to inexperience, fatigue, and/or highly conditioned behaviors, among other factors) may be elevated to higher interactive levels when even the subtlest details of their gestures, some of which they may be barely conscious, are embraced and brought to life. In shattering the logic of routine musical behaviors, an artist may create an openness to heightened experience in the same way that a Zen koan or meditative practice frees the mind from ordinary associations. The principle is somewhat akin to what chaos theorists call "sensitive dependence upon initial conditions," although such a transformational catalyst may emerge at any moment in a performance.[14]

From the perspective of collective consciousness, a single ensemble member invoking transcendence can also enliven group transcendence through the field effect of consciousness. The enhanced connection one artist achieves with the collective field of consciousness stimulates the flow of this consciousness, particularly when artists and listeners are receptive to this flow, within each individual awareness. There may also be a physiological entrainment at work here, where the brain-wave coherence in a single improviser can motivate this coherence in ensemble members.

Once the ensemble is integrated as a self-organizing holon, it becomes a catalyst for impacting this transformation in listeners. It does this through both heightened sensitivity to listener influences and heightened capacity to transmit integral, transcendent values. This is a delicate juncture in the improvising system, because of the contrasting types of information and processes involved: players generate musical ideas, listeners respond to them. Yet, as Paul Berliner states, "performers and listeners form a communication loop in which the actions of each continuously affect the other."[15] How is this loop formed? How does the exchange of these contrasting types of information lead to collective, transcendent unity?

Here we begin with the premise that sufficient engagement on the part of listeners in the musical ideas of artists must occur before listener transcendence is possible. This means that listeners must be familiar enough, or intuitively resonant, with the musical language being spoken for it to have meaning. But familiarity must be balanced with novelty. Excessive familiarity or predictability, because it promotes a clear sense of what is going to follow, dilutes the need for listeners to inhabit the edge of the localized present that mediates transcendence in improvised music. In this sense, listeners are as susceptible as artists to conditioned patterns, which manifest in attachments to familiar terrain, and when their projected expectations or even desires are excessively fulfilled, the very same object-referral dullness that inhibits artists may undermine listeners' capacities to invoke deeper experiences. However, with not enough familiarity, listeners become alienated; they lack the grounding to stay at the edge of that temporal cliff. It must always be remembered that listeners infer implication and realization processes just as do artists, even if, unlike artists, who generate ideas, listeners can only passively experience the flow. This is not to suggest that listeners infer the exact slate of implications from any given realized moment that players do; it would be absurd to think that this would be the case with even experienced players with similar backgrounds and styles. However, presuming enough familiarity with the style or stylistic mix at hand for engagement, listeners can be intimately drawn into the process. They can be captivated by the fine line artists walk between predictability and surprise, the interactions between musicians, and the spontaneous discoveries of new treasures. When an improviser is able to sustain activity at this inner-directed threshold, the listener is drawn into the heightened experience of the present, as the optimal vantage point from which to experience this process.

The more listeners are integrated into the improvised music system, the more they are capable of then feeding back their unique types of information to players, thus supporting the self-organizing nature of the system. The sheer captivation that is characteristic of transcendence can be clearly felt by improvisers. This may manifest in, depending on the type of music and type of audience, profound stillness, absence of fidgeting and coughing, or resonant movement and perhaps verbal displays of approval. Moreover, there may be reason to speculate that listeners who are deeply engaged can also inform, through deep transpersonal involvement in the performance, the implication fields of artists and on a very subtle level influence musical decisions. Buckminster Fuller preferred to speak extemporaneously rather than preparing his lectures: "my spoken thoughts are greatly affected by subconscious feedback from my audiences."[16]

In this way, listeners can thus be active, dynamic participants in the improvised music system, shedding new light on jazz pianist Denny Zeitlin's acknowledgment that "an audience can be tremendously helpful in reaching that ecstatic state . . . it is really quite magical when that happens."[17]

When artists and listeners merge, they form a self-organizing tier whose receptivity to environmental influences is heightened. However, this brings us to a juncture in the macrohierarchy at which two very important differences impact systematic integration. Up till now, each integrative level may clearly be seen to involve heightened receptivity in consciousness—whether in that of the individual improviser, the individual-ensemble collective, or the individual-ensemble-audience collective—to parts-to-whole expressions, as well as whole-to-parts feedback from the enlivened whole. But because now the emergent whole includes physical aspects (including performance space, acoustics, temperature, humidity, weather, etc.), it appears that the emergent whole differs fundamentally from those which preceded it. While this whole encompasses a greater array of localized information, it does not appear to comprise a greater intersubjective field of consciousness—simply because the new components are objective rather than subjective—that will feed back this wholeness to constituent human components. In other words, players play and engage in parts-to-whole/whole-to-parts feedforward/feedback loops, listeners listen and similarly uphold these loops, but inanimate environmental influences exist as static information that is integrated not through enlivened receptivity on the part of the environment but on the part of artists and listeners. The newly upholstered seats, lighting fixtures, dust balls under the stage, or moist air molecules on humid days are neither inspired, in other words, by peak performances and any degree of coherence or integration among human participants, nor capable of feeding this back to them.

But might strata of consciousness and reality exist that are not only transcendent of the human neurophysiology but, in fact, underlie seemingly inanimate physical dimensions of a time and place? Here is where worldview considerations that extend far beyond music come into play. From the perspective of the nonduality premise, construed in either its general or strong interpretations, consciousness or spirit is primary in the broader scheme of creation. Therefore, there is no facet of reality that is not a manifestation of consciousness/spirit, which can manifest in various ways at subtle scales, the perception and understanding of which is dependent upon the level of consciousness of the perceiver. The archetypal impulses previously considered may be one manifestation, the "subtle energies"[18] that healers in various traditions claim to access may be another. The panpsychism that, as David Skrbina illuminates, has been pervasive in Western thought, for which correlates across the globe are abundant, sheds additional light on the question. Panpsychism—embraced in one form another by not only ancient thinkers such as Thales, Heraclitus, Plato, and Aristotle, but in more recent eras Bacon, Spinoza, Newton, Leibniz, James, and Whitehead—holds that matter and consciousness are inseparable at all scales of creation, one is not foundational to the other. In short: "All things have mind or mind-like quality."[19] While it does not necessarily follow that all aspects of creation—from electrons to mountain ranges to asteroids—are conscious entities, the premise that they are facets of spirit or cosmic intelligence, or inextricably linked thereto, poses extraordinary implications for the range of influences that may be enlivened in collective improvised performance.

At this point consideration might extend to the strata of discarnate entities or intelligences, to which perception may open up in higher states and stages of consciousness, which is found in wisdom traditions across the globe—including not only Abrahamic and Asian mystical lineages but shamanic and indigenous traditions.[20] Christopher Bache, in his preparations to enliven the collective consciousness in his university classroom teaching, invokes "the guardians" of the place, institution, and discipline, surmising that "where there is organization in the physical world there is also organization in the spiritual world."[21] University of Arizona psychologist Gary Schwartz has conducted compelling empirical studies that suggest the presence of such entities and their capability of transmitting veridical information to receptive individuals.[22]

Whether one is inclined to embrace or reject these possibilities, I believe the case that is emerging for their validity must be at least seriously considered, particularly when situated within a broader mosaic of cultural, historical, empirical, and theoretical considerations. Here let us not forget the compatibility of the idea of discarnate entities with the other features of consciousness—that it is physically transcendent, nonlocal, intersubjective, and interactive with subtle scales of the material world—for which empirical support is increasingly available. Therefore, when Evan Parker acknowledges the important influence of "the precise emotional, acoustic, psychological and other less tangible atmospheric conditions" of a time and place of performance,[23] improvisation-based insights may contribute to a more complete understanding of what these "less tangible atmospheric conditions" might entail. This points to another example of how the arts may help bridge the realms of science and spirituality.

Jung's interest in the *I Ching*, the Taoist "Book of Changes," due to its capacity to divine answers to questions based on the determination of the particular constellation of forces at any given time, pushes us further toward transcendent domains. Jung found it "astonishing" that the "hidden qualities of the moment become legible in the hexagram" obtained by "manipulating bundles of yarrow stalks or by throwing three coins. The runic stalks of coins fall into the pattern of the moment."[24] Might these patterns be further examples of the very transcendent forces acknowledged by mystics? Reflecting on the notion of *zeitgeist*, usually translated as the "spirit of the times," physicist and Nobel laureate Werner Heisenberg surmises that this is likely "a fact as objective as any fact in natural science," one that is informed by the interplay of "features of the world which . . . independent of time, are in this sense eternal"[25] and the relative, culturally shaped forms in which the artist works.

If, indeed, the physical world is ultimately a manifestation of spirit or eternal consciousness, then the artists-listeners-environment collective represents a far more vast composite whole—one that indeed is capable of both sensitivity to and assimilation of profound parts-to-whole expressions, and the feeding back of this enlivened integration to those parts—than if understood as solely the addition of inanimate, localized information to the artists-listeners level (which in itself is not insignificant). The nonduality thesis makes possible and favors the first, more expansive conception, thus underscoring the capacity of the improvised music system to harness the precise, interior-exterior constellations of a given time and place, and yield a kind of transformational impact that is not possible in nonimprovised settings. Therefore, when Nachmanovitch talks of an enlivenment of "a quality of energy in the room that is very personal and particular to those people, that room and that moment,"[26] he may be referring to a localized integration that is underpinned by an even more vast confluence of forces.

Might interpretive performance invoke some aspect of this enlivened intersubjective field? Bennett Reimer, in fact, describes this experience as key to the spiritual aspects of the interpretive performance that is central to conventional musicianship.[27] What the foregoing analysis underscores, however, is that because collective improvisatory performance unites artists and listeners—and beyond—in the actual generation of musical ideas, it is a different order of intersubjectivity. Interpretive performance is incapable of transforming subtle influences of participants and environment into musical ideas as these have already been fashioned by the composer. Therefore, consistent with our distinctions between kinds of creative processes, I think of improvisatory integration as *primary intersubjectivity*, and that invoked in interpretive performance *secondary intersubectivity*. Both are important as indicators of peak states within their respective realms, and the emergence of large improvising groups that harness this capacity will be an important development of the integral musical era. And as interpretive performers gain improvisatory and meditative grounding, as characteristic of the emergent integral musical paradigm, their capacities for this merging will increase and contribute to the revitalization of European classical repertory and offshoots thereof that would not otherwise be possible.

Let us close by examining how this transformational impact unique to improvisation extends beyond the real-time experience of participants in the improvised music event and, over time, catalyzes corresponding transformation in education and society at large.

Impact on the Broader Society

The four levels of the improvised music system—individual artist, ensemble, audience, and environment—comprise those facets directly involved in a given performance episode. If we look at the impact of transformational performances over time, we can extend this model to include further levels. Two that are of particular relevance to this book are education and society. Artists and listeners who directly experience the transformational impact will be inspired to explore further avenues for this kind of experience and development, which will likely entail both creativity development through, among other things, engagement with improvised music, and consciousness development through meditation and related practices and studies. As members of the broader society they will transmit these values in their correspondingly broadened visions, activities, and pursuits. And because they are likely participants in the educational world, possibly in multiple ways (e.g., either as current or former students or teachers, parents, members of school boards, friends of other parents with students in schools, etc.), they will also transmit these values to this all-powerful force (education) for either transforming or perpetuating the status quo in society at large. Unfortunately, as noted in previous chapters, conventional education succumbs to the latter. But if a jazz-driven integral revolution, which let us keep in mind means jazz writ large and thus encompasses trans-stylistic as well as style-based improvisation, could take hold in music, it could then influence corresponding change in the academy at large. At this point, two streams of transformation extending from the improvising ensemble to society might be identified—one encompassing direct flow from ensemble to society via transformational episodes in particular performances, the second flowing through the educational world via transformational development over time.

An important part of the emergent vision that is transmitted will be the intersubjective or collective dimensions of consciousness that are enlivened through collective improvisation practice. As previously emphasized, this directly correlates with enlivenment of intersubjective consciousness through large group meditation practice, empirical support for which we have seen suggests profound benefits might result for society at large in the form of reduced crime, accidents, and illness. Improvised music can thus promote interest in one of the most promising innovations of our times, and possibly shed light on the mechanics that underlie the effect.

Here it is interesting to note parallels between the two phenomena in their respective kinds of parts-to-whole and whole-to-parts interplay. Collective consciousness enlivened in meditation might be seen from a parts-to-whole vantage point as an emergent property of individuals invoking self-Self union in silence. However, from a whole-to-parts perspective, the collective field might be seen as a localized, or differentiated, manifestation of cosmic intelligence. Individual consciousness, then, is not foundational to collective consciousness but, in fact, a differentiated manifestation of it.

The same principle holds in collective improvisation. The enlivened intersubjective field from a parts-to-whole perspective may be understood as an emergent phenomenon informed by the individual consciousnesses of the various participants. Yet from a whole-to-parts perspective, individual consciousness can be seen as a manifestation of the collective.

An integral framework illuminates that all of these realities hold, thus underscoring the significance of these two kinds of human interaction. Were enlivened intersubjective consciousness through collective meditation and improvisation to be understood solely as emergent phenomena, a compelling argument for these activities could be made. But when we also recognize that they also comprise a conduit for the cosmic creative intelligence that gives rise to the entire universe to not only flow, but perhaps even flow more intensely, the stakes are raised in light of the prospects for ceding centrality to these modes of experience in our educational and societal systems.

In chapter 12, these ideas will be considered further in the context of the participatory role of human consciousness in the broader evolutionary scheme. Meanwhile, the next phase in our journey takes us into another manifestation of the parts-to-whole/whole-to-parts interplay that is embodied in jazz, this having to do with the mechanics of style evolution on both individual and collective scales.

Chapter 8

Individuation

An Integral View of Personal and Collective Style Evolution

The jazz tradition has always placed great emphasis on the cultivation of a distinctly personal voice. Yusef Lateef has based his teaching in this principle: "I try to get students to be themselves, because that's when new and interesting things will be presented and given to the culture. That's the nature of this music, African American music, to sound like yourself."[1] Or as Thelonious Monk would insist, "Play yourself!" which was not only at the heart of this icon's philosophy, but as Robin Kelly conveys in his landmark biography of this twentieth-century musical master, he also "understood it as art's universal injunction."[2]

But what does it mean to play or sound like yourself? How is this facet of artistic expression developed? What is its significance in not only artistic practice but also overall creativity and consciousness development and thus integral education?

This chapter responds to these questions from the vantage point of individuation, which was approached in chapters 2 and 3 as the emergence of a distinctly personal style within a discipline that is informed by the interior-exterior spectrum that comprises the human being and reality. While, as noted previously, important similarities might be drawn between individuation, particularly from a Jungian standpoint, and enlightenment in that both involve integration of interior and exterior domains, we will reserve the term *enlightenment* to refer to this integration in life at large, and *individuation* to its manifestation, and thus the emergence of a distinctly personal voice that is informed by transcendent content, within a particular discipline. In so doing, new light is shed on the capacity for individuation to render the domain a vehicle for the broader kind of development.

We begin with a consideration of individuation as a self-organizing process, whereby the enlivenment of self-motivational and self-navigational faculties through process-rich integral learning environments promotes a kind of autodidactic development that is not likely in creativity-deficient conventional educational settings. The very mechanics that underlie the emergence of a personal voice on an individual scale are then viewed as identical to those that govern collective style evolution. The chapter closes with a consideration of several different musical identities and their varying degrees of conduciveness to individuation, with the Contemporary Improviser Composer Performer profile that characterizes the pantheon of master artists in jazz and European classical (in earlier times) traditions seen as exemplary.

Individuation as a Self-organizing Process

The idea that individuation unfolds of its own accord, providing suitable conditions are present in learning models, poses important educational ramifications given the dynamic and rapidly expanding nature of the contemporary knowledge base. Howard Gardner emphasizes two important points in framing his theory of Multiple Intelligences that are closely related to individuation. "The first is that not all people have the same interests and abilities; not all of us learn in the same way." The second is "one that hurts: that nowadays no one person can learn everything that there is to learn. Choice is therefore inevitable."[3] It is thus not surprising that Gardner endorses "process-rich" learning environments, whose self-organizing properties are rooted in an intrinsic principle to individuation within a discipline: No stronger impetus for self-driven growth is to be found than when individuals begin to glimpse the sprouting of a personal voice within their work. An integral perspective enables us to probe this in depth, with the following premises as a guide.

First, individuation is rooted in the core evolutionary impulse that governs the entire creation. The self-referential, curving back of cosmic creative intelligence onto itself, generating primordial vibrations that form the building blocks of creation, initiates an evolutionary trajectory that proceeds from undifferentiated to differentiated wholeness (or at more localized scales, less-differentiated to more-differentiated wholeness). Individuation is thus a condition whereby the infinite spectrum (differentiation) of relativistic influences that comprise a practitioner's life and experience unite with transcendent (wholeness) influences, which include archetypal impulses, to yield a personal style that is both richly distinct yet also deeply transformative.

From this vantage point, personal individuation is but a further stage of differentiation along a vast continuum that might be seen as beginning with the "big bang" that is hypothesized to have taken place around 14 billion years ago. This was followed by the formation of the earth around 10 billion years after that, followed by the first signs of biological life roughly a billion years later. The first animals appeared about 600 million years back, the first mammals 200 million years ago, with the first appearance of the genus *Homo sapiens* 2.5 million years in the past. Humans who resemble current humans appeared 200,000 years ago; movement from hunting and gathering to agrarian, industrial, and postindustrial ages occurred over the past 10,000 years, with the stages (construed from the vantage point of certain Western societies) of cultural evolution—modern, postmodern, and integral—manifesting over the past few centuries. Personal individuation, then, is simply the product of the very confluence of interior and exterior forces that have comprised the core evolutionary thrust in the cosmos from time immemorial in the particular style or creative voice of a single practitioner in a field. The impulse to individuate is intrinsic to the cosmos and the human psyche that is a facet of the cosmic intelligence; it is part and parcel of what Brian Swimme and Thomas Berry call the great "flaring forth" of creation from the primordial wholeness.[4] Articulating a cosmological correlate to Jean Gebser's notion of "ever-present origin," they muse: "If in the future, stars would blaze and lizards would blink in their light, these actions would be powered by the same numinous energy that flared forth at the dawn of time." This "originating power," that I propose from a strong nondual standpoint as the self-referential dynamics by which cosmic intelligence folds back on itself, "is not simply located there at that [primordial] point in time, but is rather a condition of every moment of the universe, past, present, and to come."[5]

Second, individuation entails construction of a process-structure channel in the psychophysiology that enables the flow of transcendent, archetypal content into creative expression. We have so far considered the whole-to-parts/ parts-to-whole function of the process realm, with meditation upholding the first, and improvisation and composition the second. Now we can delineate these WP/PW functions within the structural realm, with the upward integration of archetypal content in the individual voice as exemplary of the first, and as the second, the transformational impact of subsequent expression, which as Jung states leads awareness "back to the wellsprings of life."[6]

Third, archetypal content must be expressed creatively to be fully integrated; otherwise it lies dormant in the psyche. This is not to deny that some degree of integration occurs through dreams and passive exposure to the arts, literature, and other archetypally rich domains. However, creative expression is the most powerful means for this integration in that it entails both penetration to deeper realms of consciousness and also the wrestling of transcendent, archetypal content in surface forms, or, to again invoke Jung, the "fashioning of archetypal content in the language of the present."[7]

Fourth, different kinds of archetypal content exist, for each of which is required a different kind of surface outlet for expression. This need not be interpreted in a dualistic manner, in which discrete archetypal structures exist in transcendent realms and appear intact in discrete forms in the manifest world. Rather, as per our earlier analysis, archetypal phenomena exist at less-differentiated realms of a continuum, or chain of creation—what Wilber, paraphrasing Arthur Lovejoy, has called the "Great Nest of Being"—that also includes a highly differentiated surface.[8] There is no clear point at which surface phenomena may be differentiated from transcendent underpinnings, a principle that underlies the coevolutionary, participatory interaction between surface and archetypal realms. It is, nonetheless, not only helpful to conceive of transcendent and surface domains as provisionally discrete, and possible to do so without losing sight of the fluid nature of these inner-outer boundaries. When we thus refer to these realms, I am talking about interconnected regions within an unbroken wholeness. And inasmuch as all phenomena therefore consist of archetypal content, some—as I have been arguing is the case for the arts—are particularly rich in such content. Individuation is thus a relative term, denoting a higher degree of archetypal integration than less-individuated practice within a field.

Fifth, when a given archetypal impulse is integrated, the time frame for which is indeterminate and highly variable according to personal disposition, one experiences a kind of satiation with that content, and is thereby intuitively drawn to new terrain and sources of nourishment. At this point, the practitioner invokes a style shift, which will be seen as the very process that frames collective style shifts. In this regard, style phases may be understood as underpinned in "archetypal pockets," perhaps akin to what chaos theorists call "attractors," which are phases of evolution or states in a system that possess a kind of inner stability and integrity.[9] Style periods may also be seen as examples of "dissipative structures," the phrase Nobel laureate in chemistry Ilya Prigogine coined to describe forms, the most prominent example he cited to be biological systems, that emerge from an entropic or chaotic environment.[10] Nothing appears more chaotic than the infinite morass of influences that shape style evolution, within which the archetypal impulse emerges as a kind of galvanizing structure.

Here is where the need for educational systems to be rich in options and resources is all-important; any sort of institutional incentive, whether in the form of grades, awards, or even monetary incentives, pales compared to the sheer force of archetypally driven, individuative thrust for growth. This is not to suggest that institutional structures are not necessary, but rather a balance between carefully designed curricular models that aim toward the needs of the majority and flexibility is needed to accommodate this powerful educational momentum.

Sixth, individuation unfolds through cycles of Direct Creative Experience, Reflection, and Craft. Direct Creative Experience (DCE) involves whatever activity one engages with, which could be jazz, scientific research, meditation, interpersonal interaction, marketing strategies, classroom teaching, and so on. Reflection involves the rumination on the meaning and purpose of a given creative activity, assessment of one's level of performance in that activity, and identification of strategies for further growth. Reflection promotes autodidactic tendencies because it is here where practitioners fathom the deeper meaning of their work and how this relates to the day-to-day processes and materials they work with. This directly informs the subsequent phase of Craft, which pertains to those areas of further practice and study that are deemed necessary for further growth. In jazz, this might entail the mastery of certain harmonic structures, or technical skills on one's instrument. In physics, improved mathematical skills. In sports, better conditioning. And if one's primary discipline is to serve as a vehicle for expression of extradisciplinary influences, then craft must be seen as not only a discipline-specific venture (musicians practice scales, accountants balance spreadsheets), but also as an interdisciplinary (life experience, travel, relationships, health) and transdisciplinary (spiritual practice) enterprise, each function comprised of corresponding faculties. Thus, craft from an integral standpoint is more adequately and fully summarized to span the technical, theoretical, philosophical, historical, and transpersonal resources that are necessary for self-transcending expertise in a domain. We will shortly examine how these extradisciplinary areas are transformed into the discipline-specific expression.

The deeper and more expansive the DCE, the broader is the corresponding platform for reflection and self-driven pursuit of craft. This development can be thought of as consisting of two facets that give additional shape to Csikszentmihalyi's notion of autotelic, or self-organizing learning.[11] As considered earlier: Self-motivational tendencies enable practitioners to invest the intensive work on a daily basis to acquire the skills needed to construct an adequate channel for the archetypally rich, creative expression that characterizes individuation. No impetus is stronger than the perception of one's creative expressions as a direct mirror of one's inner and outer worlds, and as creative development as the means— one that is increasingly experienced as a core evolutionary thrust in the psyche as individuation develops—for integrating these worlds. Second is the enlivenment of self-navigational faculties that direct practitioners to terrain needed at a given stage of growth, and the resources to master that terrain. Jazz musicians, even if their formative growth has often been considerably informed by mentoring relationships with elders in the lineage, are masters at designing their own daily practice regimes, technical drills, models for harmonic studies, and approaches to historical knowledge.

Individuals whose experience is confined to Level I, domain-specific creativity will have weaker interior motivational impetus as well as self-navigational instincts for exploring further Level I terrain, let alone Levels II (A and B) and III connections (review chapter 2).

It is important to emphasize that the cycles of DCE, Reflection, and Craft do not always occur in discrete, sequential phases, one after the other. Reflection can occur during DCE. Some aspect of craft development may occur during reflection and DCE. DCE and Reflection may occur in the pursuit of craft. However, some balance of each of these phases of activity is essential for the individuation process. And different individuals will find themselves driven toward different balances between the three areas at different phases in their growth. There will be times when extensive immersion in craft is needed, other times when highly exploratory creativity is needed with minimal attention to craft aside from basic maintenance work. There may even be times when extensive reflection is called for that has individuals step back from musical engagement in order to take stock of the deeper meaning and purpose that underlies the considerable demands and sacrifices of musical development.

Art and Individuation

Might the arts be uniquely conducive to individuation? While one can imagine an argument in support of this point, more important is the principle that individuation, albeit to varying degrees, is possible in any field and that the arts, and particularly improvisation-based musical art and its nested synergies, may enhance this development across disciplines. A core principle here is the abstract nature of much artistic material, notably musical sound, combined with the aesthetic rather than practical function of the activity. Recall the distinctions drawn in chapter 2 between problem solving and aesthetic creativity. Problem-solving creativity, as found in much of the sciences, pertains to observations and theorizing about existing phenomena with the practical purpose of maximizing understanding of the physical environment for the improvement of life. Geologists study rocks, physicists probe subatomic phenomena, anthropologists investigate the origins and developments that shape human societies. Problem solving can also be thought of in terms of discovery.[12] Musicians, painters, and sculptors not only solve problems, but also manipulate and meld the materials of their disciplines in ways that are shaped by untold influences from all aspects of life and thus serve as powerful expressive vehicles that are imbued with transcendent as well as relativistic qualities. In no other area of creativity are mental, physical, emotional, intuitive, intersubjective, intercultural, transpersonal faculties integrated as they are in the arts (particularly when primary creativity is central). A level of differentiated wholeness, and thus emergence of the uniquely personal voice, is possible in the arts that is not in fields outside of the arts.

The point, however, is not that only artists can individuate, but that individuation is vivified in the arts. Moreover, engagement with the arts can enhance individuation in any field and thus must be granted an important place in educational and social policies. The notion of arts as a catalyst for individuation therefore gives further substance to the growing chorus of arts advocacy voices that urge—even as arts are among the first areas to be cut in educational systems—that this realm assume centrality. "Imaginative and intuitive thought," reflects Estelle Jorgensen, "the ability and willingness to see others' perspectives, value, and care genuinely for others as one cares for wisdom" are among the many important contributions of the arts in an "information-driven and technology-driven world."[13] I believe that growth of individuation, as the emergence of a deeply grounded personal voice and thus impetus for meaning, provides an interior platform that uniquely supports these kinds of attributes.

The arts can also both help individuals arrive at the general field that most fulfills their archetypal needs and forge a personalized pathway within that field. And as will now be considered, when the inner needs of a particular artist align with the inner needs of society at a given era, the emergent style structures that define the voice of the artist also define those of the collective voice. At this point, individuation gives rise to innovation.

Innovation and Collective Style Evolution

"The culturally important individual," wrote art historian Walter Abell, "the one whom we regard as the great artist, poet, seer, or philosopher," will embody influences that include not only "individual psychology" but also "social psychology, its economic and sociological concomitants, and if one wishes to press so far back, the biological, geographical, geological, and other foundations of history." Moreover, this individual will "be one whose psychic faculties include an acute responsiveness to collective psychic states."[14]

Abell's words describe what we will call the *innovator*, that rare individual whose expressions have a transformational impact upon an entire genre. The innovator does not consciously attempt to transform a field, but rather, as a spontaneous aspect of the individuation process, happens to achieve this kind of impact due to the alignment of his or her interior, archetypal needs and outer creative expression with those of the collective community and society. Just as individuals have personal archetypal needs at a given point in time, so do communities and the broader society. When an artist whose personal individuation needs fulfill those of the collective, this artist's transformation in personal style resonates with, and is therefore hailed by the community. A collective style shift results from the personal style shift of the innovator that does not usually result from the style shift of the individuator. Here I should emphasize that I am not talking about fads that may come and go, but rather about enduring style developments whose significance may only be recognized long after the fact.

Style evolution is therefore not simply a chance phenomenon, where some approach emerges within the constant stream of activity in a given era and domain and suddenly catches on. Nor is it generally the result of conscious efforts on the part of individuators to innovate. Style evolution, as noted earlier, is the product of a wide array of underlying musical, extramusical, and transcendent factors, and while individuators who also innovate play an important role in this development, this role involves as much dissolving egoic attachments and becoming a conduit for the larger forces as it is the purposeful invention of something new. Innovation unfolds from the very innocence that underpins the individuation of which it is a subset. Abell attributes the impact Giotto had in painting in the evolution of "realism of the late Middle Ages and the Renaissance" to "the emergence into consciousness and gradual clarification . . . of a primordial mode of vision to which all the artists of the epoch were similarly disposed."[15] Giotto's work was innovative not because he consciously sought to alter the collective landscape of artistic practice, but because the particular kinds of expression he needed to work with for his own evolution aligned with the collective disposition and receptivity to those very forms.

Although individuation may manifest in either conservative or novel style structures, innovation will always usher in new terrain. Here it is important to emphasize, however, that most instances of individuation will occur through contemporaneous rather than past-based style structures, where practitioners evolve a distinct voice within the overarching style parameters that have been established in that era by prior innovation. Because creative artists are receptive to the interior-exterior influences of their times, it is only natural that they evolve creative voices that are informed by those factors. When Bud Powell, Charlie Parker, Dizzy Gillespie, Thelonious Monk, and other innovators laid groundwork for bebop; throngs of practitioners in that era could then individuate in that innovative form of jazz. It served as an attractor, to return to the complex systems principle, within the overall scheme of style development. Occasionally, however, practitioners may have interior needs for archetypal imagery that is most accommodated by past style structures. In such cases, the path to individuation will lead away from contemporary structures in a seemingly retrogressive direction. While this will generally not position the practitioner as innovator, one who thus effects large-scale transformation, the resultant expressions, because genuinely grounded in an inner, archetypal thrust, will nonetheless be infused with a timeless, transcendent power and depth.

By the same token, the work of practitioners whose retrogressive or seemingly progressive orientations are driven by superficial forces—for example, fashion, recognition, economics, aesthetic ideology, social environment—will lack this kind of artistic substance, regardless of the stylistic era that informs it. Attempts to sound "contemporary" or to forge new terrain without interior grounding, not to mention adequate skills, will be empty, as will be politically driven efforts to revive the canon—a point that a number of writers have made in response to the so-called neoconservative movement in jazz that took hold in the 1980s. "This music that was once so continually innovative," wrote Eric Nisenson, "has now become so reactionary and staid."[16] Although I do not share in total Nisenson's and others' analysis of this wave and identification of its primary culprits, I share their view of politically mediated aesthetics—whether manifesting in conservative or innovative attempts—as serious impediments to genuine artistic evolution.[17]

The distinctions and relationship between innovation and individuation are illuminated by a look at two historically renowned jazz saxophonists, Stan Getz and John Coltrane, who were roughly, until Coltrane's premature death, contemporaries of each other. While Getz evolved a richly personal sound, he remained relatively immune to the drastic upheavals jazz saxophone playing underwent during his lifetime.[18] I am thus inclined to categorize Getz as an artist who achieved a high degree of individuation, but who did not emerge as a major innovator, particularly in terms of his influence on the broader musical world. Coltrane, on the other hand, exemplified both individuation and innovation, the latter evidenced by his pivotal role in several transformations in jazz. In no way is this to denigrate the work of Getz, whose playing it might be added Coltrane adored, nor his importance in the history of jazz. It is simply to distinguish between two very high degrees of artistic development.

Coltrane not only redefined the technical and conceptual horizons of the saxophone, but also that of the entire jazz idiom, within a relatively short time span. Coltrane took tonal jazz to its harmonic limits in compositions such as "Giant Steps," "Countdown," "Moment's Notice," and "Lazy Bird," where rapid modulation to distant keys presented unprecedented challenges and new expressive possibilities for improvisers. When jazz needed to open up from harmonic constraints to allow for greater interactive freedom, Coltrane and his legendary quartet—featuring drummer Elvin Jones, pianist McCoy Tyner, and bassist Jimmy Garrison—responded with groundbreaking modal formats. The quartal harmonies and melodic shapes, and rhythmic and interactive concepts evolved in this ensemble continue to be foundational elements in contemporary jazz. His legendary "sheets of sound" and extended saxophone-drums duets with Jones, and later Rashied Ali, defined new textural and intensity levels in the music. At the same time, his infusion of Indian and other non-Western musical and extramusical influences, including spirituality, further expanded the horizons of jazz practice and culture. Coltrane's subsequent excursions into free jazz provided further artistic leadership in the idiom.

When we look at Coltrane's life, within and outside of the arts, we find that he embodied the extraordinary conditions that are often found in the lives and work of major innovators. He was driven by deep spiritual convictions that were informed by study and practice of Eastern and Western contemplative disciplines. He viewed his art as a force for elevating the spiritual condition of mankind, thoroughly committed, as Nisenson describes "this last great jazz innovator" to "a search for the ultimate essence of music and the mind of God."[19] He possessed unusual reserves of energy that enabled him to practice constantly and develop the virtuosity necessary to mold the harmonic, melodic, rhythmic, and textural elements of music into new forms that expressed the cultural and transcendent currents of the times. In sum, Coltrane was a profound embodiment of artistic innovation due to the fact that each phase of his outer growth was driven by internal evolution, and his outer creativity ushered in important transformations in practice in jazz and beyond. As he penetrated into the most sacred spaces within his being and innocently manifested the corresponding imagery, the power of these expressions resonated in the collective awareness, and in at least three different junctures, new eras in jazz were ushered in. Moreover, that Trane's influence extended to other musical genres—including popular and concert music worlds—indicates the power and depth of his contributions.

Individuation and Identity

This is not to suggest that Coltrane, particularly once he began to realize the impact of his music on the broader field, remained oblivious to his role as innovator and was not driven to further this impact. Even if his innovations originated in an innocent commitment to individuate, to dig as deep as he could into his interior reservoir and cultivate a personal voice regardless of how that would manifest, it is likely that he at some point cultivated an identity as an innovator. This is very different from conscious attempts to innovate that are ungrounded in inner impulse to first individuate. Whether on track to individuate or having gained a glimpse of taking the next step of innovation, the establishment of a corresponding identity, a sense of self in relationship to a given field, is essential to success. This provides an overarching framework for inspiration and guidance that enables one to invest time and energy in necessary development. If an aspiring athlete, biologist, educator, or law enforcement officer is to engage in the necessary daily work over a period of years to gain competency, he or she must identify as a potential individuator in the respective area. The same holds with music. This is not to deny the possibility of this identity construction becoming so firmly established that, instead of the career pathway becoming a vehicle for line-specific individuation within a broader scheme of creativity-consciousness development, it inhibits that growth through object-referral attachments to the line. An example is when practitioners become so obsessed with their work that they fail to lead a balanced life. Accordingly, identity construction must be balanced by identity dissolution, all of which points to the value of parts-to-whole/whole-to-parts integral process breadth where improvisation-based creative growth coexists with meditation-based consciousness development.

The following four musical identities, which are general templates within which personalized subidentities of course may evolve, will be examined from the standpoint of their capacities to promote individuation. In concluding that three of the four identities are prohibitive to individuation, this is not to dismiss any of them, or any other musical pathway, as viable *destinations* that might be arrived at through the individuation process. Rather, it is to distinguish between the goal and the path, which are not always the same, and to emphasize that a destination that entails limited process-structure scope, while not equipped to serve as an integral avenue, if arrived at through process/structure-rich integral avenues is as viable as one that is process/structure-rich. In other words, growth toward individuation calls for grounding in a kind of process-structure breadth that is unimpeded by materialist-shaped, conventional models of musical growth and corresponding identities. However, having gained this grounding and evolved an individual voice, that voice may lead practitioners to a wide range of areas, including specialized focus in those that may not have qualified as pathways but certainly qualify as individuated destinations. While most musicians will retain some form of diverse engagement as a result of their journey, as this is the natural tendency of creative development, it is important to acknowledge capacities for those who eventuate in more specialized profiles. This, however, must not be conflated with the highly specialized profiles that are reached through highly specialized pathways; these are decidedly nonintegral.

Four Musical Identities

The four identities are as follows: Interpretive Performance Specialist, Freelancer, Mainstream Jazz Musician, and Contemporary Improviser-Composer-Performer—the first three of which are limiting to individuation/innovation, and the last of which is highly conducive to this integral creative goal.

Interpretive Performance Specialist

The Interpretive Performance Specialist (IPS), whose creative focus is confined to playing music composed by others, is as noted the most prevalent identity in musical academe. Because it encompasses the narrowest process range and is most bound by structuralist/materialist tendencies, it is therefore the least conducive to individuation when it is the primary orientation in musical development. As just established, this is not to say the IPS may not be part of, or even the sole, destination reached when a musician individuates through a process/structure-rich course of musical development. Nor is it to suggest that some degree of individuation is not possible in this form of music making—individuation to some extent, as is the case with creativity and improvisation, is possible in all activity. However, compared to what is possible through a broader process spectrum, the prospects for IPS-based individuation are conspicuously limited. A look at why the IPS identity is limited as a primary pathway will reinforce principles encountered previously.

The IPS exclusively engages in music through performance of composed-notated repertory, meaning that contact with basic musical elements is confined to largely fixed syntactic/nonsyntactic parameters. IPSs cannot generate or meld syntactic elements—they cannot invent or alter harmonic, melodic, or rhythmic materials—and are only allowed relatively small creative latitude within the realm of a few nonsyntactic parameters: timbre, dynamics, and tempo (not a syntactic rhythmic element). Accordingly, IPSs have limited inner mechanisms for a broader spectrum of musical influences, let alone extramusical influences, to meld with musical structures and evolve an individual voice that is the reflection of the totality of exterior and interior aspects of their time and place. This is not to deny that some IPSs evolve extraordinarily personal styles of interpretation, nor to suggest that this is not of value. Rather that, in terms of the degree of individuation that is possible in music, the IPS profile is the most deficient in this regard. Recall our categorization in earlier chapters of interpretive performance as a secondary form of musical creativity, with improvisation and composition as primary.

Another limitation is the integration of transcendent experience. As considered earlier in our distinctions between transcendence and integral transcendence, it is not that the IPS does not invoke episodes of flow or peak experience, but that he or she lacks adequate channels, the second-person process-structure matrix rooted in contemporary improvisation and composition, through which this experience may flow and inform the individual voice within a first-second-third-person synthesis.

Not only does IPS confinement (when, as is most common, is not arrived at through process-structure breadth) limit practical musical opportunities and overall artistic fulfillment, it also breeds ethnocentric tendencies as it lacks the means by which practitioners transcend category. All music is seen through the object-mediated lens of the IPS paradigm. When arrived at through an IPS pathway, the IPS, although evolving extraordinary competency, is prone to all these limitations. However, when arrived at through the broader Contemporary Improviser-Composer-Performer pathway, the IPS will have access to a foundation in which these limitations may be transcended.

The Freelancer

The Freelancer (FL) identity may be construed broadly to mean the musician with a fairly diverse skill set who makes a living through a variety of musical functions. An important feature of the FL profile is that his or her opportunities for musical expression are most often mediated by external forces, which might include the composer who has created the music the FL plays, the conductor or band leader of the ensemble that plays it, the producer of the recording of it, the promoter who books the performance, and so on, rather than internally driven. In other words, Freelancers have limited capacities to create their own music free from exterior constraints and to let their inner voices unfold of their own accord. A version of the FL identity is particularly pertinent to the present discussion, the musician who has grounding in interpretive performance skills and mainstream jazz. Thus, for example, the freelance trumpet player might play in a symphony orchestra, brass quintet, do studio work, play the solo chair in jazz big band and perhaps a salsa group. All of these are fine outlets, and this kind of skill set may seem directly in line with the diverse nature of today's musical world. Upon closer inspection, however, we realize that a common kind of constraint is found in all of these musical situations: the process spectrum is confined to emulative work, even if it involves improvisation, which will always be style specific. In other words, the opportunity to experience the penetration beyond familiar syntactic/non-syntactic configurations through creative exploration and thus the organic unfolding of the individual voice may possibly be almost as foreign to the Freelancer as it is to the Interpretive Performance Specialist.

Again, the problem is not with this musical identity as destination that is arrived at through a process/structure-rich program of development that leads to individuation. The problem is when it serves as both default pathway and goal.

Mainstream Jazz Musician

A third profile that is found in musical academe is the Mainstream Jazz Musician, involving the musician whose focus is conventional jazz improvisation, composition, and arranging terrain. While the process breadth of the MJM appears to be formidable, and certainly surpasses that of the IPS and some FLs, once again we encounter the constraint whereby creative engagement is confined to preordained familiar configurations of syntactic and nonsyntactic elements. As such, individuation is limited, not because any given artist might individuate, following a broader process set, as what in retrospect might be labeled Mainstream Jazz Musician, but because this destination is imposed—either by institutional or personal ideologies or practical circumstances—at the outset. And, lest one succumb to confused notions of tradition, while nowadays Bud Powell, Monk, Bird, and Dizzy Gillespie might be viewed as exemplars of the jazz mainstream, their work was not driven by this identity in their times. Rather, it was driven by a fourth identity that is optimally conducive to individuation and innovation; the Contemporary Improviser-Composer-Performer (CICP).

Contemporary Improviser-Composer-Performer

We can gain a fairly complete grasp of the significance of the CICP profile by reiterating the musical practice axiom encountered earlier: Musicians improvise, compose, and perform in the language of their times.

Inherent in this single statement is a description of the process-structure breadth that has been the driving force for centuries of musical creativity—from that of Bach, Mozart, Beethoven, Clara Schumann, and Franz Liszt to Ellington, Coltrane, Monk, Gillespie, Jane Ira Bloom, and Wynton Marsalis. Several elements are explicit, others implicit. Primary and secondary creative processes are explicit, as is the structural principle that stresses the importance of contemporary practice. Moreover, if we think of the present not as a default destination but as an entryway that leads to the totality of tradition, we can infer additional important aspects in the axiom. There is not only an important place for past study and practice in the CICP profile, thus ancillary engagement, but past and present can coexist in a nonlinear, interactive way. Granted, most CICPs will express themselves in contemporaneous materials; that is the natural evolutionary thrust that gave rise to the arts and drives artistic development. But with this foundation, the destinations are unlimited, as established earlier. This holds for those who arrive at scholarly specializations: as we will consider in chapter 10 as characteristic of "Integral Musicology." While all musical inquiry (artistic and scholarly) will be grounded in CICP foundations, which thereby radically alters the center of what comprises musicology, this does not rule out the possibility of an individual arriving at a conventional focus through this wide-angled approach. The expanded set of tools will enable greater insights into such areas.

Most significant are the ramifications extending from the CICP profile for artistic individuation and innovation as it will be the driving force in the postmodern and integral syntheses that mark the current era of musical practice. As noted previously, the great jazz innovators were CICPs, many of which rejected the label *jazz* because of the extent to which it was construed not as an entryway to the broader musical landscape, but as a preordained destination, one that would be defined not by the exploratory thrust that enabled the current jazz paradigm to evolve to its current status, but by emulative tendencies that would aim at replication of established norms. This was the impetus for the formation in the 1960s of the Association for the Advancement of Creative Musicians, which we have already encountered, and will see further as we turn to an integral exploration of jazz, as among the closest embodiments of integral musical principles to have yet appeared due to the commitment of its founding visionaries to the transcendence of boundary, as well as embrace of interior-spiritual as well as outer dimensions of creative development.[20] Indeed, the parts-to-whole creative process breadth inherent in the CICP profile invites corresponding engagement with meditation and related practices and studies that uphold a complementary whole-to-parts function in artistic evolution; the jazz tradition provides us with a strong cadre of exemplars in this regard.

We close the chapter with a look at a new understanding of multicultural or global musicianship that is uniquely embodied in the CICP identity and the integral principles in which it is based.

Integral Transcultural Musicianship

That today's musicians face an excess of riches is an understatement of epic proportions.[21] While on one hand they have access to a seemingly infinite range of influences that might inform the evolution of the individual voice, on the other they are confronted with enormous challenges. Two in particular point to the value of an integral approach. One is what might be called *modernist futility*, the other *postmodern frivolity*. The basis for modernist futility is that it takes much of a lifetime to master even a single genre, thus rendering substantive competency in more than one or perhaps a few others highly unlikely. At best, one can succumb to superficial skimming, which characterizes postmodern frivolity, where one cobbles together a bit of this and a bit of that, with little of substance resulting. We will consider parallel challenges and tendencies in the contemporary spiritual landscape in chapter 12, where the overwhelming variety of pathways and practices available can lead to similar superficiality.

An integral approach sheds new light on these contemporary ordeals by redirecting our attention, regarding the musical instance at hand, from the musical surface to the deeper dimensions of creativity and consciousness that are the source of genuine synthesis. Here two primary goals of contemporary global or transcultural musicianship, which is synonymous with integral musicianship, must be placed front and center in order to understand the integral conception of this goal. First, the primary goal of such musicianship is not to become proficient in multiple genres, but rather to cultivate the ability to infuse influences from whatever genres or sources are needed as appropriate to one's interior needs. A by-product of this will be the establishment of an intimate relationship with the broader musical landscape as an organic extension of one's own being. Here let us reiterate that the central current of the musical world lies not in the infinite array of tributaries, but in their melding, and that this melding is as much an interior affair as an exterior one. A look at any tradition reveals that this, in fact, is how the tradition evolved in the first place, through the confluence of diverse streams that crystallized in the work of innovating artists.

Stemming from this first musical goal are heightened capacities for fulfilling another, the ability to interact with musicians from diverse cultural, racial, ethnic, and stylistic backgrounds, including those who may have made little or no headway toward the broader cross-stylistic landscape, and create music of depth and beauty that is the unique product of the disparate backgrounds of those involved.

Therefore, taking up the first point, while some degree of engagement with, and thus studies in, diverse musical traditions is necessary to integral/global/creative musicianship, the primary determinant as to how this goal is achieved is not the number of genres or influences assimilated, but the extent to which musical (and extramusical) experience is organically infused as part of the individual voice. Self-transcending, deep penetration within the framework (as entryway) of one's primary tradition through emulative and exploratory approaches to improvisation and composition, rigorous studies in theory and craft, all of which are ideally complemented with meditation practice, is the basis. For at this point, receptivity to new influences is heightened, and those assimilated will be integrated deep in the musical psyche, at which point they will resonate as aspects of the profound individual voice. This is very different than the piecemeal situating of diverse influences atop a shallow foundation, the result of which may in fact diffuse whatever depth of expression might have already been possible. When infusion is grounded in integral foundations, musicians are self-driven toward study of those sources that suit their transcendent needs. Thus, while the more diverse the stylistic resources in twenty-first-century music learning environments the better, formidable global skills and aptitudes are possible without extensive multimusical exposure, let alone mastery, were this even possible. Far more important is cultivating the inner platform whereby whatever influences contacted are integrated as organic extensions of deep personal expression. Debussy genuinely appropriated Javanese gamelan influences without anything resembling formal study of that tradition, just as Coltrane assimilated influences of Indian music similarly without formal study thereof. This is not to dismiss the possibility that some musicians will be drawn to extensive study of the music of other cultures. Again, this must be driven by interior impulse.

And as capacities for organic infusion are cultivated, capacities for the second goal—which again involves dynamic, creative collaboration with musicians from diverse backgrounds—develop apace. Musicians who transcend category with tradition-specific grounding, which optimally occurs via improvisatory and compositional engagement approached through both rigorous emulative and robust exploratory work, will be uniquely positioned to interact with those coming from highly varying traditions. And due to jazz's unmatched integration of improvisation and composition, musicians with grounding in this process scope—and here let us always recall that improvisation writ large is at its basis—will often be able to meet musicians from other traditions more than halfway; in other words, integral jazz artists will be able to venture further than others into the trans-stylistic, syncretic waters where all lineages unite and come closer to foreign shores to invite collaboration.

Jazz's broad "pitchscape," encompassing modal, tonal, and post-tonal practices and rich rhythmic foundations that are grounded in what is arguably the most inherently global rhythmic culture—that of Africa— additionally promote wide-ranging collaboration from a structural perspective. A general principle may thus be inferred here—that grounding in Afrological and Eurological streams provides Western musicians a formidable interior template for global infusion and collaboration. Key features of the Afrological, as noted earlier, are improvisation and time feel–based rhythmic grounding; key features of the Eurological are compositional process and understanding of formal architecture (thus Eurological compositional skills factor more prominently than interpretive performance skills in the proposed synthesis). In no way is this to suggest a sequential progression in this development, where first the Afrological and Eurological unite and then broader influences are accessible, will hold in all cases. For some musicians, the global may initiate the trans-stylistic growth. But over time, the Afrological-Eurological nexus will for many, if not most musicians, provide optimal foundations for global integration, and twenty-first-century music curricula, at least for musicians in the West, should be designed accordingly.

Furthermore, these jazz-driven connections to the overarching landscape and the syncretic possibilities it affords invite complementary probing of deeper dimensions not only of the historical and cultural roots of the tradition that provided the point of departure for this exploration, but also the primordial dimensions of sound and its most foundational psychoacoustic manifestations in music. That this may entail cross-cultural exploration reveals an interior kind of trans-traditional exploration that complements the overt trans-traditional exploration of the contemporary musical surface. A primary reason for this for Western musicians is that the tempered tuning systems of Western music are offshoots of the pure tuning that was once central in European classical lineage and which still prevails in many other regions of the world. While arguments are sometimes advanced for the superiority of pure tuning in terms of the music-consciousness relationship in that it is based in the natural overtone series, an integral perspective, reminding us that music is inextricably linked to culture, reveals that the harmonic richness and corresponding formal architectures, compositional process by which these are wrought, and extraordinary composed-notated repertory that are unique to Western music would not have evolved were it not for the tempered system. However, as musicians and musicology fathom the music-consciousness relationship, inquiry into the pure tuning from which the tempered system emerged will transpire along with syncretic excursions in contemporary practice and potentially yield not only expanded creativity but heightened understanding of the role of music in human creativity and consciousness development. Integral jazz musicians (CICPs), therefore, may probe African, Indian, or other musical traditions that are the source of this understanding of music as the manifestation of the primordial sounds that originate deep in consciousness. Here is where complementary engagement in meditation practice, for many already an intimate partner to the systematic improvisation-based work that comprises their process scope, would further enhance their investigations, for the sound-consciousness connection calls for not only musical but spiritual broaching of that juncture.

A musical thought experiment encapsulates the previous discussion: Imagine a think tank comprised of a team of experts in music curriculum design. Their task: Design a viable twenty-first-century music curriculum that is geared toward enabling musicians to navigate meaningful and substantive pathways through the infinitely varied mosaic of styles and cross-stylistic hybrids of our times. The guiding question: Amid the innumerable genres in existence, might there be one or more that are particularly conducive to this global navigation and access? Assuming that this question would direct attention to the realm of processes and structures, I believe three conclusions would likely emerge that underscore an integral understanding. One is that a process-structure region that comes early under the "Js," were the thousands of genres to be listed alphabetically, would be unmatched in this capacity. I am of course talking about jazz. Second is that specialized interpretive performance, regardless of genre, is among the very least equipped to fulfill this requisite, due to its limited process range. Therefore, among the multitude of models that might comprise the center of musical study, the prevailing one—with all appreciation of its positive aspects—is most deficient. A third conclusion, however, points to an exciting resolution to the quagmire that unites these two waves. That is, while jazz may be unmatched as a gateway, no single genre contains everything that today's musicians need. Therefore, what is needed is a revamped foundation rich in process-structure breadth from which openings at both core and upper-structure levels to other regions are carefully integrated, thus leading to more advanced studies in style-specific domains, including jazz, European classical music, and any of the infinite possibilities, including style-specific and trans-stylistic, that are available and which might vary from school to school. Jazz is a leading source for these foundational skills, a point to be explored further in chapter 10.

Finally, the difference between genuine establishment of the Contemporary Improviser-Composer-Performer identity and superficial engagement in these processes, as say from an embellished Interpretive Performance Specialist standpoint, cannot be emphasized strongly enough. The CICP identity means that the artist experiences the entire musical world and world at large through the lens of the creative artist who transforms the infinite array of influences into a profoundly personal voice. The embellished IPS identity may gain fulfillment and performative benefits from occasional, or even regular, experiences with improvising and composing, but if the primary orientation of the musician is interpretive performance, the kinds of reflection, self-driven study, and the host of understandings—musical and extramusical—regarding the connection between music and creativity and the broader world will still lack an interior basis from which to blossom. We will return to this point when we consider the school of music of the future, in which the CICP identity will be central, in chapter 10.

Summary

We have considered the mechanics of individual style development, or individuation, to be indistinguishable from those that govern collective style development. In both realms, transcendent impulses combine with sociocultural influences and musical materials to yield surface style features. The personal voice of individuated musicians contributes to the collective voice, and when individuation gives rise to innovation in a given musician's evolution, the very emergent features that define his or her realization of a new personal style period resonate in the collective consciousness and usher in a new style period. Innovation, while realized by only a relatively few artists in a given era, does not represent an attainment superior to individuation, or is it a goal that is consciously chosen. Rather, it is the exact same spontaneous unfolding of deep structures that merge with exterior structures as gives rise to individuation, but which in the case of the innovator happen to align or resonate with the needs of the collective consciousness of the time and place.

By distinguishing between four profiles and their capacities for individuation (and potential innovation), we gained a more nuanced understanding of the limitations of conventional musical study and the possibilities inherent in an integral approach. Capacities for individuation or innovation are least in the most process-deficient profile, the Interpretive Performance Specialist, and optimal in the Contemporary Improviser-Composer-Performer profile that in today's world is exemplified in jazz artists who approach their genre as writ large—as a self-transcending vehicle for broader musical and extramusical creativity and consciousness development. Therefore, while the CICP profile need not eventuate in musical terrain that is either explicitly or implicitly definable as jazz per se, it must be grounded in that terrain in order to have access to the fullest breadth of global fusion possible.

Having considered in some depth the process and structural mechanics that underpin style development in general, and the process-structure region called jazz in particular, we are now ready to embark upon a more complete investigation of the jazz idiom from an integral vantage point.

Chapter 9

Jazz

An Integral Reading

What Is Jazz?

Louis Armstrong's famous response to this question over a half century ago—"Man, when you got to ask what is it, you'll never get to know"—conveyed, in his inimitable way, the ontologically elusive nature of the genre.[1] Combining highly emotive expressive nuances that can only be mastered aurally with a vibrant creative core and extraordinary technical virtuosity that has invited assimilation of influences from around the world, jazz has always eluded definition. Bebop, now considered a quintessentially mainstream form of jazz, was considered a radical development when it first appeared in the late 1940s.[2] Not long after that, free and modal jazz took the music in even more divergent directions, all of which were accompanied by an ever escalating infusion of classical, popular, folk, indigenous, and global elements that continues to this day. The not infrequent reference to jazz as the "first world music" is thus not unwarranted.[3]

While the pantheon of jazz masters has largely embraced this syncretic thrust, the jazz community has often been riddled by sparring between conservatives and progressives about what ought and ought not to be included under the heading.[4] Andre Hodeir's characterization of these debates, while offered in the early 1970s, is as timely now as it was then. Reflecting on tendencies to sharply define the boundaries of the idiom—"each of us has been a classifier"—and to exclude that which is deemed as anomalous by using "familiar surroundings [as a] shield against fear," his characterization of the prevailing response is blunt: "We wage a preventive war, destroying the enemy before he can destroy us. . . . anything that cannot immediately be assimilated to an already familiar and admired model is destroyed before it can affect our sensibility in any way."[5]

These sensibilities are particularly dominant in academic jazz studies, which has inherited the notion of styles as fundamentally discreet compartments within a fractured musical landscape from overall musical studies and fragmentary patterns in education at large. Inasmuch as jazz education will be central to the arts-driven and music-driven transformation of academe, and by extension society, this field will need to adopt an integral understanding of musical genres in general, and jazz and particular, as self-transcending gateways to a broader musical and extramusical wholeness if this transformation is to take place. A reply to the "What is Jazz?" question from an integral vantage point reveals not only a more complete understanding of how the idiom exemplifies these principles, but also how this understanding of jazz is in many ways fundamental to understanding the evolutionary thrust of the broader musical landscape. As established in earlier analyses, not all tributaries extend equally far into the central musical ocean, and when we step back from categories and view the landscape in terms of process-structure regions, it becomes evident that jazz looms large in the topography of contemporary musical practice. If the transcend portion of the transcend-and-include precept does not enable in itself an exceptionally strong endorsement of jazz as a predominant global tributary, a consideration of what is included as well all the more illuminates its unique expanse. Central features of jazz are central features of global musical practice.

Therefore, while mainstream jazz aficionados may tend to react to this self-transcending perspective as one that poses threats to the preservation of the idiom's distinctive musical, cultural, and spiritual roots (a similar stance to that held by purists in the European classical field), I believe the analysis presented in this chapter shows the opposite to be true—that these roots are revitalized through this broader integration and creative exploration, enabling their significance to be celebrated to an even greater degree. The point, nonetheless, is not to advocate jazz in any of its forms as an a priori destination for all musicians and listeners, but rather as a process-structure gateway that is unmatched in its capacities for the trans-stylistic syncretism that is central to integral musical practice. When all is said and done, there is no discernible point at which jazz or any idiom begins and the rest of the musical landscape begins, the realization of which entails a radical shift in conception of style region and landscape alike. That the great jazz innovators invoked this realization and viewed their particular tributary as a robust avenue for broader exploration underscores the extent to which the resources for such are uniquely inherent in the jazz tributary. An integral reading of jazz is based in the ongoing negotiation between tributary and musical ocean just as an integral understanding of consciousness views the personal self as a wave atop the infinite ocean of the transcendent Self.

The chapter begins with an overview of jazz's core features as illumined through the first-, second-, and third-person perspectives that are central to integral theory. Process and structure dimensions, as well as the modern/postmodern/integral trajectory, are correlated with each perspective, with an integral awareness of jazz keenly illuminating the idiom's first-second-third-person synthesis. Examination follows of how the synergistic interplay within the idiom's process and structure dimensions renders the vehicle the aforementioned global gateway. Atop an underlying Afrological, archetypal thrust, African American and Eurological streams unite and invite broader global infusion. We will see that jazz's process-structure tapestry yields a fluid and transparent conduit, exemplary of the arts, that is uniquely receptive to the flow of transcendent, archetypal impulses. As these manifest and drive style evolution in jazz, they also drive style evolution in the broader musical world.

The chapter closes with reflections on how this rich process-structure tapestry provides a model template for parts-to-whole and whole-to-parts engagement that can inspire application across fields.

Jazz from First-, Second-, and Third-person Perspectives

Third-person: Modernism

The viewpoint Hodeir eschews earlier clearly reflects a third-person, objective-exterior awareness. Here jazz is defined largely in terms of mainstream approaches to improvising and composing and seen as but one among myriad discrete style areas in the musical world. This may be correlated with a modernist evolutionary phase, in which structural concerns supersede process or transcendent dimensions. Emulative processes that reinforce discipline-specific grounding predominate; exploratory activity that stretches the boundaries of what might constitute jazz is subordinated. Differentiation thus succumbs to dissociation, a primary example of which is the tendency to "wage a preventive war" in order to "shield" jazz from foreign influences. Both jazz education and European classical training can be seen as rooted in this conception within their respective domains.

Second-person/third-person Synthesis: Structural Postmodernism

When third-person awareness expands to include a second-person understanding, jazz's interobjective and intersubjective dimensions come into focus. Key to both is an expanded process scope that now includes a robust exploratory component, which in turn enables intradisciplinary (interobjective) connections to the broader musical landscape, and interdisciplinary (intersubjective) connections to the broader sociocultural knowledge base. Hence, the (third-person) modernist perspective opens up to the (second-person) postmodern, which from an integral vantage point may be understood in terms of two possible streams. When exploratory processes become dissociated from the emulative-exploratory interplay, a conventional or astructural postmodern conception and its preoccupation with intersubjective considerations (knowledge as relative, culturally constructed) and subordination of discipline-specific structural criteria (e.g., the idea of a canon) prevails. When the dissociation of the exploratory is restored to a more healthy differentiated status, thus involving emulative-exploratory balance, what might be called structural postmodernism, where both intersubjective and objective criteria are deemed important, ensues.

From the standpoint of second-/third-person synthesis, the theme of freedom as a driving force for the evolution of jazz is underscored.

First-second-third-person: Integral Synthesis

When awareness opens up to include a first-person perspective along with second/third-person process-structure grounding, hence characterized as integral, jazz is most fully understood as an interior-exterior, self-transcending phenomenon. Here meditation, as a primary first-person epistemology, is seen as an important aspect of the jazz process scope due to the manner in which it underpins the second-person process matrix. The first-person structure realm includes the archetypal domain, from which the subtle, vibratory impulses that underpin overlying expressions originate. It is from the integral vantage point that style categories are understood not as self-confining destinations but as tributaries that flow into a unified central current whose creative and expressive locus lies in the interstices between style streams. This does not diminish the importance of style-specific engagement, styles being the source of important skills and musical treasures, but rather repositions the focus to reflect integral musical practice. Whereas the conventional, modernist approach to jazz places style categories at the center, and dissociative (as opposed to constructive or structural) postmodern practice marginalizes styles, an integral understanding, even if decentering style categories, situates them in dynamic relationship with trans-stylistic creative work.

One of the important ramifications of the integral reading has to do with the broader understanding it enables of the liberation theme, or the quest for freedom. The conventional perspective, reflective of second-/ third-person synthesis, views the impetus for liberation as largely compensatory, driven by a reaction to the oppression that African American culture had to endure throughout its history. And from this second-person understanding, it was only natural that a music would emerge with corresponding features—for example, an improvisatory core, ample solo space for individual musicians to shine, and rich syncretic tendencies—which would allow high degrees of personal creative expression. From an integral vantage point, these correlations not only hold, but are also placed in a broader light where first-person transcendent, archetypal forces are recognized as contributing to the freedom impulse. As we will see later in the chapter, the revolutionary developments in jazz in the 1960s—a period when not only "free jazz" emerged but so did other important kinds of liberation in the genre and overall musical world—all of which of course cannot be considered apart from corresponding social upheavals, coincide with the comprehensive archetypal analysis that Richard Tarnas has presented. Directly in line with the nonduality thesis that acknowledges intimate connection between human consciousness and the cosmic wholeness, Tarnas convincingly shows that these musical and cultural developments align directly with the Uranus-Pluto conjunction of the time. Uranus is the planetary correlate to the archetypal qualities of change, rebellion, freedom, liberation, reform and revolution, and unexpected breakup of structures; Pluto to those of creation and destruction; birth, death, and rebirth; degeneration and regeneration.[6]

While not all readers may embrace these correlations, their compatibility with conventional analyses of the period is noteworthy. Consider, for example, Judy Lochhead's characterization of free jazz in terms of liberation from "tonal harmonic structure, hierarchical textures, metrical rhythmic structures, sectional form." Qualities such as "negation of the status quo, new modes of organization, chaos as a creative force, and randomness and unpredictability [as catalysts for] emancipation"[7] clearly underscore how closely intertwined music and societal evolution can be. But whereas a conventional reading of this turbulence might tend toward understanding it largely as a result of the broader social transformations, an integral reading enables a more expansive, coevolutionary perspective where music and society are seen as part of a broader totality, and where the birthing of archetypal impulses from the cosmic wholeness, in which individual and collective consciousness are subsumed, are seen as the driving force for change.

An important musical manifestation of this at that critical, mid-twentieth-century historical moment of the 1960s were further strides in the convergence of Afrological and Eurological streams that jazz uniquely straddles. As will be considered from the vantage point of both jazz's pitch and rhythmic languages and their interaction and the idiom's process scope, the role of the Afrological as foundational and the Eurological as a more differentiated stream became more solidified at this time, yielding a richly coevolutionary Afrological-Eurological synthesis to characterize the genre. Not only did important structural "Africanisms,"[8] as LeRoi Jones terms them, such as rhythmic time feels and modality (which by no means are unique to Africa) blossom in contemporary formats, but multiple improvisatory languages came into being that would provide an infrastructure for important further growth not only in the genre but in the overall musical landscape as well. Let us have a more detailed overview of Afrological and Eurological features prior to embarking on the broader analysis.

Processes, Structures, Styles, and Streams: Jazz-driven Afrological and Eurological Coevolution

To reiterate an earlier point, whereas George Lewis appropriated these terms to describe two contrasting improvisatory movements in the second half of the twentieth century, I have been using them in a broader, though not-unrelated sense, as delineations of predominant culturally and creatively mediated streams in the overall musical world.[9]

Features of the Afrological Stream

> *Process*: Improvisation, particularly in collective formats, is the predominant primary creative process.

> *Structure*: Pitch, modality.

> *Rhythm*: Unmetered pulse, time feel

> *Form*: Cyclic, or structurally open, improvised time feel.

> *Constituent styles*: Jazz (and its various types), Blues, Rhythm and Blues,

> Hip-Hop, Rap, Funk, Salsa, Afro-Cuban, Afro-Brazilian, innumerable other genres and subgenres.

> *Other features*: Dissolution of division between performer and creator, performer and listener.

Core archetypal impulse: Cyclic conception of time and
change; freedom and creativity, spontaneity.

Features of the Eurological Stream

Process: Composition is the predominant primary creative
process, interpretive performance of compositions the
predominant secondary and overall creative process.

Structure: Pitch, tonality.

Rhythm: Pulse, meter, multi-meter.

Form: Architectural.

Constituent styles: Renaissance, Baroque, Classical, Romantic,
Impressionist, Neoclassical, Serial, Postmodern concert
music.

Other features: Division of labor between creator (composer)
and performer. Clear division between musician and
listener in music-making events.

Core archetypal impulse: Linear, teleological conception of
time and change, architectural form.

Improvisation is central to the Afrological while composition is central to the Eurological. This is not to deny the important role improvisation played in earlier stages of the Eurological lineage, nor the signs of
its resurgence in that tradition in the late twentieth century. Indeed, this
resurgence prompted Lewis to coin the term Eurological in the first place,
and his argument that this improvisatory wave was shaped far more than
recognized by Afrological improvisatory sensibilities is an important one.
However, in the broader scheme of musical practice, the more significant contribution to world musical culture in the Eurological tradition is
its compositional process. Nor in these correlations do I intend to deny
the considerable compositional aspect of jazz, a genre largely based in
Afrological practice but with not-insignificant Eurological aspects. Here
similar reasoning applies, with jazz composition owing a significant debt
to the European tradition even if the jazz approach to the process would
take on unique dimensions in its incorporation of improvisation as an
essential aspect of the resultant work. Therefore, just as contemporary
Eurological improvisatory contributions were considerably shaped by
Afrological influence, jazz's compositional contributions were similarly
impacted by Eurological influence.

Corresponding to its improvisatory core, Afrological formal structures are cyclic in nature. Modality, where entire pieces (or sections of pieces) are based in a single scale or mode, predominates.[10] Rhythmic time feels originating in drumming traditions are central. Corresponding to its compositional core, the Eurological structural features of tonality and rich architectural forms evolved. A quasi-hierarchical scheme will be advanced where the process-structure scope of jazz, viewed in terms of the nested synergies encountered in chapter 3, situates the Eurological atop the Afrological, enabling an important interplay between the two streams that enables them to coevolve.

Inasmuch as we have already delved fairly extensively into the jazz process realm (chapters 2, 3, and 5), we will first look at important aspects of jazz's structural scope that support this synthesis. Just as we saw the alignment of improvisation and composition processes, with improvisation as the foundation, to yield a framework whereby these and other processes could interact and evolve synergistically, we will now see how the alignment of time feel–based rhythm and modality, as uniquely facilitated through cyclic or pulse-driven open forms, provide a framework atop which tonality and architectural form can interact and coevolve synergistically. As the analysis proceeds, it is important to keep in mind the transparency principle iterated earlier: that the combination of fluidity and integrity in the jazz structural scope yields a conduit that is highly receptive to the flow of transcendent, archetypal impulses in an upward or whole-to-parts direction that enables important developments not only in jazz but the overall musical world to manifest.

Criteria for Archetypal Richness

Recalling our previous analyses, the archetypal phenomenon is best understood in the context of undifferentiated, cosmic wholeness giving rise to the infinitely diverse creation, with archetypal impulses emerging as dynamic constellations of transcendent energy at primordial regions of this differentiation scheme and shaping overlying phenomena. The archetypal understanding advanced here is compatible with any worldview in which surface manifestations of phenomena are underpinned in underlying or interior strata of consciousness or spirit. Therefore, subtle energies accessed by healers, Hindu *devatas* or laws of nature, indigenous spirits or intelligences, and interpretations of quantum physics that hold mind and matter on foundational scales are, as Jung put it, "one and the same thing," may be seen as different kinds of descriptions of the same underlying stratum of creation that shapes overlying expression.

Although all surface dimensions of life are informed by archetypal energy, the transcendent integrity of the archetypal impulse often dissipates in the density and highly differentiated nature of the exterior world. Some phenomena, however, are uniquely capable of retaining the transcendent power of the archetype even amid this differentiation, and these are deemed archetypally rich. Awareness, when encountering archetypally rich expressions, is reminded of the transcendent origins it shares in common with the archetypal impulse and, to once again invoke Jung's imagery, is led by the deepest springs of life. Archetypal energy might be thought of as a kind of transcendent bubble that forms at primordial levels of creation, and while usually dissipating as it approaches the surface, manages to retain its form in certain areas of life that are conducive to the coexistence of its delicate, primordial nature and outer turbulence. The arts are general examples of archetypally rich phenomena, with jazz being particularly endowed with these properties.

Let us go into this by revisiting principles encountered in chapter 3. Recall there the idea that the undifferentiated unity of cosmic wholeness contains subjective, processual, and objective impulses in unmanifest form, with the process impulse as the first fluctuation, and thus primordial manifestation, from this wholeness. This is the *devata* impulse, the divine feminine archetype, that which drives, and seeks, outlets rich in collective, improvisatory creativity. Next is structure, the masculine archetype, which drives and seeks outlets rich in object-mediated expression, which pertains to composition. So, along the process line of musical engagement, we find corroboration with the principle introduced in chapter 6 that composition is a differentiated line extending from an improvisatory ancestor. And because each stage of differentiation does not exclude but includes prior differentiation(s), composition coexists with what is commonly understood today as an improvised music line, also a differentiation from the same common improvisatory, archetypal ancestor shared with compositional creativity. This sheds light, from the perspective of primary creative processes, on the argument that the Afrological underlies the Eurological in terms of archetypal emergence and differentiation, the understanding of which lays groundwork for understanding how the two waves might coevolve.

A similar conclusion may be drawn from an archetypally informed structural perspective. As cosmic intelligence curves back on itself and generates the primordial frequencies that become musical sounds, the archetypal thrust for structural differentiation begins with the emergence of rhythmic and pitch languages. Rhythm is most foundational in this scheme, which manifests first in the drumming-based time feels from which Black Atlantic Rhythm came into being. Eurological rhythmic features such as the use of meter and tempo to delineate large-scale architectural forms are further differentiations of the rhythmic impulse. In the realm of pitch, modality is most foundational, and later we will consider how pure tuning systems enable a kind of modal, melodic nuance not possible in tempered systems, which are oriented to the tonal system—which is a further differentiation and eventually separate evolutionary line from the modal—and its unmatched harmonic richness. Along both rhythmic and pitch structural lines, we again see that the Afrological underlies the Eurological, the understanding of which in turn enables us to appreciate jazz, the genre that unites the process-structure totality to an extent unmatched by any other, as a site where the unique features of the two streams can coexist and coevolve.

Several primary indicators of archetypally rich surface developments may be noted. One is *transformed consciousness*, as in the experience of euphoria Jung notes as characteristic of archetypal expression. Second is the *transparent* and *fluid* nature of archetypally rich phenomena, an example of which to be shortly examined is the swing time feel central to jazz. Third is the *cross-parametric* nature of archetypally rich evolutionary transitions, as characteristic of the musical and sociocultural turbulence of the 1960s where upheavals in rhythm, pitch, and other dimensions of jazz are suggestive of the birthing of a common, underlying impulse that differentiated along multiple parameters. This illuminates the principle that, even if the archetypal impulse manifests in diverse overlying phenomena, it must always be understood as the intrinsic thrust in the cosmic wholeness to evolve toward greater differentiation within its unity and therefore one that can catalyze evolution among highly differentiated surface elements (e.g., pitch and rhythmic languages and their subcomponents). The transcendent archetypal impulse is perennially shaping surface developments and seeking outlets for its expression. Therefore, the same impulse as it approaches the manifest stratum of creation may parse into the realms of highly distinct pitch, rhythm, and nonsyntactic (e.g., timbre, density, dynamics) parameters and exert transformational impact. The innovations of the 1960s along these lines may be a primary example, and a strong case might be made that because these involved the birthing of more overt Africanisms, the African American psyche and its uniquely rich, though at times tragic, cultural history provided an ideal conduit for the archetypal impulses to incubate, sustain their upward thrust, and then, when conditions aligned—including those planetary—manifest in sound. And because all humanity is linked to the collective consciousness in which archetypal impulses originate, key aspects of African American music would not only resonate and become predominant in American music but also in global musical consciousness. An integral analysis expands the support for William Banfield's assertions that "Blues and jazz could only have come from Black people" and that black music is "*the game changer*" in the contemporary musical world.[11]

This sheds light on a fourth indicator of archetypal richness, one that is unique to the African American experience. This is the capacity for musical elements to survive and remain intact despite extraordinarily hostile conditions. No more dramatic example is to be found than in the key Africanisms that survived the holocaust of slavery—most prominent of which is an aspect of jazz that is often regarded as most characteristic of the idiom: rhythm.

Jazz Rhythm

The Time Feel

The basic component of jazz rhythm is what improvising musicians commonly call "time feel," or "groove."[12] Time feels of one kind or another are central aspects of Black Atlantic Rhythm.[13] They are among the traditional musical Africanisms that would survive the unthinkable atrocities of slavery. Despite the "weird and unbelievably cruel" conditions that had to be endured, states Jones, "all over the New World there are still examples of pure African traditions that have survived three hundred years of slavery and four hundred years of removal from their source."[14] For musical practices to not only have retained their integrity amid such circumstances, but to also have strongly influenced other traditions, is among a number of criteria that are suggestive of rich archetypal underpinnings. In other words, they are uniquely imbued with transcendent properties that resonate deeply with artists and listeners alike across times and places. Rhythm is a primary example.

"The pervasiveness of this influence," notes Pressing in affirming this point, "suggests that there is something special about such rhythm—something intrinsic, apparently going beyond the historical lineages of the music to U.S.-based capitalist audio product dispersal."[15] Surmising that "there are evidently structural and psychological reasons that Black Atlantic rhythm has this inspirational capacity," which includes a "cathartic quality to this rhythm, making it viable in achieving a personal sense of release," and also acknowledging that jazz is "the most structurally sophisticated African American music built [upon them]," Pressing's assessment is notably consistent with the archetypal premise being advanced.[16] Let us make some general observations about the structure of the time feel with this perspective in mind.

Time feels, as noted in chapter 6, are cyclical and thus invite inner-directed temporal conception; improvisation is thus the primary vehicle through which the time feel elicits transcendence (although composition can and does occur using time feels). Furthermore, as they manifest in today's music, time feels may be generalized to consist of interactions between the basic beat or pulse of the music and the way certain parts of the beat, and of the measure (groupings of beats), are accented. We will shortly go into swing as a particular and central kind of jazz time feel. But first let us have an overview of the basic time feel structure, which can be thought of in terms of three layers: pulse and meter, melodic line atop the pulse, and accents/articulations.

Layer 1: Pulse is a regular succession of rhythmic beats at equidistant intervals that are generally grouped, in jazz as in much of Western music, into metric units of either 4 or 3. However, extensive use of other metric cycles, significantly informed by diverse traditions from around the world, has been steadily on the rise in recent decades.

Layer 2: Atop the pulse is the improvised melodic line, which enlivens the time feel by establishing a 2:1 relationship between pulse and melody note. For every pulse, two melody notes sound, to provide a kind of counterpoint between the underlying beat and the overlying melody. This is not to suggest other rhythmic relationships are not possible; in fact, there are no limits to the rhythmic possibilities within a time feel. However, the 2:1, or eighth-note relationship, is central to establishing the basic groove or time feel, and thus has emerged as a foundational rhythmic practice atop which infinite variety is possible.[17]

Layer 3: The third layer of the time feel consists of accents, ornaments, and inflections which are applied to the melodic line, as well as other parts (e.g., percussion, or comping instruments).[18] These are important indicators of time feel because they define what part of the beat and what part of the measure are structurally important. Two very different time feels can have the exact same pulse, meter, and overlying melody and harmonic sequence; it is the placement of accents, articulations, and embellishments that distinguish one feel from another. Applied to two prominent time feel types in jazz: Accents on the downbeat of eighth-note couplings are characteristic of even eighth-note feels, whereas accents on the upbeat along with a more lilting quality, whereby the first of any two successive eighth notes is slightly longer (particularly at medium and slow tempos) than the second, characterize the swing feel. It is important to emphasize that within each of these general time feel categories a wide variety of accent placements, and thus constituent time feels, are possible. David Elliott, in one of the relatively few attempts to systematically analyze the time feel phenomenon, attributes the effect of the time feel to "the pattern of accents the rhythm section gives to the constituent beats of the metronomic pulse, and perhaps most importantly, the characteristic rhythms, timbres and accents that occur *between* the pulses."[19] Through "playing around it [the time], 'stretching it,' or cutting across it with rhythms and accents indigenous to the particular feel . . . the result is a continuous tension, and exquisitely balanced dynamic; a regular, coherent pattern that implies its own continuation."[20] Fred Hersch notes that there can "be ten, fifteen kinds of time" resulting from the way the pulse is articulated. "You can set a metronome here and, by playing with an edge or playing behind it or right in the center, you can get all kinds of different feelings. That's what makes it come alive."[21]

Evident in the preceding analysis are facets of the time feel structure that are conducive to transformed consciousness. Its propulsive rhythmic drive consisting of strong underlying pulse and rich variations atop that pulse is contagious and elicits full-bodily engagement; here it is important to remember that time feels originate in drumming and dancing traditions. Surface transparency and fluidity, moreover, exemplifies the capacities unique to the arts considered in chapter 2 to enable upward flow and integration of archetypal imagery.

Let us now examine how these characteristics are evident in the time feel that is most definitive of jazz.

Swing

Richard Waterman urges exploration of the "mechanisms by which jazz, supported perhaps by cultural understandings and psychological sets, establishes itself as a musical medium of communication, through its quality of *swinging*," and particularly the resultant effect "of euphoria." Until this happens, "jazz will resist definition."[22]

As stated before, the swing feel—to begin with its surface features— contrasts with even eighth-note feels in the lilting quality of its eighth notes, which are not equal in duration, and tendencies to accentuate the second of any two successive eighth notes rather than the first. Any such generalization must be regarded as an approximation and need not be taken as absolute; for instance, not all accents occur on the upbeat as this would be rigid and predictable. The same holds for note durations. J. A. Progler's work, building upon the "participatory discrepancies" theory first introduced by Charles Keil, is particularly informative in its attempts to penetrate to the core of this elusive aspect of jazz and quantify the ratio between two successive swing eighth notes.[23] But this reveals common attempts to notate swing eighth notes as triplets, for example, as problematic because not only are swing eighth notes not exactly triplets, the relationship between first and second notes in any couplet changes according to tempo. Swing eighth notes, for example, are more even (equal in duration) at faster tempos. Moreover, particularly at medium and slow tempos, eighth note conception will vary within a given phrase.[24]

A look at the polyrhythmic foundations of swing—particularly its three against two, or 3:2, relationships that are directly inherited from African music—may shed light on principles underlying the durational, phrasing, and articulation issues.

3:2 Polyrhythms

Paul Berliner attributes to the coexistence of 3:2 polyrhythms in African music a "playful ambiguity" resulting from the adopting of "different rhythmic viewpoints or frames of reference for apprehending and organizing the multilayered cyclical parts," these parts seeming "to begin and end at different points along their cycles. When listeners shift perspectives from the duple to the triple handclapping accompaniment—framing the music in terms of the slower delineation of time—the bell, shaker and drums parts alter in stress, phrasing, and shape."[25]

Elsewhere I have proposed that the walking bass line that constitutes a core aspect of swing contains both triple and duple rhythmic groupings, thus embodying the polyrhythmic concept.[26] My analysis centers on a 12/8 pattern from West Africa that has turned up in much music of South America and the Caribbean, undoubtedly transported to the West by enslaved peoples centuries ago. Figure 9.1, informed in part by the work of John Chernoff,[27] provides a brief analysis and hands-on example for readers fluent with musical notation that illustrates these polyrhythmic relationships that I propose are at the heart of swing.

The top line of the 12/8 pattern is that traditionally played by the bell part, the bottom line that of the hand clap and rattle part. Sing the rhythm in the top line and tap the pulse that the line suggests; you will likely feel that the three-beat cycle is implied. Then sing the bottom line

Figure 9.1. West-African Polyrhythmic Patterns Possibly Seminal to Swing (after Chernoff).

and tap the implied pulse, which will likely be felt as a four-beat cycle with each beat corresponding to each note. Alternate back and forth so that each line becomes familiar. Now continue tapping the four-beat pulse of the bottom line, which again is identical to the rhythm itself, and sing the top line at the same time. This may take a bit of work, not only because of the top line's syncopated rhythm but because of its implicit three-beat feel, which at first may feel awkward against the four-beat cycle of the bottom line. However, when this is performed accurately, the resultant polyrhythmic groove may begin to elicit the transformed consciousness or "euphoria" to which Waterman refers. Sense of meter is obscured yet sense of forward motion is heightened, yielding a transparent surface that is conducive to transcendent impulses.

The next step reveals why the bottom, hand clap/rattle line may be where the walking bass line of swing originates. Sing this line twice while tapping the top line, then sing it twice through alone, and then continue alternating between the two, ideally without pausing between the two iterations and establishing a strong flow. When the line is sung alone, try to feel it not as the monorhythmic, four-beat cycle first encountered, but as part of the polyrhythmic framework—the only difference being that the top line does not sound externally but is heard internally. When the bottom line by itself is felt as imbued with this buoyant, propulsive quality, which is clearly different than the effect of the monorhythmic conception, it *swings*.

I commonly assign this exercise to an undergraduate musicianship class consisting largely of classical music students who have had little or (usually) no practical contact with jazz or non-Eurological music. They do this standing up as their bodies need to move. I emphasize that rhythm needs to be embodied, it needs to flow through the entire psychophysiology, for the time feel to be effectively realized. What I notice among even the most seemingly stiff students is that, when they perform the polyrhythm accurately, they seem to begin to feel the groove in ways that are discernible to others.

Let us continue our analysis by noting two kinds of 3:2 polyrhythmic relationships. One is that just considered, manifesting over the course of an entire measure, with as we just saw every four notes of the walking bass/rattle–hand clap line felt in terms of both four- and three-beat cycles. A second kind of 3:2 polyrhythmic relationship manifests in each beat and manifests directly in the jazz group. Here, in other words, every note of the walking bass line simultaneously contains triple and duple subdivision implications, each of which is distributed to different parts of the ensemble. The triplet pattern manifests in the jazz drum set, with the bass drum directly iterating or implying the rhythm, and the ride cymbal implying a triplet pattern (generally conceived as quarter note and eighth note coupling for each beat). The duplet pattern manifests in the improvised (or composed) eighth note (could also be sixteenth note) melodic lines played by horn players, pianists, guitarists, and other melodic instruments that are important to an authentic swing concept. It is not that other rhythmic relationships are not possible or permitted—swing invites an unlimited rhythmic range—but that the eighth note/sixteenth note rhythm is foundational to establishing, or enlivening, the feel in the consciousness of performers and listeners. In other words, the transcendent, archetypal qualities of the swing impulse gain an adequate channel through which to flow when these surface structures—the triple and duple rhythmic relationships authentically conceived and executed—are in place.

Testimonies among musicians and listeners bear this out. Carmen Lundy compares the rhythmic affect of swing to the spiritual affect of rhythm in African American church services. In church, the spirit comes "through the music, and much of it has to do with rhythmic pulse. In jazz, it's the same thing."[28] Guitarist Emily Remler's statement that "if the rhythm section is really swinging, it's such a great feeling, you just want to laugh"[29] is consistent with the euphoria or elation associated with Jung's notion of archetypally rich expressions, as is the observation of a drummer Paul Berliner interviews who compares the inner sensations from jazz's rhythmic grooves to the intensive pleasure of lovemaking: "I felt so good I just started grinning and laughing."[30]

In conjunction with these transcendent, transformational qualities are clear indications of the highly malleable and fluid aspects of this rhythmic feature that, while retaining an integrity that clearly demarks swing, vary greatly from one individual to another. "A half century of jazz," Hodeir remarks, "has taught us that swing has hundreds of guises. Frankie Trumbauer did not swing like John Coltrane" nor did "Louis Armstrong [swing] like Roy Eldridge," yet amid these highly individualized differences something that is clearly discernible as swing may still be identified.[31] Once again, we see indicators of the transparency principle that suggests—to reiterate Pressing's characterization of Black Atlantic Rhythm in general, and which we now apply to swing in particular—there is "something special" about this element.

Closely related is an important further manifestation of the transparency principle that emerged in the turbulence of the 1960s, involving an increased sense of unmetered pulse, or as it is commonly termed—playing across the bar line. The drummer Tony Williams, who burst onto the scene at an early age in Miles Davis' legendary quintet of the time, was pivotal in establishing as a central facet of contemporary jazz drumming phrasing that at once retained a strong sense of pulse, momentum and improvisatory buoyancy yet obscured the sense of rigid metrical divisions.[32] Again, one need only look at African music for the underlying roots of this concept. Chernoff compares the Western idea of meter, where the rhythmic organization of a piece is usually delineated with a major pulse "every two, three or four beats,"[33] with that of African music where the simultaneous sounding of multiple rhythmic patterns obscures the sense of meter yet contributes to the music's drive. Paul Berliner adds that "the compelling interplay of . . . a kaleidophonic array" of parameters including "pitch, timbre and hardness of attack" keep "the music in a perpetual state of excited motion."[34] Instead of a clear hierarchy of beats within a cycle, a sense of forward motion prevails that blurs the sense of metric groupings. Movement in this direction by playing over the bar line among jazz musicians in the mid-1960s is suggestive of yet another Africanism, one clearly aligned with the archetypal thrust toward greater freedom, that was unearthed in the sociocultural turbulence of this time.

Here it is important to also note the role of African influences in the motoric rhythms used by twentieth-century European classical composers such as Igor Stravinsky, where often through mixed meters that would obscure the sense of any particular grouping, the effect of unmetered pulse would be achieved. Jazz and its swing time feel played a role in transmitting this and other Africanisms to the European tradition.

Related to playing across the bar line is what is called *time feel layering*, where jazz rhythmic sections—drums, bass, piano, and/or guitar—explore the different subdivisions of the feel, as in moving back and forth between "four" and "two" feels, not only between sections in a piece but sometimes sustaining ongoing vacillation between them. This variance in the density levels of the music—when moving to a two feel, the bassist frees up from the constancy of walking bass lines—further illustrates key aspects of transparency in that the swing impulse still retains strong integrity even when iterated with decreased note activity.

Exterior and interior aspects of swing thus come into view. The preceding rhythmic analysis illuminated its surface, or exterior features, which represent the third-person level. The second-person perspective acknowledges the African and African American origins and evolution of the time feel, how Afrological sensibilities—for example, collective improvisatory, drumming-based music making, inseparable from dance and ritual—endured extraordinary hardship and slavery-driven migration and manifested in musical structures and practices that are not only predominant in the West but globally as well. And the just-mentioned transcendent experiences, which can be understood as both process-mediated—for example, as resulting from inner-directed, improvisatory time conception—and structure-mediated as resulting from the upward flow of archetypal imagery. Accordingly, the entire first-second-third person framework can be seen as upholding the transparency principle.

Having examined this principle from the standpoint of jazz's rhythmic core, let us now examine it through the idiom's combined rhythm-pitch framework. As we have intimated, developments in the jazz pitch realm may be seen as contributing to its rhythmic evolution, and vice versa.

Rhythm-pitch Interplay: Cross-parametric Evolution 1

Where in jazz's pitch spectrum do we find the transparency principle embodied? Where, in other words, the coexistence of fluidity and dynamism with structural integrity elicits the flow of archetypal impulses in surface structures, and where undifferentiated underlying structures contain overlying potentialities in seed form that will eventually differentiate.

This brings us to the blues, the quintessential core of African American music—and indeed American music at large—whose roots can be directly traced to the field hollers, ring shouts, work songs, and spirituals through which African American culture preserved important Africanisms in both pitch and rhythmic (as well as other) forms.

Blues: An Integral Perspective

An integral perspective invites a more expansive understanding of the blues than usually prevails, one that reveals inherent in it the transparency and undifferentiated-to-differentiated-wholeness principles just cited. The blues contains in seed form both pitch and rhythmic impulses that differentiate into respective streams and constituent streams. In other words, just as we considered earlier each note of the walking bass line as a kind of 3:2 poly-rhythmic composite structure from which triple and duple aspects are distributed in different parts of the ensemble, blues is at once a pitch and rhythmic structure whose evolution over time has given rise to more differentiated pitch and rhythmic languages. Blues provided a kind of incubation chamber within the rhythmic domain for swing to eventually emerge, from which as we saw even eighth-note feels would subsequently emerge, partly through contact with Afro-Cuban/Brazilian music, and partly through interior receptor sites within the jazz rhythmic domain (e.g., the Bell rhythm considered earlier). Blues also provided an incubator in the pitch domain for modal and tonal lines to differentiate.

However, where an integral perspective may deviate somewhat from convention is in viewing blues as essentially a modal framework that would then give rise to tonal differentiation. Modality, which is generally construed as entire pieces or large sections based in a single mode, is more closely aligned with the Afrological stream. Tonality, defined by functional harmonic structures (e.g., dominant to tonic chord resolutions) that often modulate from one key area to another, is Eurological. Just as we saw, from a process vantage point, jazz's Afrological improvisatory foundations would support differentiation and integration of both improvisatory and Eurologically rooted compositional aspects, jazz's Afrological modal foundations—as embodied in blues—similarly promote integration and differentiation of modal and Eurological tonal elements.

At first glance, the characterization of blues as modal may seem problematic, for at least two reasons. One is that it employed aspects of functional harmony suggestive of tonality fairly early on. Second is that as blues evolved, it tended to incorporate more complex tonal structures rather than modal structures.[35] Nonetheless, I concur with Joachim Berendt's view that "modality is inherent in jazz from the beginning. All of archaic blues, the rich store of Black folk-music, is modal."[36] A closer look into this illuminates principles important to the transparency principle by which central Africanisms, driven by interior, archetypal forces and exterior musical and sociocultural forces, are integrated into the musical landscape via the jazz structure scope (and to be considered below structure-process scope).

To begin, the modal properties of blues bear some resemblance to those of Hindustani *raga* formats and Arabic modal structures in their cyclic forms and their grounding in a single, nonmodulating pitch center.[37] A single blues scale can be used to improvise on basic blues forms, and invites a preponderance of pitch-bending inflections along with the scale's coexisting natural thirds and flatted thirds—the second considered a "blue note"—that may be driven by a quest for a differentiated melodic spectrum not provided by the tempered scale and its division of the octave into only 12 chromatic tones. The harmonic richness of Western pitch languages is the result of tempering the intervallic relationships that occur naturally between tones as they occur in the overtone series, which gives rise to a scale that is divided into 12 equally distributed notes. This not only enables a wide array of vertical configurations, or chords, that accentuate and embellish a given key area—comparable to a modal center—but also, unlike what is possible in pure tuning modality, also enables temporary and enduring deviation, or modulation, between proximal and distant key centers that would be important to large-scale architectural forms in the European classical tradition. Pure tuning, on the other hand, enables division of the octave into more than 12 tones, giving rise to a melodic richness not possible in tempered systems. It is not unreasonable to speculate that the blue notes and pitch inflections that are important features of blues are driven by a search for more nuanced, or differentiated, pitch options than the tempered system provides.

Furthermore, even in blues' functional harmonic structures that are suggestive of tonality, important differences may be noted, including the V-IV-I cadence—which is generally not found in European tonal music—and the dominant IV chord, which would not be analyzed as a secondary dominant structure, but as a "blues IV chord."[38] Therefore, it is likely that these basic vestiges of tonality and even the more elaborate tonal manifestations of blues that would emerge toward the middle of the twentieth century are due to the bulk of musical influences available to early jazz musicians in the late nineteenth and early twentieth centuries being largely tonal, in the forms of ragtime, marches, church hymns, and European classical music. It was therefore inevitable for blues to invite some degree of tonal syncretism. Sociological forces might also be noted as possible factors in this, where a lingering postslavery, sociomusical oppression may have afforded early jazz musicians less creative latitude than they would find later; hence, greater impetus toward tonal orientation. "The awareness of modality in jazz was gradually suppressed," as Berendt puts it, "beginning with New Orleans and even more so with the advent of the Chicago style of the twenties."[39]

This perspective may shed new light on, and possibly begin to resolve, the seemingly anomalous emergence of modality in the broader jazz pitchscape of the 1960s. Whereas modality in the European classical tradition preceded tonality, in jazz the opposite occurred (viewing jazz here in terms of its commonly identified developmental periods). The advent of what jazz historians generally acknowledge as "modal jazz" would not come until after a good half century of tonal jazz. At first this may appear to be a regression that defies evolutionary movement from less differentiated to more differentiated structures, with tonality seen as embodying the second. But if we view the situation similarly to that of blues, which in any case might be seen as the locus for this very modal-tonal evolution, the situation is not anomalous at all. Just as early blues musicians had access to largely tonal resources, including tempered tuning, and thus the blues took on surface tonal elements atop their modal foundations, jazz musicians up until the 1960s had largely tonal resources at their disposal in the broader scheme of their music making (where blues was part of a larger palette that also included repertory from Broadway shows and other popular music). It would require the mid-twentieth-century confluence of sociocultural turbulence, a sufficient degree of evolution in jazz pitch languages where musicians might be inclined to pursue new frontiers, and planetary alignments conducive to the corresponding archetypal propulsion that would allow the modal impulses that were always there—always waiting for a surface outlet to arise—to finally manifest.

Still, the question remains as to why an apparently less differentiated structure emerging chronologically after a more differentiated structure could be seen as an evolutionary progression rather than regression. Here several lines of response reinforce the idea of transparency in the jazz pitch space enabling archetypal impulses to flow upward and shape evolution at the surface.

First, pure tuning modality is not less differentiated than tempered tuning tonality; it is simply different. "We should give up the prejudice," states Alain Danielou, "that sees in the harmonic [tonal] form a development or 'progression' from the modal form, with the accompanying notion that 'progression' implies 'progress.' "[40] Rather, these represent two fundamentally distinct pitch systems, each of which has differentiated along its own parameters (with modality viewed here from a pure tuning standpoint).[41] And thus, as seen before with blues and its inflections, it may well be that in the expansion of the pitch space from its tonal constraints, jazz musicians were on a deep level driven by the archetypal impulse to differentiate in pure tuning modal outlets, but because these were unavailable, the closest option was tempered modal frameworks. Had jazz musicians access to other tuning systems more conducive to traditional modal systems and their microtonal aspects, the jazz pitch landscape may have turned out very differently. That not being the case, the tempered tuning modality of the Euro-American landscape would need to suffice.[42]

Second, pitch languages are among a broader spectrum of musical parameters, among which became prominent in the developments of the 1960s were new rhythmic, timbral, formal, and interactive dimensions that represented extraordinary differentiation of the jazz surface and arguably required a kind of "simplification" of the jazz pitchscape to take hold. The turbulence in multiple spheres of life during that time, which must always take into account planetary alignments, yielded conditions particularly suitable for the inherent modality of the blues, as well as its Afrological rhythmic and expressive aspects—underlying all of which is a primordial fusion of pitch, rhythmic, and other potential language structures in undifferentiated, seed form—to take their next evolutionary strides. Again, the dynamism, fluidity, transparency of the musical surface, now adding cross-parametric integration (subdivided into intra- and inter-parametric aspects), are key indicators of archetypally rich birthing. Intra-parametric differentiation can be seen in the modal pitchscape as its quartal harmonies, those built largely by fourths, merged with aspects of the tertial structures, those built in thirds, of tonality. The voicings of the chords derived from the Dorian mode in Miles Davis' "So What" is a classic example.[43] Intra-parametric rhythmic differentiation is evident in the more overt uses of polyrhythms, playing across the bar line, and layering of time feel considered earlier. But it is in the inter-parametric interplay of all of these elements that the principle of archetypal emergence is most vivid, where a unified, transcendent structure deep in the psyche of a culture differentiates into a radiantly vibrant musical surface characterized by diverse and highly evolved facets. When we also consider timbral evolution and other developments such as new formal structures and instrumental roles and combinations—and here we see openings to Eurological influence—that came into being with the concurrent advent of free jazz during that explosive time, the argument for an underlying archetypal template that could support this breadth is reinforced. And this is all before we take into account the expansion within the process realm of improvisation and composition, to be examined shortly. At which point modality takes on entirely new significance as a key aspect of the evolution of the idiom, one that involves further differentiation of the Afrological core and corresponding confluence with Eurological other streams. Therefore, even if one accepts the notion that tempered tuning modality is less differentiated than tonality, in the broader scheme of things, the totality of the jazz spectrum became more differentiated with the advent of modality.

It is also important to emphasize that modality in jazz did not supplant tonality, it coexisted with it—a clear example of the integral transcend-and-include principle. This is very different from the kind of postmodern (astructural) creative aesthetic that prevailed in contemporary Western classical music circles during the same time, which might be characterized as transcend-and-discard in that exploration of new possibilities would be pursued that decidedly rejected past terrain. Jazz creativity was driven by the integration—often within the work of a single artist—of present exploration and past emulation that exemplifies the integral vision. Therefore, as the jazz pitchscape underwent transformation, modality was among an array of streams that would emerge and coexist with others, including tonal, post-tonal, and all kinds of hybrids. Pieces such as Coltrane's "Impressions" exemplified the modal period, where instead of two chords per measure that moved rapidly between highly distant key areas in pieces such as "Giant Steps" and "Lazy Bird," frameworks consisting of 1 chord per 8 or 16 measures opened up new compositional, and more significantly, improvisatory horizons. Free jazz abandoned preordained pitch structures and while often inviting atonal explorations was even more significant in opening up, as just noted, new timbral, formal, and interactive horizons. Meanwhile, neither the blues nor other standard forms would disappear amid these developments but rather would continue to evolve, and be played in their original forms, apace. The blues, moreover, might be thought of as a kind of archetypally rich foundation that would retain vital nutrients that would inform these broader excursions.

That this inclusive vision continues to this day is noteworthy given the virtual explosion of creative options open to jazz and other contemporary musical artists. Here the transparency principle takes on expanded dimensions. Just as we saw jazz's rhythmic realm to invite upward flow of transcendent impulses through its combination of fluid dynamism and strong integrity, now we can see its pitch-rhythm integration to uphold the same evolutionary function and contribute to the integral confluence—in notable distinction to the astructural postmodern tendencies to reject the past—that is central to contemporary musical practice.

To summarize and further elaborate on this analysis from a first-second-third-person integral perspective: Expanded third-person features now include pitch-rhythmic syntactic languages and timbral/textural (and other) nonsyntactic languages, with modal foundations in the first evolving concurrent with tonal developments, and with all aspects coexisting synergistically as a vibrant, exquisitely fluid and transparent musical surface. The sociocultural upheavals—and thus second-person forces—of the 1960s, the musical manifestations of which included modality coming to the surface and further transparency in swing, made conditions for transparency and upward archetypal integration even more ideal. Further examination of this turbulence in terms of a quest for freedom and liberation, key aspects to the inception of jazz, reveals a powerful link between second-person and first-person considerations.

From a largely second-person standpoint, the move from tonality to modality enabled a freeing up from what in retrospect might be seen as uniform and predictable structural boundaries, such as static density, dynamic, and formal parameters. This promoted new kinds of exploration that were consistent with the sociocultural milieu dominated by the breaking down of boundaries of all kinds—from the questioning of social codes, protests against war and other governmental policies, to the quest for racial and gender equality. It would be inevitable that a creative art form such as jazz would reflect these developments by seeking outlets for their musical manifestation. Free jazz would take these even further.

A first-person, transdisciplinary understanding acknowledges validity in all of these considerations and also extends the analytical scope to include the role of transcendent, archetypal forces as playing a catalyzing role in musical evolution. Now the nonlinear evolutionary break from tonality to modality, and the freedom imperative, can be seen as also driven by the pushing upward of archetypal impulses—in which pitch, rhythmic, and improvisatory dimensions are unified—in the quest for surface outlets for their expression. As stated earlier, for any given archetypal impulse there are particular surface features that will facilitate its expression, and an important aspect of style evolution is the flow of transcendent impulses toward these outlets or the closest ones available. Thus, it is not that these archetypal forces suddenly came into being in the '60s; they were there exerting their influence all along. However, as Tarnas convincingly argues, correlations between planetary alignments and human behavior can be noted throughout history, and the Uranus-Pluto conjunction—associated qualities of which as seen earlier include freedom, liberation, and dissolution and rebirth—of this time period is consistent with its second-person sociocultural revolutionary and third-person musical developments. The point is not that planetary alignments cause the changes, but that they are part of a broader constellation of forces that shape archetypal prevalence and corresponding creative expression during a given era.[44] This nondual, individual-cosmos perspective expands and reinforces the transparency argument.

We now extend our cross-parametric inquiry to reintegrate the process realm, which enables a fuller sense of the surface transparency that enables these qualities to manifest.

Rhythm-pitch-process Reintegration:
Cross-parametric Evolution 2

The emergent rhythmic (further growth of swing and even eighth-note feels, unmetered pulse, time feel layering) and pitch (modal and tonal evolution) developments of the 1960s could not come about without corresponding expansion in jazz's process realm. Bringing improvisation and composition back into the discussion furthers our task of understanding jazz's process-structure richness and its importance in the emergent postmodern and integral synthesis. Figure 9.2 illustrates by uniting the nested synergies of the process spectrum first encountered in chapter 3 with its structural counterpart in the rhythm-pitch domain. From the undifferentiated realm of consciousness, where subjective, process, and objective realms exist as unmanifest potentialities, emerge process and structure lines and their respective musical differentiations.

Recall along the process line our earlier consideration of how core processes of meditation (part of the integral process scope in all fields) and improvisation give rise to the various more differentiated and nested interactions (meditation-improvisation-composition, meditation-improvisation-composition-performance, etc.). This yields a robust conduit for flow of awareness in parts-to-whole and whole-to-parts directions.

The analysis in the previous section enables us to add a structural differentiation line and its nested interactions. From the core structures of rhythm and pitch emerge the differentiation of time feels and modality, followed by swing and even eighth-note feels and the coexistence of modality and tonality, and so on. Note the inclusion at the most differentiated level of Eurological rhythm, which pertains to the pulse and meter (and later mixed meter) elements that would uphold large-scale architectural forms. Here it should be emphasized that more differentiated aspects did not always manifest later chronologically but rather are integrated within the jazz-inspired structure scope later. Therefore, even though Eurological rhythm largely predates swing (at least in the form we have come to know it, and until its twentieth-century coexistence with Eurological rhythm), the eventual emergence of swing enabled a framework in which the Eurological could be subsequently situated as part of a richly differentiated musical surface with which it could interact synergistically. The integral transparency principle, by which awareness and archetypal imagery flow upward into surface outlets through the combination of fluidity and integrity, and then back to the source, is now seen as upheld by not only rhythm-pitch elements (particularly swing and modality) interacting synergistically but also the richly differentiated process scope (particularly improvisation).

When knowledge systems are aligned according to the less differentiated to more differentiated evolutionary trajectories of their constituent areas, awareness has access to a conduit through which it may flow and not only embrace all areas as part of a unified whole, but in so doing to understand them as inextricably linked to one another and the cosmic

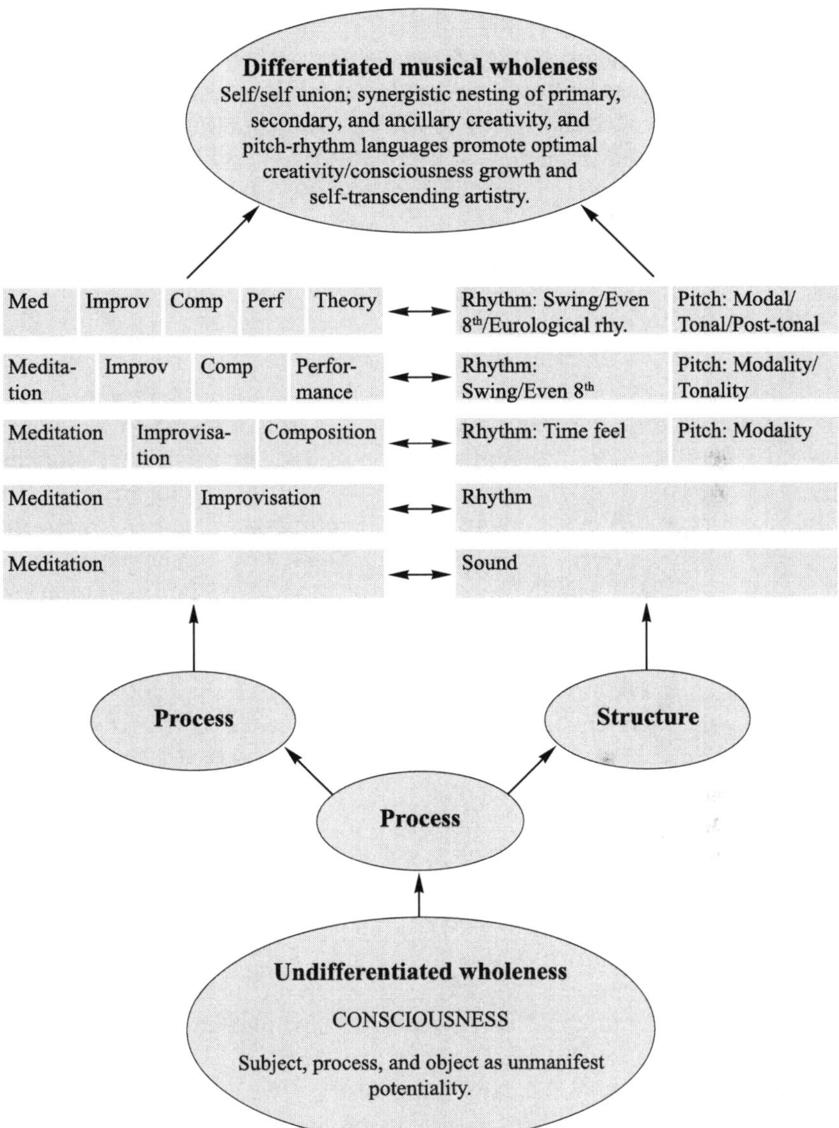

Figure 9.2. Jazz's Process-structure Scope and Great Nest of Musical Being.

wholeness. Not only are they understood as differentiated manifestations of the undifferentiated cosmic wholeness, but as pathways which in their optimally differentiated forms permit reconnection with that wholeness, thereby rendering it more differentiated. In this way, creativity and consciousness development, and the frameworks—such as jazz—that promote this, can be seen as, in addition to the untold enrichment in sense of meaning and purpose they bring to individual life, upholding the participatory function of human consciousness in cosmic evolution. And when this alignment is absent, as in conventional approaches to musical study and education at large, these farther dimensions of human creative and spiritual development are precluded.

Improvisation Revisited

The importance of the improvisation line in this integration is underscored when we view it in terms of four distinct improvisatory streams that began to differentiate, with occasional bouts of ideologically driven dissociation, in the 1960s. First was the continuation of a mainstream pathway, which adhered to bebop and standard repertory, largely of tonal orientation. Second was the emergence of modal jazz improvisation, in which new melodic and harmonic shapes (e.g., pentatonic scales, quartal harmonies, chromatic approaches to modality), interactive relationships, and textural facets emerged. As the earlier noted challenges of navigating highly sophisticated chord sequences receded to the background (at least temporarily), musicians were able to attend to additional facets of the music. Free jazz represented a third improvisatory pathway that furthered this broader exploration by removing almost all preordained improvisatory constraints. Where modal jazz might still accommodate, to some degree, musicians deploying idiomatic tonal practices in appropriate contexts—for example, improvisation on a Dorian mode for extended passages does not require total relinquishing of approaches to that mode as it relates to the fast-moving II chord in tonal contexts—free jazz was far less amenable to this.[45] Free jazz also involved the exploration of alternatives to the traditional practice of sequences of solos atop cyclic harmonic (tonal or modal) rhythmic forms. The very concept of the soloist as set apart from an accompanying ensemble began to give way to an approach to ensemble roles in which, paradoxically, everyone is a soloist and no one is a soloist. In other words, any given member of an ensemble might assume a foreground role at any given time, which could last for only a brief instant or at times be lengthy, and there would also be extended periods where all ensemble members would assume roughly equal degrees of prominence.

Free jazz gave rise to free improvisation, a fourth pathway that, while arguably situated beyond the boundaries of jazz, was as Lewis convincingly shows, influenced by jazz far more than often meets the eye, even if its surface manifestations might not always suggest such a connection.[46] Whereas free jazz often would generally involve more or less conventional jazz instrumentation, with, despite notable creative excursions, performers often upholding quasi-conventional roles and the music often guided by a jazz-rooted identity, free improvisation is undertaken from a stylistically open vantage point. Of course, one can argue that the dispositions of the musicians will always mediate the resultant music and thus the absence of preordained parameters more aptly describes the intention than the reality. On the other hand, given that any two or more musicians will bring different backgrounds to the music making reveals that, even if improvisers are never entirely free from their conditioning, collective freely improvised music may traverse areas that no single member of the ensemble would broach were he or she playing alone. This latter principle makes it inevitable that important jazz-driven interactive dynamics as well as rhythmic practices that have long predominated the broader landscape will make their way into free improvisation, which is consistent with Lewis' argument. It also supports my argument that all contemporary improvisers will benefit from systematic grounding in these practices regardless of their perceived stylistic/trans-stylistic destinations.

Needless to say, the boundaries between free jazz and free improvisation can often be nebulous, as are those between mainstream and modal improvising. By drawing these general distinctions, however, we can gain a sense of the extraordinarily differentiated scope of the improvisation process line. Furthermore, that each stage of improvisatory evolution would both transcend and include its predecessor enabled jazz to uphold a central aspect of integral musical practice that the European classical tradition, even as it saw improvisation begin to reenter its horizons in the latter half of the twentieth century, would relinquish. In other words, the four improvisatory streams spawned in jazz would coexist, and even while some musicians would come to focus on one or another, many engage with all of them in one way or another. The European classical paradigm is driven by a much more linear sense of evolution, more akin to the sciences than the arts or spirituality, where new developments replace those prior.

The coexistence of diverse improvisatory streams reveals nested synergies within improvisation itself, an inherent aspect of which is connections to diverse areas of the musical landscape. Clearly evident in the identification of the four streams are connections to wide-ranging rhythmic and pitch (modal, tonal, post-tonal) structural sources. As powerful are connections to improvisation's processual sibling, composition, which would be key to the idiom's bridging Afrological and Eurological facets.

Composition in Jazz and Beyond

The vast majority of jazz musicians are composers as well as improvisers. We can identify the same kind of progression of compositional activity in the idiom as we did with improvisation. In its most basic form, compositional activity in jazz manifests in the song-form framework, as in the creation of "heads" that serve as vehicles for improvisation. While this kind of compositional activity may not be as elaborate as that involved in the writing of a string quartet, big-band composition, or symphonic work, it still involves the discontinuous act of generating and notating ideas, selecting one or more as seminal, followed by the development of the idea or ideas into a coherent structure that is to stand on its own as musical statement, and which is to be performed at another time and place. Moreover, jazz composition in recent decades has involved greater exploration of extended forms, often through the larger instrumentation afforded by the jazz big band, usually numbering around 18 or 20 musicians, and with increasing work being done with symphony orchestra formats and other ensembles not commonly associated with jazz. Jazz musicians, therefore, increasingly self-identify as composers as well as improvisers, and as the music moves into these larger forms and forces, it is only natural that the compositional achievements unique to the European classical tradition be regarded as seminal and important sources of guidance. Again, we encounter important means by which jazz straddles both Afrological and Eurological streams, which is further supported by not only the rich differentiation in the process realm but also that of the structure realm that is inevitable in the improvisation-composition nexus.

However, not only will Eurological composition strongly impact the evolution of jazz composition and thus the jazz idiom, but in turn jazz composition will strongly influence Eurological composition and thus that of the broader idiom. The centrality of improvisation in the emergent compositional conception is key, which will spawn at least three different developments. First is the incorporation of the time feel and thus prominent use of the rhythm section as important facets of contemporary musical meaning and vitality and thus essential to the twenty-first-century compositional landscape. However, it is anticipated that the exclusive reliance on the rhythm section for time feel articulation found in much jazz will give way to new approaches to time feels in emergent formats. However, this will require new models of musicianship training; whereas string or woodwind sections in today's symphony orchestra might be assigned parts that are playable by musicians without time feel grounding as long as the groove is upheld by rhythm sections, if the rhythm section is absent, so is the groove without players who possess adequate skills in this area.

Second is the incorporation of the conventional solo format in the emergent compositional contexts, which as already has happened in the jazz big band, promotes the merging of jazz approaches to formal architecture with classical approaches. In other words, the statement of basic thematic material that in European composition is followed by composed development when followed by an improvising soloist provides a very different kind of formal development. This, as common in jazz big band writing, may then be followed with further compositional development resulting in a bridging of two compositional paradigms.

Third is the exploration of even further approaches to improvisation that go beyond soloists and involve sections, or even entire ensembles, engaging in improvisatory creativity at strategic points in compositions. A relatively small but not insignificant lineage of more expansive approaches to large jazz ensemble composition, as evident in the work of Sun Ra, Anthony Braxton, Cecil Taylor, Karl Berger, and Graham Collier, exemplifies this approach within more-or-less conventional jazz ensemble formats, which invites promising possibilities in ensembles traditionally associated with Eurological composition.[47]

The latter approach provides a glimpse of ways the boundaries between improvisation and composition may begin to blur, which will be a facet of the integral era (which will still include improvisation and composition in more-or-less intact forms as well). Whereas the fashioning of improvisatory passages within composed-notated pieces as just considered points in this direction from a compositional standpoint, improvisatory conducting systems such as those devised by Butch Morris and Walter Thompson, in which the conductor provides cues that guide the music making, represent strides in this direction from an improvisatory standpoint.[48] At the most radical end of the spectrum, one for which precursors are relatively scant, will be the emergence of large improvising ensembles that, while possibly performing at times with preordained improvisatory constraints or even some composed-notated passages, create spontaneously with nothing planned in advance. Having created one of the few and largest examples of this at the University of Michigan, I can attest to both its enormous challenges and even more enormous rewards. I describe it as a high-risk, high-yield approach to music making, where there is no middle ground: either it fails miserably due to the susceptibility of the approach to utter chaos, or succeeds magnificently when all members fuse into a coherent, magical, and transformational entity that is capable of a power and beauty only possible through improvisation.

For free improvisation on this scale to work, ensemble members will need not only technical proficiency, and strong style-specific and trans-stylistic improvising skills, but also an "interactive intelligence" that is specific to the challenges of a group this large. Systematic improvisatory studies that include multiple approaches to improvising, composition, performance, and various theoretical studies, combined with systematic meditation practice, provides an optimal foundation for success in this format. The importance of meditation cannot be overstated due to not only the value of heightened presence, but also the enlivenment of collective consciousness, in this approach. Jazz, then, not only spawns the improvisatory-compositional continuum that gives rise to the large, collective improvising ensemble, it also provides more of the extended skill set needed to excel within it than any other genre. When, as in the case of compositional skills, the jazz foundation is augmented by Eurological studies, and as in the case of rhythmic training, engagement with various non-Western musical traditions, the outlines of a twenty-first-century music curriculum, and school of music begin to come into view. This will be the topic of the next chapter.

What is important here is that this format, which will not replace others but coexist with them in the integral era, may be thought of as the culmination of the jazz-inspired, differentiated musical wholeness, where highly diverse tributaries inform real-time musical expression, nested synergies in the skill set and musical terrain are enlivened, and archetypal influences flow and exert their transformational influences on musicians and listeners and environment alike.

From Afrological Core to Global Synthesis

The expansion of the nested synergies framework to include both process and structure realms further underscores the argument made earlier (chapters 2 and 3) for the centrality of African American music in general, and jazz and particular, to American musical culture, and also its significance within world musical culture. The deep archetypal impulse in consciousness exerting an upward thrust to differentiate in improvisatory, and then improvisatory and compositional activity (and other processes), and in Black Atlantic Rhythm and then other rhythmic structures, and in modally rooted blues and then more diverse pitch languages, could only incubate in the African American psyche and then find expression in black music. From this foundation, the exquisite compositional treasures, with their ornate architectures and tonal and post-tonal intricacies of the Eurological could reconnect with their improvisatory heritage, and join forces with the Afrological in providing an unmatched vehicle that would invite infusion of other streams and deliver a template to the musical world that exemplifies the integral syncretism.

Indeed, although it is important to recognize the horizontal coevolutionary exchange between key aspects of Afrological and Eurological streams, it is also important to recognize the vertical relationship whereby only atop the foundations of the first will the second evolve to its fullest—in turn enabling the Afrological to also reach heights that would otherwise be unattainable—and yield its important contributions to global musical practice. To attempt the reverse argument, that the Eurological is foundational, or even that of shared footing, would have to address the enormously problematic division of labor of that lineage, surpassed only by the virtual extinction of improvisation as a result. These problems become more apparent as we turn to the prospects of postmodern and integral inroads being navigated in the European classical lineage.

Eurological Stream: Postmodern Inroads and Integral Prospects

Much of our focus has been on jazz-driven openings toward musical postmodern and integral practice, with some consideration of integration of Eurological contributions in this context. What about inroads in this direction directly extending from the Eurological lineage?

This question will clarify distinctions between postmodern and integral stages and illuminate why the Eurological stream is capable of only astructural postmodern growth, with structural postmodern and integral not possible without the restoration of its prior process template (but now in expanded form), nor embrace of important facets of the contemporary structure scope such as Black Atlantic Rhythm.

A look at shortcomings inherent in Eurologically based postmodern readings of musical practice illuminates this point. Often citing the appropriation of non-Eurological influences by Stravinsky, Milhaud, Ravel, and other late nineteenth- or early twentieth-century European composers as preliminary examples of postmodern excursions, this conception is limited due to its structural orientation and neglect of process. In no way is this to suggest that the compositional creativity among these composers was deficient, or ought to be downplayed in importance, in the subsequent analyses. Indeed, many of the works that define this period, with Stravinsky's *Rite of Spring* perhaps iconic among them, arguably represent the most extraordinary examples of composed-notated repertory to ever appear. Rather, it is to call attention to patterns in practice and analysis that reflect a predisposition toward structure at the expense of process and thus limit the extent of even postmodern practice and understanding, let alone that of the integral. In short, the composed work serves as a lens through which the musical world is viewed and interpreted, reflecting a decidedly modernist, rather than postmodern, vantage point.

Here the fact comes to the fore that improvisation, often in collective formats, was central to much of the music being mined, whereas the formats to which foreign influences are transported exclude improvisation. Hence, a clash between the Eurological division of labor model, where composers create, performers perform, and the Afrological improvised-music paradigm, where creator and performer, and time and place of creation and performance, are one and the same. Even if it might be argued that composers engage in some kind of genuine, postmodern, cross-cultural infusion in their compositional activity, it is difficult to imagine that performers who perform their notated scores, as well as listeners—both constituencies comprising the musical majority—invoke anything near that kind of experience. Rather, the bulk of the impact is a lateral expansion of the reigning modernist paradigm. And given the distinctions between improvising and composing, as delineated in chapters 6 and 7, the extent to which even composers invoke postmodern experience is subject to question. Again, the point is not to question the quality of the music, or to suggest that the kinds of infusion are disingenuous, but simply to illuminate that this is perhaps more adequately deemed late modernist rather than postmodern activity. Therefore, assertions such as that of the musicologist Glenn Watkins, that the aforementioned examples of syncretism reveal the "European musical tradition . . . [to be] the paradigmatic example of musical ecumenicalism," while aiming to counter accusations of ethnocentrism, may in fact do more to fuel than refute such accusations.[49]

Once again we encounter the Matrix of Materialism and, as manifesting in music, its exclusive orientation toward the masterwork as the measure of all things. At the core of this thinking is the view of improvisation not as an expressive means in its own right, but—at best—a subspecies of composition, and an underdeveloped one at that. An integral understanding, which as we have emphasized always includes interiors as well as exteriors, enables us to understand this sensibility as an example of third-person, exterior/objective confinement. Just as scientific materialism reduces human consciousness to, or at best understands it through the lens of a physical substrate, conventional/modernist musicology reduces music to a body of composed-notated art objects. Second-person, inter-subjective considerations are confined to those that can be explicated from the third-person orientation, and thus the conflation of the limited cross-cultural infusion noted earlier for genuine postmodern practice. Collective improvisation, embodying not only second-person art making, but also the second-person core of the arts within the spirituality-art-science, first-second-third-person trinity, is the benchmark of postmodern musical practice and beyond. It enables us to posit as a correlate to the master-work, the *master-process*.

It would not be until the mid-twentieth century when improvisation began to make its reentry into Eurological practice and, therefore, that claims for a postmodern era in the lineage might be justified. Leading this wave, for which George Lewis provides a comprehensive survey, were composers such as Robert Ashley, Christian Wolff, Lukas Foss, Earle Brown, and John Cage who, seeking new frontiers, began providing greater creative latitude to performers.[50] Even here, however, residual modernist tendencies reveal just how deeply ingrained was the structuralist/materialist orientation in this tradition. For one thing, it is important to realize that the Eurological improvisatory wave was, while not insignificant, miniscule in comparison to the overarching interpretive-performance thrust in this tradition. That this is still the case over a half-century later, even as this Eurological improvisatory wave has grown considerably, underscores this point. Second, Eurological postmodern strides were constrained by lingering distinctions between "high and low" art that directly contradicted the dissolution of such distinctions that was a core postmodern precept. Instead, clear boundaries prevailed regarding what kinds of musical sources may and may not have been legitimately explored. John Cage's sentiments about jazz, deviating from greater receptivity evident earlier, are reflective of this orientation. Confiding that he "could do just fine without jazz," Cage was candid in his aversion to appropriation of influences from this and other non-Eurological idioms that he nonetheless saw were valued by his contemporaries: "Jazz per se derives from serious music. And when serious music derives from it [jazz], the situation becomes rather silly."[51]

Aside from suggesting that Cage's ostensible commitment to wide-ranging musical exploration and liberation from conventional norms may not have been as deep as many have been led to believe, this remark reflects two layers of the ethnocentrism that still runs deep in conventional Eurological circles. The first is likely obvious, in his referencing the Eurological as "serious" in order to distinguish it from jazz and presumably all or most other music, that one can only conclude he deems not serious. The second may be less obvious but no less misguided, in his assertion that jazz originates in ("derives from") the Eurological. Not only does this reflect a structural bias, but also a process bias, with neither emblematic of postmodern conception.

Here an interesting twist might also be noted: Whereas Stravinsky, Ravel, Milhaud, and other Eurological composers, even if their appropriations were confined to the compositional, embraced jazz and other non-Eurological sources, the resurgence of improvisation later in the century in that lineage tended to be confined within Eurological boundaries. Hence, where the former creative efforts were informed by structural expansion and processual contraction, the latter were shaped by processual expansion and structural contraction. A more robust postmodern paradigm would see growth along both parameters, as well as the transcendence of ethnocentric patterns. The aversion to the term *improvisation* among some of the prominent Eurological postmodernists, with Cage a primary culprit, might also be noted, where as Lewis points out terms such as *indeterminacy* and *intuition* were used to distance emergent paradigms from Afrological improvisatory practice.[52]

These patterns are consistent with the use of subtly discriminatory, yet nonetheless powerful, language—sometimes called *exnomination*—that reifies the prevailing ethnocentrism. By using headings that are inclusive in principle yet exclusive in practice, ethnocentric assumptions become even more deeply entrenched than if overtly biased language were used. For now the exclusion of non-Eurological sources is conveyed as so obvious that it need not be stated. Common examples include "Art Music" and "Western Art Music," which while suggestive of a wide range of genres, usually are meant to include only European classical music and its direct contemporary offshoots. The heading "New Music," which was coined a few decades into the twentieth century to herald a fundamental break from conventional Eurological practice while viewing itself as charting the next evolutionary era in that lineage, is a particularly relevant example in light of the present discussion of postmodern inroads. Though at face value suggestive of a celebration of the explosive diversity of forms spawned by the ever-increasing global confluence of the time, the moniker in fact is more striking in the musical scope it excludes—which Robert Walser succinctly identifies as much "of the music most 20th- [and now twenty-first-] century people have cared about"—than what it actually encompasses.[53] While most every music school or department offers coursework, ensembles, and supports research that comes under the New Music banner, the vast majority of this activity remains confined to Eurological terrain, defined in terms of both process- and structure-horizons. One would be hard-pressed to hear jazz, blues, hip-hop, or any of the infinite instances of multiethnic fusion, as current or "new" as much as this music is, at an academic New Music concert. Improvisation remains almost as foreign in these performances as in an all-Mozart recital.

And until fairly recently, much of the compositional activity that transpired in the academic musical sector confined itself to a small portion of the Eurological structural scope. Rather than the organic interaction seen in jazz of modal, tonal, and post-tonal content, along with conventional and exploratory rhythmic forms, much of academic New Music compositions appear to be driven by an "ethos of aversion," where pitch centers and pulse-based rhythm were subject to an unwritten taboo, in favor of atonal pitch languages and highly abstract timbral fabrics— what, recalling Leonard Meyer's terminology, might be termed nonsyntactic elements, which many listeners, and in retrospect, more than a few composers and performers, found alienating. Once again, strict conceptual divides between high and low art, even amid an avowed exploratory thrust, precluded the infusion of pitch and rhythmic elements—hence, syntactic elements—from non-Eurological traditions, the cross-cultural mining of which Stravinsky and his contemporaries savored, that might have been the source of rich vitality, particularly when combined with the interesting nonsyntactic explorations that were occurring in the musical world at large. But in stark contrast to the postmodern undermining of aesthetic hierarchies, much compositional work under the auspices of New Music remained constrained by a rigidly hierarchical, modernist aesthetic. William Bolcom, Pulitzer Prize–winning composer who through much of his career sustained an openness to wide-ranging musical influences as well as an active performance career, recalls "ideological struggles in music making" due to the prominence of serial compositional practices that eschewed conventional pitch languages and bred an obsession with mathematically generated atonal pitch sets. "It was taboo to be tonal at all. And you had to pretend that you had some kind of [post-tonal pitch] system."[54] Concurrent tendencies for composers to no longer be active as performers, again deriving from the division of labor noted earlier, contributed to a "big wasteland of twentieth-century unperformable music."[55]

Susan McCrary does not mince words in her critique of these tendencies and the role of the academy in perpetuating them. Noting that the academic institutions that have "provided a shelter for alienated artists for the last forty years has also encouraged them to pursue increasingly abstract, mathematically based, deliberately inaccessible, modes of composition," she also identifies in this a "curious reversal," where "the relentless serial noise of Schoenberg's protest against the complacent bourgeoisie has become the seat of institutionalized order." As a result, "attempts by younger composers to communicate, to become expressive, are dismissed as noise—the noise of human emotion and social response."[56]

The point here is not to categorically dismiss all music coming from academic composition departments and that which is devoid of conventional aspects of pitch and rhythm, or which might be based in mathematically generated pitch sets. Indeed, one of the compelling aspects of art is its capacity to yield powerful expressions even when exterior forces, either self-induced or externally imposed, impede creative options. And thus, when viewed on a piece-by-piece basis, one would not need to look far for substantive and important work in the academe compositional sphere. Furthermore, even if an integral reading of the musical world suggests that the pitch-rhythmic domain that Meyer delineated as syntactic, even when construed across cultures and taking into account the infinite diversity of pitch-rhythmic languages, indeed comprises the central structural locus of musical expression, this does not mean that in the course of individuation a given artist may not gravitate toward work that focuses on nonsyntactic elements. We will explore this more shortly. However, when taken as a whole, as a movement, one must acknowledge some degree of validity in these observations, which point to the significant extent to which creative exploration and decision making—where and where not one might look for acceptable sources and outlets of expression—has been mediated by deep-seated, structuralist/materialist patterns that are decidedly uncharacteristic of postmodern development. Pressing lends support to the pervasiveness of these tendencies when he compares the expressive impact of polymetric rhythmic practices employed by late twentieth- and early twenty-first-century Euroclassical composers that are not rooted in Afrological time feels to those that are, ascribing to the latter "heightened power to evoke emotion and affect in the (listener)."[57]

If the postmodern wave is to truly take hold and give way to an integral era, it is essential that these patterns are identified and addressed. A telling manifestation of their deep-rooted nature is found in the realm of improvisation pedagogy, a look at which underscores the manner in which aesthetics and praxis dynamically interact and inform each other. Viewing this first from a Eurological lens: Preliminary forays into improvisation among Interpretive Performance Specialists in this tradition around the mid-twentieth century were both facilitated by—and also in turn fueled—the narrow structural horizons that prevailed. With syntactic elements subordinated, the prevalence of nonsyntactic materials offered Eurological improvisers inviting gateways whereby successful improvisatory attempts could be made early on. In other words, the generation of musical ideas utilizing variety in timbre, or dynamics, or density levels, is not nearly as precise an endeavor as improvising with harmonic, melodic, and rhythmic materials and thus can nonetheless yield convincing statements with far less preparation. I myself have devised a system of improvisation study based on this principle geared for classical musicians who have never improvised.

Competent syntactic improvisation, on the other hand, requires extensive study, and while approaches like mine situate the nonsyntactic as syntactic entryway, this does not ensure musicians will cross this bridge. This is in no way to suggest that syntactic improvisation is superior, or to deny the achievements of artists who have developed nonsyntactic work to extraordinary heights that have entailed as extensive a program of study and practice as syntactic improvisers. It is simply to denote an inherent entryway in the musical materials that were in vogue and how this enabled musicians to circumvent a kind of training without which the twentieth-century Eurological improvisatory stream would remain confined to a notably limited spectrum compared to what was possible. In my improvisatory work with many fine Eurological performers, I can attest that without syntactic study, their backgrounds as interpretive specialists render them significantly disadvantaged when it comes to the skill set needed to thrive and find meaning in today's musical world. Even when they overcome inbred fears about improvising, and conditioned reliance on conductors and notated scores for pulse and pitch parameters, and manage to embrace the improvisation process, a further step remains to be taken. Yet again, this time from the angle of pedagogy, we see forces that allow for, at best, a partial, postmodern paradigm within the Eurological tradition and, so long as this lineage views itself apart from the overarching musical world, preclude its further development.

Integral arts historian Michael Schwartz' observations about postmodern limitations in general artistic practice underscore these points as they apply to music:

> While unparalleled in its creative outpour and brilliance, postmodern exhibition art, as a whole, has been overcharged in the masculine drives of Eros and agency—the Eros of newness and growth over the Agape of embracing existing world spaces

and showing any possibilities of relative harmony and health therein; and with the agency of the artist (or the viewer-critic) regularly taking precedence over communion, clear communication, and community.[58]

Jazz as Connecting Thread

In returning to jazz as a galvanizing force in the broader musical world, it is important to acknowledge that the Afrological has not been immune to these patterns. Founded as we have seen upon an exploratory thrust, the Association for the Advancement of Creative Musicians provided a community and practical infrastructure where African American musicians could pursue genuine postmodern and integral strides. However, as Lewis notes, there was a sense among some musicians engaged in this project that, due to the same aversion to the syntactic and favoring of the nonsyntactic seen in Eurological New Music circles, the emulative was sometimes overshadowed by the exploratory. Early AACM member Phillip Cohran, for example, lamented that "most of the guys that came into the AACM wanted . . . to play 'out' because it didn't require any discipline. Later on they developed tremendous discipline, but at the time it was just playing notes. That didn't do it for me."[59] The postmodern quest for new horizons can only go so far before it yields to the integral synthesis.

Here, however, a significant distinction between this important twentieth-century movement and its Eurological New Music counterpart points to the unique capacities in jazz to catalyze postmodern and integral growth. That is, the AACM was not predicated on the supremacy of a given creative or cultural line, but rather a commitment to digging deep into the untold creative resources of the overarching musical landscape and harnessing the transformational power of music that has manifested in cultures across the globe and across history. That the AACM was strongly Afrological in its musical and demographic points of departure, even to the point of largely excluding non–African American musicians, does not in any way contradict this statement, but in fact underscores it. As an initiative by and for African American musicians, it is only natural that the entryway into the musical landscape, for an excursion that would ultimately transcend boundaries, be through that particular cultural/ethnic/creative framework. Furthermore, that this entryway happened to comprise a structure-process scope uniquely conducive to this journey—namely, that entailing improvising and composing within significant portions of the syntactic/nonsyntactic spectrum of the musical world, coupled with spiritual engagement as directly related to the creative process, underscores a very different kind of exploratory impetus.

That, moreover, many in the AACM world eschewed the term *jazz* due to the structuralist/materialist implications the term often conjured up—for example, rather than denoting an ongoing process of growth, a return to past forms and rigid compartments—indicates not the style aversion of quasi-postmodern New Music but the style transcendence characteristic of an integral musical vision.

A subsequent project that was deeply informed by the AACM exemplifies similar principles. Karl Berger's Creative Music Studios, founded in the 1970s in Woodstock, New York, sought to transcend divisions and utilize music as a transformational agent. Again, while the term *jazz* was avoided due to limiting connotations, a significant number of the faculty had strong jazz grounding. And consistent with the integral principle that the function of style category is to inform a cross-stylistic synthesis, it is this grounding that enables CMS to, within its short life span, make significant contributions to this synthesis. "Theoretically I've always known that music is some sort of universal language, but now we're beginning to see the practice of it," Berger concludes as he marvels at the range of musical, cultural, and geographical backgrounds that would converge at CMS. Featuring artists/instructors such as Naná Vasconcelos from Brazil, Trilok Gurtu from India, Ismet Siral from Turkey, Aïyb Dieng from Senegal, powerful and magical kinds of interactions would often result. He adds that "the idea is not so much to combine styles but to look at the elements common to all the different forms of music,"[60] such as pitch and rhythmic languages, and allow the creative process to organically weave these together.

As Robert Sweet points out in his book on CMS, meditation and other kinds of spiritual practice were also important aspects of this project,[61] which, when combined with a robust process-structure matrix, upholds the whole-to-parts (meditative/silence-driven) and parts-to-whole (improvisation/composition-driven) interplay that is characteristic of integral musical understanding and practice. Once in place, wide-ranging and genuine fathoming of diverse musical traditions, theoretical terrain, and spiritual foundations is possible that could not take place otherwise.

If these developments are to transpire on a broader scale, entirely new educational models will be needed for musicians and audiences alike. Musicians need to acquire integral skill and aptitude sets, listeners will similarly need grounding in the practices and understanding that enable them to reap the transformational rewards of the arts that uniquely stem from improvisation-based musical art. The very improvisation-compositional process alignment and Afrological-Eurological-Global structural alignment that will constitute musical training must also be integrated into general education coursework in ways appropriate to non-practitioners in order that a more sophisticated cultural awareness evolves in society. And if the spiritual dimensions of the idiom are to be fully fathomed, consciousness study and development—approached both through practice and analysis—must become a prominent aspect of the twenty-first-century musical and overall educational landscape. Chapter 11, exploring this from a nondual, integral vantage point, will draw distinctions between postmodern inroads already evident in the burgeoning contemplative studies movement and what integral approaches might look like that are very much like those drawn above between postmodern and integral musical understanding.

Summary

An integral reading of jazz brings together insights from conventional jazz scholarship and considerations that do not commonly enter into music research, particularly regarding the interior dimensions and forces that shape the evolution of the genre, which in turn were seen as important to the evolution of the broader musical landscape. The nonduality premise central to an integral worldview provides an ideal framework for such investigation as it accommodates the idea of transcendent, archetypal impulses as underpinning surface developments. The archetypal principle can thus be understood from the standpoints of individual consciousness, collective or intersubjective consciousness, and planetary alignments in the cosmological domain—at which point dissolution of boundaries between interior and exterior reality necessitate a newfound conception of wholeness for which these language-bound categorizations are not adequate. When coupling this structure-mediated nonduality premise with the strong nonduality conception, (which is process mediated) that sees individual and cosmic improvisatory creativity as rooted in the same self-referential mechanics of consciousness, a yet broader understanding of the self-transcending capacities inherent in jazz is possible. For these give rise to the nested synergies and integral transparency principles that promote, respectively, the process-mediated and structure-mediated flow of awareness and archetypal content in whole-to-parts and parts-to-whole directions. The swing time feel, modality, the blues as undifferentiated incubator that would deliver these to the musical world, take on new significance from an integral vantage point.

Therefore, in light of the foundational purpose for human existence, and by extension engagement in any given discipline, which is to connect with the cosmic wholeness from which all of creation manifests—we gain further understanding of jazz as unmatched in its exemplification of this principle.

Part III

———————————

Change

Overview

This final section explores the issue of paradigmatic change on three fronts—musical study, education at large, and society. Chapter 10 explores what an integral school of music might look like and the many ways it would differ from conventional schools, while in many instances subsuming aspects of the latter within a vastly expanded and reconfigured framework. This would allow the jazz-inspired integral template to take hold and in turn inform education at large, change-oriented parallels with which are explored in chapter 11. Here striking similarities between the ordeal of integrating, or more aptly, reintegrating improvisation in musical study and the more recent (re)integration of meditation in the educational world reveal insights into the multidimensional nature of reform strategies.

Chapter 12 takes these reflections on paradigmatic transformation to a societal scale, with the moment-to-moment dynamics of creative improvisation within a small jazz group seen as a microcosm of the kind of improvising that needs to happen on a global scale. Jazz is seen as a vehicle for centering three kinds of anomalies, each more radical than its predecessor, related to the creativity-consciousness relationship, laying preliminary groundwork for what post-integral understandings of music and human potential might look like.

Chapter 10

The Music School of the Future

I close by recommending free improvisation in general and in every respectable form to all those for whom [music] is not merely a matter of entertainment and practical ability, but rather principally one of inspiration and meaning in their art. This recommendation, to be sure, has never been so urgent as now, because the number of people whose interest belong to the former category and not to the latter has never been so great. Even if a person plays with inspiration, but always from a written score, he or she will be much less nourished, broadened, and educated than through the frequent offering of all of his or her powers in a free fantasy practiced in the full awareness of certain guidelines and directions, even if this improvisation is only moderately successful.

—Johann Hummel, *Ausführliche theoretisch-practische Anweisung zum Piano-Forte-Spiel*[1]

The Music School of the Present

As apt as these observations about the pedagogical and creative benefits of improvisation may have been in Hummel's early nineteenth-century musical world, they are all the more so in the early part of the twenty-first. As the primary means for artistic expression and navigating the confluence of musical streams that is increasingly characteristic of our musical era, improvisatory skills have never been more important than at the present moment, and as the musical world progresses from modern and postmodern to integral eras, the need for this foundation will only increase. Although this may seem self-evident, colleagues from fields outside of music are often surprised to learn how elusive it remains in musical academe: The division of labor that for nearly two centuries has engulfed European classical music—the lineage in which musical study is largely centered—has, in deeming interpretive performance the primary occupation of the musical majority and relegating composition to a distinct minority, rendered improvisation virtually extinct in this tradition and, with jazz studies as a notable exception, musical training overall. Hummel's remarks, made in 1828, came at a time when improvisation, once a central expressive modality for the majority of musicians in the European tradition, had begun to fade from common practice. As unthinkable as it might be for an art student to graduate never having created a single painting, sculpture, design, print, or video installation, let alone having compiled a collective portfolio of such work, the parallel to this is the norm in music. That, moreover, most interpretive performance specialists (whether students, faculty, or professionals) are terrified at the very prospect of spontaneously creating music of their own—which is tantamount to heart surgeons who are possessed of a fear of blood, or skydivers of a fear of heights—speaks to the extent to which the academic approach to the discipline has become detached from the creative core of the tradition to which it ostensibly claims homage. "Of all the arts," laments Charles Fowler, "music is taught in the least creative way. From kindergarten through graduate school, music is presented to students as a preexisting body of literature with which the student must become familiar." Therefore, while "the study of music, we often hear, develops creative self-expression, the rhetoric is seldom matched in practice. . . . As far as students are concerned, composers are dead people, and music is a finished art."[2]

Despite the ever-escalating wave of appeals for reform that have been issued over the past half-century, and even with the addition of coursework—usually relegated to the periphery—in areas such as jazz, world music, and music technology, what Fowler describes as "the special problems"[3] of music persist at a time when the gulf between musical studies and the musical world has never been wider, nor the need for it to be bridged more urgent. As I have asserted numerous times, the problem is not the European classical repertory, nor the interpretive and analytical traditions it has spawned, but the extent to which the paradigm has become engulfed in an object-mediated aesthetic and praxial orientation that, deviating sharply from its historical roots, not only precludes creativity within the field, but as important, across genres and disciplines. From the standpoint of integral evolutionary trajectories, the expansion of the reigning modernist/ethnocentric orientation in the direction of postmodern/worldcentric and integral/cosmocentric would not only deepen appreciation for the treasures of the Eurological past, whose greatness is beyond debate, but also that of the many treasures found in a wide array of musical cultures, the greatness of which is also beyond debate. An integral approach to reform transcends and includes conventional practices, thus revealing the capacity for change to be, despite prevailing fears to the contrary, a win-win proposition. And perhaps ironically, "the field of music learning," as I have argued elsewhere, "contains within the very tradition it seeks to preserve the comprehensive, creative blueprint which it seeks (yet finds so elusive) to integrate."[4]

I believe the integral musical vision provides a powerful blueprint for the school of music of the future to not only fulfill its conventional aspirations for excellence within the European classical model but to accomplish something far broader—to bring to the world a musical paradigm that exemplifies the unifying and transformational capacities unique to this area of the arts. Centered in systematic approaches to improvisation (which include multiple approaches to improvisation, composition, performance, and theoretical inquiry) and meditation that uphold the parts-to-whole and whole-to-parts trajectories that support optimal creativity and consciousness development, the emergent paradigm will see jazz, which is unmatched in not only this process scope but in its richly integrative structural underpinnings, move from the periphery to front and center stage. This new role for jazz, however, will not position the idiom as self-confining destination, which is essentially that which has been upheld by European classical music, but as self-transcending tributary that flows into the broader musical ocean and its richly syncretic currents. In so doing, groundwork is laid in music for an integral, creativity-consciousness template that has the capacity to impact corresponding reform in education and society at large.

This chapter provides a glimpse of what such a school might look like. It begins with an overview of how conventional and integral models of musical study differ along numerous parameters, including their very different roles for creativity, approaches to basic musicianship, ensemble and private instruction frameworks, and organizational structures. A brief analysis of the two models from the standpoint of the Four Quadrants will illuminate not only surface manifestations of these differences, but that they are grounded in interior premises that will need to be addressed if the needed change is to be achieved. Limited penetration to underlying assumptions is a key reason why, as intimated earlier, reform has been minimal—confined to horizontal embellishment of the prevailing model rather than vertical transformation—despite ever-escalating concerns about the viability of the prevailing approach.

The chapter then presents three approaches to change that progress toward an integral paradigm. The first involves simply making the present model more flexible, providing students greater options to access the important foundational skills that the conventional approach has relegated to the fringes. The second takes the further step of actually beginning to reconstruct the curricular core around these foundational skills, with a new approach to basic musicianship oriented toward the skill set of the Contemporary Improviser-Composer-Performer profile a central development. The third expands upon this reconceived core and introduces a framework called the Integral Learning Environment that unites a wide range of areas of study—including improvisation, composition, performance (including principal instrument studies and ensemble), rhythm, aural skills, keyboard, movement, meditation, theory, history, and aesthetics—within a single laboratory setting that will comprise roughly half of the credit load for music undergraduates in their first two years. This does not replace entirely all conventional areas during that time—students will still take private instruction and ensembles, albeit encompassing much expanded terrain—but yields an integrative and creative foundation that has the capacity to transform all areas of musical engagement.

This sets the stage for consideration of the new kind of thinking and discourse needed for change in this direction to occur, and its ramifications for not only musical study but education at large. For if musical academe can emerge as a site where the jazz-inspired integral vision might take hold, the potential is considerable for that vision's embrace by the broader academy and, by extension, overall society.

Overview of Conventional and Integral Music Schools

Figure 10.1 launches our investigation by outlining important distinctions between conventional and integral schools of music. To briefly comment on these considerable differences, beginning with the central artistic profile: Whereas the conventional model aims toward the Interpretive Performance Specialist, and thus secondary and ancillary creativity at the exclusion of primary, the integral is oriented toward the Contemporary Improviser-Composer-Performer in which the entire creative spectrum is anchored in the primary processes of improvising and composing. Recalling our prior analysis, improvising and composing are primary because they enable creative engagement with syntactic and nonsyntactic elements in fluid and diverse forms, where performance enables creative engagement with only a few nonsyntactic elements such as timbre and tempo (the others fashioned, often centuries and continents removed from one's time and place).[5]

Conventional music school	Integral music school
Central artistic profile: Interpretive Performance Specialist in European classical repertory.	**Central artistic profile:** Contemporary Improviser-Composer-Performer whose work traverses diverse horizons.
Creativity: Secondary (performance) and ancillary (theoretical) creativity prevail; primary (improvising and composing) absent for most students and faculty.	**Creativity:** Primary creativity at center for all students and faculty, with appropriate distribution of secondary and ancillary creative engagement.
Musicianship core: Heavy emphasis in theory courses on four-part writing and analysis from European common practice period, with corresponding aural skills orientation focusing on dictation and sight-singing. Rhythmic training largely absent, particularly with contemporary focus. Improvising and composing (part-writing is not composing!) absent.	**Musicianship core:** Hands-on, creative, integrative, and contemporaneous emphasis (present as lens to past). Rhythmic training centered in Black Atlantic Rhythm, mastered in conjunction with improvisation, is as high priority as harmonic and melodic development. Harmonic fluency gained primarily through contemporary keyboard realization, with writing following keyboard practice, and all materials approached in conjunction with improvisation and composition. Contemporary five-part writing replaces four-part writing in core.
Ensembles: Large conducted bands, orchestras, and choirs comprise central experience for most students. Chamber music secondary.	**Ensembles:** Bands, orchestras, choirs, chamber ensembles situated in broader continuum at the center of which are small creative music ensembles for which students improvise and compose and perform, and large improvising ensembles.
Private instruction: Focus on interpretive performance of classical repertory. Isolated from other areas of study. Aims toward specialized skills on principle instrument.	**Private instruction:** Places interpretive skills within broader context, includes work in improvisation, aural skills (particularly aural transposition), and composition.
Technology: Weakly integrated and poorly understood in terms of pedagogical and aesthetic strengths and limitations.	**Technology:** Carefully integrated and understood in terms of pedagogical and aesthetic strengths and limitations.
Curriculum discourse: Minimally informed by pedagogical theory or contemporary musical world.	**Curriculum discourse:** Strongly grounded in pedagogical theory and contemporary musical world.

Figure 10.1. Primary Differences Between Conventional and Integral Schools of Music *(continued on next page).*

Conventional music school	Integral music school
Spirituality: Largely absent in terms of institutional acknowledgement.	**Spirituality:** Prevalent aspect of integral school, with abundant coursework in meditation and related practices and studies and openness to this domain in culture of field.
Central research orientation: Structural and historical aspects of repertory comprise focus. Inquiry into creative process largely absent. Conventional musicology riddled by false division between Historical (Eurological) and Ethnomusicology (everything else) areas.	**Central research orientation:** Cognitive and transformational dimensions of the creative process central. Structural and historical inquiry conducted through process-based lens. Spirituality/consciousness-based inquiry, including inquiry into music/cosmos connections. "Integral Musicology" transcends divisions between previous Historical and Ethnomusicological areas; instead "All music is world music."
Organizational structure: Faculty grouped in clearly demarked compartments (e.g theory, history, performance) reflective of conventional curricular and research divisions.	**Organizational structure:** Faculty no longer grouped within conventional divisions, rather in self-selecting pods according to teaching and creative affinities.
Public school music teacher training: Aims to replicate Interpretive Performance Specialist profile. Highly dependent on methods classes for teaching skills.	**Public school music teacher training:** Aims to produce contemporary improvisers-composers-performers. Pedagogical development rooted in artistic development; methods classes build on comprehensive foundations.
Arts outreach/advocacy: Driven by notion of European classical music as the pinnacle of humanity's artistic achievements. Views audience as passive receptors.	**Arts outreach/advocacy:** Driven by celebration of the diversity of the musical world as the core roles, and transcendent richness, of music and the arts in their many forms in human development and the importance of societies being in touch with the art forms of their own culture as a foundation for multi-cultural embrace. Everyone is regarded as musical/artistic, with integral advocacy initiatives involving both passive exposure and direct engagement in art-making.

Figure 10.1. *Continued.*

Core musicianship studies, where musical paradigms are arguably most firmly grounded, will differ greatly between the two approaches. Whereas the conventional musicianship core places heavy emphasis on more passive study of eighteenth- and nineteenth-century European materials, with four-part writing in the style of J. S. Bach chorales receiving particularly extensive attention,[6] integral musicianship studies involve vastly altered content and process dimensions. From a process perspective, hands-on, creative, integrative, and contemporaneous approaches (present as lens to past) are favored where possible, not at the exclusion of analytical, localized, and past studies, but as broad and lively gateways that enhance assimilation. Therefore, harmonic fluency in the integral model is gained primarily through contemporary keyboard realization, with writing following keyboard practice, and all materials approached in conjunction with improvisation and composition. Contemporary five-part writing replaces eighteenth-century four-part writing in the core. Whereas rhythmic training is largely absent in the conventional approach, particularly as it manifests in the contemporary musical landscape, rhythmic training in the integral, particularly with its grounding in what Jeff Pressing has termed Black Atlantic Rhythm, is regarded as high a priority in the musicianship core as harmonic and melodic development.[7]

Private instruction, an area considered so foundational to musical study that it is rarely considered as subject to new approaches, even in curriculum reform discourse, will expand its horizons in the integral paradigm. Conventional private lessons focus on interpretive performance and corresponding technical and expressive issues; integral private instruction places these concerns within a broader context that also includes improvisation studies and the kinds of technical development related to it (which can significantly enhance interpretive skills). Although private instruction will continue to play an important role in the integral paradigm, there will be less dependence on this modality as aspects of it are distributed throughout the broader curriculum.

Ensembles are the face of conventional musical study, with large wind bands, orchestras, and choirs generally considered the central groups. While smaller, chamber music ensembles are regarded by many faculty as even more important to musical development, they do not generally occupy the same curricular space or status and are thus vastly more peripheral to the culture of most schools and the field at large. The same is true for jazz ensembles—large and small—and the various other kinds of groups that have emerged in musical academe in recent decades. In the integral approach, the ensemble experience will expand radically, whereby conventional groups—large and small—are situated within a broader range of possibilities with new kinds of ensembles, directly reflecting musical practice, emerging as central. Two in particular will be the small creative music ensemble in which students improvise, compose, perform, and arrange, and the large improvising ensemble that harnesses the collective dynamics of consciousness between performers and listeners alike.

The shift from conventional to integral ensemble paradigms will be among the most dramatic aspects of the transformation in the field. In order to appreciate this, it is important to note the close, paradigm-confirming relationship between ensembles and private instruction in the conventional framework: Students develop formidable, albeit specialized, skills on their respective instruments in their individual lessons, which thereby enables the ranks of ensembles to be filled with highly competent instrumentalists who uphold strong performance levels in the various groups. Here we see a kind of correlate to the idea of tributaries, considered earlier in terms of musical styles, that flow into a central musical ocean—with a significant and highly problematic difference. Because the focus is on interpretive performance in both private lessons and ensemble, these tributaries are not self-transcending but self-confining. The reigning paradigm is reified, with formidable power dynamics at play as ensemble directors vie for territory and students. Conductors of conventional large ensembles, understandably, are loathe to allow students greater latitude in their ensemble options since this means they will no longer be guaranteed the best players. Yet as the musical landscape recognized in musical academe expands, this latitude becomes increasingly imperative.

In the case of the wind band (wind ensemble, symphonic band), the virtual absence of professional ensembles of this nature (with the exception being military bands) makes it particularly difficult to justify its centrality. A common argument, one that is not entirely without merit, is that important gains in overall musicianship are nonetheless made through the experience of playing in a fine wind band. Even from the conventional standpoint in which this argument is based, however, it is difficult to imagine how these benefits would not be far overshadowed by increased emphasis on chamber music over large group playing. When, moreover, the case is viewed from an integral standpoint, in which primary creativity rather than secondary (that which prevails in both large and small classical ensembles) is central, both of the prior arguments are moot. If the ensemble experience gained in musical study is to align with that of the musical world, the small creative music ensemble—in which all members improvise and compose—must assume front and center stage.

This does not mean, however, large ensembles are to be jettisoned, but that this aspect of musical academe must be reenvisioned and restructured from its foundations on up in order to reflect a more realistic distribution. While I believe the emergent ensemble format will look radically different from the present one in terms of surface features (range of ensemble options, range of music making that occurs, rehearsal hours per week, etc.), I believe a model is possible that enables the diversity needed while still achieving high quality in traditional areas. A symphony orchestra consisting largely of improvisers-composers-performers will not only be capable of broader programming, it may well be capable of a higher level of inspiration, vitality, and depth when it comes to playing Mozart, Beethoven, and Ravel—as important to the integral paradigm as to the conventional one—than currently achieved. Here the jazz pianist Keith Jarrett's frustrations when he returned to playing classical repertory with symphony orchestras might be noted. He found the majority of the musicians to be profoundly unfulfilled and disconnected from music as a transformational phenomenon. Exceptions were those who had outlets for primary creativity.[8]

Technology has become a buzzword synonymous with progress in musical study in many fields. In the conventional model, it is either completely ignored or ceded little importance by faculty whose musical horizons are largely oriented toward historical moments which long predate today's technological advances. The result is confusion and ambivalence, at best, and at worst outright rejection of this important aspect of contemporary musical life. Part of these concerns are justified, however, in that technology is often advocated with little attention to its aesthetic ramifications, which one can see are highly problematic in a lineage whose locus is a repertory that was created for acoustic instruments and in which, with notable exceptions, technologically enhanced renditions generally do not achieve the impact possible with conventional instruments. However, dissenting voices tend to remain silent on this account due to fears of being perceived as outmoded.

An integral perspective dispels this confusion by recognizing three important perspectives and functions regarding technology—pedagogical, creative, and aesthetic—and by underscoring both strengths and limitations in corresponding discourse. Technology offers important ways of rendering all aspects of the pedagogical enterprise more efficient and thus should be embraced in this capacity. Technology also opens up new creative pathways in which conventional boundaries, including those between improvisation and composition, may be transcended and give rise to powerful and transformational possibilities that otherwise might not be possible. At the same time, it is also important to emphasize that technological development in music when undertaken without corresponding aesthetic development is as prone to the same problems as technological explorations in general when undertaken apart from corresponding consciousness development. In music, a delicate psychoacoustic resonance has evolved over the centuries that is important to the transformational aspects of performance; richly expressive, transcendent responses may be elicited from the bow moving across the string, or the air being blown into the shakuhachi, and the overtone-rich vibrations that are produced and processed by the auditory cortex. It may not be enough to simply reproduce the surface sonorities and pitches digitally to deliver this kind of experience, just as technological manipulation of biological systems at their genetic core may be problematic without an expanded consciousness that may illuminate the broader ramifications of this exploration. Explorations and applications of music technology need to be connected with the creative and spiritual thrust that has driven musical evolution.

Music research is an area that will undergo tremendous upheaval in the shift from conventional to integral models. The conventional orientation in musicology—as elucidated by John Sloboda, David Elliott, and Christopher Small—toward the art object and its structural features and historical and cultural contexts will be situated within a broader spectrum of inquiry that is centered in the cognitive and transformational dimensions of the creative process. "There is a vast body of literature on the musical compositions which figure prominently in our art culture," states Sloboda, "but most of this deals with the product of composition, not the process."[9] In addition to a shift in the object of study will be a shift in the skill set of the musicologist. The ancillary creativity, in other words, that comprises scholarship will be positioned as an outgrowth of primary (improvisatory and compositional) and secondary (performance) creativity. The foundations for what I propose as Integral Musicology are therefore the very foundations for integral musicianship: meditation and improvisation as, respectively, whole-to-parts and parts-to-whole vehicles for creativity and consciousness development, atop which the various differentiated areas of musical inquiry and practice are synergistically integrated. This does not preclude the emergence of the scholar who specializes in research into any given area, conventional or not, but it means that such research will be grounded in a broader spectrum of experience than generally occurs conventionally. Current divisions between Historical Musicology, which deals with European classical tradition, and Ethnomusicology, which deals with all else, will dissolve in the expansion of the object-mediated model to include process- and self-mediated, interior dimensions. The driving force of the integral model will be to illuminate the important contours of the contemporary musical landscape so that improvisers-composers-performers may navigate pathways through it. Guided by the axiom "all music is world music," musicology will comment on musical regions as much as process-structure tributaries that flow into today's syncretic ocean as they will on these tributaries as discrete, isolated areas.

The role of the curriculum committee will undergo considerable change in the move toward the integral framework, and as we will explore, will be a foundational galvanizing force for that change. Curricular deliberations will be strongly informed by pedagogical theory, the needs of an ever-changing musical landscape, questions regarding sustainability along ecological, economic, sociocultural, and other parameters, and the biggest questions related to human creative and spiritual potential. Whereas conventional curriculum committees tend to operate from a status quo conception that holds the existing model as the norm against which new ideas are assessed, the emergent curriculum committee will subject prevailing and new ideas and strategies alike to ongoing critical scrutiny.

In the realm of organizational structure, the division of labor that is definitive of the past two centuries of European classical music and around which conventional schools are organized (e.g., separate areas of performance, conducting, theory, history) will open up to the more expansive Contemporary Improviser-Composer-Performer template as an organizing principle. This will enable the dissolution of conventional divisions and the grouping of faculty according to collaborative affinities. As will be explored later in the chapter, new musicianship frameworks will invite involvement among multiple faculty, which will be among the criteria by which faculty are situated in localized units within a school.

Spirituality represents yet another significant new development that will be seen in the integral music school. Riding the wave of recently emerging contemplative studies and consciousness studies movements in higher education at large, with a Spirituality in Music Education project now also underway, all of which of course reflect the growing interest in a spirituality that transcends borders in society at large, it is inevitable that this interest manifests in overt ways in a field as conducive to this as music. Instruction in meditation practice and related practices and studies will exist not just as extracurricular but be integrated into the curriculum.

Music teacher training will be grounded in a far more expansive conception of both the monumental importance of the public school music teacher in not only musical but the broader educational and societal transformation, and the radically new kind of preparation that is required of this individual. While the Music Education area of musical studies is arguably where the most comprehensive dialogues take place regarding reform in the field, thinking and efforts have largely been confined to embellishment of the Interpretive Performance Specialist profile—hence, horizontal rather than vertical change. In the integral approach, aspiring music teachers will be Contemporary Improvisers-Composers-Performers who are not only in touch with a wide range of music but, due to this process-structure scope, have extraordinary tools to evolve a profoundly transformative pedagogical voice. The rich pedagogical instincts inherent in the CICP profile will enable entirely new approaches to teacher training methods classes.

Finally, integral approaches to outreach and advocacy will differ from those that prevail. Whereas conventional efforts to advocate the importance of music tend to view European classical music as the center, the integral approach is driven by the need to enliven an appreciation of the broader landscape, with emphasis that individuals should be grounded in the music of their own culture as gateway. In contrast to the clear divisions between "high" and "low," and between musician and nonmusician—in other words, who makes music and who does not, the integral approach celebrates the transcendent richness in all music and the inherent musicality in every individual.

This overview of distinguishing features of the two models will be illuminated by a brief review of the Four Quadrant analysis presented earlier in order to more fully grasp how the paradigms differ. This will shed light on the multitiered nature of the frameworks and why change needs to occur in exterior and interior dimensions alike if the integral vision is to be realized.

Four Quadrant Analysis

Let us begin by delineating the broad scope of the Contemporary Improviser-Composer-Performer profile. Recalling our prior analysis (chapter 2) that traced this in terms of clockwise, cumulative movement of awareness (exterior to interior, or parts to whole): CICPs engage with the full spectrum of syntactic and nonsyntactic elements in diverse and fluid forms and thus transcend and include third-person, discipline-specific engagement (Upper Right) within an intradisciplinary, second-person scope (Lower Right). In other words, the stylistic point of departure opens up to the overall musical landscape. This self-transcending movement continues as awareness, due to the very same process breadth, opens up to interdisciplinary, sociocultural influences (Lower Left, also second-person) of the world at large, which further promotes emergence of the individual voice. Now Afrological and Eurological and other major musical streams are understood as rich culturally mediated phenomena, an understanding that then, as awareness opens up to first-person, transdisciplinary domains (Upper Left), becomes grounded in the contrasting temporal foundations of the respective core processes (Afrological-improvisation, Eurological-composition) as different pathways to transcendence. Self-referral awareness, for which meditation practice is a primary tool, predominates over object-referral tendencies toward conditioned attachments, and thus provides an interior receptivity to this parts-to-whole integration. Optimal creativity and consciousness development—as measured by inventiveness, interactivity, individuation in the first domain and self-realization, diversity, and heightened critical inquiry faculties in the second—is enjoyed by individuals and collective communities of integral CICPs.

From the very framework that enables this delineative analysis, a diagnostic analysis, equally important to paradigmatic change, is possible. As we have seen, inhibition of creativity underlies a host of problems that have been summed up as a "creativity/diversity/critical inquiry crisis." Subsequent analysis enables an elaboration on that crisis in terms of four pathologies that are inherent in, and perpetuated by, the conventional approach. Extending from the core problem of process or epistemological dearth, what I call *epistemopathology*, are *ethnopathological, theopathological,* and *ecopathological* tendencies.

Beginning again with the Upper Right and proceeding in a clockwise direction: Epistemopathology is the reduction of the process scope to secondary and ancillary creativity and the structural expanse to syntactic and nonsyntactic elements in style-specific configurations. Therefore, musical engagement is reduced to an Upper-Right, exterior-objective affair. Without adequate process breadth, contact with basic elements in the more fluid and diverse forms that characterizes intradisciplinary awareness correlative of the Lower Right—that where the entryway genre serves as tributary to the broader musical world—is not possible. Dissociation of the specialized interpretive performance process at this juncture in the system not only instills the epistemopathological pattern but makes inevitable the other three deficiencies, most immediately evident of which is the ethnopathological.

The ethnopathological assessment is due to the inextricable link between music and culture, and the default monocultural conception of the model. Without means to creatively engage with the broader landscape, musicians' capabilities to forge genuine connections to other musical cultures are limited—connections that are optimally established when diverse influences are seen as informing the personal creative voice. Inasmuch as the creative voice evolves not only through musical infusion but extramusical infusion, the very inaccess to basic elements in diverse and fluid configurations that precludes Lower-Right, intramusical engagement also precludes Lower-Left, sociocultural awareness. As seen in chapter 2, creativity-rich experience promotes the melding of musical elements and extramusical elements in awareness, key to individuation. This would enable intimate connections with not only diverse musical lineages but the diverse cultures in which they originate. Absent creative process diversity, no such connections are possible, further strengthening the ethnocentrism intrinsic to the conventional model.

This ethnocentrism is further reified by confinement of time conception to the linear, monocultural dimensions of the Eurological, composed-music-based paradigm, even if participants do not compose but only perform compositions of others in this system. When improvisation and composition are approached through the diverse options provided by the contemporary musical world, which would thus include both Afrological and Eurological and possibly other approaches, awareness becomes open to two fundamentally distinct and culturally mediated types of temporal cognition that are important to multiethnic awareness. Absence of these processes further promotes ethnocentrism, which now can be understood as limited integration of an important Lower-Left/Upper-Left nexus, defined as such due to the close link between temporality and consciousness.

Squarely illuminated by limited access to the Upper-Left, interior realm, are theopathological tendencies that are inherent in the conventional paradigm. It is not that interpretive performers do not invoke transcendent experience; they, in fact, invoke at times powerful transcendent experiences, which are to be celebrated. It is because these temporary, transformational glimpses—or states—are not grounded in creative diversity and thus lack a conduit through which this experience may flow, be informed, and critically examined, from an all-quadrants perspective. It is as if awareness skips from Upper-Right to a momentary Upper-Left orientation, and, much like the experience of the religious fundamentalist, renders the practitioner inclined to view his or her pathway as the only or at least superior avenue to this experience. Instead of self-referral, or self-Self union, in which awareness transcends object-referral attachments and realizes the univesality of the experience, now it clings to the path. Whereas the religious fundamentalist is bound by all manner of scriptural authority, the interpretive performance specialist is bound by a vast treasury of "musical scriptures" in the form of composed-notated repertory. Rigid distinctions between "high art" and "low art" inevitably result. Foreign musical influences are rejected as tainted, or less pure, when in fact, were transcendence grounded in creative diversity, not only would a reverence for the broader influences result, but also a process means for critically examining the framework. Here we can see that theopathological tendencies become closely linked with those ethnopathological, a point underscored in Bruno Nettl's entertaining though sobering comparison of schools of music to rigidly hierarchical and evangelical religious orders. The primary purpose of such schools is the "initiation of [its] graduates into a priesthood whose task is to missionize, to promulgate art music and urge society to replace other kinds of music with it."[10] Predicated on the idea that European classical music is "the serious music of society, the music associated with eternal and spiritual values," graduates are impelled to join an "army willing to defend a beleaguered position [where] art music is losing ground to other kinds of music."[11]

When listeners encounter this model, even as seemingly passive onlookers (although in chapter 7 we will consider listeners as dynamic ensemble members in improvised performance), they are indoctrinated into these very patterns that constrain artistic awareness of its practitioners. They sense the creative and ethnological horizons of the performers, and whether they are in touch with the pulse of the time and place—regardless of what kind of music is performed—and on some level apprehend that as truth. In appealing for a more expansive model, this is in absolutely no way to suggest that there will be no place for an "all-Chopin recital," or for that matter, an "all-Ellington" concert, in the integral aesthetic paradigm. The problem with the conventional approach does not lie, nor will it be resolved, in any single performance. Rather, it lies in the overarching, ongoing orientation that is perpetuated over time as graduates of the conventional model go out into the world and project the values of the conventional worldview as members of symphony orchestras, chamber music groups, music teachers, arts board members and through other activities.

What about ecopathological tendencies? At first glance, the argument that the conventional model might promote such may seem untenable given the considerable interest in the classical music world in environmental issues—at least this is my experience, and if I am wrong this only underscores my point. I believe that when we look at this as a continuum that extends directly from the previously noted epistemo-, ethno-, and theopathological patterns, the case however may be made. Beginning with the absence of collective improvisatory music making and the severing of the individual from the immediate musical ecology (as we saw, improvisation represents a primary modality for enlivening intersubjective consciousness), we can also see a disconnection from the broader ecology of the overarching musical world and its diverse cultural roots. A disconnection from the spiritual ecology that is uniquely possible through improvisatory and compositional creativity is then evident. Here we come to a dimension of spiritual experience in which awareness opens up to subtle energies, existing at similarly subtle strata of consciousness as, if not ontologically synonymous with, the transcendent, archetypal influences considered earlier. When this is contacted through primary creativity, particularly that which is improvisatory and collective, one senses a level of intimacy and communion with the physical environment that is only possible when one actually transforms its subtle impulses into musical expressions. A degree of "ecological intelligence" is established that is not possible in the absence of this creative channel and the various layers of musical, cultural, spiritual ecologies to which the natural (biological) ecosphere is intimately linked. When artistic creativity is grounded in improvisation, a uniquely intimate connection with the environment is possible that exemplifies that which will be need to be invoked by large portions of the society if it is to deal with today's environmental challenges.

Granted, the ecopathological tendencies inherent in the model may be less pronounced than the other three—when viewed from the standpoint of the experiences of the musicians themselves. But when one considers the capacity of the arts to inform listener awareness, the ramifications become more apparent. Consider, for example, the impact of the marginalization, if not outright exclusion, of the all-important African American dimensions of contemporary American and much global practice, not only for African Americans but for all Americans. Whether or not one subscribes to the view that I and others hold regarding the African American foundations of American musical culture, one cannot deny that at the very least this stream is equal in importance to the Eurological. When such an enormous part of one's cultural identity is denied in the study and practice of music in its (the culture's) music schools, the transformational function of the arts is undermined in the awareness of listeners. And let us always keep in mind that this manifests in both process realms (e.g., improvisation) and structural realms (e.g., rhythm and its interaction with pitch languages). It is not that European and other musical genres are inherently devoid of this transformational capacity, but that individuals generally need transformational grounding in the expressions of their time and place if they are to fathom deeply those of other times or places. When this is compromised, the sense of wholeness, meaning, and purpose, and enlivenment of the self-driven impulse to growth—recalling Jung's description of the function of art that takes awareness back to "the deepest springs of life,"[12] and Wilber's of how art inspires us to find our "higher possibilities"[13]—that is intrinsic to the arts is undermined. This will be the basis for transformation of patterns of consumption, the kinds of businesses one supports, inner awareness of outer surroundings, and the other kinds of change that will be needed for ecological sustainability.

And when the ramifications of the conventional musicianship model for underprivileged urban and other communities are considered, the eco-pathological patterns—which of course exacerbate and are exacerbated by the other three—become all the more pronounced. Because the sense of wholeness that the arts can help foster—the "development of knowledge, self-esteem, and creative imaginations,"[14] as Karlton Hester describes what features lay dormant in the absence of viable arts programs and exposure for inner-city youth—is also threatened by the litany of other problems inherent in poverty and marginalization.

Once again, arts paradigms transmit their respective values systems as well as their treasures to the populace. Although there appears to be no dearth of exhortation for arts advocacy activity coming from musical academe, rarely do we see "outreach" complemented by the equally important "inreach" work that needs to be done in order that the aforementioned kinds of pathologies, which in fact may exacerbate the very obstacles to the arts advocates seek to overcome, are not perpetuated. When listeners encounter musicians who only play music created by others, are out of touch with the vibrancy of contemporary forms and the cultural diversity of the times, and endorse the transformational power of the arts from a single stylistic vantage point, they are being told a very small part of the story, not all of which is even true, of the arts. Integral Arts Advocacy combines the self-critical dynamism of inreach with a much more expansive and inclusive outreach platform that speaks more deeply to the diverse constituencies of our world.

Many will find this assessment harsh. However, I believe this is precisely the kind of diagnostic work that must be done if the kind of change that is needed, and possible, is to occur. Where there is pathology there is also potential for healing. Musical academe has excelled as a site where a tiny, yet beautiful and important, slice of musical practice has flourished, where on any given evening fine and occasionally extraordinary performances of European classical repertory can be heard throughout the world. Now the time has come for the horizons of the field to open up, not only through horizontal expansion but vertical transformation, which means fathoming of the musical shadow that has eluded attention. And as alarming as adherents of the conventional musicianship model might find insinuations that it is inherently ethnocentric, constrained by and perpetuates the same mechanisms that yield religious fundamentalism, and possibly even contributes to alienation from the environment, the integral perspective may provide even greater cause for alarm in revealing the inhibition of creativity at the heart of these pathologies to entail the inhibition of a cosmic, evolutionary thrust in a field that is uniquely equipped to channel that thrust. Here it must be emphasized that the ramifications of inhibited creativity extend far beyond limited means for personal expression and perhaps curtailed professional opportunities, or even the previously mentioned deficiencies. Inhibition of creativity skews the balance between the first-, second-, and third-person realities—or subject, process, and object; or spirituality, art, and science—that we saw in previous chapters to uphold an evolutionary function in every instant and location in time and space. Once again we return to the strong non-duality thesis that, central to the integral account being advanced, links creativity and consciousness on individual and cosmic scales. Music, due to its improvisatory foundations, is unmatched in and beyond the arts as exemplary of this principle. Constructing an arts model around secondary creativity essentially excludes the artistic impulse from the equation, and instead of harnessing the self-transcending power of nested synergies inherent in arts engagement rooted in primary creativity, the field is riddled by nested fissures that not only make fragmentation and stasis inevitable within the field, but also result in the litany of shortcomings identified that are projected to the world. By shifting the guiding orientation from Interpretive Performance Specialist to Contemporary Improviser-Composer-Performer, the spirituality-art-science balance could be restored at macro and micro scales.

The integral framework is unmatched in its capacities to both penetrate to the heart of the shadow yet at the same time delineate a new vision of unprecedented scope and excitement that situates the best of conventional practice within a far broader approach. And because of the transformational potential in music illuminated in an integral reading of the field, if musical study could invoke the change needed it could emerge as a catalyst of unprecedented force for change in the broader educational and societal arenas. The thinking here is somewhat reminiscent of Buckminster Fuller's assessment of the prospects for humanity. As noted in the introduction to this volume, Fuller proposed that there will be no middle ground, that the degree of transformation required for even just survival will be so enormous that it will catapult civilization to an entirely new evolutionary era. I believe the same holds for musical studies: as long as the field remains entrenched in a model that finds itself increasingly distanced from the musical world, its very survival is in question. If it achieves the reform needed to rectify this divide, the field will not only flourish but emerge as a healing force for all of education and humanity.

A look at three approaches to reform sheds light on this admittedly bold assertion.

Three Approaches to Change

Change Strategy #1: Option-rich Curricula

The first approach is the simplest and roughly corresponds to an astructural postmodern musical worldview. Involving opening up greater freedom and flexibility within existing curricular models, it requires neither the creation of a single new course, nor a single new faculty appointment, although these might be organic outgrowths of the approach. The basic idea is that most every school has a moderately diverse array of resources to offer students, but the intractability of the present curricular framework, particularly at the core level (generally the first two years), precludes students from accessing these resources nearly as fully as they might. As emphasized several times by now, the conventional model was not designed with a diverse musical world in mind and attempts to rectify the situation by adding to the existent foundations offer minimal improvement. They may even exacerbate the problem by perpetuating a fragmented, exclusionary, and creatively deficient musical worldview; while the new offerings may exemplify new values, that they are relegated to the fringes reifies the conventional foundations as the norm in the minds of students. Through greater options, students would be better able to chart their pathways, take responsibility for their education, and become more in touch with their particular learning styles and musical goals.

The approach might also free up faculty who otherwise were constrained by covering required classes to explore new approaches that align with student interests. In this way, the model becomes self-organizing: instead of being governed by the inertia of convention and special interests, it now expands the forces to which it must respond as it moves forward. Outmoded content and epistemologies might fall to the wayside and allow innovative frameworks that are not only vibrant with contemporary relevance, but renewed perspectives on past treasures as well. With an astute administration, resources might then be deployed in the direction of emergent areas to which students gravitate, and those directed toward conventional areas whose enrollments might be in decline could be diminished. While this approach to change may seem astonishingly self-evident to colleagues in the business world, musical academe has distanced itself from this thinking and instead allowed itself to be driven by a host of extraneous factors that have often excluded the best interests of students.

From an integral perspective, among the primary benefits of the option-rich approach is not so much that it will lead to an integral curricular framework, which is unlikely, but that it has the capacity to enliven awareness about core musical and educational issues that will be important to arriving at that framework. Here the importance of sustaining new levels of dialogue, which are ideally informed by corresponding literature, in conjunction with reform proposals cannot be emphasized strongly enough. Otherwise, faculty are prone to habituated fears and assumptions that the educational experience might be compromised if students are given freedom. One also hears the extraordinary claim that the needed diversification has already been achieved in the field. This "mission accomplished" perspective reflects a limited understanding that fails to see the difference between the embellished Interpretive Performance Specialist identity, where improvising and composing are—at best—primary creativity ornaments to a secondary creativity foundation, and the Contemporary Improviser-Composer-Performance identity in which the artist integrates the entire primary, secondary, and ancillary scope through the lens of a profoundly personal artistic voice. The concern that diversification might dilute conventional skills, while perhaps the more reasonable of the two, is no less misguided. These are part of a broader inventory (see inset at the end of this chapter) of prominent conceptual challenges posed by the integral musicianship paradigm. Enlivened and sustained dialogue would likely reveal diversity to be core to the nature of arts and artistic development, it is the evolutionary norm and central to self-transcending depth. Diversity is more than a luxury, or even a politically correct or ethical goal to be sought once conventional "foundations" are solidly in place: Diversity is central to what it means to be an artist and needs to be a predominant facet of artistic development, which must begin with diversification of the process scope from the curricular foundations on up, accompanied by a shift in individual and cultural identity from Interpretive Performance Specialist to Contemporary Improviser-Composer-Performer.

Enlivened dialogue would also promote a more nuanced and critical look at both new proposals and existing structures. If option-rich curricula are no panacea, neither are significant portions of what students are currently required to take. In no way is this to deny the brilliance of some aspects of conventional musical study, particularly in the high level of interpretive skills that it promotes. However, to deny the gulf between this and contemporary musical practice, and the fragmented, creativity-deficient, and ethnocentric patterns that the model perpetuates would be to overlook one of the most problematic areas in all of higher education. Proposals for opening up the curriculum for options that are accompanied by rationale and dialogue that brings out this range of perspectives would make the most significant contributions to change in an integral direction.

But regardless of what kinds of pathways students might be able to forge through any such approach, there will be need for design of new curricular models that more directly embody integral features. This brings us to a second approach to change, that involving a new core musicianship class that provides foundational skills for the Contemporary Improviser-Composer-Performer.

Change Strategy #2: Integral Basic Musicianship—
Foundations for a New Core Curriculum

At the University of Michigan, I designed what appears to be among the very first jazz-based musicianship classes to be approved to fulfill core curriculum (first two years) requirements.[15] Second-year classical music majors may opt to continue the conventional track or take my class, which covers a wide range of harmonic, melodic, and rhythmic material through the primary creative processes of improvisation and composition, with secondary and ancillary engagement structured in close alignment with the primary process foundation. Jazz, European classical, and other musical traditions comprise the sources of musical materials, with strong emphasis on developing skills that enable access to the central syncretic current of the musical world. Style-specific and trans-stylistic improvisation study, strong emphasis on Black Atlantic Rhythm, extensive keyboard realization work (required of all students regardless of principal instrument), composition, multiple types of aural skills development, movement, preliminary exposure to meditation, writing and analysis comprise the spectrum of activities covered with this self-transcending aim in mind.

While jazz factors considerably in various areas of the class, it is important to emphasize the strategies by which this emerged, as well as how these very strategies invite integration of wide-ranging sources. Two questions frame the approach:[16]

1. Stepping back from the stylistic and disciplinary categories that prevail in musical study, what are the skills—in
terms of processes and structures—required for today's
musicians to navigate successful, meaningful, and transformative pathways within the current kaleidoscope of
possibilities that characterize the musical world?

2. With a predilection toward hands-on, creative, integrative, and contemporaneous sources when possible, what
are the richest stylistic regions for the skills identified?

So in other words, we first withdraw from the prevailing categories
and identify what students need to know and be able to do, and then
return to the realm of category for the strongest sources of those needs.
In response to the first question, improvising, composing, performing,
fluency with contemporary pitch and rhythmic languages; highly developed technical, aural, and conceptual faculties; capacities for moving
freely across genres in order to inform a richly personal artistic voice, to
adapt to new developments, and for collaborating with musicians from
highly disparate backgrounds are among the important skills commonly
identified. While, in response to the second question, no single genre
possesses the totality of skills needed by today's musicians, jazz looms
large, particularly when construed *writ large*, as a foundation that supports a range of growth that is unmatched by any other genre. Jazz is
thus uniquely equipped as the basis for a twenty-first-century musicianship paradigm due to both its own process-structure expanse and that to
which it opens up. Here let us reemphasize that for Western musicians,
jazz's capacity to unite Afrological and Eurological streams atop its African American foundations provides an ideal template for further global
integration. Hence the contemporaneous principle whereby a predilection
for current resources does not reflect a disregard for the treasures of the
past, but rather recognizes that these treasures are optimally fathomed
through a present-based entryway. The self-transcending principle, then,
not only extends across cultural and geographical boundaries but historical ones as well.

It should therefore be clear that, even with the recognition of jazz
as central, the guiding profile here is not what was termed in chapter 8
the Mainstream Jazz Musician, who aims to replicate stylistic norms, but
the Contemporary Improviser-Composer-Performer, who aims to transcend and include stylistic norms. Harnessing the synergistic interactions
and breadth of the skill set encompassed in a systematic approach to
improvisation, which let us recall includes primary, secondary, and ancil-

lary creative processes, the CICP is also the guiding profile for the entire integral musical study enterprise. Here it might be noted that while primary and secondary creativity are explicit in the CICP profile, ancillary engagement is implicit, and therefore, even areas seemingly unrelated to contemporary creativity, such as scholarly research into age-old repertory, may be profoundly informed by its scope.

The question then becomes how to organize this broad range of engagement and study into a coherent system. Here is where Alfred North Whitehead's three-stage "rhythm of learning," consisting of what he called romance, precision, and generalization stages, provides a uniquely effective framework for foundational musicianship skills.[17]

STAGE I: ROMANCE

Stage I, corresponding to romance, begins with improvisation using non-syntactic elements—density, dynamics, silence, timbre, texture—as catalysts. The basic idea here is to initiate generation of musical materials with minimal external constraints, so that students from the outset begin to draw from their internal imagery. A characteristic exercise involves creating variety within whatever elements are specified (e.g., "create a short solo piece that utilizes a wide range of dynamics and density"). Most conventional improvisation training begins and ends with syntactic parameters, which nowadays usually means jazz, which has the effect for many students of obstructing the creative flow. The problem for novice improvisers at the college level is that this approach asks them not only to make music for the first time without the aid of notation, it also asks them at the same time to create with entirely new language structures (time feels and corresponding melodic and rhythmic conceptualization). Rather than becoming emotionally engaged, students become inhibited, and rather than experiencing improvisation as an expressive outlet for inner imagery, this approach denies that imagery and forces them to generate ideas through a foreign language, which in many cases they have hardly even heard. The initial exercises are invaluable as entryways for classical musicians who have had little or no improvisatory experience as well as expanding the horizons of competent jazz improvisers.[18]

Though the emphasis at this stage is on process and its corresponding generation of ideas, one need not presume that compelling musical results, even with beginners' early attempts, will be altogether absent. Such results sometimes occur within the very first sessions, producing an all-important self-confidence that is necessary to skill development. Moreover, groundwork is laid for later forays into syntactic improvisation by virtue of the fact that when syntactic elements are generated, even if in bits and pieces as by-products of the nonsyntactic approach, students gain glimpses of areas that they need to work on in order to better be able to express themselves. For example, students whose early excursions bring them into some sort of time feel, or pitch region in which they realize they have minimal tools, will not only establish a kind of intimate connection with these areas given that they, in a sense, stumbled upon them on their own, but they will also gain a clear picture of what to work on next. Here again we return to the cycles of Direct Creative Experience, Reflection and Craft, and the self-organizing (self-motivational, self-navigational) aspects of creativity-based education.

The power therefore of beginning with nonsyntactic elements is that it provides just enough in the way of constraints to elicit and direct a flow of ideas, yet it is open enough to not impose theoretical, technical, or conceptual obstacles that might impede the all-important flow. Here it is important to realize how this approach differs from "free" or entirely open improvising formats, which are also highly useful in improvisatory development (I also use them early on, but not as primary formats). However, when novice improvisers are given absolutely no parameters, the absence of catalysts and landmarks can shut down the flow. Accomplished improvisers who are uncomfortable with open formats for perhaps different reasons tend to resort to tried-and-true clichés, which often sound contrived and out of place in these contexts. The nonsyntactic parameters provide just enough structure to elicit from beginners and accomplished syntactic improvisers what is necessary for them to be able to take advantage of the unique expressive power of open frameworks, where spontaneous interaction and inner-directed conception are at their zenith, and can yield highly magical moments.

I might also add that the series of nonsyntactic exercises I have devised extend from the basic exercises just described to highly advanced exercises that place virtuosic demands on students. For example, a later exercise involves a single musician developing four contrasting motives, creating a kind of self-contained counterpoint by alternating between one and the other, eventually merging the four ideas. However, stage I in this class, whose intention is to launch beginners and begin to expand the horizons of experienced improvisers, is well served by more basic exercises.

Rhythmic training also begins in stage I, with preliminary exercises derived from Indian rhythmic solfège; students chant syllables that designate patterns of 2s, 3s, 4s, and 5s, and clap designated polyrhythms. These exercises serve to develop inner pulse, polyrhythmic skills and odd-meter skills. Preliminary concepts from Black Atlantic Rhythm are introduced, although this important domain is broached more systematically in stage

II (partly because many classical students have trouble with sustaining basic pulse and thus are invited to begin their improvisatory journeys with European rhythmic conceptions).

Stage I also involves theoretical study of the basic elements (identification of nonsyntactic and syntactic parameters), an introduction to implication-realization theory, and an overview of pedagogical principles (hands-on learning, proper sequential organization, creativity, etc.). Graphic composition, where students sketch out pieces that are to be realized through improvisation, is included in this phase.

Aural skills at this stage include singing and aural transposition, which involves taking a pattern in a single key and working it out by ear in multiple keys. This is an intensive, high-yield activity that not only cultivates the strong ear-to-hand coordination essential for improvisation but in so doing also promotes exceptional dexterity on an instrument.

Movement, meditation, sound awareness, and listening are also part of this section. Movement is usually done in conjunction with rhythmic training, where students incorporate different types of body motion while they chant and clap the rhythmic patterns. Meditation is usually a guided relaxation or breath awareness practice, and students are encouraged to explore systematic instruction at local meditation centers. Sound awareness consists of musical meditations to cultivate deep listening skills, as well as the other types of aural skills listed earlier. The aural, rhythmic, and contemplative facets of stage I are sustained through the other two stages of the course.

It should also be emphasized that all students in the class are grouped into small "creative music ensembles" in which they fulfill a variety of creative projects—involving improvisation, composition, arranging, performance—that incorporate the various knowledge areas studied in the class. We will later consider this as the central ensemble format in the integral school of music, which will also include a wide variety of other groups.

STAGE II: PRECISION

Stage II, corresponding to Whitehead's Precision, begins with modality, which is the pitch framework through which students also first encounter time feels. We thus divide stage II into two sections; IIA deals with modality and rhythmic syntax, IIB with tonality. Here we begin our engagement with Black Atlantic Rhythm with even eighth-note feels since that is more closely aligned with their backgrounds in classical music, and to a lesser extent, popular music (most students are exposed to some degree to popular genres). Swing follows, requiring sustained engagement throughout the course of the year for fluency to begin to manifest.

Students with jazz experience also benefit from these exercises in that often most of their improvising has been done in tonal formats. Thus, even though these students will immediately exhibit greater fluidity (which is not necessarily true in stage I) with these formats, they will continue to expand their horizons. Moreover, in that constraints from stage I (density, registral variety, motivic development) are imposed on the modal formats in part II, experienced jazz improvisers will be more than adequately challenged here. Students also compose in modal formats in this phase, with an emphasis on adhering to principles of melodic construction such as effective contour, distribution of leaps and steps, motivic development, and handling of dissonance.

An important learning vehicle is introduced in stage II that is central throughout the remainder of the course: keyboard realization, with vocalization. In other words, all students accompany themselves at keyboard while they sing given passages that embody particular concepts. In the integral model, virtually no pitch element is dealt with which is not realized at the keyboard.

Aural musicianship also takes on new dimensions at this stage, moving into progressively more challenging patterns, including those involving chromaticism and larger intervallic shapes. Transcription also comes into play, where students learn by ear recorded solos of master improvisers. Both of these modes of aural skills make considerable use of the voice, as students must sing patterns prior to working them out on their instruments.

Stage IIB introduces tonality. Following a review of key signatures and intervals for students needing this, the class departs radically from conventional approaches to tonality by replacing four-part writing in the style of Bach chorales with five-part, contemporary harmonic idioms, based on jazz and pop structures, that are learned first through keyboard realization prior to written application. The five-part harmonic texture is based in the seventh-chord structure, as with a four-note voicing played in the right hand and the bass note in left. When chord extensions and alterations are introduced, the additional notes replace expendable chord tones (e.g., the thirteenth replaces the fifth) as per standard practice, to retain the five-note format. The class does not entirely do away with four-part European common practice exercises but situates them much further along the continuum of priorities, based in the principle that most of what today's students need to know regarding tonal materials can be gained through the contemporary five-part format. Parallels are drawn frequently between contemporary and Eurological tonal practices; the V7/II chord functions the same way in Ellington or Charlie Parker as it does in a

Bach chorale; the French augmented sixth chord is the same as a jazz subV7(b5), even if the resolutions differ. A continuum from diatonic to nondiatonic harmonic materials emerges that, including applied chords and richly altered extended harmonies, matches if not exceeds the expanse of conventional approaches, while situating this within a contemporary, process-rich context that integrates keyboard realization, writing, improvisation, composition, and rhythmic time feels. An entirely new level of fluency is possible.

Keyboard realization is key. I have found that students who are not piano principals, including some who have not touched the keyboard prior to taking my course, are able to realize chromatically rich harmonic sequences in multiple keys—playing only from chord symbol or function—by the end of their second term. Having internalized these sounds in hands, hearts, and ears, and integrating them with a wide array of other processes, provides tools directly applicable to the creative engagement of the twenty-first-century CICP.

Stage III: Generalization

Stage III of the Integral Learning Environment musicianship sequence involves creating with the tools gained in previous sections. Although creative application is central to the approach from its outset, now students are invited to let their creativity flow in ways that are not constrained by the parameters of the class (occasional wide-open excursions, by the way, are structured into the system at prior points). This allows new levels of highly personalized integration of skills, and sets the stage for both further, self-driven growth, and also access to more advance resources of a given institution, which might include advanced studies in jazz improvisation and composition, analysis of European classical repertory, orchestration, or historical studies.

Let us now examine how a third approach to change harnesses the openings established in this class in a broader format called the Integral Learning Environment.

Change Strategy #3: The Integral Learning Environment

The previously mentioned class is situated at Michigan within an otherwise conventional curricular framework, meaning that while students take it to fulfill second-year music theory and aural skills requirements, they also take private lessons, ensembles, music history, and other coursework to fill out the rest of their load. Inherent in the class are connections that extend organically from its hands-on, creative, and integrative orientation to wide-ranging areas that might be harnessed to promote integral strides across the curriculum. Here is where what I envision as the Integral Learning Environment (ILE) represents a paradigmatically different approach to not just a single course but a significant portion of the curriculum. The idea is similar to the class just discussed: housed within a single framework are diverse learning modalities and knowledge areas, with students engaged in ensembles (in addition to robust hands-on individual engagement such as keyboard realization) that put what they learn to direct use in live performance. But ILE takes the idea to a new scale, encompassing aspects of private instruction, music history, and ensembles so that the synergistic interplay of areas often approached in isolation can give rise to entirely new ways of musical knowing and expression, all the while rendering the curriculum more efficient, flexible, and self-organizing for the benefit of students and faculty alike.

The challenge in all educational disciplines—that of how to address the ever-expanding knowledge base without extending years of schooling—will never be solved through curricular accretion; it will only be solved through integration, through synthesis of carefully examined existing and new areas into a coherent whole. ILE is rich in capacities to achieve this synthesis due to its creative breadth, self-transcending contemporaneous thrust, and integration.

It is not that ILE need necessarily encompass the totality of study within its horizons; while the idea could be implemented in a variety of ways, I envision it as a six- to eight-credit class that is cotaught and is offered for first- and second-year students. Atop this reformed core students would then have foundations that enable wide-ranging pursuits in the curricular upper structure.

Let us first explore this by looking at connections to the study of the applied instrument that is central to conventional approaches and will continue to play an important role in the integral era. Here aural transposition and transcription studies noted earlier are a primary example due to their rigorous, high-yield/low-overhead nature. In other words, once the assignment is given, the role of the instructor immediately recedes to the background; it is up to students to do the work, which while intensive, lays groundwork of enormous value for multiple areas of engagement. Extensive ear-hand coordination and technical prowess extending from this work is particularly valuable for improvising, composing, and performing—the entire primary and secondary creative process scope. A progressive sequence of this kind of work might allow aspects of private instruction to be absorbed within the ILE framework, thus freeing up students and faculty to devote attention to other areas.

In no way is this to suggest that private instruction is dispensable, nor that virtuosity is any less important in the integral approach than the conventional: if anything, it will be more important. What is needed, however, is to step back from conventional categories, as noted earlier, and take inventory of what students will need to be able to do, and then determine the richest sources of these skills. On their principal instruments they will need to produce beautiful sounds, in tune, and develop extraordinary dexterity. Aural transposition and transcription are exceptionally powerful tools that contribute to this mastery, and if these are more appropriately administered in a class rather than the private lesson, then the first seeds of integration are sewn. Rendering students and faculty less dependent upon private instruction will also help with the budget as this is among the most costly modes of instruction in all of higher education. I believe that many private instructors would relish the idea of smaller contingents of private students and the opportunity to be involved in other kinds of teaching.

The same principle holds for historical knowledge and the broader range of concerns that fall within musicology (e.g., theory, cultural studies, cognition). Though the integral musicianship class clearly covers much that conventionally is ascribed to music theory, important seeds are also planted for broader musicological studies that could easily blossom in ways that further free up the curriculum through more efficient, and arguably effective, approaches. Here it should be emphasized that Integral Musicology, while including virtually everything that is encompassed in conventional musicology, not only vastly expands the scope but situates study of the creative process, which has been largely ignored in the conventional approach, at the forefront. The primary task of Integral Musicology, with integral musicologists being Contemporary Improvisers-Composers-Performers, is to illuminate the interior and exterior dimensions of contemporary creative musicianship—how CICPs navigate their ways through today's global melding, the interplay of Afrological, Eurological, and other musical currents; consciousness and spirituality; evolution of the individual voice; stages of musical evolution (modern, postmodern, integral), among an infinitude of other areas. An important parallel with integral instrumental instruction may be noted here: Whereas the conventional focus is on performance of music created by others, the primary purpose of instrumental virtuosity in the integral model is to fashion a vehicle that serves one's own improvising and composing, with the mastery of traditional repertory a secondary goal. And where the conventional musicological focus is on the historical and structural aspects of music created by others, integral musicology primarily seeks to shed light on the cognitive, cultural, and transformational dimensions of contemporary creative practice. Musical traditions are broached as tributaries that flow into the musical ocean prior to being considered in isolation. Because these areas would be seen as organically connected to the creative process and creative development, conditions for meaning and assimilation might be significantly heightened if they were part of the expanded framework of the Integral Learning Environment. And again, ILE would absorb part of an area of study conventionally approached in isolation.

Here the need for minimizing the time undergraduate students spend in lecture formats cannot be overstated. It is not that there is no place for this learning modality, nor that colleagues who are quite brilliant at it do not exist. It is that its effectiveness for students who do not come to it with heightened receptivity based in hands-on, creative, integrative, and contemporaneous foundations is questionable. By resituating lecture and largely analytical classes from the core curriculum to among a slate of upper-structure electives that students may choose according to their interests and learning styles, and instead enlivening entryways to these knowledge areas through ILE, instructors may likely appreciate teaching the very same students who may have been falling asleep in their classes a year or two prior.

Ensemble is yet another area that could be integrated within the ILE framework. The aforementioned small Creative Music Ensemble, consisting of four to six members, in which students improvise, compose, arrange, and perform is a format that is arguably the most predominant in musical practice. It has been the central framework in jazz since the idiom's inception, with large ensembles playing a secondary, though not unimportant, role in the evolution of the music and clearly peripheral today, and of course has been predominant in all forms of popular music throughout history. Even contemporary chamber music groups in the classical world are moving in this direction. Why should this not be the central format in musical study? Predicated on the CICP profile, this ensemble provides a direct outlet for the totality of primary, secondary, and ancillary creativity to manifest in live performance. This is after all the reason why musicians invest the tremendous amounts of time and energy needed to gain requisite skills—to share these with the world through performance. In a single stroke, by situating this real-world ensemble format at the core, ILE not only provides a framework for diverse and integrative skill development but makes considerable strides in aligning the curriculum and culture of musical study with the actual musical landscape.

ILE will also give rise to a very new kind of ensemble experience, the large improvising ensemble that harnesses the collective dynamics of consciousness among players and listeners that results in extraordinary transformational experience for all involved. At Michigan I have designed one of the few such ensembles in existence and anticipate that this will be an important new wave in the coming integral era, when unprecedented numbers of the population will be engaged with meditation and spiritual development and will deeply resonate with improvisation-based musical art as among the vehicles for this in the arts. This format not only places demands on systematic improvisation skills of its members that are as, if not more, formidable than the small ensemble format, it also invites its members to be engaged with meditation practices that cultivate listening and sensitivity to enlivened individual and collective transcendence. Engagement in small ensembles, and the skill set of ILE, will thus directly inform and flow into the large ensemble experience, which represents a kind of localized manifestation of self-transcending tributaries that flow into the overarching musical ocean.

A wide range of other ensembles will also be part of the integral school of music, although conventional large and small groups—in which interpretive performance is central—will move from the center to a more peripheral status for the majority of students. Not only will rehearsal time be reduced but these groups will not be required of all or most music students as they are now, simply due to the sheer breadth of skills students will need to gain. This is not to suggest that the quality of these groups will necessarily suffer, nor that they will be confined to the interpretive performance focus. As more and more students are launched on the CICP pathway, thus bringing more advanced skills to these ensembles, these groups will be able to accomplish more in less rehearsal time. They will also be able to program more diverse repertory, which may be a factor in attracting students who otherwise might opt for other experiences, as well as bolster audiences.

New scheduling systems will come into play in the ensemble paradigm as music schools align performance experiences with the musical world while striving to also retain traditional excellence. One promising approach may be to have conventional ensembles sustain a reduced weekly rehearsal schedule and then undergo periods of more intensive work—say for three weeks at a time—during which the performance level can escalate.

ILE will also give rise to new conceptions of music teacher training. Conventional approaches are fundamentally flawed from an integral perspective due to the inherently narrow and fragmented model of musicianship (division of labor) that prevails, as well as the inevitable split between musicianship and pedagogical expertise. Even with the best of intentions, no amount of methods classes will compensate for the limited musical perception (the aforementioned creativity-diversity-critical inquiry crisis) inherent in the Interpretive Performance Specialist profile; today's musical world calls for an entirely new skill set and musical understanding. From an integral perspective, the answers to all questions pedagogical and the source of all teaching expertise resides in the music, not in techniques of teaching that are gained in teacher education classes. More particularly, the historically central Contemporary Improviser-Composer-Performer is the means by which core musical, and thus pedagogical, insights are gained. Now, this is in no way to suggest that there is no need for teacher training coursework. Rather, that aspiring music teachers need to be grounded in the CICP pathway in order for this coursework to prepare them for success in the emergent integral musical landscape of our times.

Were ILE to be offered as a six- to eight-credit class in the first two years, roughly half the credit load for students enrolled, students could then complement it with private instruction, other ensembles, and electives. The curricular upper structure, roughly the second two years, could then be comprised of further coursework in a variety of areas—including more advanced studies in theory, history, jazz, orchestration, counterpoint, meditation and consciousness studies, among others. The upper structure might even be generally divided into two approaches to many of these areas, the first being hybrid classes, followed by domain-specific approaches. For example, in the area of orchestration—a hybrid approach might juxtapose work of Ravel, Stravinsky, Ellington, and Gil Evans, which would connect nicely to domain-specific orchestration that focuses on specific traditions. Counterpoint or harmony could similarly begin with hybrid approaches that draw from both European and jazz approaches and then be followed by coursework that delves extensively into advanced practices within the respective lineages. In this way, a whole-to-parts flow that begins in the integral musicianship class and is further cultivated in ILE continues to manifest in the third and fourth years of study. This in no way is to stipulate that students would have to follow the hybrid-to-specialized approaches at the upper-structure level; upon completion of ILE they would have skills that would enable wide-ranging pathways that include proceeding directly to domain-specific advanced studies.

Finally, ILE opens up promising possibilities for collaborative teaching, which in turn will allow new organizational structures to emerge in schools of music. While the majority of faculty in an integral school of music will be Contemporary Improvisers-Composers-Performers, each colleague may still have one or more areas of particular expertise that complement those of their peers. Inasmuch as the ILE will involve an expanded class schedule, this suggests fertile ground for team-teaching by colleagues with complementary orientations. Consider, as one among many possibilities, an ILE that consists of 30 students and which meets 8 hours per week. This could easily justify team teaching by three colleagues who round out their loads with other teaching.

And from this kind of collaborative teaching new organizational structures could emerge. Instead of grouping faculty according to out-moded specializations, now they could be grouped according to creative and coteaching affinities. The sky may indeed be the limit when it comes to ways in which the ILE framework might be implemented.

Although it is likely not difficult to see how the Integral Learning Environment, were it to be established and effectively implemented, could vastly transform the kind of skill set and understanding that is possible in musical study, a point that may not be so evident cannot be emphasized strongly enough: Without a corresponding shift in the overall culture of musical academe, as well as in the identity of its participants, from the reigning Interpretive Performance Specialist to the Contemporary Improviser-Composer-Performer orientation, it will all be for naught. For as long as secondary creativity remains the guiding thrust, even if it occupies a far reduced percentage of overall musical engagement, the self-organizing and diverse properties of musical growth—arguably the most important goals of any viable educational model—will fail to blossom. Music students need to view their growth through the process-structure lens of the musical world they live in, not one that has long come and gone, if they are to be driven to gain the tools they need—as well as cultivate a genuine multiethnic musical embrace.

Let us now turn to how the integral musicianship vision might take hold in order that it may evolve and exert its transformational impact throughout the field and beyond. Key here is the merging of jazz and music education, the area of musical academe that concerns itself not with preparation of professional performers, for example, those who will join symphony orchestras and the like, but rather with training of school music teachers and research into music learning and teaching. While therefore often viewed as a peripheral figure in the aesthetic hierarchy of the field, I believe the music educator may be the individual capable of the greatest transformational impact on twenty-first-century culture. I therefore resonate deeply with Harold Best when he asserts that the "music education degree—not the performance degree, or any other kind of music degree—is the first among equals, if not the centrally important degree. Its candidates should be the most carefully selected, the most elegantly and comprehensively trained."[19] I believe the fulfillment of this vision will come when the preparation of the twenty-first-century music educator is grounded in the jazz-inspired, integral musicianship paradigm—where the self-transcending breadth and depth of the Contemporary Improviser-Composer-Performer profile enables a transmission of artistic, musical, and spiritual knowledge in a classroom that is scarcely imaginable from the current Interpretive Performance Specialist perspective. In order for this to manifest in teacher training curricula, Music Education and Jazz Studies must forge a union.

The Jazz/Music Education Nexus as Key to Integral Change

Music schools are typically divided into the primary areas of performance (with subdivisions according to instrument and function—e.g., strings, winds, brass, voice, piano, conducting), theory, history, and music education, with secondary areas including areas such jazz, music technology, world music, and popular music. Music education occupies a curious place within this scheme in that it falls fairly low within the aesthetic hierarchy, with music educators, as Nettl observes, "often seen as philistines who," in their efforts to prepare students for a more diverse musical world, "do not wish to teach [them] the best music and the highest values."[20] As a result, music education faculty often find themselves caught in a conundrum, where any aspirations they might entertain toward a new vision for the twenty-first-century music teacher are tempered by pressures from performance faculty who want to see music teachers that continue the pipeline that fuels interpretive performance specialization. That an ever-escalating wave of appeals for reform over the past half-century has been generated from music education ranks, or at least with the music teacher in mind, yet yielded minimal results, underscores this predicament and the stasis that has long prevailed in the field.

As chronicled by Terese Volk, these appeals have included symposia at Tanglewood, Yale, Wesleyan, and the University of Michigan, curricular recommendations articulated by organizations such as the National Association of Schools of Music, Music Educators National Conference, College Music Society, and International Society for Music Education, publications such as the *National Standards for Arts Education*, and curricular initiatives such as the Comprehensive Music Project (CMP) and Manhatanville Music Curriculum Program (MMCP), within the second of which I was an undergraduate music student.[21] Parallel events in Europe may also be noted, often under the guise of Rhythmic Music Education, a heading that reflects awareness of the pervasiveness of Afrological rhythmic practices in the musical world.[22] Regular conferences of the International Society for Music Education have often focused on ways to expand the horizons of music teacher training to better reflect the diverse horizons of the musical world.

Still, substantive reform remains elusive and I believe a Jazz/Music Education alliance could break the impasse. As we have seen, jazz embodies diversity and offers the aspiring music teacher unmatched tools for this kind of growth. This point, however, does not inform music education reform dialogues nearly as much as it might. It is not that jazz is excluded from these dialogues, but that it is relegated to the smorgasbord of genres that might be included in the expanded palette. As a result of which, a process-structure region—which happens to be called jazz—that inheres foundational properties is, even with newfound expressions of the need to break free from lingering discriminatory tendencies, still confined to the periphery.

A review of how integral and conventional conceptions of multicultural musicianship differ will shed light on the roots of this central problem and how it may be addressed.

Multicultural Musicianship: Conventional and
Integral Perspectives Revisited

Recall distinctions drawn in chapter 8 between the conventional view of multicultural musicianship as a horizontal expansion of the Interpretive Performance Specialist paradigm and the jazz-inspired vision of multicultural musicianship as inherent in the Contemporary Improviser Composer Performer profile. Any genuine multicultural synthesis is impossible without this grounding. Here is where use of the term itself invites superficial conceptions by suggesting this is something to be added to the existing paradigm when, in fact, it represents an intrinsic facet of musical artistry—providing that artistry is grounded in adequate process scope. I therefore concur with Barbara Lundquist's acknowledgment of the problematic nature of the term *multicultural* and use it, as she does, with caution. I also believe the integral perspective has important things to offer what she observes as a "multiplicity of perspectives and objectives observable in multicultural music education, the lack of clarity of its goals, and the differences among its adherents."[23] For example, when the enterprise is grounded in the CICP process expanse, the daunting exterior issue of the degree and kind of multicultural avenues that need to be represented in a learning environment finds its resolution internally. Every student will diversify in his or her own way, and the task of the educational institution is first to establish a process-rich environment—hence the CICP identity and its grounding in systematic improvisation studies (which integrates multiple approaches to improvisation, composition, performance, and various kinds of theoretical inquiry)—and then provide as great a variety of multicultural resources as possible. Multicultural musicianship, then, becomes not so much the amassing of skills in diverse musical sources as the establishment of an interior relationship with, and perception of, the broader musical world as a reservoir of tools for artistic individuation, or the evolution of the personal creative voice. Multicultural musical aspirations from an integral perspective are thus more aptly characterized as transcultural in that the practical and conceptual apprehension of today's music diversity is rooted in transcendence of surface boundaries. When this perspective of the musical world is enlivened through adequate process-breadth, no dearth of exterior resources will be severe enough to preclude students from finding what they need. And when, through inhibition of creativity, this inner thirst to diversify remains dormant, even the greatest excess of exterior resources will not cultivate a genuine multicultural/transcultural awareness.

Jazz, as the contemporary genre in which the CICP profile is most prevalent, is not only the embodiment of this essential aim, it is synonymous with the concept. Again, there is reason why the idiom has been termed the first world music. When, as is the case in much multicultural musicianship literature, jazz is listed as among the areas of the musical world that need to be integrated, or at least accessed, as students diversify, a principle central to the whole enterprise is being overlooked.[24] Embellishment of the Interpretive Performance Specialist profile is not only incapable of fulfilling multicultural/transcultural aspirations, it may even impede such efforts by reifying interpretive performance—which let us recall is secondary creativity—as the erroneous center, and the peripheral role of other musical sources that may be based in primary creativity. Advocacy that fails to acknowledge this key point—and I do not believe it is unreasonable to direct this charge at much of the literature on the topic—actually inhibits movement in this direction by confining it to a superficial maneuver that leaves the monocultural conceptual, curricular, and cultural foundations of the field intact. And therefore, when Terese Volk states that "music education," in response to the various exhortations for change she identifies, "moved quickly to incorporate all musics in the curriculum" in a commitment to serving "the needs of a pluralistic society," it is important to emphasize that she could be talking only about horizontal modification of the conventional model, not the vertical transformation of its foundations that is needed.[25]

One also senses that much of the commentary on multiculturalism is made not by practitioners who have invoked this internal shift themselves and invested in the extensive training in order for it to manifest in their music making, but rather by well-intentioned colleagues who, driven perhaps by a yearning for a social justice that has been inhibited in their Interpretive Performance Specialist upbringing, seek ways for music teachers to meaningfully impact an increasingly diverse student constituency whose cultural expressions are often marginalized. As music school faculty, including those in charge of teacher training, move from IPS to CICP backgrounds, this otherwise noble impetus for multicultural progress will become more grounded in the deep principles that underlie this all-important aspect of contemporary musical life.

Shifting the Orientation Internally and Externally

Here are several ways the Jazz/Music Education alliance could begin to rectify the situation. The first involves the stronger collective voice that would emerge and provide greater curricular autonomy. Though jazz degree programs, relatively new to musical academe, have tended to achieve a modicum of such autonomy, music education—due to the inertia of political, ideological, and hierarchical patterns—has very little, particularly at the core level.[26] Music schools remain riddled by a highly centralized approach to the core curriculum that, while flying directly in the face of much educational thought, allows for little creativity among faculty in its various areas, all of which have very different needs. Music education faculty, as much as they might like to fashion a core curriculum more relevant to their students needs, do not enjoy that latitude. In noting this, I do not necessarily mean to rule out the idea of a curricular core that might accommodate much or all these areas, and in fact, as I have been arguing, one based in the CICP skill set could serve this function admirably. But not only is the present core grounded in an outmoded musical conception, it is rigidly imposed upon most of the field. Since jazz studies has managed to circumvent this pattern, a Jazz/Music Education alliance might enable aspiring music teachers to similarly benefit, whereby they could be enhanced by the broadened skill set inherent in jazz, particularly when approached from an integral vantage point as jazz *writ large*. This might even catalyze a broader and more gradual exodus from the conventional core.

Unfortunately, jazz has not generally been approached integrally, as we saw in chapter 5, and thus while even its conventional skill set would significantly enhance the development of the music teacher, even greater benefits intrinsic to the art form remain to be gained. However, leading to a second benefit of the alliance, music education may help bring these out. Here it might be noted that music education has been a site for far more robust critical inquiry than has transpired in jazz education. Even with an ever-rising tide of jazz education materials and literature in recent decades, philosophical activity is scarce: this book, in fact, despite its broader aims, may be among the very first attempts at a philosophy for the field.[27] Music education, to the contrary, has been much more fertile ground for philosophical activity, even if it has not manifested in corresponding curricular and cultural reform. This could contribute greatly to the liberation from jazz education's prevailing modernist orientation and help illuminate the postmodern and even integral potentialities inherent in the jazz tradition.[28] It is not that music education has firmly established itself at these further evolutionary stages—the field may be reasonably characterized as straddling modernist and postmodern orientations—but that its critical inquiry tools could initiate a process whereby jazz studies penetrates more deeply into the nature of jazz itself, as a result of which the integral vision comes into view for both fields. Jazz education, for example, has been minimally receptive to and thus informed by the music and vision of the Association for Advancement of Creative Musicians (AACM), considered in previous chapters (5 and 9) to be among the closest embodiments of musical integralism in not only African American musical culture but the broader musical landscape.[29] The philosophical vitality of music education could help jazz education unearth this and other treasures within its own lineage.

The first stride in this symbiotic relationship might come in the expansion of jazz's inherent creative process spectrum to include trans-stylistic approaches to improvising and composing that enable transcendence (and inclusion) of style-specific boundaries. "Rock, classical, folk and jazz are all yesterday's titles," observed Ornette Coleman. "I believe that the music world is getting closer to a singular expression, one with endless musical stories of mankind."[30] This calls for a wider range of improvisatory approaches than prevails in conventional jazz education, and for which thinking in music education is highly conducive as exemplified in the work of Maud Hickey, Lenore Pogonowski, Bennett Reimer, Jackie Wiggins, and others. Here improvising and composing are construed from a trans-stylistic vantage point, which when integrated with the strong style-specific grounding of jazz, both of which are embodied in the integral musicianship framework, provides a formidable foundation to meet today's multicultural/transcultural needs.

At the same time, music education could benefit from this same confluence with jazz due to limitations in the (astructural) postmodernism that, while allowing liberation from modernist rigidity, would succumb to a rigidity of its own that, perhaps ironically, inhibits capacities for navigating the very contemporary kaleidoscope it celebrates. Here a key impediment is the postmodern "leveling" considered earlier, by which important topographies that are the source of key skills go unrecognized.[31] Important features of mainstream jazz, including its tonal and modal improvisatory parameters and Black Atlantic Rhythm, are among the topographies that are enormously important and fertile gateways to the broader musical world, yet do not gain the recognition they warrant in postmodern music education discourse. As noted earlier, it is not that this discourse in any way rejects these musical developments, but that it fails to see and argue for their foundational nature.

To understand the leveling problem more fully: As intimated before, most music education faculty, including many of those who most ardently endorse change, are products of the interpretive performance paradigm they seek to alter if not overthrow. It is thus understandable that in liberating from one oppressive musical regime, or what inspired by Nettl one might call "theocracy," colleagues are understandably loathe to fall prey to another.[32] As a result, a view of the musical world prevails as a spectrum of infinitely diverse and equally important music, devoid of contours. Reflecting an "egalitarian view of social justice," Bennett Reimer insightfully notes, "the arts need to be leveled" in order that notions of canon or any other "elitist device intended to raise one tradition, that of the ruling class and its culture, above all others" are circumvented. The musical postmodern idea that "there are many traditions in the arts, none of which is superior to others"[33] is remarkably similar to Ken Wilber's identification of a broader cultural "flatland" that is also endemic to postmodern thought.

As a result, jazz is considered as just another genre, one that falls early under the "Js" in the alphabet. Despite being unmatched in its integration of primary creative processes, robust rhythmic foundations, and other features central to the emergent global synthesis, jazz eludes consideration as a source of foundational skills. Because these practices and synthesis are foreign to the Interpretive Performance Specialist profile, postmodern leveling is inevitable among even the most ardent reform agents who come from this background. As category-bound as the model it seeks to overthrow, this orientation, despite its ostensibly egalitarian thrust, fails to penetrate deep into the process-structure scopes of various musical regions and instead remains caught up in the conventional compartmentalization that is the source of the long-standing curricular gridlock. That a particularly broad and deep process-structure region within the overarching twentieth- and twenty-first-century musical wholeness is called *jazz* is as relevant to contemporary musical practice and development as whether or not planetary temperature elevation is called *climate change* or *global warming*. What is relevant are the ecological and musical realities in question—which in music involves an unmatched creative process scope that is intimately united with rigorous methodologies for craft development and essential rhythmic foundations, all of which have come into being largely through African American experience, culture, and practice and which provide avenues that open up to a wider array of transcultural possibilities than ever before available.

The ramifications of this for musical studies reform parallels an argument I will develop further in the context of spiritual pluralism; as long as we ignore the important richly contoured topographies of the knowledge base, whether spiritual or musical, we allow the dictates of political correctness to impede a possibility whose benefits equal if not outweigh any risk otherwise averted—that of one or another area emerging as exemplary of unifying properties that may illuminate these in areas in which they might otherwise have remained hidden from view. And thus, where Phillip Goldberg has pointed out the uniquely ecumenical portrayal of nonduality in Hindu Vedanta as a catalyst for illuminating that foundation in other traditions, and in many cases helping practitioners in the West rediscover their spiritual heritage, postmodern sensibilities preclude this viewpoint.[34] I believe that a strong case may be made for jazz as playing the same role in the musical world.

A look at two important developments in the quest for reform in musical study will illustrate the limitations of postmodern leveling and how a jazz-inspired integral vision might rectify them. One is the Comprehensive Musicianship Project launched in the 1970s, which sought to broaden and integrate the various areas that comprise musicianship.[35]Another is the *National Standards for Arts Education*, which was published in 1994 and proscribes specific parameters of achievement in music, theater, dance, and visual arts for levels K–12. An integral analysis sheds light on why, despite these initiatives, the field remains as deeply entrenched in the conventional Interpretive Performance Specialist orientation as ever.

Comprehensive Musicianship and National Standards for Arts Education

Let us begin by recalling the previously considered protocol for an integral musicianship core, the design of which consists of two conceptual strategies. First is the stepping back from conventional stylistic and disciplinary categories and identifying what students need to know. Second is to then seek the best sources for this knowledge as measured by their creative, hands-on, integrative, and contemporaneous aspects. Both the Comprehensive Musicianship Project (CMP) and National Standards for Arts Education (NSAE) are driven by strong intentions exemplary of the first step, as indicated in their delineation of a broader skill set than conventional curricula provide or aim toward. However, when looked at through an integral jazz lens, important oversights are evident in how these initiatives approach both steps that I believe are reflective of postmodern leveling.

The lack of attention to rhythm, and particularly the all-important advent of Black Atlantic Rhythm, is immediately conspicuous. Limited recognition of the integrative properties of improvisation and composition is another. Although NSAE situates these primary creative processes among its nine skill areas for music, it fails to acknowledge their capacities to not only integrate other processes, but content as well. This is key to solving the challenge facing every field of an ever-expanding knowledge base. Among the thousands upon thousands of musical genres in the world, jazz—to reiterate once more a central theme in this chapter—is not only unmatched in its integration of improvisation and composition, it is also the primary source of Black Atlantic Rhythm. It also encompasses a wide swath of the musical world's pitchscape in its modal/tonal/post-tonal expanse, which too is integrated atop its improvisatory and compositional foundations. With this integrative, hands-on, creative, and contemporaneous foundation provided by jazz, connections to European classical music and its important resources, as well as those of many other lineages, could be harnessed to cultivate a truly broad kind of musical development that includes the best of the conventional spectrum and far more. That jazz's self-transcending capacities extend not only to the broader musical landscape but the overall, interdisciplinary knowledge base as well are also noteworthy as these directly address the final two of the nine standards. Unfortunately, an inbred aversion to recognizing the unique contributions of a given style has precluded mining the idiom for these important principles.

Among the facets of the integral protocol that is particularly helpful in this analysis is its whole-to-parts approach to the knowledge base. Here I frame the whole-to-parts concept not with meditation as the anchor but rather a smaller part of that continuum; the principle is nonetheless consistent with the broader conception. Stepping back from conventional categories, the approach first guides our fathoming of the knowledge base in terms of processes and structures—highly general areas. Then within the process realm, it directs us toward the primary (improvising and composing), secondary (performing), and ancillary (theorizing, historicizing) creative processes previously identified. Within the structure realm, it first directs us to pitch and rhythmic considerations, and then within each of these areas to constituent realms. It is difficult to imagine that something as prevalent as time feel or groove could be overlooked by the National Standards were this approach to be followed. Nor the integrative properties of the primary process components.

I would also add that the skill sequence listed within these parameters in the NSAE is weak in essential parts-to-whole properties, with little latitude given for exploratory creativity without preordained boundaries. Instead, students from early on are asked to improvise and compose within detailed constraints that are, in my view, often not only unrealistic to achieve but prohibitive to the developmental flow, which must always balance emulative and exploratory modalities, that is characteristic of improvisatory and compositional growth.

Thus, while it is important to emphasize that no single style source, or process-structure region, includes all of what today's students need, it is also important to recognize those whose process-structure richness open up connections to the broadest terrain. It is only logical to place these at the foundation. Jazz is uniquely equipped to provide foundational skills that could fulfill the aims of the Comprehensive Musicianship Project and National Standards for Arts Education. Were the CMP from its inception in the 1970s to have been formulated around jazz as self-transcending gateway, the vertical transformation of musical studies that has long been desperately needed might well have taken hold by the 1990s, at which point the NSAE might have taken radically different form. A jazz/music education alliance grounded in integral principles could shed light on these patterns and enable these important initiatives to blossom to their fullest extent.

Bennett Reimer and David Elliott as Important Integral Precursors

Another benefit of the jazz/music education alliance might be the illumination of a broader vision in which prevailing tensions are, if not completely reconciled, at least shown to be not as pronounced as often thought. The long-standing debates between two leading music education thinkers—David Elliott and Bennett Reimer—may be a primary example. Both have made important contributions that might be seen as preliminary integral strides and I believe recognition of this may help transform perceived conflicts into opportunities for progress.

We have already considered Reimer's critical identification of limiting postmodern patterns as important to conceptual groundwork conducive to the integral vision. Reimer is also a strong advocate of improvisation and composition and has intimated a more nuanced perspective than usually advanced that recognizes distinctions between the areas in order that their unique contributions may be more effectively understood and harnessed.[36] Reimer acknowledges spiritual dimensions of the creative process that are consistent with the integral vision, which include recognition of a kind of collective merging in group performance that is very much in line with the field aspect of consciousness discussed in previous chapters.[37] Although, as noted, interpretive performers do not merge with each other and audiences in the actual creation of musical ideas, which I term a primary intersubjective field effect, they are capable of enlivening a secondary field effect that exemplifies peak interpretive performance and the capacities for which will be enhanced when interpretive performers gain improvisatory grounding.

Elliott, advancing perhaps the most compelling argument for improvisation and composition prior to the present integral analysis, also lays important preliminary groundwork for an integral approach. Elliott makes three other important contributions in this regard. One is his recognition of Csikszentmihalyi's "flow" as an important measure of fulfillment, meaning, and creative engagement and expression, at which point music education discourse opens up to interior dimensions. While Elliott subscribes to a materialist view of consciousness in his earlier writing on this topic, a position that he may since have abandoned, the fact that he brings this transformational aspect of consciousness into the discourse is significant.[38] Second is his giving shape to the notion of rhythmic time feel, providing, as discussed in chapter 9, an important precursor to Pressing's notion of Black Atlantic Rhythm and other investigations of this structure, that is so pervasive in contemporary musical practice. While it is difficult to imagine a more important aspect of musicianship training, it remains anomalous to conventional curricula; theoretical investigation of the sort that Elliott initiates will play an important role in rectifying this problem. Third is that Elliott identifies a stage model of multicultural/transcultural development that moves from superficial, exterior appropriation toward a more substantive kind of assimilation that is consistent with the integral precept that multicultural musicianship is a natural outgrowth of being a musician in a diverse world.[39]

Perhaps ironically, however, Elliott, while arguing vigorously from an ostensibly postmodern vantage point, in two ways appears somewhat bound by modernist thinking. One is in his conception of creativity. Although he rightly positions creative application and engagement as central, his view of creativity as largely an object-mediated endeavor in my view is incomplete and thereby reduces the range of creativity-based educational strategies. By object-mediated, I refer to Elliott's emphasis that an action may be deemed creative only through the assessment of its concrete result: "It is the tangible outcome or product that has priority in determinations of creativity."[40] While certainly products of creativity enter into the equation, overshadowed in this thinking are both the intrinsic value of doing, regardless of tangible result, that is evident in Reimer's more process-oriented conception, and the interior, transformational dimensions of creative engagement. Creativity from an integral perspective is not just an exterior affair that can solely be measured accordingly, a perspective that reflects a partial parts-to-whole understanding; it is also an interior phenomenon that is rooted, as we have seen from a more complete parts-to-whole perspective, in the integration of personal self and transcendent Self. And when the phenomenon is viewed from a whole-to-parts perspective, even silent meditation practice and its experience of pure consciousness, devoid of all content save for awareness itself, can be regarded as a kind of creative activity.

More directly relevant to the integral framework for creativity development I have been delineating, the all-important need for stylistically open, creative exploration to complement style-specific creativity is also marginalized, if not rejected outright, in Elliott's object-mediated viewpoint. Margaret Barrett underscores this concern in her consideration of children's creativity: If "a competent or proficient level of musicianship is a prerequisite for creative endeavor" according to the model posited by Elliott (and significantly informed by Csikszentmihalyi's ideas on the topic), we run the risk of ignoring or devaluing the significant benefits of "children's musical play" that occurs "beyond the institutional boundaries of the classroom" and, one might reasonably presume in most instances to occur prior to any such levels of attainment.[41] I would add that richly exploratory "children's musical play" is an essential aspect of creative development at all stages of growth, and that a closer look at the musical landscape, as per Elliott's important axiom that musical study be grounded in musical practice, would reveal this key pedagogical facet to be evident in real world musical praxis. It is hopefully clear, however, how this broader view differs from notions of creativity as an "anything goes" affair, and here I concur with Elliott in his rejection of such notions in revealing creative development to, in fact, require rigorous study and practice. But an integral conception also sees the need for a robust exploratory component to complement this grounding. Therefore, whereas a modernist, object-mediated conception focuses on the emulative, and the postmodern champions the exploratory, the integral unites both as essential to creative development.

Further suggestive of a modernist orientation in Elliott's work is his sharp critique of Reimer's emphasis that music education be grounded in an aesthetic rationale. Inferring in Reimer's aesthetic vision an exclusively object-mediated (and thus work-centered or modernist) orientation, a possible overinterpretation that in itself may be subject to question, Elliott rails against the idea of "Music Education as Aesthetic Education" altogether in his argument for a "praxial" approach that is based in Small's notion of "musicking."[42] In other words, aesthetics for Elliott appears to be an inherently structural, object-mediated phenomenon, and hence his appeal for corresponding liberation thereof. But what about a postmodern aesthetics or an integral aesthetics that recognizes process as important an aesthetic pillar as object? Elliott's arguable confinement to a modernist conception hinders his capacity to recognize important openings to both in not only Reimer's work but his own.

Here a curious irony may be noted in their contrasting views of creativity and aesthetics, and the exchange that has resulted between them: Whereas Elliott's praxial approach implies a process-mediated aesthetics (even if he might eschew the term), his view of creativity tends to be more object-mediated. Whereas Reimer's aesthetic vision may be more object-mediated, his view of creativity is more process-mediated. Thus, where Elliott vigorously challenges Reimer's aesthetic orientation as neglecting the art process, Reimer suggests in response that Elliott overcompensates by replacing one extreme with another, thereby overemphasizing the art process. An integral reading of these debates expands the framework and enables us to step back and realize that both are talking about different angles of the same phenomenon. Clearly, both value both process and object/structure dimensions as important and thus their perspectives may be seen as not in fundamental conflict but as driven by the need to highlight facets that may not receive the attention they warrant. I might add that in terms of the integral point that change needs to involve not only enormous shifts in curricular models, organizational structures, but also individual and cultural identity—hence the IPS orientation opening up to the CICP—Reimer and Elliott exhibit a fuller grasp of this than the majority of reform advocates. In essence, recalling our analysis of integral evolutionary dynamics in chapter 4, Elliott's and Reimer's ideas need not be seen as *dissociative* in relationship to each other but as a more evolutionary *differentiation* within a broader, inclusive wholeness that is blossoming in the field.

Furthermore, an integral perspective reveals the need for artificial divisions, resulting in part from category-bound thinking, to be transcended: Creativity and aesthetics are not separate realms. One cannot simultaneously posit, as Reimer's position might be reasonably characterized, process-mediated creativity and object-mediated aesthetics, nor, as Elliott's might be, object-mediated creativity and process-mediated aesthetics. An integral understanding reminds us that creativity and aesthetics, as well as diversity, critical inquiry, spirituality, and the host of other phenomena intrinsic to the arts, are inextricably linked aspects of an unbroken wholeness.

Both Elliott and Reimer are nonetheless to be applauded as important integral precursors in a field that is positioned, but does not always live up to the corresponding responsibility, to play an enormously important role in not only the transformation of musical study but education at large. An alliance between jazz education and music education would help illuminate their advocacy for the return of the primary creative processes of improvisation and composition to their rightful central status as important to the formulation of an integral music education, and thus overall musical studies vision. It would be but a relatively small step, at least conceptually, to complement this parts-to-whole thrust with a whole-to-parts meditation based trajectory. At which point, the stage would be set for a more full-blown integral musicianship paradigm in which the broader dimensions unique to jazz would have the opportunity to blossom. Whereas jazz education and music education, particularly when broached separately, occupy lower rungs of the aesthetic hierarchy of musical study, when uniting and emerging as a powerful voice and source of vision for the future, they may not only begin to catalyze change in musical academe but could establish a site for conversations important to change in education at large.

Breaking the Impasse

The need for a new discourse in the field, even among those who may be identified as "change agents," cannot be overstated. In order to underscore this need, I would like to address an issue that is, at once, the most provocative, challenging, and potentially divisive in the field, yet at the same time absolutely crucial to the kind of change needed and which may, in fact, provide a kind of wake-up call to the field. I am talking about race, the complexities of which may be unmatched in music and musical study given the inextricable link between music, ethnicity, and culture. Nor are the opportunities for progress in this area so profoundly evident as in music.

Karlton Hester sets the stage for this exploration:

> Race has always mattered in America and the consequences of racism are far reaching. Racism has always affected the way many Americans think and feel about certain music. Bigotry has limited the growth and development of music in America. How much greater contribution could African American musicians such as Louis Armstrong, Duke Ellington, Art Tatum, Charlie Parker, Charles Mingus, John Coltrane, and countless other innovators have made in their musical quests with institutional support and respect equivalent to that given the composers of European dodecaphonic music? What would the range of possibilities for rap music be if the music and creative arts programs had not been abducted from inner city school programs? Had "jazz" remained a function of the African American community, how might the music have affected the development of knowledge, self-esteem, and creative imaginations of young people who are now desperately seeking positive African American role models?[43]

When we consider the ramifications of these words for musical studies in higher education, which by any account can only be assessed as extraordinary, what is arguably the most difficult and important question to be confronted in this field, one that appears rarely if ever articulated head on, becomes inevitable.

Is musical academe racist?

In order to respond to this question, I would like to propose distinctions between "racism" and "ethnocentrism" in hopes of a more nuanced, and perhaps slightly less charged (were that even possible), discussion of this topic. Ethnocentrism entails conditioned, unexamined thinking and behavior that privilege the perspectives and practices of a given ethnic or cultural orientation with limited or no awareness of how it excludes or marginalizes other racial, ethnic, or cultural orientations. Racism is the conscious privileging of a given racial, ethnic, or cultural orientation with at least some modicum of awareness of how it excludes or marginalizes other racial, ethnic, or cultural orientations. Therefore, to return to the exnomination tendencies rampant in the field as but one among many possible examples, the use of the headings "Art Music" or "New Music," while one is not consciously aware of the extent to which they exclude while appearing to include, is an ethnocentric behavior. It is inherited from a system that has long been immune to self-critical inquiry and all but the most astute individuals within interpretive performance ranks or related research areas will not think twice about using these headings to refer to particular areas of practice even if they may be sympathetic to broader musical horizons. One will even hear these ethnocentric headings invoked among vocal advocates for reform.

At what point might ethnocentrism take the next step and become racist? When one is alerted to the hidden discriminatory nature of this language yet continues its use. More overt examples of racism by now have already been discussed, even if that term had not been used, and need not be inventoried further. The main principle is that where there is ethnocentrism there is the possibility for racism, and musical academe clearly exhibits both. Even the organizational structures of music schools might be cited as an example of these tendencies, where most all areas within European classical music are labeled according to instrument (e.g., strings, winds) or process (conducting, theory), yet jazz—which utilizes all instruments used in European classical music (even if a few are less common in jazz) and ironically is the most process-rich of all areas—is labeled according to its genre. What is the effect of this? In being designated as "jazz," not only are the idiom's unique musical attributes obscured in yet another example of the previously considered leveling, but the genre is also stigmatized as something "foreign" to the presumed, yet unlabeled, European classical norm. In not labeling the European focus, its unquestioned centrality is reinforced, particularly to the susceptible student who has little reason to suspect that such tendencies are the result of anything but the best of intentions. The division in musicology between "historical musicology"—the emphasis of which is on European classical music—and "ethnomusicology" is another example of the same impetus to separate from the "pure, native species" the "invasive species" that may threaten its integrity (but in fact can elevate it if dynamics of artistic evolution were properly understood).

Few custodians of the conventional musicianship paradigm will deny or decry the phenomenon of racism in American history, past and present. But when it comes to the possibility that the musical model that they have inherited and perpetuate may contribute to that deplorable behavior, most are largely oblivious, and may likely reject any such insinuation vehemently. Though everyone will decide for themselves where they individually might fall, if at all, on the preceding ethnocentrism-racism continuum, I do not believe there is any question that the field at large encompasses its full range. Among the ironic aspects of the situation is that most every college or university regularly issues strong proclamations of commitment to diversity, and that while music is a field uniquely equipped to play a leadership role in these efforts, musical academe arguably lags behind most other fields when it comes to this important principle. It is difficult to imagine another field of academic study that is more monocultural in its orientation. (Again, relegating various kinds of non-European music to the fringes is not to be confused with genuine diversification.) I therefore view the present moment as both one of great urgency in addressing a pressing issue and also one of great opportunity. For the ethnopathological roots of racism are inextricably linked to the other three pathologies, and a full-scale commitment to addressing the racism issue—and it cannot be overemphasized that nothing less than an integral, multitiered approach will suffice—could therefore address the entire spectrum and catalyze an unprecedented transformation in the field.

An important site where this new thinking and dialogue needs to take place is the curriculum committee.

Integral Music Curriculum Committee and
Diversity-driven Discourse

The first task of the curriculum committee that sets its sight on diversity is to clarify the concept. From an integral standpoint, diversity is construed broadly, including not only the all-important racial, ethnic, cultural, and gender-based demographic criteria that generally dominate diversity discourse, but also the equally important diverse epistemologies or ways of knowing and experiencing, including spiritual practice and perspectives, individuals of varied backgrounds bring to a learning environment. To welcome individuals of diverse racial-ethnic-cultural-gender backgrounds but to exclude their forms of knowledge and creative expression represents a notably superficial approach to this important issue. The next step is to identify the musical manifestation of exemplary diversity, which is the jazz-inspired Contemporary Improviser-Composer-Performer profile. As a powerful vehicle for creativity to open to consciousness, integrating diverse ethnic, racial, cultural, and other influences along the way, the CICP template embodies the highest ideals of diversity in music. And inasmuch as a diagnostic function must always complement delineative inquiry when paradigmatic change is at stake, diversity-driven musical discourse must also illuminate the Interpretive Performance Specialist model as the antithesis of this goal.

By now, the primary differences between the models have been well examined, with a concise overview clearly underscoring their connections to the diversity theme. Whereas the CICP vision is multicultural and transcultural, the IPS is monocultural and often resistant to broader influences. Whereas the CICP framework is creatively rich, comprehensive, and integrative, the IPS is creatively deficient, specialized, and fragmented even within that specialized orientation (e.g., by narrowing the scope to only secondary and ancillary engagement and then fragmenting that engagement). Whereas the CICP approach is contemporaneous, which is inherently conducive to diversity, the IPS is past-based, which is not.

Diversity-driven discourse might illuminate further distinctions that may not be so immediately evident. Whereas the CICP approach cultivates self-sufficiency through its varied, integrative, and creative modes of engagement, the IPS breeds dependency upon exterior, institutional resources. Here the intimate relationship between exploratory creativity and rigorous emulative studies embodied in jazz is key, rendering aspiring CICPs less dependent upon teachers and more capable of devising their own studies, and sustaining rigorous self-driven practice regimes, to attain the needed skills—which then allows them to gain more of the all-important knowledge that can only come from teachers/mentors and other exterior resources. And just as creatively and epistemologically diverse models promote greater self-sufficiency than their opposites, they also promote the enlivenment of intrinsic pedagogical instincts and aptitudes. Conventional models of teacher education, lacking this artistic breadth, tend to be highly dependent upon methods classes in attempts to deliver necessary teaching skills; a CICP foundation would enable entirely new kinds of teacher formation strategies to emerge that harnesses the inherent pedagogical potential in contemporary creative artistry. For this reason, the aspiring music teacher must gain as extensive a grounding in the CICP skill set and vision as those students who aim to pursue careers not as teachers but as professional, practicing artists.

Although most curriculum committee members in the early stages of the transformation process will not be CICPs, it will be important that they attempt to view the musical landscape through that lens. Deliberations driven by the diversity imperative will assist them in committing to the deep work that this requires. By deep work, I am talking about intensive introspection into the roots of the conventional musical worldview and its many manifestations. Committee members will need to closely examine their use of language and how exnomination practices— for example, the use of phrases such as Art Music and New Music that are inclusive in theory but exclusive in practice—reinforce conventional patterns that preclude diverse embrace. They will need to recognize that conventional organizational structures (e.g., separate departments of theory, history, performance) are directly configured according to the division of labor in European classical music and thus serve as diversity-resistant pillars at the heart of the model. It will also be important that curriculum committee members recognize the extent to which worldviews are physically embodied and that change needs to occur on this level as well. My experience has been that many musicians who are grounded only in European classical music have great difficulty internalizing and authentically executing African American stylistic nuances, while musicians who come up through African American traditions, particularly jazz, more readily excel with European nuance. This is likely due to the greater creative diversity inherent in jazz as well as its grounding in Black Atlantic Rhythm, the origins of which are deeply tied to drumming and dance. This points to yet another reason why jazz needs to occupy a central place in the curriculum for all music students.

The inset passage provides an inventory of prominent features of integral, CICP-based musical study that are particularly challenging even to ardent advocates of reform who are products of IPS backgrounds. This will help in centering key issues and also underscoring the need for personal transformative work if collective change is to occur. It will be particularly helpful for collective reflection on this inventory to be undertaken by the committee.

Musical paradigm blindness: Among the biggest challenges to the Interpretive Performance Specialist musical worldview posed by the integral musicianship paradigm and its Contemporary Improviser-Composer-Performer foundations include:

- The idea of alternative musical worldviews (to one's own) in general, and specifically those not grounded in composed-notated works but in other structures (e.g., Black Atlantic Rhythm) and processes (improvisation) as the basis for meaning, expression, transcendence, and transformation.

- The idea of styles as self-transcending entryways to a broader musical wholeness, which can only be accessed through process breadth, rather than self-confining destinations. That the central aesthetic pulse of the musical world lies in the confluence of genres rather than genres as discrete style compartments.

- The centrality of black music in American culture and its fundamental gateway properties vis-à-vis the broader musical landscape; the idea that musical training grounded in black music, with jazz at the center, could enable equal or even greater skills and understanding in European classical music for those inclined than generally attained in the conventional model.

- The possibility of contacting basic musical elements in fluid and diverse forms (only possible through improvisation and composition) as a basis not only for the evolution of a distinctly personal voice, but also unique kinds of musical understanding.

- The idea that genuine integration of musical disciplines—such as performance, theory, and history—that are ordinarily approached separately is not possible without improvisation at the foundation. Comprehensive Musicianship requires improvisation at the core of the curriculum and cultural identity.

- The difference between cursory engagement with improvisation and composition, as embellishments of the Interpretive Performance identity, and the establishment of a Contemporary Improviser-Composer-Performer identity in which these primary creative processes are central, thus providing a vastly different and broader lens through which one perceives the musical world and the world at large.

- The degree of self-sufficiency possible in the CICP profile, and the degree of exterior, institutional dependence inherent in the conventional IPS paradigm.

- Black Atlantic Rhythm as a preeminent American musical phenomenon that is of equal, if not greater prominence, in American and global musical culture as musical compositions.

- Jazz's structural richness (the idiom's process breadth is easily grasped even if often eluding attention).

- How a process-weak framework (e.g., interpretive performance specialization) may promote ethnocentrism and a musical fundamentalism similar to religious fundamentalism;

> how transcendent experience in such frameworks may, furthermore, reify such tendencies.

- Why critical inquiry faculties are inevitably compromised in the interpretive specialist paradigm.

- How arts advocacy initiatives centered in interpretive performance specialization may undermine arts awareness in overall population and thus exacerbate marginalization of the arts.

- How decentralization of European classical music in the curriculum and broadening of the skill set might actually enhance the vitality, sustainability, and even skill level in this very tradition.

- Why decentralization of European classical music need not be construed as a devaluation of that tradition.

- The idea of a model of musicology whose primarily aim is to illuminate the creative, diverse, and transformational dimensions of contemporary creative artistry rather than music created by others, at other times and places.

- The idea of private instruction whose primary aim is to cultivate skills that serve a musician's improvisatory and compositional activity rather than mastery of music created by others, at other times and places.

Curriculum committee dialogue rooted in the diversity imperative would also transform the nature of the committee's purpose and its members' obligations. Conventional curriculum committees tend to be passive, confined to activities such as vetting proposals for new classes and degree programs, and acting on student petitions to substitute courses outside of curricular requirements for those that are included in it. In my 25-years-plus of serving on such committees, and consulting with them at a variety of institutions, rarely have I seen such deliberations informed by significant conversance with literature on learning and teaching. As a result, an unspoken assumption prevails that the conventional model is essentially sound—that it is grounded in careful consideration of pedagogical principles, is continually monitored in light of its relevance to the overarching musical landscape, this monitoring exemplifies vigorous critical inquiry that is uniquely possible in the academic environment and places the best interests of students as the highest priority. Accordingly, any deviations from the model set in place must be subject to the highest degree of scrutiny.

The fact is, the conventional curricular model and corresponding curricular deliberations are weakly grounded in pedagogical principle, severely distanced from contemporary musical practice, reflect a minimal degree of critical inquiry about both the viability of the framework or the discourse itself, and tend to be driven more by the self-interests of departments than student needs. A curriculum in the arts that inhibits creativity, undermines self-sufficiency, promotes ethnocentrism and racism, and reifies an aesthetic-spiritual exclusivity that is rooted in inner mechanics notably similar to religious fundamentalism can hardly be seen to serve the best interests of students. If the finely honed peer review framework that upholds at least a modicum of critical scrutiny in academic research were to be applied to curricular discourse, I do not believe the conventional music curriculum would withstand this process. Indeed, it is even difficult to imagine what a peer-reviewed, or peer-reviewable, endorsement of the conventional curriculum might look like.

A diversity-driven curriculum dialogue that is informed by an integral vision will also help colleagues place the current paradigm in an evolutionary perspective that helps celebrate its positive aspects. The basic principle is that the very evolutionary thrust toward differentiated wholeness that catalyzes movement in the CICP direction is that which not only gave rise to the extraordinary European classical repertory in the first place, but also the IPS profile that has engulfed the system. It is just that the IPS profile is the result of differentiation taking the extreme step of dissociation. But to rectify this does not mean jettisoning the interpretive performance line, rather the situating of it in a larger context. The shift in change discourse from horizontal modification of the creativity-deficient, self-confining IPS model to the creativity-rich, self-transcending CICP paradigm is thus one of the most pressing issues in the field.

I believe it is evident that diversity-driven discourse, particularly when undertaken from an integral perspective, has the capacity to connect with virtually every area and concern of musical academe. Here it is important to recognize that any of the four pathologies might serve as a catalyst for curricular discourse that intersects with the other three; a commitment to rectifying the creativity crisis, for example, would directly connect with ethnopathological, theopathological, and ecopathological challenges and illuminate ways these could be rectified. Again, where there is pathology there is also potential for paradigmatic change. Given the fact that most every college and university issues regular proclamations of commitment to diversity, combined with the inherent potential in music to assume leadership in this area, despite the diversity crisis in musical academe, the prospects for this particular theme to catalyze a discourse that leads to unprecedented change are promising indeed. I believe, moreover, that it is only a matter of time before higher administrative leadership that is truly committed to diversity, upon realizing that a unit on their campus with unique transformational potential in this area not only fails to realize that potential but arguably impedes diversity progress, intercedes in order to help the field break the impasse.

Finally, a diversity-driven curricular conversation rooted in integral principles will invite colleagues to step back from the field of music and contemplate the biggest questions about not only the purpose of education, but the nature and purpose of the human being and relationship to the cosmic wholeness. At which point, the significance and urgency of fundamentally reforming the conventional paradigm in musical studies will likely become even more apparent. For music is a region within the arts that is unmatched in its creative vitality, its capacity to touch deeply and unite individuals and communities across the globe, its conductivity to spiritual practice, and—when perceived through a nondual, integral lens—its direct embodiment of the primordial vibrations that emanate from cosmic intelligence as it engages in the *lila*, or improvisatory play, that gives rise to the infinite diversity of creation. Diversity-driven curricular discourse that is integrally informed would reveal the potential to align musical study in this vision, for which jazz is uniquely equipped as a Western gateway, and usher in a transformation that could send ripples throughout the educational world and society. Though conventional musical study tends to be severed from important dialogues about education and the world around us, an integral approach to the field could become a site where cutting-edge discourse about the nature of human creativity and consciousness, its relationship to the challenges of our times, and ways it may be cultivated transpire on a regular basis. From a field that, like overall education and society at large, lacks a compelling vision for sustainability and growth, a profound template might emerge that fills this lack on a cross-disciplinary scale.

A look at the issue of paradigmatic change in the broader academy will shed light on how overarching receptivity to the contributions of a jazz-inspired integral revolution in music might be fostered.

Chapter 11

Paradigmatic Change and the
Twenty-first-century Academy

It is easier to move a cemetery than change a curriculum.

—Woodrow Wilson[1]

Anyone who has spent much time on a curriculum committee knows all too well the truth in Wilson's remark. And if the jazz-driven integral transformation of musical study is to catalyze similar reform in education at large, curricular models will not only need to undergo change but the entire educational enterprise must be overhauled from the ground level on up. The enormity of this task cannot be underestimated when considering that, paralleling tendencies in music, there has been no dearth of appeals for reform in the academy at large, yet, as former Harvard president Lawrence Summers observes, "education changes remarkably little over time."[2] This assessment echoes the sentiments of a growing number of reform advocates, and as apt as it may be from the standpoint of horizontal change, it is all the more so when it comes to the vertical change that will characterize the integral educational revolution. Whereas horizontal change involves expansion or modification of the prevailing third-person, objective orientation, with perhaps some movement into second-person approaches, vertical reform involves the integration of these atop the first-person foundations of consciousness. At this point, the interior-exterior divide that has long confined the learning and teaching enterprise to but a tiny slice of what it could and needs to be will be bridged.

Why the abiding stasis, or what Robert Zemsky describes as an educational "logjam"?[3] While there is no denying the political, economic, ideological, and cultural factors that contribute to the long-standing inertia, I believe two equally significant obstacles may be identified. One is the lack of a compelling vision or template that might guide the field from its current moorings in a new direction. Second is the lack of an adequate conversation within individual institutions and the field at large that would, as it were, enliven critical awareness of the educational enterprise, its enormous importance in a world beset with challenges, and thus not only receptivity to but a commitment to finding alternatives—a conversation that, in other words, would transform a culture of stasis to one of change. In order to "break the logjam," not only will "a kind of dislodging event (or set of events),"[4] as Zemsky puts it, be necessary; it will also be necessary to articulate a compelling vision for the future and identify the patterns and premises of the prevailing approach through penetrating thinking and discourse.

This chapter explores the delineative and diagnostic capacities of the jazz-inspired integral vision as a catalyst for institutional change. It begins by exploring striking parallels between challenges in advocating improvisation in music and meditation in education at large. That improvisation and meditation alike were central in earlier eras within their respective knowledge domains (music and intellectual life), yet both are conventionally marginalized and treated as anomalous, underscores the extent to which education has deviated from the very traditions to which it pays homage.

We then continue our examination of meditation-improvisation parallels from what might seem to be an unlikely perspective—that of the emergent contemplative/consciousness studies movement in higher education. While the integration of meditation in college and university classrooms is the driving force for this movement, which we will examine in terms of four stages, salient principles apply to the integration of improvisation in jazz's journey in the academy. In the first, modernist stage, meditation is relegated to extracurricular status, just as was improvisation in the time prior to formal jazz education. A subsequent postmodern stage sees the beginnings of integration of meditation in scattered coursework. An "early integral" stage sees the design of curricular models, such as the BFA in Jazz and Contemplative Studies at the University of Michigan, that provide students more extensive grounding in meditation practice. Here improvisation and meditation come together, laying groundwork for a subsequent "late integral" stage involving designing the entire educational edifice around the parts-to-whole/whole-to-parts interaction and corresponding all-quadrants creativity and consciousness development.

Next, and perhaps the most important aspect of the chapter, is a framework for catalyzing entirely new dialogue and thinking about the educational enterprise that I call Deep Inquiry. Here a sequence of guiding questions directs attention from modernist to postmodern and then integral educational visions, laying conceptual groundwork on individual and collective scales for practical strategies.

The chapter closes with a look at the variety of ways the fruits of the new conversation and thinking may be harvested. These include utilizing existing themes such as diversity, interdisciplinary learning, creativity/innovation, arts advocacy, athletics, and sustainability as integral entryways, establishment of an integral education pilot program, and creation of a national consortium to galvanize integral reform activity into a collective voice. Here is where an astute administration has the opportunity to assume an unprecedented kind of leadership and contribute to the paradigmatic educational, and in turn, societal change called for in our times.

Tales of Two Epistemologies:
Meditation and Improvisation (Re)enter the Academy

If, as already seen, the incorporation of second-person improvisation practice in musical study has met with resistance, one can only imagine the challenges involved in introducing first-person meditation practices within the largely third-person orientation of the broader academy. At least improvisation, even if more challenging to evaluate than notated composition, can be assessed through some semblance of conventional protocols since it involves the production and organization of sound. Meditation takes place in silence and is far more elusive when it comes to both integration and assessment in college and university classrooms. We will shortly see that this hurdle can be fairly easily overcome, however. More important to the discussion at the moment is that both improvisation and meditation represent expansion of the epistemological spectrum, which from the third-person, object-mediated orientation of the conventional academy means significant obstacles will be encountered.

This point is underscored by the fact that both epistemologies were central to past eras in their respective knowledge systems yet are still approached as "foreign invaders." It is common knowledge that Bach, Handel, Beethoven, Mozart, and most of the great icons in the European classical tradition were, like their contemporary counterparts in jazz, improvisers as well as composers and performers. Were curricular dialogues in musical academe grounded in this fact, it is difficult to imagine that this process scope would remain so elusive in the field. Less well known is a parallel kind of epistemological contradiction, where as the philosopher Pierre Hadot has elucidated, the systems of rational, logical thought and analysis that are attributed largely to ancient Greek and Roman schools of philosophy, and which the academic world regards as its roots, are but part of an exploratory scope whereby thinkers utilized contemplative methodologies to transcend the realm of ordinary mental functioning and penetrated to more silent and subtle intuitive ways of knowing. Showing that "a profound difference exists between the representations which the ancients made of *philosophia* and the representation which is usually made of philosophy today," Hadot illuminates the dietary, discursive, meditative, and contemplative practices among the ancients that were "intended to effect a modification and transformation in the subject who practiced them."[5] Thus, while there is "no denying the extraordinary ability of the ancient philosophers to develop theoretical reflection on the most subtle problems of the theory of knowledge, logic, or physics," it is also important to recognize interior, first-person engagement that complemented this third-person exterior inquiry.[6]

Just as the art objects that comprise the European musical canon originated in a robust creative thrust in which improvisation, now marginalized, was central, the objective approaches to knowing that predominate the academy originated in a much broader epistemological scope in which contemplative experience, similarly marginalized, was central. While on one hand these parallels might be perceived pessimistically as further indications of the intractability of the current educational paradigm, an integral analysis may provide reason for a more sanguine outlook: Not only does advocacy of these epistemologies entail a return to past roots, it involves one in which these practices may be approached in more differentiated and evolved ways that do not conflict with prevailing third-person learning, but in fact may enhance both it and the contemplative (and improvisatory) methodologies alike.

The first point—that contemplative education can enhance conventional educational aspirations, or improvisation can enhance conventional musical aspirations—is not nearly as radical as the second, that the integration of contemplative and improvisatory practices into the academy may enable a kind of evolution in these epistemological traditions to transpire that might not otherwise be possible. If anything, the opposite concern might seem the more obvious problem, and one that has eluded the gaze of neither contemplative nor jazz educators—that the extrication of meditation practices and jazz from their traditional contexts, and subsequent introduction into an academic climate that is notoriously devoid of spiritual and artistic vitality, might compromise the integrity of these practices. A common criticism of conventional jazz education is that, while students at many schools develop high degrees of competency, their playing lacks feeling and authenticity—or as Hal Galper has put it, "players that are more theoretically proficient than expressive." With the demise of jazz clubs, jazz sessions, and the kind of grounding in not only the musical but cultural dimensions of the music that could happen in the "university of the streets," important compromises have thus resulted in academic jazz studies. "By embracing neo-European classical methodology," Galper continues with an emphasis on the cultural, "a true, historically valid jazz methodology based on African oral teaching concepts has never developed."[7] Although contemporary contemplative education has not been in place nearly as long as jazz education, at least in anything resembling the codified format of the latter, the parallels between removing meditation from the context of ashrams, monasteries, or even local meditation centers, and jazz from its traditional settings are quite evident.

While there is no denying the validity of these concerns, I believe the solution is not to retreat from the academic integration of contemplative and improvisatory practices but rather to follow a twofold path: First is to render academic practice more authentic via retaining ties to contemplative and improvisatory traditions, and second is to harness the analytic, cross-traditional, and critical faculties of the academy so that tradition-specific and trans-traditional spiritual and artistic engagement may coexist and coevolve.

Having broached this issue previously in the context of music and evolution of musical academe, let us now examine it through the lens of the contemplative studies movement. In so doing, we gain a more complete grasp of the manner in which systematic meditation provides a whole-to-parts template for the academic landscape of the future, and how the improvisation-driven parts-to-whole thrust complements that growth.

Four Stages of Contemplative/Consciousness Studies

The integration of meditation and related practices and studies into the educational world represents what is arguably among the most radical innovations of our times and can be seen in terms of four stages.

In what might be called the "precurricular" or modernist stage, contemplative activity occurs outside of college and university classrooms in formats such as religious clubs and prayer and meditation groups. This stage correlates fairly readily with the modernist stage of sociocultural evolution, with interior engagement largely a tradition-specific endeavor (e.g., campus religious meetings) that, reflective of the centrality of the first-person/third-person split, is kept far apart from classroom practice. We need not be distracted here by questions regarding distinctions and/ or common ground between religious and contemplative practice (e.g.: Do meetings of campus religious groups that solely involve discussion and social activities constitute contemplative practice?). Most important is that anything that might broach the contemplative dimension was generally relegated to an extracurricular status. The exterior-interior divide is thus kept intact.

Interesting parallels might be cited with jazz's early incursions into musical academe, where, as considered in chapter 5, the music was often banned from not only the curriculum but even from being played in the music buildings where these curriculums were housed. Music students often had to resort to after-hours jam sessions after the faculty had gone home.

The beginning of the "early curricular" or postmodern stage of contemplative or consciousness studies might arguably be correlated with the Contemplative Practice Fellowship Program of the American Council of Learned Societies. Launched in 1997, this initiative involved the incorporation of meditation and related practices and studies in credit-bearing academic coursework.[8] It is not that integration of contemplative practices in coursework was entirely absent prior to this time (I had been involved in this integration for at least a decade), but that the ACLS initiative, and subsequent formation of the Association for Contemplative Mind in Higher Education, galvanized those already engaged in this work into a collective voice, and also provided resources to help those interested to get started in this area. In this stage, most of this work has been generally confined to isolated pockets—in other words, single, elective courses— rather than course clusters or programs, although some movement in the latter realm has begun to take hold.[9]

Several features may be noted that define postmodern contemplative education. First is the tendency to extricate practice from its traditional settings, an approach that was likely inevitable given the complex nature of the integration of this work in an academic world not keenly receptive to such. If anything broaching spirituality, religion, or mysticism has long been considered taboo, relinquishing of any such associations was not only wise but likely essential. Second is the recognition of a broad swath of practices that are identified as contemplative with little attempts to differentiate them in terms of types, effectiveness, and results. While this approach has positive aspects in its pluralism and inclusiveness, it also has limitations in inviting a kind of "anything goes" sensibility. Third is the emphasis on the use of contemplative practices as tools for stress-reduction and cognitive sharpening, while their potential as vehicles for spiritual and transformative growth remains subordinate. These concerns aside, the importance of this first wave of entry into the academic curricular landscape cannot be overstated.

It is interesting to note that whereas meditation and contemplative studies entered the curricular stream through a postmodern orientation that is consistent with the overarching postmodernism of the academy at large, jazz's entrance into the curricular stream, many years before the ACLS project, retained its modernist leanings. In other words, improvisation was largely confined to style-specific frameworks and exploration of trans-stylistic possibilities was minimal. This was undoubtedly shaped by the overarching modernism of musical academe. However, jazz's confluence of improvisatory and meditative practices renders it an ideal vehicle for movement in an integral direction. This is the principle behind my design of what appears to be the first curriculum at a mainstream institution to significantly incorporate contemplative practice—the BFAJCS degree program at the University of Michigan—indicative of movement to a third phase of contemplative/consciousness studies education, which I think of as "early integral." Students in the BFAJCS program take twenty to twenty-five credits of contemplative-oriented coursework, involving practice and theory, in addition to a full slate of jazz and overall musical studies. The curriculum thus uniquely spans the first-second-third-person realms that are central to the integral worldview. The model is characterized as "early integral" primarily because in a fully integral model, all coursework will be grounded in integral principles, where in the BFAJCS track, consistent with the patterns at most mainstream institutions where students majoring in a given area take coursework throughout the institution, only a portion of the curriculum is so grounded.[10]

Nonetheless, aspects of the curriculum embody important principles that will be central to a full integral approach and it is thus useful to view the fourth stage of contemplative/consciousness studies through this lens. Key here are the systematic approaches to improvisation and meditation at the heart of the BFAJCS track, as a result of which a number of the aforementioned concerns, corresponding to each process line, are addressed. Improvisation, confined to style-specific approaches in the prior stage, is now approached in both style-specific and trans-stylistic frameworks, as are the host of other practices (composition, performance, theory, etc.) that comprise the systematic improvisation continuum. The same holds with the systematic meditation continuum, where as wide a range of practices as in the prior postmodern stage are acknowledged, but now they are differentiated according to specific parameters and organized into a coherent system where a more nuanced understanding of their benefits is possible and questions regarding integrity of practice may now be answered.

Having already explored the systematic improvisation spectrum at length, let us explore the systematic approach to meditation in greater depth, as it reveals important aspects of the stage four, integral educational model. We will not entirely ignore its improvisatory partner, however, as the interaction of the two epistemological prongs is key to the broader picture. Following a brief focus on the first, we will resume drawing connections between them.

Key Features of a Stage Four, Integral Approach to Contemplative/Consciousness Studies

Recall that a systematic approach to meditation spans a continuum that is anchored in the experience of pure consciousness uniquely invoked in silent, sitting meditation and includes any number of contemplative methodologies, such as contemplative approaches to reading, writing, movement, nature communion, and creative arts. While it is important to recognize that different individuals will walk different pathways en route to creativity and consciousness development, I believe that most individuals—when it comes to the consciousness entryway to this wholeness—will benefit from some degree of silent meditation practice along with some degree of active contemplative engagement and thus, fully aware that there may well be exceptions, I advance this general framework. Let us bear in mind that one of the primary tasks of the academy in delineating curricular frameworks is to approximate the needs of the majority and provide as much flexibility as possible to accommodate the needs of the minority. I thus offer the following analysis in this spirit.

In order to help students and faculty discover further direction within the wide range of systematic meditation options, I have taken an additional step, already encountered, in distinguishing between formal, quasi-formal, and nonformal practices in order that students and faculty may gain a clearer sense of the benefits and limitations unique to the different approaches.[11] By formal practice I mean engagement with the methodologies and conceptual resources of a contemplative lineage, thus enabling grounding not only in systematic instruction but also a theoretical and cultural context. Generally speaking, formal practice will include silent, sitting meditation as an anchor to a broader contemplative spectrum that may include somatic, breathing, dietary, and other practices. Further benefits of formal practice frameworks include participation with communities of practitioners, availability of expert instruction, and access to the retreats or intensives that most serious practitioners attest are important to their growth.

Quasi-formal engagement involves learning meditation from books, or DVDs, or academic classrooms where practices are, almost necessarily to a certain extent, extricated from traditions. Nonformal engagement involves the broader array of practices that may be construed as contemplative, such as reading, writing, creative arts, but may not be necessarily approached with contemplative intention. Nor are nonformal methodologies, generally speaking, approached in conjunction with corresponding consciousness-based theoretical models (e.g., models of mind, how transcendence is invoked within the discipline, and development over time)—at least not the extent that is found in formal engagement. One can see that nonformal engagement corresponds with the more active forms of contemplative practice that complement the silent meditation anchor in the systematic meditation approach. We can thus conclude that systematic meditation practice might ideally comprise some combination of formal and nonformal practice.

In no way is this to entirely dismiss the place of quasi-formal practice, particularly when resources for formal engagement are limited, or perhaps when it is elected due to the inclinations of a given individual. It is simply to distinguish between the many possibilities available so that students and faculty can forge meaningful, diverse, and manageable pathways. At institutions in vicinities where formal practice resources (e.g., local meditation centers) are not as readily available, quasi-formal instruction may be the only option, which could nonetheless be inspired or informed by formal approaches when faculty possess this grounding. Most important is that whatever avenues are selected result from exposure to diverse possibilities and critical examination thereof. Though postmodern contemplative studies has established openings and receptivity to a diverse range of practice, its failure to differentiate between the various possibilities may ultimately limit the tools that students might gain to navigate their ways through this very spectrum. The situation precisely parallels that of the postmodern "leveling" of the musical landscape considered in the previous chapter, where liberation from the exclusive centrality of European classical music by a growing contingent of educators has rendered them loathe to allow another to take its place. As a result, jazz—even with its powerful, self-transcending properties that enable musicians to navigate meaningful trans-traditional pathways—remains marginalized. I do not propose a particular spiritual lineage as a self-transcending, contemplative counterpart to jazz. I do propose, however, as a framework that is conducive to this goal the interplay of formal and nonformal grounding that comprises the systematic meditation continuum.

Let us now turn to the benefits of both systematic meditation and systematic improvisation, as these shed further light on the delineative and diagnostic aspects of the parts-to-whole/whole-to-parts integral process template and the contributions they make to paradigmatic change.

Parallel Benefits from Systematic Meditation and
Systematic Improvisation Engagement

The first benefit has to do with what might be termed "integrity of practice." As noted earlier, engagement with a formal meditation tradition promotes regularity of practice, interaction with a contemplative community, access to expert instruction, and advanced programs. Grounding in an improvisatory tradition such as jazz similarly promotes capacities to interact with musical communities and direct contact with master practitioners and authentic practices and structures.

Directly extending from this grounding are a host of skills that are characteristic of creativity and consciousness development. In chapter 2, we identified three primary aspects of creative development to be inventiveness, interactivity, and individuation. Consciousness development includes growth of self-awareness, diversity awareness, and critical inquiry faculties, within each parameter a wide range of constituent faculties might be included.

A third category of benefits includes what I call *integral threads* that are woven between direct experience and intellectual analysis and lay rich groundwork for the very cognitive development that has long been central, even if out of balance, in the conventional academy. Viewing this first from the standpoint of meditation: Key here is that formal, systematic practice involves various kinds of analytical studies—for example, mechanics of practice, nature of mind, cultural connections, developmental trajectories, among others—that are central in many meditation lineages. When this terrain is broached in the context of tradition-specific contemplative affiliation, there is an interior, organic link between direct, first-person transcendent experience, due to its richly meaningful and transformational nature, that instills entirely new kinds of third-person intellectual connections. When, in other words, students experience the noetic depth that Alfred Lord Tennyson describes as the "clearest of the clearest, the surest of the surest,"[12] a powerful bond, and corresponding receptivity, is established with the many theoretical, cultural, and historical aspects of the framework within which that experience is invoked.

Here the importance of a conceptual foundation to contemplative development cannot be overemphasized. Inner experience and outer understanding are not separate realms of growth, but coevolutionary aspects of contemplative evolution. Wilber emphasizes that even though it is possible to invoke peak episodes—"states"—of higher levels of development, these will be understood only through the lens of one's present stage. Explaining that it is not enough to sit down to meditate and "hope for the best," Tibetan Buddhist teacher Traleg Rinpoche emphasizes the importance of "a conceptual framework that is based on a correct view" that grounds one's practice. "We need to have a comprehensive view of our human nature, our place in the scheme of things, and our relationship to the world in which we live and to our fellow sentient beings."[13] In no way should this passage be taken to suggest, even when Rinpoche also states that "our meditation should be informed" by these considerations, that awareness is directed to the realm of these or other concepts during actual meditation practice.[14] No, we allow the mind to go the other way, toward the pristine silence of pure consciousness. What is important is the overall context within which students take up meditation; when this happens within the theoretical, cultural, and historical foundations of a formal tradition, which also involves a strong community of practitioners, systematic instruction, and advanced programs, a degree of integrity and effectiveness of practice, as well as development, is possible that is difficult to achieve otherwise.

It is one thing to invoke higher states from a conceptually neutral perspective, or, say, a materialist standpoint and interpret them as the result of particular kinds of neurological firing; it is quite another to understand them from a nondual integral perspective as attunement with the ground of all Being, of all Creation. It is even possible that peak episodes without proper conceptual understanding may be confusing, as in the luminous perceptual phenomena that might accompany causal experience, or the extraordinary oneness of nonduality. This understanding may be key for these temporary states to become enduring stages.

And when glimpses of, and subsequent grounding in higher stage experience are invoked within the context of a lineage, rich integral threads are woven internally between diverse areas of knowledge. Parallels with improvisatory development are abundant, for these same threads may be woven between peak improvisatory experience and areas critical to broader musical development. To whatever extent lingering stereotypes of early jazz musicians as unschooled, innocent of musical notation, and lacking in theoretical understanding are even marginally accurate, they are clearly dispelled by the wide-ranging and exceptional fluency of today's jazz musician. And when we recall the principle of nested synergies, where improvisation underpins and interacts with the full range of primary, secondary, and ancillary creative processes to yield a richly differentiated and integrative scope of technical, theoretical, and creative faculties, we see the musical manifestation of integral threads as enormously compelling.

A fourth kind of benefit stemming from systematic meditation and improvisation studies has to do with enhanced abilities to navigate pathways across, respectively, contemporary spiritual and musical landscapes. Just as the central pulse of the musical world, as already seen, lies in the interstices between genres rather than the discrete categories that pervade academic and commercial conceptions, the central pulse of the spiritual world may be similarly construed as residing not in the language-bound categories of religious denominations but in the terrain in which they intersect, which is interior, even if the entryways are exterior. This may be further illustrated by recalling the notion encountered earlier in the context of music: Here styles or traditions are seen as self-transcending tributaries that flow into the central musical ocean that is their source and in which other tributaries merge. In connection with that source, and with other tributaries that lead to it, music becomes a powerful vehicle for creativity and consciousness development. Recall also, however, that the importance of grounding in tributaries is not diminished in this account but, in fact, underscored, for these are the source of essential skills and great music. Additionally, contact with the broader musical ocean can in turn enhance tradition-specific engagement.

The same holds for spiritual life, even if the situation is somewhat more complex. Tradition-specific grounding provides tools that promote forging meaningful pathways through the contemporary kaleidoscope of spiritual pathways. This calls for what Robert Forman calls a trans-traditional spiritual awareness, one that is open to and appreciative of the diversity of possibilities, yet also sufficiently grounded so that one does not get swept up in the ever-rising tide of options. Sustaining balance between these poles is easier said than done. One need not look far to find individuals who, cloistered within the confines of a single lineage, remain either largely oblivious to the broader spiritual mosaic, or perhaps prone toward denigrating views of traditions other than their own. At the opposite extreme are contemplative aspirants who succumb to a kind of "spiritual promiscuity," flitting about from one approach to another. Many shallow wells do not yield water, recalling a Zen proverb.

What kind of guidance might the integral perspective provide to help seekers arrive at a viable balance? Recognizing that an extraordinarily wide range of possibilities exists, I do not believe it is unreasonable to surmise as follows: First, that most individuals will gravitate toward, and gain from, some degree of exposure to diverse spiritual perspectives. Second, however, is that for most this will manifest in grounding in regular practice within a primary tradition, with possible secondary supplementation coming from other traditions. This supplementation may take the form of inspirational or theoretical literature, occasional attendance at trans-traditional gatherings, or practices that complement but do not interfere with the primary practice. For example, one might engage in a tradition-specific meditation practice and complement it with *hatha yoga* practice from another source, and perhaps nature mysticism from another. Every individual has different needs at different times and thus needs to forge his or her own way. However, the value of a solid foundation cannot be overstated in this endeavor and here contemporary thinkers such as Forman, Phillip Goldberg, and Elizabeth Lesser may offer timely wisdom in advocating grounding in a formal tradition as a basis for broader excursions.

Although this perspective may seem to be ultra-conservative, it is important to emphasize the delicate nature of trans-traditional spiritual activity and why many traditions frown on any kind of involvement whatsoever with other pathways, including even reading literature or attending an informational or inspirational talk. Why? For one thing, it can lead to confusion or naïvely informed tendencies to gravitate between forms and, as noted earlier, end up with minimal grounding in any. Second, it can involve the opening up of awareness to subtle energies that do not readily meld. Engagement in a tradition is a multidimensional endeavor that may involve enlivenment of different planes of spiritual intelligences, which while ultimately may enable profound growth, are not conducive to casual mixing and matching pathways. My personal inclination is to regard methodologies for navigating interior realms as delicate, even sacred structures that have evolved over long periods of time and therefore are to be approached in their purest forms. Concerns about modifying these practices or melding them with others are perhaps something akin to those regarding genetic manipulation of the food supply, or other life forms, where exterior technological advances made without corresponding growth of interior awareness, and subsequent interior-exterior integration, enable meddling at foundational levels of the biosphere that may result in serious health and environmental consequences that are not immediately apparent.

The interplay between tradition-specific and trans-traditional grounding also upholds a two-way critical inquiry function. On one hand, the firm foundation of a primary pathway can facilitate scrutiny of potentially superficial offshoots or hybrids. In turn, the situating of the primary pathway within the broader spiritual confluence can enhance critical investigation of that primary avenue through exposure to both parallel and conflicting perspectives. Encountering descriptions of higher states and stages of consciousness from diverse lineages that are consistent with accounts from one's own can be tremendously inspiring and reinforce one's devotion. Encountering premises or experiences that may appear divergent may elicit a kind of questioning that would not other-wise transpire.

The trans-stylistic merging of the contemporary spiritual landscape is at once an extraordinarily exciting and liberating phenomenon as well as a highly complicated one to be taken seriously. I believe the cultivation of the capacity to therefore effectively sustain tradition-specific grounding with carefully formulated, and complementary trans-traditional engagement *as appropriate to one's needs*, is among the most important educational priorities of our times. It is the basis for what might be called a twenty-first-century "spiritual intelligence," which might be seen as an important aspect of diversity intelligence. Just as creative musicians with tradition-specific and trans-traditional foundations develop a thirst for exposure to and reverence for diverse musical and cultural influences, spiritual aspirants with corresponding foundations can cultivate that same thirst and reverence for diverse spiritual pathways. When, as exemplified in jazz, global creative and spiritual openings are catalyzed by a single domain, the degree of diversity awareness evolves exponentially through the synergistic relationship of artistic and spiritual lines. Now conventional framing of diversity as the capacity for mere "tolerance" is seen as but the crude beginnings of a far broader and deeper diversity awareness, in which individuals see the diversity of social, artistic, and spiritual fabrics as essential aspects of their own being and evolution. Oppression or marginalization of any individual or group is essentially an impediment to one's own, and everyone's, creative and spiritual evolution.

This leads to a final parallel between systematic meditation and systematic improvisation engagement and growth. This is the nondual pinnacle of human development identified by the world's wisdom traditions, and which we have seen provides a deeper understanding of creativity and consciousness alike. Human consciousness is a manifestation of cosmic wholeness, human creativity is a manifestation of cosmic creativity. The synergistic interplay between deep spiritual and creative grounding enlivens this awareness in practitioners, whereby each becomes an avenue to the other. Recall our early working definition of creativity and consciousness: Creativity is an exterior entryway to creativity-consciousness wholeness, consciousness an interior entryway. As this wholeness grows in one's awareness, receptivity increases to possible practical and transformational applications of this understanding such as collective meditation projects to enliven intersubjective consciousness and its capacity to radiate profound coherence in the environment.

What are the prospects of harnessing the educational benefits of the systematic meditation/improvisation interplay, and thus the jazz-inspired integral vision, in today's colleges and universities, where these benefits can in turn be transmitted to society?

Inasmuch, as noted earlier, the defining feature of the full integral evolutionary stage is that the entire curriculum, and arguably the entire institution, would be created from an integral perspective, it may appear that any such transformation is unlikely any time soon at a mainstream educational institution. However, the establishment of the new approach even in small pockets at otherwise conventional institutions could make significant preliminary contributions to the broader transformation. In this regard, integral educators may have much to learn from the several alternative institutions whose conceptual frameworks align, albeit to varying degrees, with an integral perspective. These include California Institute of Integral Studies (CIIS), JFK University, Maharishi University of Management (MUM), and Naropa University, all of which are accredited at undergraduate and graduate levels. That each differs as much from each other as from its conventional counterparts underscores the variety of forms an integral educational paradigm may take. Naropa University is Buddhist-inspired, CIIS and MUM are inspired by Vedantic lineages, and while Naropa and CIIS foster more pluralistic cultures of practice, all students and faculty at MUM engage in a uniform set of practices. Benefits in each orientation may be noted; pluralism allows for individuals to chart their own contemplative pathways, uniformity enables a kind of collective grounding and depth that, much like in an ashram or monastery where an entire community follows a shared routine, would not be possible otherwise. Even if contemplative pathways in mainstream institutions will necessarily be forged according to the unique constraints encountered by faculty innovators, an awareness of the unique features of the alternative schools may significantly enhance these efforts.

At the basis for all of these developments is the need for a new kind of dialogue and thinking to take hold in a university setting that renders individuals and the collective culture a vibrant climate for paradigmatic change. Let us turn to a format I call Deep Inquiry that is designed for this purpose.

Deep Inquiry: Gateway for Integral Academic Discourse

Deep Inquiry is a systematic framework that invites colleagues to pause, reflect, and come to terms with their deepest and most passionate convictions about the ultimate purposes and potentials of education as well as the extent to which many, if not most, colleagues have become disconnected from these convictions. As a result, personal fulfillment and growth have been limited, and the kind of change that is needed in our educational systems at this juncture in history is significantly impeded. I believe the formation of a Deep Inquiry Group (DIG) that is committed to this expanded dialogue has the capacity to significantly cultivate receptivity to paradigmatic change.

The DIG framework consists of a sequential progression of questions that seek to restore this connection by directing thinking and discourse from the prevailing third-person, objective/exterior orientation toward first-second-third-person integral synthesis. The questions correspond with modern, postmodern, and integral perspectives and aim to catalyze critical examination of conventional and nonconventional assumptions alike in order to both promote receptivity to change in general, and advance the alternative, integral vision in particular.

While there is no denying that Deep Inquiry is rooted in its own sets of assumptions—those of the nondual, integral worldview—I believe that its capacity to catalyze self-critical inquiry will aid both colleagues who may ultimately embrace them as well as those who will not in their quest to find more meaning in the educational process. As I emphasize in Level III inquiry, the biggest questions regarding the nature of the human being and reality can be responded to from diverse perspectives. I believe most colleagues, even if not all embrace the integral vantage point, agree that open dialogue and juxtaposition of diverse viewpoints can only enhance the vitality of the learning environment. For the growing majority that are committed to change, even if they might not agree about what that might look like, this enhanced conversation is even more critical. "Without new thinking based on deep dialogue," assert Matthew Bronson and Ashok Gangadean, efforts at change will, at best, be constrained by "new dogmas, new taxonomies, new ideological schisms that merely replicate, rather than intervene in the turf wars and real wars that embody the cultural pathologies of late modernity."[15]

Deep Inquiry engages us in articulating a vision and practical ramifications that help us break free from these tendencies. When engaged with in collective formats, Deep Inquiry invites, in addition to conventional modes of discourse (e.g., discussion and debate), the use of alternative approaches as well, including the Council practice that originates in Native American traditions and has also been used extensively in Quaker meetings, and the closely related Bohmian dialogue articulated by the physicist David Bohm. In these approaches, individuals speak only when moved from a deep inner impulse, and rather than engaging in linear exchange—where one person makes a statement, another replies—viewpoints are expressed from the heart in a nonlinear manner, allowing deep convictions to flow not only from individual awareness but for collective consciousness to reveal its insights as appropriate at a given time and place and for a given group.[16]

First-second-third-person Questions as Catalysts

The Deep Inquiry framework catalyzes three levels of discourse that are guided by three primary questions, and corresponding supplemental questions to be considered shortly:

LEVEL I: third-person inquiry (conventional/modern): What is the nature and purpose of learning within in a given field?

LEVEL II: second-person/third-person inquiry (postmodern): What is the nature and purpose of education at large?

LEVEL III: first-second-third-person inquiry (integral): What is the nature and purpose of the human being who is being educated?

In other words, DI begins with the kind of conversation that generally prevails, which is largely geared toward third-person, discipline-specific concerns. It then moves to the question of what constitutes the scope and purpose of education at large, a topic broached far less frequently in the highly compartmentalized conventional academy. Connections are then made from this second-person inquiry to prior third-person considerations. A probing follows of a realm that is virtually off-limits, that regarding the nature of the human being who is being educated, and thus first-person terrain and questions related to Ultimate Reality and Meaning. Similarly, the investigation of first-person reality does not occur in isolation but connects back to second- and third-person considerations. This is where the supplemental questions come into play, as these aim to situate any set of concerns within the whole in order to help individuals arrive at a vision that exhibits optimal coherence. Although the progression generally proceeds along a parts-to-whole trajectory, the feeding back of each subsequent level of discourse to prior ones, which is particularly vivid in the broaching of URAM terrain, upholds a complementary whole-to-parts trajectory.

LEVEL I INQUIRY: THIRD-PERSON, DISCIPLINE-SPECIFIC ORIENTATION

Primary guiding question: What is the nature and purpose of learning within in a given field?

Supplementary questions:

1. What is the process-structure expanse—what do students need to know and how is this knowledge to be gained—that is generally encompassed in your field in order to achieve competency?

2. What philosophical or theoretical principles, ideally cited in educational literature, support this educational perspective and approach?

3. What paradigmatically different approaches might be identified, and what are their supporting theoretical/philosophical premises?

4. What is your particular philosophy regarding learning and teaching in your field, and how well does your teaching, particularly in its process-structure scope, align with that?

5. What do you regard as the primary factors in shaping your educational worldview?

6. What are the ramifications of the conventional viewpoint and your viewpoint on the challenges, as you see them, facing individuals and society in the twenty-first century?

7. If you had complete freedom to design your own approach to your discipline, what would that look like?

Commentary: One might presume that, if nothing else, there would be no dearth of discipline-specific dialogue and thinking in conventional academe that tackles the preceding questions. However, a look at the parameters of discipline-specific discourse within the Deep Inquiry framework reveals that even here conventional discourse falls short. As a result, the entirely reasonable viewpoint that many would advance in response to the primary question—that the nature and purpose of education within a field is to promote expertise in the field—remains disconnected from broader educational questions. This will likely begin to change when colleagues contemplate supplementary questions. In asking them to define the knowledge base in their field in terms of processes and structures, DI begins to direct awareness beyond language-bound categories and their associations toward what actually constitutes knowledge and knowing. By having them then articulate underlying educational principles that support this spectrum, DI illuminates how much of what happens in the classroom flies in the face of much learning theory. In asking them to identify paradigmatically different approaches, DI engages them in an important aspect of critical inquiry not commonly addressed. Juxtaposing contrasting paradigms can uphold a powerful critical function. Through inviting individuals to articulate their own philosophy of learning as pertaining to their field, and to contemplate what sort of model they might design if given creative latitude, this critical inquiry shifts from the field as an external phenomenon to their own work. Even at this level of inquiry colleagues will begin to see discrepancies between educational practice and educational vision.

Level II Inquiry: second-person/third-person synthesis

What is the nature and purpose of the overall educational enterprise? In other words, is education primarily a vocational enterprise, to prepare graduates to enter the workforce? Or might a broader purpose be identified, one that aims toward a broader kind of human development? If so, what comprises that development?

Supplementary questions:

1. What is the process-structure expanse that is generally encompassed in the field of education?

2. How well aligned is the process-structure expanse with the prevailing sense of educational goals (e.g., as might be articulated in the mission statement of the institution)?

3. What philosophical or theoretical principles, and corresponding literature, support this approach?

4. What might be identified as a paradigmatically different approach from that which prevails, and what are its supporting theoretical/philosophical premises and corresponding literature?

5. What is your personal philosophy of education and how well does your teaching, particularly in its process-structure scope, reflect that vision?

6. What do you regard as the important factors in your education and life experience that shape your educational philosophy?

7. What insights unearthed in Level II inquiry may have influenced your perspective on Level I inquiry and practice?

8. What are the ramifications of the conventional viewpoint and your viewpoint on the challenges, as you see them, facing individuals and society in the twenty-first century?

Commentary: With Level II inquiry, we move from consideration of the nature and purpose of study in a given field to consideration of the nature and purpose of education at large. To be sure, Level II questions will likely have come up in Level I inquiry, which points to the interconnectedness, and parts-to-whole/whole-to-parts nature of the Deep Inquiry process. Questions such as whether education ought to be primarily vocational or something broader place the expanded dialogue front and center and begin to elicit receptivity to Level III dialogue.

I suspect that most colleagues, particularly when given an opportunity to step back from day-to-day practice, would express a view of education as more than just preparation for the workforce, but rather as a means of promoting a broader kind of growth in students. Even colleagues who may lean toward vocational emphasis in the major field may hold a more expansive vision of education at large and thus argue vehemently that it is important that students gain a more well-rounded education. What is lacking, however, in the conventional visioning process is the clear articulation of just what comprises this well-rounded education, how it is achieved, and how the domain-specific is reconciled with the cross-disciplinary. This is where, once colleagues take a stab at this in response to the purpose of education question, the supplementary questions are of value.

Nowadays, there is much talk about creativity, interdisciplinary thinking, self-sufficiency, environmental awareness, and cross-cultural sensitivity as important attributes of a sound education. However, since opportunities for faculty to really dig into the question of broader purposes are limited, to be able to hold it in awareness at length and penetrate deep into its many layers, this ever-longer list of educational attributes becomes more a litany of self-satisfying buzzwords than genuine catalysts for educational practice. There is little talk about how these qualities are cultivated, which would be a spontaneous aspect of Level II Deep Inquiry, even without the supplementary guiding questions.

With these questions, the kind of centering that is needed for genuine change occurs. If the process-structure question illuminated a limited scope on a discipline-specific level, it underscores this problem when viewed from a cross-disciplinary level given the fact that, while structure changes across fields (e.g., biology and anthropology and economics deal with very different content) in conventional academe, epistemology (lectures, reading, writing, discussion) does not. At this point, colleagues need to come to terms with a gulf between educational aspiration and educational reality: few would argue that creativity is cultivated without creative activity, or that multiethnic or environmental awareness are cultivated without hands-on engagement that promotes these kinds of growth.

But what about the liberal arts curriculum that allows students to partake of coursework in the arts, sociology, environmental studies, and other areas that correspond to many of the attributes listed?

Here is where the supplementary questions help identify important differences between even the most liberal of conventional educational models and integral approaches. First, the process-structure diversity of integral models is distributed throughout the curriculum; one does not engage creatively, say, in one or two art classes over the course of four years in order to fulfill this dimension of human development. The same holds true with community engagement, environmental studies, and many other areas. Interdisciplinary awareness leads to a second point. Whereas conventional models attempt interdisciplinarity largely through juxtaposition of self-confining approaches (fields approached in isolation), integral approaches both juxtapose and synthesize through self-transcending approaches to all fields. At this point, the most distinguishing feature of the integral is placed front and center: methodologies such as meditation for inner experience and development.

Level II inquiry helps center this important distinction as soon as creativity enters the discussion. One cannot significantly broach the domain of creativity without broaching the domain of consciousness. When colleagues are asked to identify theoretical/philosophical principles corresponding to their vision of education, they will inevitably be reminded of this intimate connection. When they are asked to identify alternative educational models, they will encounter further reminders. When they are asked to assess the process-structure scope of the conventional model and how well it is aligned with their ever-unfolding vision, they will thus see this as important terrain. When, furthermore, they fully cross the interior-exterior divide and engage in Level III Deep Inquiry, they will see that an education without the contemplative dimension—as radical a departure from conventional pedagogy as this is—is as difficult to imagine as the inclusion of this realm might be for present-day educational conservatives who are so strongly inclined to reject it. Recall from the introduction my recounting feedback from colleagues who waged an all-out assault on the

Jazz and Contemplative Studies proposal at Michigan, including one who, despite a specialization in music of 200 years ago, proclaimed that "this will set the school back 50 years," and another who claimed one could "do the same thing [as meditation] with Prozac!" Level III inquiry, moreover, may well stretch the horizons of many contemplative educators in that it broaches some of the biggest questions of human and cosmic existence— taking us once more into the realm of Ultimate Reality and Meaning.

LEVEL III: FIRST-PERSON ORIENTATION

What is the nature and purpose of the human being who is being educated? In other words, is the human being a physical or a spiritual entity? Or put another way, is human consciousness reducible to a physical substrate, epiphenomenal to that substrate, or transcendent of that substrate? What happens when we die? Is there a purpose to human existence? God, or cosmic intelligence? These are among a host of "big questions" that have occupied thinkers from time immemorial and which need to assume a more central place in educational discourse in order for integral paradigmatic change to manifest.[17]
Supplementary questions:

1. What are the factors or influences that shape your responses to these questions?

2. What philosophical or theoretical principles support them?

3. What might be identified as a paradigmatically different worldview, and what are its supporting theoretical/philosophical premises?

4. How well does your worldview, and particularly its process-structure scope, align with your educational vision?

5. How might insights unearthed in Level III inquiry impact on your Level II and I thinking and practice?

6. What are the ramifications of the conventional worldview (of the human being and cosmic totality) and your worldview on the challenges, as you see them, facing individuals and society in the twenty-first century?

Commentary: Having reflected deeply on the nature and purpose of education within a field, and then within education at large, the probing of the nature and purpose of the human being who is being educated broaches terrain—including that of spirituality, mysticism, and religion—that far extends beyond what usually transpires in academic circles. To be sure, this may be problematic even for many colleagues disposed toward substantive reform, including those in contemplative education circles. Why, then, is this inquiry necessary? Is it not possible for education to cross the interior-exterior divide through the integration of contemplative practices alone, leaving this sort of theoretical speculation to be taken up outside of the walls of the academy? And what about church-state boundaries?

Here we return to the axiom introduced early on, that the degree of change possible is directly predicated on the degree of "swinging" between the localized concerns of a particular field and inquiry into the most far-reaching questions about Ultimate Reality and Meaning—in essence, the scope of Deep Inquiry. For this will open up an unprecedented kind of conceptual space from which new vistas of exploration and practical application of potentialities inherent in human creativity and conscious-ness may be possible in education and beyond. This inquiry will also enliven a kind of critical dynamism in which individuals transcend com-mon, language-bound associations and begin to access deep underlying principles that may be obscured by conventional attachments. Aversion to this kind of inquiry, even among those who may otherwise be ardent advocates of reform, is rooted in a limited vision of the human being and the role of the university to cultivate full human potential. To turn back at this point in the Deep Inquiry journey is to relinquish the opportunity to assume an unprecedented kind of educational leadership, one that is urgently needed in today's world. Level III Deep Inquiry is for those who are driven by this need.

An integral approach to this inquiry both stretches the outer bound-aries of the discourse and illuminates formidable nuance within those boundaries, in so doing enabling participants to come to terms with pat-terns and perspectives that might otherwise elude awareness. In so doing, potential common ground is identified that might unite highly divisive perspectives that are often polarized beyond any hopes of conciliation. The long-standing divide between spirituality and science is, of course, a primary example. Realizing that the ideal of bridging these worldviews is predicated on integral assumptions that not everyone shares, it is important to emphasize that, although I approach the process through an integral lens, Deep Inquiry has the capacity to enable colleagues of all perspectives to come to terms with their personal convictions about what education might potentially be and how current practice may or may not align with those convictions. I view this as the primary purpose of the process, and believe the vitality of the educational enterprise would increase considerably were this to occur among conservatives and progressives alike. Though I strongly believe that the materialist worldview, and materialist educational approaches, are unsustainable and pose grave threats on a planetary scale, I believe the academic would benefit tremendously if colleagues who nonetheless hold such materialist perspectives were to engage in a deep, critical examination of their platform and its ramifications, and come away from the process with their convictions fortified. It is imperative that any collective discourse that is catalyzed by Deep Inquiry yield a space for conservative and progressive voices alike.

I nonetheless believe that the process would not only mobilize the growing population of educators who are inclined toward change in an integral direction, but even transform some within the conservative ranks. This is due to the fact that most participants in the educational world do not subscribe to an overarching materialist worldview regardless of their educational predilections. This was borne out in UCLA researchers Helen and Alexander Astin's landmark study of spirituality in higher education. Though few eyebrows may have been raised when their findings showed considerable spiritual interest among the student population, when they also revealed this to be virtually matched among the faculty, the expectations of many were clearly challenged.[18] In other words, consistent with the large percentage of the overall population for whom spirituality is important, so it is with a sizeable percentage of the faculty. Whereas students expressed frustration at its exclusion from the educational process, faculty expressed ambivalence or confusion over how it might be integrated.

When I first learned of these findings, I found myself even more disappointed about the weak integrity that pervades the educational enterprise. Were the majority of colleagues materialists, which of course is their very right, at least there would be some coherence between individual convictions (at least among the faculty) and the overarching educational orientation. But now the realization that most faculty do not teach according to their deepest convictions about the nature of the human being and the cosmic wholeness, but are simply puppets of an inherited, paradigm-blind system, provided me with an even deeper cause for distress. I view this as a crisis as enormous as any other in our world because it reduces the transformational potential of education—which is predicated on teachers sharing with students their most exciting, passionate, and far-reaching ideas about human potential and reality—to essentially the ingestion of data. Even those instances where faculty manage a much more substantive type of engagement falls far short of what is possible in terms of transformational possibilities. The educational enterprise has been hijacked by the ideological special interests of a distinct minority.

Deep Inquiry might help the spiritual majority come to terms with this divide between worldview and educational practice, thereby promoting change whereby Level III insights feed back to Level II and I practices and reform. It might also accomplish a more dramatic kind of transformation among the aspiritual minority, where adherents of a materialist worldview who nonetheless embrace nonmaterialist educational approaches—for example, hands-on, active, creativity-based, interactive learning—might be compelled to consider that the roots of the conventional practices they reject may be traced to broader premises about the nature of the human being, and even cosmic reality, that may also be subject to question. Again, the primary purpose of Deep Inquiry is to facilitate coherence between overarching worldview and educational practice. Whether this results in a shift to an integral educational vision, which I believe is inevitable, is a secondary consideration; any such change will come from the coherence established in the first place.

Level III inquiry may also shed light on the reasons for this schism between worldview and practice. The church-state boundary that has rightly been established in order that the religious perspectives of any single denomination or lineage are not imposed on students and faculty provides an obvious starting point. An integral perspective provides a more nuanced view of this policy and its ramifications, where a general principle that was clearly necessary at a certain historical juncture has been interpreted, wittingly or not, far more broadly than needed, and perhaps than originally intended. In other words, in relegating discipline-specific religious or spiritual practice to outside the academy, the educational world has taken the extreme step of removing any kind of interior experience from academic culture and practice. Coupled with this fortification of the exterior-interior divide, and arguably underlying it, would be the increasingly prominent role of science—and its materialist conception known as scientism—in the educational world.

Here is where Deep Inquiry might unearth a second insight, having to do with the extent to which the removal of spirituality from education has fueled extremist tendencies in both science and religion. In other words, when any component of the spirituality-art-science trinity is either excessively privileged or marginalized, the entire system is thrown out of kilter and creativity and consciousness development is impaired. When the three domains are in balance, they are realized as self-transcending gateways to a wholeness of experience and understanding that is informed by all three; integral science includes art and spirituality, integral spirituality embraces science and art, integral art unites science and spirituality. Creativity and consciousness development is optimal when grounded in this wholeness. The categorical removal of spirituality (at least in part via church-state boundaries) combined with the marginalization of the arts allowed a scientific paradigm to overtake the academic world that radically oversteps its bounds and represents a kind of fundamentalism that is as problematic as that which may be identified from any other domain. And perhaps ironically, this paradigm has fueled the very religious fundamentalism that it so ardently, and rightly, seeks to counteract. An understanding of this point, for which I believe Level III Deep Inquiry is uniquely equipped, is essential to paradigmatic change in the twenty-first-century academy.

Tales of Two Fundamentalisms

The two fundamentalist platforms may be best understood in terms of two cosmic narratives, or accounts of the nature of the universe and the human being. One is well known from the highly publicized debates between so-called creationists and evolutionists—the notion that God created the world 10,000 years ago or less, humans lived alongside dinosaurs, and that the geological record and all other indicators of a far more vast planetary timescale are erroneous.[19] A second one is less recognized, yet exerts enormous influence in academic practice, which holds that the universe is fundamentally a physical phenomenon, devoid of meaning and purpose, in which the human being emerged as a random outgrowth. Recall Steven Weinberg's view that "the more the universe seems comprehensible, the more it seems pointless," and the corresponding conception of the human being as a kind of "a farcical outcome of a chain of accidents reaching back to the first three minutes."[20]

As long as these are the only two options, education and society will remain riddled by an unnecessary war between two profoundly unsatisfying, and in my view sadly impoverished, worldviews. Happily, these are not the only two options, and the integral nondual vision provides a framework that reveals them as instances of extreme forms of dissociation that have occurred within important lines of human development—one known as religion, the other science—on the path toward differentiation. One has dissociated in the form of a spirit-contorted cosmic narrative devoid of reason, the other a material-based narrative devoid of spirit. Deep Inquiry provides a framework that helps penetrate beyond these superficial conceptions by inviting colleagues to stop, carefully ponder what is being claimed, and step back from the highly charged and divisive category-bound associations that prevail. In the absence of this kind of discourse, any quest for a more nuanced perspective, where for example one might subscribe to some notion of cosmic intelligence—or what Chinese call Tao, Indians Brahman, Andean shamans Ushai, Native Americans Great Spirit, to name just a few—as well as evolutionary dynamics that govern differentiation much as Darwin has proposed in the biological realm, is quashed by the polarization that prevails. Even to suggest, as in David Loye's idea of a "second-Darwinian revolution," that a broader view of evolutionary dynamics might be inferred in Darwin's work that invites spiritual-physical synthesis is risky business in the highly charged climate of scientism that is pervasive in higher education.[21]

Through the combination of the central status of science in the academy and the smokescreen resulting from debates with religious extremists, science has been fairly immune to critical inquiry and oblivious to its own extremism from within its own ranks and beyond. A look at some manifestations of this will underscore the point.

Evolutionary Theory Is Not a Theory of Life's Origins

I commonly display the following statement by Karen Armstrong to students—undergraduate and graduate alike—and have even done so with faculty colleagues at professional academic conferences, and am continually amazed at how oblivious most are to its egregious nature. Part of the reason this is so elusive is that many recognize her, and rightly so, as among the most important commentators on the phenomenon of religious fundamentalism of our times. It is therefore easy to miss the fundamentalism in her remark: "Christian fundamentalists reject the discoveries of biology and physics about the origins of life and insist that the Book of Genesis is scientifically sound in every detail."[22]

It is not that religious fundamentalists do not reject the findings of science, or don't tout their scriptural accounts as incontrovertible. The problem has to do with Armstrong's reference to "discoveries of biology and physics about the origins of life": Not only do no such discoveries exist, neither do corresponding theories that have received even a modicum of acceptance. Physics offers in the Big Bang a highly plausible and fairly well-accepted theory (at least within the scientific community) about how the material world as we know it came into being 14 billion years ago (minus perhaps the few minutes, as Weinberg might remind us, it took for the fundamental particles to take form); this, however, is not a theory of the origins of life. Biology in Darwin's natural selection offers a highly plausible and widely accepted (again, at least within the scientific community) account of how biological life evolved over the millennia; it is not a theory of how life originated in the first place. The question of how life emerged parallels the question of how consciousness emerged in terms of elusiveness from the materialist vantage point, with the nondual, integral perspective holding that the underlying assumption—that life and consciousness emerged from a material substrate—may be fundamentally flawed. Were science to advance a theory of the origins of life that achieved near the consensus in the field as Big Bang and evolutionary theories, or Einstein's relativity theory, it would entirely dwarf the prior theories in significance. It would equal in significance discovery of life on another planet, or a cure for all cancers, or ways to reverse global warming. That this obviously has not happened, yet the assumption prevails that it has, or is perhaps not far off, represents an extraordinary degree of hubris that— as a kind of fundamentalism in itself—only fans the flames for further fundamentalism. Exemplifying Wilber's "pressure cooker" effect, [23] the stronger the reductionist proclamations from materialist scientists, where the human being is viewed as nothing but, to reinvoke Francis Crick, a "pack of neurons," the more that religious extremists cling to their equally skewed misinterpretations of scripture and denominational dogma in a misguided compensatory response. Any prospects for productive dialogue to ensue between the diverse viewpoints are dashed.

Yet the biologist Richard Dawkins, among the most eloquent adherents of the materialist worldview, goes to great lengths to argue that science is inherently immune to fundamentalist tendencies. His central point is not unreasonable—science is evidence-driven, religion is faith-driven.[24] Here, however, an integral perspective promotes a more nuanced view of these concepts. First, evidence is different in different spheres of reality. Third-person, empirical evidence, where science excels, is part of a broader spectrum that also includes what might be called aesthetic, or second-person creative evidence, the stuff of the arts, and the interior, subjective first-person evidence of spiritual experience. As noted earlier, the integral approach brings all three into the mix, thus allowing the exterior empirical methodologies to which scientific materialists confine their investigation and assessment of reality to be informed by creative and interior realms as well. Here is where an integral perspective illuminates the meaning in Einstein's famous words—"science without religion is lame, religion without science is blind"—which as Dawkins rightly points out ought not link Einstein with a conventional religious conception.[25] Religion in this context pertains to interior, subjective experience, without which scientific inquiry is ungrounded. Embodying what Wilber calls "quadrant absolutism,"[26] science confined to only right-hand, exterior quadrants is somewhat like a baseball team moving in the home run fences when it comes up to bat, and then moving them back when it takes the field. This delimiting of the playing field to perspectives compatible to one's own position is a key aspect of fundamentalism.

It is also important to keep in mind that empirical findings that are compatible with a materialist viewpoint may also be compatible with an integral one; for example, mind-brain connections do not "prove" consciousness is reducible to brain any more than they might prove the opposite—that mind is primary. To arbitrarily interpret such findings to support one's foregone conclusions about the nature of reality is a fundamentalist maneuver. Where this materialism becomes even more evident is when materialists, even while privileging third-person methodologies, conveniently filter out third-person research that does not fit their conclusions. Again—conspicuously absent in much materialist advocacy is serious consideration of the fact that thousands of studies support psi and related capacities of consciousness; materialists often either entirely ignore this body of work, or categorically dismiss it as flawed or fraudulent.[27] As argued earlier, it is not that every single one of these studies ought to be assumed as beyond reproach, as is the case with any kind of research, but that even a tiny fraction would be enough to topple the materialist regime. Given the coherence of these findings with the broader matrix of criteria pointing in an integral direction—which include the universality and historicity of the claims (including by an increasing number of formerly skeptical scientists), the large percentage of the population who report corresponding experiences, and the fact that materialism is such a demographically and historically minority viewpoint—I believe the onus is on materialists to systematically rule out this research through a comprehensive review of it in its entirety. That this is admittedly no small task may reveal it to be more than a logistical obstacle to this genuine scientific obligation, it may indeed represent another strong indicator of the extremism inherent in the materialist position. I also believe the previously asserted axiom that correlates worldview with exploration of future possibilities underscores the point that as much as the integral view of consciousness requires empirical support, the disproving of it requires equal or greater support if the materialist alternative is to be taken seriously.

Level-line Fallacy

Though scientific fundamentalists are quick to argue that their primary quarrel is with religious fundamentalists and not the totality of spiritual engagement, "even mild or moderate religion," as Dawkins put it, "helps to provide the climate of faith in which extremism naturally flourishes."[28] This statement is a clear example of what Wilber calls a "level-line fallacy."[29] In other words, because of low-level development within a given line—which Dawkins rightly notes is the case with fundamentalist behavior along the religious line—the extremist (and thus equally fundamentalist) response is to dismiss the line entirely, a classic case of throwing the baby out with the bathwater. From this standpoint, however, one could just as soon alter Dawkins' statement ever so slightly—"Even mild or moderate *science* helps to provide the climate of faith in which extremism naturally flourishes"—to advance an argument to eradicate science.

An integral perspective elevates the thinking to a more inclusive and nuanced perspective that critiques limited development in any area but also realizes the source of fundamentalism lies not in the line in which it occurs but in the differentiation within that line taking the extreme step of dissociation—scientific and religious fundamentalism being among the primary examples. The solution, then, is not to eliminate the line but deepen engagement in it, an approach that runs starkly counter to the rising tide of materialist exhortations that humanity would be better off were religion to somehow disappear.

This point is underscored when one notes tendencies among scientific fundamentalists to provide inventories of the atrocities committed in the name of religion while failing to recognize those resulting from scientific practice. Two obvious examples of the latter are the creation of increasingly lethal weaponry and ecological devastation. As everyone has known for decades, not only do enough nuclear weapons exist to destroy the planet many times over, but chemical and biological warfare may wreak as much havoc. It has also long been common knowledge that rampant use of antibiotics makes it highly likely that some strain-resistant virus will eventually appear that causes a pandemic of unthinkable proportions. The point is not to advocate a retreat from scientific and technological innovation in order to avoid future abuse any more than a retreat from religion is the solution to extremism in that domain. Rather, what is needed are deeper and more expansive science and religion paradigms in order that destructive by-products of these core forms of human creativity are far overshadowed by their positive aspects. That this deepening would involve the merging of the two realms underscores the irony in the current debates, where two developmental lines vie for power oblivious to the fact that a power far greater than what is conceivable in their respective fundamentalist imaginations would come from a marriage with their perceived adversary. Both realms, as Wilber succinctly puts it, "need to grow up."[30]

That this is urgently needed may be particularly evident when one considers genetic science as a further area of scientific practice that may be deeply problematic if not spiritually grounded. The probing and manipulation of foundational levels of biological existence, whether involving genetic modification of the food supply or creation of new life forms, may result in consequences far beyond our imagination. "Up to now," writes Nobel laureate George Wald, "living organisms have evolved very slowly, and new forms have had plenty of time to settle in. Now whole proteins will be transposed overnight into wholly new associations, with consequences no one can foretell." Moving forward in this direction may be not only "unwise but dangerous," potentially breeding "new animal and plant diseases, new sources of cancer, novel epidemics."[31]

Here is where I believe grounding in meditation and corresponding practices that enable awareness to navigate these realms in nuanced ways, as well as awareness of the insights from wisdom traditions that may provide important guidance, needs to be considered as important to twenty-first-century scientific method. Hari Sharma and Christopher Clark, for example, report on the concept of *ojas* in the Indian system of ayurvedic medicine as a substance that exists at the junction point between "consciousness and matter," thus described as the "lamp at the door" that shines both inward and outward, which is essential to health.[32] This is somewhat reminiscent of the concept of the transcendent, archetypal impulse in artistic creativity, for which surface outlets are needed for its expression and integration. When subtle levels of biological existence are altered, the sequential flow and integration of essential forms of energy and vibrational frequencies may be inhibited. Just as the integral musicologist needs to have strong grounding in improvisation and meditation in order to have an adequate foundation for fathoming and commenting on surface activity in the musical world, the integral biophysicist must have grounding in meditation and genuine exposure to arts in order to fathom the biophysical world. The days when science and technological development can proceed without corresponding development of creativity and consciousness are long over.

Nonetheless, materialists remain steadfast about keeping anything resembling spiritual or religious perspectives apart from discourse about sustainability. "It should be blindingly obvious," Sam Harris remarks about religious extremism, "that beliefs of this sort will do little to help us create a durable future for ourselves—socially, economically, environmentally, or geopolitically."[33] Although Harris is obviously right on this account, he fails to acknowledge that if science clings to its own extremism and privileges only its mainstream perspectives and approaches, the world faces an equally serious problem—that of addressing sustainability from the same paradigm that gave rise to it. Scientific beliefs that categorically rule out transcendent dimensions of reality, and thus possible avenues of exploration that will be important to addressing the global ecological crisis, will "do little to help us create a durable future."[34]

I similarly applaud Dawkins, with the same caveat, in his critique of religious fundamentalists' tendencies to hide behind their "holy books"[35] regardless of any degree of contradicting evidence, which just as readily applies to musical fundamentalists who hide behind their scores (created by others) against the evidence of the creative foundations of contemporary (and age-old) musical practice. What Dawkins and many scientific materialists need to recognize, however, is not only that they too have their holy books, but in fact they may be less aware of their dogmatic function than their religious and musical counterparts because of compromised critical inquiry faculties that are inherent in dominant paradigms. Thomas Kuhn notes that periods of "normal science," of which the materialist model is a primary example, tend to be characterized by a relaxing of the critical vigilance that led up to the establishment of the given paradigm. Attempting to "force nature into the preformed and relatively inflexible box that the paradigm supplies, those [phenomena] that will not fit into the box are often not seen at all."[36] Nor is the box itself. The deeply entrenched and unexamined materialist assumptions of the human being and cosmos as fundamentally physical phenomena, perpetuated not in a single holy book but in a multitude of literature, fly just as much in the face of evidence as young Earth arguments do in the face of the fossil record and broader geological findings. Therefore, when Harris describes "religious faith [as] the one species of human ignorance that will not admit of even the possibility of correction [and as] sheltered from criticism in every corner of our culture,"[37] he could just as well be speaking of scientific faith in the academic community. The fact that he does not, however, may suggest an even deeper level of entrenchment and paradigm blindness to have engulfed science than religion—at least religious fundamentalists are aware of their fundamentalism (and perhaps even proud of it). Scientific materialists, much like musical materialists, deny that fundamentalism in their domain is possible.

Four Pathologies Revisited: Fathoming the Scientific Shadow

A consideration of the various pathologies that are intertwined in materialist ideology points us in the direction of the roots of the shadow. Just as we saw in the case of musical materialism in chapter 4, extending from a core epistemological crisis, or epistemo-pathology—the narrowing of the modalities of engagement—ecopathological, ethnopathological, and theopathological tendencies are inevitable. Viewing these here as we did previously in terms of the Four Quadrants: Ecopathology, as just considered, involves desecration of the inextricable link between subjective interiors and the exterior world. In materialist science that rejects interiors, this is analyzable as Upper-Right absolutism or dissociation. Ethnopathology involves the privileging of a culturally mediated epistemology (Western) in the investigation of the natural world and rejection of others, analyzable here as limited Lower-Left awareness. Theopathology is the uncritical privileging of a mono-epistemological and mono-quadratic cosmic narrative, which in the case of scientific fundamentalism in its rejection of interiority involves confinement to Upper-Right, exterior epistemologies and perspectives. One might even argue from a strong nondual integral vantage point that because the self-referential awareness that underlies individual creativity is a manifestation of the same self-referential creativity on a cosmic scale, knowledge systems deficient in improvisatory and meditative experience are inherently theopathological. Exclusionary, fundamentalist tendencies are an inevitable by-product of interior fragmentation resulting from process-deficient engagement.

Whereas musical study has managed through its materialism/fundamentalism to distance itself from the broader musical world and its explosive diversity and creativity, education at large through its scientific materialism/fundamentalism has distanced itself from a society in which interest in spirituality and religion is as strong as ever. Although this has tended to befuddle materialists, Deep Inquiry may shed light on why this interest is unlikely to dissipate anytime soon, and more importantly, why it represents an evolutionary thrust that, if more fully harnessed, could give rise to entirely new levels of scientific, artistic, and spiritual understanding. This may be the basis for a degree of sustainability and flourishing that is beyond the materialist imagination.

I have to admit that I cringe a bit as I write these words, not in fear of vehement outcries from members of the mainstream science community, which is a given, but in fear that my critique of extremist tendencies will be taken as a rejection of science per se. Nothing could be farther from the truth. "Science as an enterprise is something I highly value," states Michael Lerner as he spearheads a movement of Spiritual Progressives. But—echoing my position—"scientism as a worldview is a belief system that has no greater rational status than any other belief system," a point that has largely eluded the scientific mainstream.[38] That at least three major professional organizations have been formed to offer scientists "safe haven" for open investigation of anomalous phenomena suggests that my uneasiness is not unfounded. It also provides optimism that what the physicist William Tiller calls a "second Copernican revolution"[39] may loom on the horizon—providing education can break the impasse.

Awe as an Opening for Reconciliation

What are the prospects for these tendencies to be overcome, the contrasting worldviews reconciled, and openings forged to an integral synthesis? Here Dawkins may point to a possible avenue, even if he opts not to pursue it as such. I am talking about the sense of awe he and other scientists feel for the cosmos—even if not Kosmos—that some describe as a kind of "religiosity." "What I see in Nature," wrote Einstein, "is a magnificent structure that we comprehend only imperfectly, and that must fill a thinking person with a feeling of humility."[40] Though Dawkins emphatically distinguishes any sense of religiousness inferred in such testimony as "light years away" from the conventional sense of religion, an integral perspective invites a broader and more inclusive viewpoint. This is that the very self-reflexive consciousness that is at the basis of Einstein's and many other scientists' transformational experience may be the very link between individual and cosmic wholeness that is the driving force for the emergence of what happen to be called "science" and "religion" alike. "Beings endowed with self-awareness become, precisely in virtue of that bending back upon themselves, immediately capable of rising into a new sphere of existence," wrote the twentieth-century Christian mystic Teilhard de Chardin. "Abstract thought, logic, reasoned choice and invention, mathematics, art, the exact computation of space and time, the dreams and anxieties of love, are simply the bubbling up of the newly-formed life-centre as it explodes upon itself."[41]

Science is an object-mediated channel for self-reference in its orientation toward the physical world, art is process-mediated in its orientation toward creativity and intersubjectivity, and spirituality self-mediated in its orientation toward the innermost dimensions of the knowing subject. But when self-referral engagement is intact in each of these domains, they transcend their surface boundaries and unite. And when this engagement is compromised, through epistemological dearth, then each line is subject to object-referral dissociation from the broader unity it is capable of leading to. And, therefore, the abhorrent dissociation from the differentiation of true religion that has given rise to religious fundamentalism has its parallel in the abhorrent dissociation from the differentiation of true science that has given rise to materialism.

Accordingly, instead of attributing the religious impulse to mass hysteria or poor educational systems, as materialists are often inclined to do, Deep Inquiry might help illuminate its roots in the primordial evolutionary thrust of cosmic creativity—the basis for the very science that materialists mistake as the only valid expression of that creativity—to find outlets for its expression. Religion, like art and science, is rooted in the core tendency toward union with the cosmic wholeness, and has unfortunately succumbed at times to the same dissociation from this core impulse as the other areas. Even amid these fundamentalist/dissociative obstacles, individuals find ways to give authentic expression to this intrinsic aspect of the nondual relationship between individual and cosmos.

Deep Inquiry could aid this realization by illuminating the limitations of language.

The term *religion*, for example, need not be confined to churches, scriptures, and denominations, but could be taken back to its foundational impulse—which is to "bind back to the source"—just as yoga means "union with the divine." Why is it so difficult to see the common ground in these descriptions of wholeness, as well as appreciate the infinite diversity of ways individuals and cultures have sought to invoke it through the ages? An integral perspective neither falls into the simplistic "all religions are the same" thinking, which stems from limited parts-to-whole engagement, nor does it lose sight of the fact that they unite in a shared quest for wholeness, ignorance of which is indicative of incomplete whole-to-parts engagement. The arts have important contributions to make in this transcendence of superficial categories. The Nigerian musician/scholar Fela Sowande provides guidance for this when he defines religion as "the inner awareness of the factual dynamic relationship between the individual on one hand and the Cosmos and World of Nature on the other," and then art as "the meaningful expression of that relationship in any medium whatsoever."[42] If art is an expression of "man's awareness and understanding of himself in relationship to a dynamic Universe of which he is an integral and indispensable unit,"[43] then surely science can be thought of similarly, just proceeding from a different epistemological entryway, as can religion with its unique processes as yet another entryway to wholeness. As we begin to understand the various means of human creative expression as driven by a cosmic impulse, we are able to recognize the sometimes childish creation narratives—whether articulated by religious fundamentalists or scientific materialists—as attempts, however absurd, at the same quest for meaning.

Buddhist Fundamentalism?

We are also able to identify the blind alleys that sometimes lure thinkers into highly narrow and rigid perceptions. Owen Flanagan's argument that Buddhism is unique among the world's wisdom traditions in the coherence between its view of the human being "and the way science says we ought to see our selves and our place in the world" is a primary example.[44] Indicative of the misinterpretation of the doctrine of *anatta*, or "no self," an aspect of what Wilber calls "Boomeritus Buddhism," Flanagan sells both science and Buddhism short in trying to reduce the second to the already-reductionist misconception that pervades the first. *Anatta* properly understood refers to the illusory and ever-changing nature of the personal self, not the absence of an eternal, transcendent Self. Perhaps most conspicuous in Flanagan's analysis is his failure to acknowledge Buddhist doctrines such as karma, reincarnation (which presumes something very soul-like), or the pantheon of gods and spiritual entities that, in fact, reveal it to share profound points of intersection with other religions, and depart equally as profoundly from the materialist science to which he subscribes. Instead, he recounts discussions with the Dalai Lama and His Holiness' apparent deference to science, which has been deeply misunderstood, in order to support the Buddhism-materialism nexus. The Dalai Lama clearly endorses karma and reincarnation, and although less explicit in his acknowledgment of discarnate entities and spiritual planes of reality, one can only surmise from his Tibetan lineage that these are also central to his worldview.

Still, Flanagan somehow manages to evade the issue of reincarnation altogether. And thus while insisting that "there are no souls, or non-physical minds" or dimensions of consciousness that would transmigrate in the reincarnation process, or "divine beings," or any of the other "supernatural concepts that have no philosophical warrant," but which are central Buddhist precepts, he nonetheless insists on the compatibility of Buddhism and materialist science.[45] This is eerily reminiscent of the materialist orientation in European classical music, where the sense seems to prevail that once the repertory was created and the ultimate musical truth was told, there was no longer a need for the majority of musicians to engage in the creative processes by which that repertory first came into existence and from which a dynamic, ever-evolving musical understanding might be possible. In science, the creative scientific method rooted in observation, deep introspection, and experiment that produced certain kinds of understandings of the natural world, so it seems, could similarly fall by the wayside once the physicalist truths were established in that discipline. As we saw with biologist Dawkins and neuroscientist Harris, elaborate arguments—this time from the philosopher Flanagan—as to the immunity of science to the same kind of dogma that is presumably inevitable in religion only underscore the degree of this dogma. The fact that even empirical findings (e.g., psi) from the realm of science itself contradict the materialist, self-confining stance of scientism, further emphasize the incoherence in this argument.

Stephen Batchelor is another self-proclaimed Western Buddhist who shares Flanagan's privileging of the same scientism as the most viable account of truth, as evidenced in his viewing the "strongest argument against gods, spirits, and tantric divinations [to be] found in the existence of the electricity grid, brain surgery, and the Declaration of Human Rights."[46] The idea these are intrinsically incompatible is a typical materialist-fundamentalist maneuver that the emergent integral science (or integral spirituality) reveals as unnecessarily dualist and misguided. But at least Batchelor exhibits a modicum of self-critical humility. "However tempting it is for me to dismiss the existence of gods and spirits as outdated nonsense, I need to be aware of the equally tenuous foundations of my own beliefs about the Big Bang, evolution by natural selection, or the neural foundations of consciousness." Again, we see an unnecessary polarization between phenomena that are conventionally perceived as incompatible, yet which the integral nondual perspective readily accommodates within a broader synthesis, the first pertaining to Upper-Left, interior dimensions, the second to Upper-Right, exterior reality. Nonetheless, recalling a conversation with an elderly, lifelong Tibetan Buddhist about these matters, Batchelor offers a remarkable concession rare among either scientific or religious materialists: "I believed these things on much the same grounds that he believed in disembodied gods and spirits. Just as I unquestionably accepted the authority of eminent scientists, so he accepted the authority of eminent Buddhist teachers."[47]

I believe that against a backdrop of Level III Deep Inquiry, where the biggest questions about the nature of the human being and cosmic reality are not only centered but investigated through the multiple lenses of empirical, philosophical, phenomenological, theoretical, and historical perspectives, these dichotomies would be exposed. This would allow participants to entertain the possibility of more expansive and inclusive visions and also to introspect into the domain-specific shadows that, left unchecked, inevitably undermine such expansiveness and inclusivity, and therefore, paradigmatic change.

Along these lines, a jazz-inspired perspective might help further defuse some of the charge inherent in talk about evolution. Did life forms evolve or differentiate completely as a kind of free improvisation, governed by no underlying principles and proceeding only by moment-to-moment adaptations, as might be associated with the neo-Darwinian perspective? Or might this development have been grounded in some kind of *a priori* principles, comparable to the "chord changes" and "rhythmic languages" atop which jazz musicians improvise, perhaps associated with a neo-Lamarkian perspective? Or some combination of both, in which the improvising both adheres to pregiven structures yet also alters these in a participatory way? Once again we encounter the issue of ontological pregivens with which integralists have wrestled, and while generally subscribing to some degree of the existence of such, have expressed confusion and ambivalence about (review the analysis at the end of chapter 4). Jazz-inspired Deep Inquiry, in addition to helping the educational world break free of its conventional polarizations, could also aid the integral community in reclaiming its nondual, integral roots.

Transcendence of superficial associations and divisions is also enhanced when Deep Inquiry goes beyond conventional analytical processes and debates and is grounded in meditation practice and nonlinear, discursive methodologies such as the Council and Bohmian dialogue protocols mentioned earlier. Now individuals begin to enliven deep intuitive faculties about their deeper nature, purpose, and those of the cosmic totality. Futile and shallow debates over Creationism, Intelligent Design, or Evolution can now give way to authentic and transformative introspection and interaction that exemplifies the highest ideals of Ultimate Reality and Meaning inquiry. Closely related polarizations between liberals and conservatives and spiritual-but-not-religious and devoutly religious identities might similarly begin to dissolve and open up genuine opportunities for mutual exchange and growth. In so doing, groundwork is established for newfound educational exploration and application.

Questions still remain, however, regarding how this newfound spiritual/religious—or creativity and consciousness—awakening might manifest in the educational world. I believe that the revisiting of the principles and policies by which interiority has been relegated to outside the academy may be a fruitful place to look.

Church-State Boundaries Reconceived

Recall my previous thoughts regarding the schism between the large percentage of not only the broader population but the academic population that hold strong spiritual beliefs, and the role of church-state boundaries, or an unnecessarily extreme conception of them, in promoting this gulf. If religion had to be excluded, then an aversion to anything that smacks of interiority is somewhat understandable. However, a more nuanced understanding of religion *writ large*, as well as availability of trans-traditional entryways, might have driven more faculty to find alternative and acceptable pathways to access religious ground.

Here it must be emphasized that church-state boundaries are in certain ways quite vague. We know that a public institution cannot endorse a particular faith, nor require students to engage in its practices. We know that schools *can* teach *about* religion as a kind of cultural-historical phenomenon. But what is not nearly so clear is the extent to which a public educational institution might yield an environment where students may engage in actual religious practices of their choosing.[48] And here an important point is noteworthy: any such legal thresholds have almost always been broached through some kind of tension between religious fundamentalist, or at least tradition-specific, agendas and scientific secular norms, the second of which are inevitably scientism-tinged.[49] What might be possible if church-state boundaries were broached through the lens of integral spirituality and integral science perspectives, where labels and divisions of all kinds—religion, spirituality, science, creativity, consciousness—are conceived to denote entryways to a broader unity?

I believe that this is precisely what will be possible with the contemplative/consciousness studies movement considered earlier, and why it is important for that movement to make the transition from its current postmodern orientation toward an integral approach. As noted, the interplay of trans-traditional and tradition-specific grounding is key, with the second generally compromised in much of this work to date. As the tradition-specific component becomes more prominent, boundaries between what is contemplative and what is religious in nature will blur. One might argue that this has been the case with this work since its inception, but inasmuch as those instances of tradition-specific grounding have usually involved Eastern lineages, and largely Buddhist ones to boot, nowhere near the politically charged climate exists that might elicit immediate protests were Abrahamic, and particularly Christian engagement, involved. However, I believe that as this all-important crossing of the exterior-interior educational divide progresses, coupled with the increased reconnection with the contemplative roots of Abrahamic lineages that has been growing in strength since the latter half of the twentieth century, student and faculty interest in integrating genuine practice and wisdom from these traditions will grow apace. And that this is to be welcomed as fully as are Eastern, indigenous, nature-based and other aspects of the vast majority of traditions available, even if some do not at first glance appear "religious" in nature.

At first glance, this approach might invite two very different reactions. One, coming from both many contemplative educators and the scientific and educational mainstream, is that it flies in the face of church-state boundaries, and that—presuming contemplative studies is really here to stay (many educators of course would rather see it disappear)—engagement with only those contemplative traditions that are clearly nonreligious in nature ought to be allowed in mainstream public institutions. By contrast, a second reaction, coming from religious conservatives, is that now, at long last, they will be able to advance their beliefs.

I believe both are rooted in narrow thinking. For one thing, the idea that some clear criteria might be identified by which a contemplative practice might be seen as religious or not is questionable. The situation might be more aptly understood as a highly gradual continuum of what appear—according to quite arbitrary and conditioned assumptions—to be more overtly religious and less overtly religious kinds of engagement. Few would deny that Bible study with corresponding prayer is religious. But is reading of Buddhist, Taoist, or Vedantic texts with corresponding meditation practice any less religious? One might reply that meditation by simply following one's breathing is essentially different, in terms of religiosity, than contemplating or seeking to invoke Christ in prayer. But when one begins to look at the deeper experiences linked with the practices and how they are described—for example, realization of Buddha-mind, or Christ consciousness—these superficial distinctions quickly fade away. What about communion with nature inspired by shamanic teachings, in which attunement to transcendent dimensions of the physical world and consciousness are central? The fact is, all of these constitute religious practice, and all need to be embraced as part of the twenty-first-century educational palette of options from which students (and faculty) may choose as they navigate their developmental pathways. Therefore, instead of shying away from the term *religion*, the time has come to plunge full out into it from an integral perspective so that fundamentalist tendencies—in religion, science, and education at large—might be dispelled and practice rendered deeper and more authentic.

This is why fundamentalist religious embrace of any such openings in the educational landscape will be counteracted by the nature of these openings. For religious practice in the emergent environment will encounter a requisite for any approach to retain its place in the emergent educational environment that fundamentalists are ill-equipped to address and by which they will be denied a place: critical juxtaposition of tradition-specific engagement and trans-traditional inquiry. It will not be enough to engage in one's practice(s) and studies separate from the broader community; rather, practitioners will need to interact with and intellectually engage in critical reflection on how their particular tributary flows into the trans-traditional melding—which means not only other spiritual lineages but the broader tapestry of the knowledge base. Tradition-specific science—biology, physics, chemistry, neuroscience—must open its horizons not only to the broader intradisciplinary (science as a whole), interdisciplinary (science within the humanities and arts) spectrum, but also the transdisciplinary realm of consciousness, spirituality, religion, and mysticism. Fundamentalist science that falls short of this will face the same fate as fundamentalist religion. Arguments for the categorical rejection of interior dimensions of reality will be viewed as extreme as categorical rejection of the fossil record, or against the significant common ground—as well as differences—between spiritual pathways, and will not survive in the emergent environment. Nor will tradition-specific musical practice that is devoid of the self-transcending processes of improvisation and composition and thus succumbs to fundamentalism in that domain. The arts, and particularly improvised jazz musical art, have much to offer in this transformation due to inherent grounding in this process spectrum and thus conversance with the idea of discipline as gateway rather than self-confining destination.

Therefore, while Deep Inquiry at first glance may appear to unacceptably risk the possible incursion of religious fundamentalist viewpoints in the educational environment, upon closer inspection it might actually provide among the most effective tools for diffusing these belief systems—even if this might mean also diffusing the equally rigid ideologies of those harboring the anti-religious concerns in the first place. If in this diffusion practitioners might, instead of rejecting their previously dogmatic (and thus self-confining) frameworks, deepen their engagement to realize them as self-transcending, the academic world could actually become a site for rendering previously superficial spiritual/religious and scientific practice more authentic. That this deepening might hold as well for approaches to contemplative practice in the current contemplative studies movement speaks to the power of the Deep Inquiry framework.

Our worldview determines where we look and where we do not for avenues to sustainability and progress; the farthest-reaching capacities of human creativity and consciousness will only be cultivated with conceptual backdrops of corresponding breadth. Scientific and religious fundamentalism not only dramatically narrow the scope of this backdrop, but do so through conspicuously weak rationales that exemplify the worst, not the best, of these important domains of human endeavor. While the academic world has managed to keep one sort of fundamentalism safely outside its borders, it has become so engulfed in and blinded by the other that it not only significantly undermines its capacity to realize its full potential in educating the whole human being, but also its capacity to assume a much-needed leadership in a world desperately in need of a new guiding vision. Deep Inquiry has the capacity to bring limiting tendencies in conventional discourse to individual and collective awareness and lay conceptual groundwork for the most exciting and awe-inspiring transformation imaginable in an area of society long immune to even moderate reform. This, and only this, will break up the academic logjam that has held the field back from realization of this potential.

Harvesting the Fruits of Deep Inquiry

How might the revitalized discourse catalyzed through Deep Inquiry be transformed into practical initiatives? After all, it is one thing for a new kind of conversation to transpire; it is another to put it into action, particularly when the kind of action needed represents such a degree of paradigmatic departure from the conventional educational worldview. Following are some thoughts about how this might be achieved.

Top-down and Bottom-up Approaches

First of all, any movement forward must entail the interplay of top-down and bottom-up approaches to reform. The first is administration-driven, the second driven by faculty, students, and staff. A key strategy that can be fairly easily deployed by the administration is to elevate customary rhetoric about change and innovation to a new level, one that faculty have not yet heard and thus have not had the opportunity to tune out. This can be framed as the difference between vertical and horizontal change. As has been pointed out at length, horizontal change entails embellishment of prevailing approaches, vertical entails overhauling the model from its foundations. The argument can be made that is not to enough to approach innovation through an academic lens; the challenges of today's world are too enormous. Administrators can, with the support of a Deep Inquiry

Group, establish a new level of exploration that steps back and examines the educational enterprise and human potential not through an academic lens but through a human developmental lens that does not shy away from spiritual questions.

A bottom-up correlate to this new conversation could be a curriculum that embodies the emergent vision. Deep Inquiry will likely underscore the need for a much broader epistemological base that encompasses meditation and other practices for creativity and consciousness development. The BFA in Jazz and Contemplative Studies curriculum provides a template for such a model that could be implemented on a cross-campus scale. It is up to the faculty to design such a model; it is up to the administration to create the receptivity on the campus for such initiatives, and to stimulate excitement about a kind of educational reform of potentially historical significance. To reiterate a point from the previous chapter—the curriculum is the bloodstream of the university, it is the river through which its values flow throughout the educational arena and to society at large. The curriculum also defines the identity of the university. It is not enough to have innovation occurring in isolated coursework, this must coalesce in a curricular pathway in which students can focus, and it must be given a name in order to assert its importance both within and beyond the academy. No mainstream institution, even with the burgeoning contemplative/consciousness studies movement, has broken the ice with a full-blown commitment to large-scale curricular implementation of this work. An extraordinary opportunity awaits the astute administration that, committed to not only "individuation," where excellent work and a modicum of originality is sustained, but a degree of "innovation" that, as exemplified by John Coltrane in jazz, foundationally alters the broader knowledge base in a way that, in integrating inner and outer realms of knowing and development, has not yet come from the academic world and is urgently needed in the world at large.

The innovating academy is one that transcends itself. It transcends the inherited notion of what it means to be educated and redefines not only the goal but the process by which it is arrived at. Any divide between the "farther reaches of human nature," to invoke Maslow's phrase from the title of his landmark book, and the farthest reaches of education is a result of individuals, no matter how progressive their rhetoric, represents a clinging to an old and obsolete conception of education and view of change through that lens. This will all but ensure the existing model remains in place. The innovator closes this gap and, in inspiring others to rise to this level, is capable of breaking the logjam.

New Faculty Appointments and Re-deployment in Paradigmatically New Areas

Just as considered in musical studies reform, both new appointments of faculty with expertise in the emergent integral terrain as well as incentives for faculty development are further ways administrators can make important contributions to change. Astute administrators at higher echelons of the institution, moreover, such as presidents and provosts, will not depend on lower-ranking leadership to identify key agents of change within their respective units where potential contributions, perhaps because of limited administrative vision at localized levels, go unrecognized. They will, instead, remain on the alert for this kind of work and find ways when they discover it to allow its transformational impact to be channeled. This may involve re-deploying faculty so that part of their load straddles a new area, and may require transcendence of conventional organizational hierarchies. When I established the Program in Creativity and Consciousness Studies at the University of Michigan, a campus-wide initiative, the pivotal connection that made this happen was between me and the senior vice-provost. Leadership in my home unit played a minimal role in this development and may well not have generated the support necessary for it to transpire. When I joined the University of Michigan faculty in 1987, I formed a faculty improvisation ensemble with several top classical artists who had limited or no experience in this process, which greatly enlivened receptivity to some of the new horizons I wished to broach. Faculty meditation groups and consciousness/spirituality discussion groups, of which the Deep Inquiry framework is an example, are important counterparts in the overall academy.

Curriculum Committees and Departments Reconceived

In order for strides in this direction to be made, it will be necessary to reconceive the nature and role of the curriculum committee, a closely related area that also eludes attention even within reform dialogues. While curriculum committees uphold an important vetting function, they all too often squelch curricular innovation through entrenchment in the outmoded notion of education as largely a third-person affair. They are bound by notions of rigor that are more akin to "rigor mortis." Howard Gardner replies to such critics of reform by distinguishing between the "sophomoric 'multiple-choice-cum-isolated fact' mentality" that conflates "superficial conformity" with "genuine rigor."[50]

Curriculum committees also tend to be strongly influenced by the self-interests of departments. Asserting that "departments are the source of much evil in universities," David Helfand, former professor of astronomy at Columbia University and president of Quest University, does not mince words in his assessment of this prominent impediment to change. "They waste enormous amounts of time and emotional energy by arguing about space, faculty lines, and resources, while walling off disciplines from innovative approaches to knowledge and restricting students and faculty alike to narrow, often outmoded paths of inquiry."[51] When departments thus place representatives on curriculum committees, the result is not unlike congressional lobbyists who in many instances exert strong influence to uphold their self-interests, which in the educational world means departmental interests rather than those of the students and institution at large.

From an integral perspective, the solution to the problem is not to dissolve departments, nor curriculum committees, but to transform their composition, functions, and identities. Just as faculty and students need to evolve a self-transcending view of their respective fields, so do departments. Curriculum committees, in turn, need to both embrace a broader vision of education and relinquish some of their authority. One strategy might be to require that curriculum committee members, during their tenure, publish peer-reviewed work on learning and teaching, with an emphasis on educational reform, in order to retain their spot on the committee. Or, perhaps more radically, only allow those engaged in such research to cast votes. Non-publishing (on learning) colleagues could still vet and offer commentary. (Here it is important to note that faculty publishing, with the exception of colleagues in education, rarely deals with learning and teaching but rather is oriented to intellectual or creative research in their field. In other words, biology, physics, sociology, and art professors do not get tenure by publishing about teaching these areas or broader educational visions but rather through engaging in the fields as practitioners.) While there is no denying it might be difficult in many academic areas and institutions to actually populate curriculum committees under these constraints, this might provide an extraordinary impetus for change. For now, those with a vested interest in stasis would have to earn the right to uphold this stance, in so doing gaining important skills that might either render their conservative platform substantive, or elicit a newfound openness to change.

Mining Existing Avenues to Change

Administrators and faculty could also harness receptivity and openings to paradigmatic change through existing areas or themes on their campuses. For example, most every institution lays claim to a commitment to diversity, which is usually construed in terms of racial, ethnic, cultural, and gender demographic balance. In recent years diversity dialogues have increasingly broached the realm of epistemology, at which point fertile openings to creativity and interior methodologies such as meditation, hence the integral parts-to-whole/whole-to-parts process scope, are readily identified. Interdisciplinary and integrative education is another important emergent theme; integral approaches provide compelling conceptions whereby interdisciplinarity is situated within a transdisciplinary spectrum.

Arts advocacy initiatives have begun to spring up in higher education, among the most prominent of which recently may be one launched at the University of Michigan in 2011. It is important that upper administrators, as they attend these events and promote this work, realize that they may be able to play an important role in holding arts units to their convictions. For example, as I conveyed in a letter to the leaders of the Michigan initiative, it is disingenuous to proclaim the importance of the arts as a vehicle for fostering creativity while academic approaches to musical arts are predicated on the inhibition of creativity. As important as arts "outreach" is arts "inreach," where a field critically examines its own patterns and premises as much as it seeks to advance its mission. Upper administrators could help elevate weak levels of self-critical inquiry, which can prevail as readily in the arts as any other field.

Sustainability is another area that is open to integral approaches, which bring in an interior dimension to this theme and reveal the importance of addressing it not only in its ecological manifestation but also economic, cultural, and spiritual dimensions. Faculty, student, and staff well-being is another area of great importance on college campuses that is directly addressed by, and thus open to, an integral educational vision.

Another promising albeit provocative area through which important integral entryways might be made is athletics. Conventionally, athletics is confined to a monodimensional, love-hate relationship with the broader academy. Everyone loves their football, basketball, hockey, and softball teams when they win. Yet when programs falter for a few years in a row, coaches begin to fear for their jobs even if the kind of teaching they provide is exceptional. From a conventional perspective, athletics is regarded as an academically suspect area, at best a necessary evil that perhaps promotes school spirit and may help overall recruiting, and at worst a realm that is inherently at odds with the educational mission and needs to be seriously curtailed.[52]

An integral understanding of both education and sports reveals a very different picture, one that calls for the role of athletics to be more deeply fathomed in order that its extraordinary educational treasures may be harnessed and transmitted to the broader institution. Think about it: Sports is unsurpassed in its capacities for mind-body integration and heightened states of consciousness or flow, exemplifying first-person experience.[53] Its rich interactive capacities exemplify second-person, intersubjective engagement. Its rigorous analytical and craft dimensions, involving careful attention to detail, sophisticated conceptual understanding, and cultivation of extraordinary technical abilities, equal if not exceed the third-person aspects of most fields. When, moreover, we view these first-, second-, and third-person domains not in isolation but as part of an interactive system, a synthesis that characterizes peak athletic performance, we see rich self-transcending capacities whereby sports opens its horizons to untold vistas of the broader knowledge base. In offense-defense team sports such as basketball, hockey, soccer, football, tennis, and lacrosse, a strong improvisatory component may be noted that is quite similar to that of jazz. Where jazz musicians spontaneously invent within the constraints of chord changes and rhythmic time feels and the moment-to-moment developments of ensemble members, athletes improvise within the constraints of their respective games and the moment-to-moment exchanges with teammates and opponents. This is not, however, to rule out the improvisatory dimensions of sports such as baseball, golf, track, and gymnastics—improvisation manifests in subtler ways in these formats.

Just as music, from an integral perspective, is more than a form of entertainment but a powerfully transformational mode of human creativity, sports when similarly viewed from an integral vantage point exhibit these kinds of properties. When it comes to situating the domain within the first-second-third person, spirituality-art-science trinity, sports can be seen as a highly sophisticated art form, comprising—as do the arts per se—multitudinous constituent forms, all of which provide powerful gateways to the inner-outer synthesis that defines an integral vehicle for creativity-consciousness development. The academic world would do well to look to this area as an important avenue to the university of the future.

In no way is this to overlook the excesses that have been all too common in the culture of intercollegiate athletics, ranging from recruiting violations to fraudulent attempts at academic eligibility to cover-ups of poor and sometimes criminal behavior by student athletes. And one can only applaud the work of the NCAA in addressing many of these problems. But to view college sports only through a conventional lens is to succumb to the worst kind of third-person confinement and overlook an important gateway for paradigmatic innovation.

Formation of Consortia

The formation of consortia for the advancement of integral education will be important to this change. Just as, like many new fields, jazz education began in small and marginalized pockets in music schools and benefited significantly from the formation of the now-defunct International Association for Jazz Education, International Association of Schools of Jazz, and most recently Jazz Education Network, the evolution of integral education from small and isolated pockets will similarly be enhanced by corresponding organizations. These organizations serve as a collective voice that asserts the importance of the respective emergent areas and provide inspiration and, by facilitating networking between colleagues at different institutions, information exchange. They indicate to astute administrators that this is an area that might warrant support and offer inroads for innovation and leadership. And less receptive colleagues, upon noticing that the existence of these broader networks forming around this work, may not be so readily inclined to dismiss it as the wayward deviations of just one or a few fringe faculty at their particular institutions.

A number of such organizations might be cited at the time of this writing. An integral education group exists within Integral Institute, which is the primary overarching body advocating integral thought. The Association for Contemplative Mind in Higher Education is another. I have recently cofounded the Consortium for Consciousness Studies in Higher Education (CCSHE) with the aim of galvanizing the few handfuls of programs (not just individual coursework) that are focusing on this work into a collective voice and also a forum for collaboration.

Educational Reform Yields Societal Reform

As noted early on, the educational world has the capacity to mirror and reify the worldview of society, or it can usher in a new worldview. Unfortunately, conventional education has succumbed to the first, not only becoming deeply entrenched in the materialist tendencies of the industrial age but perpetuating these in its classrooms, research laboratories, and concert halls. It is difficult to imagine how anyone could argue that materialism is a viable worldview for either our schools or our society. Operating without a sustainable blueprint, our world plunges closer and closer to a critical juncture in which the consequences of this lack loom ever larger on the horizon. Integral Theory offers such a blueprint, one that is quite well suited to the academic world in that it embraces, albeit in a much expanded framework that extends current academic boundaries, the best of what conventional education has to offer. The jazz-inspired integral vision, moreover, offers a kind of delivery system to bring the integral template into the academic arena, not only exemplifying its epistemological breadth, but exemplifying the liberation of thinking from conventional confinement through a wide-ranging swinging between disparate poles. This very swinging, which offers educational institutions so poised opportunities for unprecedented leadership, also has much to offer society at large as it wrestles with the extraordinary challenges of this historical moment.

Chapter 12

Planet Earth Takes a Solo

"Giant Steps," "Lazy Bird," "Countdown," and "Moment's Notice" are among a wave of compositions from John Coltrane's late tonal period that posed unprecedented challenges for musicians when it came to improvising on the harmonic structures of these pieces. Requiring the navigation of chord sequences that moved rapidly between distant key areas, these pieces made it difficult for improvisers to rely on past conventions and necessitated new strategies that were appropriate to the new kinds of "changes," as jazz musicians refer to harmonic sequences. Coltrane's subsequent forays into modal and free jazz called for, albeit involving different musical parameters, further expansion of the improvisatory palette. Transposing this principle to a global scale, the improvising ensemble called "humanity"—consisting of over seven billion members—needs to invoke new ways of thinking and action as it navigates its way through the "chord changes" of unprecedented complexity and scope that are unique to our time. Nuclear proliferation and other kinds of weapons buildup, terrorism, climate change and its host of ecological consequences, economic instability, wide-scale poverty and disease, food and water shortages, nationally and internationally divisive political tensions, and overpopulation are some of those most commonly cited. A jazz-inspired integral framework not only brings unmatched tools for identifying and understanding the roots of these challenges, it also excels in illuminating the potential for transforming this moment in history into opportunities for growth.

But if this to occur, an important first step is to take stock of this extraordinary moment in planetary history and the precarious nature of the present circumstances. If solutions to any single area remain elusive, the challenges become exponentially daunting when one considers them as part of an interconnected matrix of crises, which might be seen as a negative version of the nested synergies at the core of the jazz creativity-consciousness spectrum. Just as the synergistic interaction between improvisation, composition, performance, arranging, and various kinds of theoretical inquiry yields a notably rich template for engagement and growth, the flaring up of conditions within any given problem area can exacerbate conditions in other areas. The 2008 earthquake in poverty-ridden Haiti, where an already weak economic and social infrastructure made the consequences of this natural disaster far worse than they might have been, is what in retrospect—without in any way downplaying the magnitude of this catastrophe and the resultant suffering that continues to this day—may turn out to be a relatively localized example. Without dwelling on possible doomsday scenarios, it does not require an excessive stretch of the imagination to contemplate instances involving far more widespread instances of cross-parametric crisis confluence that are not confined to a particular country or region of the world. Never before have the chronological windows for action been smaller, nor has the need for action been more urgent.

If these challenges are to be transformed into opportunities for progress, not just in terms of material existence but also along intellectual, creative, cultural, and spiritual lines, it is important to embrace the present moment with the heightened presence of the creative improviser. To put the current situation out of our minds and hide behind our day-to-day routines, which is all too common in the developed world where circumstances for many are deceptively stable, is to succumb to a weak form of improvisatory engagement. To wake up to the situation and invest time, finances, and other resources in addressing environmental, medical, and social causes represents a higher level of improvisatory creativity. As does exploring new vistas in science and technology for potentially important breakthroughs that might be key to sustainability. Or supporting political candidates who bring dynamic, progressive visions that are driven by the sense of urgency called for in the present moment.

An even more complete improvisatory engagement, moreover, is possible that recognizes the need for both exterior approaches as well as interior understanding and solutions—in other words, outer social action informed by inner spiritual communion and growth. This describes the Integral Improviser, one who embraces the circumstances of our times with both a sense of urgency yet also a comprehensive vision and sense of evolutionary opportunity and joy. The Integral Improviser recognizes the enormity and complexity of the challenges at hand, yet also the possibility that the quest to meet these challenges may enable not only mere survival but new vistas of growth in areas ranging from health, prosperity, creativity, intelligent use of the environment, education and human rights for all, spiritual progress, and—last but not least—global peace. The emergent spirituality movement in the latter part of the twentieth century has placed increasing emphasis on spiritual growth as not just an interior affair but also an inner-outer synthesis that is predicated on robust engagement with the issues of the times. The time has come for this principle to be the guiding force for the twenty-first century, planetary integral improvising ensemble.[1]

In chapter 6, we considered the internal mechanics that underlie peak improvisatory performance, where moment-to-moment temporal conception enables the transformation of ideas that might have been initially conceived as products of linear (albeit localized) past-present-future causal chains to present events that are generators of future possibilities. Or in other words, these events are *centered*. When exclusively conceived as products of predecessors, events or perceptual phenomena occupy the periphery of one's awareness. When awareness shifts and events are centered, they are experienced as generators of new possibilities—which does not preclude simultaneous awareness of relationship to past events, but frees us from binding attachments to the past. This thereby enables a kind of clearing of the creative slate and receptivity to radically new, and even anomalous, possibilities, that might have, in less robust improvisatory engagement, remained far outside one's horizon of expectations.

These very kinds of improvisatory transformations also manifest on a planetary scale and pose extraordinary ramifications for Ensemble Earth's navigating the chord changes at hand. Never before has the capacity been more crucial for not only individuals but also communities and even nations to liberate from the inertia of the past and view the present as an opportunity for newfound creativity and progress. Inherited patterns of energy consumption need to give rise to more efficient and prudent patterns. Inherited patterns whereby terrorism and violence are automatically countered with further violence need to give rise to a more expanded slate of strategies for peace. Countries, regions, ethnicities, and communities that have been ravaged by generations of conflict, often involving horrendous brutality against one another, need to break free from the endless cycles of retribution that sustain these conflicts and engage in the present moment as the ground for a new future vision. Love, forgiveness, and compassion, then, can be seen as having improvisatory roots.

As present centering capacities are enlivened, entirely new strategies may emerge, at which point the question arises—which comes first, the heightened improvisatory experience of the present, or the new strategies? The answer is that either may serve as transformational, creative catalyst, at which point both can work together for maximal results. Heightened experience of the moment, in other words, represents an expansive stage of consciousness in which we have optimal access to acquired resources— our inner repository of skills, information, influences, and intuitions—as well as receptivity to the infinite possibilities that might be perceived in our surroundings. And by the same token, new possibilities can catalyze this transformation from ordinary to heightened consciousness for those who are open to these possibilities. The transformation needed in our times calls for both parts-to-whole and whole-to-parts engagement.

In this light, let us review three important manifestations of the creativity-consciousness relationship that are anomalous in both conventional dialogues about sustainability, and even, albeit to a lesser degree, integral discourse, that jazz can help center. I believe that if this centering can occur in integral circles, followed by the same positioning in the educational world, this would catalyze an openness in broader sectors of society to an entirely new vision of human creative and spiritual potential. Integral thinkers such as Ken Wilber, Andrew Cohen, and Steve MacIntosh have suggested that some sort of World Federation will emerge and guide humanity in the transition that is to come.[2] Development of creativity and consciousness must be central to any charter or constitution that such a body might adopt, and it is incumbent upon the integral community to establish a more secure grounding in these premises.

The three forms of anomaly centering involve integral understandings of creativity and consciousness on individual, collective, and cosmic scales. As we will see, from each kind of understanding extend practical ramifications that may give rise to entirely new approaches to sustainability and progress in response to the challenges of our times.

Three Manifestations of the
Creativity-Consciousness Relationship Centered by Jazz

Individual Creativity and Consciousness

The first instance of jazz-driven anomaly centering involves the creativity-consciousness relationship as it manifests on an individual scale. At first glance, it might be argued that this is already fairly well centered, as interest in meditation and transcendent or peak experience of various kinds, which are core to the integral vision, is at an all-time high even in mainstream society. However, what has not yet been centered in either circle are the self-referential mechanics that underlie the meditation-improvisation relationship. As we have explored, in meditation, undertaken in silence, the self curves back on the Self, unimpeded by ordinary kinds of mental, physical, emotional, and sensory engagement, and thus relativistic objects of perception. In creative activity, the self curves back on the Self while fully engaged with objects—whether they be the chord changes of jazz, economic theories, ecological strategies, pathways of social action, or any of the innumerable ways humans create. This understanding illuminates important differences between meditative and active transcendence that enhance our awareness of how these modes of engagement complement each other. At this point we gain a theoretical basis for the interplay of parts-to-whole creativity and whole-to-parts meditation practices—always bearing in mind that the entire process spectrum is *writ large* (e.g., meditation as a continuum, improvisation as a continuum)—that are central to the jazz-inspired, integral template for creativity-consciousness growth. From this enhanced conceptual awareness the prospects for implementation in educational and broader settings, including the business world, social service agencies, environmental organizations, medicine, the military, and government are increased.

Collective, Intersubjective Creativity and Consciousness

A second manifestation of the creativity-consciousness relationship that an integral understanding of jazz helps center is the enlivened experience of collective consciousness that is invoked in group creative formats; in other words, the uniting of players, listeners, and environment into a self-organizing unity. We have examined this experience as not only a *sense* of interconnectedness, but as contact with an ontologically veridical, intersubjective field aspect of consciousness to which individual consciousness is linked. We have seen that an ever-growing body of empirical findings into nonlocal and intersubjective consciousness supports this understanding, which is also consistent with the accounts of consciousness posited by most if not all of the world's wisdom traditions.

Christopher Bache, in his compelling commentary on enlivening collective consciousness in his university classroom teaching, provides examples of an instance of intersubjectivity that uniquely parallels that invoked in jazz.[3] Reflecting his notion of a "group mind" or "class mind," a student recounts:

> All of us who have been in your class feel a deep connection
> to one another. We don't know what it is. We only know that it
> is there . . . something binding us together. We were sensitive
> to each other's thoughts and feelings. There were times when
> I could pick up bits and pieces of people's thoughts.[4]

More far-reaching ramifications extend from the possibility that large groups of meditators gathering for extended practice can radiate coherence and calm in the environment, thereby reducing crime, accidents, and illness.[5] The basic principle is that individual consciousness, or the personal self, is but a facet of collective consciousness, which is the transcendent Self, and therefore all human behavior manifests against, and is informed by, this transcendent, collective backdrop. If the collective field is permeated by stress, tendencies toward outer stressful behavior are greater; if the field is more harmonious and coherent, so will be thinking and action. Because meditation involves the merging of the personal self with the transcendent, collective Self that is the source of creation, it promotes collective harmony. When meditation is practiced in large groups, the effect is magnified by a "group dynamics of consciousness," in the words of Maharishi Mahesh Yogi, the foremost exponent of this idea in recent times. Due to the "indomitable influence of coherence in national consciousness" that results from establishment of large groups in a given country, "collective stress is eliminated, negativity is neutralized, national creativity is enlivened, and all aspects of national life function increasingly in harmony with Natural Law." In turn, this generates "a profoundly nourishing influence for the whole world family."[6]

It is difficult to imagine a more powerful vehicle for what Llewellyn Vaughn-Lee calls the "return of the divine feminine and the world soul." "In denying the feminine her sacred power and purpose we have impoverished life in ways we do not understand." Without an understanding of the "interconnectedness of life, how all the parts relate to one another, we cut our world off from the source that alone can heal, nurture, and transform it."[7] Maharishi attributes the transformative impact of collective meditation practice to the enlivenment of the interaction of *Gyan Shakti*, the power of silence, and *Kriya Shakti*, the power of action, in the collective consciousness that is the source of creation. "We bow down to this great moment when Mother Divine is expressing to us that performance that is the nourishing power of the world."[8]

Roger Nelson, researching the collective meditation phenomenon independently as part of his Global Consciousness Project, provides further corroboration for this effect by measuring field enlivenment through random number generators that respond to atypical coherence. Following the 9/11 terrorist attacks, a particularly large group of meditators gathered in Iowa with the intention to "meditate together and create an influence of stability and peace." When the largest number had gathered on September 26, the random number streams showed a deviation from expectation that was "steady and unusually strong, leading to a final result that has a chance likelihood of about 1,000 to 1."[9] Robert Oates and others have proposed that the establishment of these groups throughout the world might even be an antidote to terrorism and larger global conflicts.[10]

To be sure, this second type of anomaly arguably dwarfs the first in the extent to which it challenges conventional academic, and thus materialist, assumptions about the nature of the human being, human potential, and reality. It is one thing to bring transcendence and even meditation practices into the picture in attempts to cultivate this experience—ideas that might be accepted apart from any kinds of ontological claims about interior or spiritual dimensions of the human being and reality. One can ascribe to a materialist worldview and reap significant benefits from meditation. The idea of collective mind is a very different story, as it represents the beginnings of an account of the human being that is much more compatible with the world's spiritual traditions than that of the materialist worldview that has had the academic sciences—and thus the academy at large—so firmly within its grip. If the possibility that dimensions of consciousness exist that transcend the physical is problematic to the contemporary academy, the idea of an intersubjective consciousness poses challenges of an even higher order for it begins to point in the direction of nondual mysticism that holds individual consciousness and cosmic wholeness are inseparable.

And neither are these ideas and supportive findings, although compatible with the integral worldview, as centered in integral discourse as they might be. This is not to suggest that concepts such as Jung's collective unconscious, Emerson's Oversoul, Teilhard de Chardin's noosphere, and Sheldrake's morphic fields are absent in integral literature.[11] Rather, that the idea of deep intersubjectivity—which Christian de Quincey emphasizes transcends language-bound communication and symbol exchange—has not been placed at the forefront near to the extent that is possible and needed, where it might serve as a platform for further theoretical investigation and practical application.[12] Though there is no denying that the prospects of enlivening harmony in the environment through collective meditation is a bold proposition, it needs to be placed front and center in our thinking if it is to be critically examined and potentially embraced. For it represents not only a lateral expansion of conventional strategies, but also a paradigmatically new, vertically innovative approach to sustainability. This does not mean conventional interventions, such as diplomacy and prudent economic and ecological policies that are undertaken not with self-interests but with the whole in mind, will be unnecessary. Rather, these need to be pursued as part of a broader matrix of strategies, which might be seen as a global version of the top-down, bottom-up, or parts-to-whole/whole-to-parts interplay that lies at the heart of individual creativity-consciousness development. Conventional interventions are top-down, parts-to-whole, linear approaches; collective meditation represents a bottom-up, whole-to-parts, nonlinear approach; the full spectrum is necessary. But until the idea of a collective, intersubjective consciousness is centered, any further application will be limited.

The centering of intersubjectivity also brings us closer to the doorstep of an even more far-reaching, jazz-inspired conception of the creativity-consciousness relationship—which is the inextricable link between creativity and consciousness on individual and cosmic scales.

Nondual, Cosmic Creativity, and Consciousness

Here we encounter once again the age-old premise of nonduality or unity—that human consciousness is inextricably linked to the universal consciousness that is the source of creation—that has been central to most of the world's wisdom traditions. Within this general nonduality premise we have identified a strong nonduality premise that holds individual creative and spiritual experience and development as rooted in the very same self-referential mechanics that underlie how cosmic intelligence creates the infinitely diverse universe. Richard Tarnas, in his book *Cosmos and Psyche*, captures both viewpoints when he states that "the cosmos . . . appears to be informed by some kind of pervasive creative intelligence . . . with which human intelligence is intimately connected . . . and in which it can consciously participate."[13] The "participatory turn"[14] in contemporary spiritual discourse represents one of the most exciting frontiers being explored, and the strong nonduality premise enables new perspectives on this frontier. The idea is generally framed from the perspective that spiritual pathways are not comprised solely of preexisting terrain that lie waiting to be discovered, which thus invites claims of exclusivity (e.g., one avenue to spiritual reality may be superior to another), but in fact are forged and created through the experiences and development of individual spiritual aspirants. The strong nonduality thesis enables us to take this thinking a step further and affirms that, therefore, individual creativity and consciousness evolution contributes to the evolution of the cosmos itself.

At this point, the prior two anomalies take on entirely new meaning from both conceptual and practical vantage points. Now improvisatory and meditative engagement are seen as not only localized vehicles for growth but, in fact, vehicles for enlivening the very mechanics of creativity and consciousness *through which the cosmos creates*. As considered earlier, the stakes are raised when it comes to excluding these from educational and social systems. As, if not more profoundly, collective meditation and collective improvisation represent not only frameworks for the melding of individual minds (and hearts and bodies) in a localized oneness, but represent an even more intensified enlivenment of the mechanics of cosmic creativity. We will shortly consider practical ramifications of this that extend far beyond reduced violence, accidents, and illness, as important as these results may be.

De Quincey underscores the significance of this new understanding of intersubjectivity when he asks whether or not collective consciousness emerges from subjectivity, or whether or not the opposite might hold. In other words, is collective mind an emergent phenomenon from the level of individual mind, or might intersubjectivity be foundational, of which individual consciousness is a subsequent differentiation? In arguing for the second of these, which it must be added does not rule out the capacity for individual mind to also inform collective consciousness, he articulates a vision compatible with the strong nonduality premise.[15] If all of creation is a manifestation of universal, cosmic intelligence curving back on itself and generating untold strata of differentiation, intersubjective consciousness—a more intensified and nonlocal manifestation of cosmic self-reference—can be seen as a more primary level of differentiation of which individual consciousness—a more localized manifestation of cosmic self-reference—is a further differentiation.

But mention of group dynamics of consciousness, among the more dramatic examples of the capacity in human consciousness to enliven the cosmic intelligence and thus coevolutionary nature of reality, is not prominent in participatory literature, or as seen, in integral literature, let alone the educational circles where this centering, if the shift is to significantly manifest in society, must take place. I view this as a result of predominantly parts-to-whole discourse that tends to fall short in fathoming the whole, and either wholesale absence, or at most, notably weak whole-to-parts inquiry that proceeds from inadequate nondual grounding. As we have considered earlier, at the moment one invokes the nonduality premise, a core precept to Integral Theory that often eludes integral discourse, one makes a commitment to full probing of the biggest questions of human and universal existence, Ultimate Reality and Meaning. An important part of which is a cosmic narrative that provides an account of the "flaring forth" of the infinitely differentiated manifestations of reality.

As argued previously, while concerns about URAM inquiry are understandable, even more problematic is an aversion to it, which in arbitrarily privileging the metaphysical assumption that such inquiry is neither authentically possible nor productive, progress in harnessing the participatory potential of human consciousness is impeded. In other words, if human consciousness is indeed inextricably linked to the cosmic intelligence, a precept that one would presume to be central to any participatory transpersonal vision and certainly to anything that lays claim to being considered integral, then any limitations regarding the extent to which the ultimate questions of existence are apprehensible to human understanding pale compared to what indeed may be fathomed. Weak parts-to-whole inquiry that never quite reaches the nondual whole, along with limited whole-to-parts attempts, significantly inhibit any subsequent participatory conception. Exemplifying the first approach, Ferrer's characterization of participatory spiritual foundations as "one ocean with many shores" may be then seen as arrived at, as it were, by land.[16] But the self-referential link between creativity and consciousness on individual and cosmic scales, again which is absent even in participatory and integral discourse, directs us to also proceed from the ocean itself. In short, an integral conception of the participatory turn enables, if not requires, the two approaches to coexist, parts-to-whole and whole-to-parts, in robust capacities.

When the nonduality premise is fully centered, the complementary functions of these approaches and thus a more complete conception of the participatory nature of human creativity and consciousness in cosmic evolution are possible. This gives rise to what might be considered a "post-integral" understanding of Ultimate Reality and Meaning, which by now we can declare is synonymous with individual and cosmic creativity and consciousness, for which music in general, and jazz in particular, are positioned to play important roles in bringing to the forefront of educational and societal conversations.

Music as Post-integral Catalyst

Let us use the notion of intersubjective consciousness, now understood as a manifestation of cosmic intelligence, as a post-integral gateway. A continuum of possibilities extending from collective meditation practice directs our attention toward post-integral frontiers. If this kind of collective practice can, as studies suggest, radiate coherence and harmony in an environment resulting in reduced crime, accidents, and illness, might further potentialities exist from this enlivenment of the cosmic intelligence that gives rise to all of creation? For example, might this coherence extend to weather and climate, to mention two areas where pressing challenges loom, widely predicted water scarcity perhaps foremost among them? And if this is possible, might it also extend to planetary geothermal processes, as in volcanoes and earthquakes?

There is no denying the radical nature of this kind of speculation and the apparent difficulties in providing either theoretical or empirical rationales that might support it. However, when we take into account the matrix of considerations and findings that suggest age-old conceptions of consciousness as nonlocal, intersubjective, and interactive with matter (what we saw in chapter 4 as *psychokinesis*), notions of consciousness as reducible to a material substrate, or at best, epiphenomenal to it, begin to yield to more expansive conceptions, including the understanding of consciousness as primary, even to matter, in the broader scheme of creation. At which point, the very notion of what is radical needs to be revisited, because what may ultimately turn out to be the most radical notion of our lifetimes may be the materialist account that has been handed down to many of us as ultimate truth and which has spawned untold problems in our world.

How might jazz deliver a post-integral understanding of reality and inform corresponding practical explorations?

Here we return to the three-tiered, vertical model of tradition considered first in chapter 3 (not to be confused with the four competing understandings of the jazz tradition examined in chapter 5). Recall that the surface tier consists of trans-traditional navigation of contemporary pathways, informed by the melding of streams uniquely enabled by the integral skill set (Contemporary Improviser-Composer-Performer). The middle tier consists of the tributaries, or the musical lineages, that inform (and are in turn informed by) this melding. The underlying tier consists of engagement with traditions, or aspects thereof, in which the understanding of musical sound as primordial vibration that originates in the most foundational and subtle frequencies of cosmic intelligence is preserved. Western traditions such as jazz, European classical, popular and much folk music, because they are based in the tempered scale, may not be nearly as fertile ground for this kind of inquiry as non-Western lineages, with Indian music a primary example. In this regard, interest among jazz musicians in Indian music due to its rhythmic and spiritual dimensions, as in its connection to meditation, might be seen as both emblematic of an integral musical pathway and laying groundwork for subsequent post-integral explorations and growth. The point is not that Indian music is the only source for exploration of the primordial nature of sound and its connection with consciousness and cosmic intelligence that distinguishes the post-integral model; other lineages might be grounded in this knowledge as well. Most important is that in the post-integral musical era, musicians will not only engage in the contemporary confluence and dynamic interplay with traditional tributaries that fuel and are nourished by that, but also some form of explorations into the most foundational realm of spiritual psycho-acoustics, the totality of this engagement informing musical understanding and practice.

In going into this underlying tier of musical tradition, it is important to emphasize how widespread is the idea of music as a manifestation of universal principles. "The concept of the harmony of the spheres," as we are reminded by the German physicist Hans Kayser, "is as old as the first awakening of mankind to consciousness."[17] This idea is undergoing a revival. "What we call music in our everyday language," wrote the Sufi musician and mystic Hazrat Inayat Khan, "is only a miniature, which our intelligence has grasped from the music or harmony of the whole universe which is working behind everything, and which is the source and origin of nature."[18] Noting that "it was not until the Renaissance that God became portraiture, prior to that he had been conceived of [as] sound or vibration," the composer/musicologist Murray Schafer points to deep roots of the association between music and the "sonic materials of the universe."[19]

Generally framed from a structural vantage point, an integral reading of jazz makes possible a richer investigative lens that consists of both process and structure facets. From a process standpoint, the self-referential core of improvisation provides, as considered in chapter 4, a parts-to-whole lens to the self-referential core of cosmic improvisation, the *lila* or play of creation in which the one generates the many. We can thus paraphrase the philosopher Henryk Skolimowski's assertion that "we create because the Cosmos creates through us"[20] by stating that we "improvise because the Cosmos improvises through us." In other words, the spontaneous, self-referential curving back of the cosmic intelligence onto itself that gives rise to all of creation is more clearly embodied in improvisatory creativity than any other form. And from this primordial improvisatory core emerges more differentiated improvisatory and compositional creative streams, whose manifestation appears most vivid in the realm of music, and jazz in particular.

From a structural standpoint, jazz's archetypally rich rhythmic and pitch foundations point us to the origins of musical sounds at the junction point between unmanifest, undifferentiated cosmic intelligence and the faintest stirrings of the manifest, differentiated world noted earlier. This provides a contemporary context that is compatible with the long-held idea that musical pitch systems are intimately linked to the cosmic order—from the structure of the solar system and orbits of the planets to the subatomic world. Kayser notes Kepler's role in elevating this from "mere faith" to being aligned with "scientific thinking." In his *Harmonices Mundi*, "Kepler shows that between the mutual velocities of the planets there exists a great number of musical harmonies. He discovered his famous Third Law of Planetary Motion through typical harmonical thinking, the so-called octave reduction."[21] The German musicologist Wilfried Krüger and the French nuclear physicist Jean Charon, notes Joachim Berendt, proposed correlations between "the eight electrons of the oxygen atom shell and the eight protons of the oxygen atom nucleus" and the major scale, as well as between the spins of particles and half and whole tones.[22] Along the same lines, the British chemist John Newlands in 1864 correlated musical intervals with the periodic table of the elements.[23]

The Time Theory in Indian music, consistent with this thinking, is predicated on the notion that the intervallic structures of the *ragas* correspond to frequencies in the daily cycle, and thus by playing certain *ragas* at certain times one can radiate harmony and other effects in the environment. This bears similarities with ancient Greek and Roman ideas. "Thousands of years before the advent of the profession of music therapy," Edith Boxhill notes, "the shaman or medicine man of many cultures was aware of the curative power of music and used it directly in healing." This power was recognized by Pythagoras, who "prescribed specific musical intervals and modes to promote health," and by Plato, who "linked music to the moral welfare of the nation in *Laws*."[24]

Here a variety of further claims and studies might be noted. Tompkins and Bird in their classic book *The Secret Life of Plants* report findings indicating certain kinds of plants respond differently to particular kinds of music.[25] Masaru Emoto's studies of the effect of music on the patterns of ice crystals suggest some capacity for music to affect the physical environment.[26] More provocative claims, while difficult to substantiate, let alone for many to swallow, include accounts reported by Ravi Shankar in his autobiography of master musicians from ancient times who, knowing what *raga* to play at what time of day combined with extraordinary expressive and technical skills, were able to "bring rain, melt stones, cause flowers to blossom, attract ferocious wild animals—even snakes and tigers—to a peaceful, quiet circle in a forest around a musician. To us, in the modern, materialist age," Shankar reflects, "all this seems like a collection of fables, but I sincerely believe that these [capacities] were all feasible, especially when one considers that these great musicians were not just singers and performers, but also great yogis."[27]

Charles Diserens reports on similar effects, where particular *ragas* would allegedly elicit peaceful or hostile behavior, end droughts, and affect the growth of plants.[28] Alain Danielou distinguishes within this musical tradition between *marga* rules, which are "universal and unchangeable," and *desi* principles, "which vary endlessly according to place and time." Affirming these transformational capacities, he asserts, "The power of a music constructed according to *marga* rules is extraordinary, its influence over animate and inanimate things unlimited. There is no sort of transformation in the structure or appearance of things that cannot be achieved through the influence of organized sounds."[29] The overlying two tiers of tradition noted previously may thus be seen as engagement with *desi* principles, the underlying one with *marga* rules.

What is to be made of these kinds of claims? From a conventional, materialist standpoint, the tendency is to categorically dismiss them. From an integral standpoint, they are neither categorically dismissed nor blindly embraced, but positioned within a broader spectrum of possibilities and findings where they may be critically examined and then either mindfully set aside or viewed as avenues for further exploration. Here the unique critical inquiry capacities inherent in the integral framework, which include first-second-third-person approaches, dwarf that which are possible from the exclusively third-person materialist vantage point, which is even limited within the third-person domain.

Beginning with an integral third-person, object-mediated (but not object-bound) perspective, such claims are juxtaposed with a large slate of phenomena, both those which are conventionally accepted and not, in order that the various findings or propositions may bump up against each other, which helps perceivers liberate from conditioned assumptions that might arbitrarily rule out one or another possibilities. Here, then, the intimate relationship between sound, consciousness, and matter that is implicit in the prior claims is positioned side by side with findings that are also suggestive of this relationship (e.g., the ten or so categories of psi research). Bearing some compatibility with the idea that sound may impact weather, McTaggart reports on indigenous interventions where shamans induced rain in draught-ridden regions.[30] The physicist Roger Nelson points to preliminary findings that corroborate with this.[31] When, for example, we couple this with the extensive psychokinesis work that has been done, perhaps the most dramatic of which is the Stanford physicist William Tiller's work with meditating subjects altering the pH balance in a solution through mere intention, this may not be as far-fetched as it seems.[32]

From an integral second-person, process-mediated perspective, critical inquiry into these possibilities is driven by diverse epistemologies. Improvisation, composition, meditation, and theoretical inquiry—the process spectrum of integral jazz—are primary examples. Process diversity promotes critical analysis by helping investigators liberate from conditioned assumptions through the often turbulent movement from different kinds of awareness inherent in process-rich engagement. Moving from analytical investigation to improvisatory exploration to compositional development of ideas over time shakes practitioners out of complacent, status quo thinking. And when we add meditation to the process scope, a kind of first-person, self-mediated inquiry is possible that is not otherwise, where the experience of pure consciousness provides direct experience of a realm of perception that is preverbal, thus transcendent of language, assumptions, and expectations.

In short, the synergistic interplay of first-second-third-person modes of critical engagement allow a degree of critical reflection that is simply not possible through materialist approaches that deny the very existence of first-person reality, tend to confine themselves to third-person investigation, and to be weak in second-person approaches. Now practitioners can directly observe the delicate juncture between pure, wakeful awareness and the faintest stirrings of thought, thereby developing conversance with the manner in which perspectives are both constructed according to the conditioning of one's environment and yet also dissolved, at which point one is optimally able to discern between ideas that endure due to deeper as compared to more superficial ontological substance. Individuals are now positioned to make more informed choices when it comes to worldview, as opposed to blindly inheriting perspectives that are exclusive, fear-driven, and devoted more to preserving the status quo than a genuine, open quest for knowledge.

It is imperative that room for this new vision of the human being and critical inquiry protocol be found in our educational systems if it is to manifest in the world at large. Our worldview dictates where we look for solutions and how we pursue them. There is no greater priority in education than in training individuals in methods for dynamic, critically rich approaches to worldview construction and dissolution. Swinging hard, far and wide, between familiar terrain and far-reaching possibilities, from the intricate and intensive pursuit of skills in craft and rigorous analysis to wide-ranging exploratory excursions, jazz art provides a template for this expanded kind of critical inquiry. From this, informed choices may be made as to where we look for solutions to present challenges, and how to transform them into opportunities for growth.

Although some—materialists and nonmaterialists alike—may find the ideas broached here startling, if this is due to lack of prior exposure, then this kind of excursion into new territory might be embraced as part of creative development. And when we think deeply about climate change, thus realizing that conventional, linear solutions alone are extremely unlikely to address this problem, might the possibility that human consciousness might impact weather and climate, however preposterous it might seem, pose ramifications that, however seemingly implausible, cannot be ignored? Dean Radin, in a delightfully provocative reflection on future applications that might extend from a nondual, integral understanding of consciousness, muses about a coming era in which "specialized human intention teams [are formed] to regulate the global climate."[33] In my view, any discomfort over these possibilities pales when examining materialist-driven explorations of possible future interventions and explorations of human potentialities. Here again, on a broader scale, we encounter the need to distinguish novelty from innovation, with the first resulting from the inertia of differentiation but prone to dissociation, and the second genuinely grounded in interior principles that promote evolutionary movement toward differentiated wholeness.

The inventor Ray Kurzweil, in his book *The Age of Spiritual Machines*, predicts that genetic engineering and nanotechnology will in the not too distant future render distinctions between carbon-based human beings and artificially created intelligent entities moot. Not only will people "have relationships with automated personalities and use them as companions, teachers, caretakers, and lovers,"[34] but also entities that are either technologically enhanced or completely technologically generated may have capacities for spiritual experiences. The basic premise, predicated on the notion that what we think of consciousness is reducible to or epiphenomenal to neurobiological activity, is that by reverse engineering the human physiology, technology is rapidly moving toward a time when every aspect of the human body may be artificially replicated. "Regardless of the nature or derivation of a mental experience, spiritual or otherwise," Kurzweil reflects, "once we have access to the computational processes that give rise to it, we have the capacity to understand its neurological correlates."[35] At which point these correlates may be replicated synthetically in new self-conscious entities that "claim to be conscious," claims that eventually "are largely accepted."[36] Kurzweil and others view emergence of such entities as part of a line of technological development that at some future point will give rise to a "singularity," where intelligent machines are capable of creating even more intelligent machines—what David Chalmers describes as AI+ (Artificial Intelligence plus) giving rise to AI++, initiating a chain of increasingly super-intelligent systems that would represent "one of the most important events in the history of the planet."[37]

Although there is good reason, when considering the full spectrum of research into human consciousness at hand, to doubt—Kurzweil's and

Chalmers' arguments to the contrary notwithstanding—whether the full emotional, creative, spiritual, and certain cognitive aspects of human intelligence can be replicated artificially, what is important to consider is the materialist vantage point that underpins this kind of exploration, which is likely to nonetheless yield some sort of results even if short of those claimed. In other words, as science and technology advance and gain the capacity to fathom realms of creation that raise untold ethical and spiritual questions, is there no reason for concern about negative consequences—which Kurzweil and Chalmers are both quick to admit— to these sorts of excursions?

Kurzweil himself underscores such risks when he acknowledges the prospects, perhaps bordering on inevitability, of the design of self-replicating nanoviruses that could cause unthinkable kinds of destruction. Chalmers acknowledges possibilities no less chilling than the "end of the human race, an arms race of warring machines, and the destruction of the planet." It would thus be imperative in our pursuit of this kind of development to proceed "very carefully, by building appropriate values into machines, and by building the first AI and AI+ systems in virtual worlds."[38] And while there is little reason to doubt that the vast majority of individuals pursuing cutting-edge research and application in genetic engineering and related areas that probe the foundational aspects of the human psychophysiology may have the best of intentions in their commitment to finding cures for diseases, ending poverty, and other enhancements to the quality of life attributed to these developments, it takes only a few individuals with less noble intentions to utilize this knowledge in catastrophic ways. We have reached a point when anything short of self-transcending, integral science is undertaken at great risk; the time has come for the emergence of such an integral approach to science, one that is informed by the most comprehensive understanding of human creativity and consciousness, thus a science that intersects profoundly with art and spirituality. This will require a foundational change in the way science is conceived within and beyond the academic world.

Here it might be emphasized that, while I have argued for the need for wide-ranging exploration—jazz-inspired swinging between familiar and radical terrain—in order to break free from conditioned patterns in all fields, this is not to suggest compromised critical examination, let alone practical implementation, related to areas explored. Once again, tradition-specific and trans-traditional engagement and domains coevolve. The three-tiered model of post-integral engagement, and its first-second-third-person domains inspired by jazz, provide a robust framework for critical inquiry that continually juxtaposes traditional insights with new possibilities. Jazz thus exemplifies the capacity for art making as not only a powerful, expressive, transformational vehicle in its own right, but also as a key agent for this urgently needed science-spirituality synthesis. And just as leading innovators in jazz throughout much of its history—including Duke Ellington, Charles Mingus, Max Roach, Dizzy Gillespie, John Coltrane, and Muhal Richard Abrams—rejected the label due not to the musical and cultural richness it represented but the self-confining connotations that ran counter to their self-transcending creative explorations, the time has come for similar transcendence of categories in scientific and spiritual circles so that these important areas of endeavor can unite as well as strengthen their respective integrities.

As a whole, the scientific community, which is housed largely in the academic world, lags far behind—albeit with notable exceptions—the spiritual community, which lies outside the academy, in this regard. Indeed, it is not without great risk that an academic scientist will proclaim the fulfillment of scientific practice to be when whatever entryway is pursued—whether it is physics, chemistry, evolutionary biology, or neuroscience—opens up its boundaries to intersect with the realms of art and spirituality. Yet this is the integral paradigm that needs to guide all fields of inquiry, and one need look no further than the musical world to find in jazz a potent source of inspiration and guidance for this expanded and inclusive vision. Let us recognize this treasure in our midst and harness its transformational resources in order that humanity may take its next evolutionary strides.

Notes

Introduction

1. Mirra Alfassa was the longtime spiritual guide and partner of the twentieth-century sage Sri Aurobindo, and is commonly referred to as "the Mother." She is quoted here in Allan Combs' *Consciousness Explained Better*, 135.

2. In *The Weather Makers*, Tim Flannery suggests that even if all carbon emissions were to cease now, results would not be evident for another 75 years. Needless to say, this does not bode well. Other thinkers on this topic are more sanguine, while sharing the sense of urgency for action. Lester Brown, for example, in *Plan B 4.0: Mobilizing to Save Civilization* outlines a number of strategies that he believes would ensure sustainability. The philosopher Ken Wilber and spiritual teacher Andrew Cohen engage in an interesting dialogue on humanity's prospects for survival in *EnlightenNext* magazine, June 2011.

3. R. Buckminster Fuller, *Utopia or Oblivion*.

4. In addition to the commentary to this effect one will likely find from most major spiritual teachers, see also Edmund Bourne, *Global Shift*; Peter Russell, *Waking Up in Time*; Hardin Tibbs' vision as reported in Ross Robertson, "Dreams of an Eco-Spiritual Futurist"; Jean Houston's chapter "Jump Time Is Now" and Barbara Marx Hubbard's chapter "A Vision for Humanity," in *The Mystery of 2012: Predictions, Prophecies and Possibilities*.

5. Ken Wilber, "Introduction to Integral Theory and Practice," 1.

6. Ibid., 1, 3.

7. Perhaps the most comprehensive account in support of this is George Lewis' *A Power Stronger Than Itself*. See also Peter Westbrook's, *The Flute in Jazz: Window on World Music*.

8. The transcend and include principle is found in much of Wilber's writing; see for example Wilber, "Introduction to Integral Theory and Practice," *Sex, Ecology, Spirituality*, and *Integral Spirituality*.

9. See, for example, Jenny Boyd, *Musicians in Tune*; Lewis Porter, *John Coltrane: His Life and Music*; Paul Berliner, *Thinking in Jazz*; and David Borgo, *Sync or Swarm: Improvising Music in a Complex Age*, for discussion of this point.

10. Robert O'Meally, "Introductory Notes," in *Uptown Conversation*, 1.

11. This comment is attributed to Woodrow Wilson and is frequently invoked as a rallying cry against, as well as a barb, at the entrenchment of conventional education.

12. I go into this in Ed Sarath, *Music Theory Through Improvisation: A New Approach to Musicianship Training*.

13. John Sloboda has written extensively on this orientation; see his "Composition and Improvisation," *The Musical Mind*, 102,

14. Ibid. Also see David Elliott, *Music Matters*.

15. See, for example, Terese Volk, Music, Education, and Multiculturalism.

16. Ed Sarath, "A New Look at Improvisation," *Journal of Music Theory*.

17. This is the Integral Basic Musicianship, Jazz 220-221 course sequence, offered for second-year music majors at the University of Michigan School of Music.

18. Sarath, "A New Look at Improvisation."

19. See Mirabai Bush for a good synopsis of this initiative in her foreword to the 2005 issue of *Teachers College Record* devoted to Contemplative Education. Also, see Ed Sarath, "Meditation, Creativity, and Consciousness: Charting Future Terrain within Higher Education," in the same issue.

20. See Jensine Andresen, "Meditation Meets Behavioral Medicine," *Journal of Consciousness Studies*.

21. These comments were forwarded by email to the full music faculty listserve.

22. See Robert Forman, *Grassroots Spirituality*. He also formed an organization called The Forge predicated on trans-traditional spiritual principles, http://www.theforge.org.

23. An exception to this is those individuals who live in monasteries or ashrams in which total immersion in a given pathway is not only appropriate, it epitomizes spiritual engagement along the ascetic pathway.

24. Wilber in his *Integral Spirituality*, 114, quotes Traleg Rinpoche on this point.

25. While there may be some similarity here with Noam Chomsky's idea of deep linguistic structures, he does not argue for these as originating in transcendent dimensions of consciousness.

26. See Maharishi Mahesh Yogi, *Celebrating Perfection in Education*, 150.

27. Phillip Goldberg, *American Veda: How Indian Spirituality Changed the West*.

28. Emerson is quoted in ibid., 36. In other words, with some forms of Buddhism as a possible exception, Taoists, Jews, Christians, Muslims, Native American, shamans and practitioners from other spiritual lineages might just as readily make this statement.

29. Wilber stresses the nonduality premise, but it is not highly prevalent in much integral literature, including many articles in the *Integral Journal of Theory and Practice*.

30. Reported in John S. Hagelin et al., "Effects of Group Practice of the Transcendental Meditation Program on Preventing Violent Crime in Washing-

ton, D.C.; Results of the National Demonstration Project to Reduce Crime and Improve Governmental Effectiveness in Washington, D.C., June–July, 1993," *Social Indicators Research.*

31. Peer-reviewed journals include Journal of Conflict Resolution, Journal of Mind and Behavior, and Social Indicators Research.

32. See David Orme-Johnson et al., "International Peace Project: The Effects of the Maharishi Technology of the Unified Field," *Journal of Conflict Resolution* for an account of decreased fighting in the Middle East correlating with group meditation programs set up in the vicinity.

33. Thomas Kuhn, The Structure of Scientific Revolutions.

34. For example, Wilber and other integralists acknowledge ideas such as Teilhard de Chardin's *noosphere,* and Rupert Sheldrake's *morphic fields,* but overall mention of intersubjective consciousness is otherwise infrequent.

35. URAM, http://www.scranton.edu/faculty/uram/s.

36. Steve MacIntosh, Integral Consciousness and the Future of Evolution, 195.

Chapter 1. The AQAL Framework

1. Wilber, "Introduction to Integral Theory and Practice," 2.

2. Wilber, Sex, Ecology, Spirituality.

3. The strong nonduality precept is inspired by Maharishi Mahesh Yogi's *Apaurusheya Bhāshya* and his notion of the self-interactive dynamics of consciousness. See his *Celebrating Perfection in Education.*

4. Sean Esbjörn-Hargens and Michael Zimmerman, *Integral Ecology,* 7.

5. See Wilber, Sex, Ecology, Spirituality.

6. Sean Esbjörn-Hargens et al., eds. Introduction, in *Integral Education,* 2.

7. The Quadrants first appeared in Ken Wilber's *Sex, Ecology, Spirituality.*

8. See Wilber, *Integral Spirituality,* for excellent commentary on all-quadrants integration and spiritual development.

9. See ibid., for discussion of how first-second-third-person perspectives correlate to the Four Quadrants.

10. Ibid.

11. Ibid.

12. See Sean Esbjörn-Hargens, "An Overview of Integral Theory: An All-Inclusive Framework for the 21st Century," in *Integral Theory in Action.*

13. Leonard Meyer, *Style and Music Theory, History, Ideology,* 340. This taxonomy is useful for much but not necessarily all of music. At first glance, objections from a postmodern vantage point may seem to be the most valid. In other words, twentieth-century musical explorations at times resulted in music without melody, harmony, and rhythm, at least as conventionally construed, at which point one might argue that the textural or timbral aspects of the music—while what Meyer called "nonsyntactic"—assumed a "syntactic" function. An integral perspective allows for such a modification. However, that postmodern ideologies

from the mid-twentieth century that suggested tonality and rhythm were obsolete have clearly been proven misguided in both contemporary jazz and classical circles affirms the integral applicability of Meyer's precepts.

14. Berliner, *Thinking in Jazz*, 392.

15. At issue here is not the degree to which this integration may or may not have been achieved by any given individual but the fact that a blueprint has been established around the improvisation-meditation interplay that shows great promise for integral growth.

16. Howard Gardner, Frames of Mind: The Theory of Multiple Intelligences.

17. Wilber stresses this important point at length throughout his recent work, perhaps the most forceful articulation of which is *Integral Spirituality*.

18. Arthur Koestler, *Janus*. See also Wilber, *Integral Spirituality*.

19. Wilber, *Integral Spirituality*.

20. Michael Murphy and Rhea White, *In the Zone: Transcendent Experience in Sports*.

21. See Wilber, "Introduction to Integral Theory and Practice."

22. Heide Göttner-Abendroth, *The Dancing Goddess*, 47–48.

23. See Lewis, *A Power Stronger Than Itself*.

24. Jeff Pressing, "Black Atlantic Rhythm: Its Computational and Transcultural Foundations," *Music Perception*.

25. Guthrie Ramsey, *Race Music*, 163.

26. See, for example, Llewellyn Vaughn-Lee, *The Return of the Feminine and the World Soul*.

27. Richard Tarnas, *Cosmos and Psyche*, 491.

28. Wilber, "Introduction to Integral Theory and Practice," 2, emphasis in original.

Chapter 2. Improvisation-driven Growth of Creativity and Consciousness

1. See Ken Wilber et al., Integral Life Practice: A 21st-Century Blueprint for Physical Health, Emotional Balance, Mental Clarity, and Spiritual Awakening.

2. Wilber, Integral Spirituality.

3. I base this assessment on the following considerations: First are Wilber's major books, which while on occasion are powerful endorsements of the transformational aspects of the arts, do not devote relatively speaking much attention to the area, nor to creativity. A look at the indices of these books confirms this point. Second is the *Journal of Integral Theory and Practice*, in which notably few articles deal with creativity and the arts. Third are otherwise fine collections of essays in two important collections: *Integral Theory in Action*, edited by Sean Esbjörn-Hargens, and *Integral Education: New Directions for Higher Learning*, edited by Esbjörn-Hargens et al. In no way is this a critique of the authors or editors of these volumes but simply an observation about an orientation in integral discourse that has not yet opened up to creativity and the arts near to the extent the theory calls for.

4. Wilber et al., Integral Life Practice.

5. See, for instance, Ken Wilber's remarks in his foreword to *The Mission of Art*, by Alex Grey, in Wilber, *Collected Works*, vol. 4.; and Michael Schwartz' "Frames of AQAL, Integral Critical Theory, and the Emerging Integral Arts," in *Integral Theory in Action: Applied, Theoretical, and Constructive Perspectives on the AQAL Model*.

6. I have gone into these distinctions in depth in Ed Sarath, "A New Look at Improvisation," *Journal of Music Theory*.

7. Mihalyi Csikszentmihalyi, *Creativity: Flow and the Psychology of Discovery and Invention*, 71.

8. This closely corresponds to what I have also called formal meditation practice in Sarath, "Meditation, Creativity, and Consciousness."

9. See, for example, Robert Sternberg, ed., *Handbook of Creativity*, where discussion of transcendent dimensions of creativity are scarce. For exceptions, see Mihalyi Csikszentmihalyi, *Flow: The Psychology of Optimal Experience*; Abraham Maslow, *The Farther Reaches of Human Nature*; Ruth Richards, ed., *Everyday Creativity and New Views of Human Nature: Psychological, Social and Spiritual Perspectives*.

10. Sternberg, ed., *Handbook of Creativity*.

11. See, for example, Maud Hickey, "Creativity Research in Music, Visual Art, Theatre, and Dance," in Richard Colwell and Carol Richardson, *The New Handbook on Music Learning and Teaching*. See also Elliott, *Music Matters*, 216, for similar assessment that emphasizes a product and exterior novelty.

12. See Robert Forman, *The Problem of Pure Consciousness*, 8, and Charles Alexander and Ellen Langer, eds., *Higher Stages of Human Development*, 313.

13. Daniel Dennett, *Consciousness Explained*, 106.

14. Volk, *Music, Education, and Multiculturalism*, 194.

15. John Dewey, *How We Think*.

16. Ibid.

17. Betty Anne Younker, "Critical Thinking," in Colwell and Richardson, eds., *The New Handbook of Research on Music Teaching and Learning*, 167.

18. Kuhn, *The Structure of Scientific Revolutions*.

19. Meyer, *Style and Music Theory, History, Ideology*, 340. As noted previously, this taxonomy is useful for much but not necessarily all of music.

20. See Alain Danielou, *Music and the Power of Sound: The Influence of Tuning and Interval on Consciousness*.

21. The interview with Ligeti first appeared in *Jazz Magazine* 484 (September 1998). It may be found at: http://dothemath.typepad.com/dtm/györgy-ligeti-interviewed-by-benoît-delbecq-.html

22. Carol Gould and Kenneth Keaton, "The Essential Role of Improvisation in Musical Performance," *The Journal of Aesthetics and Art Criticism*.

23. In other words, while at the heart of all creativity is some degree of improvisatory activity, a valid and important point that Keaton and Gould nicely underscore and which is further illuminated in the present analysis, a parametric analysis reveals the idea that improvisation in jazz does not fundamentally differ

from that of interpretive performance misguided. Even in instances where jazz musicians may compromise moment-to-moment spontaneity with a reliance on stockpiled phrases—which even in the most extreme cases still comprises but part of a given improvisation—creative manipulation of syntactic elements still occurs that is categorically not possible in interpretive performance, as well as a creative manipulation of a wide range of nonsyntactic elements. In distinguishing between primary and secondary creativity according to syntactic and nonsyntactic elements accessed, we can see clearly that the two forms not only differ in degree, but also differ in kind.

24. I am indebted to Professor Robert Anderson of the University of Michigan Medical School for this fitting description of paradigms with weak self-critical facets.

25. See Sarath, *Music Theory Through Improvisation*, for specific exercises, particularly chapter 1.

26. George Lewis, "Improvised Music since 1950: Afrological and Eurological Perspectives," *Black Music Research*.

27. Csikszentmihalyi, *Creativity*, 19.

28. Quoted in Michael Levin and John S. Wilson, "No Bop Roots in Jazz: Parker," *Downbeat*.

29. Berliner, *Thinking in Jazz*, 202.

30. Jorge Ferrer, Marina Romero, and Ramon Albaveda describe transdisciplinarity as creative "application of any relevant perspective across disciplines with an awareness of their paradigmatic assumptions" in their chapter "Integral Transformational Education," in *Integral Education*, 82.

31. See Basarab Nicolescu, *Manifesto of Transdisciplinarity*, for an excellent account of transdisciplinarity that does broach transcendent domains.

32. Forman, *The Problem of Pure Consciousness*, 8.

33. Alexander and Langer, eds., *Higher Stages of Human Development*, 313.

34. C. G. Jung, *The Spirit in Man, Art, and Literature*, 82.

35. Wilber, *Collected Works*, 394.

36. Jung, *The Spirit in Man, Art, and Literature*, 123.

37. C. G. Jung, *On the Nature of the Psyche*, 125.

38. David Bohm, *Wholeness and the Implicate Order*, 9.

39. Samuel Floyd, *The Power of Black Music: Interpreting Its History from Africa to the United States*, 85.

40. Koestler, *Janus*, 150.

41. Susanne Langer, *Philosophy in a New Key: A Study in the Symbolism of Reason, Rite, and Art*, 206–207.

42. Maslow, *The Farther Reaches of Human Nature*.

43. Csikszentmihalyi, *Creativity*, 113.

44. Quoted in Imants Baruss, *Science as a Spiritual Practice*, 105.

45. Ibid.

46. Quoted in Ibid., 112.

47. Daniel Belgrad, *The Culture of Spontaneity*.

Chapter 3. Meditation-driven Growth of
Creativity and Consciousness

1. Alexander and Langer, eds., *Higher Stages of Human Development*, 314.

2. Swami Durgananda, *The Heart of Meditation: Pathways to a Deeper Experience*, 5.

3. Hari Sharma and Christopher Clark, *Contemporary Ayurveda*, 18.

4. Following are excellent sources that deal with benefits of meditation practice and corresponding neurobiological research. Jensine Andresen, "Meditation Meets Behavioral Medicine," *Journal of Consciousness Studies*; James Austin, *Zen and the Brain*; Richard Davidson, "Long-term Meditators Self-induce High Amplitude Gamma Synchrony during Mental Practice," *National Academy of Sciences Review*; Candace Pert, *Molecules of Emotion: The Science Behind Mind-Body Medicine*; Fred Travis and R. Keith Wallace, "Autonomic and EEG Patterns during Eyes-Closed Rest and Transcendental Meditation (TM) Practice: The Basis for a Neural Model of TM Practice"; C. N. Alexander, M. V. Rainforth, and P. Gelderloos, "Transcendental Meditation, Self-actualization, and Psychological Health," *Journal of Personality and Social Psychology*; R. W. Cranson et al., "Transcendental Meditation and Improved Performance on Intelligence-related Measures: A Longitudinal Study," *Personality and Individual Differences*; T. Emarvahdana and C. D. Tori, "Changes in Self-concept, Ego Defense Mechanisms, and Religiosity Following Seven-day Vipassana Meditation Retreats," *Journal for the Scientific Study of Religion* 36.

5. See Daniel Goleman, *The Meditative Mind: The Varieties of Meditative Experience*, and also the website for the Contemplative Mind in Society, www. contemplativemind.org, where a "contemplative tree" vividly illustrates a comprehensive overview of the wide variety of meditation practices available.

6. Durgananda, *The Heart of Meditation*.

7. Sharma and Clark, *Contemporary Ayurveda*, 19.

8. I first made this argument for silent meditation as a kind of anchor in "Meditation in Higher Education: The Next Wave?" and refined it in "Meditation, Creativity, and Consciousness: Charting Future Terrain within Higher Education." It is further developed in chapter 11 of this book.

9. Integral Methodological Pluralism is a basic principle in Wilber et al.'s *Integral Life Practice*.

10. See Elizabeth Lesser, *The New American Spirituality: A Seeker's Guide*, and Durgananda, *The Heart of Meditation*, for commentary on the possible ups and downs of meditation-driven growth.

11. These are sometimes referred to as "lower self" and "higher self." Maharishi Mahesh Yogi: "Lower self is that aspect of the personality that deals with only the relative aspect of existence . . . the mind that thinks, the intellect that decides, the ego that experiences. The higher Self is that aspect of the personality that never changes [and is] the very basis for the entire field of relativity, including the lower self." Quoted in Alexander and Langer, eds., *Higher Stages of Human Development*, 319.

12. Owen Flanagan's *The Problem of the Soul* is an example of such materialist tendencies, where the notion of *anatman*, or no self—which I believe is originally and most genuinely intended to refer to the dissolution of the personal self—is misunderstood as the absence of an aspect of consciousness that transcends the physical, which corresponds to what in most traditions is some form of soul. With this reasoning Flanagan concludes that Buddhism is unique among the world's wisdom tradition in its alignment with science, the extremism in this religious and scientific privileging being underscored when he conveniently neglects consideration of reincarnation and other aspects of Buddhist thought and experience that are decidedly rejected by the very scientific paradigm he exalts. Aurobindo offers an interesting commentary on the broader Buddhist worldview that might have given rise to this misunderstanding: "Buddha, it must be remembered, refused always to discuss what was beyond the world. But from the little he said, it would appear that he was aware of a Permanent beyond similar to the Vedantic Para-Brahman, but which he was quite unwilling to describe. The denial of anything except a negative state of Nirvana was a later teaching, not Buddha's." In A. S. Dalal, *A Greater Psychology: The Psychological Thought of Sri Aurobindo*, 375.

13. Quoted in Dalal, *A Greater Psychology*, 336.

14. Lama Anagorika Govinda, *Foundations of Tibetan Buddhism*, 74.

15. Alexander and Langer, eds., *Higher Stages of Human Development*, 314.

16. Travis and Wallace, "Autonomic and EEG Patterns," 416.

17. Alexander and Langer, eds., *Higher Stages of Human Development*, 314.

18. Govinda, Foundations of Tibetan Buddhism, 80.

19. Ellen Langer, *Mindfulness*.

20. Alexander and Langer, eds., *Higher Stages of Human Development*, 309.

21. Travis and Wallace, "Autonomic and EEG Patterns."

22. Ervin Laszlo, *Introduction to Systems Philosophy*, 195.

23. Ibid.

24. Travis and Wallace, "Autonomic and EEG Patterns," 403.

25. Ken Wilber, *One Taste: The Journals of Ken Wilber*.

26. Forman, *The Problem of Pure Consciousness*, defines the pure consciousness event as "wakeful though contentless (unintentional) consciousness," 8.

27. William Stace, *Mysticism and Philosophy*, 121.

28. Alexander and Langer, eds., *Higher Stages of Human Development*, 317, emphasis mine.

29. Ibid.

30. Govinda, *Foundations of Tibetan Buddhism*, 80.

31. Ibid.

32. Forman, *The Problem of Pure Consciousness*, 8.

33. Alexander and Langer, eds., *Higher Stages of Human Development*, 318.

34. Murphy and White, *In the Zone*, 118–119.

35. Ibid., 125.

36. Berliner, *Thinking in Jazz*, 392.

37. The ephemeral nature of transcendent experience is one of James' common observations in his classic work, *The Variety of Religious Experience*.

38. Murphy and White, *In the Zone*, 151.

39. Alexander and Langer, eds., *Higher Stages of Human Development*, 314.

40. Ibid, 314.

41. C. G. Jung, "Two Essays on Analytical Psychology," 275. Among Jung's clearest accounts of individuation are those found in *The Archetypes and the Collective Unconscious* and *On the Nature of the Psyche*.

42. Jung, *The Archetypes and the Collective Unconscious*, 40.

43. Harold Coward, *Jung and Eastern Thought*, 161.

44. Ibid., 161.

45. Ibid. Jung cites the great Christian mystic Meister Eckhart as an exemplar and analyzes "this new state of consciousness born of religious practice" much as it would be characterized from traditional Eastern vantage points. "[O]utward things no longer affect an ego-bound consciousness, thus giving rise to mutual attachment, but (rather) an empty consciousness gives rise to another influence. This 'other' influence is no longer felt as one's own activity, but as that of a non-ego which has the conscious mind as its object," 162.

46. Jung, *The Archetypes and the Collective Unconscious*, 275.

47. Victor Mansfield, *Head and Heart: A Personal Exploration of Science and the Sacred*, 121.

48. Ibid.

49. Jung, *The Spirit in Man, Art, and Literature*, 82.

50. This argument appears in Ed Sarath, "Improvisation and Curriculum Reform," in *The New Handbook of Research Music Teaching and Learning*.

51. Csikszentmihalyi, *Creativity*, 113.

52. Wilber et al., *Integral Life Practice*.

53. Alexander and Langer, eds., *Higher Stages of Human Development*, 315.

54. Ibid.

55. These important findings are summarized in Ken Wilber, Daniel Brown, and Jack Engler's Introduction, 49–59, in Wilber's *Collected Works*.

56. Wilber, Integral Spirituality.

57. Wilber, Introduction to *Collected Works*, 49.

58. Andresen, "Meditation Meets Behavioral Medicine"; Austin, *Zen and the Brain*; Davidson, "Long-term Meditators"; Travis and Wallace, "Autonomic and EEG Patterns"; and Roger Walsh and Susan Shapiro, "The Meeting of Meditative Disciplines and Western Psychology."

59. Fred Travis, Alarik Arenander, David DuBois, "Psychological and Physiological Characteristics of a Proposed Object-referral/Self-referral Continuum of Self-awareness," *Consciousness and Cognition*.

60. Alexander and Langer, eds., *Higher Stages of Human Development*, 314.

61. Travis, Arenander, and DuBois, "Psychological and Physiological Characteristics," 416.

62. Ibid., 416–417.

63. Ibid.

64. Alexander and Langer, eds., *Higher Stages of Human Development*, 319.

65. Ibid., 320.

66. Ibid., 322.

67. Gary Schwartz, *The Sacred Promise: How Science Is Discovering Spirit's Collaboration with Us in Our Daily Lives.* Among the classic accounts of subtle intelligences is The Findhorn Gardens: Pioneering a New Vision of Man and Nature in Cooperation, from the Findhorn Community. Also see Wolfgang Weirauch, ed., *Nature Spirits and What They Say: Interviews with Verena von Holstein.* From a somewhat different angle, more directly related to the educational world, is an account of an experience John Dewey had where he seemed to visit another plane of existence and gain specific information about a kind of utopian educational model. This is reported in William Schubert's, Love, Justice and Education: John Dewey and the Utopians.

68. W. Y. Evans-Wentz, ed., *Tibetan Yoga and Secret Doctrines*, 211.

69. Ibid., 75.

70. Alexander and Langer, eds., *Higher Stages of Human Development*, 323.

71. Quoted in Craig Pearson, *Supreme Awakening: Experiences of Higher States of Consciousness*, 231.

72. Quoted in ibid., 235.

73. Durgananda, *The Heart of Meditation*, 5–6.

74. Wilber, *Integral Spirituality*, 241.

75. Ibid., 89.

76. Ibid., 248.

77. Ibid.

78. Combs, *Consciousness Explained Better*, 146.

79. Maharishi Mahesh Yogi has revived the Gandharva Veda tradition based in this principle.

80. Danielou, *Music and the Power of Sound.*

81. Ananda K. Coomaraswamy, "Lila," *Journal of the American Oriental Society.*

82. Peter Westbrook, "Unstruck Sound and Forgotten Truth," *Ultimate Reality and Meaning*, 113.

83. Lao Tse, *Tao Teh Ching*, 61.

84. John Anthony West, *Serpent in the Sky: The High Wisdom of Ancient Egypt*, 33.

85. Westbrook, "Unstruck Sound and Forgotten Truth."

86. The Abhinavagupta passage is from Paul Muller-Ortega, *The Triadic Heart of Siva*, 118, emphasis mine.

87. Maharishi Mahesh Yogi explains the self-referential principles of creation as the interplay of three aspects of consciousness that interact at cosmic and individual scales. These are knower (*rishi*); process of knowing, or self-referential curving back (*devata*); and object of knowing (*chandas*). In his *Apaurusheya Bhāshya*, commentary on Rig (Rk) Veda, he locates this self-referential interac-

tion, and ensuing dynamics of creation, within a single syllable of the Vedic literature. "AK (the first syllable of Rk Veda) describes the collapse of fullness of consciousness—A collapses within itself to its own point value, K. This collapse, which represents the eternal dynamics of consciousness knowing itself, occurs in eight successive stages." In other words, the syllable A represents *rishi*, the collapse of A represents the *devata* value, and K represents the *chandas* value. The resultant syllable AK is the first sound emerging from this interaction, and as these interactions continue, they result in the "eight syllables of the first Pada, which emerge from and provide a further commentary on the first syllable of Rk Veda, AK. These eight syllables pertain to the eight Prakrti or eight fundamental qualities of intelligence, which constitute the divided nature of pure consciousness." In Kai Druhl, "Consciousness as the Subject and Object of Physics: Toward a New Paradigm for the Physical Sciences," *Modern Science and Vedic Science*, 156.

88. Maharishi Mahesh Yogi, *Celebrating Excellence in Education*, 166–167.

89. Ibid., 155.

90. Jung, *On the Nature of the Psyche*, 125.

91. See Joachim Berendt, *The World Is Sound: Nada Brahma*, and Danielou, *Music and the Power of Sound*, for excellent accounts of this.

92. See Alfred North Whitehead, *Process and Reality*, and Bohm, *Wholeness and the Implicate Order*.

93. Andrew Cohen, *Being and Becoming: Exploring the Teachings of Evolutionary Enlightenment*, 76.

94. Coomaraswamy, "Lila," 101.

95. William S. Sax, "The Ramnagar Ramlila: Text, Performance, Pilgrimage," *History of Religions*, 129.

96. Tagore quoted in Edward C. Dimock, "Lila," *History of Religions*, 159.

97. Maharishi Mahesh Yogi, *Celebrating Excellence in Education*, 165.

98. Arthur Lovejoy, *The Great Chain of Being*.

99. Henryk Skolimowski, *Let There Be Light: The Mysterious Voyage of Cosmic Creativity*, 131.

100. Ibid., 234.

101. Wilber, *Integral Spirituality*, 240.

102. Ibid., 234.

103. Jorge Ferrer, *Revisioning Transpersonal Theory: A Participatory Vision of Human Spirituality*, 133.

104. Ibid.

105. Henryk Skolimowski, *The Participatory Mind*; David Skrbina, *Panpsychism in the West*. Skrbina makes an impressive case for the prevalence in Western thought of the conventionally anomalous idea that some aspect of mind, subjectivity, or consciousness is inherent in all phenomena—including those of the physical word. The view that "all things have mind or mind-like quality" (2) is evident in one way or another in the thought of not only ancient thinkers such as Thales, Heraclitus, Plato, and Aristotle, but in more recent eras Bacon, Spinoza, Newton, Leibniz, James, and Whitehead. It's compatibility with the previous

account of *lila* in Vedanta is clear, with the latter possibly resolving differences between idealism and panpsychism as articulated by Christian de Quincey in *Radical Knowing: Understanding Consciousness through Relationship*. Whereas, according to de Quincey, materialism is incapable of explaining how mind emerges from matter, idealism is incapable of explaining how matter emerges from mind. Panpsychism thus fulfills this gap. But, in fact, the self-referential curving back of cosmic intelligence onto itself is compatible with both idealism and panpsychism platforms.

106. Michael Zimmerman, "The Final Cause of Cosmic Development: Non-dual Spirit or the Second Law of Thermodynamics?," 203.

Chapter 4. Integral Evolutionary Dynamics

1. Wilber, *Integral Spirituality*, 185.

2. According to Jung, the shadow "personifies everything that the subject refuses to acknowledge about himself and yet is always thrusting itself upon him directly or indirectly—for instance, inferior traits and other incompatible tendencies," in *The Archetypes and the Collective Unconscious*, 284–285.

3. Wilber, *Integral Spirituality*, 124–127.

4. Ibid., 137–139.

5. See Susanne Cook-Greuter, *Postautonomous Ego Development: A Study of Its Nature and Development*; Carol Gilligan, *In a Different Voice: Psychological Theory and Women's Development*; and Jane Loevinger, *Paradigms of Personality*.

6. See Amit Goswami, *The Self-Aware Universe: How Consciousness Creates the Material World*, for an excellent overview of philosophies of mind.

7. Ken Wilber, *The Marriage of Sense and Soul: Integrating Science and Religion*, 13.

8. Ibid., 13.

9. Ibid.

10. Ibid.

11. Ken Wilber, "From Modernity to Postmodernity," *Collected Works*, vol. 4, 601.

12. While the qualifiers *astructural* and *structural* are admittedly not without their limitations, I believe by keeping salient principles in mind any confusion may be avoided. My use of the term astructural correlates with deconstructive, and structural with constructive (which is what Wilber uses). Why not just use the more conventional terminology? Because this invites even further confusion in musical circles, where the "constructivist" perspective—which holds that knowledge is not absolute but constructed by individuals and their unique sociocultural circumstances—that is commonly invoked directly correlates, and thus clashes, with the deconstructive postmodern platform. Hence, my use of the term astructural is an attempt to circumvent this problem. Granted, this does not resolve the further problem that, while astructural postmodernism eschews

ascribing inherent value or meaning to the structural features of the art object, it then replaces these with relativistic, sociocultural structures to which it cedes privilege as meaning-markers. Inasmuch as conventional postmodernists do not see these latter criteria as structures, although integralists do (or at least those who subscribe to the perspective I advance), I have chosen to err in this direction as the lesser of two evils.

13. Stephen Jay Gould, *Rock of Ages*, 5.

14. Francis Crick and Christof Koch, "Towards a Neurobiological Theory of Consciousness," in *The Nature of Consciousness*, 277.

15. Francis Crick, *The Astonishing Hypothesis*, 236.

16. Steven Weinberg, *The First Three Minutes*, 131–132.

17. Steven Weinberg, *Dreams of a Final Theory: A Scientist's Search for the Ultimate Laws of Nature*, 53.

18. John Searle, "Reductionism and the Irreducibility of Consciousness," in *The Nature of Consciousness*, 451. See also Judith Hooper, *The Three-Pound Universe*, 17; Goswami, *The Self-Aware Universe*.

19. John Searle, *The Mystery of Consciousness*, 17–18.

20. Hooper, *The Three-Pound Universe*.

21. David Chalmers, *The Conscious Mind: In Search of a Fundamental Theory*, 25.

22. Ibid., 357.

23. Antonio Damasio, *The Feeling of What Happens: Body and Emotion in the Making of Consciousness*; 82; Chalmers, *The Conscious Mind*, 22–27.

24. Fred Alan Wolff, *The Spiritual Universe: One Physicist's Vision of Spirit, Soul, Matter, and Self*, 10.

25. Edward Kelly et al., in *Irreducible Mind: Toward a Psychology of the 21st Century*, for example, note common attempts of materialists to disprove the "objective significance" of mystical experience by identifying and thus reducing them to biological correlates, resulting in "facile and triumphant neurologizing about 'God Spots' and the like [which comprise] a long and dismal history" of these tendencies, 518. William James even noted these tendencies as far back as 1902 in his *The Varieties of Religious Experience*: Having no means to explain these states, medical materialism's attempts to discredit them by associating them with "nerves and liver is altogether illogical and inconsistent" (30).

26. Robert Jahn and Brenda Dunne, *The Margins of Reality*, 90.

27. Ibid., 182.

28. Ibid., 197.

29. Hyman is quoted in Dean Radin, *The Conscious Universe*, 5. Also see Dean Radin, *Entangled Minds: Extrasensory Experiences in Quantum Reality*, for an investigation of psi from the standpoint of quantum mechanics.

30. Radin, *The Conscious Universe*, 5.

31. Ibid., 6.

32. Elizabeth Mayer, *Extraordinary Knowing: Science, Skepticism, and the Inexplicable Powers of the Human Mind*, 191–192.

33. William Tiller, *Psychoenergetic Science: A Second Copernican-Scale Revolution*.

34. Http://www.perceptualstudies. University of Virginia Health Center.

35. Jenny Wade, *Changes of Mind: A Holonomic Theory of the Evolution of Consciousness*, 23–26.

36. Sharma and Clark, *Contemporary Ayurveda*, 147–148.

37. Rupert Sheldrake, *Morphic Resonance: The Nature of Formative Causation*.

38. Rupert Sheldrake, *Dogs Who Know When Their Owners Are Coming Home*.

39. Daryl Bem, "Feeling the Future: Experimental Evidence for Anomalous Retroactive Influences on Cognition and Affect," *Journal of Personality and Social Psychology*.

40. Tarnas, *Cosmos and Psyche*.

41. Schwartz, *The Sacred Promise*.

42. Quoted in David Ray Griffin, *Parapsychology, Philosophy, and Spirituality*, 24.

43. Etter's comment is found in Christopher Bache, *The Living Classroom: Teaching and Collective Consciousness*, 91–92.

44. Mansfield, *Head and Heart*, 39.

45. See, for example, Antonio Damasio, *Descartes' Error: Emotion, Reason, and the Human Brain*; Dennett, *Consciousness Explained*; and J. Allan Hobson, *Consciousness*. Damasio's interpretation of the following passage from Descartes as "unequivocally" confirming a dualist perspective is telling re my point. Descartes affirms the existence of a "soul [that is] entirely distinct from body . . . and even if the body were not, the soul would not cease to be what it is." Concluding that "this is Descartes' error: the abyssal separation between body and mind," Damasio proceeds to emphasize the outmoded nature of this viewpoint (249). But what if Descartes is speaking from a direct experience of discarnate consciousness, or witnessing characteristic of subtle awareness, what Vedantins call *Turyatit*, which could easily be described in language that suggests an absolute ontological schism but in reality denotes a particular condition of consciousness where subjectivity is experienced as detached from the body within a broader spectrum of subjective-objective unity? And what about the body of contemporary research into discarnate consciousness as cited earlier in the chapter?

46. Prominent parameters of conventional creativity research include psychometric, biometric, and historiometric angles of consideration; see Sternberg, ed., *Handbook of Creativity Research*.

47. The Buddhist doctrine of *annata*, or *anatman*, translates as "no self," and is also read as "no soul." I believe there is good reason to think that the first interpretation is more reliable in that it is consistent with the illusory and ever-changing nature of the relativistic or egoic self. Among the problems with the latter interpretation is that it is incompatible with the notion of rebirth or reincarnation, which is overlooked by contemporary writers such as Owen Flanagan, *The Problem*

of the Soul, and Sam Harris, "Killing the Buddha," *Shambhala Sun*, who assert that Buddhism may be uniquely aligned with a (materialist) science worldview.

48. Sean Esbjörn-Hargens, Jonathan Reams, and Olen Gunnlaugson, eds., Introduction, *Integral Education: New Directions for Higher Learning*, 2.

49. Wilber, *Integral Spirituality*, 193.

50. Ibid., 195.

51. Ron Miller, *What Are Schools For*, 74.

52. Ibid., 81.

53. Ibid., 87.

54. Ibid., 90.

55. Esbjörn-Hargens, Reams, and Gunnlaugson, Introduction.

56. Alfred North Whitehead, *The Aims of Education*, 18.

57. Ibid., "If Methuselah was not a well-educated man, it was not his own fault or that of his teachers" (63).

58. Ibid., 92.

59. John Dewey, *Experience and Education*.

60. Jerome Bruner, *The Process of Education*, 196.

61. Ibid., 6.

62. Carl Rogers, *Dialogues*, 180.

63. Maxine Greene, *Releasing the Imagination: Essays on Education, the Arts, and Social Change*, 32–33.

64. Ibid., 184.

65. Gardner, *Frames of Mind*.

66. Howard Gardner, *Intelligence Reframed: Refining the Theory*.

67. Helen Astin and Alexander Astin, *Spirituality in Higher Education: A National Study of College Students' Search for Meaning and Purpose*.

68. See Mirabai Bush, Foreword, *Teachers College Record*, for an excellent account of the ACLS project.

69. bell hooks, *Teaching to Transgress: Education of the Practice of Freedom*, 206.

70. Esbjörn-Hargens, Reams, and Gunnlaugson, Introduction. *Integral Education*.

Chapter 5. Jazz and the Academy

1. Maslow, *The Farther Reaches of Human Nature*, 56.

2. The Harvard meeting was chronicled in a special issue of *Negotiation Journal*, Michael Wheeler, ed., "Improvisation and Negotiation."

3. Maslow, *The Farther Reaches of Human Nature*, 56.

4. Ibid., 95.

5. Ibid., also see Maslow's *Religion, Values, and Peak Experiences*.

6. LeRoi Jones, *Blues People*, 1. Karlton Hester, *Bigotry and the Afrocentric "Jazz" Evolution*, 537.

7. Bruno Nettl, *Heartland Excursions: Ethnomusicological Reflections on Schools of Music*.

8. Lake is quoted in Lewis, *A Power Stronger Than Itself*, 264.

9. Brubeck is quoted in Antonio J. Garcia, "Dave Brubeck: His Music Keeps Us Here," *Jazz Educators Journal*, 41. See also James Lincoln Collier, *Jazz: The American Theme Song*, for discussion of obstacles confronted by jazz educators in advocating jazz studies in the academic world. George E. Lewis illustrates this point in "Improvised Music since 1950" where he conveys the condescending attitudes of twentieth-century Eurological (Euroclassical) composers and even improvisers toward jazz. See also Daniel Murphy, "Jazz Studies in American Schools and Colleges: A Brief History," *Jazz Educators Journal*, 34–38. Also see Martin Williams, "Recognition, Prestige, and Respect: They're Academic Questions," in *New Perspectives on Jazz*.

10. Directory of Music Faculties at Colleges and Universities, United States and Canada (College Music Society).

11. For example, *Journal of Black Music Research*, *Ethnomusicology Journal*, and other academic and commercial presses have provided outlets for jazz scholarship. In my view, however, this only nominally offsets the orientation of other prominent research journals that have been less receptive to this research, particularly prior to the 1990s.

12. National Association of Schools of Music curricular guidelines. Also see *National Standards for Arts Education: What Every Young American Should Know and Be Able to Do in the Arts*.

13. Murphy, "Jazz Studies in American Schools and Colleges."

14. Montreux, Switzerland's Jazz Academy and Lisbon, Portugal's Hot Club are examples of community jazz schools in Europe. Source: International Association of Schools of Jazz Directory.

15. The IAJE began as National Association of Jazz Educators, then became International Association of Jazz Educators, and then the International Association of Jazz Education. The organization declared bankruptcy in 2007.

16. For more information on the IASJ, see http://www.iasj.com.

17. The trend to hire highly visible jazz musicians has an interesting history. In the 1960s and 1970s, before many schools had jazz departments, these kinds of appointments were made through departments of African American Studies or some area outside of music. See Eric Porter, *What Is This Thing Called Jazz?*, and Paul Austerlitz, *Jazz Consciousness: Music, Race, Humanity*.

18. The basic principle here is that jazz musicians improvise, compose, and perform, thus embodying the three pillars of music making that might be identified as core to Western musical practice, including of course the European classical tradition. See Elliott, *Music Matters: A New*. That the majority of music majors and professional orchestral musicians focus on interpretive performance of Euroclassical music indicates a sharp deviation from that tradition. Composition students and professional concert music composers generally have strong performance skills, and many engage in improvising as part of the composing process, indicating a process breadth that begins to approximate that of the jazz musician.

19. Representative John Conyers from Michigan spearheaded this proclamation, which was introduced at the 100th Congress, first Session, as H. Con. Res. 57, on March 3, 1987. Expressing the sense of Congress respecting the designation of jazz as a rare and valuable American treasure, the measure refers to jazz as "a multifaceted art form which continues to birth and nurture new stylistic idioms and cultural fusions and . . . a true international language adopted by musicians around the world as a music best able to express contemporary realities from a personal perspective." The resolution was passed by the House of Representatives on September 23, and by the Senate December 4 of that year.

20. David Baker, "IAJE President's Message," *Jazz Educators Journal*. I might add that I have taught a sophomore basic musicianship class for 15 years that appears to be one of the few instances of a jazz offering fulfilling core curriculum requirements (first two years).

21. College Music Society's Directory of Music Faculties at Colleges and Universities, United States and Canada.

22. Nettl, *Heartland Excursions*, 93.

23. Eric Nisenson, *Blue: The Murder of Jazz*.

24. Graham Collier remarks that "it would seem that the 40 years and more that have passed since bebop's heyday would have left more of a mark than a jazz-funk groove or a bossa nova bass line" in "Jazz Education in America," *Jazz Changes*, 9. The point is not that there is no place for jazz-rock or bossa novas, but that so much else has also happened, which, because it is less "currently fashionable," has not made its way into jazz programs. The eminent bassist Charlie Haden, another advocate for an expanded vision of jazz education, echoes Collier's sentiments; in his address to the IAJE in Anaheim in 1998 he strongly urges greater emphasis on individuality and creativity. Allan Chase spoke to the same point as part of a panel discussion at the 1999 meeting in New Orleans, which also included Graham Collier and myself; Graham Collier, "The Shape of Jazz to Come," *Jazz Changes*. See also Nisenson's *Blue*.

25. Lateef is quoted in an October 2004 article in *Downbeat* entitled "Jazz Musicians on Education," 102.

26. Quoted in Graham Collier, *Interaction*, 26.

27. Lewis, *A Power Stronger Than Itself*, 280.

28. Ibid., 28.

29. Metheny's remarks are published in the *International Association of Schools of Jazz Newsletter*, emphasis in the original.

30. Ibid.

31. "I used exotic scales—scales from every culture," stated Dennis Sandole, an early teacher of Coltrane. Porter, *John Coltrane*, 51.

32. David Liebman, Self-Portrait of a Jazz Artist: Musical Thoughts and Realities, 177.

33. Quoted in Porter, *John Coltrane*, 37.

34. Ross Russell, *Bird Lives: The High Life and Hard Times of Charlie Parker*.

35. For example, Ingrid Monson, *Saying Something: Jazz Improvisation and Interaction*; Porter, *What Is This Thing Called Jazz?*; Porter, *John Coltrane*; Berliner,

Thinking in Jazz, and Lewis, *A Power Stronger Than Itself*, comment on the importance of spirituality in one way or another. Nonetheless, analytical models are scarce in the literature.

36. John Sloboda, "Composition and Improvisation," in *The Musical Mind*, 102.

37. A field aspect of consciousness is explored in Lynne McTaggart, *The Field: The Quest for the Secret Force of the Universe*. Also see Lynn Mason et al., "Exploratory Study: The Random Number Generator and Group Meditation," *Journal of Scientific Exploration*, Radin, *The Conscious Universe*.

38. William Banfield, *Cultural Codes: Makings of a Black Music Philosophy*, 183.

39. O'Meally, "Introductory Notes," 1.

40. See Impact Jazz, for example. Http://www.impactjazz.com. Also John Kao's *Jamming*; Frank Barrett, "Creativity and Improvisation in Jazz and Organizations: Implications for Organizational Learning," *Organization Science*; and Ed Sarath, "Jazz Lessons for the Boardroom," *Newsday*.

41. Wheeler, "Improvisation and Negotiation."

42. Paul Haidet, "Jazz and the 'Art' of Medicine: Improvisation in the Medical Encounter," *Annals of Family Medicine*.

43. Kabir Sehgal, *Jazzocracy: Jazz, Democracy, and the Creation of a New American Mythology*.

44. Daniel Fischlin and Ajay Heble, eds., *The Other Side of Nowhere: Jazz, Improvisation, and Communities in Dialogue*.

45. David P. Brown, *Noise Orders: Jazz, Improvisation, and Architecture*.

46. Lewis's *A Power Stronger Than Itself* provides an exhaustive history of the AACM.

47. Abrams is quoted in ibid., 231.

48. Coltrane is quoted in Porter, *John Coltrane*, 232.

49. Daniel Fischlin, " 'See clearly . . . feel deeply': Improvisation and Transformation: John McLaughlin Interviewed by Daniel Fischlin," *Critical Studies in Improvisation*.

50. Lorentz is quoted in Gleick, *Chaos*, 20.

51. Ibid.

Chapter 6. Invention: Improvisation and Composition as Contrasting Pathways to Transcendence

1. Steve Lacy, *Findings: My Experience with the Soprano Saxophone*, 21.

2. Sarath, "A New Look at Improvisation."

3. Sloboda, "Composition and Improvisation," 102.

4. Bruno Nettl, "Thoughts on Improvisation: A Comparative Approach," *The Musical Quarterly*, 6.

5. Berliner, *Thinking in Jazz*, 36; chapter 2 is titled "Composing in the Moment." While elsewhere Berliner, in considering that the "compositional condi-

tions" of jazz may differ in degree from those of notated composition due to the "multiple tasks" (497)—split-second decisions, interactive variables, irreversibility of the processes—he stops short of considering the processes as differing in kind.

6. Elliott, *Music Matters*, 170.

7. This has been called the "motive explanation"; see Lewis, "Improvised Music since 1950." See also Gould and Keaton, "The Essential Role of Improvisation in Musical Performance."

8. Phillip Alperson, "Thoughts on Improvisation," *Journal of Aesthetics and Art Criticism*, 27.

9. Luciano Berio, *Two Interviews*, 81.

10. Such aleatoric methods can involve both composer and performer indeterminacy. Exemplifying the former is John Cage's use of the *I Ching* in composing *Music of Changes* (1951), where musical materials were determined through the throwing of dice. Stockhausen's or Earle Brown's strategies of giving latitude to performers in determining structural dimensions of a piece provide examples of the latter. The temporality involved in either compositional approach differs greatly from that of conventional, determinate composition, but if the process involves discontinuity and some degree of reflection on what will or might follow, then the conditions of the proposed definition, and their purpose of distinguishing improvisation and composition, are satisfied.

11. Ellen Dissanayake, in *Art and Intimacy*, and Steven Mithen, in *The Singing Neanderthals*, both suggest that music's origins lie in the cooing of mothers with their infants. Darwin's thoughts on the mating origins are expressed in this statement from *The Descent of Man*: "It seems probable that the progenitors of man, either the males and females of both sexes, before acquiring the power of expressing mutual love in articulate language, endeavored to charm each other with musical notes and rhythm" (880).

12. See International Society for Improvised Music, http://www.isimprov. org, which I founded in 2004.

13. See Eugene Narmour, *The Analysis and Cognition of Basic Melodic Structures: The Implication-Realization Model*.

14. Jonathan Kramer, *The Time of Music*, 22.

15. These concepts first appeared in Sarath, "A New Look at Improvisation."

16. See ibid. for more on the notion of timescape, and reversible temporal conception.

17. Kramer, *The Time of Music*, 52.

18. Parker is quoted in David Borgo, *Sync or Swarm*, 57

19. Hints of this point serving as a possible portal into a new aesthetic paradigm are found in Phillip Alperson, "Thoughts on Improvisation"; Bruno Nettl, "Thoughts on Improvisation: A Comparative Approach," *The Musical Quarterly*; Estelle Jorgenson, *Transforming Music Education*; and Bennett Reimer, *A Philosophy of Music Education*. It is interesting to note that thinking in this direction appears to be more prominent outside of jazz research circles rather than inside those circles. This may reflect an assumption among jazz researchers that improvisation is a phenomenon so intrinsic to jazz that ontological inquiry is, by now,

unnecessary, whereas those outside of the field come to it far less encumbered by orthodox tendencies. In my view, the absence of penetrating inquiry into improvisation is a serious limitation in jazz research.

20. Sarath, "A New Look at Improvisation."

21. Christian Wolff et al., "Improvisation, Heterophony, Politics, and Composition,"135.

22. Stephen Nachmanovitch, Free Play: The Power of Improvisation in Life and Art.

23. The terms *retensive* and *protensive* originate in Edmund Husserl's phenomenology of time conception. *On the Phenomenology of the Consciousness of Internal Time (1893–1917)*. See also David Lewin, "Music Theory, Phenomenology, and Modes of Perception," *Music Perception*, and Izchak Miller, *Husserl, Perception, and Temporal Awareness*.

24. Noam Sivan, "Improvisation in Western Art Music: Its Relevance Today," doctoral dissertation, Julliard School of Music. Sivan offers one of the finest overviews of the history of improvisation in European classical music. It is thus not surprising that his ontological and pedagogical approaches to the subject are strongly composition-based. "As soon as a musical improvisation is not confined to the practice room and is experienced by at least one listener, it is subject to the same organizational principles that govern written composition" (75)—meaning, in Sivan's view, overarching formal relationships. While this perspective will be of use in both expanding, as well as focusing, the creative horizons of many improvisers, it is partial in its neglect of moment-to-moment decision-making strategies that reflect as keen a creative awareness yet yield formal designs, which in many instances may only be appreciated in retrospect, that are unique to improvisatory creativity.

25. Erik Christensen, *The Musical Timespace: A Theory of Music Listening*, 48. See also Barbara Barry, *Musical Time*, and Jonathan Kramer, *The Time of Music*.

26. Jean Gebser, *The Ever-Present Origin*, 456.

27. It should be noted however that Gebser, *The Ever-Present Origin*, 456, does make mention of select indigenous or what he calls "primordial" musical traditions that "have been discovered only in the last decade [hence the 1940s]" such as "the songs of the Canary Islands as well as several from the Andes." He does not, however, deal with the improvisatory aspects of these traditions nor the possible relationship of that to their "timelessness."

28. Kramer, *The Time of Music*, 23.

29. Ibid., 25.

30. Transformation of temporal experience is commonly noted as a feature of transcendence. See for example Mihalyi Csikszentmihalyi, *Flow*; Eckhart Tolle, *The Power of Now: A Guide to Spiritual Enlightenment*; and Ed Sarath, "A New Look at Improvisation."

31. Kramer, in *The Time of Music*, models distinctions between linear and nonlinear temporality with the Markov chain from information theory. Lower-

order Markov processes involve relationships between fewer antecedent events and are thus more nonlinear; higher order processes are more linear due to their linkage with more predecessors. While a zero-order Markov relationship is theoretically possible, which would involve the conception of an event with absolutely no connection to its predecessors, generally there will be some degree of relationship in improvised event chains between a moment and its near past. Thus there is some overlap between each event and temporally adjacent events, consistent with Thomas Clifton's idea of the present as a "horizon" that fades into the past and future as portrayed in his book *Music as Heard.*

32. Quoted in Derek Bailey, *Musical Improvisation,* 72.

33. See David Clarke's "Structural, Cognitive and Semiotic Aspects of the Musical Present," *Contemporary Music Review,* for example. It is curious to note that the research into the length of the present that Clarke cites delineates outer but not inner limits of present conception—in other words, having to do with the longest possible time span that might encompass a present moment. Similarly, Kramer, *The Time of Music,* and Clifton, *Music as Heard,* treat the present as a span or horizon, not as a point. This might reflect the orientation in music theory toward composition conception and its expanding temporal thrust. William James, not a music theorist, has surmised about the shortest temporal boundaries in psychology.

34. See Sarath, "A New Look at Improvisation," for more on event cycle frequency.

35. See Elliott, *Music Matters,* and Maud Hickey, "Creativity Research in Music."

36. Polansky is quoted in Wolff et al., "Improvisation, Heterophony, Politics, Composition," 137.

37. Maharishi Mahesh Yogi, *Celebrating Excellence in Education.*

38. Ibid.

39. See Sarath, *Music Theory Through Improvisation,* chapter 1, for examples of these silence studies.

40. Austin, *Zen and the Brain,* 112.

41. Therefore, in response to Sivan's suggestion in "Improvisation in Western Art Music" that improvisation is unique in its capacity to "penetrate into the subconscious mind of the musician" (37), I might qualify this and suggest that improvisation and composition offer contrasting avenues into the subconscious.

42. Jeff Pressing, "Improvisation: Methods and Models," in *Generative Processes in Music.*

43. I am assuming here a conventional approach to jazz improvisation, in full recognition of the work of Ornette Coleman, late-period John Coltrane, Cecil Taylor, and many others who have explored improvising approaches within the jazz idiom that were not based on conventional harmonic-rhythmic sequences.

44. Nettl, "Thoughts on Improvisation: A Comparative Approach."

45. I formed a 20-plus member improvising ensemble at the University of Michigan whose terrain, ranging from entirely free-form (no referent)

improvisation to jazz to the use of graphic scores, covers much of the continuum mentioned. As one might imagine with an ensemble of this size, the closer the group ventures toward the completely improvisational end of the spectrum, the more critical it is for each member to have an understanding of temporal concerns and how they are linked to interactive capacity.

46. David Cope, *New Directions in Music*, 142.

47. Ibid., 144.

48. See Carl Phillip Immanuel Bach, *Essay on the True Art of Playing Keyboard Instruments*; Johann Joachim Quantz, *On Playing the Flute*; and Carl Czerny, *A Systematic Introduction to Improvisation on the Pianoforte*.

49. Again, the interesting yet in my view shortsighted argument that improvisation in jazz and more overt improvisatory genres differs not in kind but only in degree has been put forth by Carol Gould and Kenneth Keaton, "The Essential Role of Improvisation in Musical Performance."

50. Herbert Simon, "The Architecture of Complexity," *Proceedings of the American Philosophical Society*, 106.

51. Kramer, *The Time of Music*, 56.

52. Gilbert Rouget's *Music and Trance* is seminal in revealing how widespread the transcendence-music linkage is around the globe. Although Rouget challenges the notion that transformed consciousness might consistently result from particular musical structures, he does consider this relationship to be among an array of factors (another important one being the disposition of the practitioner toward transcendence) leading to such experiences.

53. John Coltrane's solo on "Impressions" is from a recording of the same name. Oliver Nelson's "Stolen Moments" solo is on his recording *Blues and the Abstract Truth*.

54. Parker is quoted in Borgo, *Sync or Swarm*, 57.

55. Sarath, "A New Look at Improvisation," 23–27.

56. Brahms is quoted in Willis Harmon and Howard Rheingold, *Higher Creativity: Liberating the Unconscious for Breakthrough Insights*, 41.

57. Mozart is quoted in ibid., 33.

58. Paul Hindemith, *A Composer's World: Horizons and Limitations*, 71.

59. Judith Becker, "Hindu-Buddhist Time in Javanese Gamelan Music," in *Explorations in the Study of Time*, 162.

60. Ibid., 169.

61. Ibid.

62. John Broomfield, *Other Ways of Knowing: Recharting Our Future with Ageless Wisdom*, 73.

63. Dorothy Lee, "Codifications of Reality: Lineal and Nonlineal," in *The Nature of Human Consciousness*, 132.

64. Ibid., 138.

65. Kramer, *The Time of Music*, 24.

66. Christopher Small, *Music of the Common Tongue*.

67. Wilber, *Integral Psychology*.

68. Kramer, *The Time of Music*, 24–25.

69. Göttner-Abendroth, *The Dancing Goddess*, 47–48.

70. Ibid., 26.

71. Elliott, *Music Matters*, 26.

Chapter 7. Interaction: A Systems View of the Improvisation Process

1. Nachmanovitch, *Free Play*, 99.

2. Michael Murphy, *The Future of the Body*, 151.

3. Ibid.

4. Jackson is quoted in Berliner, *Thinking in Jazz*, 394.

5. Williams is quoted in ibid.

6. David Borgo makes an excellent and extensive exploration of improvisation from a complex systems perspective in his *Sync or Swarm: Improvising Music in a Complex Age*. While my appropriation is far less extensive, it is unique in its bringing consciousness into play from both localized, transformational angles and also intersubjective field angles.

7. For further reading on systems thought, see Ludwig von Bertalanffy, *Perspectives on General Systems Theory*; Ervin Laszlo, *Introduction to Systems Philosophy*; James Gleick, *Chaos*; Arthur Koestler, *Janus*.

8. Peter Senge et al., *Presence: An Exploration of Profound Change in People, Organizations, and Society*.

9. Borgo, *Sync or Swarm*, 127.

10. Frank Barrett, "Creativity and Improvisation in Jazz and Organizations: Implications for Organizational Learning," *Organization Science*.

11. Koestler, *Janus*.

12. Ervin Laszlo, *Introduction to Systems Philosophy*.

13. Borgo, *Sync or Swarm*, 89–121.

14. Gleick, *Chaos*, 23.

15. Berliner, *Thinking in Jazz*, 459.

16. Fuller, *Utopia or Oblivion*, 115.

17. Zeitlin's comment is found in Dominic Milano, "The Psychology of Improvisation," *Keyboard Magazine*, 35.

18. See International Society for the Study of Subtle Energies and Energy Medicine, http://www.issseem.org.

19. Skrbina, *Panpsychism in the West*, 2

20. Numerous sources may be cited here that point to the same reality. University professor Christopher Bache, *The Living Classroom*, approaches the topic from the perspective of the classroom teacher. Gary Schwartz in *The Sacred Promise* reports on his empirical studies suggestive of contact with discrete spiritual intelligences or entities. *The Findhorn Gardens* chronicles contact with nature spirits made by founders of the Findhorn community in northern Scotland. Gilbert

Rouget's *Music and Trance* considers transformations in consciousness throughout the world's musical traditions, which in many instances is thought by practitioners to involve the periodic invocation of spirits that inhabit the psychophysiology for ritualistic and healing purposes. The *Tibetan Book of Living and Dying* by Sogyal Rinpoche is a classic account of the existence of *bardos* or planes of existence where the departed soul encounters different kinds of beings.

21. Bache, *The Living Classroom*, 102.

22. Schwartz, *The Sacred Promise*.

23. Evan Parker is cited in Bailey, *Musical Improvisation*, 97.

24. Jung, *The Spirit in Man, Art, Literature*, 57.

25. Werner Heisenberg, *Physics and Philosophy: The Revolution in Modern Science*, 109.

26. Nachmanovitch, *Free Play*, 101.

27. Reimer, *A Philosophy of Music Education*, 113–115.

Chapter 8. Individuation: An Integral View of the Personal and Collective Style of Evolution

1. Lateef, "Jazz Musicians on Education," 104.

2. Robin D. G. Kelly, *Thelonious Monk: The Life and Times of an American Original*, 452.

3. Gardner, *Multiple Intelligences*, 10.

4. Brian Swimme and Thomas Berry, *The Universe Story: From the Primordial Flaring Forth to the Ecozoic Era*.

5. Ibid., 17.

6. Jung, *The Spirit in Man, Art, and Literature*.

7. Ibid.

8. Although it is important to recognize that the archetypal principle as presently construed is not fully compatible with Arthur Lovejoy's conception of a Great Chain of Being, an idea which he concludes is "a failure . . . an experiment in thought carried on by many great and lesser minds, which by now can be seen to have an instructive negative outcome." Arthur Lovejoy, *The Great Chain of Being*, 329.

9. Gleick, *Chaos*, 237.

10. Ilya Prigogine and Isabelle Stengers, *Order Out of Chaos*, 12–14.

11. Csikszentmihalyi, *Creativity*, 113.

12. Ibid.

13. Jorgensen, *Transforming Music Education*, 73.

14. Walter Abell, "Toward a Unified Field of Aesthetics," in *Aesthetics Today*, 458, 459. Abell's remarks are rooted in Jung's premise that "the work of art has its source not in the personal unconscious of the poet, but in a sphere of unconscious mythology whose primordial images are the common heritage of mankind." Jung, *The Spirit in Man, Art, and Literature*, 80. By "personal unconscious," I believe

Jung refers to something like what I am calling the personal self, and by "primordial images," he refers of course to his concept of archetypes.

15. Abell, "Toward a Unified Field of Aesthetics," 447.

16. Nisenson, *Blue*, 1.

17. For example, I do not share the common perception of Wynton Marsalis as among the primary instigators of the neoconservative movement.

18. An example of this point is found on Getz's recording of Chick Corea's modal composition, "Litha," where Getz in my view sounds a bit dated.

19. Nisenson, *Blue*, 1.

20. Lewis, A Power Stronger Than Itself.

21. Gunther Schuller surmised along these lines in his keynote address at the Jazz Education and Music Education symposium held in Corfu, Greece in October 2009, which was convened by the International Association of Schools of Jazz and International Music Council.

Chapter 9. Jazz: An Integral Reading

1. "Louis the First," Interview with Louis Armstrong, *Time Magazine*, February 21, 1949, 52.

2. For accounts of the revolutionary nature of bebop, see LeRoi Jones, *Blues People*; George Lewis, *A Power Stronger Than Itself*, Eric Porter, *What Is This Thing Called Jazz?*; and Scott DeVeaux, *The Birth of Bebop: A Social and Musical History*.

3. Jazz has always been a richly syncretic idiom, but the pace at which jazz expanded its boundaries, which escalated notably with the advent of free and modal jazz around the 1960s, seems to have progressed with time. See Paul Austerlitz, *Jazz Consciousness: Music, Race, Humanity*, for a comprehensive account of the Caribbean influence on jazz. For general overviews of jazz's eclectic strides, see: Eric Nisenson, *Blue*; Robert Sweet, *Music Universe, Music Mind*; Ingrid Monson, "Oh Freedom: George Russell, Miles Davis and Modal Jazz," in *In the Course of Performance: Studies in the World of Musical Improvisation*; George Lewis, *A Power Stronger Than Itself*; Eric Porter, *What Is This Thing Called Jazz?*; Ronald Radano, *New Musical Figurations: Anthony Braxton's Cultural Critique*; and Graham Lock, *Blutopia: Visions of the Future and Revisions of the Past in the Work of Sun Ra, Duke Ellington, and Anthony Braxton*.

4. Nisenson, *Blue*.

5. Andre Hodeir, *The Worlds of Jazz*, 108.

6. Tarnas, *Cosmos and Psyche*, 94–99.

7. Judy Lochhead, "Hearing Chaos," *American Music*, 239.

8. Jones, *Blues People*.

9. Lewis, *A Power Stronger Than Itself*.

10. Informative accounts of modality in jazz are provided by Keith Waters, "What Is Modal Jazz?," *Jazz Education Journal*, and Ingrid Monson, "Oh Freedom."

11. Banfield, *Cultural Codes*, 183.

12. David Elliott, "Structure and Feeling in Jazz: Rethinking Philosophical Foundations," *Bulletin of the Council for Research in Music Education*, 95.

13. Pressing, "Black Atlantic Rhythm."

14. Jones, *Blues People*, 13.

15. Pressing, "Black Atlantic Rhythm," 286.

16. Pressing, "Black Atlantic Rhythm," notes, "Had history been different, it is difficult to imagine a similar global impact based on, for example, the layered structures of Thai course music, or the hocketing of Guillaume de Machaut," 291.

17. Hal Crook, *Ready, Aim, Improvise*, provides a clear analysis of the eighth note line conception. Also see Liebman, *Self-Portrait of a Jazz Artist*, 59, on this point.

18. Elliott, "Structure and Feeling in Jazz: Rethinking Philosophical Foundations," 95.

19. Ibid, 97.

20. Ibid.

21. Berliner, *Thinking in Jazz*, 151.

22. Richard Waterman is quoted in Leroy Ostransky, *Understanding Jazz*, 41–42.

23. J. A. Progler, "Searching for Swing: Participatory Discrepancies in the Jazz Rhythm Section," *Ethnomusicology*, makes an attempt at quantifying Keil's concept. Charles Keil, "The Theory of Participatory Discrepancies: A Progress Report," *Journal of Ethnomusicology*.

24. Some writers estimate the relationship between successive swing eighth notes to be more in the equal vicinity of 1.5 to 1 than the equally divided 2:1 ratio of the triplet configuration. (These ratios should not be confused with the 2:1 melody to bass line relationship of the second layer of the time feel). See Progler, "Searching for Swing." I believe that while it may be productive to seek to delineate these kinds of mathematical correlations, it is important to emphasize their partial and provisional nature (e.g., ratios may change with tempo) and to not overlook the dynamic nature of the time feel, where even within a single measure, and a sequence of measures, swing may be iterated in continually new ways while still maintaining a consistency of feeling of the music.

25. Berliner, *Thinking in Jazz*, 151.

26. Sarath, *Music Theory Through Improvisation*, 128–135.

27. John Chernoff, *African Rhythm and African Sensibility*, 86.

28. Carmen Lundy is quoted in Berliner, *Thinking in Jazz*, 392.

29. Emily Remler is quoted in ibid., 389.

30. Ibid. An interesting issue is raised here regarding the relationship of transformed consciousness and specific musical features. Gilbert Rouget, after his extensive, cross-cultural survey of the music-trance relationship in his book *Music and Trance* and Judith Becker, who later adds insights from contemporary neuroscience to this inquiry in her book *Deep Listeners*, are both inclined to think that direct correlations between type of music and transformed conscious-

ness appear to be inconclusive. However, I believe that exploration of possible mechanisms, as suggested in Theresa Olson-Sorflaten's and others' research, may reveal a more nuanced understanding of the music-consciousness relationship that illuminates specific connections between elements and resultant experience while still allowing for listeners' individual backgrounds to play a key role as well.

31. Hodeir, *The Worlds of Jazz*, 109.

32. Recordings of Davis' such as *Miles Smiles* and *E.S.P.* are good examples.

33. Hodeir, The Worlds of Jazz, 42.

34. Berliner, *Thinking in Jazz*, 148.

35. A prominent example is what is sometimes called Bird Blues, inspired by Charlie Parker's composition "Blues for Alice," involving a much faster harmonic rhythm than typical blues:

F | Em7(b5) A7 | Dm7 G7 | Cm7 F7 | Bbmaj7 |Bbm7 | Am7 D7 | Abm7 Db7 | Gm7 | C7 | Fmaj7 Dm7 | Gm7 C7 ||

36. Berendt, *The World Is Sound*, 223.

37. An excellent account of correlations with the blues and Arabic and African structures is found in a document called "Roots and Branches of Jazz," published by the Society for Preservation and Propagation of Eastern Arts.

38. Thus, the IV dominant seventh in blues is not analyzed as a secondary dominant chord but more as a kind of diatonic chord within the blues pitch space, sometimes called a "Blues IV chord." See Mark Levine, *The Jazz Theory Book*, 220.

39. Berendt, *The World Is Sound*, 223.

40. Danielou, *Music and the Power of Sound*, 59–60.

41. See Danielou, "Relations to a tonic, the modal music of India," in his book *Music and the Power of Sound* for a comprehensive analysis.

42. Here it might be tempting to argue that, particularly with the increasing access to diverse musical practices of recent decades, eventually jazz musicians would find such an alternative. However, the fact that this would require different instruments for the most part, notably in the case of the piano, points to a further reason why this has not happened.

43. The Dmin7 chord is voiced with a second-inversion G major triad above the D root, providing extensions of the eleventh and thirteenth, resolving to an F major triad atop the D root.

44. Tarnas, *Cosmos and Psyche*, 86.

45. For an instructive account of free jazz, see Ekkehard Jost, *Free Jazz*.

46. Lewis, *A Power Stronger Than Itself*.

47. Ibid.

48. Butch Morris led the 30-plus member London Improvisers Orchestra in his system of "conduction" at the 1996 London Jazz Festival. Walter Thompson has created a system called Sound Painting that consists of over 600 gestures that specify a wide range of pitch, rhythmic, textural, and interactive parameters. See Jeffrey Agrell, *Improvisation Games for Classical Musicians*.

49. Watkins' comment is found in *Pyramids at the Louvre: Music, Culture, and Collage from Stravinsky to the Postmodernists*, 465, which is otherwise an extraordinarily comprehensive account of cross-cultural influences and collage through a twentieth-century, Eurological lens. However, asserting to those who are "eager to promote the cause of Third World musics and popular arts of every stripe" that the appropriation of diverse influences in this lineage reflects "the same cultural relativism that the multiculturalists now claim to have discovered," Watkins' viewpoints unwittingly underscore the intractability of the modernist/structuralist orientation that remains securely in place in musical academe and large sectors of Eurological musical practice.

50. Cage is quoted in Lewis, *A Power Stronger Than Itself*.

51. Ibid.

52. Lewis' comments are in Borgo, *Sync or Swarm*, 86.

53. Walser's remarks are from his foreword to Christopher Small's *Music, Society, Education*, x.

54. Marilyn Shrude, "Teaching Composition in Twenty-First Century America: A Conversation with William Bolcom," *American Music*, 177.

55. Ibid., 174.

56. McCrary's remarks are in her afterword in Jacques Attali's *Noise: The Political Economy of Music*, 153.

57. Pressing, "Black Atlantic Rhythm," 308.

58. Schwartz, "Frames of AQAL, Integral Critical Theory, and the Emerging Integral Arts," 245.

59. Phillip Cohran is quoted in Lewis, *A Power Stronger Than Itself*, 125.

60. Berger's statement is found in Joachim Berendt, *The World Is Sound*, 213. For an inspiring and informative account of the Creative Music Studios, see Robert Sweet, *Music Universe, Music Mind*.

61. Sweet, *Music Universe, Music Mind*.

Chapter 10. The Music School of the Future

1. Quoted in V. Goertzen, "By Way of Introduction: Preluding by 18th- and 19th-century Pianists," *Journal of Musicology—A Quarterly Review of Music History, Criticism, Analysis, and Performance Practice*, 305. Original from Johann Hummel, *Ausführliche theoretisch-practische Anweisung zum Piano-Forte-Spiel* (second ed.).

2. Charles Fowler, *Strong Arts, Strong Schools: The Promising Potential and Shortsighted Disregard of the Arts in American Schooling*, 124.

3. Ibid.

4. Ed Sarath, "Is the Paradigm Shifting without Us?," *International Journal of Music Education*, 36.

5. Meyer, *Style and Music Theory, History, Ideology*, 340.

6. Prominent textbooks include Dorothy Payne and Stefan Kostka, *Tonal Harmony*, and Edward Aldwell and Carl Schachter, *Harmony and Voice Leading*.

7. Pressing, "Black Atlantic Rhythm."

8. See Ian Carr, *Keith Jarrett: The Man and His Music*, 154–155, for an account of the pianist's disappointments when he returned to playing classical repertory with symphony orchestras. He found the majority of the musicians to be profoundly unfulfilled and disconnected from music as a transformational phenomenon. Exceptions were those who had outlets for primary creativity.

9. Elliott, *Music Matters*; Sloboda, "Composition and Improvisation," 102.

10. Nettl, *Heartland Excursions*, 138–139.

11. Ibid., 134, 139.

12. Jung, *The Spirit in Man, Art, and Literature*, 82.

13. Wilber, *Collected Works*, 394.

14. Hester, *Bigotry and the Afrocentric "Jazz" Evolution*, 532.

15. This is the two-term Jazz 220-221 Integral Basic Musicianship sequence at Michigan. Other schools may allow coursework in jazz or improvisation after the conventional four-term theory sequence to fulfill core electives, but generally do not allow jazz—despite its exceptional core skill set—to fulfill requirements in the first two years.

16. See Sarath, preface to *Music Theory Through Improvisation*, vii–xv.

17. Whitehead, *The Aims of Education*.

18. Sarath, *Music Theory Through Improvisation*, chapter 1.

19. Harold M. Best, "Creative Diversity, Artistic Valuing, and the Peaceable Imagination." *Arts Education Policy Review*, 95.

20. Ibid., 59.

21. Volk, *Music, Education, and Multiculturalism*.

22. See for example, *Rhythmic Music Education*, edited by Jan Ole Traasdahl. published by Danish Music Council, which is a report on a 1996 congress held in Copenhagen.

23. Barbara Reeder Lundquist, "Music, Culture, Curriculum, and Instruction," in *The New Handbook for Research in Music Education*, 626–627.

24. As, for example, Volk, *Music, Education, and Multiculturalism*, may sometimes tend to do.

25. This is confirmed by her confusing statement that despite "the fact all musics were accepted in the music curriculum, there was little evidence of multicultural approaches in music theory, history, or even music education methods." But where, then, would multicultural approaches have been implemented? Elsewhere she confirms the self-evident fact that ensembles and private lessons are devoid of this, which essentially covers the bulk of the curriculum. Volk, *Music, Education, and Multiculturalism*,111.

26. For example, jazz majors, as is the case at the University of Michigan, may take one year of the two-year classical theory and history sequences, enabling them to focus on the broad skill set required in jazz artistry earlier on. Music education majors could benefit considerably from this template.

27. Prior to the present book, no book-length philosophical perspective on jazz education appears evident. The short-lived *Jazz Changes* magazine, for which I wrote a regular column, that was put out by the International Association of

Schools of Jazz (not to be confused with the now-defunct International Association for Jazz Education) was perhaps the strongest source of jazz education philosophical discourse. Graham Collier's *Interaction*, David Borgo's *Sync or Swarm*, and George Lewis' *A Power Stronger Than Itself* touch on jazz education at times, in the context of a broader commentary on the music.

28. See, for example, David Elliott, *Music Matters*; Bennett Reimer, *A Philosophy of Music Education*; and Estelle Jorgenson, *Transforming Music Education*. Also, important collections such as David Elliott, ed., *Praxial Music Education*, and the section on philosophy in the *New Handbook for Music Education Research*, Richard Colwell and Carol Richardson, eds.

29. See Lewis, *A Power Stronger Than Itself*.

30. Ornette Coleman's remarks are found in Sweet, *Music Universe, Music Mind*, 23.

31. Reimer, *A Philosophy of Music Education*, 20.

32. Again, Nettl's *Heartland Excursions* provides an entertaining/sobering comparison of musical study to a religious order.

33. Reimer, *A Philosophy of Music Education*. Echoing sentiments Wilber has articulated at length in framing the integral vision, Reimer lays important groundwork for musical reform by illuminating the flagrantly contradictory, self-privileging, and incoherent aspects of the postmodern platform. On one hand, "denying, if not ridiculing, the notions of truth and progress," and "abandoning reason as foundational in human affairs," yet on the other, depending on this very reasoning to make its own claims that "the 'truth' about the human condition has been reached," postmodernism is a primary example of a viewpoint that, while nonetheless yielding important insights about the extent to which meaning is culturally constructed, is notably deficient in its self-transcending and thus self-critical capacities.

34. Goldberg, *American Veda*.

35. See "Contemporary Music Project," *Music Educators Journal* 59, 9 (May 1973): 33–48; William J. Mitchell, "Under the Comprehensive Musicianship Umbrella," *Music Educators Journal*; Laura Kautz Sindberg, "The Wisconsin CMP Project at Age 21," *Music Educators Journal*.

36. Reimer, *A Philosophy of Music Education*.

37. Ibid., 113–115.

38. In a personal conversation in the fall in 2009, Elliott strongly retracted his materialist analysis in *Music Matters* and recognized this as a kind of blind alley that he was led to due to the prevalence of materialist thinking on the topic in academic circles.

39. Elliott, *Music Matters*, 135.

40. Ibid., 216.

41. Margaret Barrett, "A Systems View of Creativity," in *Praxial Music Education*, 185.

42. Elliott, *Music Matters*, 29–36.

43. Hester, *Bigotry and the Afrocentric "Jazz" Evolution*, 532.

Chapter 11. Paradigmatic Change and the
Twenty-first-century Academy

1. This remark has been paraphrased to convey an even more poignant commentary on educational stasis: Changing a curriculum is like moving a cemetery.

2. Lawrence Summers, "The 21st Century Education," *New York Times*, Education Life, January 22, 2012.

3. Robert Zemsky, *Making Reform Work: The Case for Transforming American Higher Education*, 181.

4. Ibid.

5. Pierre Hadot, *What Is Ancient Philosophy?*, 2, 6.

6. Ibid., 3.

7. Hal Galper, "Jazz in Academia: Another Look," *Jazz Changes*, 8.

8. Bush, Foreword.

9. See Sarath, "Meditation in Higher Education: The Next Wave?"

10. See Sarath, "Jazz, Creativity, and Consciousness: Blueprint for Integral Education" and "Meditation, Creativity, and Consciousness: Charting Future Terrain within Higher Education."

11. Sarath, ibid.

12. Quoted in Alexander and Langer, eds., *Higher Stages of Human Development*, 313.

13. Wilber, Integral Spirituality, 114.

14. Ibid.

15. Ashok Gangadean and Matthew Bronson, "Encountering the (W)hole: Integral Education as Deep Dialogue," in *Integral Education: New Directions for Higher Learning*, 149.

16. I am indebted to my colleague Martha Travers at the University of Michigan whose extensive use of these dialogic frameworks has enlightened me to their power. I believe the Deep Inquiry framework uniquely harnesses this power.

17. Two excellent sources for "big questions" are Zoe Sallis, Ten Eternal Questions: Wisdom, Insight, and Reflection for Life's Journey, and Lama Surya Das, The Big Questions: How to Find Your Own Answers to Life's Essential Mysteries.

18. Helen and Alexander Astin, Spirituality in Higher Education: A National Study of College Students' Search for Meaning and Purpose.

19. Richard Dawkins, in *The God Delusion*, provides vivid testimony of creationist accounts, as in the belief of a Harvard-trained geologist that "the Earth was less than 10,000 years old," 284.

20. Steven Weinberg, *The First Three Minutes*, 131–132.

21. Affirming a theme central to integral sustainability, Loye argues that the conventional, neo-Darwinian account has fallen "tragically short" in promoting the understanding of the emergence of "higher brain, mind, and consciousness, which characterizes of the emergence of our species and our impact on this

planet" and is needed in our time. David Loye, "Telling the New Story: Darwin, Evolution, and Creativity versus Conformity in Science," in Ruth Richards, ed., *Everyday Creativity and New Views of Human Nature* (Washington, DC: American Psychological Association, 2007), 154–155.

22. Karen Armstrong, *The Battle for God: A History of Fundamentalism*, x.

23. Wilber calls this the "pressure cooker" effect, *Integral Spirituality*, 182.

24. Dawkins, *The God Delusion*, 282–283.

25. Ibid., 15.

26. Wilber, Integral Spirituality, 234.

27. Dean Radin, in *The Conscious Universe*, delves into these dismissive tendencies fairly extensively. See in particular his chapter "A Field Guide to Skepticism."

28. Dawkins, *The God Delusion*, 303.

29. Wilber, *Integral Spirituality*, 183–186.

30. Ibid., 193.

31. George Wald, "The Case against Genetic Engineering," in *The Recombinant DNA Debate* (reprinted from *The Sciences*, Sept./Oct. 1976 issue).

32. Sharma and Clark, *Contemporary Ayurveda*, 30.

33. Sam Harris, Letter to a Christian Nation, xii.

34. Here it should be emphasized that Harris' worldview, very unlike that of Dawkins and most materialists, appears open to transcendent dimensions of reality and he writes with insight into meditation practices, even if practical exploration of possibilities such as harnessing the harmonizing effects of collective consciousness are prominent in his writing.

35. Dawkins, *The God Delusion*, 282.

36. Kuhn, *The Structure of Scientific Revolutions*, 24.

37. Sam Harris, *The End of Faith: Religion, Terror, and the Future of Reason*, 223.

38. Michael Lerner, *The Left Hand of God: Healing America's Political and Spiritual Crisis*, 150.

39. Tiller, *Psychoenergetic Science*.

40. Einstein is quoted in Dawkins, *The God Delusion*, 15.

41. Teilhard de Chardin, *The Hymn of the Universe*, 93.

42. Sowande is quoted in Bill Cole, *John Coltrane*, 21.

43. Ibid., 29.

44. Owen Flanagan, *The Problem of the Soul*, 208.

45. Ibid., vii–viii.

46. Stephen Batchelor, *Confessions of a Buddhist Atheist*, 200.

47. Ibid., 198.

48. See, for example, Conrad Cherry et al., *Religion on Campus*, 14–16, for commentary on Supreme Court rulings that allowed religious clubs to exist and be funded on state university campuses. See also Warren E. Nord, *Religion and American Education: Rethinking a National Dilemma*.

49. Cherry et al., *Religion on Campus*.

50. Gardner, *Multiple Intelligences*, 182.

51. David J. Helfand, former professor of astronomy at Columbia University and president of Quest University, makes this remark in "Where Tradition Goes to the Back of the Class," *New York Times*, Education Life, January 22, 2012, 13.

52. See, for example, John Thelin, *Games Colleges Play: Scandal and Reform in Intercollegiate Athletics*.

53. See Murphy and White, *In the Zone*, for one of the best accounts of the interior and creative dimensions of athletics.

Chapter 12. Planet Earth Takes a Solo

1. Maharishi Mahesh Yogi has described this in terms of living "200 per cent of life," and outlined seven core premises for his international movement that included care for the environment, eradication of poverty, and world peace. He also instituted meditation in prison programs.

2. Steve MacIntosh discusses this possibility in *Integral Consciousness and the Future of Evolution*, as do Ken Wilber and Andrew Cohen, in "The Guru and the Pandit: Eros, Buddha, and the Spectrum of Love: Dialogue between Ken Wilber and Andrew Cohen," *EnlightenNext* magazine.

3. Bache, *The Living Classroom*, 44.

4. Ibid.

5. Lynne McTaggart, *The Field: The Quest for the Secret Force of the Universe*; Sharma and Clark, *Contemporary Ayurveda*; Bache, *The Living Classroom*; Robert Oates, *Permanent Peace: How to Stop War and Terrorism—Now and Forever*.

6. Maharishi Mahesh Yogi, *Constitution of India Fulfilled through Maharishi's Transcendental Meditation*, 43–44.

7. Vaughn-Lee, *The Return of the Divine Feminine and Return of the World Soul*, 1, 3, 4.

8. Maharishi Mahesh Yogi, press-conference.globalgoodnews.com/archive/december/07.12.02.htm.

9. Reported by Bache, *The Living Classroom*, 243 n. 49.

10. Oates, *Permanent Peace*.

11. See, for example, Wilber, *Sex, Ecology, Spirit* and *Integral Spirituality*, and Bache, *The Living Classroom*.

12. De Quincey, *Radical Knowing*.

13. Tarnas, *Cosmos and Psyche*, 489.

14. Jorge Ferrer and Jacob Sherman, eds., introduction to *The Participatory Turn: Spirituality, Mysticism, Religious Studies*, 1.

15. De Quincey, *Radical Knowing*, 184–185.

16. Jorge Ferrer, *Revisioning Transpersonal Theory: A Participatory Vision of Human Spirituality*, 133.

17. Hans Kayser's quote is found in Berendt, *The World Is Sound*, 63.

18. Hazrat Inayat Khan, *The Music of Life*, 70.

19. Murray Schafer, *The Soundscape: Our Sonic Environment and the Tuning of the World*, 10.

20. Skolimowski, *The Participatory Mind*.

21. Berendt, *The World Is Sound*, 63.

22. Ibid.

23. Ibid, 71.

24. Edith Boxhill, *Music Therapy for Living: Principles of Normalization Embodied in Music Therapy*, 1.

25. Peter Tompkins and Christopher Bird, *The Secret Life of Plants*.

26. Masaru Emoto, *The Hidden Messages of Water*.

27. Ravi Shankar, *My Music, My Life*, 28–29.

28. Charles Diserens and Harry Fine, *A Psychology of Music*, 45.

29. Danielou, *Music and the Power of Sound*, 59.

30. Lynn McTaggart, *The Field*, 210. See also her *The Intention Experiment: Using Your Thoughts to Change Your Life and the World*, 184, for discussion of Roger Nelson's findings suggestive of a consciousness-weather relationship, and also shamanic practices that have seemed to exhibit these properties.

31. McTaggart, *The Intention Experiment*.

32. Tiller, *Psychoenergetic Science*.

33. Dean Radin, "A Brief History of the Potential Future," in *Mind Before Matter: Visions of a New Science of Consciousness*, 173.

34. Ray Kurzweil, *The Age of Spiritual Machines*, 279.

35. Ibid., 151.

36. Ibid., 180.

37. David Chalmers, "The Singularity: A Philosophical Analysis," *Journal of Consciousness Studies*," 10,

38. Ibid., 63.

Bibliography

Abell, Walter. 1961. "Toward a Unified Field of Aesthetics." In *Aesthetics Today*, ed. Morris Phillipson. New York: Meridian. 432–465.

Agrell, Jeffrey. 2008. Improvisation Games for Classical Musicians. Chicago: GIA.

Aldwell, Edward, and Schachter, Carl. 1978. *Harmony and Voice Leading*. New York: Harcourt Brace Jovanovich.

Alexander, Charles, and Langer, Ellen, eds. 1990. *Higher Stages of Human Development*. New York: Oxford University Press.

Alexander, C. N., Rainforth, M. V., and Gelderloos, P. 1991. "Transcendental Meditation, Self-actualization, and Psychological Health." *Journal of Personality and Social Psychology* 57: 950–964.

Alperson, Phillip. 1984. "Thoughts on Improvisation." *Journal of Aesthetics and Art Criticism* 43: 17–29.

Andresen, Jensine. 2000. "Meditation Meets Behavioral Medicine." *Journal of Consciousness Studies* 7, no. 11/11: 17–74.

Armstrong, Karen. 2000. *The Battle for God: A History of Fundamentalism*. New York: Random House.

Astin, Helen, and Astin, Alexander. 2003. Spirituality in Higher Education: A National Study of College Students' Search for Meaning and Purpose. Los Angeles: UCLA, Higher Education Research Institute.

Attali, Jacques. 1985. *Noise: The Political Economy of Music*. Minneapolis: University of Minnesota.

Austerlitz, Paul. 2005. *Jazz Consciousness: Music, Race, Humanity*. Middletown, CT: Wesleyan University Press.

Austin, James. 1998. *Zen and the Brain*. Cambridge, MA: MIT.

Azzara, Christopher. 2002. "Improvisation." In *The New Handbook of Research on Music Teaching and Learning*, ed. Richard Colwell and Carol Richardson. New York: Oxford University Press. 171–187.

Bach, Carl Phillip Immanuel. 1949 (1759). *Essay on the True Art of Playing Keyboard Instruments*. Trans. W. J. Mitchell. New York: W.W. Norton; original edition, Berlin: G. L. Winter.

Bache, Christopher. 2008. *The Living Classroom: Teaching and Collective Consciousness*. Albany: State University of New York Press.

Bailey, Derek. 1980. *Musical Improvisation.* New York: Prentice Hall.

Baker, David. 2002. "IAJE President's Message." *Jazz Educators Journal* 15, no. 5: 4.

Banfield, William C. 2010. *Cultural Codes: Makings of a Black Music Philosophy.* Lanham, MD: Scarecrow Press.

Barrett, Frank. 1998. "Creativity and Improvisation in Jazz and Organizations: Implications for Organizational Learning." *Organization Science* 9, no. 5: 605–622.

Barrett, Margaret. 2005. "A Systems View of Creativity." In *Praxial Music Education,* ed. David Elliott. New York: Oxford University Press. 177–195.

Barry, Barbara. 1990. *Musical Time.* Stuyvesant, NY: Pendragon.

Baruss, Imants. 2007. *Science as a Spiritual Practice.* Charlottesville, VA: Imprint Academic.

Batchelor, Stephen. 2010. *Confessions of a Buddhist Atheist.* New York: Spiegel and Grau/Random House.

Becker, Judith. 1981. "Hindu-Buddhist Time in Javanese Gamelan Music." In *Explorations in the Study of Time,* ed. J. T. Fraser, Nathaniel Lawrence, and David Park. New York: Springer Verlag.161–172.

———. 2004. *Deep Listeners: Music, Emotion, Trancing.* Bloomington, IN: Indiana University Press.

Belgrad, Daniel. 1998. The Culture of Spontaneity: Improvisation and the Arts in Postwar America. Chicago: University of Chicago Press.

Bem, Daryl. 2011. "Feeling the Future: Experimental Evidence for Anomalous Retroactive Influences on Cognition and Affect." *Journal of Personality and Social Psychology* 100: 407–425.

Berendt, Joachim-Ernst. 1991. *The World Is Sound: Nada Brahma.* Rochester, VT: Destiny.

Berio, Luciano. 1985. *Two Interviews.* New York: Marion Boyars.

Berliner, Paul. 1994. *Thinking in Jazz: The Infinite Art of Improvisation.* Chicago: University of Chicago Press.

Bertalanffy, Ludwig von. 1975. *Perspectives on General Systems Theory.* New York: George Braziller.

Best, Harold M. 1994. "Creative Diversity, Artistic Valuing, and the Peaceable Imagination." *Arts Education Policy Review* 95, no. 5: 2–8.

Bohm, David. 1981. *Wholeness and the Implicate Order.* London: Routledge.

———. 1996. *On Dialogue.* London: Routledge.

Bonshek, Anna. 2001. *Mirror of Consciousness: Art, Creativity, and Veda.* Delhi: Motilal Barnarsidass.

Borgo, David. 2005. Sync or Swarm: Improvising Music in a Complex Age. New York: Continuum Books.

Bourne, Edmund, 2008. *Global Shift: How a New Worldview Is Transforming Humanity.* Oakland, CA: New Harbinger.

Bowman, Wayne. 1998. *Philosophical Perspectives on Music.* New York: Oxford University Press.

Boxhill, Edith. 1989. *Music Therapy for Living: Principles of Normalization Embodied in Music Therapy.* St. Louis: MMB Music, Inc.

Boyd, Jenny. 1992. *Musicians in Tune: Seventy-Five Contemporary Musicians Discuss the Creative Process*. New York: Fireside/Simon and Schuster.

Broomfield, John. 1997. *Other Ways of Knowing: Recharting Our Future with Ageless Wisdom*. Rochester, VT: Inner Traditions International.

Brown, David P. 2005. *Noise Orders: Jazz, Improvisation, and Architecture*. Minneapolis: University of Minnesota Press.

Brown, Leonard L. 2010. *John Coltrane and Black America's Quest for Freedom*. New York: Oxford University Press.

Brown, Lester. 2009. *Plan B 4.0: Mobilizing to Save Civilization*. New York: W.W. Norton.

Bruner, Jerome. 1960. *The Process of Education*. Cambridge, MA: Harvard University Press.

Bush, Mirabai. 2005. Foreword. *Teachers College Record* 108, no. 9: 1721–1722.

Carr, Ian. 1991. *Keith Jarrett: The Man and His Music*. London: Paladin/Harper Collins.

Chalmers, David J. 1996. *The Conscious Mind: In Search of a Fundamental Theory*. New York: Oxford University Press.

———. 2010. "The Singularity: A Philosophical Analysis." *Journal of Consciousness Studies* 17: 7–65.

de Chardin, Teilhard. 1965. *The Hymn of the Universe*. New York: Harper and Row.

Chernoff, John Miller. 1979. *African Rhythm and African Sensibility*. Chicago: University of Chicago Press.

Cherry, Conrad; DeBerg, Betty A.; Porterfield, Amanda. 2001. *Religion on Campus*. Chapel Hill: University of North Carolina Press.

Christensen, Erik. 1996. *The Musical Timespace: A Theory of Music Listening*. Aalborg, Denmark: Aalborg University Press.

Churchland, Patricia. 1998. "Can Neurobiology Teach Us Anything about Consciousness?" In *The Nature of Consciousness: Philosophical Debates*, ed. N. Block, O. Flanagan, and G. Guzelder. Cambridge, MA: MIT. 127–139.

Clarke, David. 1989. "Structural, Cognitive, and Semiotic Aspects of the Musical Present." *Contemporary Music Review* 3: 111–131.

Clifton, Thomas. 1983. *Music as Heard*. New Haven: Yale University Press.

Cohen, Andrew. 2010. *Being and Becoming: Exploring the Teachings of Evolutionary Enlightenment*. Lenox, MA: EnlightenNext.

Cohen, Andrew, and Wilber, Ken. 2011. "The Guru and the Pandit: Eros, Buddha, and the Spectrum of Love: Dialogue between Ken Wilber and Andrew Cohen." *EnlightenNext*: 47, 46.

Cole, Bill. 1993. *John Coltrane*. New York: Da Capo.

College Music Society. *Directory of Music Faculties at Colleges and Universities, United States and Canada*. Missoula, MT: College Music Society, 2007.

Collier, Graham. 1994. "Jazz Education in America." *Jazz Changes* 1, no. 1: 3–22.

———. 1996. *Interaction*. Berlin: Advance Music.

———. 2000. "The Shape of Jazz to Come." *Jazz Changes* 7, no. 3: 6–11.

Collier, James Lincoln. 1993. *Jazz: The American Theme Song*. New York: Oxford University Press.

Combs, Allan. 2009. *Consciousness Explained Better: Toward an Integral Understanding of the Multi-faceted Nature of Consciousness.* St. Paul, MN: Paragon House.

"Contemporary Music Project." 1973. *Music Educators Journal* 59, 9 (May): 33–48

Cook-Greuter, Susanne. 1999. Postautonomous Ego Development: A Study of Its Nature and Development. PhD dissertation.

Coomaraswamy, Ananda K. 1941. "Lila." *Journal of the American Oriental Society* 61: 98–101.

Cope, David. 1989. *New Directions in Music.* Dubuque: WC Brown.

Cortwright, Brant. 2007. *Integral Psychology: Yoga, Growth, and Opening the Heart.* Albany: State University of New York Press.

Coward, Harold. 1985. *Jung and Eastern Thought.* Albany: State University of New York Press.

Cranson, R. W.; Orme-Johnson, D. W.; Guckenbach J.; Dillbeck, M. C.; Jones, C. H.; Alexander C. N. 1991. "Transcendental Meditation and Improved Performance on Intelligence-related Measures: A Longitudinal Study. *Personality and Individual Differences* 12: 1105–1116.

Crick, Francis. 1995. *The Astonishing Hypothesis.* New York: Touchstone/Simon and Schuster.

Crick, Francis, and Koch, Christof. 1998. "Towards a Neurobiological Theory of Consciousness." In *The Nature of Consciousness: Philosophical Debates*, ed. N. Block, O. Flanagan, and G. Guzelder. Cambridge, MA: MIT. 277–292.

Crook, Hal. 2002. *Ready, Aim, Improvise.* Berlin: Advance Music.

Csikszentmihalyi, Mihalyi. 1990. *Flow: The Psychology of Optimal Experience.* New York: Harper and Row.

———. 1996. *Creativity: Flow and the Psychology of Discovery and Invention.* New York: Harper Perennial.

Czerny, Carl. 1983 (1836). *A Systematic Introduction to Improvisation on the Pianoforte.* Trans. A. L. Mitchell. New York: Longman; original edition, Vienna: Cassel.

Dalal, A. S. 2001. *A Greater Psychology: The Psychological Thought of Sri Aurobindo.* New York: Tarcher/Putnam.

Damasio, Antonio. 1994. *Descartes' Error: Emotion, Reason and the Human Brain.* New York: Avon Books.

———. 1999. *The Feeling of What Happens: Body and Emotion in the Making of Consciousness.* New York: Harcourt.

Danielou, Alain. 1995 (1943). *Music and the Power of Sound: The Influence of Tuning and Interval on Consciousness.* Rochester, VT: Destiny.

Davidson, Richard. 2004. "Long-term Meditators Self-induce High Amplitude Gamma Synchrony during Mental Practice." *National Academy of Sciences Review* 101, no. 46: 16309–16373.

Dawkins, Richard. 2006. *The God Delusion.* New York: Houghton Mifflin.

Dennett, Daniel. 1991. *Consciousness Explained.* Boston: Back Bay.

DePraz, M. Varela; Vermersch, F.; and Vermersch, P. eds. 2003. *On Becoming Aware: Advances in Consciousness Research.* Amsterdam: Jonathan Benjamin.

DeVeaux, Scott. 1997. *The Birth of Bebop: A Social and Musical History*. Berkeley: University of California Press.

Dewey, John. 1991 (1933). *How We Think*. Buffalo: Prometheus Books.

———. 1938. *Experience and Education*. New York: MacMillan.

Dillbeck, Michael. 1991. "The Bhagavad Gita: A Case Study in Vedic Psychology." *Modern Science and Vedic Science* 4, no. 2: 96–134.

Dimock, Edward C. 1989. "Lila." *History of Religions* 29, no. 2: 159–173.

Diserens, Charles M., and Fine, Harry. 1939. *A Psychology of Music*. Cincinnati: Cincinnati College of Music.

Dissanayake, Ellen. 2000. *Arts and Intimacy: How the Arts Began*. Seattle: University of Washington Press.

Druhl, Kai. 1997. "Consciousness as the Subject and Object of Physics: Toward a New Paradigm for the Physical Sciences." *Modern Science and Vedic Science* 7, no. 1: 143–164.

Swami Durgananda. 2002. *The Heart of Meditation: Pathways to a Deeper Experience*. South Fallsburg, NY: SYDA Foundation.

Elliott, David. 1987. "Structure and Feeling in Jazz: Rethinking Philosophical Foundations." *Bulletin of the Council for Research in Music Education* no. 95: 3–38.

———. 1995. *Music Matters*. New York: Oxford University Press.

———, ed. 2005. *Praxial Music Education: Reflections and Dialogues*. New York: Oxford University Press.

Emoto, Masaru. 2004. *The Hidden Messages of Water*. Hillsboro, OR: Beyond Words Press.

Emarvahdana, T., and Tori, C. D. 1997. "Changes in Self-concept, Ego Defense Mechanisms, and Religiosity Following Seven-day Vipassana Meditation Retreats." *Journal for the Scientific Study of Religion* 36: 194–206.

Esbjörn-Hargens, Sean. 2010. "An Overview of Integral Theory: An All-Inclusive Framework for the 21st Century." In *Integral Theory in Action: Applied, Theoretical, and Constructive Perspectives on the AQAL Model*, ed. Sean Esbjörn-Hargens. Albany: State University of New York Press. 33–61.

———, ed. 2010. *Integral Theory in Action: Applied, Theoretical, and Constructive Perspectives on the AQAL Model*. Albany: State University of New York Press.

Esbjörn-Hargens, Sean; Reams, Jonathan; Gunnlaugson, Olen, eds. 2010. *Integral Education: New Directions for Higher Learning*. Albany: State University of New York.

Esbjörn-Hargens, Sean, and Zimmerman, Michael. 2009. *Integral Ecology: Uniting Multiple Perspectives on the Natural World*. Boston: Shambhala.

Evans-Wentz, W. Y., ed. 1967. *Tibetan Yoga and Secret Doctrines*. New York: Oxford University Press.

Ferrer, Jorge. 2002. *Revisioning Transpersonal Theory: A Participatory Vision of Human Spirituality*. Albany: State University of New York Press.

Ferrer, Jorge; Romero, Marina; Albaveda, Ramon. 2010. "Integral Transformative Education: A Participatory Proposal." In *Integral Education: New Directions for Higher Learning*, ed. Sean Esbjörn-Hargens, Jonathan Reams, and Olen Gunnlaugson. Albany: State University of New York Press.

Ferrer, Jorge, and Sherman, Jacob, eds. 2008. *The Participatory Turn: Spirituality, Mysticism, Religious Studies.* Albany: State University of New York Press.

Findhorn Community. 1975. *The Findhorn Gardens: Pioneering a New Vision of Man and Nature in Cooperation.* San Francisco: Harper and Row.

Fischlin, Daniel. 2010. " 'See clearly . . . feel deeply': Improvisation and Transformation: John McLaughlin Interviewed by Daniel Fischlin." *Critical Studies in Improvisation / Études critiques en improvisation* 6, no. 2: 1–9.

Flanagan, Owen. 2002. *The Problem of the Soul.* New York: Basic Books.

Flannery, Timothy. 2003. *The Weather Makers: How Man Is Changing the Climate and What It Means for Life on Earth.* New York: Atlantic Monthly Press.

Floyd, Samuel A. 1995. *The Power of Black Music: Interpreting Its History from Africa to the United States.* New York: Oxford University Press.

Forman, Robert, ed. 1990. *The Problem of Pure Consciousness.* New York: Oxford University Press.

———. 2004. *Grassroots Spirituality.* Charlottesville, VA: Imprint Academic.

Fowler, Charles. 1996. *Strong Arts, Strong Schools: The Promising Potential and Shortsighted Disregard of the Arts in American Schooling.* New York: Oxford University Press.

Fuller, R. Buckminster. 1969. *Utopia or Oblivion: The Prospects for Humanity.* New York: Bantam.

Galper, Hal. 1996. "Jazz in Academia: Another Look." *Jazz Changes* 1, no. 2: 8–9.

Gangadean, Ashok, and Bronson, Matthew. 2010. "Encountering the (W)hole: Integral Education as Deep Dialogue." In *Integral Education: New Directions for Higher Learning*, ed. Sean Esbjörn-Hargens, Jonathan Reams, and Olen Gunnlaugson. Albany: State University of New York Press.

Garcia, Antonio J. 2001. "Dave Brubeck: His Music Keeps Us Here." *Jazz Educators Journal* 34, no. 3: 39–45.

Gardner, Howard. 1983. *Frames of Mind: The Theory of Multiple Intelligences.* New York: Basic Books.

———. 1993. *Multiple Intelligences: The Theory in Practice.* New York: Basic Books.

———. 1999. *Intelligence Reframed: Refining the Theory.* New York: Basic Books.

Gebser, Jean. 1953 (1949). *The Ever-Present Origin.* Trans. Noel Barstad with Algis Michunas. Columbus, OH: University of Ohio Press.

Gilligan, Carol. 1993. *In a Different Voice: Psychological Theory and Women's Development.* Cambridge, London: Harvard University Press.

Gleick, James. 1987. *Chaos.* New York: Viking.

Goertzen, V. 1996. "By Way of Introduction: Preluding by 18th- and 19th-century Pianists." *Journal of Musicology—A Quarterly Review of Music History, Criticism, Analysis, and Performance Practice* 14, no. 3: 299–337. Original from Hummel, Johann. 1829. *Ausführliche theoretisch-practische Anweisung zum Piano-Forte-Spiel* (second ed.). Vienna: Tobias Haslinger.

Goldberg, Phillip. 2010. *American Veda: How Indian Spirituality Changed the West.* New York: Harmony/Random House.

Goleman, Dan. 1996. *The Meditative Mind: Varieties of Meditative Experience.* New York: Penguin.

Goswami, Amit. 1993. *The Self-Aware Universe: How Consciousness Creates the Material World.* New York: Tarcher.

Göttner-Abendroth, Heide. 1991. *The Dancing Goddess: Principles of a Matriarchal Aesthetic.* Trans. Maureen T. Krause. Boston: Beacon Press.

Gould, Carol, and Keaton, Kenneth. 2000. "The Essential Role of Improvisation in Musical Performance." *The Journal of Aesthetics and Art Criticism* 58, no. 2: 143–148.

Gould, Stephen Jay. 1999. *Rock of Ages: Science and Religion in the Fullness of Life.* New York: Ballantine.

Lama Anagorika Govinda. 1969. *Foundations of Tibetan Buddhism.* York Beach, ME: Samuel Weisner.

Greene, Maxine 1985. *Releasing the Imagination: Essays on Education, the Arts, and Social Change.* San Francisco: Jossey-Bass.

Griffin, David Ray. 1997. *Parapsychology, Philosophy, and Spirituality.* Albany: State University of New York Press.

Hadot, Pierre. 2002. *What Is Ancient Philosophy?* Cambridge, MA: Harvard University Press.

Hagelin, John. 1987. "Is Consciousness the Unified Field? A Field Theorist's Perspective." *Modern Science and Vedic Science* 1, no. 1: 29–88.

———, et al. 1999. "Effects of Group Practice of the Transcendental Meditation Program on Preventing Violent Crime in Washington, D.C.; Results of the National Demonstration Project to Reduce Crime and Improve Governmental Effectiveness in Washington, D.C., June-July, 1993." *Social Indicators Research* 47: 153–201.

Haidet, Paul. 2007. "Jazz and the 'Art' of Medicine: Improvisation in the Medical Encounter." *Annals of Family Medicine* 5, no. 2.

Harmon, Willis, and Rheingold, Howard. 1984. *Higher Creativity: Liberating the Unconscious for Breakthrough Insights.* New York: Tarcher.

Harris, Sam. 2004. *The End of Faith: Religion, Terror, and the Future of Reason.* New York: W.W. Norton.

———. 2006. "Killing the Buddha." *Shambhala Sun*, March: 73–75.

———. 2006. *Letter to a Christian Nation.* New York: Alfred Knopf.

Hartranft, Chip. 2003. *The Yoga Sutra of Patanjali.* Boston: Shambhala.

Heisenberg, Werner. 1958. *Physics and Philosophy: The Revolution in Modern Science.* New York: Harper and Row.

Helfand, David J. 2012. "Where Tradition Goes to the Back of the Class." *New York Times*, Education Life, January 22: 13.

Hester, Karlton. 2009. *Bigotry and the Afrocentric "Jazz" Evolution.* San Diego: University Readers.

Hickey, Maud. 2002. "Creativity Research in Music, Visual Art, Theatre, and Dance." In *The New Handbook on Music Learning and Teaching*, ed. Richard Colwell and Carol Richardson. New York: Oxford University Press. 398–415.

Hindemith, Paul. *A Composer's World: Horizons and Limitations*. Cambridge, MA: Harvard University Press.

Hobson, J. Allan. 1999. *Consciousness*. New York: Scientific American Library.

Hodeir, Andre. 1972. *The Worlds of Jazz*. New York: Grove.

Hooper, Judith. 1992. *The Three-pound Universe*. Los Angeles: Tarcher.

hooks, bell. 1994. *Teaching to Transgress: Education as the Practice of Freedom*. New York: Routledge.

Houston, Jean. 2009. "Jump Time Is Now." In *The Mystery of 2012: Predictions, Prophecies and Possibilities*. Boulder: Sounds True.

Hubbard, Barbara Marx. 2009. "A Vision for Humanity." In *The Mystery of 2012: Predictions, Prophecies and Possibilities*. Boulder: Sounds True.

Husserl, Edmund. 1991. *On the Phenomenology of the Consciousness of Internal Time (1893–1917)*. Trans. J.B. Brough. Dordrecht, Netherlands: Kluwer Academic Publishers.

Jahn, Robert, and Dunne, Brenda. 1987. *The Margins of Reality*. San Diego: Harcourt and Brace.

James, William. 1962 (1892). *Psychology*. New York: Penguin; original edition, New York: Henry Holt.

———. 1962 (1902). *The Varieties of Religious Experience*. New York: Penguin; first edition, New York: Longman, Green and Co.

Jones, LeRoi. 1963. *Blues People: Negro Music in White America*. New York: Harper Collins/Perennial.

Jorgensen, Estelle R. 2003. *Transforming Music Education*. Bloomington, IN: Indiana University Press.

Jost, Ekkehard. 1994. *Free Jazz*. New York: Da Capo.

Jung, C. G. 1956. *Two Essays on Analytical Psychology*. Trans. R. F. C. Hull. New York: Meridian Books.

———. 1990 (1959). *The Archetypes and the Collective Unconscious*. Princeton: Princeton University Press, Bollingen.

———. 1960. *On the Nature of the Psyche*. Princeton: Princeton University Press, Bollingen.

———. 1961. *The Spirit in Man, Art, and Literature*. Princeton: Princeton University Press, Bollingen.

Kahn, Hazrat Inayat. 1988. *The Music of Life*. New Lebanon, NY: Omega.

Kao, John. 1996. *Jamming*. New York: Harper Collins.

Keil, Charles. 1995. "The Theory of Participatory Discrepancies: A Progress Report." *Journal of Ethnomusicology* 39, no. 1: 1–19.

Kelly, Edward F.; Kelly, Emily W.; Crabtree, Adam; Gauld, Alan; Grosso, Michael; and Greyson, Bruce. 2007. *Irreducible Mind: Toward a Psychology for the 21st Century*. Lanham, MD: Rowman and Littlefield.

Kelly, Robin D. G. 2009. *Thelonious Monk: The Life and Times of an American Original*. New York: Free Press.

Koestler, Arthur. 1979. *Janus*. New York: Vintage.

Kramer, Jonathan. 1988. *The Time of Music*. New York: Schirmer.

Kuhn, Thomas. 1962. *The Structure of Scientific Revolutions*. Chicago: University of Chicago Press.

Kurzweil, Ray. 1999. *The Age of Spiritual Machines*. New York: Viking.

Lacy, Steve. 1994. *Findings: My Experience with the Soprano Saxophone*. Paris: CMAP, Outre Mesure.

Lao Tse. 1961. *Tao Teh Ching*. Asian Institute Translation. New York: St. John's University Press.

Langer, Ellen. 1989. *Mindfulness*. New York: Da Capo.

Langer, Susanne. 1948. Philosophy in a New Key: A Study in the Symbolism of Reason, Rite, and Art. New York: Mentor.

Lateef, Yusef. 2004. "Jazz Musicians on Education." *Downbeat*, October, 102.

Laszlo, Ervin. 1972. *Introduction to Systems Philosophy*. New York: Torchbook.

Lee, Dorothy. 1974. "Codifications of Reality: Lineal and Nonlineal." In *The Nature of Human Consciousness*, ed. Robert Ornstein. New York: Viking. 128–142.

Lerner, Michael. 2006. The Left Hand of God: Healing America's Political and Spiritual Crisis. New York: Harper Collins.

Lesser, Elizabeth. 1999. *The New American Spirituality: A Seeker's Guide*. New York: Random House.

Levin, Michael, and Wilson, John S. 1994. "No Bop Roots in Jazz: Parker." *Downbeat* 61, no. 2: 24–26. Originally published September 9, 1949.

Levine, Mark. 1995. *The Jazz Theory Book*. Petaluma, CA: Sher Music.

Lewin, David. 1986. "Music Theory, Phenomenology, and Modes of Perception." *Music Perception* 3, no. 4: 327–392.

Lewis, George. 2008. *A Power Stronger Than Itself: The AACM and American Experimental Music*. Chicago: University of Chicago Press.

Lewis, George E. 1996. "Improvised Music since 1950: Afrological and Eurological Perspectives." *Black Music Research* 16 (Spring): 91–119.

Liebman, David. 1996. *Self-portrait of a Jazz Artist: Musical Thoughts and Realities*. Berlin: Advance Music.

Lochhead, Judy. 2001. "Hearing Chaos." *American Music* 19, no. 2: 210–246.

Lock, Graham. 2000. *Blutopia: Visions of the Future and Revisions of the Past in the Work of Sun Ra, Duke Ellington, and Anthony Braxton*. Durham: Duke University Press.

Loevinger, Jane. 1987. *Paradigms of Personality*. New York: W. H. Freeman and Company.

Lovejoy, Arthur. 1964. *The Great Chain of Being*. Cambridge, MA: Harvard University Press.

Loye, David. 2007. "Telling the New Story: Darwin, Evolution, and Creativity versus Conformity in Science." In *Everyday Creativity and New Views of Human Nature*, ed. Ruth Richards. Washington, DC: American Psychological Association. 153–173.

Lubriel, Luis. 2009. "Integral Music Performance and Pedagogy." *Journal of Integral Theory and Practice* 4, no. 3: 87–108.

Lundquist, Barbara Reeder. 2002. "Music, Culture, Curriculum, and Instruction." In *The New Handbook of Research on Music Teaching and Learning*, ed. Richard Colwell and Carol Richardson. New York: Oxford University Press. 626–647.

MacIntosh, Steve. 2007. *Integral Consciousness and the Future of Evolution: How the Integral Worldview Is Transforming Politics, Culture, and Spirituality*. St. Paul, MN: Paragon House.

Maharishi Mahesh Yogi. 1969. *Bhagavad Gita: A New Translation and Commentary*. Penguin: New York.

———. 1997. *Celebrating Perfection in Education*. New Delhi: Maharishi Vedic Publications.

———. 1999. *Constitution of India Fulfilled through Maharishi's Transcendental Meditation*. New Delhi: Vedic Vishwa-Vidyalaya.

Mansfield, Victor. 2002. *Head and Heart: A Personal Exploration of Science and the Sacred*. Wheaton, IL: Theosophical Press.

———. 2008. *Tibetan Buddhism and Modern Physics*. West Conshohocken, PA: Templeton.

Maslow, Abraham. 1948. *Motivation and Personality*. New York: Harper.

———. 1968. *Toward a Psychology of Being*. New York: D. Van Nostrand.

———. 1970. *Religion, Values, and Peak Experiences*. New York: Penguin.

———. 1971. *The Farther Reaches of Human Nature*. New York: Penguin.

Mason, Lynne; Patterson, Robert P.; and Radin, Dean I. 2007. "Exploratory Study: The Random Number Generator and Group Meditation." *Journal of Scientific Exploration* 21: 295–317.

Mayer, Elizabeth L. 2007. *Extraordinary Knowing: Science, Skepticism, and the Inexplicable Powers of the Human Mind*. New York: Bantam.

McCarthy, Marie. 2009. "Exploring the Spiritual in Music Teacher Education: Group Musical Improvisation Points the Way." *The Mountain Lake Reader* 5: 12–23.

McTaggart, Lynne M. 2002. *The Field: The Quest for the Secret Force of the Universe*. New York: Harper Collins.

———. 2007. *The Intention Experiment: Using Your Thoughts to Change Your Life and the World*. New York: Free Press.

Mell, Margaret. 2010. Mind, Body, and Spirit: In Pursuit of an Integral Philosophy of Music Teaching and Learning. PhD dissertation.

Metheny, Pat. 2001. Keynote Address. *International Association of Schools of Jazz Newsletter* (Summer): 3–8.

Meyer, Leonard. 1989. *Style and Music Theory, History, Ideology*. Philadelphia: University of Pennsylvania Press.

Milano, Dominic. 1984. "The Psychology of Improvisation." *Keyboard Magazine* 10, no. 10: 30–35.

Miller, Izchak. 1984. *Husserl, Perception, and Temporal Awareness*. Cambridge, MA: MIT.

Miller, Ron. 1990. *What Are Schools For? Holistic Education in American Culture*. Brandon, VT: Holistic Education Press.

Mitchell, William J. 1969. "Under the Comprehensive Musicianship Umbrella." *Music Educators Journal* 55, no. 7: 71–72, 75.

Mithen, Steven. 2006. *The Singing Neanderthals: The Origins of Music, Language, Mind, and Body*. Cambridge, MA: Harvard University Press.

Monson, Ingrid. 1996. *Saying Something: Jazz Improvisation and Interaction*. Chicago: University of Chicago Press.

———. 1998. "Oh Freedom: George Russell, Miles Davis and Modal Jazz." In *In the Course of Performance: Studies in the World of Musical Improvisation*, ed. Bruno Nettl and Melinda Russell. Chicago: University of Chicago Press. 149–168.

Montouri, Alphonso. 2003. "The Complexity of Improvisation and the Improvisation of Complexity: Social Science, Art, and Creativity." *Human Relations* 56, no. 2: 237–255.

Montouri, Alphonso, and Purser, Robert. 1994. "Miles Davis in the Classroom: Using the Jazz Ensemble Metaphor for Enhancing Team Learning." *Journal of Management Education* 21–31.

Muller-Ortega, Paul Eduardo. 1989. *The Triadic Heart of Siva: Kaula Tantricism of Abhinavagupta in the Non-dual Shaivism of Kashmir*. Albany: State University of New York Press.

Murphy, Daniel. 1994. "Jazz Studies in American Schools and Colleges: A Brief History." *Jazz Educators Journal* 26 (Fall): 34–38.

Murphy, Michael. 1992. *The Future of the Body*. New York: Tarcher.

Murphy, Michael, and White, Rhea. 1995. *In the Zone: Transcendent Experience in Sports*. New York: Penguin.

Music Educators National Conference. 1994. *National Standards for Arts Education: What Every Young American Should Know and Be Able to Do in the Arts*. Reston, VA: Author.

Nachmanovitch, Stephen. 1990. *Free Play: The Power of Improvisation in Life and Art*. Los Angeles: Tarcher.

Naidus, Beverly. 2009. *Arts for Change: Teaching Outside the Frame*. Oakland: New Village Press.

Narmour, Eugene. 1990. *The Analysis and Cognition of Basic Melodic Structures: The Implication-Realization Model*. Chicago: University of Chicago Press.

Nettl, Bruno. 1974. "Thoughts on Improvisation: A Comparative Approach." *The Musical Quarterly* 60, no. 1:1–19.

———. 1995. *Heartland Excursions: Ethnomusicological Reflections on Schools of Music*. Urbana: University of Illinois Press.

Nicolescu, Basarab. 2002. *Manifesto of Transdisciplinarity*. Albany: State University of New York Press.

Nisenson, Eric. 1997. *Blue: The Murder of Jazz*. New York: Da Capo.

Nord, Warren E. 1995. *Religion and American Education: Rethinking a National Dilemma*. Chapel Hill: University of North Carolina Press.

Oates, Robert. 2002. *Permanent Peace: How to Stop Terrorism and War—Now and Forever*. Fairfield, IA: Institute for Science, Technology, and Public Policy.

Olson-Sorflaten, Theresa. 1995. Increased Personal Harmony and Integration as Effects of Maharishi Gandharva Veda Music on Affect, Physiology, and Behavior: The Psychophysiology. PhD dissertation, Maharishi International University.

O'Meally, Robert; Edwards, Brent Hayes; and Griffin, Farah Jasmine, eds. 2004. *Uptown Conversation: The New Jazz Studies*. New York: Columbia University Press.

Orme-Johnson D.; Alexander, C.; Davies, J.; Chander, H.; and Larimore, W. 1988. "International Peace Project: The Effects of the Maharishi Technology of the Unified Field." *Journal of Conflict Resolution* 32, no. 4: 776–812.

Orme-Johnson, David; Dillbeck, M.; Wallace, R. K.; and Landrith, G. 1982. "Inter-subject EEG Coherence: Is Consciousness a Field?" *International Journal of Neuroscience*16: 203–209.

Ostransky, Leroy. 1977. *Understanding Jazz*. Englewood Cliffs: Prentice Hall.

Palmer, Parker. 1998. *The Courage to Teach*. San Francisco: Jossey-Bass.

Payne, Dorothy, and Kostka, Stefan. 2000. *Tonal Harmony*. New York: McGraw Hill.

Pearson, Craig. 2011. *Supreme Awakening: Experiences of Higher States of Consciousness*. Fairfield, IA: Maharishi University of Management Press.

Pert, Candace. 1997. Molecules of Emotion: The Science behind Mind-Body Medicine. New York: Touchstone.

Porter, Eric. 2002. *What Is This Thing Called Jazz?* Berkeley: University of California Press

Porter, Lewis. 1998. *John Coltrane: His Life and Music*. Ann Arbor: University of Michigan Press.

Pressing, Jeff. 1987. "Improvisation: Methods and Models." In *Generative Processes in Music*, ed. John Sloboda. London: Oxford University Press. 129–176.

Pressing, Jeff. 2002. "Black Atlantic Rhythm: Its Computational and Transcultural Foundations." *Music Perception* 19, no. 3: 285–310.

Prigogine, Ilya, and Stengers, Isabelle. 1984. *Order Out of Chaos*. New York: Bantam.

Progler, J. A. 1995. "Searching for Swing: Participatory Discrepancies in the Jazz Rhythm Section." *Ethnomusicology* 39, no. 1: 21–54.

Quantz, Johann Joachim. 1996 (1752). *On Playing the Flute*. Trans. E. R. Reilly. New York: Schirmer; original edition, Berlin: Johann Frederick Voss.

de Quincey, Christian. 2005. *Radical Knowing: Understanding Consciousness through Relationship*. Rochester, VT: Park Street.

Quinn, Robert. 1996. *Deep Change: Discovering the Leader Within*. San Francisco: Jossey-Bass.

Radin, Dean. 1997. *The Conscious Universe*. San Francisco: Harper.

———. 2006. *Entangled Minds: Extrasensory Experiences in Quantum Reality*. New York: Paraview Pocket Books.

———. 2007. "A Brief History of the Potential Future." In *Mind Before Matter: Visions of a New Science of Consciousness*, ed. Trish Pfeiffer and John E. Mack. Winchester, UK: O Books/John Hunt.

Radano, Ronald M. 1996. *New Musical Figurations: Anthony Braxton's Cultural Critique*. Chicago: University of Chicago Press.

Ramsey, Guthrie. 2003. *Race Music: Black Cultures from Bebop to Hip Hop*. Berkeley: University of California Press.

Reimer, Bennett. 2003. *A Philosophy of Music Education: Advancing the Vision*. Chicago: University of Chicago Press.

Rentschler, Matt. 2006. "Introducing Integral Art." *Journal of Integral Theory and Practice* 1, no. 1: 41–49.

Richards, Ruth, ed. 2007. *Everyday Creativity and New Views of Human Nature: Psychological, Social, and Spiritual Perspectives.* Washington, DC: American Psychological Association.

Robertson, Ross. 2011. "Dreams of an Eco-Spiritual Futurist: A Conversation with British Sustainability Strategist Hardin Tibbs." *EnlightenNext* 47: 52–63.

Rogers, Carl. 1961. *On Becoming a Person.* Boston: Houghton-Mifflin.

———. 1989. *Dialogues.* Boston: Houghton-Mifflin.

Rouget, Gilbert. 1985. *Music and Trance.* Chicago: University of Chicago Press.

Russell, Peter. 1992. *Waking Up in Time: Finding Inner Peace in Times of Accelerating Change.* Novato, CA: Origin.

Russell, Ross. 1973. *Bird Lives: The High Life and Hard Times of Charlie Parker.* New York: Da Capo.

Sallis, Zoe. 2005. *Ten Eternal Questions: Wisdom, Insight, and Reflection for Life's Journey.* San Francisco: Chronicle Books.

Sarath, Edward. 1995. "Is the Paradigm Shifting without Us?" *International Journal of Music Education* no. 25: 29–37.

———. 1996. "A New Look at Improvisation." *Journal of Music Theory* 40, no. 1: 1–39.

———. 2002. "Improvisation and Curriculum Reform." In *The New Handbook of Research on Music Teaching and Learning,* ed. Richard Colwell and Carol Richardson. New York: Oxford University Press. 188–198.

———. 2003. "Meditation in Higher Education: The Next Wave?" *Innovative Higher Education* 27: 215–234.

———. 2005. "Jazz Lessons for the Boardroom." *Newsday,* May 15.

———. 2006. "Meditation, Creativity, and Consciousness: Charting Future Terrain within Higher Education." *Teachers College Record* 108, no. 9: 1816–1841.

———. 2007. "Improvisation, Consciousness, and the Play of Creation: Music as a Lens into Ultimate Reality and Meaning." *Ultimate Reality and Meaning* 30, no. 1: 54–77.

———. 2010. "Jazz, Creativity, and Consciousness: Blueprint for Integral Education." In *Integral Education: New Directions for Higher Learning,* ed. Sean Esbjörn-Hargens, Jonathan Reams, and Olen Gunnlaugson. Albany: State University of New York Press.

———. 2010. *Music Theory through Improvisation: A New Approach to Musicianship Training.* New York: Routledge.

Sax, William S. 1990. "The Ramnagar Ramlila: Text, Performance, Pilgramage." *History of Religions* 30 (November): 129–153.

Schafer, R. Murray. 1997. *The Soundscape: Our Sonic Environment and the Tuning of the World.* Rochester, VT: Destiny Books.

Schubert, William H. 2009. *Love, Justice and Education: John Dewey and the Utopians.* Charlotte, NC: Information Age Publishing.

Schwartz, Gary E. 2011. *The Sacred Promise: How Science Is Discovering Spirit's Collaboration with Us in Our Daily Lives.* New York: Atria.

Schwartz, Michael. 2010. "Frames of AQAL, Integral Critical Theory, and the Emerging Integral Arts." In *Integral Theory in Action: Applied, Theoretical, and Constructive Perspectives on the AQAL Model*, ed. Sean Esbjörn-Hargens. Albany: State University of New York Press. 229–252.

Searle, John R. 1997. *The Mystery of Consciousness*. New York: New York Review of Books.

———. 1998. "Reductionism and the Irreducibility of Consciousness." In *The Nature of Consciousness: Philosophical Debates*, ed. N. Block, O. Flanagan, and G. Guzelder. Cambridge, MA: MIT. 451–459.

Sehgal, Kabir. 2008. *Jazzocracy: Jazz, Democracy, and the Creation of a New American Mythology*. Mishawaka, IN: BetterWorld Books.

Senge, Peter; Scharmer, C. Otto; Jaworski, Joseph; Flowers, Betty Sue 2004. *Presence: An Exploration of Profound Change in People, Organizations, and Society*. New York: Currency Doubleday.

Shankar, Ravi. 1968. *My Music, My Life*. New York: Simon and Schuster.

Sharma, Hari, and Clark, Christopher. 1998. *Contemporary Ayurveda: Medicine and Research in Maharishi Ayurveda*. Philadelphia: Churchill Livingstone.

Shear, Jonathan. 2006. *The Experience of Meditation*. St. Paul, MN: Paragon House.

Sheldrake, Rupert. 1999. *Dogs That Know When Their Owners Are Coming Home*. New York/London: Random House.

———. 2009. *Morphic Resonance: The Nature of Formative Causation*. Rochester, VT: Park Street.

Shrude, Marilyn. 2010. "Teaching Composition in Twenty-first-Century America: A Conversation with William Bolcom." *American Music* 28, no. 2: 173–190.

Simon, Herbert. 1962. "The Architecture of Complexity." *Proceedings of the American Philosophical Society* 106.

Sindberg, Laura Kautz. 1998. "The Wisconsin CMP Project at Age 21." *Music Educators Journal* 85, no. 3: 37–39, 42.

Sivan, Noam. 2009. Improvisation in Western Art Music: Its Relevance Today. PhD dissertation. Julliard School of Music.

Skolimowski, Henryk. 1994. *The Participatory Mind*. New York: Penguin.

———. 2010. *Let There Be Light: The Mysterious Voyage of Cosmic Creativity*. New Delhi: Wisdom Tree.

Skrbina, David. 2005. *Panpsychism in the West*. Cambridge, MA: MIT.

Sloboda, John. 1985. "Composition and Improvisation." In *The Musical Mind*, ed. John Sloboda. New York: Oxford University Press.

Small, Christopher. 1994. *Music of the Common Tongue*. London: Calder Riverrun.

———. 1996. *Music, Society, Education*. Hanover, NH: Wesleyan University Press.

Smith, Page. 1990. *Killing the Spirit: Higher Education in America*. New York: Viking.

Society for Preservation and Propagation of Eastern Arts. 1987. "Roots and Branches of Jazz." Provo: Eastern Arts.

Sogyal Rinpoche. 1993. *The Tibetan Book of Living and Dying*. San Francisco: Harper Collins.

Stace, William. 1970. *Mysticism and Philosophy*. London: Macmillan.

Sternberg, Robert, ed. 1999. *Handbook of Creativity*. New York: Cambridge.

Summers, Lawrence. 2012. The 21st-Century Education. *New York Times*, Education Life. January 22.

Lama Surya Das. 2006. *The Big Questions: How to Find Your Own Answers to Life's Essential Mysteries*. New York: Rodale Books.

Sweet, Robert. 1996. *Music Universe, Music Mind*. Ann Arbor: Arborville.

Swimme, Brian, and Berry, Thomas. 1992. *The Universe Story: From the Primordial Flaring Forth to the Ecozoic Era*. New York: Harper Collins.

Tarnas, Richard. 2006. *Cosmos and Psyche: Intimations of a New World View*. New York: Viking.

Tart, Charles. 2009. *The End of Materialism: How Evidence of the Paranormal Is Bringing Science and Spirit Together*. Oakland, CA: New Harbinger.

Thelin, John R. 1996. *Games Colleges Play: Scandal and Reform in Intercollegiate Athletics*. Baltimore: Johns Hopkins University Press.

Tiller, William. 2007. *Psychoenergetic Science: A Second Copernican-Scale Revolution*. Walnut Creek, CA: Pavior Publishers.

Tolle, Eckhart. 1999. *The Power of Now: A Guide to Spiritual Enlightenment*. Novato, CA: New World Library.

Tompkins, Peter, and Bird, Christopher. 1973. *The Secret Life of Plants*. New York: Harper and Row.

Traasdahl, Jan Ole, ed. 1996. *Rhythmic Music Education*. Copenhagen: Danish Music Council.

Travis, F.; Arenander, A.; and DuBois, D. 2004. "Psychological and Physiological Characteristics of a Proposed Object-referral/Self-referral Continuum of Self-awareness." *Consciousness and Cognition* 13: 401–420.

Travis, Fred, and Wallace, R. Keith. 1999. "Autonomic and EEG Patterns During Eyes-closed Rest and Transcendental Meditation (TM) Practice: The Basis for a Neural Model of TM Practice." *Consciousness and Cognition* 8: 302–318.

Vaughn-Lee, Llewellyn. 2009. *The Return of the Feminine and the World Soul*. Inverness, CA: The Golden Sufi Center.

Volk, Terese M. 1998. *Music, Education, and Multiculturalism: Foundations and Principles*. New York: Oxford University Press.

Wade, Jenny. 1996. *Changes of Mind: A Holonomic Theory of the Evolution of Consciousness*. Albany: State University of New York Press.

Wald, George. 1979 (1976). "The Case against Genetic Engineering." In *The Recombinant DNA Debate*, ed. David Jackson and Stephen Stich. Upper Saddle River, NJ: Prentice Hall. 127–128. Reprinted from *The Sciences*, September/October 1976 issue.

Walsh, R., and Shapiro, S. 2006. "The Meeting of Meditative Disciplines and Western Psychology." *American Psychologist* 61, no. 3: 227–239.

Waters, Keith. 2000. "What Is Modal Jazz?" *Jazz Education Journal* 33, no. 1: 53–55.

Watkins, Glenn. 1994. *Pyramids at the Louvre: Music, Culture, and Collage from Stravinsky to the Postmodernists*. Cambridge, MA: Belknap Press of Harvard University Press.

Weinberg, Steven. 1977. *The First Three Minutes*. New York: Basic Books.

———. 1993. *Dreams of a Final Theory: The Scientist's Search for the Ultimate Laws of Nature*. New York: Vintage Books.

Weirauch, Wolfgang, ed. 2004. *Nature Spirits and What They Say: Interviews with Verena Stael von Holstein*. Edinburgh: Floris.

West, John Anthony. 1993. *Serpent in the Sky: The High Wisdom of Ancient Egypt*. Wheaton, IL: Quest Books/Theosophical Publishing House.

Westbrook, Peter. 1997. "Universal Elements in Musical Cosmology." *Cosmos* 13: 21–47.

———. 2007. "Unstruck Sound and Forgotten Truth." *Ultimate Reality and Meaning* 30, no. 1: 93–120.

———. 2008. *The Flute in Jazz: Window on World Music*. Silver Spring, MD: Harmonia Books.

Wheeler, Michael, ed. 2005. "Improvisation and Negotiation." *Negotiation Journal* 21, no. 4: 415–423.

Whitehead, Alfred North. 1929. *The Aims of Education*. New York: Free Press.

———. 1929. *Process and Reality: An Essay in Cosmology*. New York: MacMillan.

Wiggins, Jackie. 2001. *Teaching for Musical Understanding*. New York: McGraw Hill.

Wilber, Ken. 1995 (rev. 2000). *Sex, Ecology, Spirituality*. Boston: Shambhala.

———. 1998. *The Marriage of Sense and Soul: Integrating Science and Religion*. New York: Broadway Books.

———. 1999. "Foreword to *The Mission of Art*, by Alex Grey." *Collected Works*. Vol. 4. Boston: Shambhala.

———. 1999. *One Taste: The Journals of Ken Wilber*. Boston: Shambhala.

———. 2000. *Integral Psychology*. Collected Works. Vol. 4. Boston: Shambhala.

———. 2006. *Integral Spirituality: A Startling New Look at the Role for Religion in the Modern and Postmodern World*. Boston: Shambhala.

———. 2006. "Introduction to Integral Theory and Practice." *Journal of Integral Theory and Practice* 1, no. 1: 1–40.

Wilber, Ken; Patten, Terry; Leonard, Adam; and Morelli, Marco. 2008. *Integral Life Practice: A 21st-Century Blueprint for Physical Health, Emotional Balance, Mental Clarity, and Spiritual Awakening*. Boston: Integral Books.

Williams, Martin. 1990. "Recognition, Prestige, and Respect: They're Academic Questions." In *New Perspectives on Jazz*, ed. David N. Baker. Washington, DC: Smithsonian Institution. 113–119.

Wolff, Christian; Polanski, Larry; Don, Kui; Asplund, Christian; and Hicks, Michael. 2007. "Improvisation, Heterophony, Politics, Composition: Panel Discussions with Christian Wolff, Larry Polanski, Kui Don, Christian Asplund, and Michael Hicks." *Perspectives of New Music* 45, no. 2: 133–140.

Wolff, Fred Alan. 1999. *The Spiritual Universe: One Physicist's Vision of Spirit, Soul, Matter, and Self*. Needham, MA: One Moment Press.

Younker, Betty Anne. 2002. "Critical Thinking." In *The New Handbook of Research on Music Teaching and Learning*, ed. Richard Colwell and Carol Richardson. New York: Oxford University Press. 162–170.

Zemsky, Robert. 2010. *Making Reform Work: The Case for Transforming American Higher Education*. New Brunswick, NJ: Rutgers University Press.
Zimmerman, Michael. 2010. "The Final Cause of Cosmic Development: Nondual Spirit or the Second Law of Thermodynamics?" In *Integral Theory in Action: Applied, Theoretical, and Constructive Perspectives on the AQAL Model*, ed. Sean Esbjörn-Hargens. Albany: State University of New York Press. 203–251.
Zull, James. 2006. "Key Aspects of How the Brain Learns." *The Neuroscience of Adult Learning: New Directions for Adult and Continuing Education*, ed. Sandra Johnson and Kathleen Thompson, 110 (Summer): 3–10.